Public School Law
Teachers' and Students' Rights

SIXTH EDITION

Stephen B. Thomas

Kent State University

Nelda H. Cambron-McCabe

Miami University, Ohio

Martha M. McCarthy

Indiana University

Boston • New York • San Francisco • Mexico City • Montreal
Toronto • London • Madrid • Munich • Paris • Hong Kong
Singapore • Tokyo • Cape Town • Sydney

Executive Editor and Publisher: *Stephen D. Dragin*
Series Editorial Assistant: *Anne Whittaker*
Marketing Manager: *Darcy Betts*
Production Editor: *Mary Beth Finch*
Composition Buyer: *Linda Cox*
Manufacturing Buyer: *Linda Morris*
Production Management and Composition: *Progressive Publishing Alternatives*
Cover Administrator: *Joel Gendron*

For related titles and support materials, visit our online catalog at www.pearsonhighered.com

Between the time website information is gathered and then published, it is not unusual for some sites to have closed. Also, the transcription of URLs can result in typographical errors. The publisher would appreciate notification where these errors occur so that they may be corrected in subsequent editions.

Library of Congress Cataloging-in-Publication Data

Thomas, Stephen B.
  Public school law : teachers' and students' rights / Stephen B. Thomas,
Nelda H. Cambron-McCabe, Martha M. McCarthy. — 6th ed.
        p.   cm.
  Includes bibliographical references and index.
  Author's names appear in different order in previous ed.; Nelda H.
Cambron-McCabe name appears first.
  ISBN-13: 978-0-205-57937-2
  ISBN-10: 0-205-57937-X
  1. Students—Legal status, laws, etc.—United States.   2. Teachers—Legal
status, laws, etc.—United States.   I. Cambron-McCabe, Nelda H.   II. McCarthy,
Martha M.   III. Title.

  KF4119.M38 2009
  344.73'0793—dc22

                                                              2008003419

Printed in the United States of America

10 9 8 7 6 5 4 3 2 1   RRD-VA   12 11 10 09 08

**Allyn & Bacon
is an imprint of**

www.pearsonhighered.com   ISBN-10: 0-205-57937-X
ISBN-13: 978-0-205-57937-2

Contents

Preface

The sixth edition of *Public School Law: Teachers' and Students' Rights* provides a comprehensive treatment of the evolution and current status of the law governing public schools. The content of all chapters has been updated, and some new sections have been added to capture emerging issues of legal concern.

Since World War II, lawmakers have significantly reshaped educational policy. Most school personnel are aware of the burgeoning litigation and legislation, and some are familiar with the names of a few landmark Supreme Court decisions. Nonetheless, many teachers and administrators harbor misunderstandings regarding basic legal concepts that are being applied to educational questions. As a result, they are uncertain about the legality of daily decisions they must make in the operation of schools. Information provided in this book should help alleviate concerns voiced by educators who feel that the scales of justice have been tipped against them.

Public School Law differs from other legal materials currently available to educators because it addresses legal principles applicable to practitioners in a succinct but comprehensive manner. Topics with a direct impact on educators and students are explored, and the tension between governmental controls and the exercise of individual rights is examined within the school context. The analysis of specific school situations relies on applicable constitutional and statutory law and judicial interpretations of these provisions. Implications of legal mandates are discussed, and guidelines are provided for school personnel.

We have attempted to present the material in a nontechnical manner, avoiding the extensive use of legal terms. However, the topics are thoroughly documented through extensive notes that appear at the bottom of pages should the reader choose to explore specific cases or points of law in greater detail. These notes provide additional information on selected cases and should assist the reader in understanding specific concepts. Also, a glossary of basic terms and a table of Supreme Court cases are provided at the end of the book.

A few comments about the nature of the law might assist the reader in using this book. Laws are not created in a vacuum; they reflect the social and philosophical attitudes of society. Moreover, individuals who have personal opinions and biases make laws. Although we may prefer to think that the law is always objective, personal considerations and national political trends do have an impact on the development and interpretation of legal principles.

Also, the law is not static but rather is continually evolving as courts reinterpret constitutional and statutory provisions and legislatures enact new laws. In the 1960s and early 1970s, courts and legislative bodies tended to focus on the expansion of personal rights through civil rights laws and constitutional interpretations favoring the individual's right to be free from unwarranted governmental intrusions. However, since 1975 judicial rulings have supported governmental authority to impose restraints on individual freedoms in the school context in the interest of the collective welfare. While the themes of educational equity and individual rights, which dominated litigation earlier, remain important, efforts to attain educational excellence have generated a new genre of legal activity pertaining to teachers' qualifications and performance standards for students. Moreover, the educational agendas promoted by the religious and political right, such as prayer in public schools and curriculum censorship, have provoked substantial legal activity.

Throughout this book, much of the discussion of the law focuses on court cases because the judiciary plays a vital role in interpreting constitutional and legislative provisions. Decisions are highlighted that illustrate points of law or legal trends, with particular emphasis on recent litigation. A few cases are pursued in depth to provide the reader with an understanding of the rationale behind the decisions. Reviewing the factual situations that have generated these controversies should make it easier for educators to identify potential legal problems in their own school situations.

As we complete this book, judicial decisions are being rendered and statutes are being proposed that may alter the status of the law vis-a-vis teachers and students. Additionally, some questions confronting school personnel have not yet been addressed by the Supreme Court and have generated conflicting decisions among lower courts. It may be frustrating to a reader searching for concrete answers to learn that in some areas the law is far from clear.

In spite of unresolved issues, certain legal principles have been established and can provide direction in many school situations. It is important for educators to become familiar with these principles and to use them to guide their decisions. While the issues generating legal concern will change over time, knowledge of the logic underlying the law can make school personnel more confident in dealing with questions that have not been clarified by courts or legislatures.

We have attempted to arrange the chapters in logical sequence for those reading the book in its entirety or using it as a text for school law courses. An introductory chapter establishes the legal context for the subsequent examination of students' and teachers' rights, and a concluding chapter provides a summary of the major legal principles. Subheadings appear within chapters to facilitate the use of this book for reference if a specific topic is of immediate interest. The reader is encouraged, however, to read the entire text because some topics are addressed in several chapters from different perspectives, and many of the principles of law transcend chapter divisions.

For example, litigation involving various aspects of teachers' rights has relied on precedents established in students' rights cases; the converse also has been true. Throughout the text, various sections are cross-referenced to alert the reader that a particular concept or case is discussed elsewhere in the book. Taken together, the chapters provide an overall picture of the relationship among issues and the applicable legal principles.

Although the content is oriented toward practicing educators, the material should be of equal interest to educational policymakers because many of the legal generalizations pertain to all educational personnel. In addition, this book should serve as a useful guide for parents who are interested in the law governing their children in public schools. Given its comprehensive coverage of students' and teachers' rights, this book also is appropriate for use as a basic text for university courses or in-service sessions.

The material should assist school personnel in understanding the current application of the law, but it is not intended to serve as a substitute for legal counsel. Educators confronting legal problems should always seek the advice of an attorney. Also, there is no attempt here to predict the future course of courts and legislatures. Given the dynamic nature of the law, no single text can serve to keep school personnel abreast of current legal developments. If we can provide an awareness of rights and responsibilities, motivate educators to translate the basic concepts into actual practice, and generate an interest in further study of the law, our purposes in writing this book will have been achieved.

Acknowledgments

A number of individuals contributed to the completion of this book. We are extremely grateful to our students who reacted to various drafts of the chapters and assisted in checking citations. Our sincere thanks go to the following education graduate students: Michelle Walker-Glenn, Miami University; Justin Bathon, Janet Rumple, Lei Wang, and Ran Zhang, Indiana University; and Lindsy Hitesman, Kent State University. Also, the following law students from Indiana University provided valuable assistance in reviewing drafts of chapters, locating legal materials, and verifying citations: David Amaya, Camille Johnson, Matthew Kelley, Katherine Nolan, and Emily Richardson. We would also like to thank the reviewers of this edition of the text: Andrew DeSanto, Neumann College; Carl Lashley, University of North Carolina, Greensboro; Marcelle Lovett, University of North Florida; Robert S. McCord, University of Nevada, Las Vegas; Linda M. Morford, Eastern Illinois University; Agnes E. Smith, University of South Alabama; Joseph Torres, New Mexico State University. This book would not have been completed without the support of our families who offered constant encouragement as they do in all our professional endeavors. Their contributions simply cannot be measured.

1

Legal Framework
of Public Education

The authority for the establishment and control of American public education, which served approximately 48,000,000 students in the 2005–2006 school year,[1] is grounded in law. State and federal constitutional and statutory provisions provide the framework within which school operational decisions are made. Policies and practices at any level of the educational enterprise must be consistent with legal mandates from higher authorities. The overlapping jurisdictions of federal and state constitutions, Congress and state legislatures, federal and state courts, and various governmental agencies (including local school boards and school-based councils) present a complex environment for educators attempting to comply with legal requirements. In an effort to untangle the various legal relationships, this chapter describes the major sources of law and how they interact to form the legal basis for public education. This overview establishes a context for subsequent chapters in which legal principles are discussed more fully as they apply to specific school situations.

State Control of Education

The Tenth Amendment to the United States Constitution stipulates that "the powers not delegated to the United States by the Constitution, nor prohibited by it to the states, are reserved to the states respectively, or to the people." The Supreme Court has recognized that this Amendment was intended "to allay fears that the new national government might seek to exercise powers not granted, and that the states

---

[1]National Center for Education Statistics, *Number and Types of Public Elementary Secondary Schools from the Common Core of Data* (Washington, D.C.: U.S. Department of Education, 2007), available at http://nces.ed.gov/pubs2007/pesschools06/tables/table_7.asp.

might not be able to exercise fully their reserved powers."[2] Since the United States Constitution does not authorize Congress to provide for education, the legal control of public education resides with the state as one of its sovereign powers. The Supreme Court repeatedly has affirmed the comprehensive authority of the states and school officials "to prescribe and control conduct in the schools" as long as actions are consistent with fundamental federal constitutional safeguards.[3] The state's authority over education is considered comparable to its powers to tax and to provide for the general welfare of its citizens. Although each state's educational system has unique features, many similarities are found across states.

Legislative Power

All state constitutions specifically address the legislative responsibility for establishing public schools. Usually the legislature is charged with providing for a uniform, thorough and efficient, or adequate system of public education. In contrast to the federal government, which has only those powers specified in the United States Constitution, state legislatures retain all powers not expressly forbidden by state or federal constitutional provisions. Thus, the state legislature has plenary, or absolute, power to make laws governing education.

Courts have recognized the state legislature's authority to raise revenue and distribute educational funds, control teacher licensure, prescribe curricular offerings, establish pupil performance standards, and regulate other specific aspects of public school operations. Moreover, states can mandate school attendance to ensure an educated citizenry. At the present time, all 50 states require that students between specified ages (usually 6 to 16) attend a public or private school or receive equivalent instruction. In addition, legislatures are empowered to create, reorganize, consolidate, and abolish school districts, even over the objections of affected residents.[4]

Legislatures also can authorize other school governance arrangements, such as state-funded charter schools that operate outside many regulations on the basis of a charter granted by the state or local board of education or other entities. The charter school movement has been characterized as one of the fastest-growing education reform efforts nationally. Since 1991, 40 states and the District of Columbia have enacted laws authorizing charter schools, usually specifying a cap on the number of charters granted to existing public or private schools or groups starting new schools.

---

[2]United States v. Darby, 312 U.S. 100, 124 (1941).

[3]Tinker v. Des Moines Indep. Sch. Dist., 393 U.S. 503, 507 (1969). *See also* Knight v. Alabama, 476 F.3d 1219 (11th Cir. 2007) (finding that tax provisions of the state constitution did not violate the Federal Constitution in that the challenged tax policies were not undermining the desegregation process to a level that would even remotely trigger the Fourteenth Amendment), *cert. denied*, 127 S. Ct. 3014 (2007).

[4]State laws, however, can place restrictions on school district boundaries. *See, e.g.*, State v. Bd. of Educ., 741 S.W.2d 747 (Mo. Ct. App. 1987).

As of September 2007, 4,147 schools operated as charter schools and served over 1.24 million children (over 2 percent of all schoolchildren).[5]

In some instances, when state laws are subject to several interpretations, courts are called on to clarify legislative intent. If the judiciary misinterprets the law's purpose, the legislature can amend the law in question to clarify its meaning. However, if a law is invalidated as abridging state or federal constitutional provisions or federal civil rights laws, the legislature must abide by the judicial directives. Additionally, a state's attorney general may be asked to interpret a law or to advise school boards on the legality of their actions. Unless overruled by the judiciary, the official opinion of an attorney general is binding.

Although the state legislature cannot relinquish its law-making powers, it can delegate to subordinate agencies the authority to make rules and regulations necessary to implement laws. These administrative functions must be carried out within the guidelines established by the legislature. Some states are quite liberal in delegating administrative authority, whereas other states prescribe detailed standards that must be followed by subordinate agencies. It is a widely held perception that local school boards control public education, but local boards have only those powers conferred by the state. Courts consistently have reiterated that the authority for public education is not a local one, but rather is a central power residing in the state legislature. School buildings are state property, local school board members are state officials, and teachers are state employees. Public school funds, regardless where collected, are state funds.

State Agencies

It has been neither feasible nor desirable to include in statutes every minor detail governing public schools; all states except Wisconsin have established a state board of education that typically supplies the structural details to implement broad legislative mandates. In most states, members of the state board of education are elected by the citizenry or appointed by the governor, and the board usually functions immediately below the legislature in the hierarchy of educational governance.

Accreditation is an important tool used by state boards to compel local school districts to abide by their directives. School districts often must satisfy state accreditation requirements as a condition of receiving state funds. Though accreditation models vary, it is common for states to assess student outcomes as well as establish minimum standards in areas such as curriculum, teacher qualifications, instructional materials, and facilities. In some states, different grades of school accreditation exist, with financial incentives in place to encourage local schools to attain the highest level. Beginning in the mid-1980s, there has been a movement toward performance-based accreditation under which a school's performance is assessed against predicted outcomes calculated for the school in areas such as pupil achievement, absenteeism, and student retention.

---

[5]Moreover, California operated 710 charter schools, while Arizona, Florida, Ohio, and Texas each had over 300. Center for Education Reform, *National Charter School Data* (Washington, D.C.: Center for Education Reform, 2007), available at www.edreform.com/_upload/CER_charter_numbers.pdf.

Within legislative parameters, the state board of education can issue directives governing school operations. In some states, rules pertaining to such matters as proficiency testing for students and programs for children with disabilities are embodied in state board rules rather than state law. Courts generally have upheld decisions made by state boards of education, unless the boards have violated legislative or constitutional mandates.[6] State boards of education, however, cannot abrogate powers delegated by law to other agencies, such as local school boards or councils.

In addition to the state board, generally considered a policy-making body, all states have designated a chief state school officer (often known as the superintendent of public instruction or commissioner of education) to function in an executive capacity. Traditionally, the duties of the chief state school officer (CSSO) have been regulatory in nature. However, other activities, such as research and long-range planning, may be part of this role. In some states, the CSSO is charged with adjudicating educational controversies, and citizens cannot invoke judicial remedies for a grievance pertaining to internal school operations until such administrative appeals have been exhausted. When considering an appeal of a CSSO's decision, courts will not judge the wisdom of the decision or overrule such a decision unless it is clearly arbitrary or against the preponderance of evidence.[7]

Each state also has established a state department of education, consisting of educational specialists who provide consultation to the state board, CSSO, and local school boards. State department personnel often collect data from school districts to ensure that legislative enactments and state board policies are properly implemented. Furthermore, most state departments engage in research and development activities to improve educational practices within the state.

Local School Boards

Although public education in the United States is state controlled, it is for the most part locally administered. All states except Hawaii have created local school boards in addition to state education agencies and have delegated certain administrative authority over schools to these local boards. Nationwide, there are approximately 14,200 local districts, ranging from a few students to several hundred thousand.[8] Some states, particularly those with a large number of small school districts, have established intermediate or regional administrative units that perform regulatory or service functions for several local districts.

As with the delegation of authority to state agencies, assignment of powers to local school boards is handled very differently across states. Some states with a deeply

[6]Wilt v. Ohio State Bd. of Educ., 608 F.2d 1126 (6th Cir. 1979) (upholding the state board's authority to compel a school district to be annexed to a neighboring district because it failed to meet minimum state standards; and reasoning that the annexed district had no federal constitutional right to remain in existence).

[7]*See, e.g.,* Botti v. S.W. Butler County Sch. Dist., 529 A.2d 1206 (Pa. Commw. Ct. 1987).

[8]National Center for Education Statistics, *Number and Types of Public Elementary and Secondary Agencies, 2005–2006* (Washington, D.C.: U.S. Department of Education, 2007), available at http://nces.ed.gov/pubs2007/pesagencies06/tables/table_6.asp.

rooted tradition of local control over education give local boards a great deal of latitude in making operational decisions about schools. In states that tend toward centralized control of education, local boards must function within the framework of detailed legislative directives. State legislatures retain the legal responsibility for education and can restrict the discretion of local boards by enacting legislation to that effect.

The citizenry within the school district usually elects local school board members.[9] The United States Supreme Court has recognized that the Equal Protection Clause requires each qualified voter to be given an opportunity to participate in the election of board members, with each vote given the same weight as far as practicable.[10] When board members are elected from geographical districts, such districts must be established to protect voting rights under the "one person, one vote" principle. If "at-large" elections result in a dilution of the minority vote, an abridgment of the federal Voting Rights Act may be found.[11]

The state legislature can specify the qualifications, method of selection, and terms and conditions of local school board membership. Board members are considered public school officers with sovereign power and policy-making authority, in contrast to school employees, who are hired to implement directives.[12] Public officers cannot hold two offices if one is subordinate to the other, cannot have an interest in contracts made by their agencies, and in some states cannot occupy more than one paid office. Generally, statutes stipulate procedures that must be followed in removing public officers from their positions. Typical causes for removal include neglect of duty, illegal performance of duty, breach of good faith, negligence, and incapacity.

A local board must act as a body; individual board members are not empowered to make policies or perform official acts on behalf of the board. School boards have some discretion in adopting operational procedures and policies, but they are legally bound to adhere to such procedures once established. Although courts are reluctant to interfere with decisions made by boards of education and will not rule on the wisdom of such decisions, they will invalidate any board action that is arbitrary, capricious, or outside the board's legal authority (i.e., an *ultra vires* act).

School board meetings and records must be open to the public.[13] Most states have enacted "sunshine" or open meeting laws, acknowledging that the public has a right to be fully informed regarding the actions of public agencies. Certain exceptions to open meeting requirements are usually specified in the laws. For example, in many

[9]In some cities, school board members are appointed by the mayor. But in a few states, local board members are appointed by other agencies, such as the city council or county board of supervisors.

[10]Hadley v. Junior Coll. Dist., 397 U.S. 50 (1970).

[11]42 U.S.C. § 1971, *et seq.* (2007). Section 1973 states that "no practice or procedure shall be imposed or applied ... in a manner which results in a denial or abridgment of the right ... to vote on account of race. ... " *See, e.g.,* Moore v. Itawamba County, Miss., 431 F.3d 257 (5th Cir. 2005).

[12]*See, e.g.,* Barrow v. Greenville Indep. Sch. Dist., 480 F.3d 377 (5th Cir. 2007) (noting that the superintendent serves in an advisory role to the school board, but the board has the policy-making authority).

[13]However, a New Jersey court has indicated that handwritten notes used by the board secretary to prepare the official minutes were not public records. *See* O'Shea v. W. Milford Bd. of Educ., 918 A.2d 735 (N.J. Super. Ct. App. Div. 2007).

states, school boards can meet in executive session to discuss matters that threaten public safety or pertain to pending or current litigation, personnel matters, collective bargaining, or the disposition of real property. Although discussion of these matters may take place in closed meetings, statutes usually stipulate that formal action must occur in open meetings.[14]

Local school boards hold powers specified or implied in state law and other powers considered necessary to achieve the purposes of the express powers. These delegated powers generally encompass the authority to determine the specifics of the curriculum offered within the school district, raise revenue to build and maintain schools, select personnel, and enact other policies necessary to implement the educational program pursuant to law. Courts have recognized that even without specific enabling legislation, local boards have discretionary authority to establish and support secondary schools, kindergartens, and nongraded schools; alter school attendance zones; and close schools. Local boards also can contract with private companies to provide various services and even manage total school operations, although such matters at times will qualify as required subjects for collective bargaining.

Some local school board decisions (e.g., minimum length of instructional time[15]) have been challenged as beyond the board's lawful scope of authority. Unless school boards act in violation of state or federal law, courts usually defer to boards' decisions (e.g., upholding community service requirements as a prerequisite to receipt of a high school diploma[16]). Additionally, local school boards cannot delegate their decision-making authority to other agencies or associations.

School-Based Councils

Since the mid-1980s, the objective of decentralizing many operational decisions to the school level (i.e., site-based management) has been increasingly important. Therefore, school councils have become more prevalent. Where school-based councils have been created and delegated authority in certain domains (e.g., curriculum, personnel), their decisions have the force of law.[17] Only if councils act beyond their

[14]*See, e.g., In re* Kansas City Star Co., 73 F.3d 191 (8th Cir. 1996) (holding that a closed session between the desegregation monitoring committee and school board did not violate the Missouri Sunshine Act).

[15]*Compare* Morgan v. Polk County Bd. of Educ., 328 S.E.2d 320 (N.C. Ct. App. 1985) (upholding the decision to lengthen the school day and term) *with* Johnston v. Bd. of Trs., 661 P.2d 1045 (Wyo. 1983) (holding that a school district's practice of compressing the school week into four days violated the state law requiring the school year to be 175 days).

[16]*See, e.g.,* Herndon v. Chapel Hill-Carrboro City Bd. of Educ., 89 F.3d 174 (4th Cir. 1996); text accompanying note 74, Chapter 3.

[17]Under the Chicago School Reform Act, 105 ILCS 5/34-2.2(c) (2007), the local school council is authorized to appoint a principal without school board approval. Under Kentucky's Education Reform Act, KRS 160.345(2)(h) (2007), superintendents must forward all principal applicants who meet statutory requirements to the site-based school council, not simply the ones the superintendent recommends and supports, Young v. Hammond, 139 S.W.3d 895 (Ky. 2004). Massachusetts's Education Reform Act, Mass. Gen. Laws ch. 71, § 59B (2007), lodges the responsibility for hiring and firing of teachers and other building personnel with school principals under the supervision of the superintendent.

scope of authority or impair protected rights will their decisions be invalidated by the judiciary.

The 1990 Kentucky Education Reform Act entails major changes in school funding, curriculum, and governance, including the creation of school-based councils with authority for policy decisions affecting school sites. Whereas local school boards retain many of their traditional powers—such as establishing schools, setting tax rates and budgets, and maintaining facilities—the school-based councils are authorized to hire the building principal, select textbooks, and make policy decisions in other areas such as curricular offerings, staff assignments, and student discipline. Determining the respective spheres of authority of local boards and school-based councils has created some tension. In 1994, teachers challenged a local board's action in requiring school-based councils to obtain board approval before implementing school improvement plans. Noting some overlap in duties between local boards and school councils, the Kentucky Supreme Court reasoned that the state did not delegate to local boards approval authority over council decisions pertaining to school improvement plans.[18] The court reasoned that the state law granting school-based councils independent policy-making powers constituted a clear delegation of legislative authority to the school level.

Although school district boards of education and, in some jurisdictions, school-based councils are authorized to perform discretionary duties (i.e., those involving judgment), school employees (e.g., superintendents, principals, teachers) can perform only ministerial duties necessary to carry out policies. Hence, a superintendent can recommend personnel to be hired and propose a budget, but the school board, or in some instances the school council, must make the actual decisions.[19]

Federal Role in Education

Unlike state constitutions, the United States Constitution is silent regarding education; hence, individuals do not have an inherent federally protected right to an education.[20] The Constitution, however, does confer basic rights on individuals, and these rights must be respected by school personnel. Furthermore, Congress exerts control over the use of federal education aid and regulates other aspects of schools through legislation enacted pursuant to its constitutionally granted powers.

United States Constitution

A constitution is a body of precepts providing the system of fundamental laws of a nation, state, or society. The United States Constitution establishes a separation of powers among the executive, judicial, and legislative branches of government. These three branches form a system of checks and balances to ensure that the intent of the Constitution is respected. The Constitution also provides a systematic process for

[18]Bd. of Educ. v. Bushee, 889 S.W.2d 809 (Ky. 1994).

[19]*See* text accompanying note 36, Chapter 8.

[20]San Antonio Indep. Sch. Dist. v. Rodriguez, 411 U.S. 1 (1973).

altering the document, if deemed necessary. Article V stipulates that amendments may be proposed by a two-thirds vote of each house of Congress or by a special convention called by Congress on the request of two-thirds of the state legislatures. Proposed amendments then must be ratified by three-fourths of the states to become part of the Constitution.

Since the United States Constitution is the supreme law in this nation, state authority over education must be exercised in a manner consistent with its provisions. In 1958, the Supreme Court declared: "It is, of course, quite true that the responsibility for public education is primarily the concern of the states, but it is equally true that such responsibilities, like all other state activity, must be exercised consistently with federal constitutional requirements as they apply to state action."[21] The Supreme Court has interpreted various constitutional guarantees as they apply to educational matters. Although all federal constitutional mandates affect public education to some degree, the following provisions have had the greatest impact on public school policies and practices.

General Welfare Clause.   Under Article I, Section 8, of the Constitution, Congress has the power "to lay and collect taxes, duties, imposts and excises, to pay the debts and provide for the common defense and general welfare of the United States." In 1937, the Supreme Court declared that the concept of general welfare is not static: "Needs that were narrow or parochial a century ago may be interwoven in our day with the well-being of the nation. What is critical or urgent changes with the times."[22] Although historically this clause has been the subject of much debate, the Supreme Court has interpreted the provision as allowing Congress to tax and spend public monies for a variety of purposes related to the general welfare.[23] The Court has stated that it will not interfere with the discretion of Congress in its domain, unless Congress exhibits a clear display of arbitrary power.[24]

Using the general welfare rationale, Congress has enacted legislation providing substantial federal support for research and instructional programs in areas such as science, mathematics, reading, special education, vocational education, career education, and bilingual education. Congress also has provided financial assistance for the school lunch program and for services to meet the special needs of various groups of students, such as the educationally and culturally disadvantaged. In addition, Congress has responded to national health and safety concerns with legislation such as the 1980 Asbestos School Hazard Detection and Control Act and the 1988 Indoor Radon Abatement Act, which require the inspection of school buildings and, if necessary, remedial action to assure the safety of students and employees. More recently, the federal government, in passing the Children's Internet Protection Act, attempted to protect the welfare of minors by policing the suitability of materials made available

[21]Cooper v. Aaron, 358 U.S. 1, 19 (1958).

[22]Helvering v. Davis, 301 U.S. 619, 641 (1937).

[23]*See, e.g., Helvering, id.*; United States v. Butler, 297 U.S. 1 (1936).

[24]*Helvering*, 301 U.S. at 644–645.

electronically.[25] Among the act's provisions is the requirement for public libraries and schools receiving federal funds to install Internet filtering software to block children's access to indecent material. In 2003, the Supreme Court upheld this law in *United States v. American Library Association*, concluding that filtering information did not violate the First Amendment rights of library patrons and that the act was a valid exercise of the spending power of Congress.[26]

Commerce Clause.   Congress is empowered to "regulate commerce with foreign nations, among the several states, and with Indian tribes" under Article I, Section 8, Clause 3, of the Constitution. Safety, transportation, and labor regulations enacted pursuant to this clause have affected the operation of public schools. Traditionally, courts have favored a broad interpretation of "commerce" and an expanded federal role in regulating commercial activity to ensure national prosperity. Interpreting congressional powers to regulate commerce, in 1985 the Supreme Court held that a municipal mass transit system was subject to the minimum wage and overtime requirements of the federal Fair Labor Standards Act (FLSA).[27] This decision, *Garcia v. San Antonio Metropolitan Transit Authority*, overturned a precedent established in 1976 when the Court limited congressional authority to enforce federal minimum wage requirements in areas of "traditional" state governmental functions.[28] Concluding that attempts to identify such state functions that would be immune from federal requirements had been unworkable and inconsistent with established principles of federalism, the Court in *Garcia* found nothing in the FLSA destructive of state sovereignty.

Obligation of Contracts Clause.   Article I, Section 10, of the Constitution stipulates that states cannot enact any law impairing the obligation of contracts. Administrators, teachers, and noncertified personnel are protected from arbitrary dismissals by contractual agreements. School boards enter into numerous contracts with individuals and companies in conducting school business. The judiciary often is called on to evaluate the validity of a given contract or to assess whether a party has breached its contractual obligations.[29]

First Amendment.   The Bill of Rights, comprising the first 10 amendments to the United States Constitution, safeguards individual liberties against governmental encroachment.[30] The most preciously guarded of these liberties are contained in the

---

[25]20 U.S.C. § 9134(f) (2007); 47 U.S.C. § 254(h)(5) (2007).

[26]539 U.S. 194 (2003).

[27]469 U.S. 528 (1985).

[28]Nat'l League of Cities v. Usery, 426 U.S. 833 (1976).

[29]*See, e.g.*, Columbus Indep. Sch. Dist. v. Five Oaks Achievement Ctr., 197 S.W.3d 384 (Tex. 2006) (concluding that defendant should have had the opportunity to argue that the school district had waived its immunity when sued for breach of contract).

[30]Several of the original states were reluctant to ratify the Constitution without the promise of a statement of individual liberties. *See* Robert Rutland, *The Birth of the Bill of Rights, 1776–1791* (Chapel Hill: University of North Carolina Press, 1955), Chapters 7 and 8.

First Amendment, which stipulates that Congress may not enact any law that respects an establishment of religion; prohibits the free exercise of religion; abridges the freedoms of speech or press; restricts the right to peaceably assemble; or prohibits the right to petition the government to redress grievances.

The religious freedoms guaranteed by this amendment have evoked a number of lawsuits challenging governmental aid to and regulation of nonpublic schools and contesting public school policies and practices as advancing religion or impairing free exercise rights. Cases involving students' rights to express themselves and to distribute literature have been initiated under First Amendment guarantees of freedom of speech and press. Moreover, teachers' rights to academic freedom and to speak out on matters of public concern have precipitated numerous lawsuits. The right of assembly has been the focus of litigation involving student clubs and employees' rights to organize and engage in collective bargaining.

Fourth Amendment.   This amendment guarantees the right of citizens "to be secure in their persons, houses, papers, and effects against unreasonable searches and seizures." The Supreme Court has recognized that the basic purpose of the Fourth Amendment is "to safeguard the privacy and security of individuals against arbitrary invasions by governmental officials."[31] This amendment has frequently appeared in educational cases involving everything from drug-testing programs; searches of students' lockers, cars, and persons; coercively administered pregnancy tests; and the search of a student's computer files when linked to an educational institution's network system. A few cases have involved alleged violations of school employees' Fourth Amendment rights by school officials.

Fifth Amendment.   In part, this amendment provides that no person shall be "compelled in any criminal case to be a witness against himself, nor be deprived of life, liberty, or property without due process of law; nor shall private property be taken for public use, without just compensation." Several cases have addressed the application of the self-incrimination clause in instances where teachers have been questioned by superiors about their activities outside the classroom. The Fifth Amendment also has been used in educational litigation to protect citizens' rights to appropriate compensation for property acquired for school purposes. Due process litigation concerning schools usually has been initiated under the Fourteenth Amendment, which pertains directly to state action. However, cases in the District of Columbia (involving topics such as desegregation and discipline) have relied on due process guarantees of the Fifth Amendment, because the Fourteenth Amendment does not apply in this jurisdiction.

Ninth Amendment.   The Ninth Amendment stipulates that "the enumeration in the Constitution, of certain rights, shall not be construed to deny or disparage others retained by the people." This amendment has appeared in educational litigation in

---

[31]Camara v. Mun. Court of City and County of S.F., 387 U.S. 523, 528 (1967).

which teachers have asserted that their right to personal privacy outside the class-room is protected as an unenumerated right. Furthermore, grooming regulations applied to teachers and students have been challenged as infringing on personal rights retained by the people under this amendment.

Fourteenth Amendment.   The Fourteenth Amendment is the most widely invoked constitutional provision in school litigation since it specifically addresses state action. In part, the Fourteenth Amendment provides that no state shall "deny to any person within its jurisdiction, the equal protection of the laws." This clause has been signifi-cant in school cases involving alleged discrimination based on race, national origin, sex, and ethnic background. In addition, school finance litigation often has been based on the Equal Protection Clause, although with very little success.[32]

In addition, the Due Process Clause of the Fourteenth Amendment, which pro-hibits states from depriving citizens of life, liberty, or property without due process of law, has played an important role in school litigation. Property rights are legitimate expectations of entitlement created through state laws, regulations, or contracts. Com-pulsory school attendance laws confer on students a legitimate property right to attend school, and the granting of tenure gives teachers a property entitlement to continued employment. Liberty rights include interests in one's reputation and fundamental rights related to marriage, family matters, and personal privacy. In addition, the Supreme Court has interpreted Fourteenth Amendment liberties as incorporating the personal freedoms contained in the Bill of Rights.[33] Thus, the first 10 amendments, originally directed toward the federal government, have been applied to state action as well. Although the principle of "incorporation" has been criticized, Supreme Court precedent supports the notion that the Fourteenth Amendment restricts state interfer-ence with fundamental constitutional liberties. This principle is particularly important in school litigation since education is a state function; claims that public school poli-cies or practices impair personal freedoms (e.g., First Amendment free speech guaran-tees) are usually initiated through the Fourteenth Amendment.

The federal judiciary has identified both procedural and substantive compo-nents of due process guarantees. *Procedural due process* ensures fundamental fair-ness if the government threatens an individual's life, liberty, or property interests. Minimum procedures required by the United States Constitution are notice of the charges, an opportunity to refute the charges, and a hearing that is conducted fairly. In comparison, *substantive due process* requires that state action be based on a valid objective with means reasonably related to attaining the objective. In essence, sub-stantive due process shields the individual against arbitrary governmental action that impairs life, liberty, or property interests.

Since the Fourteenth Amendment protects personal liberties against unwar-ranted state interference, private institutions, including private schools, are not subject

[32]*See, e.g.*, San Antonio Indep. Sch. Dist. v. Rodriguez, 411 U.S. 1 (1973).

[33]*See, e.g.*, Cantwell v. Connecticut, 310 U.S. 296, 303 (1940); Gitlow v. New York, 268 U.S. 652, 666 (1925).

to these restrictions. For private school policies and practices to be challenged successfully under the Fourteenth Amendment, there must be sufficient governmental involvement in the private school to constitute "state action."[34] To date, this has not occurred, although the Supreme Court may have opened the window for possible future inclusion when it determined that state athletic associations (typically private corporations) are entwined with state government and therefore are involved in state action.[35]

Federal Legislation

Congress is empowered to enact laws to translate the intent of the United States Constitution into actual practices. Laws reflect the will of the legislative branch of government, which, theoretically, in a democracy represents the citizenry. Because the states have sovereign power regarding education, the federal government's involvement in public schools has been one of indirect support, not direct control.

Funding Laws. Federal legislation affecting public education was enacted just prior to ratification of the Constitution. The Ordinances of 1785 and 1787, providing land grants to states for the maintenance of public schools, encouraged the establishment of public education in many states. However, it was not until the mid-twentieth century that Congress began to play a significant role in stimulating targeted educational reform through its spending powers under the General Welfare Clause.

The most comprehensive law offering financial assistance to schools, the Elementary and Secondary Education Act of 1965 (ESEA), in part supplied funds for compensatory education programs for economically disadvantaged students attending public and nonprofit private schools.[36] With passage of ESEA, federal aid to education doubled, and the federal government's contribution increased steadily until reaching its high point of 9.8 percent of total public education revenue in 1980. The federal share then declined to the 6 to 7 percent range for a period of time, but by 2003–2004 exceeded 9 percent once again.[37]

Congress and federal administrative agencies have exerted considerable influence in shaping public school policies and practices through categorical funding laws and their accompanying administrative regulations. Individual states or school districts have the option of accepting or rejecting such federal assistance,

---

[34]*See, e.g.*, Rendell-Baker v. Kohn, 457 U.S. 830 (1982).

[35]*See* Brentwood Acad. v. Tenn. Secondary Sch. Athletic Ass'n, 531 U.S. 288 (2001). *See also* Tenn. Secondary Sch. Athletic Ass'n v. Brentwood Acad., 127 S. Ct. 2489 (2007) (finding no due process violation as appropriate procedures were followed, notwithstanding minor procedural irregularities).

[36]Ariz. State Bd. for Charter Schs. v. United States Dep't of Educ., 464 F.3d 1003 (9th Cir. 2006) (determining that for-profit schools were not eligible for funding under the ESEA or IDEA, notwithstanding reference in both laws to charter schools).

[37]National Center for Education Statistics, *Revenues for Public Elementary and Secondary Schools* (Washington, D.C.: U.S. Department of Education, 2006), available at http://nces.ed.gov/programs/digest/d06/tables/dt06_158.asp.

but if categorical aid is accepted, the federal government has the authority to prescribe guidelines for its use and to monitor state and local education agencies to ensure fiscal accountability.[38]

Much of the federal categorical legislation enacted during the 1960s and 1970s provided funds to assist school districts in attaining equity goals and addressing other national priorities. For example, the Bilingual Education Act of 1968 and the Education for All Handicapped Children Act of 1975 (which became the Individuals with Disabilities Education Act of 1990) have provided federal funds to assist education agencies in offering services for students with special needs. Although in the 1980s Congress shifted away from its heavy reliance on categorical federal aid by consolidating some categorical programs into block grants with reduced funding and regulations, aid for economically disadvantaged and English-deficient students and children with disabilities has remained categorical in nature.

In 2002, President George W. Bush signed into law the No Child Left Behind Act (NCLB), the most comprehensive reform of the ESEA since it was enacted in 1965.[39] The law, directed at improving the performance of public schools, pledges that no child will be left in a failing school. Specifically, the law requires states to implement accountability systems with higher performance standards in reading, mathematics, and science along with annual testing of all students in grades 3 through 8. Furthermore, assessment data must be categorized by poverty, ethnicity, race, disability, and limited English proficiency. The law greatly expands choices for parents of children attending schools that do not meet state standards. If students are in a school that has been identified as low performing, students must be given the option of attending a better school within the district, including a charter school. For students attending persistently failing schools (i.e., failure to meet the state standards in three of the four preceding years), the school district must permit the students to use federal funds to obtain supplemental educational services (e.g., tutoring, after-school or summer programs) from either public or private providers. Persistently failing schools not only lose funding as students select other schools but also face mandated reconstitution if they do not make adequate yearly progress.

The NCLB's emphasis on high-stakes testing to assess whether schools have made appropriate annual progress has been the source of controversy[40] as has the treatment of children with disabilities and LEP students in such testing programs. Some critics of the law contend that the public school curriculum has been narrowed to focus too much on the subjects being tested under accountability mandates. Also, variations across states in the rigor of the mandatory exams and the selection of passing scores have been controversial.

---

[38]*But see* William Penn Sch. Dist. v. Dep't of Educ., 902 A.2d 583 (Pa. Commw. Ct. 2006) (finding insufficient bases for requiring a repayment of $18,000 for alleged discrepancies in the district's National School Lunch Program account).

[39]20 U.S.C. § 6301 *et seq.* (2007).

[40]*See* Sharon L. Nichols and David C. Berliner, *Collateral Damage: How High-Stakes Testing Corrupts America's Schools* (Cambridge, MA: Harvard Education Press, 2007).

Civil Rights Laws.   In addition to laws providing financial assistance to public schools, Congress has enacted legislation designed to clarify the scope of individuals' civil rights. Unlike the discretion enjoyed by state and local education agencies in deciding whether to participate in federal funding programs, educational institutions must comply with these civil rights laws. Federal antidiscrimination laws are grounded in two distinct sources of federal authority. Some are enacted to enforce constitutional rights and have general application. Others are based on the federal government's authority to place restrictions on the expenditure of federal funds and apply only to recipients of federal financial assistance. Various federal agencies are charged with monitoring compliance with these laws and can bring suit against non-complying institutions. Under many civil rights laws, individuals also can initiate private suits to compel compliance and, in some instances, to obtain personal remedies.

Several laws enacted in the latter part of the nineteenth century to protect the rights of African American citizens were seldom the focus of litigation until the mid-twentieth century. Since the 1960s, these laws, particularly 42 U.S.C. Section 1983, have been used by students and teachers to gain relief in instances where their federal rights have been violated by school policies and practices. Section 1983 provides a private right to bring suit for damages against any person who, acting under the authority of state law (e.g., a public school employee) impairs rights secured by the United States Constitution and federal laws.[41] Although Section 1983 does not confer specific substantive rights (i.e., it must attach to another federal law and cannot be the basis for suit standing alone), it has been significant in school cases because it allows individuals to obtain damages from school officials and school districts for abridgments of federally protected rights.[42] However, Section 1983 cannot be used to enforce federal laws where congressional intent to create private rights is not clearly stated.[43] In addition, Section 1981 of the Civil Rights Act of 1866, as amended in 1991, prohibits race or ethnicity discrimination in making and enforcing contracts and in the terms and conditions of contractual relationships and allows for both compensatory and punitive damages.[44] It applies to all public and private schools, regardless of whether they receive federal aid.

Subsequent civil rights laws enacted since the 1960s confer substantive rights to protect citizens from discrimination. The vindication of employees' rights in school settings has generated substantial litigation under Title VII of the Civil Rights

---

[41]School boards as well as school officials are considered "persons" under 42 U.S.C. § 1983 (2007). *See* text accompanying note 197, Chapter 11.

[42]*See, e.g.,* Barrett v. Steubenville City Schs., 388 F.3d 967 (6th Cir. 2004) (finding that the superintendent violated the substitute teacher's right to direct the education of his child as protected by the Constitution and § 1983 when the superintendent refused to consider him for a full-time position because his son was enrolled in a parochial school), *cert. denied,* 546 U.S. 813 (2005).

[43]*See, e.g.,* Gonzaga Univ. v. Doe, 536 U.S. 273 (2002) (finding that Congress did not intend to create privately enforceable rights under the Family Education Rights and Privacy Act); text accompanying note 149, Chapter 3.

[44]42 U.S.C. § 1981 (2007). The Civil Rights Act of 1991, Pub. L. 102–166, expanded § 1981's protections and strengthened several other civil rights mandates.

Act of 1964, which prohibits employment discrimination on the basis of race, color, sex, religion, or national origin. Modeled in part after Title VII, the Americans with Disabilities Act of 1990 provides specific protections in employment and public accommodations for individuals with disabilities. Additionally, the Age Discrimination in Employment Act of 1967 protects employees over age 40 against age-based employment discrimination. Other civil rights laws pertain only to institutions with programs that receive federal funds, such as Title VI of the Civil Rights Act of 1964 (prohibiting discrimination on the basis of race, color, sex, religion, or national origin), Title IX of the Education Amendments of 1972 (barring sex discrimination against participants in education programs), the Rehabilitation Act of 1973 (prohibiting discrimination against otherwise qualified persons with disabilities), and the Age Discrimination Act of 1975 (barring age discrimination in federally assisted programs or activities).[45] Courts often have been called on to interpret these acts and their regulations as they apply to educational practices.

Still other federal laws offer protections to individuals in educational settings and place responsibilities on school officials. For example, the Family Educational Rights and Privacy Act guarantees parents access to their children's school records and safeguards the confidentiality of such records. This federal law also applies to both public and private educational recipients of federal financial assistance. Federal laws also protect human subjects in research projects and require parental consent before students participate in federally supported psychiatric or psychological examination, testing, or treatment designed to reveal information in specified sensitive areas.[46] Courts have played an important role in interpreting the protections included in these laws and ensuring compliance with the federal mandates.

Federal Administrative Agencies

Similar to state governments, much of the regulatory activity at the federal level is conducted by administrative agencies. The Office of Education was originally established in 1867, and it became part of the Department of Health, Education, and Welfare in 1953. In 1980, the Department of Education was created; its secretary, who serves as a member of the president's cabinet, is appointed by the president with the advice and approval of the Senate.

The primary functions of the Department of Education are to coordinate federal involvement in education activities, identify educational needs of national significance, propose strategies to address these needs, and provide technical and financial assistance to state and local education agencies. Regulations promulgated by the Department of Education to implement funding laws have had a significant impact on many schools. The department solicits public comments on proposed regulations,

[45]The Civil Rights Restoration Act of 1987, 20 U.S.C. § 1681 (2007), amended these four laws to make them applicable to entire institutions if any of their programs receive federal funds. This law was enacted in response to the Supreme Court ruling in Grove City Coll. v. Bell, 465 U.S. 555 (1984).

[46]Department of Health and Human Services, *Regulations and Policy Guidance*, 2007, available at www.hhs.gov/ohrp/.

and Congress reviews the regulations to ensure their consistency with legislative intent. The Department of Education administers regulations for over 100 different programs, ranging from services for Native American students to projects for school dropouts. The Departments of Agriculture, Labor, Defense, Justice, and Health and Human Services administer the remaining educational programs.

Through their regulatory activities, numerous federal agencies influence state and local education policies. For example, the Office for Civil Rights and the Equal Employment Opportunity Commission have reviewed claims of discrimination in public schools and initiated suits against school districts that are not in compliance with civil rights laws. The Environmental Protection Agency also has placed obligations on schools in connection with the maintenance of safe school environments. School districts can face the termination of federal assistance if they do not comply with such federal regulations.

Function and Structure of the Judicial System

Judicial decisions are usually cited in conjunction with statutory and constitutional provisions as a major source of educational law. As early as 1835, Alexis de Tocqueville noted that "scarcely any political question arises in the United States that is not resolved, sooner or later, into a judicial question."[47] Courts, however, do not initiate laws as legislative bodies do; courts apply appropriate principles of law to settle disputes. The terms *common law* and *case law* refer to judicially created legal principles that are relied on as precedent when similar factual situations arise.

Although most constitutional provisions and statutory enactments never become the subject of litigation, some provisions require judicial clarification. Since federal and state constitutions set forth broad policy statements rather than specific guides to action, courts serve an important function in interpreting such mandates and in determining the legality of various school policies and practices.

The Supreme Court has articulated specific guidelines for exercising the power of judicial review. The Court will not decide hypothetical cases and will not render an opinion on issues in nonadversarial proceedings. A genuine controversy must be initiated by a party with standing and a private right of action to sue. To achieve such standing, the party must have a "real interest" in the outcome of the case, such as having been adversely affected by the challenged practice.[48] Moreover, in determining whether a plaintiff has a private right of action under a federal statute, the courts will consider whether:

- Congress enacted the statute for the special benefit of plaintiff's class;
- The legislative history supports or opposes a private remedy;

---

[47]Alexis de Tocqueville, *Democracy in America*, rev. ed., vol. 1 (New York: Alfred A. Knopf, 1960), p. 280.

[48]Hein v. Freedom From Religion Found. Inc., 127 S. Ct. 2553 (2007) (determining that plaintiff lacked standing in a claim challenging an executive order ensuring faith-based community groups are eligible to compete for federal financial support).

- A private right of action is consistent with the underlying purpose of the statute; and
- A federal right of action would impinge on an area of law traditionally occupied by the states.[49]

Moreover, the Supreme Court will not anticipate a constitutional question or decide a case on constitutional grounds if there is some other basis for resolving the dispute. When an act of Congress is questioned, the Court attempts to "ascertain whether a construction of the statute is fairly possible by which the question may be avoided."[50] In applying appropriate principles of law to specific cases, the Court generally follows the doctrine of *stare decisis* (abide by decided cases), and thus relies on precedents established in previous decisions. On occasion, however, the Court overrules a prior opinion.[51]

Procedures vary somewhat by type of suit and jurisdiction, but a plaintiff typically initiates a suit by filing a complaint with the appropriate court clerk. After a period of discovery when evidence is gathered, the defendant may submit a motion to dismiss, arguing that the plaintiff failed to state a legal claim or that the claim was barred by the applicable statute of limitations. Furthermore, either party may request summary judgment, noting that facts of the case are not in dispute and that the party is entitled to judgment based on applicable law. If summary judgment is not granted, the plaintiff's case then is presented. Thereafter, a *directed verdict* (state trials) or *judgment as a matter of law* (federal trials) may be awarded if the plaintiff fails to establish a legal violation or if the defendant is unsuccessful in identifying a proper defense. When a directed verdict is not granted, the defendant's case is then presented, followed by closing arguments and jury instructions.

In cases argued before a judge, the trial court holds a hearing to make findings of fact based on the evidence presented, and then applies legal principles to those facts in rendering a judgment. If the case involves a jury trial, then the jury renders a verdict, identifying the prevailing party and appropriate awards. Either party may file a motion for a *judgment notwithstanding the verdict* if the party believes that the jury made an error as a matter of law. Also, either party may file a *motion for a new trial*, alleging that proper procedures were not followed, or appeal the decision to a higher court. Figure 1.1 displays the steps (civil procedure) that typically are followed at the trial court level.

Success in court is determined by the party's ability to persuade a judge or jury that the action it has taken is either allowed or required by law. Its persuasive ability is limited by the availability of creditable, admissible evidence. Notwithstanding the acceptance of a wide range of documentation and testimony, parties should not

---

[49]Cort v. Ash, 422 U.S. 66, 78 (1975).

[50]Crowell v. Benson, 285 U.S. 22, 62 (1932).

[51]For example, in 1954 the Supreme Court in Brown v. Bd. of Educ., 347 U.S. 483 (1954), repudiated the long-accepted standard of separate but equal as was supported in Plessy v. Ferguson, 163 U.S. 537 (1896), and concluded that separate schools for different racial groups were inherently unequal.

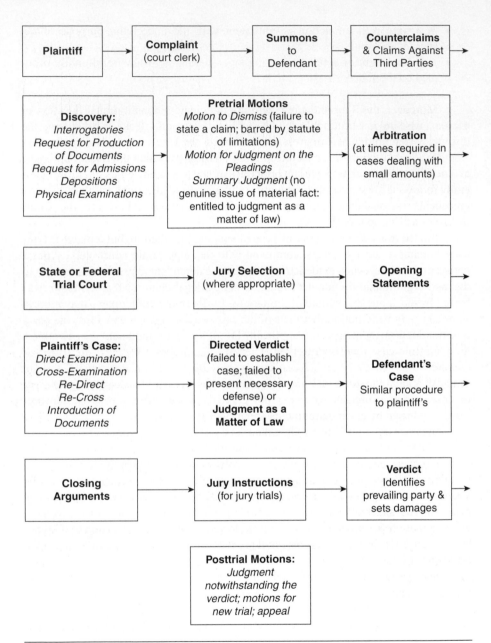

FIGURE 1.1   *Civil Procedure*

knowingly present evidence that is *incompetent* (i.e., testifying on a matter for which knowledge or expertise is lacking), *immaterial* (i.e., evidence to prove or disprove a fact that is uncontested), *irrelevant* (i.e., evidence that fails to clarify or be related to the fact or issue in dispute), or *unduly repetitious* (i.e., evidence that adds nothing new and is unnecessarily redundant).

Following a trial court decision or jury verdict, each party then must make the decision whether it is in its best interest to appeal, given the allocation of time and resources. If the original ruling is appealed, the appellate court must accept the trial court's findings of fact unless they are clearly erroneous. The appeals court reviews the written record of the evidence but does not hold a hearing for witnesses to be questioned. The appellate court may accept the trial court's findings of fact but disagree with the conclusions of law. In such instances, the case is usually remanded to the trial court for reconsideration in light of the appropriate legal principles enunciated by the appeals court.

In addition to individual suits,[52] education cases often involve class-action suits brought on behalf of all similarly situated individuals. To be certified as a class action, the suit must satisfy four rules of civil procedure:

- Numerosity—there must be a large enough number of plaintiffs that individual suits are impracticable;
- Commonality—the members of the class must have claims that include common questions of fact or law;
- Typicality—the claims of the class representatives who are named plaintiffs must be typical of the claims of other class members; and
- Adequacy of representation—the class representatives must fairly and adequately protect the interests of the entire class.[53]

If a suit is not properly certified as a class action, and the circumstances of the original plaintiff change (e.g., a student graduates from school before a judgment is rendered), the court may dismiss the suit as moot because the plaintiff is no longer being injured by the contested practice.

Various remedies are available through court action. In some suits, a court-ordered injunction is sought to compel school officials to cease a particular action or to remove restraints they have imposed on protected freedoms. For a court to issue a preliminary injunction, evidence must indicate that the complainant would likely prevail in a trial on the merits of the case. Judicial relief can take the form of a declaration that specific rights must be respected. In addition, courts can order personal remedies, such as reinstatement and removal of material from school records. Courts

---

[52]Most educational litigation involves civil suits, initiated by individuals alleging injury by another private party. Civil suits often involve claims for damages or requests for specific conduct to cease because it impairs the individual's protected rights. In contrast, criminal suits are brought on behalf of society to punish an individual for committing a crime, such as violating compulsory school attendance laws or selling drugs on school grounds.

[53]Mary Kay Kane, *Civil Procedure* (St. Paul, MN: West, 1979), pp. 226–237.

also may award damages and attorneys' fees to compensate individuals for the deprivation of their rights, and under certain circumstances require the payment of punitive damages by state officials if their conduct represents a willful or reckless disregard of protected rights.

In interpreting constitutional and statutory provisions, courts have developed various criteria to evaluate whether the law has been violated.[54] These judicially created standards or "tests" are extremely important and in some instances appear to go beyond the original intent of the constitutional or statutory provision in question. Judicial standards are continually evolving and being refined by courts. The judiciary thus occupies a powerful position in shaping the law through its interpretive powers.

Courts, however, will not intervene in a school-related controversy if the dispute can be settled in a legislative or administrative forum. The Supreme Court has emphasized that in situations involving "persistent and difficult questions of educational policies," the judiciary's "lack of specialized knowledge and experience counsels against premature interference with the informed judgments made at the state and local levels."[55] All state educational systems provide some type of administrative appeals procedure for aggrieved individuals to use in disputes involving internal school operations. Many school controversies never reach the courts because they are settled in these administrative forums. Under most circumstances, courts require such administrative appeals to be exhausted before court action is brought.

In evaluating the impact of case law, it is important to keep in mind that a judicial ruling applies as precedent within the geographical jurisdiction of the court delivering the opinion. It is possible for two state supreme courts or two federal courts to render conflicting decisions on an issue; nonetheless, such decisions are binding in their respective jurisdictions. Only decisions of the United States Supreme Court have national application.

State Courts

State courts are established pursuant to state constitutional provisions, and the structure of judicial systems varies among states. In contrast to federal courts, which have only those powers granted by the United States Constitution, state courts can review most types of controversies unless restricted by state law. State judicial systems usually include trial courts of general jurisdiction, courts of special jurisdiction, and appellate courts. All states have a court of last resort, and decisions rendered by state high courts can be appealed to the United States Supreme Court.

In most states, the court of last resort is called the supreme court or supreme judicial court. However, in New York and Maryland the highest court is the Court of Appeals, and in West Virginia it is the Supreme Court of Appeals. Courts occupying

---

[54]*See, e.g.,* Macy v. Hopkins County Bd. of Edu., 484 F.3d 357 (6th Cir. 2007) (having to decide between the "motivating factor" test and the "sole factor" test when determining whether employment discrimination was due to employee's disability), *cert. denied*, 128 S. Ct. 201 (2007).

[55]San Antonio Indep. Sch. Dist. v. Rodriguez, 411 U.S. 1, 42 (1973).

the next level in the state judicial system usually are referred to as appeals courts or superior courts. State trial courts of general jurisdiction often are called district or circuit courts, but in New York, trial courts are referred to as supreme courts of their respective counties. The most common special jurisdiction courts are juvenile, probate, domestic relations, and small claims. State judges are either elected by the voters or appointed by the governor.

Although a significant amount of public school cases involve federal law and federal courts, state courts play a particularly important role regarding areas such as the interpretation of state regulations, contracts, torts, school finance, and voucher plans, where state rather than federal constitutions and statutes are typically involved. In such matters, state high courts generally have the final say as to the permissibility of applicable state and school district policies and practices.

Federal Courts

Article III, Section I, of the United States Constitution establishes the Supreme Court and authorizes Congress to create other federal courts as necessary. The federal court system contains courts of special jurisdiction such as the claims court, tax court, and court of international trade. There are three levels of federal courts of general jurisdiction: district courts, circuit courts of appeal, and the Supreme Court. The number of federal district courts in a state is based on population. Each state has at least one federal district court; many states have two or three; and California, New York, and Texas have four each. Judgments at the district court level are usually presided over by one judge.

On the federal appeals level, the nation is divided into 12 geographic circuits, each with its own federal circuit court of appeals.[56] A thirteenth federal circuit court has national jurisdiction to hear appeals regarding specific claims (e.g., customs; copyrights, patents, and trademarks; international trade). Federal circuit courts have from 3 to 15 judges, depending on the workload of the circuit. Most circuit decisions are rendered by a panel of the court (three judges), but in some instances the entire court (en banc) will rehear a case. Although a federal circuit court decision is binding only in the states within that circuit, such decisions often influence other appellate courts when dealing with similar questions. The jurisdiction of the federal circuits is as follows:

- First: Maine, Massachusetts, New Hampshire, Rhode Island, and Puerto Rico
- Second: Connecticut, New York, and Vermont
- Third: Delaware, New Jersey, Pennsylvania, and the Virgin Islands
- Fourth: Maryland, North Carolina, South Carolina, Virginia, and West Virginia
- Fifth: Louisiana, Mississippi, Texas, and the Canal Zone
- Sixth: Kentucky, Michigan, Ohio, and Tennessee
- Seventh: Illinois, Indiana, and Wisconsin

[56]In 1981, the Fifth Circuit was divided into the Fifth and Eleventh Circuits.

- Eighth: Arkansas, Iowa, Minnesota, Missouri, Nebraska, North Dakota, and South Dakota
- Ninth: Alaska, Arizona, California, Idaho, Hawaii, Montana, Nevada, Oregon, Washington, and Guam
- Tenth: Colorado, Kansas, New Mexico, Oklahoma, Utah, and Wyoming
- Eleventh: Alabama, Florida, and Georgia
- D.C.: Washington, D.C.[57]
- Federal: National jurisdiction on specific claims

The United States Supreme Court is, of course, the highest court in the nation, beyond which there is no appeal. The Supreme Court has the ultimate authority in interpreting federal constitutional guarantees.[58] If the Supreme Court finds a specific practice unconstitutional (e.g., intentional school segregation), this judicial mandate applies nationwide. If the Court, however, concludes that a given activity does not impair federal constitutional guarantees (e.g., corporal punishment in public schools), states and local school boards retain discretion in placing restrictions on the activity. In the latter instances, legal requirements will vary across jurisdictions.

As noted previously, if the judiciary interprets a statutory enactment contrary to legislative intent, the law can be amended to clarify its purpose. Congress has done so with a number of civil rights laws in response to Supreme Court rulings. However, the legislative branch does not have this discretion in connection with constitutional interpretations. If the Supreme Court rules that a federal law conflicts with its interpretation of the United States Constitution, the law is invalidated. If Congress persists in its desire for change, a constitutional amendment is required.

The Supreme Court has original jurisdiction in cases in which a state is a party or that involve federal ambassadors and other public ministers. The Court has appellate jurisdiction in other cases arising under the Constitution or federal laws or entailing disputes between states or parties residing in different states.[59] The Supreme Court disposes of approximately 5,000 cases a year, but renders a written opinion on the merits in less than 5 percent of these cases. The Court often concludes that the topic of a case is not appropriate or of sufficient significance to warrant Supreme Court review. It requires concurrence of at least four justices for a case to be accepted, and denial of review (*certiorari*) does not infer agreement with the lower court's decision. Since the Supreme Court has authority to determine which cases it will hear, lower courts are left to resolve many issues. Accordingly, precedents regarding some school controversies must be gleaned from federal circuit courts or state supreme courts and may differ from one jurisdiction to another.

At times, an individual need not exhaust state administrative appeals before initiating a federal suit if the abridgment of a federally protected right is involved;

---

[57]Washington, D.C. has its own federal district court and circuit court of appeals; only federal laws apply in this jurisdiction.

[58]*See* Marbury v. Madison, 5 U.S. (1 Cranch) 137 (1803).

[59]*See* text accompanying notes 203–209, Chapter 11, for a discussion of Eleventh Amendment restrictions on federal lawsuits brought by citizens against the state.

however, some federal laws specify administrative procedures that must be pursued before commencing court action (e.g., Individuals with Disabilities Education Act). Suits involving federal issues also may be heard by state courts, and the United States Supreme Court may review the interpretation of federal rights by the state judiciary. Individuals have a choice whether to initiate a federal or state suit in these circumstances, but they cannot relitigate an issue in federal court if they have been denied relief in state court.

Judicial Trends

Traditionally, the federal judiciary did not address educational concerns; fewer than 300 cases involving education had been initiated in federal courts prior to 1954.[60] However, starting with the landmark desegregation decision, *Brown v. Board of Education of Topeka* in 1954,[61] federal courts assumed a significant role in resolving educational controversies. At times, courts have taken control of school district operations and have been reluctant to return authority to school boards and educators. By 1970, litigation was clearly viewed as an important tool to influence social policies, and more legal challenges to school practices were initiated in the 1970s than had been in the preceding seven decades combined.[62] Since the 1960s, courts have addressed nearly every facet of the educational enterprise. Much of this judicial intervention has involved the protection of individual rights and the attainment of equity for minority groups.

There has been a notable shift in the posture of the federal judiciary during the past two decades. In the 1960s and early 1970s, federal courts expanded constitutional protections afforded to individuals in school settings, but since the 1980s the federal judiciary has exhibited more deference to the decisions of the legislative and executive branches and greater reluctance to extend the scope of civil rights. Judicial deference to policy makers nurtures diverse standards across states and local school districts. When the Supreme Court strikes down a practice under the Constitution, standards become more uniform nationally, but when the Court defers to local boards, standards vary, reflecting local perspectives.

The Rehnquist Court and Roberts Court, with their strong federalism stance, are redefining the balance of power between the federal government and states. In sharply divided decisions, the Supreme Court has strengthened states' sovereign immunity by precluding federal lawsuits against states unless Congress has abrogated state immunity through legislation enacted to enforce the Fourteenth Amendment. Such congressional intent, however, must be explicit in the federal legislation and enacted to protect a suspect class from state action. For example, the Court has

---

[60]John Hogan, *The Schools, the Courts, and the Public In*terest (Lexington, MA: D.C. Heath, 1985), p. 11.

[61]347 U.S. 483 (1954). *See also* United States v. W. Carroll Parish Sch. Dist., 477 F. Supp. 2d 759 (W.D. La. 2007) (determining that Court supervision will be retained until the vestiges of prior race discrimination have been eliminated).

[62]William Bennett, "Excessive Legalization in Education," *Chicago Daily Law Bulletin* (February 22, 1988), p. 2.

held that Congress exceeded its authority in imposing liability on states under the Age Discrimination in Employment Act[63] and the Americans with Disabilities Act.[64] These acts did not involve a suspect class nor were they enacted to address irrational employment discrimination by states. The new federalism limits suits against states, but school districts will not benefit from the immunity unless they are considered an arm of the state for Eleventh Amendment purposes.[65]

Although the debate will likely continue over whether courts have the competence to play a key role in shaping educational policies and whether it is legitimate for courts to play such a role, without question courts do influence school policies. Despite some deceleration in federal litigation, the volume of school cases is still substantial, far outstripping school litigation in any other nation.

Conclusion

Public schools in the United States are governed by a complex body of regulations that are grounded in constitutional provisions, statutory enactments, agency regulations, and court decisions. Since the mid-twentieth century, legislation relating to schools has increased significantly in both volume and complexity, and courts have played an important role in interpreting statutory and constitutional provisions. Although rules made at any level must be consistent with higher authority, administrators and teachers retain considerable latitude in establishing rules and procedures within their specific jurisdictions. As long as educators act reasonably and do not impair the protected rights of others, their actions will be upheld if challenged in court.

School personnel, however, cannot plead "ignorance of the law" as a valid defense for illegal actions.[66] Thus, educators should be aware of the constraints placed on their rule-making prerogatives by school board policies and federal and state constitutional and statutory provisions. Subsequent chapters of this book clarify the major legal principles affecting teachers and students in their daily school activities.

---

[63]Kimel v. Fla. Bd. of Regents, 528 U.S. 62 (2000).

[64]Bd. of Trs. v. Garrett, 531 U.S. 356 (2001).

[65]*See* text accompanying note 203, Chapter 11. *See, e.g.*, Crenshaw v. Eudora Sch. Dist., 208 S.W.3d 206 (Ark. 2006) (finding that school districts were political subdivisions of the state, not arms of the state, and thus were not entitled to Eleventh Amendment immunity in a case dealing with the rights of noncertified employees to receive overtime compensation under the Fair Labor Standards Act).

[66]*See* Wood v. Strickland, 420 U.S. 308 (1975).

2

Church/State Relations

Efforts to identify the appropriate relationship between government and religion have generated substantial controversy in our nation, and since the mid-twentieth century, schools have provided the battleground for some of the most volatile disputes. This chapter provides an overview of the constitutional framework, the evolution of legal activity, and the current status of church/state relations involving education.

Constitutional Framework

The First Amendment to the United States Constitution stipulates in part that "Congress shall make no law respecting an establishment of religion or prohibiting the free exercise thereof." Although this amendment was directed toward the *federal* government, the Fourteenth Amendment, adopted in 1868, specifically placed restrictions on *state* action impairing personal rights. In the twentieth century, the Supreme Court recognized that the fundamental concept of "liberty" embodied in the Fourteenth Amendment incorporates First Amendment guarantees and safeguards these rights against state interference.[1] Since education is primarily a state function, most church/state controversies involving schools have been initiated through the Fourteenth Amendment.

Constitutional scholars continue to debate whether the framers of the religion clauses intended to sever civil and sectarian affairs or merely to prohibit religious discrimination and governmental promotion of a particular sect, but the ultimate responsibility for interpreting the restrictions imposed by the First Amendment on governmental action resides with the United States Supreme Court. Judicial standards to assess claims under the Establishment and Free Exercise Clauses and their interaction with free speech guarantees are still evolving.

In the first major Establishment Clause decision, *Everson v. Board of Education*, the Supreme Court in 1947 reviewed the history of the First Amendment and

---

[1]*See* Cantwell v. Connecticut, 310 U.S. 296, 303 (1940); Gitlow v. New York, 268 U.S. 652, 666 (1925).

concluded that the Establishment Clause (and its Fourteenth Amendment application to states) means:

> Neither a state nor the Federal Government can set up a church. Neither can pass laws which aid one religion, aid all religions, or prefer one religion over another. . . . In the words of Jefferson, the clause against establishment of religion by law was intended to erect "a wall of separation between church and state."[2]

Thomas Jefferson's "wall of separation" metaphor[3] was used widely by the federal judiciary for more than 30 years following *Everson*, even though this phrase does not appear in the First Amendment. During this period, the Establishment Clause seemed to be accorded greater weight than the Free Exercise Clause, with courts often supporting the notion that church/state "separation must be complete and unequivocal."[4]

In a 1971 case, *Lemon v. Kurtzman*, the Supreme Court articulated a tripartite test to assess Establishment Clause claims.[5] To withstand scrutiny under this test, usually referred to as the *Lemon* test, governmental action must (1) have a secular purpose, (2) have a primary effect that neither advances nor impedes religion, and (3) avoid excessive governmental entanglement with religion. This three-part test was used consistently in Establishment Clause cases involving school issues until 1992.[6] However, Supreme Court justices increasingly have voiced dissatisfaction with this test,[7] and few recent Supreme Court Establishment Clause rulings have relied solely on *Lemon*. Support for church/state separation seems to be waning, even in school cases where separationist doctrine has been the strongest.

Some Supreme Court justices favor an *endorsement* standard under which governmental action will be struck down if an objective observer would view it as having the purpose or effect of endorsing or disapproving religion,[8] and on occasion the Supreme Court has applied a *coercion* test, which requires direct or indirect governmental

---

[2]330 U.S. 1, 15-16 (1947) (quoting Reynolds v. United States, 98 U.S. 145, 164 (1878)).

[3]This metaphor is traced to a statement made by Thomas Jefferson in 1802 in a letter refusing a Baptist association's request for a day to be established for fasting and prayer in thanksgiving for the nation's welfare. *See* Robert Healey, *Jefferson on Religion in Public Education* (New Haven, CT: Yale University Press, 1962), pp. 128–140.

[4]Zorach v. Clauson, 343 U.S. 306, 312 (1952). *See also* Sch. Dist. of Abington Twp. v. Schempp, 374 U.S. 203, 219–220 (1963).

[5]403 U.S. 602 (1971). *See also* Walz v. Tax Comm'n, 397 U.S. 664 (1970) (assessing "excessive entanglement" for the first time in rejecting an Establishment Clause challenge to the tax exempt status of church property).

[6]*See* Lee v. Weisman, 505 U.S. 577 (1992); *infra* text accompanying note 21. Although the Supreme Court applied *Lemon* in school cases for more than two decades, it abandoned *Lemon* in the early 1980s in a non-school Establishment Clause case. *See* Marsh v. Chambers, 463 U.S. 783 (1983) (relying on tradition to uphold the use of public funds to pay a chaplain to open state legislative sessions with a prayer).

[7]*See* Lamb's Chapel v. Ctr. Moriches Union Free Sch. Dist., 508 U.S. 384, 398 (1993) (Scalia, J., concurring) (comparing the *Lemon* standard to a "ghoul" that rises from the dead "after being repeatedly killed and buried").

[8]*See, e.g.*, County of Allegheny v. ACLU, 492 U.S. 573 (1989); *infra* text accompanying note 48.

coercion on individuals to profess a faith.[9] Even in recent decisions where the Supreme Court has still given lip service to the more stringent *Lemon* test, the excessive entanglement prong of the test has been folded into a consideration of practices' primary effects; the phrase "excessive entanglement" has been noticeably absent in Supreme Court opinions involving Establishment Clause issues. Some lower courts are attempting to cover all bases by reviewing government action under multiple standards, including the *Lemon* test, the endorsement standard, and the coercion test (see Figure 2.1).[10]

Whereas the Establishment Clause is used primarily to challenge governmental advancement of religion, lawsuits under the Free Exercise Clause usually focus on secular (nonreligious) government regulations alleged to have a coercive effect on religious practices. In establishment cases, the legality of the governmental action itself is at issue, but in free exercise claims, individuals often accept the secular nature of the government regulation but assert that it burdens their religious exercise.

To evaluate free exercise claims, the judiciary traditionally applied a balancing test including an assessment of whether practices dictated by a sincere and legitimate religious belief were impeded by the governmental action, and if so, to what extent. If such an impairment was substantiated, the judiciary then evaluated whether the government action served a compelling interest justifying the burden imposed on the exercise of religious beliefs. Even with such a compelling interest, the judiciary still required the government to attain its objectives through the means least burdensome on free exercise rights.

In the most significant school case involving a free exercise claim, *Wisconsin v. Yoder*, the Supreme Court exempted Amish children from compulsory school

The government actions or practices will violate the Establishment Clause if they:	
<ul><li>have a religious (sectarian) purpose</li><li>advance or impede religion</li><li>create excessive government entanglement with religion</li></ul>	*Lemon Test*
<ul><li>have a purpose or effect of endorsing or disapproving religion</li></ul>	*Endorsement Test*
<ul><li>place direct or indirect government coercion on individuals to profess a faith</li></ul>	*Coercion Test*

FIGURE 2.1 *Judicial Standards to Evaluate Challenged Government Action under the Establishment Clause*

[9]*See Weisman*, 505 U.S. 577.

[10]*See, e.g.,* Newdow v. U.S. Congress, 328 F.3d 466 (9th Cir. 2002); Doe v. Beaumont Indep. Sch. Dist., 240 F.3d 462 (5th Cir. 2001); Koenick v. Felton, 190 F.3d 259 (4th Cir. 1999); Stark v. Indep. Sch. Dist. No. 640, 123 F.3d 1068 (8th Cir. 1997); Hsu v. Roslyn Union Free Sch. Dist. No. 3, 85 F.3d 839 (2d Cir. 1996).

attendance upon successful completion of eighth grade.[11] Although noting that the assurance of an educated citizenry ranks at the pinnacle of state functions, the Court nonetheless concluded that parents' rights to practice their legitimate religious beliefs outweighed the state's interest in mandating two additional years of formal schooling for Amish youth. The Court declared that "a state's interest in universal education, however highly we rank it, is not totally free from a balancing process when it impinges on fundamental rights and interests."[12] The Court cautioned, however, that its ruling was limited to the Amish who offer a structured vocational program to prepare their youth for a cloistered agrarian community rather than mainstream American society.

In a 1990 decision, the Supreme Court modified this balancing test, ruling that the government does not have to demonstrate a compelling interest to defend a criminal law that burdens the free exercise of religious beliefs. The case was initiated by two employees who had been fired for misconduct and subsequently denied unemployment benefits because they ingested peyote at a religious ceremony of the Native American Church. Distinguishing this case from *Yoder*, which involved a combination of free exercise rights and parental rights, the Court majority concluded that without such a "hybrid" situation, individuals cannot rely on the Free Exercise Clause to be excused from complying with a valid criminal law prohibiting specific conduct.[13]

Courts not only apply different criteria to assess claims under the Free Exercise and Establishment Clauses, they also impose different remedies for violations of the two clauses. If government activity abridges the Establishment Clause, the unconstitutional activity must cease. If government action is found to impair the Free Exercise Clause, accommodations to enable individuals to practice their religious beliefs may be required, but the secular policy or program would not have to be eliminated.

Troublesome church/state controversies involve competing claims under the Free Exercise and Establishment Clauses because both "are cast in absolute terms, and either of which, if expanded to a logical extreme, would tend to clash with the other."[14] The controversies become even more complex when Free Speech Clause

---

[11]406 U.S. 205 (1972).

[12]*Id.* at 214.

[13]Employment Div. v. Smith, 494 U.S. 872 (1990). Responding to this ruling, in 1993 Congress enacted the Religious Freedom Restoration Act, 42 U.S.C. § 2000bb, to reinstate the compelling interest requirement, even if the government burden results from a rule of general applicability. But the Supreme Court subsequently invalidated this law because it overstepped congressional authority by proscribing state conduct beyond the reach of the Fourteenth Amendment. *See* City of Boerne v. Flores, 521 U.S. 507 (1997). Congress again responded in 2000 by enacting under its spending powers the more narrowly drawn Religious Land Use and Institutionalized Persons Act (RLUIPA), requiring a compelling governmental interest for states to impose a substantial burden on institutionalized persons' religious exercise, 42 U.S.C. § 2000cc et seq. (2007). *See* Cutter v. Wilkinson, 544 U.S. 709 (2005) (rejecting an Establishment Clause challenge to RLUIPA), *on remand,* 423 F.3d 579 (6th Cir. 2005) (finding RLUIPA to be a permissible Spending Clause law that is not barred by the Tenth Amendment).

[14]Walz v. Tax Comm'n, 397 U.S. 664, 668–669 (1970).

protections are implicated. Accommodations to free exercise and free speech rights can be interpreted as advancing religion in violation of the Establishment Clause, but overzealous efforts to guard against state sponsorship of religion can impinge on protections under the Free Exercise and Free Speech Clauses. This tension among First Amendment guarantees has complicated the judiciary's task in assessing claims regarding the role of religion in public schools and government relations with sectarian schools.

Religious Influences in Public Schools

From colonial days until the mid-twentieth century, Protestant materials and observances were prevalent in many public schools. In two precedent-setting decisions in the early 1960s, the Supreme Court prohibited public schools from sponsoring daily prayer and Bible reading, concluding that such activities advance religion in violation of the Establishment Clause.[15] The Court reasoned that the students' voluntary participation in the religious activities was irrelevant. The fact that daily devotional activities were conducted under the auspices of the public school was sufficient to abridge the First Amendment.

In a number of subsequent decisions, the Supreme Court affirmed without an opinion or declined to review decisions in which federal appellate courts struck down state laws calling for voluntary spoken prayer in public schools, a school board's attempt to permit student-led prayers in school assemblies, and state-condoned devotional activities initiated by teachers.[16] The courts found little constitutional distinction between these practices and the state-imposed devotionals that the Supreme Court barred under the Establishment Clause in the early 1960s. However, these rulings have not resolved some issues pertaining to religious influences in public education. Is the constitutional violation lessened if students rather than teachers initiate the devotional activities? If religious observances are occasional rather than daily, is the threat of an Establishment Clause impairment reduced? Can religious speech be distinguished from other types of speech in applying restrictions?

Silent Prayer Statutes

Students have a free exercise right to engage in *private* devotional activities in public schools as long as they do not interfere with regular school activities. Indeed, it would

---

[15]Sch. Dist. of Abington Twp. v. Schempp, 374 U.S. 203 (1963); Engel v. Vitale, 370 U.S. 421 (1962).

[16]*See* Ingebretsen v. Jackson Pub. Sch. Dist., 88 F.3d 274 (5th Cir. 1996) (Mississippi law authorizing student-initiated prayer); Jaffree v. Bd. of Sch. Comm'rs, 705 F.2d 1526 (11th Cir. 1983) (teacher-initiated devotional activities); Jaffree v. Wallace, 705 F.2d 1526 (11th Cir. 1983), *aff'd mem. in part*, 466 U.S. 924 (1984) (Alabama voluntary prayer law); Karen B. v. Treen, 653 F.2d 897 (5th Cir. 1981), *aff'd mem.*, 455 U.S. 913 (1982) (Louisiana voluntary prayer law); Collins v. Chandler Unified Sch. Dist., 644 F.2d 759 (9th Cir. 1981) (student-led prayers in school assemblies).

be difficult to monitor whether students were engaging in silent prayer. Controversies have focused on state laws or school board policies that condone silent devotionals, thus placing the stamp of public school approval on such activities.

In 1985, the Supreme Court rendered its first and only opinion to date on this issue in *Wallace v. Jaffree*, invalidating a 1981 Alabama silent prayer law under the Establishment Clause.[17] Since a 1978 Alabama law already authorized a period of silent meditation in public schools, the Court majority concluded that the only logical reason for adding the phrase "or voluntary prayer" in the 1981 amendment was to encourage students to pray. But the Court indicated that laws calling for silent meditation or prayer in public schools without a legislative intent to impose prayer might withstand scrutiny under the Establishment Clause.

Therefore, the constitutionality of laws authorizing a moment of silence for prayer or meditation in public schools, which currently are on the books in a majority of the states, remains to be resolved on a case-by-case basis, and courts have rejected most recent challenges to such laws. For example, a high school teacher who was fired for refusing to comply with Georgia's law challenged the constitutionality of the statute that requires each public school teacher to conduct a minute of quiet reflection at the opening of the school day. In upholding the statute, the appeals court concluded that the provision had the secular purpose of providing an opportunity for pupils to reflect on the upcoming day.[18]

The Fourth Circuit also upheld a Virginia silent prayer statute as being neutral toward religion since students were not encouraged to pray during the moment of silence. The contested law stipulates that each school board shall establish the daily observance of one minute of silence in all classrooms so that pupils may "meditate, pray, or engage in other silent activity which does not interfere with, distract, or impede other pupils in the . . . exercise of individual choice."[19] The appeals court reasoned that the law provides a neutral medium—silence—during which students can be involved in sectarian or secular activities. Unlike the Alabama law struck down in *Jaffree*, which was clearly intended to return prayer to public schools, the appeals court reasoned that Virginia's law was enacted to provide time for quiet reflection—a good management strategy to settle students.

[17]705 F.2d 1526 (11th Cir. 1983), *aff'd*, 472 U.S. 38 (1985). Although several state practices were contested in this case, the Supreme Court addressed only the silent prayer statute. *See supra* note 16 for the disposition of the other issues.

[18]Bown v. Gwinnett County Sch. Dist., 112 F.3d 1464 (11th Cir. 1997). *See also* the No Child Left Behind (NCLB) Act of 2001, 20 U.S.C. § 6061 (2007) (specifying that no federal funds can be appropriated under the act to be used for policies that prevent voluntary prayer and meditation in public schools).

[19]Brown v. Gilmore, 258 F.3d 265, 270 (4th Cir. 2001) (quoting Va. Code Ann. § 22.1-203). *See also* Croft v. Perry, No. 3:06-CV-434-M, 2008 U.S. Dist. LEXIS 369 (N.D. Tex. Jan. 2, 2008) (upholding a Texas law requiring each school to observe a minute of silence for students to "reflect, pray, meditate, or engage in any other silent activity that is not likely to interfere with or distract another student," as satisfying the *Lemon* test). *But see* Sherman v. Twp. High Sch. Dist. 214, No. 07-6048, 2007 U.S. Dist. LEXIS 84440 (N.D. Ill. Nov. 15, 2007) (issuing a preliminary injunction prohibiting a school district from implementing an Illinois law that requires all public schools to observe a moment of silence; finding claims that the law is unconstitutionally vague and violates the Establishment Clause, likely to succeed on their merits).

School-Sponsored versus Private Devotionals

Cases have focused primarily on devotionals during the school day or in school-sponsored events,[20] and the most controversial issues currently revolve around whether the Establishment Clause concerns are eliminated if students initiate and lead such devotionals. In short, what constitutes private religious expression in the public school context that does not trigger Establishment Clause restrictions? Federal courts have provided some mixed signals regarding student-led graduation devotionals and prayers in other school events.

Weisman and Its Progeny. The Supreme Court's seminal 1992 decision, *Lee v. Weisman*, provided the impetus for a wave of legislative activity pressing the limits of the Establishment Clause. In this five-to-four decision, the Supreme Court held that a Rhode Island school district's policy, which permitted principals to invite clergy members to deliver invocations and benedictions at middle and high school graduation ceremonies, abridged the Establishment Clause.[21] The Court majority reasoned that the policy had a coercive effect; students felt peer pressure to participate in the devotionals that were conducted at the school-sponsored graduation ceremony. The Court was not persuaded that the voluntary nature of graduation exercises eliminated the constitutional infraction; students should not have to make a choice between attending their graduation ceremony and respecting their religious convictions.

Rather than reducing devotional activities in public school graduations, the Supreme Court's decision had the opposite impact. Negative reactions to this ruling resulted in school authorities and students finding creative strategies to include prayers in graduation ceremonies.

In some districts, baccalaureate services, which had not been held for many years, were reinstated. To pass constitutional scrutiny, such baccalaureates cannot be sponsored by the public school, but students, churches, or other groups can rent space from the school district to conduct the religious services.[22] In a Wyoming case, the federal district court ruled that students could rent the high school gym for a baccalaureate program because the event was not school sponsored, even though the school band performed and the district's graduation announcements mentioned the baccalaureate program.[23]

---

[20]In addition, prayers at school board meetings have been controversial. Striking down such prayers, *see* Doe v. Tangipahoa Parish Sch. Bd., 473 F.3d 188 (5th Cir. 2006), *vacated en banc with instructions to dismiss,* 494 F.3d 494 (5th Cir. 2007) (finding that those challenging the invocations did not have standing to bring suit); Coles v. Cleveland Bd. of Educ., 171 F.3d 369 (6th Cir. 1999).

[21]505 U.S. 577 (1992). Although the majority opinion applied a coercion test, four of the justices who joined the majority also signed concurring opinions in which they asserted that coercion would be sufficient to abridge the Establishment Clause, but it is not a necessary prerequisite. *Weisman,* 505 U.S. at 599 (Blackmun, J., joined by Stevens & O'Connor, J. J., concurring); 505 U.S. at 609 (Souter, J., joined by Stevens & O'Connor, J. J., concurring).

[22]*See, e.g.,* Verbena United Methodist Church v. Chilton County Bd. of Educ., 765 F. Supp. 704 (M.D. Ala. 1991) (holding that a school board must take all measures reasonably necessary to disassociate itself from a baccalaureate service sponsored by religious organizations and held in space rented from the school district).

[23]*See* Shumway v. Albany County Sch. Dist. No. One, 826 F. Supp. 1320 (D. Wyo. 1993).

Because of the prohibition on *school-sponsored* religious activities, most post-*Weisman* controversies have involved *student-led* devotionals. In some school districts the graduation ceremony has been designated a forum for student expression, so students' messages (including religious references) are not subject to review and do not bear the stamp of school approval. The Ninth Circuit upheld an Idaho school district's policy that prohibited school authorities from censoring students' graduation speeches and allowed student speakers (chosen by academic standing) to select a poem, reading, song, prayer, or any other presentation of their choice.[24] Finding the ceremony a forum for student expression, the court reasoned that the student speakers were selected based on secular criteria and were not advised to include devotionals in their remarks.

However, in another Ninth Circuit case, the appeals court upheld a California school district's refusal to allow students to deliver their proselytizing graduation speeches that had been submitted to the school principal for review in accordance with school policy. Unlike the Idaho case, the California school district had a clear policy retaining school control of the graduation ceremony. Thus, the court found censorship of the proposed religious speeches appropriate to avoid an Establishment Clause violation.[25] The key distinction is whether the school has explicitly created a forum for student expression in the graduation ceremony or has retained control over students' graduation speeches.

Student Elections to Authorize Prayers.   Especially volatile controversies surround having students decide by election to include student-led devotionals in graduation ceremonies and other school activities. The Fifth Circuit upheld the practice of allowing students to vote whether to have nonsectarian graduation prayers selected and delivered by students, reasoning that the student election removed school sponsorship.[26] But the Third and Ninth Circuit appellate courts reached an

---

[24]Doe v. Madison Sch. Dist. No 321, 147 F.3d 832 (9th Cir. 1998), *vacated and remanded en banc*, 177 F.3d 789, 792 (9th Cir. 1999). Although the full appellate court vacated the panel decision because the plaintiff had graduated, the contested policy remained in force. *See also* Doe v. Sch. Dist., 340 F.3d 605 (8th Cir. 2003) (broadly interpreting what constitutes private, rather than school-sponsored, religious expression in finding no Establishment Clause violation in a school board member's unscheduled recitation of the Lord's Prayer in the graduation ceremony); Goluba v. Sch. Dist., 45 F.3d 1035 (7th Cir. 1995) (holding that student-initiated recitation of the Lord's Prayer five minutes before the high school graduation ceremony did not represent the school and thus did not violate an injunction prohibiting school personnel from authorizing, conducting, sponsoring, or intentionally permitting prayers during the graduation ceremony).

[25]Cole v. Oroville Union High Sch. Dist., 228 F.3d 1092 (9th Cir. 2000). *See also* Lassonde v. Pleasanton Unified Sch. Dist., 320 F.3d 979 (9th Cir. 2003) (upholding school in requiring student to remove religiously proselytizing parts of his graduation speech that was part of the school-controlled ceremony; the student could announce that his speech had been involuntarily altered and could make an original version available after the ceremony). For a discussion of students' free expression rights, see Chapter 4.

[26]Jones v. Clear Creek Indep. Sch. Dist., 930 F.2d 416 (5th Cir. 1991), *vacated and remanded*, 505 U.S. 1215 (1992*), on remand*, 977 F.2d 963 (5th Cir. 1992). *See also* Tanford v. Brand, 104 F.3d 982 (7th Cir. 1997) (rejecting a challenge to invocations and benedictions at university commencement, finding no coercion on adult students who have the maturity to choose among competing beliefs).

opposite conclusion, holding that school authorities could not delegate decisions to students that the Establishment Clause forbids school districts from making.[27]

In a 2000 decision, *Santa Fe Independent School District v. Doe*, the Supreme Court found an Establishment Clause violation in a Texas school district's policy authorizing student-led devotionals before public school football games.[28] The controversial policy, and an identical graduation policy, authorized two elections—one to determine whether to have invocations and the second to select the student to deliver them. Revised policies removed the "nonsectarian, nonproselytizing" restriction on the prayers but noted that if judicially enjoined, the prior policies with this restriction would automatically be in effect.[29] The Fifth Circuit reaffirmed its position upholding student-initiated graduation prayers but held that the football game policy abridged the Establishment Clause, noting that such events occur more often, involve a more diverse age span of students, and cannot be justified to solemnize sporting events.

Addressing only the football game policy, the Supreme Court rejected the school district's assertion that having students decide to include invocations at the athletic events and to select a classmate to lead the devotionals removed school sponsorship. The Court majority declared that student-led expression at a school event on school property and representing the student body under the supervision of school personnel could not be considered private speech.[30] Even though the ultimate choice of speakers and content was made by the students, the school authorized the student election in the first place. The degree of school involvement gave the impression that the devotionals at issue represented the school, leading the Court to conclude that the practice entailed both perceived and actual endorsement of religion. The majority reasoned that the current policy had a sham secular purpose and, like previous initiatives in the school district, was intended to promote Christian religious observances in school-related events.[31]

---

[27]ACLU v. Black Horse Pike Reg'l Bd. of Educ., 84 F.3d 1471 (3d Cir. 1996); Harris v. Joint Sch. Dist. No. 241, 41 F.3d 447 (9th Cir.1994), *vacated and remanded with directions to dismiss as moot*, 515 U.S. 1154 (1995). *See also* Comm. for Voluntary Prayer v. Wimberly, 704 A.2d 1199 (D.C. 1997) (striking down a voter initiative that had the clear purpose of fostering prayer in public schools); Ingebretsen v. Jackson Pub. Sch. Dist., 88 F.3d 274 (5th Cir. 1996) (striking down a Mississippi law that allowed student-initiated prayers in all school assemblies, sporting events, commencement ceremonies, and other school-related events as sweeping too broadly by permitting student-led prayers at virtually all school activities. For legal challenges to a similar Alabama law, *see infra* text accompanying note 33.

[28]168 F.3d 806 (5th Cir. 1999), *aff'd*, 530 U.S. 290 (2000).

[29]*Id.*, 168 F.3d at 812–813. The policies were modified to eliminate "prayer" from the titles and to add references to student-led "messages" and "statements" in addition to "invocations."

[30]530 U.S. at 310. The Court emphasized that it is necessary to carefully review the history and context of the challenged action in determining its facial validity. *Id.* at 317.

[31]*Id.* at 307–309. The school district had a history of Christian observances in its schools. Parents initially filed suit in this case in 1995, complaining of numerous proselytizing activities (e.g., teachers promoting Christian revival meetings and chastising children of minority faiths) in addition to the school district's practice of allowing students to read overtly Christian prayers at graduation ceremonies and home football games.

Noting that the purpose of the Bill of Rights is to shield certain subjects from the political process, the Court held that the use of student elections intensifies the lack of representation of minority views, ensuring that they will never be heard. While rejecting the argument that Establishment Clause concerns can be eliminated by delegating decisions to students, the majority emphasized that only state sponsorship of devotionals violates the Establishment Clause; nothing in the Constitution prohibits public school students from voluntarily praying at school.

The *Santa Fe* decision did not settle what distinguishes protected private religious expression from unconstitutional school-sponsored devotionals. Indeed, some post–*Santa Fe* federal appellate rulings represent an expansive stance regarding the reach of the Free Speech Clause in protecting students' private religious expression in public schools. For example, the Eleventh Circuit upheld a Florida school district's policy that authorizes public school seniors to select classmates to give graduation messages and allows the speakers to choose the content, which could be religious.[32] Even though the school district's memo outlining the policy was entitled "Graduation Prayer," the court emphasized that the student elections are not to identify classmates to deliver prayers—the graduation messages are of unspecified content, which may or may not include sectarian material.

In a second Eleventh Circuit ruling, the court lifted the part of an injunction that had prohibited students from publicly expressing religious views in most public school settings in Dekalb County, Alabama.[33] The controversy started over a 1993 Alabama law, enacted in response to the *Weisman* ruling, which permitted nonsectarian, nonproselytizing, student-initiated, voluntary prayers, invocations, and benedictions during school-related events and extracurricular activities. The district court upheld graduation prayers but concluded that the remainder of the law swept too broadly, failing the *Lemon*, endorsement, and coercion standards. But the Eleventh Circuit lifted the part of the injunction prohibiting all student religious expression during school, declaring that the Establishment Clause does not require and the Free Speech Clause does not permit suppression of student-initiated religious expression in public schools or relegating it to whispers.

Although the Supreme Court vacated these appellate decisions and remanded the cases for further consideration in light of *Santa Fe*, the appeals court subsequently reaffirmed both rulings. Distinguishing the Supreme Court's condemnation of school-sponsored student prayer in *Santa Fe*, the Eleventh Circuit held that school censorship of private student religious expression also is unconstitutional and noted that all

[32]Adler v. Duval County Sch. Bd., 174 F.3d 1236 (11th Cir. 1999*), vacated with different results on rehearing en banc,* 206 F.3d 1070 (11th Cir. 2000), *vacated and remanded (for reconsideration in light of Santa Fe v. Doe)*, 531 U.S. 801 (2000), *reinstated on remand,* 250 F.3d 1330 (11th Cir. 2000).

[33]Chandler v. James, 180 F.3d 1254 (11th Cir. 1999), *vacated and remanded (for reconsideration in light of Santa Fe v. Doe)*, 530 U.S. 1256 (2000), *reinstated on remand sub nom.* Chandler v. Siegelman, 230 F.3d 1313 (11th Cir. 2000).

student religious speech in public schools should not be equated with expression *representing* the school.[34]

In light of *Santa Fe* and its progeny, courts will review the legislative history of school district policies to ascertain whether there has been a pattern of efforts to infuse devotionals in the public schools. Student religious expression may be considered private if truly student initiated, but the *Santa Fe* decision casts doubt on the legality of holding student elections to determine that student-led devotionals will be included in school-sponsored activities.

Pledge of Allegiance

More than four-fifths of the states have laws or policies specifying that the Pledge of Allegiance to the American flag will be said in public schools, and many of these provisions were enacted or amended since the terrorist attacks on September 11, 2001.[35] As discussed later, students have a right to opt out of the Pledge based on their religious or philosophical beliefs,[36] but volatile recent controversies have focused on whether the Pledge can be said in public schools *at all*, given the 1954 addition of the phrase "under God."

The Seventh Circuit upheld an Illinois law requiring daily recitation of the Pledge in public schools, as long as students can decline to participate. Regarding the Establishment Clause claim, the appeals court ruled that the "ceremonial deism" in the Pledge "has lost through rote repetition any significant religious content," so the reference to God does not represent religious coercion.[37] A Virginia federal district court reached the same conclusion in rejecting a constitutional challenge to a Virginia law requiring the recitation of the Pledge in public schools, noting that a civic religion has been recognized in our nation.[38] Even though the school district at issue in this case considered recitation of the Pledge in a citizenship reward program, the judge noted that other factors also were considered in making the citizenship awards, so there was no coercion to participate in the Pledge.

[34]*Chandler*, 230 F.3d at 1315. *See also* Prince v. Jacoby, 303 F. 3d 1074 (9th Cir. 2002) (finding a school district guilty of viewpoint discrimination against a student religious club that was not treated like other student clubs in access to school meeting rooms, school supplies, audiovisual equipment, and school vehicles); *infra* text accompanying note 89.

[35]Peyton Cooke, *Pledge of Allegiance Statutes, State by State* (June 19, 2006), available at www.firstamendmentcenter.org/analysis.aspx?id=17035; Jennifer Piscatelli, "Pledge of Allegiance," *StateNotes: Character/Citizenship Education* (Denver: Education Commission of the States, August 2003).

[36]*See* W. Va. State Bd. of Educ. v. Barnette, 319 U.S. 624 (1943); *infra* text accompanying note 116.

[37]Sherman v. Cmty. Consol. Sch. Dist. 21, 980 F.2d 437, 447–448 (7th Cir. 1992) (citing Lynch v. Donnelly, 465 U.S. 668, 716 (1984)).

[38]Myers v. Loudoun County Sch. Bd., 251 F. Supp. 2d 1262, 1267–1270 (E.D. Va. 2003) (rejecting also an Establishment Clause challenge to a state law requiring the motto "In God We Trust" to be displayed in public schools). *See also* Myers v. Loudoun County Sch. Bd., 500 F. Supp. 2d 539 (E.D. Va. 2007) (rejecting the parent's attempt to put ads suggesting vulgar alternatives to the Pledge in school publications and to distribute materials at school criticizing recitation of the Pledge, but upholding the parent's right to distribute materials on the sidewalk in front of the school).

The Ninth Circuit attracted national attention in 2002 when it rejected the "ceremonial deism" justification and declared that saying the Pledge in public schools abridges the Establishment Clause by endorsing a belief in monotheism.[39] The appellate panel applied the *Lemon,* coercion, and endorsement standards in finding an Establishment Clause violation and emphasized that the words "under God" had been inserted in the Pledge to promote religion rather than to advance the legitimate secular goal of encouraging patriotism.

The Supreme Court reversed the Ninth Circuit's decision in 2004 without addressing the constitutional claim in *Elk Grove Unified School District v. Newdow,* which symbolically was rendered on Flag Day exactly 50 years after "under God" was added to the Pledge. The majority reasoned that Newdow lacked standing to challenge his daughter's participation in the Pledge because California law deprives the noncustodial parent of the right to bring suit as "next friend" on behalf of his daughter.[40] Observing that Newdow retained the right to instruct his daughter regarding his religious views, the Court ruled that this right does not extend to curtailing his daughter's exposure to religious beliefs endorsed by her mother. In a subsequent suit, a California federal district court again ruled that the classroom recitation of the Pledge violates the Establishment Clause,[41] so the Supreme Court eventually may have another opportunity to address the substantive issue.

Religious Displays and Holiday Observances

The display of religious documents and the observance of religious holidays in public schools also remain controversial. In 1980, the Supreme Court declined to hear an appeal of a decision allowing religious holiday observances and the temporary display of religious symbols in public education,[42] but a week later, in *Stone v. Graham*, the divided Court struck down a Kentucky law calling for the posting of the Ten Commandments in public school classrooms.[43] In the first case, the historical and cultural significance of Christmas convinced the Eighth Circuit that the prudent and objective observance of this holiday in public schools does not serve to advance religion, even though songs such as *Silent Night* are sung and the nativity scene is displayed.[44] The appeals court held that the school board's policy, allowing the observance of holidays

---

[39]Newdow v. U.S. Cong., 292 F.3d 597, 607–613 (9th Cir. 2002), *judgment stayed,* No. 00-16423, 2002 U.S. App. LEXIS 12826 (9th Cir. June 27, 2002), *opinion amended and superseded by* 328 F.3d 466 (2003), *rev'd sub nom.* Elk Grove Unified Sch. Dist. v. Newdow, 542 U.S. 1 (2004).

[40]*Newdow,* 542 U.S. 1, 17–18 (2004).

[41]Newdow v. U.S. Cong., 383 F. Supp. 2d 1229 (E.D. Cal. 2005).

[42]Florey v. Sioux Falls Sch. Dist. 49-5, 619 F.2d 1311 (8th Cir. 1980).

[43]449 U.S. 39 (1980).

[44]*Florey*, 619 F.2d at 1314. *See also* Sechler v. State Coll. Area Sch. Dist., 121 F. Supp. 2d 439 (M.D. Pa. 2000) (rejecting an Establishment Clause challenge to holiday observance that allegedly was not "Christian enough"; the program included the menorah and Kwanzaa candelabra as well as Christmas carols and a Christmas tree and was designed to celebrate diversity).

with both a religious and secular basis, had the nonreligious purpose of improving the overall instructional program.

In contrast, the five-member Supreme Court majority in *Stone* was not persuaded that the Ten Commandments' cultural significance justified posting this religious document in public schools. Distinguishing the display of religious texts from the permissible use of religious literature in academic courses, the majority held that the purpose behind the Kentucky legislation was to advance a particular religious faith in violation of the Establishment Clause. The majority rejected the state judiciary's conclusion that the constitutional impairment was neutralized because the copies were purchased with private donations and carried the disclaimer that "the secular application of the Ten Commandments is clearly seen in its adoption as the fundamental legal code of Western Civilization and the common law of the United States."[45]

However, disputes over religious displays have continued. In several decisions outside the school domain, the Supreme Court has condoned the use of public funds or property to erect a Christmas display with the nativity scene,[46] display an unattended cross in the capitol square during the Christmas season,[47] and display a menorah with a Christmas tree and a sign saluting liberty in front of a government building.[48] The Supreme Court rendered two companion decisions pertaining to displays of the Ten Commandments on government property in 2005. The Court upheld the longstanding display of a Ten Commandments monument on the Texas state capitol grounds along with other monuments and artifacts that reflect the secular purpose of paying tribute to the state's history.[49] In contrast, the Court struck down the display of framed copies of the Ten Commandments in two Kentucky county courthouses, noting that several attempts to add secular items to the displays did not eliminate their initial religious purpose.[50] Although school displays of the Ten Commandments were not at issue in these cases, the Court indicated that *Stone v. Graham* still has precedential value.

---

[45]*Stone*, 449 U.S. at 41. *See also* Nartowicz v. Clayton County Sch. Dist., 736 F.2d 646 (11th Cir. 1984) (barring the use of public school bulletin boards and public address systems to announce church-sponsored activities).

[46]*See* McCreary v. Stone, 739 F.2d 716 (2d Cir. 1984), *aff'd by equally divided court*, 471 U.S. 83 (1985); Lynch v. Donnelly, 465 U.S. 668 (1984).

[47]Capitol Square Review & Advisory Bd. v. Pinette, 515 U.S. 753 (1995).

[48]County of Allegheny v. ACLU, 492 U.S. 573 (1989) (upholding the display of the menorah with the Christmas tree as celebrating religious liberty, but striking down a county courthouse display of the nativity scene with a banner proclaiming "Gloria in Excelsis Deo" as advancing the Christian faith in violation of the Establishment Clause).

[49]The monument was donated by the Fraternal Order of Eagles in 1961. Van Orden v. Perry, 545 U.S. 677 (2005). *See also* Books v. City of Elkhart County, 401 F.3d 857 (7th Cir. 2005) (upholding county's display of the Ten Commandments along with eight other historical documents).

[50]McCreary County, Ky. v. ACLU, 545 U.S. 844 (2005). *See also* ICLU v. O'Bannon, 259 F.3d 766 (7th Cir. 2001) (enjoining display of a monument with the Ten Commandments on the state capitol grounds as lacking a valid secular purpose).

Other religious displays also have been controversial in public schools. The Sixth Circuit held that the display of a portrait of Jesus in a public secondary school failed all three prongs of the *Lemon* test,[51] and the Eleventh Circuit upheld school authorities in ordering removal of religious words and symbols from murals painted for a school beautification project because the murals represented the school.[52] Also, a New York federal district court enjoined the display of a religious painting in the high school auditorium because it conveyed governmental endorsement of religion.[53] However, a federal district court in New Jersey found that inclusion of religious holidays, such as Christmas and Hanukkah, on school district calendars was designed to broaden students' sensitivity toward religious diversity and their knowledge of the role of religion in the development of civilization and satisfied the *Lemon* test.[54]

Some parents have alleged that public schools promote the religion of Wicca by observing Halloween with pictures of witches and goblins. The Supreme Court declined to review a Florida court's ruling in which the state appeals court held that the display of witches does not promote a nontheistic religion or give an impression that the public school endorses Wicca.[55] Similarly, in rejecting an Establishment Clause challenge to using a "blue devil" as a public school's mascot, the Sixth Circuit reasoned that no reasonable observer would believe that the mascot's primary effect was to advance or inhibit religion.[56]

Courts have rendered conflicting rulings on requests to include religious messages in bricks purchased for school walkways or on tiles to be hung at school. The Tenth Circuit upheld school authorities in barring religious messages on tiles that were to be hung in school by persons connected with the Columbine, Colorado, school shootings.[57] Concluding that such expression represents the school, the court found a legitimate pedagogical reason for limiting expression that could create religious divisiveness. In contrast, a New York federal district court found viewpoint discrimination in a school district's removal of bricks containing references to Jesus from the school walkway that was funded by selling bricks to community members who inscribed them with personal messages,[58] and a Virginia federal district court

---

[51]Washegesic v. Bloomingdale Pub. Schs., 33 F.3d 679 (6th Cir. 1994).

[52]Bannon v. Sch. Dist., 387 F.3d 1208 (11th Cir. 2004).

[53]Joki v. Bd. of Educ., 745 F. Supp. 823 (N.D.N.Y. 1990). *See also* Gernetzke v. Kenosha Unified Sch. Dist. No. 1, 274 F.3d 464 (7th Cir. 2001); *infra* text accompanying note 91.

[54]Clever v. Cherry Hill Twp. Bd. of Educ., 838 F. Supp. 929 (D.N.J. 1993).

[55]Guyer v. Sch. Bd., 634 So. 2d 806 (Fla. Dist. Ct. App. 1994).

[56]*See* Kunselman v. W. Reserve Local Sch. Dist., 70 F.3d 931 (6th Cir. 1995).

[57]Fleming v. Jefferson County Sch. Dist., 298 F.3d 918 (10th Cir. 2002). In some instances, community groups have sought school access for religious advertisements. *See* DiLoreto v. Downey Unified Sch. Dist., 196 F.3d 958 (9th Cir. 1999) (holding that the school could exclude religious advertisements from the fence surrounding its baseball field, which was a nonpublic forum open only for limited purposes; finding the district's fears about violating the Establishment Clause to be reasonable and not impermissible viewpoint discrimination).

[58]Anderson v. Mex. Acad. & Cent. Sch., 186 F. Supp. 2d 193 (N.D.N.Y. 2002), *remanded,* 56 Fed. Appx. 549 (2d Cir. 2003), *on remand,* 427 F. Supp. 2d 182 (N.D.N.Y. 2006).

held that a high school's fund-raising activity created a limited public forum in its "walkway of fame," so removal of bricks with Latin crosses violated the First Amendment.[59]

Religious displays are destined to remain controversial. Courts seem likely to strike down the permanent display of the Ten Commandments and other sectarian documents in public schools. But the objective recognition of religious holidays will probably withstand judicial scrutiny.[60]

Proselytization in the Classroom

Public schools must abide by Establishment Clause restrictions on governmental promotion of religious creeds. Because teachers and other school personnel are working with a vulnerable captive audience in public schools, their actions have been scrutinized to ensure that classrooms are not used as a forum to indoctrinate sectarian beliefs.

Federal appellate courts have enjoined teacher-initiated devotionals in the classroom,[61] upheld school authorities in ordering a teacher to remove religiously oriented books from his classroom library and to refrain from silently reading the Bible during school hours,[62] and upheld a school board's directive for a teacher to stop using religious references in delivering the instructional program.[63] A federal district court also held that school authorities properly instructed a teacher to cover a proselytizing shirt at school.[64] The judiciary has recognized that the Establishment Clause bars public school teachers' use of the "power, prestige, and influence" of their position to lead devotional activities.[65]

[59]Demmon v. Loudoun County Pub. Schs., 342 F. Supp. 2d 474 (E.D. Va. 2004).

[60]Federal appellate courts have rendered conflicting opinions regarding laws or board policies that recognize Good Friday as a legal holiday. *Compare* Metzl v. Leininger, 57 F.3d 618 (7th Cir. 1995) (recognizing Good Friday as a school holiday conveys an impermissible message that Christianity is favored in absence of any educational or fiscal justification for the holiday) *with* Koenick v. Felton, 190 F.3d 259 (4th Cir. 1999) (upholding state law authorizing a four-day Easter holiday that coincides with Passover as satisfying the Establishment Clause and allocating school resources appropriately, because school attendance would be low at this time).

[61]*See* Jaffree v. Bd. of Sch. Comm'rs, 705 F.2d 1526 (11th Cir. 1983). *See also* May v. Evansville-Vanderburgh Sch. Corp., 787 F.2d 1105 (7th Cir. 1986) (upholding school authorities in barring teachers from using the public school building to hold staff prayer meetings before school).

[62]However, the court enjoined the school board from removing the Bible from the school library, noting that the Bible has significant literary and historical significance. Roberts v. Madigan, 921 F.2d 1047 (10th Cir. 1990).

[63]Marchi v. Bd. of Coop. Educ. Servs., 173 F.3d 469 (2d Cir. 1999).

[64]The shirt read "Jesus 2000, J2K." Downing v. W. Haven Bd. of Educ., 162 F. Supp. 2d 19 (D. Conn. 2001). *See also* Hennessy v. City of Melrose, 194 F.3d 237 (1st Cir. 1999) (upholding termination of a fundamentalist Christian student teacher for criticizing the district's curriculum and school activities and vilifying the principal; religious beliefs cannot override compliance with reasonable school directives).

[65]Fink v. Bd. of Educ., 442 A.2d 837, 842 (Pa. Commw. Ct. 1982) (upholding teacher's dismissal for refusing to comply with superintendent's directives to cease opening classes with devotional activities).

In several cases, teachers have been discharged for proselytizing students or disregarding selected aspects of the curriculum that conflict with their religious values. For example, the Seventh Circuit upheld a school board's dismissal of a kindergarten teacher who literally interpreted the biblical prohibition against worshiping graven images, and thus refused to teach about the American flag, the observance of patriotic holidays, and the importance of historical figures such as Abraham Lincoln. The appellate court noted that the teacher enjoys the freedom to hold such beliefs but has "no constitutional right to require others to submit to her views and to forego a portion of their education they would otherwise be entitled to enjoy."[66] A New York appeals court also upheld the dismissal of a tenured teacher based on evidence that she had tried to recruit students to join her religious organization, conducted prayer sessions in her office, and used her classroom to promote her religious faith.[67] And the Fourth Circuit rejected a teacher's claim that he had a constitutional right to display in his classroom several news articles promoting Christianity and a poster publicizing the National Day of Prayer.[68]

Although proselytization of students by public school teachers violates the Establishment Clause, the Supreme Court has emphasized that it is permissible, even desirable, to teach the Bible and other religious documents from a literary, cultural, or historical perspective.[69] Responding to studies indicating that the role of religion in the development of Western civilization has been given insufficient and inaccurate treatment in textbooks and courses partly due to fear of violating the First Amendment,[70] several coalitions of national education, civic, and religious groups as well as the U.S. Department of Education have distributed materials addressing the legal status of various church/state issues in public schools.[71]

More than 1,000 public schools across 37 states use the Bible as a textbook for courses on "the Bible as Literature," supported by the National Council on Bible

---

[66]Palmer v. Bd. of Educ., 603 F.2d 1271, 1274 (7th Cir. 1979). For a discussion of teachers' wearing of religious attire in public schools, *see* text with note 113, Chapter 10.

[67]La Rocca v. Bd. of Educ., 406 N.Y.S.2d 348 (App. Div. 1978).

[68]Lee v. York County Sch. Div., 484 F.3d 687 (4th Cir. 2007), *cert. denied*, 128 S. Ct. 387 (2007) (holding that the expression was curricular in nature, so it constituted an employment dispute and not protected expression). *But see* Williams v. Vidmar, 367 F. Supp. 2d 1265 (N.D. Cal. 2005) (recognizing the legitimate pedagogical concern that teachers not promote religion in their classrooms in violation of the Establishment Clause, but allowing the teacher to proceed with his equal protection claim that he was treated differently because of his religion since his lesson plans required prior administrative approval, whereas other teachers' plans did not).

[69]*See* Sch. Dist. of Abington Twp. v. Schempp, 374 U.S. 203, 225 (1963).

[70]*See* Timothy Smith, "High School History Texts Adopted for Use in the State of Alabama," *Religion & Public Education*, vol. 15 (1988), pp. 170–190; Paul Vitz, *Censorship: Evidence of Bias in Our Children's Textbooks* (Ann Arbor, MI: Servant Books, 1986).

[71]*See* United States Department of Education, *Guidance on Constitutionally Protected Prayer in Public Elementary and Secondary Schools,* 68 Fed. Reg. 9645-01 (February 28, 2003); Pew Forum on Religion and Public Life and The First Amendment Center, *Teaching about Religion in Public Schools: Where Do We Go from Here?* (Arlington, VA: First Amendment Center, 2003).

Curriculum in Public Schools, and a number of additional school districts offer an elective high school course using the textbook *The Bible and Its Influence,* supported by the Bible Literacy Project.[72] Yet the line is not always clear between teaching about religion and instilling religious tenets in other courses. Numerous Bible study courses, particularly at the elementary school level, have been challenged as a ploy to advance sectarian beliefs. Courts have carefully evaluated curricular materials and even reviewed videotapes of lessons in determining whether such instruction fosters a particular creed. Courts have struck down programs in which private groups have controlled the hiring and supervision of personnel or the selection of curricular materials.[73] While most challenges have involved instruction pertaining to the Bible and the Christian faith, the Ninth Circuit upheld a school's use of role-playing to teach seventh grade world history students about Islam, reasoning that learning about the five pillars of Islam did not entail the practice of a religion.[74]

Performances of school choirs often have evoked controversies over alleged proselytization. A Utah choir director agreed to exempt a student from singing religious songs, but the student sought an injunction against the choir performing the songs and against holding two performances at religious sites. The Tenth Circuit accepted the school district's justification for the music, noting that a substantial amount of choral music is religious in nature and also accepted that the religious sites had superior facilities.[75] The Fifth Circuit similarly ruled that forbidding the school choir to sing religious songs would disqualify appropriate choral music, so the use of a religious song as the choir's theme song does not constitute an endorsement of religion.[76]

Some controversies over proselytization in the classroom have not challenged teachers' activities but have entailed requests for students to include sectarian materials in their presentations, artwork, or other school assignments. In most of these cases, the schools have prevailed in denying the students' requests. For example, the Sixth Circuit upheld a school district's prohibition on an elementary school student

---

[72]*See* Brenda Goodman, "Teaching the Bible in Georgia's Public Schools, *New York Times* (March 29, 2006), p. 7; David J. Hoff, "Alabama Lawmakers Push Elective on Bible's Role in History, Literature," *Education Week* (January 18, 2006), p. 21; National School Boards Association, "Curriculum," *Legal Clips* (January 11, 2007), p. 7; Cullen Schippe and Chuck Stetson, eds., *The Bible and Its Influence* (Front Royal, VA: Bible Literacy Project, 2005).

[73]*See, e.g.,* Doe v. Human, 725 F. Supp. 1499 (W.D. Ark. 1989), *aff'd mem.,* 923 F.2d 2d 857 (8th Cir. 1990); Hall v. Bd. of Sch. Comm'rs, 707 F.2d 464 (11th Cir. 1983); Herdahl v. Pontotoc County Sch. Dist., 933 F. Supp. 582 (N.D. Miss. 1996). *See also* Doe v. Beaumont Indep. Sch. Dist., 240 F.3d 462 (5th Cir. 2001) (*en banc*), *on remand sub nom.* Oxford v. Beaumont Indep. Sch. Dist., 224 F. Supp. 2d 1099 (E.D. Tex. 2002) (invalidating school district's "clergy in schools" counseling program under the Establishment Clause).

[74]Eklund v. Byron Union Sch. Dist., 154 Fed. Appx. 648 (9th Cir. 2005), *cert. denied,* 127 S. Ct. 86 (2006).

[75]Bauchman v. W. High Sch., 132 F.3d 542 (10th Cir. 1997). *But see* Skarin v. Woodbine Cmty. Sch. Dist., 204 F. Supp. 2d 1195 (S.D. Iowa 2002) (holding that high school choir's singing of *The Lord's Prayer* at graduation ceremony and rehearsals violated the Establishment Clause).

[76]Doe v. Duncanville Indep. Sch. Dist., 70 F.3d 402 (5th Cir. 1995). However, the court struck down the basketball team's policy of praying before games, practices, and pep rallies with the participation and supervision of school employees.

showing in class a videotape of herself singing a proselytizing religious song, concluding that student projects can be censored to ensure that the school is not viewed as endorsing religious content.[77] The same court backed a junior high school teacher who gave a student a zero on a report, because the student had cleared a different topic with the teacher but then wrote her report on the life of Jesus Christ. The court emphasized, however, that religious issues may be part of the instructional program, and one justice observed that the student might have raised a legitimate free speech issue if the assignment had been to write an opinion piece on any topic of personal interest and religious content had been rejected.[78]

In contrast to the above cases, the Second Circuit found viewpoint discrimination in a teacher's refusal to display one poster and censorship of a replacement poster because of religious content depicted by a kindergarten student asked to portray what he had learned about the environment. The court reasoned that even if restrictions are reasonably related to legitimate pedagogical interests in a nonpublic forum, blatant viewpoint discrimination is not allowed.[79] Also, a Michigan federal district court was sympathetic to a student's claim that the school's refusal to allow her to voice her religious opposition to homosexuality in a panel discussion on religion and homosexuality and in a subsequent student assembly speech violated free expression, equal protection, and antiestablishment rights.[80]

Equal Access for Religious Expression and Groups

In the 1960s and 1970s, it often was assumed that the Establishment Clause demanded that religious speech be barred from government forums. More recently, however, the Supreme Court has reasoned that singling out religious views for differential treatment compared with other private expression would be unconstitutional viewpoint discrimination, which abridges the Free Speech Clause.[81]

The Supreme Court started this trend in education cases in its 1981 decision, *Widmar v. Vincent*, finding no Establishment Clause violation in allowing student

---

[77]DeNooyer v. Merinelli, 12 F.3d 211 (6th Cir. 1993).

[78]Settle v. Dickson County Sch. Bd., 53 F.3d 152 (6th Cir. 1995). *See also id.* at 159 (Batchelder, J., concurring). In 2007, Texas enacted a law that allows religious beliefs to be expressed in homework, artwork, and other assignments, and stipulating that students should not be rewarded or penalized because of the religious content of their work. *See* Religious Viewpoints Anti-Discrimination Act, Tex. Educ. Code Ann. § 25.151 (2007). *See also Guidance on Constitutionally Protected Prayer, supra* text accompanying note 71.

[79]Peck v. Baldwinsville Cent. Sch. Dist., 426 F.3d 617 (2d Cir. 2005) (remanding for further consideration of the free expression issue but ruling that the lower court properly dismissed the Establishment Clause claim), *Cert. denied*, 547 U.S. 1097 (2006). *But see* C.H. v. Oliva, 226 F.3d 198 (3d Cir. 2000) (finding no violation of constitutional rights in connection with the removal of a student's religious posters, but remanding the case for the plaintiffs to have an opportunity to substantiate a viable complaint in this regard).

[80]Hansen v. Ann Arbor Pub. Schs., 293 F. Supp. 2d 780 (E.D. Mich. 2003).

[81]For elaboration on this notion, *see* Rosenberger v. Rector & Visitors, 515 U.S. 819, 890–899 (1995) (Souter, J., dissenting); Lamb's Chapel v. Ctr. Moriches Union Free Sch. Dist., 959 F.2d 381, 386 (2d Cir. 1992), *rev'd*, 508 U.S. 384 (1993).

religious groups to have access to a forum created for student expression on state-supported college campuses.[82] The Court concluded that by providing access to a range of student groups, public institutions of higher education advance a secular purpose and do not excessively entangle the state with religion. The Court focused on the expressive aspect of the student devotional activities in *Widmar*, concluding that the university's ban on religious meetings would abridge students' free speech rights.

Equal Access Act.   Below the college level, the Free Speech Clause was augmented in 1984 by the Equal Access Act (EAA), under which federally assisted secondary schools that have established a limited forum for student groups to meet during non-instructional time cannot deny school access to noncurriculum student groups based on the religious, philosophical, or political content of their meetings.[83] In 1990, the Supreme Court in *Board of Education of Westside Community Schools v. Mergens* rejected the contention that the EAA abridges the Establishment Clause by allowing student religious groups to meet, recognizing the law's secular purpose of preventing discrimination against religious and other types of private student expression.[84] The Court distinguished government speech promoting religion that is prohibited by the Establishment Clause from private religious expression protected by the Free Speech and Free Exercise Clauses.[85]

In subsequent cases, federal appellate courts have ruled that under the EAA student religious groups can require certain officers to be Christians to safeguard the spiritual content of their meetings[86] and that student activity periods during the school day are considered noninstructional time.[87] The Ninth Circuit ruled that the EAA prevails over state constitutional provisions calling for greater separation of church and state than required by the Establishment Clause[88] and in a subsequent case held that a school district violated the law by denying a religious club access to funds and fund-raising activities, school bulletin boards, and the public address system on an equal basis with other student groups.[89] A California appeals court held that a noncurriculum club, the Fellowship of Christian Athletes, would not have to be

---

[82]454 U.S. 263 (1981).

[83]20 U.S.C. §§ 4071–4074 (2007).

[84]496 U.S. 226, 249 (1990).

[85]*Id.* at 250.

[86]*See* Hsu v. Roslyn Union Free Sch. Dist., 85 F.3d 839 (2d Cir. 1996).

[87]Donovan v. Punxsutawney Area Sch. Bd., 336 F.3d 211 (3d Cir. 2003). *See also* Ceniceros v. Bd. of Trs., 106 F.3d 878 (9th Cir. 1997) (relying on the EAA to allow student religious groups to meet during lunch period since it was noninstructional time and other student groups were allowed to meet).

[88]*See* Garnett v. Renton Sch. Dist. No. 403, 987 F.2d 641 (9th Cir. 1993) (finding that the EAA prevailed over antiestablishment provisions in state law, so a student religious group could not be barred from the public school's limited forum for student meetings).

[89]Prince v. Jacoby, 303 F.3d 1074 (9th Cir. 2002). For a discussion of the Free Speech Clause issues in this case, *see supra* text accompanying note 34.

student initiated to be protected under the EAA—only its on-campus meetings would have to be initiated by students.[90]

Although there are limits on the reach of the EAA,[91] this federal law codified for secondary students the concept of equal access and equal treatment of religious expression that is currently guiding First Amendment litigation as well. Indeed, given recent interpretations of the reach of the Free Speech Clause in requiring equal treatment of private religious expression in public schools, there is some sentiment that the EAA may no longer be needed.

School Access for Community Groups.   The EAA applies *only* to secondary students, so community religious groups desiring public school access during noninstructional time must rely on First Amendment protections. Since the early 1990s, the Supreme Court has made some definitive pronouncements about protecting private religious expression from viewpoint discrimination. In *Lamb's Chapel v. Center Moriches Union Free School District*, the Court held that if secular community groups are allowed to use the public school after school hours to address particular topics (i.e., family life, child rearing), a sectarian group desiring to show a film series addressing these topics from a religious perspective cannot be denied public school access.[92]

Subsequently, the Supreme Court delivered a seminal decision, *Good News Club v. Milford Central School*, allowing a private Christian organization to hold its meetings in a New York public school after school hours.[93] The Milford School District had denied the Good News Club's request under its community-use policy that allows civic and recreational groups to use the school but not for religious purposes, contending that the club affiliated with the Child Evangelism Fellowship was engaging in prohibited religious worship and instruction. Disagreeing with the school district and the lower courts, the Supreme Court in *Milford* held that the school district's policy discriminated against religious viewpoints in violation of the Free Speech Clause. The majority reasoned that the Good News Club was merely seeking access to school facilities like other community groups and that it could not be disadvantaged based on the religious content of its meetings.

The Court's *Milford* decision seems to have erased the distinction between religious viewpoints and worship that some lower courts had drawn in condoning the use

[90]Van Schoick v. Saddleback Valley Unified Sch. Dist., 104 Cal. Rptr. 2d 562 (Ct. App. 2001). Some controversies have focused on what constitutes curriculum-related clubs, and most of these cases have not dealt with religious groups, so they are discussed in Chapter 4. *See* text accompanying note 102, Chapter 4.

[91]*See* Gernetzke v. Kenosha Unified Sch. Dist. No. 1, 274 F.3d 464 (7th Cir. 2001) (finding no EAA violation when a principal barred a student religious group from including a large cross in the group's school hallway mural, but not reaching the merits of the allegation that suppressing the sectarian symbols violated the First Amendment).

[92]508 U.S. 384 (1993).

[93]533 U.S. 98 (2001). *See also* Culbertson v. Oakridge Sch. Dist. No. 76, 258 F.3d 1061 (9th Cir. 2001) (upholding the Good News Club's right to meet in the public school after school hours, but enjoining teachers from distributing permission slips for the meetings as encouraging the religious club in violation of the Establishment Clause).

of public school facilities for community groups to discuss topics from sectarian perspectives, while not allowing use of public schools for religious worship.[94] Under the *Milford* ruling, if a public school establishes a limited forum for community meetings it cannot bar religious groups, even though students attending the school are the central participants in the devotional activities. The Court did not find a danger that the community would perceive the Good News Club's access as school district endorsement of religion. In subsequent cases, lower courts have allowed community religious groups to display literature on a table during back-to-school night, permitted flyers about sectarian meetings to be sent home with students, and required fees to be waived for religious meetings if other clubs received such waivers.[95] The Eighth Circuit held that a teacher could participate in meetings of the Good News Club held at the elementary school where she taught; the school district's restriction on such private expression represented viewpoint discrimination in violation of the teacher's free speech rights.[96]

Distribution of Religious Literature. The Supreme Court has not directly addressed the distribution of religious literature in public schools, and lower courts have rendered a range of opinions. Courts consistently have ruled that school personnel cannot give students Bibles or other religious materials,[97] and most courts have prohibited religious sects from coming to the school to distribute materials to captive public school audiences. For example, several courts have enjoined school boards from allowing the Gideon Society to visit schools and present Bibles to students who wish to accept them.[98]

Departing from this trend, the Fourth Circuit upheld a West Virginia school district's policy allowing sectarian organizations along with political groups to distribute materials, such as Bibles, in public secondary schools on a designated day

---

[94]*Compare* Bronx Household of Faith v. Cmty. Sch. Dist., 127 F.3d 207 (2d Cir. 1997) (upholding a school district's viewpoint-neutral prohibition on religious groups using the public school's limited forum for weekly worship services) *with* Bronx Household of Faith v. Bd. of Educ., 331 F.3d 342 (2d Cir. 2003), *on remand*, 400 F. Supp. 2d 581 (S.D.N.Y. 2005) (permanently enjoining school district from enforcing a ban on using school facilities for Sunday worship services), *vacated and remanded*, 492 F.3d 89 (2d Cir. 2007).

[95]See Child Evangelism Fellowship (CEF) v. Montgomery County Pub. Schs., 457 F.3d 376 (4th Cir. 2006) (holding that religious organizations must be treated like other community organizations in being allowed to distribute flyers about their after-school meetings in elementary schools); CEF v. Anderson Sch. Dist. Five, 470 F.3d 1062 (4th Cir. 2006), *on remand*, No. 8:04-1866-HMH, 2007 U.S. Dist. LEXIS 41988 (D.S.C. June 8, 2007) (finding viewpoint discrimination in the school district's denial of a fee waiver for religious group to use school facilities for meetings; requiring usage fees to be returned to CEF); CEF v. Stafford Twp. Sch. Dist., 386 F.3d 514 (3d Cir. 2004), *on remand*, No. 02-4549 (MLC), 2006 U.S. Dist. LEXIS 62966 (D.N.J. Sept. 5, 2006) (holding that religious groups must be allowed to display literature at an event where other groups were allowed to do so).

[96]Wigg v. Sioux Falls Sch. Dist. 49-5, 382 F.3d 807 (8th Cir. 2004).

[97]*See, e.g.*, Jabr v. Rapides Parish Sch. Bd., 171 F. Supp. 2d 653 (W.D. La. 2001) (finding that school principal violated the Establishment Clause by distributing New Testament Bibles to public school students).

[98]*See, e.g.*, Doe v. S. Iron R-1 Sch. Dist., 498 F.3d 878 (8th Cir. 2007); Berger v. Rensselaer Cent. Sch. Corp., 982 F.2d 1160 (7th Cir. 1993).

because the organizations were considered private entities that do not represent the school.[99] But the policy was invalidated at the elementary school level because of the impressionability of younger children and their greater difficulty in distinguishing private from school-sponsored speech. The Ninth Circuit also reversed a lower court's conclusion that flyers regarding summer camp activities could not be distributed in the public school because of the camp classes entitled *Bible Heroes* and *Bible Tales*. The appeals court reasoned that a restriction on distributing the flyers would impair the First Amendment since flyers about secular activities were allowed.[100]

Many recent controversies have focused on student requests to distribute religious publications. Like meetings of student-initiated religious groups, these requests pit Free Speech Clause protections against Establishment Clause restrictions. A 1995 Supreme Court decision involving higher education has influenced literature distribution in public schools. Concluding that a public university could not withhold support from a student religious group seeking to use student activity funds to publish sectarian materials, the Court majority ruled that religious material must be treated like other material in student-initiated publications subsidized by the university.[101] The Court held that the government's equal treatment of religious and secular private expression is not only permitted by the Establishment Clause, but in some circumstances is required by the Free Speech Clause.

Some courts addressing PK–12 controversies have similarly applied the "equal access" concept in concluding that the same legal principles govern students' distribution of religious and nonreligious literature.[102] The Seventh Circuit held that students in an Illinois school district could distribute a religious newspaper in the public school, a nonpublic forum, but could be restricted to specified times at a table near

[99]Peck v. Upshur County Bd. of Educ., 155 F.3d 274 (4th Cir. 1998). *See also* Bacon v. Bradley-Bourbonnais High Sch. Dist. No. 307, 707 F. Supp. 1005 (C.D. Ill. 1989) (upholding the Gideon Society's right to distribute Bibles on the school-owned sidewalk in front of a high school, because the sidewalk was considered a public forum for use by the general public).

[100]Hills v. Scottsdale Unified Sch. Dist. No. 48, 329 F.3d 1044 (9th Cir. 2003). *See also* Rusk v. Crestview Local Sch. Dist., 379 F.3d 418 (6th Cir. 2004) (finding no Establishment Clause violation in allowing distribution of flyers for religious and nonreligious purposes in an elementary school).

[101]Rosenberger v. Rector & Visitors, 515 U.S. 819 (1995). *See also* Christian Legal Soc'y v. Walker, 453 F.3d 853 (7th Cir. 2006) (ruling that a state-supported university could not require the Christian Legal Society, one of its recognized student organizations, to comply with the institution's affirmative action policy that withdraws benefits to any group denying equal treatment of individuals based on various characteristics including sexual orientation; such compliance abridged expressive association and speech rights of the group's members who are expected to adhere to a specific belief system regarding sexual conduct).

[102]*See, e.g.,* Muller v. Jefferson Lighthouse Sch., 98 F.3d 1530 (7th Cir. 1996) (applying the same rules to the distribution of religious and nonreligious student literature that is not sponsored by the school); M.B. v. Liverpool Cent. Sch. Dist., 487 F. Supp. 2d 117 (N.D.N.Y. 2007) (finding viewpoint discrimination in an elementary school's refusal to allow a student to distribute during noninstructional time a personal statement concerning the impact Jesus has had on her life); Slotterback v. Interboro Sch. Dist., 766 F. Supp. 280 (E.D. Pa. 1991) (finding no compelling Establishment Clause justification for a content-based restriction on student distribution of religious literature).

the school's entrance.[103] A Massachusetts federal district court more recently overturned disciplinary action against members of a religious club who were denied permission but nonetheless distributed candy canes with a religious message during the holiday season.[104] The court reasoned that the distribution during noninstructional time amounted to private speech that the school must tolerate. But the Third Circuit ruled that an elementary school did not violate a student's First Amendment speech rights by preventing him from distributing pencils and candy canes containing religious messages *during class,* noting that the student could distribute such materials before or after school and during recess.[105]

Even private expression is subject to reasonable time, place, and manner regulations. For example, an Indiana federal district court supported a school policy requiring students to give the principal advance notice of the distribution of materials and to submit a copy of the literature to the superintendent, but not for approval purposes.[106] Whereas reasonable restrictions have been upheld on how material is distributed, school districts cannot place a blanket ban on the distribution of religious literature.

Accommodations for Religious Beliefs

In addition to challenging sectarian influences in public schools, some students have asserted a right to accommodations so they can practice their religious beliefs. Conflicts have arisen over release-time programs for religious education, excused absences from public schools for religious observances, and religious exemptions from secular school activities.

Release-Time Programs

Although the Supreme Court has struck down the practice of using public school classrooms for clergy to provide religious training to public school students during the instructional day,[107] the Court has recognized that the school can accommodate religion by releasing students to receive such religious training off public school grounds. Noting that the state must not be hostile toward religion, the Court declared in 1952 that "when the state encourages religious instruction or cooperates with religious authorities by adjusting the schedule of public events to sectarian needs, it follows the best of our traditions."[108]

---

[103]Hedges v. Wauconda Cmty. Unit Sch. Dist. No. 118, 9 F.3d 1295 (7th Cir. 1993) (upholding the part of the district's policy restricting distribution of materials prepared by nonstudents to 10 or fewer copies, reasoning that it is an important part of education for students to learn to express themselves in their own words).

[104]Westfield High Sch. L.I.F.E. Club v. City of Westfield, 249 F. Supp. 2d 98 (D. Mass. 2003).

[105]Walz v. Egg Harbor Twp. Bd. of Educ., 342 F.3d 271 (3d Cir. 2003).

[106]Harless v. Darr, 937 F. Supp. 1351 (S.D. Ind. 1996).

[107]McCollum v. Bd. of Educ., 333 U.S. 203 (1948).

[108]Zorach v. Clauson, 343 U.S. 306, 313–314 (1952).

A release-time program was even upheld in a school district where students received an hour of religious instruction each week in a mobile unit parked at the edge of school property.[109] Courts have not been persuaded that offering a single choice of attending religious classes or remaining in the public school advances religion or that nonparticipating pupils are denied their state-created right to an education because academic instruction ceases during the release-time period.[110]

The Tenth Circuit held that time spent by public school students in a release-time program at a Mormon seminary program could be counted in satisfying compulsory school attendance and in calculating the school's state aid.[111] But the court enjoined the school's practice of awarding high school credit for the secular aspects of daily instruction received at the seminary, reasoning that the award of such credit would entangle school officials with the church because of the monitoring necessary to determine what parts of the courses were sectarian.

An Indiana federal district court also enjoined several features of a release-time program that was held in trailers located on public school property, with utilities supported by the school district. Nonparticipating students were required to read silently when their classmates participated in the nondenominational Christian instruction because school authorities feared that students might be deterred from attending the release-time program if they had other options, such as doing their homework.[112] The court found Establishment Clause violations in this district's effort to encourage participation in the program and in the use of school property for the religious classes.

Religious Absences

Requests for students and teachers to be excused from public schools to observe religious holidays raise particularly delicate issues, because such requests usually are made by members of minority sects. Courts have been asked to determine how far public school authorities must go in accommodating religious holidays and how far they can go before such accommodations abridge the Establishment Clause.

Most litigation in this arena has involved claims by teachers that personnel leave policies discriminate against religious absences; such claims are addressed in

---

[109]Smith v. Smith, 523 F.2d 121 (4th Cir. 1975).

[110]*See, e.g.,* Holt v. Thompson, 225 N.W.2d 678 (Wis. 1975). It appears that programs in which all students are released early from school one day a week would be easier to defend constitutionally because students would not be restricted to either remaining at the public school or attending sectarian classes.

[111]Lanner v. Wimmer, 662 F.2d 1349 (10th Cir. 1981). However, South Carolina adopted a law in 2006 allowing students to receive up to two credits for off-campus religious study. *See* S.C. Code Ann. § 59-39-112 (2007).

[112]Moore v. Metro. Sch. Dist., No. IP 00-1859-C-M/S, 2001 U.S. Dist. LEXIS 2722 (S.D. Ind. Feb. 7, 2001). *See also* Doe v. Shenandoah County Sch. Bd., 737 F. Supp. 913 (W.D. Va. 1990) (granting a temporary restraining order against Weekday Religious Education classes being held in buses—almost identical to public school buses—parked in front of the school, with instructors going into the school to recruit students).

Chapter 10. A few cases, however, have focused on students. To illustrate, the Fifth Circuit invalidated a school's policy that allowed students only two excused absences for religious holidays.[113] The court found that the school's interests in promoting regular attendance and protecting teachers from extra work were not sufficiently compelling to justify requiring students to take unexcused absences to observe several holy days and a week-long convocation of the Worldwide Church of God.

The judiciary, however, has not condoned excessive student absences for religious reasons, such as being absent one day a week, because of the overriding state interest in providing continuity in instruction. Also, courts have not been receptive to attempts to avoid school attendance altogether for religious reasons. In an early case, the Virginia Supreme Court recognized that "no amount of religious fervor . . . in opposition to adequate instruction should be allowed to work a lifelong injury" to children.[114] As discussed previously, the one judicially endorsed exception to compulsory school attendance involves Amish children beyond eighth grade, because of the uniqueness of the Amish lifestyle.[115]

Religious Exemptions from Secular Activities

Students have sought exemptions from public school activities and requirements that allegedly impair the practice of their religious tenets. In evaluating whether school authorities must honor such requests, courts have attempted to balance parents' interests in directing the religious upbringing of their children against the state's interest in ensuring an educated citizenry.

Observances. Courts have relied on the First Amendment in striking down required student participation in certain public school observances. In the landmark case, *West Virginia State Board of Education v. Barnette*, the Supreme Court ruled in 1943 that students could not be required to pledge their allegiance to the American flag in contravention of their religious beliefs,[116] overturning a precedent established by the Court only three years earlier.[117] In *Barnette*, the Court held that refusal to participate in the flag salute and the Pledge of Allegiance does not interfere with the rights of others to do so or threaten any type of disruption.

But controversy still surrounds the nature of required exemptions from the Pledge. Courts have struck down laws or policies requiring students to stand during the Pledge or mandating parental notification of nonparticipating students, reasoning that

[113]Church of God v. Amarillo Indep. Sch. Dist., 511 F. Supp. 613 (N.D. Tex. 1981), *aff'd per curiam*, 670 F.2d 46 (5th Cir. 1982).

[114]Rice v. Commonwealth, 49 S.E.2d 342, 348 (Va. 1948). For a discussion of the legal status of home education programs, *see* text accompanying note 11, Chapter 3.

[115]*See* Wisconsin v. Yoder, 406 U.S. 205 (1972); *supra* text accompanying note 11.

[116]319 U.S. 624 (1943).

[117]Minersville Sch. Dist. v. Gobitis, 310 U.S. 586 (1940).

~~such requirements coerce students into reciting the Pledge.~~[118] A federal judge enjoined implementation of a 2003 Colorado law requiring public school teachers to begin the school day with recitation of the Pledge. The law allowed for a religious exemption but required parents to request in writing for their children to be excused from participation for other reasons, which the court concluded placed a burden on the free speech rights of nonreligious conscientious objectors.[119] The legislature subsequently enacted a less prescriptive law calling for the daily recitation of the Pledge by willing students.

An Alabama case focused on a student who was paddled by his teacher and principal because he silently raised his fist in protest during the Pledge of Allegiance. The student was protesting the public chastisement of a classmate for not reciting the Pledge. Reversing the court below, the Eleventh Circuit concluded that the disciplinary action was an unwarranted infringement on the student's expression rights, since his silent protest was not disruptive; the principal and teacher were not entitled to summary judgment on qualified immunity grounds.[120] Of course, ~~students who opt not to participate can be disciplined if they create a disturbance while others are reciting the Pledge~~.

The Supreme Court has not directly addressed teachers' free exercise rights in connection with patriotic observances in public schools, but several lower courts have adopted the *Barnette* rationale in concluding that teachers, like students, have a First Amendment right to refuse to pledge allegiance as a matter of personal conscience.[121] Teachers, however, cannot use their religious beliefs to deny students the opportunity to engage in this observance. If a school district requires the pledge to be recited daily, teachers must make provisions for this observance in their classrooms. As discussed previously, whether "under God" can be said in the Pledge at all in public schools remains controversial.[122]

Curriculum Components.   Patriotic observances have not been the only source of controversy; religious exemptions also have been sought from components of the curriculum. Whereas teachers cannot assert a free exercise right to disregard aspects of the state-prescribed curriculum, the judiciary has been more receptive to students'

---

[118]*See, e.g.,* Lipp v. Morris, 579 F.2d 834, 836 (3d Cir. 1978) (striking down part of a New Jersey law requiring all students to stand during the Pledge); Frazier v. Alexandre, 434 F. Supp. 2d 1350 (S.D. Fla. 2006) (enjoining the school district's unconstitutional practices and awarding damages to a student who was publicly reprimanded for not participating in the Pledge and told he would have to get parental permission to opt out and would have to stand when others recited the Pledge); Circle Sch. v. Phillips, 270 F. Supp. 2d 616, 626 (E.D. Pa. 2003) (holding that a state law requiring parental notification of nonparticipating students violated the First Amendment).

[119]*See* Lane v. Owens, No. 03-B-1544 (PAC) (D. Colo. Aug. 15, 2003); Diane Carman, "For Denver Teen, the Republic Stands for Taking a Stand," *Denver Post* (April 16, 2004), p. B-03.

[120]Holloman v. Harland, 370 F.3d 1252 (11th Cir. 2004) (allowing the student's Establishment Clause claim that the teacher encouraged students to pray during the daily moment of silence also to proceed against the teacher and the school board).

[121]*See, e.g.,* Russo v. Cent. Sch. Dist. No. 1, 469 F.2d 623, 634 (2d Cir. 1972); Opinion of the Justices, 363 N.E.2d 251 (Mass. 1977).

[122]*See supra* text accompanying note 37.

requests for exemptions from instructional requirements. Students, unlike teachers, are compelled to attend school, and for many this means a public school. Accordingly, the judiciary has been sensitive to the fact that certain public school policies may have a coercive effect on religious practices. In balancing the interests involved, courts consider:

- The extent to which the school requirement burdens the exercise of sincere religious beliefs,
- The governmental justification for the requirement, and
- Alternative means available to meet the state's objectives.

School authorities must have a compelling justification to deny students an exemption from a requirement that impairs the exercise of sincere religious beliefs.

Most requests for religious exemptions are handled at the classroom or school level and do not evoke legal controversies. When they have generated litigation, students often have been successful in securing religious exemptions from instructional activities, such as drug education, sex education, coeducational physical education, dancing instruction, officers' training programs, and specific course assignments, if alternatives can satisfy the instructional objectives. The relief ordered in these cases has entailed the excusal of specific children, but the secular activities themselves have not been disturbed. For example, more than half of the states currently allow students to opt out of sex education instruction or require parental consent for children to participate in such instruction in public schools.[123] An Illinois federal district court also upheld a parent in keeping her children home on "opposite sex day," because students dressing as members of the opposite sex had a coercive effect on the practice of her religious beliefs.[124]

Religious exemptions have not been honored if considered unnecessary to accommodate the practice of religious tenets or if the exemptions would substantially disrupt the school or students' academic progress. In an illustrative case, the Second Circuit rejected a parent's request for his son to be exempted from a Connecticut school district's mandatory health curriculum, finding such attendance rationally related to the legitimate governmental goal of providing students important health information.[125]

---

[123]*See* David Rigsby, "Education Law Chapter: Sex Education in Schools," *Georgetown Journal of Gender and Law,* vol. 7 (2006), p. 898.

[124]The court also denied the school district's motion to dismiss the parent's defamation claim and claim of retaliation against her and her children (for her stance regarding opposite sex day) and her claim for harassment based on opposite sex day and published jokes that were offensive to women. Although the claims were allowed to proceed, the court held that the parent lacked standing to seek a preliminary injunction because the family had moved from the school district so there was no threat of continued harm. Stanley v. Carrier Mills-Stonefort Sch. Dist. No. 2, 459 F. Supp. 2d 766 (S.D. Ill. 2006).

[125]Leebaert v. Harrington, 332 F.3d 134 (2d Cir. 2003). *See also* Davis v. Page, 385 F. Supp. 395 (D.N.H. 1974) (rejecting parents' request for an exemption for their children from health and music courses and from classes whenever instructional media were used, which would disrupt the instructional program; students could be excused when audiovisual equipment was used solely for entertainment purposes).

However, the offended student was allowed to be excused from lessons on family life, physical growth, and AIDS instruction. In a widely publicized 1987 case, the Sixth Circuit rejected fundamentalist Christian parents' request that their children be excused from exposure to the basal reading series used in elementary grades in a Tennessee school district.[126] Reversing the lower court's grant of the exemption, the Sixth Circuit reasoned that the readers did not burden the students' exercise of their religious beliefs, because the students were not required to profess a creed or perform religious exercises. Courts also have denied religious exemptions for student athletes if an excusal from specific regulations might pose a safety hazard or interfere with the management of athletic teams.[127]

As discussed in Chapter 3, conservative parents' organizations have secured federal and state laws allowing students to be excused from public school activities and components of the curriculum for religious and other reasons. Thus, parents may be able to use legislation to secure exemptions for their children,[128] even if they cannot substantiate that particular instructional activities impair free exercise rights.

Religious Challenges to the Secular Curriculum

Some parents have not been content with religious exemptions for their own children and have pressed for *elimination* of various courses, activities, and instructional materials from public schools. Although courts often have been receptive to requests for individual exemptions from specific public school activities, the judiciary has not been inclined to allow the restriction of the secular curriculum to satisfy parents' religious preferences. In 1968, the Supreme Court recognized that "'the state has no legitimate interest in protecting any or all religions from views distasteful to them.'"[129]

Challenges to the public school curriculum raise complex questions involving what constitutes religious beliefs and practices that are subject to First Amendment protections and restrictions. In several cases protecting the free exercise of beliefs, the Supreme Court has adopted an expansive view toward religion,[130] but it has not yet found an Establishment Clause violation in connection with a nontheistic creed.

---

[126]Mozert v. Hawkins County Bd. of Educ., 827 F.2d 1058 (6th Cir. 1987). This case divided civil libertarians; some felt the students had legitimate free exercise rights at stake, whereas others felt that the requested accommodation would advance religion in violation of the Establishment Clause.

[127]*See, e.g.*, Menora v. Ill. High Sch. Ass'n, 683 F.2d 1030 (7th Cir. 1982); Keller v. Gardner Cmty. Consol. Grade Sch. Dist. 72C, 552 F. Supp. 512 (N.D. Ill. 1982).

[128]*See* Protection of Pupil Rights Amendment to the NCLB Act of 2001, 20 U.S.C. § 1232h (2007); text accompanying note 176, Chapter 3.

[129]Epperson v. Arkansas, 393 U.S. 97, 107 (1968) (quoting Joseph Burstyn v. Wilson, 343 U.S. 495, 505 (1952)).

[130]*See, e.g.*, Thomas v. Review Bd., 450 U.S. 707, 714 (1981); United States v. Seeger, 380 U.S. 163, 175 (1965).

However, several courts have suggested that secular religions should be subject to the same Establishment Clause standards applied to theistic religions, and the Third Circuit ruled that public school instructional modules in transcendental meditation unconstitutionally advanced a nontraditional religious belief (the Science of Creative Intelligence).[131] Also, the Ninth Circuit held that a nonprofit group had standing to proceed with an Establishment Clause challenge to magnet and charter schools using Waldorf methods that are guided by the spiritual science of anthroposophy.[132]

The Origin of Humanity

Instruction pertaining to the origin of human life on Earth has generated continuing legal disputes, some of which have elicited national attention. Historically, several states by law barred evolution from the curriculum, because it conflicted with the biblical account of creation. In the famous *Scopes* "monkey trial" in the 1920s, the Tennessee Supreme Court upheld such a law, prohibiting the teaching of any theory that denies the Genesis version of creation or suggests "that man has descended from a lower order of animals."[133] In 1968, however, the United States Supreme Court struck down an Arkansas anti-evolution statute under the Establishment Clause, concluding that evolution is science (not a secular religion), and a state cannot restrict student access to such information simply to satisfy religious preferences.[134]

Subsequently, the Supreme Court in 1987 invalidated a Louisiana statute that mandated "equal time" for creation science and evolution and required school boards to make available curriculum guides, teaching aids, and resource materials on creation science.[135] Reasoning that creationism is not science, the Court concluded that the law was intended to discredit scientific information and advance religious beliefs in violation of the Establishment Clause. The Court did not accept the argument that the law promoted academic freedom and reasoned that it actually inhibited teachers' discretion to incorporate scientific theories about the origin of humanity into the curriculum.

Despite two Supreme Court decisions, the origin of humanity continues to generate legal activity. The Ninth Circuit ruled that school districts can mandate instruction

[131]Malnak v. Yogi, 592 F.2d 197 (3d Cir. 1979). *See also* Altman v. Bedford Cent. Sch. Dist., 245 F.3d 49 (2d Cir. 2001); *infra* text accompanying note 149. The Supreme Court also has noted that "the state may not establish a 'religion of secularism' in the sense of affirmatively opposing or showing hostility to religion, thus 'preferring those who believe in no religion.'" Sch. Dist. of Abington Twp. v. Schempp, 374 U.S. 203, 225 (1963).

[132]PLANS v. Sacramento City Unified Sch. Dist., 319 F.3d 504 (9th Cir. 2003).

[133]Scopes v. State, 289 S.W. 363, 364 (Tenn. 1927). Ironically, in the same school district that generated the *Scopes* case, a federal district court in 2002 found an Establishment Clause violation in the practice of allowing Bible teaching in elementary schools, because the instruction entailed religious inculcation rather than the academic study of religion. Doe v. Porter, 188 F. Supp. 2d 904 (E.D. Tenn. 2002).

[134]*Epperson*, 393 U.S. 97.

[135]Edwards v. Aguillard, 482 U.S. 578 (1987). *See also* Daniel v. Waters, 515 F.2d 485 (6th Cir. 1975); McLean v. Ark. Bd. of Educ., 529 F. Supp. 1255 (E.D. Ark. 1982).

in evolution, rejecting a teacher's claim that teaching this "antitheistic" doctrine would violate the Establishment Clause,[136] and a Minnesota appeals court upheld reassignment of a teacher who refused to teach evolution in conformance with the biology curriculum specifications.[137] A Georgia appeals court ruled that the use of a biology text addressing evolution does not denigrate students' religious beliefs in violation of the First Amendment,[138] and a Virginia court rejected a challenge to using a science textbook that allegedly promoted a secular religion by teaching evolution as a scientific fact.[139]

The Fifth Circuit struck down a Louisiana school board's resolution requiring teachers to issue a disclaimer that the presentation of evolutionary theory is not intended to dissuade students from the biblical version of creation; the disclaimer was found to endorse a particular religious viewpoint rather than promote critical thinking.[140] More recently, a Georgia federal district court ruled that a school district could not add stickers to its new biology textbooks with a warning that evolution is a theory, not a fact, and should be considered critically. The court concluded that an informed, reasonable observer would know the stickers were intended to convey that the school board "agrees with the beliefs of Christian fundamentalists and creationists," which is an impermissible endorsement of religion.[141]

Much of the current attention is focused on efforts to introduce intelligent design (ID) in public school science classes. Advocates of ID believe that human beings are too complex to have evolved randomly by natural selection and, therefore, must be the product of a supernatural force, but they do not mention God in referring to an unidentified intelligent designer.[142] Supporters distinguish ID from creationism, accepting that Earth is older than creationists contend, although many critics of ID view it as a religious belief akin to creationism.

There has been political activity at the school district and state levels pertaining to teaching evolution and alternative theories in 40 states during the past decade.[143] For example, the Kansas State Board of Education made front-page news in 1999 when it rejected proposed science standards emphasizing evolution and adopted an

[136]Peloza v. Capistrano Unified Sch. Dist., 37 F.3d 517 (9th Cir. 1994). *See also* Webster v. New Lenox Sch. Dist. No. 122, 917 F.2d 1004 (7th Cir. 1990) (upholding the school board's prohibition on teaching nonevolutionary theory).

[137]LeVake v. Indep. Sch. Dist. No. 656, 625 N.W.2d 502 (Minn. Ct. App. 2001).

[138]Moeller v. Schrenko, 554 S.E.2d 198 (Ga. Ct. App. 2001).

[139]Johnson v. Chesapeake City Sch. Bd., 52 Va. Cir. 252 (Cir. Ct. 2000).

[140]Freiler v. Tangipahoa Parish Bd. of Educ., 185 F.3d 337, 344–347 (5th Cir. 1999).

[141]Selman v. Cobb County Sch. Dist., 390 F. Supp. 2d 1286, 1312 (N.D. Ga. 2005), *vacated with instructions for the district court to conduct new evidentiary proceedings,* 449 F.3d 1320 (11th Cir. 2006). The stickers were proposed only after the school district adopted new textbooks that covered evolution, whereas previous materials had largely ignored the subject.

[142]*See* Martha McCarthy, "Instruction about the Origin of Humanity: Legal Controversies Evolve," *Education Law Reporter,* vol. 203 (2006), pp. 453–467.

[143]*See* National Center for Science Education, "News Archive," *Events of 2005–2007* (September 8, 2007), available at www.ncseweb.org/pressroom.asp?branch=statement.

alternative set eliminating the requirement that local school districts teach or test students about evolution. By 2007, the board had changed the standards four times, reflecting several power shifts on the board, and the controversy over teaching evolution is likely to continue in Kansas.[144] Other states are considering science standards that include critically assessing evolution, including ID instruction, or "teaching the controversy," which is more politically palatable than mandating instruction about ID.

In 2004, a Pennsylvania school district attracted national attention when it required high school biology teachers to introduce students to ID as an alternative to evolution. After seven teachers complained, the school board dropped the requirement and instead instructed administrators to read a statement that evolution is a theory and to refer students to a book explaining ID as an alternative theory. Several families challenged the resolution, and the federal district court struck down the policy, reasoning that it was a ploy to put religious beliefs in the public school science curriculum.[145] Nonetheless, controversies over teaching evolution and alternative theories continue in legislative and judicial forums.

Other Challenges

Allegations are being made that other components of the public school curriculum violate the Establishment Clause because they advance "secular humanism" or "New Age theology," which critics claim disavow God and exalt humans as masters of their own destinies. In addition to evolution, central targets have been sex education, values clarification, and outcome-based education, but few aspects of the curriculum have remained untouched by such claims. Recently, inclusion of the popular *Harry Potter* series in public school libraries has been challenged because the books deal with wizardry and magic that allegedly advance the occult/satanism.[146]

Even courts that have considered nontheistic creeds to be "religions" for First Amendment purposes have not ruled that challenged public school courses and materials advance such creeds. In a 1987 case, the Eleventh Circuit reversed an Alabama federal judge's conclusion that a school district's use of several dozen home economics, history, and social studies books unconstitutionally advanced secular humanism, finding instead that the books instilled in students values such as "independent thought, tolerance of diverse views, self-respect, maturity, self-reliance, and logical decision-making."[147]

---

[144]*See* Sarah Sparks, "Evolution Debate Hints at Deeper Science Ed Problems," *Education Daily* (February 16, 2007), pp. 1–2.

[145]*See* Kitzmiller v. Dover Area Sch. Dist., 400 F. Supp. 2d 707, 747 (M.D. Pa. 2005). The board members who championed the policy were voted out of office, and the policy had been rescinded before the decision was rendered.

[146]*See* Kathleen K. Manzo, "Charmed and Challenged," *Education Week* (November 14, 2001), pp. 14–15.

[147]Smith v. Bd. of Sch. Comm'rs, 655 F. Supp. 939 (S.D. Ala. 1987), *rev'd*, 827 F.2d 684, 692 (11th Cir. 1987) (also rejecting the contention that the mere omission of Christian religious facts in the curriculum represented unconstitutional hostility toward theistic beliefs). *See also* Grove v. Mead Sch. Dist. No. 354, 753 F.2d 1528 (9th Cir. 1985) (reasoning that *The Learning Tree* does not advance an antitheistic faith).

The Eighth Circuit more recently ruled that a Missouri teacher's contract was not renewed for impermissible reasons after she sent a "magic rock" home with each student, with a letter indicating that the rock is "special and unique, just like you!"[148] The court found community complaints that the letter and rock advanced New Ageism to be the basis for the board's action rather than the asserted concerns about the teacher's grading practices. The Second Circuit also found no constitutional violations in celebrating Earth Day or in role-playing as part of a drug prevention program using peer facilitators.[149] However, it ruled that one teacher's assignment for students to construct images of a Hindu deity abridged the First Amendment and that making worry dolls amounted to preference of superstition over religion in violation of the Establishment Clause.

Sex education classes have been particularly susceptible to charges that an antitheistic faith is being advanced, but courts consistently have found that the challenged courses present public health information that furthers legitimate educational objectives and do not denounce Christianity.[150] In 2006, the Ninth Circuit reiterated that parents do not have the exclusive right to be the sole provider of sex education, and that parental interests do not prevail over the state's interests in providing important health information.[151] The judiciary has ruled that the Establishment Clause precludes the state from barring sex education simply to conform to the religious beliefs of some parents. However, courts have acknowledged that students have a free exercise right to be excused from sex education classes if such instruction conflicts with their sectarian beliefs.[152]

Because conservative citizen groups have not been successful in getting sex education barred from the public school curriculum, they have lobbied for the adoption of programs that stress abstinence between unmarried people. A Louisiana appeals court agreed with plaintiffs that one of these programs, *Sex Respect: The Option of True Sexual Freedom,* violated state law by promoting Christian doctrine and including some erroneous information.[153] The court ordered the school district to delete passages that were factually inaccurate or that dealt with the moral and spiritual implications of premarital sex, contraceptives, and sexually transmitted diseases.

[148]Cowan v. Strafford R-VI Sch. Dist., 140 F.3d 1153, 1156 (8th Cir. 1998). *See also* text accompanying note 99, Chapter 9.

[149]Altman v. Bedford Cent. Sch. Dist., 245 F.3d 49 (2d Cir. 2001).

[150]*See, e.g.,* Citizens for Parental Rights v. San Mateo County Bd. of Educ., 124 Cal. Rptr. 68 (Ct. App. 1975); Hobolth v. Greenway, 218 N.W.2d 98 (Mich. Ct. App. 1974); Smith v. Ricci, 446 A.2d 501 (N.J. 1982).

[151]Fields v. Palmdale Sch. Dist., 447 F.3d 1187 (9th Cir. 2006), *cert. denied,* 127 S. Ct. 725 (2006) (upholding school district's administration of a psychological assessment questionnaire with several questions pertaining to topics of a sexual nature). *See* text accompanying note 180, Chapter 3.

[152]*See, e.g.,* Brown v. Hot, Sexy and Safer Productions, 68 F.3d 525 (1st Cir. 1995).

[153]Coleman v. Caddo Parish Sch. Bd., 635 So. 2d 1238 (La. Ct. App. 1994). *See also* ACLU v. Foster, No. 02-1440, 2002 U.S. Dist. LEXIS 13778 (E.D. La. July 25, 2002) (ordering state officials to ensure that federal funds are not used to promote religious beliefs under the Governor's Program on Abstinence).

Conflicting rulings have been rendered regarding the rights at stake regarding curricular materials designed to promote tolerance for alternative lifestyles. The First Circuit held that an elementary school curriculum encouraging respect for gay persons and same-sex marriage did not abridge the free exercise rights of students or parental rights to direct the upbringing of their children.[154] After a Kentucky federal district court similarly rejected a parental challenge to a school district's mandatory diversity training for middle and high school students including respect for homosexuality that was not found to promote or condemn any religious beliefs, the Sixth Circuit reversed and remanded this case for additional proceedings regarding whether the policy chilled student expression of contrary views.[155] Also, a Maryland federal district court enjoined implementation of a school district's pilot sex education programs that address "sexual variation," reasoning that additional investigation was needed to ascertain whether the program constitutes viewpoint discrimination by presenting only the perspective that homosexuality is natural and a morally correct lifestyle and implying that certain religious beliefs about homosexuality are unenlightened and misguided.[156]

The content of reading series also has been contested on religious grounds. For example, the Impressions reading series, published by Harcourt Brace Jovanovich, generated numerous challenges in the late 1980s and early 1990s. The series, employing the whole language approach to reading instruction, was challenged as being morbid and depressing and promoting witchcraft based on the Wicca religion. Wicca has been recognized as a religion for the protection of free exercise rights, but both the Seventh and Ninth Circuits did not find that reading stories about witches or even creating poetic chants constituted the practice of witchcraft or advanced a pagan cult.[157]

Although courts have not condoned parental attacks on various aspects of the public school curriculum that allegedly conflict with their religious values, more difficult legal questions are raised when policy makers support curriculum restrictions for religious reasons. Since courts show considerable deference to legislatures and school boards in educational matters, conservative parent organizations have pressed for state and federal legislation and school board policies barring certain content from public schools.

---

[154]Parker v. Hurley, No. 07-1528, 2008 U.S. App. LEXIS 2070 (1st Cir. Jan. 31, 2008) (dismissing state law claims without prejudice so such claims could be reinstituted in state courts).

[155]Morrison v. Bd. of Educ., 419 F. Supp. 2d 937 (E.D. Ky. 2006), *rev'd and remanded,* 507 F.3d 494 (6th Cir. 2007).

[156]Citizens for a Responsible Curriculum v. Montgomery County Pub. Schs., No. AW-05-1194, 2005 U.S. Dist. LEXIS 8130 (S.D. Md. May 5, 2005).

[157]Fleischfresser v. Dirs. of Sch. Dist. 200, 15 F.3d 680 (7th Cir. 1994); Brown v. Woodland Joint Unified Sch. Dist., 27 F.3d 1373 (9th Cir. 1994). This series was discontinued in 1994 because of the controversies generated over its approach to teaching reading and the nature of the content selected. *See also* Counts v. Cedarville Sch. Dist., 295 F. Supp. 2d 996 (W.D. Ark. 2003) (striking down school district's policy requiring parental permission for students to check out certain library materials dealing with witchcraft and the occult).

State Aid to Private Schools

In addition to disputes over the place of religion in public schools, government relations with private—primarily religious—schools have generated a substantial
amount of First Amendment litigation. Unquestionably, parents have a legitimate
interest in directing the upbringing of their children, including their education. In
1925, the Supreme Court afforded constitutional protection to private schools' rights
to exist and to parents' rights to select private education as an alternative to public
schooling.[158] Yet, the Court also recognized that the state has a general welfare interest in mandating school attendance and regulating private education to ensure an educated citizenry, considered essential in a democracy. Some litigation has involved
conflicts between the state's exercise of its *parens patriae* authority to protect the
well-being of children and parental interests in having their children educated in settings that reinforce their religious and philosophical beliefs. If the government interferes with parents' child-rearing decisions, it must show that the intervention is
necessary to protect the child or the state.[159] Courts have upheld minimum state
requirements for private schools (e.g., prescribed courses, personnel requirements),
but the recent trend has been toward imposing outcome measures, such as requiring
private school students to participate in statewide testing programs.

Almost 12 percent of all PK–12 students in the United States are enrolled in private schools, but this ratio could change if additional government aid flows to private
education. Despite the fact that 37 states specifically prohibit the use of public funds for
sectarian purposes, about three-fourths of the states provide some public aid to private
school students, including those attending sectarian schools.[160] The primary types of
aid are for transportation services, the loan of textbooks, state-required testing programs, special education for children with disabilities, and counseling services. Some
of the most significant Supreme Court decisions interpreting the Establishment Clause
have pertained to the use of public funds for private, primarily sectarian, education.

Aid for Student Services

The Supreme Court's support of religious accommodations in terms of allowing government support for parochial school students has been consistent since 1993,[161] with some

---

[158]Pierce v. Soc'y of Sisters, 268 U.S. 510 (1925). *See* text accompanying note 2, Chapter 3, for a discussion of compulsory attendance laws.

[159]*See* Wisconsin v. Yoder, 406 U.S. 205, 214 (1972); *supra* text accompanying note 11.

[160]*See* National Center for Education Statistics, *Private School Universe Survey* (Washington, D.C.: U.S.
Department of Education, 2005); *The Regulation of Private Schools in America: A State-by-State Analysis*
(Washington, D.C.: U.S. Department of Education, 2000).

[161]*See, e.g.,* Mitchell v. Helms, 530 U.S. 793 (2000); Agostini v. Felton, 521 U.S. 203 (1997); Rosenberger
v. Rector & Visitors, 515 U.S. 819 (1995); Zobrest v. Catalina Foothills Sch. Dist., 509 U.S. 1 (1993); *infra*
text accompanying notes 166–172. *But see* Bd. of Educ. v. Grumet, 512 U.S. 687 (1994) (striking down a
legislative attempt to create a separate school district along religious lines to serve special-needs Satmar
Hasidic children whose strict form of Judaism does not allow them to be educated with non-Satmars).

evidence of the accommodationist trend much earlier.[162] Indeed, the "child-benefit" doctrine has been used to justify government aid for transportation and secular textbooks for parochial school students since the mid-twentieth century.[163] Also, the Supreme Court in 1980 upheld government support for state-required testing programs in private schools,[164] even though a few years earlier it had found aid to develop and administer state-required as well as teacher-developed tests in violation of the Establishment Clause, because such tests potentially could be used to advance sectarian purposes.[165]

Then, in 1993, the Supreme Court found no Establishment Clause violation in publicly supporting sign-language interpreters in parochial schools,[166] signaling a paradigm shift toward the use of public school personnel in sectarian schools. The Court in *Zobrest v. Catalina Foothills School District* reasoned that the aid is going to the child as part of a federal government program that distributes funds neutrally to qualifying children with disabilities under federal law. The child is the primary recipient of the aid, and the school receives only incidental benefits. The Court reasoned that unlike a teacher or counselor, an interpreter neither adds to nor subtracts from the sectarian school's environment but merely interprets material that is presented.

In the 1997 decision, *Agostini v. Felton*, the Supreme Court removed the prohibition on public school personnel providing remedial instruction in religious schools that it had announced 12 years earlier.[167] The controversy focused on Title I of the Elementary and Secondary Education Act (ESEA) of 1965, targeting educationally and economically disadvantaged students and requiring comparable services to be provided for eligible students attending nonpublic schools.[168] The Court in *Agostini*

[162]*See* Witters v. Wash. Dep't of Servs. for the Blind, 474 U.S. 481 (1986) (upholding use of federal vocational rehabilitation aid to support ministerial training); Mueller v. Allen, 463 U.S. 388 (1983) (upholding state tax benefit for educational expenses available to parents of public or private school students).

[163]*See* Bd. of Educ. v. Allen, 392 U.S. 236 (1968) (finding no Establishment Clause violation in a state law requiring public school districts to loan secular textbooks to all secondary students, including those attending parochial schools); Everson v. Bd. of Educ., 330 U.S. 1 (1947) (rejecting an Establishment Clause challenge to the use of public funds to provide transportation services for nonpublic school students).

[164]Comm. for Pub. Educ. & Religious Liberty v. Regan, 444 U.S. 646 (1980).

[165]Meek v. Pittenger, 421 U.S. 349 (1975); Levitt v. Comm. for Pub. Educ. & Religious Liberty, 413 U.S. 472 (1973).

[166]*Zobrest*, 509 U.S. 1. *See also Rosenberger*, 515 U.S. 819 (holding that the University of Virginia could not engage in viewpoint discrimination by denying a student religious organization access to student activities funds to pay an outside contractor to print its religious publications); *supra* text accompanying note 101. *But see* Gary S. v. Manchester Sch. Dist., 374 F.3d 15 (1st Cir. 2004) (holding that children with disabilities attending private religious schools were entitled to services, but not the full panoply of services available to public school students with disabilities; the generally applicable regulations do not selectively burden religious conduct).

[167]521 U.S. 203 (1997) (overturning its ruling that barred the use of public school personnel to provide Title I remedial services on sectarian school premises, Aguilar v. Felton, 473 U.S. 402 (1985), and the portion of its decision that invalidated a shared-time program under which public school classes were provided for parochial school students on parochial school premises, Sch. Dist. v. Ball, 473 U.S. 373 (1985)).

[168]The most recent reauthorization is the NCLB Act of 2001, 20 U.S.C. § 6301 (2007).

held that comparability can be achieved by allowing public school personnel to provide instructional services in sectarian schools, reasoning that under current Establishment Clause interpretations, the program's threat of increasing political divisiveness and requiring pervasive monitoring were insufficient to abridge the Establishment Clause. In both *Zobrest* and *Agostini*, the Court rejected the notion that the Establishment Clause lays down an "absolute bar to the placing of a public employee in a sectarian school."[169]

The Supreme Court in *Mitchell v. Helms* subsequently found no Establishment Clause violation in using federal aid to purchase instructional materials and equipment for student use in sectarian schools.[170] Specifically, the ruling allows the use of public funds for computers, other instructional equipment, and library books in religious schools under Title II of the ESEA federal aid program. The plurality reasoned that religious indoctrination or subsidization of religion could not be attributed to the government when aid, even direct aid, is:

- Distributed based on secular criteria,
- Available to religious and secular beneficiaries on a nondiscriminatory basis, and
- Allowed to flow to religious schools only because of private choices of parents.[171]

Conceding that the equipment at issue could be diverted for sectarian uses, the plurality asserted that the central issue is not divertibility of the aid, because government support for secular activities always frees parochial school resources for religious purposes. Instead, the plurality emphasized that the constitutional standard is whether the aid itself would be appropriate for a public school to receive and is distributed in an even-handed manner—conditions it concluded were satisfied by the aid in *Helms*. Six justices agreed that prior Supreme Court rulings barring state aid in the form of providing maps, slide projectors, auxiliary services, and other instructional materials and equipment to sectarian schools were no longer good law.[172]

There are very few rulings left that reflect the Supreme Court's separationist stance regarding state aid to nonpublic schools. In fact, the Supreme Court seems to have dismantled most of the decisions rendered during the heyday of applying the stringent *Lemon* test in the 1970s, in which it struck down various types of public assistance to private schools.

---

[169]*Agostini*, 521 U.S. at 223–224; *Zobrest,* 509 U.S. at 13.

[170]530 U.S. 793 (2000). *See also* Stark v. Indep. Sch. Dist. No. 640, 123 F.3d 1068 (8th Cir. 1997) (upholding a school district's decision to reopen a one-class school with a modified curriculum in response to a request from the Brethren sect; accommodating the parents' request that the school use no technology did not violate the Establishment Clause).

[171]530 U.S. at 809–814.

[172]*Id.* at 835–836, overturning Wolman v. Walter, 433 U.S. 229 (1977); Meek v. Pittenger, 421 U.S. 349 (1975). These six justices also supported a modification of the *Lemon* test, making it explicit that excessive entanglement is simply part of consideration of the policy's primary effect.

It must be remembered, however, that simply because courts have interpreted the Establishment Clause as allowing various types of public aid for nonpublic school students does not mean that states must use public funds for these purposes. For example, several state courts have ruled that transportation aid to private school students violates state constitutional provisions prohibiting the use of public funds for sectarian purposes.[173] Similarly, some state courts have invalidated lending textbooks to nonpublic school students under their state constitutions.[174] The California Supreme Court called the child-benefit doctrine "logically indefensible" in striking down a state law that provided for the loan of textbooks to nonpublic school students.[175]

In 2004, the Supreme Court delivered a significant decision, *Locke v. Davey,* upholding states' discretion to adopt more stringent antiestablishment provisions than demanded by the First Amendment.[176] At issue in *Locke* was the Promise Scholarship Program established by the state of Washington to provide aid to assist academically gifted students with their college expenses in public or private (including religiously affiliated) accredited institutions of higher education. To comply with a state constitutional prohibition on using public funds for religious purposes, the scholarships cannot be used for students to pursue degrees in devotional theology. Upholding the state restriction, the Supreme Court ruled that even though the use of the Promise Scholarships for pastoral degrees is *permitted* under the Establishment Clause,[177] it is not *required* by the Free Exercise Clause. In short, simply because the Establishment Clause allows an activity does not mean that a state must financially support the activity. The Supreme Court held that the Washington constitutional provision was intended to keep schools free from sectarian control, rejecting the contention that it emanated from religious bigotry as a so-called Blaine Amendment.[178]

Most of the state constitutional provisions that preclude the use of public funds for religious purposes are more restrictive than the Establishment Clause. The *Locke* decision has provided an impetus for state litigation as the limits of similar provisions are tested in other states. Indeed, one of the most significant implications of *Locke* might be its stimulation of an increase in church/state cases initiated in *state* courts.

---

[173]*See, e.g.,* Pucket v. Rounds, No. 03-5033-KES, 2006 U.S. Dist. LEXIS 3925 (D.S.D. Jan. 17, 2006), note 57, Chapter 3; Matthews v. Quinton, 362 P.2d 932 (Alaska 1961); McVey v. Hawkins, 258 S.W.2d 927 (Mo. 1953); Visser v. Nooksack Valley Sch. Dist. No. 506, 207 P.2d 198 (Wash. 1949). *See also* Healy v. Indep. Sch. Dist. No. 625, 962 F.2d 1304 (8th Cir. 1992) (terminating transportation benefits from the state for students attending a Lutheran school outside the school district did not violate students' constitutional rights).

[174]*See, e.g.,* Fannin v. Williams, 655 SW.2d 480 (Ky. 1983); Bloom v. Sch. Comm., 379 N.E.2d 578 (Mass. 1978); Elbe v. Yankton Indep. Sch. Dist. No. 63-3, 372 N.W.2d 113 (S.D. 1985).

[175]Cal. Teachers Ass'n v. Riles, 632 P.2d 953, 962 (Cal. 1981).

[176]540 U.S. 712 (2004) (interpreting Wash. Const. Art. I, § 11 (2007)).

[177]*See* Witters v. Wash. Dep't of Servs. for the Blind, 474 U. S. 481 (1986).

[178]*Locke,* 540 U.S. at 724 n. 7 (finding that Washington's constitutional prohibition on the use of public funds for religious worship, exercise, or instruction was *not* modeled on a failed constitutional amendment proposed by former House Speaker James Blaine in 1875, which allegedly reflected anti-Catholic sentiment).

Aid to Encourage Educational Choice

Tax-relief measures for private school tuition and educational vouchers have received considerable attention in legislative forums to make private schooling a viable choice for more families. The primary justification for such measures is that the aid flows to religious schools only because of private choices of parents.

Tax-Relief Measures.   Tax benefits in the form of deductions or credits for private school expenses have been proposed at both state and federal levels. Although Congress has not yet endorsed any proposals for federal income tax credits for private school tuition, a few states have enacted tax-relief provisions for educational expenses. The central constitutional question is whether such measures advance religion in violation of the Establishment Clause because the primary beneficiaries are parents of parochial school children and ultimately religious institutions.

In 1983, the Supreme Court upheld a Minnesota tax-benefit program allowing parents of public or private school students to claim a limited state income tax deduction for tuition, transportation, and secular textbook expenses incurred for each elementary or secondary school dependent. The Court majority in *Mueller v. Allen* found the Minnesota law "vitally different" from an earlier New York provision, which violated the Establishment Clause by bestowing tax benefits *only* on private school patrons.[179] The majority declared that Minnesota's "decision to defray the cost of some educational expenses incurred by parents—regardless of the type of schools their children attend—evidences a purpose that is both secular and understandable."[180]

A few other states provide such tax benefits. The Arizona Supreme Court upheld the state's tax benefit program providing a state tax credit up to $500 for contributions to school tuition organizations to support private school tuition.[181] However, most efforts to provide state tax relief for educational expenses have been defeated when placed before the voters, possibly because of the significant impact of such policies on state revenues.

Vouchers.   The debate continues over the merits of various voucher models under which public funds would flow to private schools based on parental choices. A number of New England states have had de facto voucher plans for years; school districts without high schools provide a designated amount for high school tuition in neighboring public school districts or independent private schools that the families select.

---

[179]463 U.S. 388, 398 (1983) (contrasting Comm. for Pub. Educ. & Religious Liberty v. Nyquist, 413 U.S. 756 (1973)).

[180]*Id.*, 463 U.S. at 395.

[181]Kotterman v. Killian, 972 P.2d 606, 615 (1999). *See also* Toney v. Bower, 744 N.E.2d 351 (Ill. App. Ct. 2001) (rejecting federal and state religious establishment challenges to an Illinois tax credit for a portion of PK–12 education expenses at public or private schools). Illinois, Iowa, and Minnesota provide tax deductions or credits for parents regarding educational expenses, and Arizona, Florida, Pennsylvania, and Puerto Rico allow credits or deductions to persons or groups contributing money to scholarship organizations that distribute the scholarships to qualifying students to attend public or private schools of their choice.

Yet, very few other plans were adopted until the mid-1990s, and not until 1999 did Florida become the first state to implement a statewide voucher plan allowing students attending failing public schools to use government vouchers in qualified public or private schools of their choice. Also, a few urban districts have adopted state-funded voucher plans for disadvantaged youth,[182] and privately funded scholarships are available for students to attend private schools in more than 30 major cities nationally.[183]

In 2002, the Supreme Court in *Zelman v. Simmons-Harris* resolved the conflict among lower courts regarding the participation of religious schools in state-funded voucher programs. In this five-to-four ruling, the Court upheld a scholarship program that gives choices to economically disadvantaged families in the Cleveland City School District through vouchers that can be used toward tuition at participating public or private schools.[184] No public school has elected to be involved in this voucher program, and almost all the participating private schools are church related.

The Supreme Court relied heavily on the fact that parents—not the government—make the decision for the scholarship funds to flow to private schools. The Court emphasized that the aid is completely neutral with respect to religion because the government benefits are provided to a broad group of individuals defined only by their financial need and residence in the Cleveland School District. Considering the program to be one of "true private choice" among public and private options, the Court found no Establishment Clause violation, even though 96 percent of participating students attend religious schools.[185]

Since there are no federal constitutional issues, the legality of voucher programs will be determined on the basis of state law. The Milwaukee and Cleveland programs have been endorsed by state courts,[186] but recently other programs have not fared well when challenged under state education clauses or state prohibitions on the use of public funds for religious purposes. In 2006, the Florida Supreme Court relied on the state constitution's education clause, similar to provisions in many other states, to invalidate the statewide voucher program for students attending deficient public schools.[187] The court interpreted the legislature's duty to provide for a uniform system of public

---

[182]Milwaukee offered the first program for disadvantaged students in 1990, and this program was expanded in 2006.

[183]The Children First America Foundation, established in 1994, provides vouchers to children in more than three-fourths of the states, and the Children's Scholarship Fund, founded in 1998, has provided scholarships to students attending 7,000 private schools. More than 100 private organizations nationally have invested $500 million in scholarships for students to enroll in private schools.

[184]536 U.S. 639 (2002). The voucher program is part of a larger initiative to address failing public schools by providing educational options to families including tutorial services, theme-based magnet schools, and community schools that receive additional funding and are governed by their own boards.

[185]*Id.* at 649.

[186]*See* Simmons-Harris v. Goff, 711 N.E.2d 203 (Ohio 1999); Jackson v. Benson, 578 N.W.2d 602 (Wis. 1998).

[187]Bush v. Holmes, 919 So. 2d 392, 398 (Fla. 2006) (interpreting Fla. Const., Article IX, § 1(a)).

schools as requiring all schools that receive state aid to satisfy the same standards. The court reasoned that the Florida voucher program unconstitutionally diverted public funds into separate, nonuniform, private systems that compete with and reduce funds for public education.

The Colorado Supreme Court also invalidated a pilot voucher program for low-income students attending low-performing schools, concluding that the program violated the "local control" clause of the state constitution by taking away districts' discretion in spending funds for instruction.[188] In addition, federal and state courts have upheld Maine's law that excludes religious schools from the state's tuition reimbursement program for high school students in districts that do not operate public high schools.[189] As discussed, the Supreme Court's 2004 *Locke* decision recognized that states can adopt more stringent antiestablishment measures than included in the First Amendment without exhibiting hostility toward religion, thereby strengthening the state grounds for challenging voucher programs.[190]

Despite recent judicial setbacks, several states are considering targeted voucher proposals, and some programs have been adopted.[191] Florida, Utah, and Arizona have established voucher programs for children with disabilities to attend private schools. In 2007, Utah voters rejected the most comprehensive legislative plan to date, which would have provided vouchers, varying by family income, for all Utah students to attend private schools selected by their parents.[192] In addition to state initiatives, the federal government in 2004 approved $14 million for a pilot voucher program for low-income students in Washington, D.C., to attend private schools.[193]

Even where voucher programs that include sectarian schools satisfy state constitutions, fiscal concerns may influence whether large-scale voucher initiatives are implemented, because states currently are not supporting students attending private schools. Voucher proposals will continue to be enacted and challenged, and their

---

[188]Owens v. Colo. Congress of Parents, Teachers, and Students, 92 P.3d 933 (Colo. 2004). Florida, Georgia, Kansas, Montana, and Virginia have provisions similar to Colorado's "local control" clause.

[189]Eulitt v. Me. Dep't of Educ., 386 F.3d 344 (1st Cir. 2004); Strout v. Albanese, 178 F.3d 57 (1st Cir. 1999); Anderson v. Town of Durham, 895 A.2d 944 (Me. 2006), *cert. denied,* 127 S. Ct. 661 (2006); Bagley v. Raymond Sch. Dep't, 728 A.2d 127 (Me. 1999).

[190]*See* Locke v. Davey, 540 U.S. 712 (2004); text accompanying *supra* note 176.

[191]In 2006, Ohio expanded eligibility beyond Cleveland to provide for up to 14,000 vouchers for disadvantaged students in Ohio who have attended failing "academic emergency" public schools for three years. Ohio Rev. Code Ann. § 3310.01 *et seq.* (2007).

[192]*See* Utah Code Ann. § 53A-1a-801 *et seq.* (2007). Glen Warchol, "Vouchers Go Down in Crushing Defeat," *Salt Lake Tribune* (November 7, 2007), available at www.districtadministration.com/newssummary. aspx?news=yes&postid=48679.

[193]The NCLB Act of 2001, 20 U.S.C. § 6301 *et seq.* (2007), requires school districts to provide educational options to students who attend public schools that for two or more years have not met their annual progress objectives toward the goal of 100 percent student proficiency in key subject areas. *See* text accompanying note 39, Chapter 1. Also, Congress included vouchers in the hurricane relief plan for displaced students due to such natural disasters. *See* Nella Banerjee, "Senate Votes 1.66 Billion for Storm-Displaced Pupils," *New York Times* (November 4, 2005), p. A-22.

legality will depend primarily on state courts' interpretations of state constitutional provisions. Indeed, instead of a national policy, we soon may have 50 standards regarding the legality of school vouchers.

Conclusion

Since the early 1960s, church/state controversies have generated a steady stream of education litigation, and there are no signs of diminishing legal activity in this domain. The principle that the First Amendment demands wholesome governmental neutrality toward religion has been easier to assert than to apply. Some lawsuits have involved claims under the Free Exercise Clause, but most school cases have focused on interpretations of Establishment Clause prohibitions.

From the 1960s through the mid-1980s, the federal judiciary seemed more committed to enforcing Establishment Clause restrictions in elementary and second-ary school settings than elsewhere. Since the mid-1980s, however, there seems to be greater government accommodation of religion, especially in terms of public funds flowing to religious schools. Also, religious influences and accommodations in pub-lic schools have become more prevalent. The Free Speech Clause increasingly seems to prevail over Establishment Clause restrictions in protecting religious expression in public schools. The metaphor of separation of church and state seems to have been replaced by the concepts of equal access for and equal treatment of religious groups.

The following generalizations characterize the current status of church/state relations involving schools:

1. State-imposed devotional activities in public schools, regardless of voluntary participation, violate the Establishment Clause.
2. Students have a free exercise right to engage in silent prayer in public schools, but school officials cannot encourage students to pray.
3. Prayers delivered by members of the clergy in public school graduation cere-monies violate the Establishment Clause, but student-initiated devotionals dur-ing the ceremony may be permissible under certain circumstances.
4. Holidays with both secular and religious significance can be observed in an objective and prudent manner in public schools.
5. The Ten Commandments and other religious documents cannot be posted per-manently in public schools, although some longstanding displays intended to celebrate the state's history have been allowed outside the school domain.
6. The academic study of religion is legitimate in public schools, but such instruc-tion cannot be used as a ploy to instill religious beliefs.
7. Under the Equal Access Act, if a secondary school receives federal funds and creates a limited open forum for student groups to meet during noninstruc-tional time, religious clubs cannot be denied access to the forum.
8. Religious organizations generally cannot distribute their literature in public schools, but sectarian materials prepared and distributed by students are

usually treated like other types of private student expression, subject to reasonable time, place, and manner restrictions.

9. If community groups are allowed to use public schools after school hours, groups cannot be discriminated against based on the religious content of their meetings, even groups that target children attending the schools.

10. Students can be released from public schools to receive religious instruction that is provided off public school grounds.

11. Students are entitled to excused absences to observe religious holidays if the absences do not place an undue hardship on the school.

12. Attempts to evade compulsory school attendance mandates for religious reasons have been unsuccessful, but Amish children have been excused from mandatory schooling after successfully completing the eighth grade.

13. Students can be excused from specific public school observances and activities that impede the practice of their religious beliefs as long as the management of the school or the students' academic progress is not disrupted.

14. Laws or policies requiring equal emphasis on the Genesis account of creation or instruction in intelligent design when evolution is taught violate the Establishment Clause.

15. States have a general welfare interest in mandating school attendance to ensure an educated citizenry; however, parents have the right to select private schooling for their children.

16. States can regulate private education, but unduly restrictive regulations may impair free exercise rights.

17. Direct government subsidies available only to religious schools violate the Establishment Clause.

18. Public aid for certain services that benefit the child and only incidentally benefit religious institutions (e.g., transportation to school; loan of textbooks; and provision of standardized testing, sign-language interpreters, computers, and other equipment) does not violate the Establishment Clause.

19. Tax benefits for education expenses incurred in public and private schools and voucher programs that allow public funds to flow to religious schools because of the private choices of parents do not violate the Establishment Clause.

20. States can impose more stringent state antiestablishment provisions, including restrictions on aid to religious schools, than demanded by the First Amendment.

3

School Attendance and Instructional Issues

Although U.S. citizens have no federal constitutional right to a public education, each state constitution places a duty on its legislature to provide for free public schooling, thus creating a state entitlement (property right) for all children to be educated at public expense.[1] Substantial litigation has resulted from the collision of state interests in guaranteeing the general welfare with individual interests in exercising constitutional and statutory rights. This chapter focuses on legal mandates pertaining to various requirements and rights associated with school attendance and the instructional program.

Compulsory School Attendance

At present, all 50 states compel children between specified ages, usually 6 to 16, to be educated. The legal basis for compulsory education is grounded in the common law doctrine of *parens patriae*, which means that the state, in its guardian role, has the authority to enact reasonable laws for the welfare of its citizens or the state. Parents can face criminal prosecution or civil suits for failing to meet their legal obligations under compulsory school attendance laws; furthermore, their children can be expelled for excessive truancy or judicially ordered to return to school.[2] In some

---

[1] *See* Goss v. Lopez, 419 U.S. 565 (1975).

[2] *See, e.g., In re* J.B., 58 S.W.3d 575 (Mo. Ct. App. 2001); State *ex rel.* Estes v. Egnor, 443 S.E.2d 193 (W. Va. 1994). *But see* Hamilton v. State, 694 N.E.2d 1171 (Ind. Ct. App. 1998) (holding that parents cannot be convicted of neglect under the compulsory attendance law if not served proper notice of their children's failure to attend school); State v. Self, 155 S.W.3d 756 (Mo. Ct. App. 2005) (holding that state officials failed to show that a mother purposefully caused her pregnant child to be truant); State v. Smrekar, 2000 Ohio 2609 (Ct. App. 2000) (holding that the school district presented insufficient evidence of unexcused absences to consider a student a habitual truant and impose a fine and jail sentence on the parents).

instances, truant children have been made wards of juvenile courts, with probation officers supervising their school attendance.[3]

State laws generally recognize certain exceptions to compulsory attendance mandates. A common exemption is for married students; some states emancipate married students from required school attendance because they have assumed adult responsibilities. Statutes often include other exceptions, such as students serving temporarily as pages for the state legislature and children who have reached age 14 and have obtained lawful employment certificates. In addition to statutory exceptions from compulsory attendance mandates, the Supreme Court has granted an exemption on First Amendment religious grounds to Amish children who have successfully completed the eighth grade.[4] Most other attempts to keep children out of school on sectarian or other grounds have not been successful.[5]

States generally do not compel school attendance beyond age 16, but a number of states encourage students to stay in school by conditioning a driver's license on school attendance for students under age 18. In an illustrative case, the West Virginia high court upheld such a state law as sufficiently related to the legitimate goals of keeping teenagers in school and reducing automobile accidents among children who have not exhibited responsibility.[6] School personnel must be certain, however, that they do not violate students' privacy or equal protection rights in releasing information about individuals who do not meet such prerequisites to obtaining their licenses.[7] The Federal Dropout Prevention Act of 2002, which is part of the No Child Left Behind (NCLB) Act, also encourages school districts to enact measures to keep high school students in school.[8]

---

[3]*See, e.g.,* G.N. v. State, 833 N.E.2d 1071 (Ind. Ct. App. 2005) (holding that the state need only show that absences occurred in finding a student delinquent; the student has the burden of showing that the absences were excused or based on good reasons). *But see In re Interest* of Kevin K., 742 N.W. 2d 767 (Neb. 2007) (holding that juvenile court's jurisdiction over a truant student ended because the student turned 16 and his mother authorized the discontinuance of his enrollment).

[4]Wisconsin v. Yoder, 406 U.S. 205 (1972); text accompanying note 11, Chapter 2.

[5]*See, e.g.,* Hatch v. Goerke, 502 F.2d 1189 (10th Cir. 1974) (finding the conflict between a public school's grooming restrictions and Indian traditions and religious beliefs did not justify an exemption from compulsory education mandates, but a student's expulsion without a hearing for refusing to cut his hair impaired due process rights); Johnson v. Charles City Cmty. Schs., 368 N.W.2d 74 (Iowa 1985) (refusing to exempt fundamentalist Baptist children from compulsory education); Johnson v. Prince William County Sch. Bd., 404 S.E.2d 209 (Va. 1991) (upholding school board's denial of parents' application for a religious exemption from the compulsory school attendance law because the parents failed to establish that their request was based on *bona fide* religious beliefs).

[6]Means v. Sidiropolis, 401 S.E.2d 447 (W. Va. 1990) (holding, however, that before a license is revoked, a school dropout must be provided a hearing with appropriate school officials to ascertain if the circumstances for dropping out are beyond the individual's control).

[7]*See* D.F. v. Codell, 127 S.W.3d 571 (Ky. 2003) (holding that the state law revoking driving privileges for students who drop out of school or are academically deficient violated equal protection rights by applying only to students living in counties with alternative education programs).

[8]Dropout Prevention Act, 20 U.S.C. § 6551-61 (2007). Proposals also have been made to provide parents with tax incentives for their children to graduate from high school. *See* David Hansen, "The High School Attainment Credit: A Tax Credit Encouraging Parents to Help Motivate Students to Graduate from High School," *Brigham Young University Education and Law Journal* (2006), pp. 357–377.

Alternatives to Public Schooling

States can mandate education, but it was settled in 1925 that private school attendance can satisfy such requirements. In *Pierce v. Society of Sisters* the United States Supreme Court invalidated an Oregon statute requiring children between 8 and 16 years old to attend *public* schools. The Court declared that "the fundamental theory of liberty upon which all governments in this Union repose excludes any general power of the state to standardize its children by forcing them to accept instruction from public teachers only."[9] In essence, parents do not have the right to determine *whether* their children are educated, but they do have some control over *where* such education takes place. If divorced parents have joint custody over their children, educational decisions cannot be made unilaterally by the custodial parent.[10]

Despite states' legal authority to regulate alternatives to public education, there has been a trend since the 1980s to ease personnel and curriculum requirements and to monitor the quality of private education by subjecting students to state-prescribed tests. Private schools may have to adhere to specific standards to receive state accreditation or to have their students compete interscholastically, but enrollment in *nonaccredited* private programs generally can satisfy compulsory school attendance.

Compulsory education laws in most states have been interpreted as permitting home education programs that meet state standards.[11] Estimates indicate that home education has grown from about 15,000 children nationwide in the mid-1970s to between 1.9 and 2.4 million students in 2005–2006.[12] Parents educating their children at home can be convicted of violating compulsory education laws for failing to report their children's course of study, texts, and instructors to the local school district, and parents can be required to maintain portfolios of their children's work that are subject

---

[9]268 U.S. 510, 535 (1925). *See also* Troxel v. Granville, 530 U.S. 57, 79 (2000) (recognizing extensive precedent leaving little doubt "that the Due Process Clause of the Fourteenth Amendment protects the fundamental right of parents to make decisions concerning the care, custody, and control of their children" in holding that a state's overbroad child-visitation law as applied to grandparent visitations violated a mother's fundamental right to direct the upbringing of her child).

[10]*See, e.g.*, Crowley v. McKinney, 400 F.3d 965 (7th Cir. 2005) (recognizing the noncustodial parent's rights to review his children's educational records but not to micromanage the school's educational program); Anderson v. Anderson, 56 S.W.3d 5 (Tenn. Ct. App. 1999) (holding that the primary custodial parent could not unilaterally decide that children should be home schooled). However, in some situations, one parent can be granted sole legal custody, including the authority to make all educational decisions, even though the other parent has visitation rights.

[11]*See, e.g.*, Gatchel v. Gatchel, 824 N.E.2d 576 (Ohio Ct. App. 2005); Tex. Educ. Agency v. Leeper, 893 S.W.2d 432 (Tex. 1994). *See also* State v. Trucke, 410 N.W.2d 242 (Iowa 1987) (recognizing that unclear language in the compulsory attendance law precluded conviction of home-educating parents).

[12]Brian Ray, *Research Facts on Homeschooling*, National Home Education Research Institute (July 10, 2006), available at www.nheri.org/content/view/199/. Accurate estimates are difficult to obtain because some parents may not report that their children are being educated at home.

to review by school district personnel.[13] In 2005, a Pennsylvania federal district court rejected parents' claim that the home education law's required instruction for a minimum amount of time and days in specific courses placed a substantial burden on their exercise of their religion or abridged the state's Religious Freedom Protection Act.[14]

Traditionally, a number of states required home tutors to be certified teachers or to hold baccalaureate degrees, but now only a few states specify postsecondary education for such instructors, and none requires home tutors to be state licensed.[15] Indeed, since 1980, the majority of states have reduced restrictions on home education, and no state has strengthened such regulations.[16] However, about three-fifths of the states require students educated at home to be subjected to some state-supervised form of assessment to ensure that students are mastering basic skills, representing a shift from *input* to *output* requirements.[17] In a typical case, a West Virginia federal district court rejected parents' challenge to the state law making children ineligible for home schooling if they score poorly on standardized tests and do not improve after home remediation.[18]

Some legal disputes have focused on rights of children with disabilities if their parents elect to educate them at home or in private schools. As discussed in Chapter 2, the Establishment Clause does not bar states from furnishing services for children with disabilities in private schools. However, this does not necessarily mean that education agencies must provide the services on private school premises or in the

---

[13]*See, e.g.*, Battles v. Anne Arundel County Bd. of Educ., 95 F.3d 41 (Table) (4th Cir. 1996); Hartfield v. E. Grand Rapids Pub. Schs., 960 F. Supp. 1259 (W.D. Mich. 1997); Stobaugh v. Wallace, 757 F. Supp. 653 (W.D. Pa. 1990). *But see* Brunelle v. Lynn Pub. Schs., 702 N.E.2d 1182 (Mass. 1998) (holding that mandated home visits were not essential to the approval of a home education plan); *In re* T.M., 756 A.2d 793 (Vt. 2000) (reversing order that child was in need of care and supervision, because the commissioner of education failed to order a hearing within 45 days of receipt of parents' notice of enrolling their child in home schooling).

[14]Combs v. Homer Ctr. Sch. Dist., 468 F. Supp. 2d 738 (W.D. Pa. 2006). *See also In re* Rebekah, 654 N.W.2d 744 (Neb. Ct. App. 2002) (holding that the state may require home schools to maintain a sequential program of instruction in language arts, mathematics, science, social studies, and health; parents had neglected their children by failing to provide proper home instruction).

[15]*See, e.g.*, People v. DeJonge, 501 N.W.2d 127 (Mich. 1993) (striking down the state's certification requirement for home tutors as applied to families whose religious convictions prohibit the use of certified instructors); Lawrence v. S.C. State Bd. of Educ., 412 S.E.2d 394 (S.C. 1991) (finding unreasonable the state's requirement that home tutors with only high school diplomas must pass a basic skills test). *But see* State v. Brewer, 444 N.W.2d 923 (N.D. 1989) (upholding requirement that home instructors without a college degree must pass an examination). Under North Dakota law, high school graduates can be home tutors if monitored by certified teachers during at least the first two years, N.D. Cent. Code § 15.1-23-03 (2007).

[16]*See* Brian D. Ray, *Worldwide Guide to Homeschooling* (Salem, OR: National Home Education Research Institute, 2005); Judith G. McMullen, "Behind Closed Doors: Should States Regulate Homeschooling?" *South Carolina Law Review*, vol. 54 (2002), pp. 75–109; Mary Jo Dare, *The Tensions of the Home School Movement: A Legal/Political Analysis* (Ed.D dissertation, Indiana University, 2001).

[17]*See, e.g.*, Murphy v. Arkansas, 852 F.2d 1039 (8th Cir. 1988) (upholding the test requirement for home-schooled students and rejecting parents' assertion that Arkansas Home School Act impaired privacy, free exercise, and equal protection rights by treating home education differently from private schools). *See also* Dare, *The Tensions of the Home School Movement*.

[18]Null v. Bd. of Educ., 815 F. Supp. 937 (S.D.W. Va. 1993).

children's homes as long as appropriate programs are made available elsewhere for children with disabilities.[19]

Another controversial issue is whether private school students and those who are home schooled have an entitlement to take selected courses and participate in extracurricular activities in public schools. A few states by law authorize such participation, but statutes in most states are silent on this issue. In the absence of a state law, the Tenth Circuit upheld an Oklahoma school district's prohibition on part-time enrollment except for fifth-year seniors and special education students.[20] The school district justified its policy because it could not receive state aid for part-time students, and the court found no burden on the religious liberties or parental rights of families who educate their children at home. More recently, an Indiana appeals court vacated the Indiana State Board of Education's order for a school district to enroll two home-schooled students on a part-time basis, reasoning that state law authorized local districts to deny such part-time enrollment.[21]

High school activities associations in most states govern interscholastic competition for students attending qualifying public and private schools, and some associations prohibit interscholastic participation of home-schooled pupils. One justification is to ensure that home schoolers cannot avoid academic eligibility requirements that public and private school students must satisfy. Several courts have ruled that home-schooled students do not have an equal protection right to participate in interscholastic sports or other extracurricular activities because such participation is a privilege rather than a right.[22]

With increasing interest in private schools and home-education programs, controversies seem likely to continue over public/private relationships in connection with dual enrollment, provision of special services, and extracurricular activities. The legal status of specific arrangements will depend on judicial interpretations of applicable state statutes and administrative regulations.

---

[19]*See, e.g.*, Hooks v. Clark County Sch. Dist., 228 F.3d 1036 (9th Cir. 2000); Forstrom v. Byrne, 775 A.2d 65 (N.J. Super. Ct. App. Div. 2001).

[20]Swanson v. Guthrie Indep. Sch. Dist., 135 F.3d 694 (10th Cir. 1998). *See also* Goulart v. Meadows, 345 F.3d 239 (4th Cir. 2003) (upholding county's policy prohibiting the use of its community centers for private educational activities that resulted in denial of home-school parents' request to use community centers for their classes and meetings).

[21]Ind. State Bd. of Educ. v. Brownsburg Cmty. Sch. Corp., 865 N.E.2d 660 (Ind. Ct. App. 2007). *See also* Hassberger v. Bd. of Educ., No. 00 C 7873, 2003 U.S. Dist. LEXIS 20477 (N.D. Ill. Nov. 13, 2003) (upholding school district's denial of a request for a private school student to enroll in a public school algebra course).

[22]*See, e.g.,* Pelletier v. Me. Principals' Ass'n, 261 F. Supp. 2d 10 (D. Me. 2003); Reid v. Kenowa Hills Pub. Schs., 680 N.W.2d 62 (Mich. Ct. App. 2004); Jones v. W. Va. State Bd. of Educ., 622 S.E.2d 289 (W. Va. 2005). *See also* Angstadt v. Midd-West Sch. Dist., 182 F. Supp. 2d 435 (M.D. Pa. 2002) (holding that cyber student had no property right to participate in the school district's interscholastic basketball program); Paul Batista and Lance Hatfield, "Learn at Home, Play at School: A State-by-State Examination of Legislation, Litigation and Athletic Association Rules Governing Public School Athletic Participation by Homeschool Students," *Journal of Legal Aspects of Sport,* vol. 5 (2005), pp. 213–265.

Health Requirements

State agencies have the power not only to mandate school attendance but also to require that students be in good health to protect the well-being of others.[23] In an early case, the Supreme Court rejected a federal constitutional challenge to a Texas law authorizing local school officials to condition public and private school attendance on vaccination against communicable diseases.[24] Numerous lower courts have upheld mandatory immunization, even when challenged on religious grounds, declaring that a pending epidemic is not necessary to justify such health requirements.[25] Parents have been convicted for indirectly violating compulsory attendance laws by refusing to have their children vaccinated as a prerequisite to school admission.

Some state statutes provide for an exemption from required immunization for members of religious sects whose teachings oppose the practice as long as the welfare of others is not endangered by the exemption.[26] Several courts have broadly interpreted such provisions as not requiring official church doctrine to prohibit vaccination or individuals to be church members to qualify for the religious exemption.[27] However, courts have denied parental attempts to use statutory religious exemptions for opposition to immunization based on fear of health risks[28] or beliefs that immunization is contrary to the "genetic blueprint"[29] or "chiropractic ethics."[30] The Supreme Court of Mississippi even questioned the rationale for religious exemptions from mandatory immunization. The court concluded that a statutory exemption discriminated against parents who opposed immunization for nonreligious reasons, and further held that such an exemption defeated the purpose of an immunization requirement—to protect all students from exposure to communicable diseases.[31] Most other courts have reasoned that states are empowered to enact religious exemptions but are not obligated to do so.

Although well established that school attendance can be conditioned on immunization against communicable diseases, states cannot abdicate their responsibility to educate children with such diseases. For example, courts have held that children

[23]*See, e.g.*, Kampfer v. Gokey, 955 F. Supp. 167 (N.D.N.Y. 1997) (upholding state law requiring public school students showing symptoms of a contagious disease to be sent home from school and preventing their return until checked by the school nurse).

[24]Zucht v. King, 260 U.S. 174 (1922).

[25]*See, e.g.*, Boone v. Boozman, 217 F. Supp. 2d 938 (E.D. Ark. 2002); Liebowitz v. Dinkins, 575 N.Y.S.2d 827 (App. Div. 1991).

[26]*See, e.g.*, Turner v. Liverpool Cent. Sch. Bd., 186 F. Supp. 2d 187 (N.D.N.Y. 2002); Fla. Dep't of Health v. Curry, 722 So. 2d 874 (Fla. Ct. App. 1998).

[27]*See, e.g.*, McCarthy v. Boozman, 212 F. Supp. 2d 945 (W.D. Ark. 2002); Berg v. Glen Cove City Sch. Dist., 853 F. Supp. 651 (E.D.N.Y. 1994). *See also In re* LePage, 18 P.3d 1177 (Wyo. 2001) (holding that the religious exemption was self-executing upon a written objection; the department of health could not require additional explanation as to why the requested exemption was based on the parents' faith).

[28]*See* Farina v. Bd. of Educ., 116 F. Supp. 2d 503 (E.D.N.Y. 2000).

[29]*See* Mason v. Gen. Brown Cent. Sch. Dist., 851 F.2d 47 (2d Cir. 1988).

[30]*See* Hanzel v. Arter, 625 F. Supp. 1259 (S.D. Ohio 1985) (rejecting additional claims that the immunization requirement also impaired constitutional privacy and due process rights).

[31]Brown v. Stone, 378 So. 2d 218 (Miss. 1979).

infected with acquired immune deficiency syndrome (AIDS) are protected by federal statutes barring discrimination against individuals with disabilities and have ruled that public schools must enroll children with AIDS upon certification by health officials that they pose minimal danger of infecting others.[32] Children can be denied enrollment in the regular school program if their presence poses a danger to others, but it is generally assumed that an alternative educational program (e.g., home instruction by computer) must be provided.

Some controversies have focused on children taking medications at school. Many school districts require medications to be kept in the school office and to be dispensed by designated personnel. Policies need to be explicit regarding exceptions to such regulations. In a California case, a student with severe asthma died before he could get assistance at the school office, and his mother was unaware that an exception to the medications policy would have allowed him to carry his inhaler at school. The mother was awarded damages for the school district's negligence in not informing parents of the policy exception.[33] A related issue pertains to disruptive children who need medication to keep their behavior under control. Several states have enacted laws preventing schools from forcing parents to medicate their children as a condition of attending school, and federal legislation in this regard has been introduced.[34]

Also, the recent national concern about improving childhood health and reducing obesity has prompted consideration of state and federal measures to strengthen requirements regarding physical activity for public school students and to curtail the availability of unhealthy snacks in schools.[35] For example, the beverage industry has agreed to pull high calorie drinks, including sugary sodas, from the nation's schools, and several states are following California's lead in enacting statutory provisions that require healthier snacks than currently available in public schools.[36]

Some school boards, particularly in urban areas, have addressed student health issues by establishing school-based clinics that offer services from immunization to disease diagnosis and treatment. In 2006, there were approximately 1,700 school-based health centers.[37] The most controversial aspect of the clinics has been their involvement in prescribing and dispensing forms of birth control. Several courts have upheld the authority of school boards to place condom machines in high school restrooms and

---

[32]*See, e.g.*, Doe v. Dolton Elementary Sch. Dist. No. 148, 694 F. Supp. 440 (N.D. Ill. 1988); Thomas v. Atascadero Unified Sch. Dist., 662 F. Supp. 376 (C.D. Cal. 1987). *See also* Martinez v. Sch. Bd., 861 F.2d 1502, 1506 (11th Cir. 1988), *on remand*, 711 F. Supp. 1066 (M.D. Fla. 1989) (finding the "remote theoretical possibility" of transmitting AIDS from a child's tears, saliva, and urine did not support segregation of the child with AIDS in a separate cubicle).

[33]Gonzalez v. Hanford Elem. Sch. Dist., Nos. F033659, F034555, 2002 Cal. App. Unpub. LEXIS 1341 (Ct. App. May 22, 2002).

[34]*See, e.g.,* Children's Mental Health Act of 2003, 405 Ill. Comp. Stat. 49/1-15 (2007).

[35]*See* Carol Chmelynski, "Standards Proposed for School Snacks," *School Board News* (May 2007), p. 3.

[36]*See* Cal. Educ. Code § 49431, 49431.5 (2007). Threats of litigation against the beverage industry for marketing junk food to children may have provided an impetus for the pact with anti-obesity groups. *See* Mary Otto and Lori Aratani, "Soda Ban Means Change at Schools," *Washington Post* (May 4, 2006), p. B3.

[37]*See* Cheryl Vital, Lawrence Kajs, and Patricia Travis, "Legal Issues and Responsible Practices in School Health Services," *Education Law Reporter,* vol. 218 (2007), pp. 13–19.

allow students to request condoms from school nurses, reasoning that such programs are within the boards' statutory powers to promote health services that prevent disease.[38]

Residency Requirements

In general, courts have ruled that public schools are obligated to educate school-age children who are *bona fide* residents, meaning they live in the district with their parents or legal guardian, are emancipated minors, or are adult students who live independently from their parents. In an important 1982 decision, *Plyler v. Doe*, the Supreme Court held that school districts could not deny a free public education to resident children whose parents had entered the country illegally.[39] Recognizing the individual's significant interest in receiving an education, the Court ruled that classifications affecting access to education must be substantially related to an important governmental objective to satisfy the Equal Protection Clause. The Court found that Texas's asserted interest in deterring aliens from entering the country illegally was not important enough to deny students an opportunity to be educated. Subsequently, the Ninth Circuit enjoined implementation of several sections of a 1994 California law denying free education and health care services to aliens residing in the state illegally (including the denial of free public education to children of illegal aliens).[40]

Children who are wards of the state and live in state facilities are usually considered residents of the school district where the facility is located, even if their parents live elsewhere.[41] Children with disabilities who have court-appointed guardians are entitled to support for an appropriate education where their guardians reside or from the district initiating their placement in a group facility.[42] Courts also have held

[38]*See, e.g.,* Parents United for Better Schs. v. Sch. Dist., 148 F.3d 260 (3d Cir. 1998); Curtis v. Sch. Comm., 652 N.E.2d 580 (Mass. 1995). *But see* Alfonso v. Fernandez, 606 N.Y.S.2d 259 (App. Div. 1993) (striking down a school district's program of distributing condoms without parental consent as violating parents' constitutional right to direct the upbringing of their children and their statutory right to give consent before health services are provided to their children).

[39]457 U.S. 202 (1982). For a discussion of standards of judicial review under the Equal Protection Clause, *see* text accompanying note 1, Chapter 5; note 1, Chapter 10. Even students temporarily in the district because their parents are assigned to federal installations for a short period of time are considered *bona fide* residents. *See, e.g.,* United States v. Onslow County Bd. of Educ., 728 F.2d 628 (4th Cir. 1984).

[40]Gregorio T. v. Wilson, 59 F.3d 1002 (9th Cir. 1995). The litigation was ended through a court-approved mediation signed on July 29, 1999.

[41]*See, e.g.,* Steven M. v. Gilhool, 700 F. Supp. 261 (E.D. Pa. 1988) (holding, however, that a state facility can charge tuition for children who are legal wards of another state).

[42]*See, e.g.,* Manchester Sch. Dist. v. Crisman, 306 F.3d 1 (1st Cir. 2002) (holding that fiscal responsibility is determined by state law, and under New Hampshire law the school district where the child resided prior to placement in a children's home was the sending district and thus responsible for the costs, regardless of the child's legal residency); Catlin v. Sobol, 93 F.3d 1112 (2d Cir. 1996) (interpreting New York law as assigning financial liability to the district where the parent resided; a child living in a group home since infancy while receiving parental support was not entitled to free schooling in the district of the home's location); Wise v. Ohio Dep't of Educ., 80 F.3d 177 (6th Cir. 1996) (finding that under Ohio law, state officials could seek reimbursement for special education costs where parents, who were not Ohio residents, unilaterally placed their child in an Ohio private residential facility).

that school districts cannot deny an education to homeless children being sheltered in their districts.[43]

In contrast to the judiciary's position that school boards must provide free public schooling for resident students, courts generally have not required public schools to admit *nonresident* students tuition free.[44] The Supreme Court upheld a Texas requirement allowing local school boards to deny tuition-free schooling to any unemancipated minor who lives apart from a parent or legal guardian for the primary purpose of attending public school.[45] The Court ruled that the requirement advanced the substantial state interest of assuring high-quality public education for residents (those living in a school district with the intent to remain).

Other courts similarly have upheld residency requirements, reasoning that tuition can be charged when students legally reside outside the school district, even though they may live in the district with someone other than their legal guardians.[46] When students move to another school district, they do not have a right to continue attending their former public school tuition free, although often they are allowed to complete the term in their former school.[47] As discussed in Chapter 4, several cases involving residency disputes have involved student athletes, and courts consistently have rejected efforts to establish limited guardianships to enable students to attend school tuition free for athletic reasons.

Minnesota was the first state to enact an interdistrict open enrollment plan, allowing students to apply for transfers to any public school district within the state. Transfer requests are subject to certain restrictions, such as space limitations, and participation by local districts is optional under some plans. The majority of states now allow for some type of open enrollment within districts and/or across district boundaries. Assessing a claim under an open enrollment plan, a Wisconsin appeals court found no rational basis for a school district's assertion that lack of space caused it to

---

[43]*See, e.g.,* Lampkin v. District of Columbia, 886 F. Supp. 56 (D.D.C. 1995); Orozco *ex rel.* Arroyo v. Sobol, 703 F. Supp. 1113 (S.D.N.Y. 1989). In 1987, Congress passed the Stewart B. McKinney Education for Homeless Children Act, later renamed the McKinney-Vento Homeless Assistance Act, 42 U.S.C. § 11431 (2007), providing some federal aid for the education of homeless children, including transportation to school. The most recent reauthorization in the No Child Left Behind Act of 2001, 20 U.S.C. § 6312(b)(1)(E) (2007), strengthens protections for homeless children and requires each state's plan to include a description of how services for the homeless will be coordinated and integrated with other educational services.

[44]*See, e.g.,* Joshua W. v. Unified Sch. Dist. 259, 211 F.3d 1278 (10th Cir. 2000); Bradshaw v. Cherry Creek Sch. Dist. No. 5, 98 P.3d 886 (Colo. Ct. App. 2003); Longwood Cent. Sch. Dist. v. Springs Union Free Sch. Dist., 806 N.E.2d 970 (N.Y. 2004); Blind Brook-Rye Union Free Sch. Dist. v. Baronti, 789 N.Y.S.2d 800 (App. Div. 2004).

[45]Martinez v. Bynum, 461 U.S. 321 (1983).

[46]*See, e.g., Joshua W.,* 211 F.3d 1278; Hallissey v. Sch. Admin. Dist. No. 77, 755 A.2d 1068 (Me. 2000); Graham v. Mock, 545 S.E.2d 263 (N.C. Ct. App. 2001).

[47]*See, e.g.,* Daniels v. Morris, 746 F.2d 271 (5th Cir. 1984). *See also* Clayton v. White Hall Sch. Dist., 875 F.2d 676 (8th Cir. 1989) (rejecting an equal protection challenge to an Arkansas school district's policy allowing nonresident children of certified and administrative employees, but not other employees, to attend school in the district; the policy was considered rationally related to the objective of recruiting high-quality teachers and administrators).

deny a nonresident student's transfer request when it had admitted three other nonresident students; the rejection of one student while admitting others was arbitrary and unreasonable.[48] In the absence of authorized open enrollment plans, students do not have a right to attend school outside their resident district or even outside their attendance zone within the district.[49]

In some situations, however, courts have found that there are legitimate reasons for children to live apart from their parents, such as health concerns or the need to provide a more suitable home environment.[50] The Eighth Circuit invalidated an Arkansas school district's residency requirement as abridging equal protection rights by discriminating against students living apart from their parents with no control over the situation and violating due process guarantees by creating an irrebuttable presumption that a student not residing with a parent or guardian is not living in the school district with the intent to remain.[51] More recently, a New Jersey appeals court ruled that a Korean student living with relatives in New Jersey was entitled to free public schooling under the hardship exception to the residency requirement because his parents in Korea could not care for him.[52]

Courts typically have rejected parental claims that restricting school enrollment to allegedly inadequate resident school districts is detrimental to their children's welfare and impairs protected rights,[53] but such assertions may be more successful in the future. Under the federal NCLB Act, students assigned to schools that have not met annual progress goals for two consecutive years must be offered other educational options with transportation provided.[54] A number of states are enacting similar accountability legislation that includes technical assistance and sanctions for schools and districts that are not meeting state academic standards and provides educational choices for students attending failing public schools. These measures may negate some of the traditional discretion enjoyed by school districts in establishing residency requirements for students.

---

[48]McMorrow v. Benson, 617 N.W.2d 247 (Wis. Ct. App. 2000).

[49]*See* Mullen v. Thompson, 31 Fed. Appx. 77 (3d Cir. 2002) (rejecting the assertion that students who attended Pittsburgh public schools slated to be closed had any constitutional interest in attending schools of their choice).

[50]*See, e.g.*, Major v. Nederland Indep. Sch. Dist., 772 F. Supp. 944 (E.D. Tex. 1991) (holding that a student whose negative relationship with her mother and stepfather triggered a move to live with another family must be allowed to attend school without charge in the new district as the move was not for educational reasons); Joel R. v. Bd. of Educ., 686 N.E.2d 650 (Ill. App. Ct. 1997) (holding that a student must be admitted to the public school where he resided with his aunt even though his parents lived in Mexico).

[51]Horton v. Marshall Pub. Schs., 769 F.2d 1323 (8th Cir. 1985). Also, school districts have been required to educate students where they mistakenly enrolled nonresidents. *See, e.g.*, Cohen v. Wauconda Cmty. Unit Sch. Dist. No. 118, 779 F. Supp. 88 (N.D. Ill. 1991); Burdick v. Indep. Sch. Dist. No. 52, 702 P.2d 48 (Okla. 1985).

[52]P.B.K. v. Bd. of Educ., 778 A.2d 1124 (N.J. Super. Ct. App. Div. 2001).

[53]*See* Ramsdell v. N. River Sch. Dist. No. 200, 704 P.2d 606 (Wash. 1985) (holding that denial of parents' request for their children to transfer from an allegedly inadequate school district did not abridge their children's state constitutional right to an "ample education").

[54]20 U.S.C. § 6316 (b) (2007).

School Fees

Public schools face mounting financial pressures due to escalating costs of facilities, supplies, insurance, and various services. Furthermore, intergovernmental competition for tax dollars is increasing while citizens continue to press for tax relief.[55] Thus, it is not surprising that school officials are attempting to transfer some of the fiscal burden for public school services and materials to students and their parents. Although the law is clear that public schools cannot charge *tuition* as a prerequisite to school attendance, various *user fees* have been imposed for transportation, books, and course materials.

Transportation

Several courts have distinguished transportation charges from tuition charges, concluding that transportation is not an essential part of students' entitlement to free public schooling.[56] Courts have upheld policies allowing school districts to differentiate between resident and nonresident students regarding transportation fees,[57] to impose geographic limitations on bus services and fees charged,[58] to deny transportation to an independent state-chartered school in the district,[59] and to charge for summer school transportation.[60]

In its only decision involving public school user fees, the Supreme Court in 1988 upheld a North Dakota statute permitting selected school districts to charge a transportation fee, not to exceed the school district's estimated cost of providing the service.[61] When the school district in question implemented door-to-door bus service, it

[55]*See* Zuni Pub. Sch. Dist. No. 89 v. Dep't of Educ., 127 S. Ct. 1534, 1541-1542 (2007) (upholding the U.S. Department of Education's findings that New Mexico's local aid program qualified as a program that "equalized expenditures" so the state could offset federal impact aid to individual districts by reducing state aid to those districts).

[56]*See, e.g.*, Kadrmas v. Dickinson Pub. Schs., 487 U.S. 450 (1988); Salazar v. Eastin, 890 P.2d 43 (Cal. 1995).

[57]*See, e.g.*, Fenster v. Schneider, 636 F.2d 765 (D.C. Cir. 1980) (finding a rational purpose for the school district to deny transportation services to nonresident students who had no federal constitutional or statutory entitlement to such services); Pucket v. Hot Springs Sch. Dist. No. 23-2, No. 03-5033-KES, 2007 U.S. Dist. LEXIS 41326 (D.S.D. June 6, 2007) (finding no impairment of constitutional rights during the period that the school district denied transportation to sectarian school children until a new state law authorized such services as long as additional public funds were not expended); Manbeck v. Katonah-Lewisboro Sch. Dist., 435 F. Supp. 2d 273 (S.D.N.Y. 2006) (upholding school district in denying transportation to a private school for a kindergarten student who was not of public school age). *But see* Bd. of Educ. of Stafford v. State Bd. of Educ., 709 A.2d 510 (Conn. 1997) (upholding state board's decision that local board of education was required to provide transportation for private school students, including times when the public schools were not in session).

[58]*See, e.g.*, Sch. Dist. v. Hutchinson, 508 N.W.2d 832 (Neb. 1993).

[59]*See* Racine Charter One v. Racine Unified Sch. Dist., 424 F.3d 677 (7th Cir. 2005) (finding that the charter school functioned as an independent school district surrounded by the public school district; state law does not require schools to transport students to other districts).

[60]*See, e.g.*, Crim v. McWhorter, 252 S.E.2d 421 (Ga. 1979).

[61]*See Kadrmas*, 487 U.S. 450. The Court further concluded that the law's distinction between reorganized and nonreorganized school districts did not present an equal protection violation in the absence of proof that the statute was arbitrary and irrational. Under the law, school districts have the discretion to waive any fee for families financially unable to pay, and benefits such as diplomas and grades are not to be affected by nonpayment of fees.

assessed a fee for approximately 11 percent of the costs, with the remainder supported by state and local tax revenues. Rejecting a parental challenge, the Supreme Court concluded that the law served the legitimate purpose of encouraging school districts to provide bus services. Noting that the state is not obligated to provide school transportation services at all, the Court held that such services need not be free.

In general, it appears that as long as school officials have a rational basis for their decisions, reasonable school transportation fees can be imposed. As discussed in Chapter 6, however, states do not have the same discretion regarding transportation for children with disabilities. Under federal and state laws, transportation is a related service that must be provided free if necessary for a child with disabilities to participate in the educational program.

Textbooks, Courses, and Materials

The legality of charging students for the use of public school textbooks has been contested with mixed results. Because the Supreme Court has not invalidated textbook fees under federal equal protection guarantees,[62] the legality of such fees rests on interpretations of state law. Public schools in four-fifths of the states loan textbooks to students without charge, and courts in several states, such as Idaho, Michigan, North Dakota, and West Virginia, have interpreted state constitutional provisions as precluding textbook fees.[63] However, courts in some states, such as Arizona, Colorado, Illinois, Indiana, and Wisconsin, have interpreted their constitutional provisions as permitting rental fees for public school textbooks.[64] While authorizing textbook fees, an Indiana federal district court ruled that the state student disciplinary code and federal equal protection guarantees precluded school boards from suspending students for their parents' failure to pay the rental fees.[65] Where textbook fees have been condoned, waivers generally have been available for students who cannot pay the assessed amount.

In addition to fees for textbooks, fees for courses and supplies also have been challenged, generating a range of judicial opinions. The Supreme Court of Missouri

---

[62]*See* Johnson v. N.Y. State Educ. Dep't, 449 F.2d 871 (2d Cir. 1971), *vacated and remanded*, 409 U.S. 75 (1972) (per curiam).

[63]*See* Paulson v. Minidoka County Sch. Dist. No. 331, 463 P.2d 935 (Idaho 1970); Bond v. Ann Arbor Sch. Dist., 178 N.W.2d 484 (Mich. 1970); Cardiff v. Bismarck Pub. Sch. Dist., 263 N.W.2d 105 (N.D. 1978); Randolph County Bd. of Educ. v. Adams, 467 S.E.2d 150 (W. Va. 1995). Four-fifths of the states provide free textbooks. *See* Kyle Zinth, "State Textbook Adoption," *State Notes* (Denver: Education Commission of the States, January 2005).

[64]*See* Carpio v. Tucson High Sch. Dist. No. 1, 524 P.2d 948 (Ariz. 1974); Marshall v. Sch. Dist. RE No. 3, 553 P.2d 784 (Colo. 1976); Hamer v. Bd. of Educ., 265 N.E.2d 616 (Ill. 1970); Chandler v. S. Bend Cmty. Sch. Corp., 312 N.E.2d 915 (Ind. Ct. App. 1974).

[65]Carder v. Mich. City Sch. Corp., 552 F. Supp. 869 (N.D. Ind. 1982). *But see* Ass'n for the Def. v. Kiger, 537 N.E.2d 1292 (Ohio 1989) (upholding state law authorizing school districts to withhold grades or credit if students failed to pay fees for materials used in courses; however, fees could not be collected for materials used for administrative rather than instructional purposes).

ruled that the practice of charging course fees as a prerequisite to enrollment in classes for academic credit impaired students' rights to free public schooling.[66] The Indiana Supreme Court more recently ruled that a mandatory $20 fee for all students was in effect a charge for attending school in violation of the state constitution.[67] The high courts of Montana and New Mexico interpreted their state constitutions as prohibiting fees for required courses, but allowing reasonable fees for elective courses.[68] In contrast, the supreme courts of Illinois, Ohio, and North Carolina have concluded that their state constitutions permit public schools to charge instructional supply fees for *any* courses.[69] In some cases, the concept of charging parents for materials and other supplies has received judicial endorsement, but the manner of fee collection (e.g., inadequate waiver provisions) has been invalidated.[70]

Currently, school districts in many states solicit fees from students for various consumable materials. The legality of such practices varies across states and depends primarily on the state judiciary's assessment of state constitutional provisions. Another issue receiving some attention is the imposition of fees for participation in extracurricular activities, which is discussed in Chapter 4.

The School Curriculum

The public school curriculum is controlled primarily by states and local school boards. The federal government, however, influences the curriculum through funds it provides for particular initiatives. For example, under the NCLB Act, states can apply for federal aid to strengthen reading instruction in the early grades.[71] Unlike the federal government, state legislatures exercise broad authority to impose curriculum mandates. State legislation regarding the public school curriculum has become increasingly explicit, and some laws as well as local school board policies have been challenged as violating individuals' protected rights. This section focuses on legal developments involving curriculum requirements/restrictions and instructional censorship.

[66]Concerned Parents v. Caruthersville Sch. Dist. No. 18, 548 S.W.2d 554 (Mo. 1977).

[67]Nagy v. Evansville-Vanderburgh Sch. Corp., 844 N.E.2d 481 (Ind. 2006) (invalidating the universal fee for all students, but recognizing that user fees for participating in extracurricular activities would be allowed), *on remand*, 870 N.E.2d 12 (Ind. Ct. App. 2007) (holding that parents who were prevailing parties could receive attorneys' fees).

[68]Granger v. Cascade County Sch. Dist. No. 1, 499 P.2d 780 (Mont. 1972); Norton v. Bd. of Educ., 553 P.2d 1277 (N.M. 1976). Fees for drivers' education have generated conflicting rulings. *Compare* Cal. Ass'n for Safety Educ. v. Brown, 36 Cal. Rptr. 2d 404 (Ct. App. 1994) (charging fees for drivers' education violates the free school guarantee of the state constitution) *with* Messina v. Sobol, 553 N.Y.S.2d 529 (App. Div. 1990) (upholding fees because drivers' education is not a mandatory course for high school graduation).

[69]*See* Beck v. Bd. of Educ., 344 N.E.2d 440 (Ill. 1976); Sneed v. Greensboro City Bd. of Educ., 264 S.E.2d 106 (N.C. 1980); State *ex rel.* Massie v. Bd. of Educ., 669 N.E.2d 839 (Ohio 1996).

[70]*See, e.g.,* Sodus Cent. Sch. v. Rhine, 406 N.Y.S.2d 175 (App. Div. 1978); *Sneed,* 264 S.E.2d at 114; Lorenc v. Call, 789 P.2d 46 (Utah Ct. App. 1990).

[71]20 U.S.C. § 6362 (2007).

Requirements and Restrictions

Courts have repeatedly recognized that the state retains the power to determine the public school curriculum as long as federal constitutional guarantees are respected. A few state constitutions include specific curriculum mandates, but, more typically, the legislature is given responsibility for curricular determinations. States vary as to the specificity of legislative directives, but most states mandate instruction pertaining to the Federal Constitution, American history, English, mathematics, drug education, health, and physical education. States also increasingly are requiring instruction pertaining to character education. Some state statutes specify what subjects will be taught in which grades, and many states have detailed legislation pertaining to vocational education, bilingual education, and special services for children with disabilities. State laws usually stipulate that local school boards must offer the state-mandated minimum curriculum, which they may supplement unless there is a statutory prohibition. In about half of the states, local school boards (and, in some instances, school-based councils) are empowered to adopt courses of study, but often they must secure approval from the state board of education.

Despite states' substantial discretion in curricular matters, some legislative attempts to impose curriculum restrictions have run afoul of federal constitutional rights. The first curriculum case to reach the Supreme Court involved a 1923 challenge to a Nebraska law that prohibited instruction in a foreign language to any public or private school students who had not successfully completed the eighth grade.[72] The state high court had upheld the dismissal of a private school teacher for teaching reading in German to elementary school students. In striking down the statute, the Supreme Court reasoned that the teacher's right to teach, the parents' right to engage him to instruct their children, and the children's right to acquire useful knowledge were protected liberties under the Due Process Clause of the Fourteenth Amendment.

The Supreme Court on occasion has ruled that other curriculum decisions, such as barring instruction in evolution, violate constitutional rights.[73] If constitutional rights are not implicated, however, courts will uphold decisions of state and local education agencies in curricular matters. For example, school districts increasingly have implemented community service requirements as part of the mandatory high school curriculum, and federal appellate courts have rejected allegations that such requirements represent involuntary servitude prohibited by the Thirteenth Amendment, forced expression of altruistic values in violation of the First Amendment, or impairments of parents' Fourteenth Amendment rights to direct the upbringing of their children.[74]

[72]Meyer v. Nebraska, 262 U.S. 390 (1923).

[73]*See* Epperson v. Arkansas, 393 U.S. 97 (1968) (holding that the First Amendment precludes states from barring public school instruction about evolution simply because it conflicts with certain religious views); text accompanying note 129, Chapter 2.

[74]Herndon v. Chapel Hill-Carrboro City Bd. of Educ., 89 F.3d 174 (4th Cir. 1996); Immediato v. Rye Neck Sch. Dist., 73 F.3d 454 (2d Cir. 1996); Steirer v. Bethlehem Area Sch. Dist., 987 F.2d 989 (3d Cir. 1993). *See also* Onondaga-Cortland-Madison Bd. v. McGowan, 728 N.Y.S.2d 109 (App. Div. 2001) (having students perform unpaid work on a school construction project for class credit under a work force training program did not violate New York labor law).

Courts defer to school authorities not only in determining courses of study but also in establishing standards for pupil performance and imposing other instructional requirements. For example, school districts can establish prerequisites and admission criteria for particular courses as long as such criteria are not arbitrary and do not disadvantage certain groups of students. The Fifth Circuit recognized that, absent a state law or other authoritative source entitling students to a particular course of study, students have no property right to be admitted to any class that is offered in the public school.[75]

In addition to having authority over the content of the public school curriculum, states also have the power to specify textbooks and to regulate the method by which such books are obtained and distributed. In most states, textbooks are prescribed by the state board of education or a textbook commission. A list of acceptable books typically is developed at the state level, and local school boards then adopt specific texts for their course offerings. However, in some states, such as Colorado, local boards are delegated almost complete authority to make textbook selections.[76] Courts will not interfere with textbook decisions unless established procedures are not followed or overtly biased materials are adopted.

Censorship of Instructional Materials

Attempts to remove books from classrooms and libraries and to tailor curricular offerings and methodologies to particular religious and philosophical values have led to substantial litigation. Few aspects of the public school program remain untouched by censorship activities. Although most people agree that schools transmit values, there is not always consensus regarding *which* values should be transmitted or *who* should make this determination.

Parental Challenges. Some challenges to public school materials and programs emanate from civil rights and consumer groups, contesting materials that allegedly promote racism, sexism, or bad health habits for students. But most of the challenges come from conservative parent groups, alleging that the use of instructional activities and materials considered immoral and anti-Christian impairs parents' rights to control their children's course of study in public schools.[77] As discussed in Chapter 2, courts have endorsed requests for specific children to be excused from selected course offerings (e.g., sex education) that offend their religious beliefs, as long as the exemptions do not impede the students' academic progress or the management of the school. Challenges to the courses themselves, however, have not found a receptive judicial forum. The discussion here focuses primarily on censorship of library and classroom materials.

To date, courts have not allowed mere parental disapproval of instructional materials to dictate the public school curriculum. In an early West Virginia case, parents alleged that the adopted English curriculum materials were godless, communistic, and

---

[75]Arundar v. Dekalb County Sch. Dist., 620 F.2d 493 (5th Cir. 1980).

[76]*See* Colo. Const. art. IX, § 15 (2007).

[77]Some of the best-known conservative groups that are active in this debate are the American Coalition for Traditional Values, the Christian Coalition, Citizens for Excellence in Education, Concerned Women for America, the Eagle Forum, and Focus on the Family.

profane. National attention was aroused as the protests evolved into school boycotts, a coal miners' strike, shootings, a courthouse bombing, and even public prayer calling for the death of school board members. The federal district court upheld the board's authority to determine curricular materials and rejected the parents' contention that the use of the books posed an infringement of constitutionally protected rights, but a reconstituted school board eventually eliminated the series.[78] In more recent cases, federal appellate courts similarly have been unsympathetic to claims that reading series or individual novels used in public schools conflict with Christian doctrine and advance an antitheistic creed, finding the challenged materials to be religiously neutral and related to legitimate educational objectives.[79]

While many challenges have religious overtones, some simply assert parents' rights to determine their children's education. The Supreme Court declined to review a case in which the First Circuit denied parents' claim that the school district was liable for subjecting their children to a mandatory AIDS-awareness assembly that featured a streetwise, comedic approach to the topic. The appeals court observed that "if all parents had a fundamental constitutional right to dictate individually what the schools teach their children, the schools would be forced to cater a curriculum for each student whose parents had genuine moral disagreements with the school's choice of subject matter."[80] The Ninth Circuit subsequently held that the Oregon law restructuring public schools to impose a rigorous academic program and student assessments, develop alternative learning environments, and create early childhood programs with an emphasis on work-related learning experiences did not abridge speech rights or "freedom of mind."[81] The court reasoned that nothing in the law compelled students to adopt state-approved views. The same court dismissed African American parents' complaint that their daughter suffered psychological injuries from

[78]Williams v. Bd. of Educ., 530 F.2d 972 (4th Cir. 1975). *See also* Skipworth v. Bd. of Educ., 874 P.2d 487 (Colo. Ct. App. 1994) (rejecting parental claim that public schools must teach morality).

[79]*See, e.g.*, Monteiro v. Tempe Union High Sch. Dist., 158 F.3d 1022 (9th Cir. 1998) (*The Adventures of Huckleberry Finn* and *A Rose for Emily*); Fleischfresser v. Dirs. of Sch. Dist. 200, 15 F.3d 680 (7th Cir. 1994) (*Impressions* reading series); Smith v. Sch. Comm'rs of Mobile County, 827 F.2d 684 (11th Cir. 1987) (*Homemaking Skills for Everyday Living*); Grove v. Mead Sch. Dist., 753 F.2d 1528 (9th Cir. 1985) (*The Learning Tree*); text accompanying notes 146-157, Chapter 2. *See also* Altman v. Bedford Cent. Sch. Dist., 245 F.3d 49 (2d Cir. 2001) (finding that the celebration of Earth Day in public schools did not constitute a religious ceremony, but concluding that having students construct worry dolls and images of a Hindu deity advanced nontraditional faiths in violation of the Establishment Clause). *See* text accompanying note 149, Chapter 2 for a discussion of other claims in this case.

[80]Brown v. Hot, Sexy and Safer Prods., 68 F.3d 525, 534 (1st Cir. 1995). *See also* Parker v. Hurley, No. 07-1528, 2008 U.S. App. LEXIS 2070 (1st Cir. Jan. 31, 2008) (finding that the school district's refusal of an exemption for young students from instruction recognizing differences in sexual orientation did not abridge their parents' First Amendment rights to exercise religious beliefs or their Fourteenth Amendment substantive due process rights); text accompanying note 154, Chapter 2; Akshar v. Mills, 671 N.Y.S.2d 856 (App. Div. 1998) (rejecting parents' petition for a formal hearing with the state commissioner regarding the school board resolution allowing peer presentations about AIDS after school and requiring parental permission for students to participate).

[81]Tennison v. Paulus, 144 F.3d 1285, 1287 (9th Cir. 1998).

being required to read two literary works that contained repeated use of the word *nigger*.[82]

Sometimes school districts have *not* prevailed, if shown that they acted arbitrarily or in violation of parents' or students' protected rights. For example, in a Maryland case discussed in Chapter 2, a federal district court enjoined implementation of a school district's pilot sex education program, reasoning that additional investigation was needed to determine if the materials on "sexual variation" constitute viewpoint discrimination by presenting only the perspective that homosexuality is natural and a morally correct lifestyle.[83]

Censorship by Policy Makers. Whereas courts have not been receptive to challenges to school boards' curricular decisions simply because some materials or course content offend the sensibilities of specific students or parents, the legal issues are more complicated when policy makers (e.g., legislators, school board members) support the censorship activity. Bills calling for instructional censorship have been introduced in Congress and numerous state legislatures, and policies have been proposed at the school board level to eliminate "objectionable" materials from public school classrooms and libraries.

The Supreme Court has recognized the broad discretion of school boards to make decisions that reflect the "legitimate and substantial community interest in promoting respect for authority and traditional values be they social, moral, or political."[84] Thus, the judiciary has been reluctant to interfere with school boards' prerogatives in selecting and eliminating instructional materials. The Second Circuit on two occasions upheld a school board's right to remove vulgar or obscene books from public school libraries, noting that a book does not acquire tenure and can be removed by the same authority that made the initial selection.[85] Similarly, the Seventh Circuit endorsed an Indiana federal district court's conclusion that "it is legitimate for school officials . . . to prohibit the use of texts, remove library books, and delete courses from the curriculum as a part of the effort to shape students into good citizens,"[86] unless the board flagrantly abuses its broad discretion to make curricular decisions.

[82]*Monteiro*, 158 F.3d 1022 (remanding the case for further proceedings regarding allegations that school personnel failed to respond to complaints of a racially hostile environment in violation of Title VI of the Civil Rights Act of 1964).

[83]Citizens for a Responsible Curriculum v. Montgomery County Pub. Schs., No. AW 05 1194, 2005 U.S. Dist. LEXIS 8130, at *3 (S.D. Md. May 5, 2005). *But see Parker*, No. 07-1528, 2008 U.S. App. LEXIS 2070 (1st Cir. Jan. 31, 2008); *supra* text accompanying note 80.

[84]Bd. of Educ. v. Pico, 457 U.S. 853, 864 (1982). *See also* Bethel Sch. Dist. No. 403 v. Fraser, 478 U.S. 675, 684 (1986); text accompanying note 10, Chapter 4.

[85]Bicknell v. Vergennes Union High Sch. Bd. of Dirs., 638 F.2d 438 (2d Cir. 1980); Presidents Council v. Cmty. Sch. Bd. No. 25, 457 F.2d 289 (2d Cir. 1972). For a discussion of teachers' academic freedom, *see* text accompanying note 71, Chapter 9.

[86]Zykan v. Warsaw Cmty. Sch. Corp., 631 F.2d 1300, 1303 (7th Cir. 1980). *See also* Seyfried v. Walton, 668 F.2d 214 (3d Cir. 1981) (holding that the high school drama club's performances were a part of the school program and therefore the school board could prohibit performance of the musical *Pippin* because of its explicit sexual scenes).

Although the judiciary has generally upheld school boards' authority in determining curricular offerings, the censorship of specific library books and materials has been invalidated under the First Amendment if motivated by a desire to suppress particular viewpoints or controversial ideas.[87] For example, the Fifth Circuit held that there were material issues of fact regarding whether a Louisiana school board intended to suppress ideas in removing from public school libraries all copies of *Voodoo & Hoodoo*, which traces the development of African tribal religion and its evolution in African American communities in the United States.[88] Likewise, the Eighth Circuit struck down a Minnesota school board's attempt to ban certain films from school because of their ideological content.[89] More recently, an Arkansas federal district court struck down a school district's policy requiring parental permission for students to check out certain library books dealing with witchcraft and the occult. The court found insufficient justification for the policy that stigmatized certain materials and abridged students' First Amendment rights to have access to the materials without parental permission.[90] Also, a Florida federal district court enjoined a school board's effort to remove from elementary school libraries *Vamos a Cuba!* along with 23 other books in a series about life in other countries, finding impermissible viewpoint discrimination and lack of compliance with the district's procedures for removing library materials.[91]

Despite substantial activity in lower courts, the Supreme Court has rendered only one decision involving censorship in public schools. This case, *Board of Education v. Pico*,[92] unfortunately did not provide significant clarification regarding the scope of school boards' authority to restrict student access to particular materials. In fact, seven of the nine Supreme Court justices wrote separate opinions, conveying a range of viewpoints about the governing legal principles. At issue in *Pico* was the school board's removal of certain books from junior high and high school libraries and the literature curriculum, notwithstanding the contrary recommendation of a committee appointed to review the books.

The Supreme Court narrowly affirmed the appellate court's remand of the case for a trial because of irregularities in the removal procedures and unresolved factual questions regarding the school board's motivation. Only three of the justices

---

[87]*See, e.g.*, Case v. Unified Sch. Dist. No. 233, 908 F. Supp. 864 (D. Kan. 1995) (*Annie on My Mind*); Salvail v. Nashua Bd. of Educ., 469 F. Supp. 1269 (D.N.H. 1979) (*Ms.* magazine). *See also* Minarcini v. Strongsville City Sch. Dist., 541 F.2d 577 (6th Cir. 1976) (upholding the school board's right to override faculty judgments regarding the selection of books for academic courses and the school library but finding no compelling reason for removing books that had already been placed in the library).

[88]Campbell v. St. Tammany Parish Sch. Bd., 64 F.3d 184 (5th Cir. 1995) (noting that the board's failure to consider recommendations of two committees and its vote to remove the book even though many board members had viewed only excerpts supplied by the Christian Coalition suggested unconstitutional motivation).

[89]Pratt v. Indep. Sch. Dist., 670 F.2d 771 (8th Cir. 1982) (noting that the board was inconsistent in retaining the book in the school library but banning two films based on the book).

[90]Counts v. Cedarville Sch. Dist., 295 F. Supp. 2d 996 (W.D. Ark. 2003).

[91]ACLU v. Miami-Dade County Sch. Bd., 439 F. Supp. 2d 1242 (S.D. Fla. 2006).

[92]457 U.S. 853 (1982).

endorsed the notion that students have a protected right to receive information. And even those justices recognized the broad authority of school boards to remove materials that are vulgar or educationally unsuitable and indicated that a trial might have been unnecessary if the school board had employed regular and unbiased procedures in reviewing the controversial materials. The *Pico* plurality also emphasized that the controversy involved *library* books, which are not required reading for students, noting that school boards "might well defend their claim of absolute discretion in matters of *curriculum* by reliance upon their duty to inculcate community values."[93]

Further strengthening the broad discretion of school authorities in curriculum-related censorship was the 1988 Supreme Court decision involving students' free speech rights, *Hazelwood School District v. Kuhlmeier*.[94] The Court's conclusion that expression appearing to represent the school can be restricted for educational reasons has been cited by courts in upholding states' and school boards' censorship decisions.[95] For example, the Fifth Circuit denied a claim by two students and the author of a textbook that the state's rejection of the book from the Texas State Board of Education's approved list of texts implicated the First Amendment. The court reasoned that the selection of curricular materials is governmental speech, not a forum for expression, and that the state board has wide discretion in making such decisions.[96] Also, the Eleventh Circuit upheld a Florida school board's decision to ban a humanities book because it included Aristophanes's *Lysistrata* and Chaucer's *The Miller's Tale*, which board members considered vulgar and immoral. While not addressing the wisdom of the board basing its decision on fundamentalist religious views, the court nonetheless relied on *Hazelwood* in deferring to the board's broad discretion in curricular matters.[97]

Specific issues may change, but controversies surrounding the selection of materials for the public school library and curriculum will likely persist, reflecting the "inherent tension" between the school board's two essential functions of "exposing young minds to the clash of ideologies in the free marketplace of ideas" and instilling basic community values in our youth.[98] School boards would be wise to establish procedures for reviewing objections to course content and library materials, and to do so *before* a controversy arises. Criteria for the acquisition and elimination of instructional materials should be clearly articulated and educationally defensible. Once a process is in place to evaluate complaints relating to the instructional program, school boards should follow it carefully, as courts show little sympathy when a school board ignores its own established procedures.

[93]*Id.* at 869 (1982). Following the Supreme Court's *Pico* decision, the school board voted to return the controversial books to the school libraries, thus averting the need for a trial regarding the board's motivation for the original censorship.

[94]484 U.S. 260 (1988). *See* text accompanying note 36, Chapter 4.

[95]*See, e.g.*, Borger v. Bisciglia, 888 F. Supp. 97 (E.D. Wis. 1995) (upholding school district's ban on showing R-rated films as related to legitimate pedagogical concerns).

[96]Chiras v. Miller, 432 F.3d 606 (5th Cir. 2005).

[97]Virgil v. Sch. Bd., 862 F.2d 1517 (11th Cir. 1989).

[98]Seyfried v. Walton, 668 F.2d 214, 219 (3d Cir. 1981) (Rosenn, J., concurring).

Electronic Censorship. The next wave of censorship activity is likely to focus on the electronic frontier. It was estimated in 2006 that approximately 87 percent of American teenagers had Internet access.[99] With schools increasingly making online services accessible to students, concerns are being raised about the possible transmission of sexually explicit material to minors. A number of states have enacted laws or are considering measures that would prohibit sending obscene materials over the Internet. Also, the federal government has enacted several measures to restrict minors' access to harmful materials over the Internet, but only one of these measures has survived judicial scrutiny. After the Supreme Court in 1997 ruled that the Communications Decency Act was unconstitutionally vague and overinclusive in its criminalization of some legitimate sexually explicit speech,[100] Congress enacted the Child Online Protection Act (COPA) imposing penalties for materials harmful to minors being distributed for commercial purposes through the World Wide Web.[101] Litigation challenging this law went before the Supreme Court twice, and ultimately enforcement of the law was permanently enjoined because it violated the First and Fifth Amendment rights of the Web site owners.[102] The law was found impermissibly vague and overbroad and not narrowly tailored to achieve the compelling interest of protecting minors from harmful Internet materials.

A third federal law, the Children's Internet Protection Act (CIPA), received Supreme Court endorsement in 2003.[103] This law requires libraries and school districts that receive technology funds to implement technology protection measures that safeguard students from access to harmful content and to monitor student Internet use.[104] In implementing the required Internet safety plans, most school districts are relying on filtering software and thus delegating to companies the decisions concerning what materials are appropriate for their students. The Supreme Court reasoned that unlike the two invalidated federal provisions, CIPA places a condition on the use of federal funds, which poses a small burden for library patrons, and the law does not penalize those posting materials on the Internet.[105] Nonetheless, there are

[99]*See* Amanda Lenhart, Mary Madden, and Lee Rainie, *Teens and the Internet*, PEW Internet and American Life Project (July 11, 2006), available at www.pewinternet.org/reports.asp.

[100]Reno v. ACLU, 521 U.S. 844, 877 (1997). *See also* Ashcroft v. Free Speech Coal. 535 U.S. 234 (2002) (striking down provisions of the federal Child Pornography Prevention Act of 1996 that prohibited possession or distribution of virtual child pornography; ruling that the overbroad prohibition was not sufficiently related to actual abuse of minors).

[101]47 U.S.C. § 231 (2002). The law called for violators to be fined up to $50,000 and sentenced up to six months in jail.

[102]ACLU v. Reno, 217 F.3d 162 (3d Cir. 2000), *vacated and remanded sub nom.* Ashcroft v. ACLU, 535 U.S. 564 (2002), *on remand,* 322 F.3d 240 (3d Cir. 2003), *aff'd and remanded,* 542 U.S. 656 (2004), *on remand sub nom.* ACLU v. Gonzales, 478 F. Supp. 2d 775 (E.D. Pa. 2007) (permanently enjoining the enforcement of COPA as violating the First and Fifth Amendments).

[103]United States v. American Library Ass'n, 539 U.S. 194 (2003).

[104]20 U.S.C. § 9134(f) (2007); 47 U.S.C. § 254(h)(5) (2007).

[105]*American Library Ass'n*, 539 U.S. 194. For information on state laws pertaining to Internet filtering requirements, see Lenhart, et al., *supra* note 99.

some fears that measures such as CIPA will have a chilling effect on schools using computer networks to enhance instructional experiences for students.[106] The competing governmental and individual interests affected by legislative restrictions on information distributed electronically will likely generate a stream of litigation.

Student Proficiency Testing

Acknowledging the state's authority to establish academic standards, including mandatory examinations, the judiciary traditionally has been reluctant to interfere with assessments of pupil performance. The Supreme Court has distinguished academic determinations from disciplinary actions, noting that the former "judgment is by its nature more subjective and evaluative than the typical factual questions presented in the average disciplinary decision."[107] Emphasizing that academic performance is properly assessed by professional educators who have expertise in this area, the judiciary has rejected challenges to teachers' grading practices unless they constitute extreme and outrageous conduct.

Courts have recognized that assurance of an educated citizenry is an appropriate government goal and that the establishment of minimum performance standards to give value to a high school diploma is a rational means to attain that goal. Three decades ago, only four states had enacted student proficiency testing legislation. Now all states have laws or administrative regulations pertaining to statewide performance testing programs, and the majority of states condition receipt of a high school diploma on passage of a test.

Recently, other forms of performance assessment, such as portfolios, have received attention, but machine-scorable tests continue to be used and are strongly supported by the federal government. Indeed, the NCLB Act mandates annual testing in grades 3 through 8 in reading and math and at certain grade intervals in science; requires all students in grades 10 through 12 to take a general test in core subjects at least once; and ties federal assistance and sanctions for schools to student test scores.[108] High-stakes assessments shape the instructional program, and states increasingly are evaluating educators' performance based on their students' test scores. Not

---

[106]*See* Martha McCarthy, "The Continuing Saga of Internet Censorship: The Child Online Protection Act," *Brigham Young University Education and Law Journal* (2005), pp. 83–101.

[107]Bd. of Curators v. Horowitz, 435 U.S. 78, 89-90 (1978). *See also* Regents v. Ewing, 474 U.S. 214 (1985).

[108]20 U.S.C. § 6301 *et seq.* (2007). Required testing in science went into effect in 2007–2008, but results of these tests will not be considered in adequate yearly progress goals for several years. Among professional associations, which have issued statements raising concerns about high-stakes testing programs and opposing the inappropriate use of tests to make high-stakes decisions, are the American Educational Research Association, American Evaluation Association, National Council for Teachers of English, the National Council for Teachers of Mathematics, International Reading Association, National Council for the Social Studies, and National Education Association. *See also* Sharon L. Nichols and David C. Berliner, *Collateral Damage: How High-Stakes Testing Corrupts America's Schools* (Cambridge, MA: Harvard Education Press, 2007).

surprisingly, claims are being made that teachers are limiting classroom activities to material covered on the tests and/or unfairly coaching students for the exams.[109]

Although the state's authority to evaluate student performance has not been questioned, the implementation of specific assessment programs has been legally challenged as impairing students' rights to fair and nondiscriminatory treatment. In a case still widely cited as establishing the legal standards, *Debra P. v. Turlington*, the Fifth Circuit in 1981 recognized that by making schooling mandatory, Florida created a property interest—a valid expectation that students would receive diplomas if they passed required courses. This property right necessitates sufficient notice of conditions attached to high school graduation and an opportunity to satisfy the standards before a diploma can be withheld. The court found that 13 months was insufficient notice of the test requirement and further held that the state may have administered a fundamentally unfair test covering material that had not been taught in Florida schools. The appeals court also enjoined the state from using the test as a diploma prerequisite for four years to provide time for the vestiges of prior school segregation to be removed and to ensure that all minority students subjected to the requirement started first grade under desegregated conditions.[110] However, the court held that continued use of the test to determine remediation needs was constitutionally permissible, noting that the disproportionate placement of minority students in remedial programs *per se* does not abridge the Equal Protection Clause without evidence of intentional discrimination.

On remand, the district court ruled that the injunction should be lifted, and the appeals court affirmed this decision in 1984.[111] By presenting substantial evidence, including curriculum guides and survey data, the state convinced the judiciary that the test was instructionally valid in that it covered material taught to Florida students. Also, data showed significant improvement among African American students during the six years the test had been administered, which convinced the court that the testing program could help remedy the effects of past discrimination.

Other courts have reiterated the principles established in *Debra P.* and have reasoned that despite evidence of higher minority failure rates, such testing and remediation programs are effectively addressing the effects of prior discrimination.[112] The Supreme Court declined to review a decision in which the lower courts rejected a challenge to a Louisiana school district's policy that conditioned promotion at the fourth and eighth grades on test passage, finding no property or liberty interest in

[109]*See, e.g.,* Buck v. Lowndes County Sch. Dist., 761 So. 2d 144 (Miss. 2000) (upholding nonrenewal of teachers' contracts for noncompliance with testing procedures that resulted in a reduction in the district's accreditation level).

[110]Debra P. v. Turlington, 644 F.2d 397, 407 (5th Cir. 1981).

[111]Debra P. v. Turlington, 564 F. Supp. 177 (M.D. Fla. 1983), *aff'd*, 730 F.2d 1405 (11th Cir. 1984). It should be noted that the Fifth Circuit was divided into the Fifth and Eleventh Circuits while this case was in progress.

[112]*See, e.g.,* GI Forum v. Tex. Educ. Agency, 87 F. Supp. 2d 667 (W.D. Tex. 2000); Anderson v. Banks, 540 F. Supp. 761 (S.D. Ga. 1982); Bd. of Educ. v. Ambach, 457 N.E.2d 775 (N.Y. 1983). *See also* Rankins v. La. State Bd. of Elementary and Secondary Educ., 637 So. 2d 548 (La. Ct. App. 1994) (finding no equal protection violation in requiring public, but not private, school students to pass a high school exit examination).

grade promotion.[113] Yet, courts have not clarified whether similar notice and due process protections required for tests used as a condition of receiving a diploma also must accompany tests used as a prerequisite to promotion. Most high-stakes testing programs include provisions for students who fail proficiency examinations to receive remediation and retake the tests. Courts have not agreed as to whether individual rights are abridged when students are not allowed to participate in graduation exercises because they failed the statewide proficiency examination.[114]

California students in an economically challenged community claimed that they were entitled to diplomas because they had passed all the required courses but had not been provided adequate educational resources to pass the state's high school exit examination. Reversing the court below, the state appeals court denied the claim of irreparable injury, noting that the test used as a diploma sanction was integral to the statutory scheme to raise academic standards in the state's schools, which served a significant public interest.[115] Also, several school districts have unsuccessfully asserted that they have been provided inadequate resources for their schools to make adequate yearly progress in terms of test results under NCLB. The courts have rejected the contention that the federal government must provide 100 percent of the funds necessary to devise and administer tests, improve test scores, and train teachers before it can expect schools to comply with federal requirements.[116] However, an Alaska court ruled that because the state failed to provide sufficient oversight to ensure that local districts were providing students a meaningful opportunity to acquire proficiency in the subjects tested by the state, receipt of a high school diploma could not be conditioned on passage of a proficiency exam. In short, some

[113]Parents Against Testing Before Teaching v. Orleans Parish Sch. Bd., 273 F.3d 1107 (5th Cir. 2001). Other courts have upheld the practice of conditioning grade promotion on test scores. *See* Bester v. Tuscaloosa City Bd. of Educ., 722 F.2d 1514 (11th Cir. 1984); Sandlin v. Johnson, 643 F.2d 1027 (4th Cir. 1981).

[114]*Compare* Williams v. Austin Indep. Sch. Dist., 796 F. Supp. 251 (W.D. Tex. 1992) (holding that the graduation ceremony can be reserved for students meeting all requirements, assuming that appropriate notice and instruction are provided) *with* Crump v. Gilmer Indep. Sch. Dist., 797 F. Supp. 552 (E.D. Tex. 1992) (requiring a Texas school to permit students who failed the exam but satisfied other graduation requirements to take part in the graduation ceremony, a milestone event, even though they will not receive their diplomas until they pass the test).

[115]O'Connell v. Valenzuela, 47 Cal. Rptr. 3d 147 (Ct. App. 2006) (recognizing that if students receive diplomas without demonstrating mastery of basic skills, they will not be provided the remediation they need to be productive workers and citizens). *See also* Valenzuela v. O'Connell, No. JCCP-4468 (Cal. Super. Ct. Aug. 13, 2007) (approving a settlement agreement that calls for legislation providing two years of academic assistance to students who fail to pass the exam); Californians for Justice Educ. Fund v. State Bd. of Educ., No. A114190, 2006 Cal. App. Unpub. LEXIS 8832 (Ct. App. Sept. 29, 2006) (rejecting a claim that the statewide test could not be used as a diploma sanction because the study of alternatives to the exit exam was not completed in a timely fashion).

[116]*See* Connecticut v. Spellings, 453 F. Supp. 2d 459 (D. Conn. 2006) (holding, however, that the U.S. Department of Education's denial of the state's requests for plan amendments without an adequate hearing may have violated the federal Administrative Procedures Act); Reading Sch. Dist. v. Dep't of Educ., 855 A.2d 166 (Pa. Commw. Ct. 2004). *But see* Sch. Dist. Sec'y of the U.S. Dep't of Educ., 512 F.3d 252 (6th Cir. 2008) (holding that state officials could reasonably interpret § 7907(a) of NCLB to mean that states do not have to comply with the laws requirements that are funded by the federal government; Congress must clarify if such compliance is mandatory).

students had not been accorded a meaningful opportunity to learn the material covered on the test.[117]

Most testing controversies have focused on statewide exams and usually on their use as a diploma sanction, but other test requirements also have generated some legal controversies. For example, the judiciary has upheld school district requirements that all students transferring from nonaccredited schools must take proficiency tests at their own expense.[118] In a Kentucky case, the Sixth Circuit ruled that requiring a high school student to pass equivalency exams to gain public school credit for a religious home study program did not violate rights to freely exercise religious beliefs or to equal protection of the laws.[119] Local school districts also can impose test requirements beyond those mandated by the state.[120] The Eleventh Circuit upheld a school district's ability grouping plan, under which middle school students are tracked based primarily on test scores and performance recommendations of former teachers.[121]

Given the high stakes attached to some exams, parents have requested access to questions on previously administered versions of the tests. The Ohio Supreme Court ruled that the statewide proficiency test fell under the definition of a public record, so previous exams must be disclosed to parents, except for portions owned and developed by a private nonprofit corporation.[122] But a Kentucky appeals court held that parents were not entitled to view the statewide proficiency exam to confirm their religious objections, because indiscriminate viewing by the public could jeopardize the test's reliability.[123] And a Florida appeals court held that test instruments are not student records within the state student records law, thus denying the guardian of a student who failed the statewide comprehensive achievement test access to test booklets and questions for the exam.[124] As stakes continue to increase based on test scores, the procedures and scales for scoring the exams seem likely to come under additional scrutiny.[125]

Administering proficiency tests to children with limited mastery of English and to children with disabilities has been controversial. After school districts and others

[117]Moore v. State, No. 3AN-04-9756 (Alaska Super. Ct. June 26, 2007), available at www.law.state .ak.us/unpublished/pdf/mooredecision.pdf.

[118]*See* Hubbard v. Buffalo Indep. Sch. Dist., 20 F. Supp. 2d 1012 (W.D. Tex. 1998).

[119]Vandiver v. Hardin County Bd. of Educ., 925 F.2d 927 (6th Cir. 1991).

[120]*See* Triplett v. Livingston County Bd. of Educ., 967 S.W.2d 25 (Ky. Ct. App. 1997).

[121]Holton v. City of Thomasville Sch. Dist., 490 F.3d 1257 (11th Cir. 2007) (noting that the placement of low income African American students disproportionately in lower tracks does not by itself substantiate a constitutional violation).

[122]Rea v. Ohio Dep't of Educ., 692 N.E.2d 596 (Ohio 1998).

[123]*Triplett*, 967 S.W.2d 25. *See also* Gabrilson v. Flynn, 554 N.W.2d 267 (Iowa 1996) (holding that under state law school board members can review confidential school records because they are charged with handling the district's affairs).

[124]Fla. Dep't of Educ. v. Cooper, 858 So. 2d 394 (Fla. Dist. Ct. App. 2003).

[125]*See* Russo v. NCS Pearson, 462 F. Supp. 2d 981 (D. Minn. 2006) (denying most requested relief but allowing negligence claims to proceed in connection with the allegation that uncorrected inflated scores on the SAT gave some students a competitive advantage over other students); *infra* text accompanying note 144.

challenged California's failure to make appropriate testing accommodations under NCLB for students with limited English proficiency,[126] the parties reached a settlement under which the U.S. Department of Education changed its classification of schools needing improvement to allow more accommodations for non-English speakers.

Courts in general have ruled that the state does not have to alter its academic standards for students with disabilities; they can be denied grade promotion or a diploma if they do not meet the specified standards.[127] Such children, however, cannot be denied the *opportunity* to satisfy requirements (including tests) for promotion or a diploma. A child with mental disabilities may be given the option of not taking a proficiency examination if the team charged with planning the individualized education program (IEP) concludes that there is little likelihood of the child mastering the material covered on the test. Children excused from the test requirement usually are awarded certificates of school attendance instead of diplomas.

The Seventh Circuit suggested that children with disabilities may need earlier notice of a proficiency test requirement than other students to ensure an adequate opportunity for the material on the test to be incorporated into their IEPs.[128] However, an Indiana appeals court subsequently ruled that diplomas for children with disabilities can be conditioned on test passage with three years notice of the requirement.[129] In upholding the statewide testing requirement, the court also noted that there were ample opportunities to receive remediation and retake the exam and that the plaintiff student's IEP sufficiently covered material on the test.

Students with disabilities are entitled to special accommodations in the administration of examinations to ensure that their knowledge, rather than their disability, is being assessed, but the nature of the required accommodations remains controversial. In the Indiana case cited above, the court rejected accommodations that would jeopardize the validity of the graduation test, such as reading to the student a test measuring reading comprehension, even though such accommodations were part of the student's IEP.[130] A California federal court conversely held that students

---

[126]Coachella Valley Unified Sch. Dist. v. California, No. C 05-02657 WHA, 2005 U.S. Dist. LEXIS 44825 (N.D. Cal. Aug. 5, 2005) (remanding state law challenge to the state judiciary); Coachella Valley Unified Sch. Dist. v. California, No. 05-505334 (Cal. Super. Ct. May 25, 2007) (finding decision to assess all students in English neither arbitrary or capricious, given that students are taught mainly in English and the impracticality of translating all assessment instruments into multiple languages). *See also Assessment and Accountability for Recently Arrived and Former Limited English Proficient (LEP) Students* (Non-Regulatory Guidance) (Washington, D.C.: U.S. Department of Education, May 2007).

[127]*See, e.g.,* Brookhart v. Ill. State Bd. of Educ., 697 F.2d 179 (7th Cir. 1983); Anderson v. Banks, 540 F. Supp. 761 (S.D. Ga. 1982); Bd. of Educ. v. Ambach, 457 N.E.2d 775 (N.Y. 1983).

[128]*Brookhart,* 697 F.2d at 187. *See* Chapter 6 for a discussion of federal and state protections of children with disabilities.

[129]Rene v. Reed, 751 N.E.2d 736 (Ind. Ct. App. 2001).

[130]*Id.* The Office for Civil Rights in the U.S. Department of Education has also reasoned that states can deny use of reading devices to accommodate children with disabilities on graduation exams, even though their IEPs allow use of such devices. *See* Alabama Dep't of Educ., 29 IDELR 249 (1998).

with disabilities were entitled to all accommodations in their IEPs when taking the state's graduation test, but the Ninth Circuit found parts of the order overbroad and not ready for judicial resolution because the claim rested on future harm that may or may not occur.[131] The NCLB regulations allow states to use alternative assessments for up to 2 percent of their students based on modified academic standards; such alternative assessments may be less rigorous but they must assess the same content.[132]

Specific proficiency testing programs will likely generate additional litigation on constitutional and statutory grounds. Educators can take steps to defeat legal challenges by ensuring that (1) students have the opportunity to be adequately prepared for the tests, (2) students are advised upon entrance into high school of test requirements as a prerequisite to graduation, (3) tests are not intentionally discriminatory and do not perpetuate the effects of past school segregation, (4) students who fail are provided remedial opportunities and the chance to retake the examinations, and (5) children with disabilities receive appropriate accommodations.

Educational Malpractice/Instructional Negligence

A topic prompting litigation since the mid-1970s is instructional negligence, commonly referred to as *educational malpractice*. Initial suits focused on whether students have a right to attain a predetermined level of achievement in return for state-mandated school attendance; parents asserted a right to expect their children to be functionally literate upon high school graduation. More recent cases have involved allegations that school authorities have breached their duty to diagnose students' deficiencies and place them in appropriate instructional programs. This section includes an overview of claims in which parents have sought damages from school districts for instructional negligence.

In the first educational malpractice suit to receive substantial attention, a California student in the mid-1970s asserted that the school district was negligent in teaching, promoting, and graduating him from high school with the ability to read at only the fifth-grade level.[133] He also claimed that his performance and progress had been misrepresented to his parents, who testified that they were unaware of his deficiencies until he was tested by a private agency after high school graduation. Concluding that the school district was not negligent, a California appeals court reasoned that the complexities of the teaching/learning process made it impossible to place the entire burden on the school to ensure that *all* students attain a specified reading level before high school graduation.

The New York high court subsequently dismissed what had appeared to be a successful educational malpractice suit. A state appellate court had awarded a

---

[131]Smiley v. Cal. Dep't of Educ., 53 Fed. Appx. 474 (9th Cir. 2002) (dissolving the parts of the lower court's injunction pertaining to required test waivers and alternative assessments for children with disabilities).

[132]72 Fed. Reg. 17748 (April 9, 2007).

[133]Peter W. v. San Francisco Unified Sch. Dist.,131 Cal. Rptr. 854 (Ct. App. 1976). *See* Chapter 13 for an overview of tort law pertaining to negligence suits.

former public school student $500,000 in damages against the New York City Board of Education for disregarding the school psychologist's report and erroneously instructing him for 12 years in a program for the mentally retarded—even though the student scored in the 90th percentile on reading readiness tests at ages 8 and 9.[134] Distinguishing this case from previous educational malpractice suits, the lower court noted that school personnel committed affirmative acts of negligence that placed crippling burdens on the student. Nonetheless, the New York high court by a narrow margin reversed the lower court's ruling and held that it was not the role of the judiciary to make such educational policy determinations that should be handled through the state educational system's administrative appeals. The same court later ruled that a student who was incorrectly diagnosed at age 10, after having been tested in English even though he understood only Spanish, was not entitled to damages from the child-care agency for its alleged failure to obtain suitable instruction for him to learn to read.[135] The court determined that the issue involved educational policy matters regarding which instructional programs might have been preferable and was not actionable in a negligence suit.

Other courts also have denied instructional malpractice claims, indicating a reluctance to intervene in such educational policy decisions.[136] For example, state courts have denied damages claims for a school district's alleged breach of its duty to evaluate and develop an individualized education plan for a child with multiple disabilities,[137] the alleged misclassification of a student with dyslexia,[138] a school district's alleged failure to provide remedial instruction for a student,[139] and a school district's failure to provide students with a quality education resulting in alleged intellectual and emotional harm and diminished future opportunities.[140]

---

[134]Hoffman v. Bd. of Educ., 410 N.Y.S.2d 99 (App. Div. 1978), *rev'd*, 424 N.Y.S.2d 376 (1979). *See also* Donohue v. Copiague Union Free Schs., 391 N.E.2d 1352 (N.Y. 1979) (dismissing an educational malpractice suit brought by a learning-disabled high school graduate who claimed that because of the school district's negligence he was unable to complete job applications and cope with the problems of everyday life).

[135]Torres v. Little Flower Children's Servs., 485 N.Y.S.2d 15 (1984). But on the same day, the court awarded damages in a medical malpractice suit, although the impact of the malpractice was educational. *See* Snow v. State, 485 N.Y.S.2d 987 (1984) (holding that failure to reassess a student upon learning he was deaf and continuing to instruct him in classes for the mentally deficient was a discernible act of medical malpractice rather than a mere mistake in judgment pertaining to the student's educational program).

[136]*See, e.g.*, Vogel v. Maimonides Acad., 754 A.2d 824 (Conn. App. Ct. 2000); Page v. Klein Tools, 610 N.W.2d 900 (Mich. 2000); Suriano v. Hyde Park Cent. Sch. Dist., 611 N.Y.S.2d 20 (App. Div. 1994).

[137]Keech v. Berkeley Unified Sch. Dist., 210 Cal. Rptr. 7 (Ct. App. 1984).

[138]D.S.W. v. Fairbanks N. Star Borough Sch. Dist., 628 P.2d 554 (Alaska 1981). *See also* Doe v. Bd. of Educ., 453 A.2d 814 (Md. 1982) (finding that a student misdiagnosed as having a brain injury instead of dyslexia and educated in an improper environment for seven years was not able to collect damages); Johnson v. Clark, 418 N.W.2d 466 (Mich. Ct. App. 1987) (finding that a student who was reading on a fourth grade level at graduation could not recover damages for the school's failure to assess him annually).

[139]Myers v. Medford Lakes Bd. of Educ., 489 A.2d 1240 (N.J. Super. Ct. App. Div. 1985).

[140]Denver Parents Ass'n v. Denver Bd. of Educ., 10 P.3d 662 (Colo. Ct. App. 2000). *See also* Scott v. Savers Prop. & Cas. Ins. Co., 663 N.W.2d 715 (Wis. 2003) (rejecting a school district's liability for educational malpractice where a guidance counselor's faulty advice regarding NCAA eligibility requirements resulted in a student losing a college athletic scholarship).

Although educational malpractice claims have not yet been successful, some courts have recognized limited circumstances under which plaintiffs possibly could recover damages in an instructional tort action. For example, the Maryland Supreme Court rejected parents' instructional malpractice claim for unintentional negligent acts in evaluating a child's learning disabilities and inappropriately instructing the child, but held that parents might secure damages if they could meet the formidable burden of proving that the defendants intentionally engaged in acts that injured a child placed in their educational care.[141] The Third Circuit, though not awarding monetary damages, held that a student with severe disabilities who had not progressed over the past decade was entitled to compensatory services from a New Jersey school district, because school authorities should have known that the child's individualized education program was inadequate.[142] And the California Supreme Court recognized that charter schools and their chartering school districts might be liable for failure to deliver promised instructional services, equipment, and supplies as required by law.[143] Also, a Minnesota federal court declined to dismiss a negligence suit against the College Entrance Examination Board and a national test scoring service for injuries resulting from incorrectly scoring and reporting SAT scores for some students.[144]

The increasing specificity of legislation pertaining to student proficiency standards and special education placements may strengthen the grounds for tort suits involving *placement negligence*. Also, state and federal legislation making school districts accountable for ensuring student mastery of state standards may increase school districts' potential liability. Even though it seems unlikely in the near future that public schools will be held responsible for a specified quantum of student achievement, it is conceivable that schools will be held legally accountable for diagnosing pupils' needs and placing them in appropriate instructional programs.

Instructional Privacy Rights

The protection of students' privacy rights has become an increasingly volatile issue in political forums. State and federal laws place dual duties on the government—to protect the public's First Amendment right to be informed about government activities and to protect the personal privacy of individuals. In addition, laws have been enacted to protect students from mandatory participation in research projects or instructional

[141]Hunter v. Bd. of Educ., 439 A.2d 582 (Md. 1982). *See also* Squires v. Sierra Nev. Educ. Found., 823 P.2d 256 (Nev. 1991) (finding also no triable case of breach of contract and misrepresentation against the private school where their child had been enrolled for four years and allegedly received inappropriate instruction).

[142]M.C. v. Cent. Reg'l Sch. Dist., 81 F.3d 389 (3d Cir. 1996). *See also* Anthony v. Dist. of Columbia, 463 F. Supp. 2d 37 (D.D.C. 2006) (remanding case to the hearing officer to redetermine the award of compensatory education as a remedy for violations of the IDEA).

[143]Wells v. One2One Learning Found., 141 P.3d 225 (Cal. 2006).

[144]Russo v. NCS Pearson, 462 F. Supp. 2d 981 (D. Minn. 2006).

activities designed to reveal personal information in sensitive areas. This section provides an overview of legal developments pertaining to students' privacy rights in instructional matters.

Student Records

The Supreme Court has recognized that the Constitution protects a zone of personal privacy.[145] Thus, there must be a compelling justification for governmental action that impairs privacy rights, including the right to have personal information kept confidential. Because of this right, questions about who has access to public school students' permanent files and the contents of such files have been the source of controversy.

Due to widespread dissatisfaction with educators' efforts to ameliorate abuses associated with student record-keeping practices, Congress enacted the Family Educational Rights and Privacy Act (FERPA) in 1974.[146] This law stipulates that federal funds may be withdrawn from any educational agency or institution that (1) fails to provide parents access to their child's educational records or (2) disseminates such information (with some exceptions) to third parties without parental permission. Upon reaching the age of majority, students may exercise the rights guaranteed to their parents before they turned 18.[147]

Education officials should assume that a parent is entitled to exercise rights under FERPA unless state law or a court order bars a parent's access to his or her child's records under specific circumstances.[148] Courts have recognized that joint custodial parents must have equal access to education information about their child. If copies of juvenile court proceedings are maintained by the school, these records are subject to FERPA in terms of confidentiality and accessibility to parents.

After reviewing a student's permanent file, the parent or eligible student can request amendments in any information thought to be inaccurate, misleading, or in violation of the student's protected rights. If school authorities decide that an amendment is not warranted, the parent or eligible student must be advised of the right to a hearing and of the right to place in the file a personal statement specifying objections to the hearing officer's decision.

---

[145]*See* Griswold v. Connecticut, 381 U.S. 479 (1965); text accompanying note 146, Chapter 9.

[146]20 U.S.C. § 1232g (2007); 34 C.F.R. § 99.1 *et seq*. (2007). Parents are not entitled to free copies of their children's records, but they do have a right to have them interpreted for them.

[147]The Family Policy Compliance Office was created to investigate alleged FERPA violations, 20 U.S.C. § 1232g(g) (2007). This office reviews complaints and responses from accused agencies and submits written findings with steps the agency must take to comply, 34 C.F.R. 99.65(a)(2), 99.66(b), 99.66(c)(1) (2007). For a discussion of FERPA and other privacy protections afforded to public school students, see Susan Stuart, "Lex-Praxis of Educational Informational Privacy for Public Schoolchildren," *Nebraska Law Review,* vol. 84 (2006), pp. 1158–1225.

[148]*See, e.g.,* Cherry v. LeDeoni, No. 99 CV 6860 (SJ), 2002 U.S. Dist. LEXIS 6701 (E.D.N.Y. April 8, 2002) (interpreting a school district's regulation requiring custodial parents to be informed of noncustodial parents' requests to see school records; the custodial parent has 60 days to produce a court order or other binding document to prevent such disclosure).

Individuals can file a complaint with the U.S. Department of Education if they believe a school district exhibits a custom or practice of violating FERPA provisions. The remedy for FERPA violations is the withdrawal of federal funds, and the Department of Education has enforcement authority. Some school districts have been advised to remedy their practices to conform to FERPA, but to date no district has lost federal funds for noncompliance.

The Department of Education functioned without direction from the Supreme Court until 2002 when the Court rendered two FERPA decisions. In *Gonzaga University v. Doe*, the Court held that FERPA's nondisclosure provisions do not create privately enforceable rights; Congress must create such rights in unambiguous terms.[149] Resolving the conflict among lower courts, the Supreme Court further held that since FERPA contains no rights-creating language, the law cannot be enforced through individual lawsuits for damages for the deprivation of federal rights.[150] The Court reiterated that FERPA has an aggregate rather than individual focus and the remedy for violations is the denial of federal funds to schools that exhibit a policy or practice of noncompliance. School personnel were relieved that the Court did not authorize private suits for damages to enforce FERPA, as such a ruling would have provided a significant incentive for parents to challenge student record-keeping practices in court.

In the second 2002 Supreme Court ruling, *Owasso Independent School District v. Falvo*, the Court reversed the Tenth Circuit's conclusion that peer grading practices violate FERPA.[151] The Supreme Court concluded that peer graders are not "maintaining" student records under FERPA, and even though students may call out the scores in class, they are not "acting for" the educational institution.[152] There may be educational reasons for not having students grade each others' work, but given the *Falvo* ruling, there is no legal barrier under FERPA. The Court also hinted that teachers' grade books may not be subject to FERPA, mentioning that records covered by the act are usually kept in a central repository, but it specifically declined to resolve this issue.

A student's records can be released to school employees authorized to review such information and to officials of a school where the student is transferring if the parents or eligible student are notified or if the sending institution has given prior

[149]536 U.S. 273 (2002) (overturning award of damages to a student for an alleged FERPA violation in connection with a private university's release to the state education department an unsubstantiated allegation of sexual misconduct, which resulted in the student being denied an affidavit of good moral character required of all new teachers).

[150]*See* Civil Rights Act of 1871, § 1, codified as 42 U.S.C. § 1983 (2007). For a discussion of damages remedies available under this federal law, *see* text accompanying note 178, Chapter 11.

[151]233 F.3d 1203 (10th Cir. 2000), *rev'd and remanded*, 534 U.S. 426 (2002), *on remand*, 288 F.3d 1236 (10th Cir. 2002) (granting summary judgment in favor of defendant school district and administrators).

[152]*Owasso*, 534 U.S. at 433. Although peers can call out scores, students' grades cannot be posted or disseminated in any manner that allows individual students to be identified (e.g., by name or listed in alphabetical order).

notice that it routinely transfers such records. Students' records must be disclosed if subpoenaed by a grand jury or law enforcement agency, and schools may disclose information pursuant to other court orders or subpoenas if a reasonable effort is made to notify the parent or eligible student.[153] The Sixth Circuit ruled that records related to substitute teachers' use of corporal punishment must be disclosed in a suit challenging the use of this disciplinary technique because FERPA does not prevent discovery of such records.[154] Identifiable information also can be disclosed to appropriate authorities or to advocacy groups if necessary to protect the health or safety of the student or others.[155] For example, the Seventh Circuit ruled that the Wisconsin Department of Public Instruction must provide names of students in connection with a state-designated advocacy agency's investigation of alleged abuse or neglect without first obtaining parental consent because the need to investigate suspected abuse or neglect can outweigh privacy interests.[156]

Under FERPA, certain public directory information, such as students' names, addresses, dates and places of birth, major fields of study, e-mail addresses, pictures, and degrees and awards received, can be released without parental consent.[157] Any educational agency releasing such data must give public notice of the specific categories it has designated as "directory" and must allow a reasonable period of time for parents to inform the agency that any or all of this information on their child should not be released without their prior consent. Directory data about a student cannot be released if accompanied by other personally identifiable information unless it is among the specified exceptions to the general rule against nonconsensual disclosure. The Kentucky Supreme Court ruled that disclosure of personally identifiable information pertaining to academic deficiencies or enrollment status to the Transportation Cabinet under the state's "no pass, no drive" statute did not fall within the FERPA

---

[153]20 U.S.C. § 1232g(b)(1)(J)(i) and (ii) (2007); 1232g(b)(2)(B) (2007). *See* Commonwealth v. Buccella, 751 N.E.2d 373 (Mass. 2001) (holding that a school district did not violate a student's privacy rights when it shared samples of the student's school work with police to compare his handwriting with graffiti on school property in connection with criminal charges). FERPA specifically exempts from the definition of "education records" the records of law enforcement units that the school maintains (e.g., a unit of commissioned officers or security guards that enforces the law and maintains security). *See* 34 C.F.R. § 99.8 (2007).

[154]Ellis v. Cleveland Mun. Sch. Dist., 455 F.3d 690 (6th Cir. 2006). *See also* People v. Owens, 727 N.Y.S.2d 266 (Sup. Ct. 2001) (finding no FERPA violation in prosecution based in part on records subpoenaed from educational institutions).

[155]*See, e.g.*, Doe v. Woodford County Bd. of Educ., 213 F.3d 921 (6th Cir. 2000) (upholding disclosure to coach of information that student was a hemophiliac and carrier of hepatitis B); 34 C.F.R. § 99.36 (2007). The Department of Education in 2007 issued a series of brochures to clarify that health or safety emergencies permit the disclosure of a student's unique information. *See* Frank Wolfe, "ED Releases FERPA Brochures to Deter School Violence," *Education Daily* (October 31, 2007), p. 2.

[156]Disability Rights Wis. v. State Dep't of Pub. Instruction, 463 F.3d 719 (7th Cir. 2006). *See also* Unified Sch. Dist. No. 259 v. Kan. Advocacy and Protective Servs., No. 04-1279-JTM, 2005 U.S. Dist. LEXIS 39220 (D. Kan. Dec. 11, 2005).

[157]For a complete list of directory items, *see* 34 C.F.R. § 99.3 (2007).

exceptions for nonconsensual disclosures.[158] Thus, the regulation was amended so that the notice to the Transportation Cabinet indicates only that students are not in compliance with state law.

Students' privacy rights do not preclude federal and state authorities from having access to data needed to audit and evaluate federally supported education programs. These data usually must be collected in a way that prevents the disclosure of personally identifiable information. However, FERPA was amended in 2001 in accordance with the provisions of the USA PATRIOT (Uniting and Strengthening America by Providing Appropriate Tools Required to Intercept and Obstruct Terrorism) Act to give institutions permission to disclose, without parental or student consent, personally identifiable information to representatives of the U.S. attorney general based on an order from a court of competent jurisdiction in connection with investigations of terrorism crimes.[159] A provision of NCLB also requires public secondary schools to provide military recruiters with access to personal contact information for every student.[160] Although parents can request that their records be withheld, some school districts simply submit their student directories to the military recruiters.

Composite information on pupil achievement and discipline can be released to the public as long as individual students are not personally identified.[161] Disciplinary information (number of occurrences and when they occurred without identifiable data) *must* be released to the media under some state open records laws.[162] Yet, a Florida appeals court ruled that discipline forms about incidents on school buses and surveillance videotapes of such incidents could not be disclosed to a television station even with personally identifying information redacted, because

[158]Codell v. D.F., No. 1998-CA-002895-MR, 2001 Ky. App. LEXIS 71 (Ct. App. June 22, 2001). The U.S. Department of Education contends that FERPA precludes the release of student immunization records without parental consent to comply with the Health Insurance Portability and Accountability Act (HIPAA). *See* Letter from Family Policy Compliance Office to Alabama Department of Education (February 24, 2004), available at www.ed.gov/policy/gen/guid/fpco/ferpa/library/alhippaa.html.

[159]20 U.S.C. § 1232g(j) (2007). Schools are required to record such disclosures in students' permanent files. *See* USA PATRIOT Act, 18 U.S.C. § 2332b(g)(5)(B) (2007); Stuart, "Lex-Praxis," *supra* note 147.

[160]20 U.S.C. § 1232h(c)(4)(a)(i) (2007). *See also* Rumsfeld v. Forum for Academic & Institutional Rights, 547 U.S. 47 (2006) (finding no First Amendment compelled speech violation by requiring law schools that receive federal aid to accommodate the military's recruitment message).

[161]*See, e.g.,* Laplante v. Stewart, 470 So. 2d 1018 (La. Ct. App. 1985) (finding that the public had the right to examine the rankings of schools participating in a school effectiveness study conducted by the state department of education). *But see* Sargent Sch. Dist. No. RE-33J v. W. Servs., 751 P.2d 56 (Colo. 1988) (holding that student scholastic data were exempt from disclosure under the state's open records law); Fish v. Dallas Indep. Sch. Dist., 170 S.W.3d 226 (Tex. App. 2005) (rejecting open-records request for longitudinal student performance data on the Iowa Test of Basic Skills because the requested information could be traced to students in violation of FERPA).

[162]*See e.g.,* Bd. of Trs. v. Cut Bank Pioneer Press, 160 P.3d 482 (Mont. 2007); Hardin County Schs. v. Foster, 40 S.W.3d 865 (Ky. 2001). *See also* United States v. Miami Univ., 294 F. 3d 797 (6th Cir. 2002) (holding that universities cannot release to the media personally identifiable disciplinary records, which are educational records under FERPA).

Florida law goes further than FERPA in preventing the release of such information.[163]

Several courts have addressed what constitutes an educational record. The Tenth Circuit concluded that school personnel could advise parents of harassment and assault victims regarding how they dealt with the perpetrator; disclosures to parents of victims or witnesses of the playground assaults did not comprise an educational record that would implicate FERPA.[164] A Pennsylvania court also held that parents of elementary students were entitled under FERPA to have access to notes taken by the school psychologist during interviews pertaining to allegations that a teacher had physically and emotionally abused the students.[165] And a Kentucky appeals court ruled that a special education teacher could view videotapes made in her classroom for the purpose of evaluating her own performance and improving her classroom management; both FERPA and the comparable state law provided for an exception for teachers with a legitimate educational interest in the material sought.[166] A New York appeals court also ruled that the records of students in a teacher's class would have to be disclosed (obliterating identifying data) for use by the teacher in defending charges pertaining to his reputation and competence.[167]

FERPA cannot be used by parents to assert a right to review faculty evaluations used to determine which students will be given academic honors, such as membership in the National Honor Society.[168] Also, students cannot rely on FERPA to challenge teachers' grading procedures, other than whether grades were accurately calculated and recorded.[169] The Fourth Circuit ruled that FERPA does not entitle students to see an answer key to exams to check the accuracy of their grades, because the key is not part of students' educational records.[170]

Other federal laws provide additional protections regarding the confidentiality and accessibility of student records.[171] Many states also have enacted legislation addressing the maintenance and disclosure of student records. Both state and

[163]WFTV v. Sch. Bd. of Seminole, 874 So. 2d 48 (Fla. Dist. Ct. App. 2004).

[164]Jensen v. Reeves, 3 Fed. Appx. 905 (10th Cir. 2001). *See also* Cudjoe v. Edmond Pub. Schs., 297 F.3d 1058 (10th Cir. 2002) (finding a teacher's comments about a student during a residents' meeting at her condominium complex did not rise to the level of invading privacy rights protected by FERPA or the Federal Constitution).

[165]Parents Against Abuse in Schs. v. Williamsport Area Sch. Dist., 594 A.2d 796 (Pa. Commonw. Ct. 1991).

[166]Medley v. Bd. of Educ., 168 S.W.3d 398 (Ky. Ct. App. 2004).

[167]Bd. of Educ. v. Butcher, 402 N.Y.S.2d 626 (App. Div. 1978).

[168]*See, e.g.,* Moore v. Hyche, 761 F. Supp. 112 (N.D. Ala. 1991); Price v. Young, 580 F. Supp. 1 (E.D. Ark. 1983); Becky v. Butte-Silver Bow Sch. Dist. 1, 906 P.2d 193 (Mont. 1995).

[169]*See, e.g.,* Tarka v. Cunningham, 917 F.2d 890 (5th Cir. 1990). *See also* Hurd v. Hansen, 230 Fed. Appx. 692 (9th Cir. 2007) (finding no violation of a student's due process and equal protection rights in a teacher's award of a "C" grade).

[170]Lewin v. Cooke, 28 Fed. Appx. 186 (4th Cir. 2002).

[171]*See, e.g.,* Individuals with Disabilities Education Act, 20 U.S.C. § 1415(b)(1) (2007).

federal privacy laws recognize certain exceptions to "access and disclosure" provisions. For example, a teacher's daily notes pertaining to pupil progress that are shared only with a substitute teacher are exempt from the laws. Private notes, however, become education records and are subject to legal specifications once they are shared, even among educators who have a legitimate need for access to such information.

At times there are conflicts between "freedom of information" or "right to know" provisions and federal and state laws protecting privacy rights. In general, FERPA protections of personally identifiable educational records prevail over state open records provisions.[172] For example, an Illinois appeals court upheld a school board's refusal to disclose information on students' medical and guardianship status, their receipt of free or reduced lunches, or their classification as English language learners, reasoning that such information was exempted from the state disclosure law.[173]

Since Congress, state legislatures, and the judiciary have indicated a continuing interest in safeguarding students' privacy rights in connection with school records, school boards would be wise to reassess their policies to ensure they are adhering to federal and state laws. School personnel should use some restraint, however, before purging information from student files. Pertinent material that is necessary to provide continuity in a student's instructional program *should* be included in a permanent record and be available for use by authorized personnel. It is unfortunate that school personnel, fearing federal sanctions under FERPA, have deleted useful information—along with material that should be removed—from student records. The mere fact that information in a student's file is negative does not imply that the material is inappropriate. Public school officials have a *duty* to record and communicate true, factual information about students to schools where they are transferring, including institutions of higher learning.

Pupil Protection and Parental Rights Laws

Congress and state legislatures have enacted laws to protect family privacy in connection with school research activities and treatment programs. Under federal law, human subjects are protected in research projects supported by federal grants and

---

[172]*See, e.g.,* Wall v. Fairfax County Sch. Bd., 475 S.E.2d 803 (Va. 1996) (holding that individual vote totals in a student election were scholastic records exempt from public disclosure).

[173]Chi. Tribune Co. v. Bd. of Educ., 773 N.E.2d 674 (Ill. App. Ct. 2002). *See also* Burlington Free Press v. Univ. of Vt., 779 A.2d 60 (Vt. 2001) (ruling that FERPA required withholding identifying personal information on hockey team members from the media, even though the university's response to the complaint pertaining to student hazing on the team had to be disclosed). *But see* Lindeman v. Kelso Sch. Dist. No. 458, 172 P.3d 329 (Wash. 2007) (holding that videotape recorded on school bus for safety reasons was not a record maintained for students, so it did not qualify as exempt from public disclosure under state law).

contracts in any private or public institution or agency.[174] Informed consent must be obtained before placing subjects at risk of being exposed to physical, psychological, or social injury as a result of participating in research, development, or related activities. All education agencies are required to establish review committees to ensure that the rights and welfare of all subjects are adequately protected.

In 1974, two amendments to the General Education Provisions Act required, among other things, that all instructional materials in federally assisted research or experimentation projects (designed to explore new or unproven teaching methods or techniques) be made available for inspection by parents of participating students. The amendments also stipulated that children could not be required to participate in such research or experimentation projects if their parents objected in writing. In 1978, Congress enacted the Hatch Amendment, which retained the protection of parents' rights to examine instructional materials in experimental programs and further required parental consent before students could participate in federally supported programs involving psychiatric or psychological examination, testing, or treatment designed to reveal information in specified sensitive areas pertaining to personal beliefs, behaviors, and family relationships.[175]

Several amendments have extended federal privacy protections for students and their families. Parents must be allowed to review in advance all instructional materials in programs administered by the Department of Education, and federally assisted education programs cannot require students, without prior written parental consent, to be subjected to surveys or evaluations administered by the Department of Education that reveal sensitive information about students or their families.[176] The department is charged with reviewing complaints under this law; if an educational institution is found in violation and does not comply within a reasonable period, federal funds can be withheld.

Some conservative citizen groups have pressed for a broad interpretation of the federal law, but courts usually have not agreed. The Sixth Circuit affirmed without an opinion a Michigan federal district court's ruling that a school district's decision to have a child see a school counselor (because of his problems interacting with classmates) without securing his parents' consent did not violate the parents' rights under the Hatch Amendment.[177] A Kentucky court also rejected a Hatch Amendment

---

[174]42 U.S.C. § 201 *et seq.* (2007); 45 C.F.R. § 46.101 *et seq.* (2007).

[175]20 U.S.C. § 1232h (2007); 34 C.F.R. §§ 75.740, 76.740, and 98.4 (2007).

[176]*See* the Grassley and Tiahrt Protection of Pupil Rights Amendments, 20 U.S.C. § 1232h (2007). The sensitive areas specified in the most recent amendment are political affiliations; mental or psychological problems of students or families; sexual behavior and attitudes; illegal, antisocial, self-incriminating, and demeaning behavior; critical appraisals of individuals with whom respondents have close family relationships; legally recognized, privileged relationships; religious practices, affiliations, or beliefs of the student or parents; or income (other than that required to determine eligibility for financial assistance programs). Parents must be notified at least annually of their rights under this law.

[177]Newkirk v. E. Lansing Pub. Schs., No. 91-CV563, 1993 U.S. Dist. LEXIS 13194 (W.D. Mich. Aug. 19, 1993), *aff'd mem.*, 57 F.3d 1070 (6th Cir. 1995).

challenge to the use of certain questions included in the statewide student assessment program.[178]

The Third Circuit denied New Jersey parents' claim that a voluntary survey asking students sensitive questions about their attitudes and behavior violated federal privacy protections or represented compelled speech because written parental permission was not secured for their children to participate.[179] The court reasoned that even if participation in the survey was involuntary, as the parents claimed, there was no violation because the disclosure of personal information occurred only in the aggregate and was properly safeguarded.

In a California case, parents, who had granted permission for their elementary school children to participate in a survey regarding psychological barriers to learning, later learned that the survey included some items pertaining to sexual topics and alleged that these items violated their right to privacy and to control the upbringing of their children. The Ninth Circuit affirmed the lower court's conclusion that parents do not have a free-standing fundamental right, or a right encompassed by any other fundamental right, to prevent the school from providing students important information pertaining to sex. The court emphasized that while parents have the right to select a school of their choice for their children, they do not have the right "to compel public schools to follow their own idiosyncratic views as to what information the schools may dispense."[180] Proclaiming that "schools cannot be expected to accommodate the personal, moral or religious concerns of every parent,"[181] the court found the psychological survey to be a reasonable way to advance legitimate state interests.

There is concern among educators that the federal pupil protection requirements and similar provisions being considered or enacted by many states will cause certain instructional activities to be dropped even before being legally challenged. Although these measures are couched in terms of protecting students' privacy rights by granting them *exemptions* from particular instructional activities, if a substantial number of exemptions are requested, the instructional activity may be eliminated from the curriculum.

Conclusion

The state and its agents enjoy considerable latitude in regulating various aspects of public education, but any requirements that restrict students' activities must be reasonable and necessary to carry out legitimate educational objectives. When students' or parents' protected rights are impaired, school authorities must be able to substantiate

---

[178]Triplett v. Livingston County Bd. of Educ., 967 S.W.2d 25 (Ky. Ct. App. 1997).

[179]C.N. v. Ridgewood Bd. of Educ., 430 F.3d 159 (3d Cir. 2005).

[180]Fields v. Palmdale Sch. Dist., 427 F.3d 1197, 1206 (9th Cir. 2005) (citing Brown v. Hot, Sexy & Safer Prods., 68 F.3d 525, 533-534 (1st Cir. 1995)).

[181]*Fields,* 427 F.3d at 1206.

that there is an overriding public interest to be served. From an analysis of court cases and legislation pertaining to general requirements and rights associated with school attendance and the instructional program, the following generalizations seem warranted:

1. The state can compel children between specified ages to attend school.[182]
2. Students can satisfy compulsory attendance mandates by attending private schools and, in most states, by receiving equivalent instruction (e.g., home tutoring) that is comparable to the public school program.
3. School officials can require immunization against diseases as a condition of school attendance and can allow religious exemptions to such requirements.
4. Students cannot be excluded from public school because of particular health conditions, unless school attendance would endanger the health of others.
5. Public school districts must provide an education for *bona fide* resident children (even those whose parents entered the country illegally), but children who live apart from their parents or guardians for educational purposes are not entitled to tuition-free schooling.
6. Fees can be charged for public school transportation as long as the fees are rationally related to legitimate state objectives.
7. Fees can be charged for the use of public school textbooks and for supplies associated with courses unless such fees are prohibited by state constitutional or statutory provisions.
8. The state and its agencies have the authority to determine public school course offerings and instructional materials, and such curricular determinations will be upheld by courts unless clearly arbitrary or in violation of constitutional or statutory rights.
9. School boards can eliminate instructional materials considered educationally unsuitable if objective procedures are followed in making such determinations.
10. Courts defer to school authorities in assessing student performance, in the absence of evidence of arbitrary or discriminatory academic decisions.
11. Proficiency examinations can be used to determine pupil remedial needs and as a prerequisite to high school graduation if students are given sufficient notice prior to implementation of the test requirements and are provided adequate preparation for the examinations.
12. Public schools do not owe students a duty to ensure that a specified level of achievement is attained.
13. Parents and 18-year-old students must be granted access to the student's school records and an opportunity to contest the contents.
14. Individuals do not have a private right to bring suits for damages under the Family Educational Rights and Privacy Act; the remedy for violations is the withdrawal of federal aid from the noncomplying agency.

---

[182]The notable exception to compulsory attendance pertains to Amish children who have successfully completed eighth grade. *See* Wisconsin v. Yoder, 406 U.S. 205 (1972); text accompanying note 11, Chapter 2.

15. School personnel must ensure the accuracy of information contained in student records and maintain the confidentiality of such records.
16. Parents have the right to inspect materials used in federally funded experimental projects or surveys, and students have a right to be excused from participation in such programs or activities involving psychiatric or psychological testing or treatment designed to reveal information in specified sensitive areas pertaining to personal beliefs, behaviors, and family relationships.

4

Students' Rights in
Noninstructional Matters

Students continue to test the limits of their personal freedoms in public schools, frequently colliding with educators' efforts to maintain an appropriate school environment. When controversies cannot be resolved locally, courts often are called on to address the legal issues involved. For example, what types of student expression are constitutionally protected? Under what circumstances must student-initiated groups be allowed to meet in public schools? What restrictions can be placed on student appearance? What conditions can be attached to participation in school-related activities? This chapter addresses these and other questions regarding students' rights in connection with selected noninstructional issues with an emphasis on First Amendment freedoms of speech and press and closely related association rights.

Freedom of Speech and Press

The First Amendment, as applied to the states through the Fourteenth Amendment, restricts *governmental* interference with citizens' free expression rights. The government, including public school boards, must have a compelling justification to curtail citizens' expression. The First Amendment also shields the individual's right to remain silent when confronted with an illegitimate government demand for expression, such as mandatory participation in saluting the American flag in public schools.[1] In short, the First Amendment protects decisions regarding what to say and what not to say, with no constitutional distinction between compelled speech and compelled silence.

In our nation, free expression rights are perhaps the most preciously guarded individual liberties and often are relied on to protect unpopular viewpoints. For example, the United States Supreme Court has used the First Amendment to protect

---

[1]*See* W. Va. State Bd. of Educ. v. Barnette, 319 U.S. 624 (1943); text with note 116, Chapter 2.

political protesters' right to burn the American flag[2] and the Ku Klux Klan's right to place a cross on public property.[3]

Although public school authorities traditionally were allowed to restrict student expression for almost any reason, the Supreme Court has recognized since the mid-twentieth century that students do not shed their constitutional rights as a condition of public school attendance. The Court has acknowledged that the Constitution "does not tolerate laws that cast a pall of orthodoxy over the classroom."[4] However, the Court also has stated that "the constitutional rights of students in public school are not automatically coextensive with the rights of adults in other settings," and may be limited by reasonable policies designed to take into account the special circumstances of the educational environment.[5] The collision of individual and governmental interests in the school context has generated a growing body of First Amendment litigation.

Unprotected Expression

Before applying First Amendment protections, conduct must be found to constitute expression. Only where conduct is meant to communicate an idea that is likely to be understood by the intended audience is it considered expression for First Amendment purposes.[6] Even if specific conduct qualifies as expression, it is not assured constitutional protection; the judiciary has recognized that defamatory, obscene, and inflammatory communications are outside the protective arm of the First Amendment. In addition, lewd and vulgar comments and expression that promotes illegal activity for minors are not protected in the public school context.

Defamatory Expression.   Defamation includes spoken (slander) and written (libel) false statements that expose another to public shame or ridicule and are communicated to someone other than the person defamed. Courts have upheld school authorities in banning libelous content from publications distributed at school and imposing sanctions on students responsible for such material,[7] but regulations cannot be vague or grant school officials complete discretion to censor materials considered potentially libelous.

[2]Texas v. Johnson, 491 U.S. 397 (1989). Despite their fundamental significance, free expression rights can be restricted. As Justice Holmes noted, freedom of speech does not allow an individual to yell "fire" in a crowded theater when there is no fire. Schenck v. United States, 249 U.S. 47, 52 (1919).

[3]Capitol Square Review & Advisory Bd. v. Pinette, 515 U.S. 753 (1995). *But see* Virginia v. Black, 538 U.S. 343 (2003) (upholding a statutory prohibition on cross burning with the intent to intimidate).

[4]Keyishian v. Bd. of Regents, 385 U.S. 589, 603 (1967). *See also* Shelton v. Tucker, 364 U.S. 479, 487 (1960); Sweezy v. New Hampshire, 354 U.S. 234, 250 (1957).

[5]Bethel Sch. Dist. No. 403 v. Fraser, 478 U.S. 675, 682 (1986). *See also* Morse v. Frederick, 127 S. Ct. 2618, 2621-2622 (2007); Tinker v. Des Moines Indep. Sch. Dist., 393 U.S. 503, 506-507 (1969).

[6]For a discussion of these requirements, *see Johnson*, 491 U.S. at 404; United States v. O'Brien, 391 U.S. 367, 376 (1968). In the school context, *see, e.g.*, Jarman v. Williams, 753 F.2d 76 (8th Cir. 1985) (holding that social and recreational dancing in public schools is not expression that enjoys First Amendment protection).

[7]*See* Draudt v. Wooster City Sch. Dist., 246 F. Supp. 2d 820 (N.D. Ohio 2003) (upholding school authorities' right to seize copies of the school newspaper that they reasonably believed contained defamatory material about a student).

Fair comment on the actions of public figures, unlike defamatory expression, is constitutionally protected. Public figures can establish that they have been defamed only with evidence that the comment was false and the speaker acted recklessly or with actual malice.[8] As discussed in Chapter 13, school board members and superintendents are generally considered public figures for defamation purposes, but courts have rendered conflicting opinions regarding whether teachers, principals, and coaches have assumed the risk of nonmalicious defamation.

Obscene, Lewd, or Vulgar Expression. The judiciary has held that individuals cannot claim a First Amendment right to voice or publish obscenities, although there is not a bright-line rule regarding what expression falls in this category.[9] Yet, school authorities do not have to prove that student expression is obscene for it to be curtailed. In a significant 1986 decision, *Bethel School District No. 403 v. Fraser*, the Supreme Court granted school authorities considerable latitude in censoring lewd, vulgar, and indecent student expression. Overturning the lower courts, the Supreme Court upheld disciplinary action against a student for using a sexual metaphor in a nominating speech during a student government assembly.[10] Concluding that the sexual innuendos were offensive to both teachers and students, the majority held that the school's legitimate interest in protecting the captive student audience from exposure to lewd and vulgar speech justified the disciplinary action. The Court reiterated that speech protected by the First Amendment for adults is not necessarily protected for children, reasoning that in the public school context the sensibilities of fellow students must be considered. The majority recognized that an important objective of public schools is the inculcation of fundamental values of civility and that the school board has the authority to determine what manner of speech is appropriate in classes or assemblies.[11] The majority further

---

[8]*See, e.g.*, Hustler Magazine v. Falwell, 485 U.S. 46, 52 (1988). *See also* text with note 87, Chapter 13, for a discussion of the principles of tort law governing defamation suits for damages.

[9]*See* Miller v. California, 413 U.S. 15, 24 (1973) (identifying the following test to distinguish obscene material from constitutionally protected material: "(1) whether 'the average person, applying contemporary community standards' would find that the work, taken as a whole, appeals to the prurient interests; (2) whether the work depicts or describes, in a patently offensive way, sexual conduct specifically defined by the applicable state law; and (3) whether the work, taken as a whole, lacks serious literary, artistic, political, or scientific value"). On several occasions, the Supreme Court has recognized the government's authority to adjust the definition of obscenity as applied to minors. *See, e.g.*, Ginsberg v. New York, 390 U.S. 629 (1968) (upholding a state law prohibiting the sale to minors of magazines depicting female nudity).

[10]478 U.S. 675 (1986). Throughout his speech, Fraser employed a sexual metaphor to refer to the candidate, using such phrases as "he's firm in his pants . . . his character is firm," "a man who takes his point and pounds it in," "he doesn't attack things in spurts—he drives hard, pushing and pushing until finally he succeeds," and "a man who will go to the very end—even the climax, for each and every one of you." *Id.* at 687 (Brennan, J., concurring). Fraser was suspended for two days and disqualified as a candidate for commencement speaker. However, he did eventually deliver a commencement speech, so his claim that the disqualification violated due process rights was not reviewed by the appellate court.

[11]*Id.* at 683. *See also* Anderson v. Milbank Sch. Dist. 25-4, 197 F.R.D. 682 (D.S.D. 2000) (upholding punishment of a student for saying the word *shit* within earshot of the school secretary in violation of the school's zero tolerance rule prohibiting profane or inappropriate language on campus); Pangle v. Bend-Lapine Sch. Dist., 10 P.3d 275 (Or. Ct. App. 2000) (upholding punishment of a student who distributed an underground newspaper that used vulgar and threatening language).

rejected the contention that the student had no way of knowing that his expression would evoke disciplinary action; the school rule barring obscene and disruptive expression and teachers' admonitions that his planned speech was inappropriate provided adequate warning of the consequences of the expression.

Inflammatory Expression.   The judiciary also has sanctioned regulations banning the use of inflammatory expression in public schools. Courts have differentiated fighting words and other expression that agitates, threatens, or incites an immediate breach of peace from speech that conveys ideas and stimulates discussion.[12] Although inflammatory student expression at school is not constitutionally protected, courts have not spoken in unison regarding whether such expression off school grounds can be the basis for school sanctions.[13]

The U.S. Supreme Court has not addressed the application of the First Amendment to alleged threats made by students toward classmates or school personnel, but there is a growing body of lower court litigation.[14] For example, the Ninth Circuit upheld suspension of a student for threatening to shoot a counselor, despite conflicting testimony regarding what was actually said.[15] The appeals court emphasized that threats of physical violence are not shielded by the First Amendment.

In determining if a true threat has been made, courts can consider a number of factors, such as (1) reactions of the recipient and other listeners, (2) whether the maker of the alleged threat had made similar statements to the victim in the past, (3) if the utterance was conditional and communicated directly to the victim, and (4) whether the victim had reason to believe that the speaker would engage in violence.[16] In an illustrative case, the Arkansas Supreme Court held that a student-composed rap song did not entail fighting words but was a true threat, as it contained an unconditional threat to the life of a classmate and was delivered to the targeted student who perceived it as unequivocally threatening.[17] Also finding a true threat, the Eighth Circuit reversed the lower court and upheld expulsion of a student for writing a letter threatening to rape and murder his former girlfriend. The court was convinced that

---

[12]*See* Gooding v. Wilson, 405 U.S. 518, 524 (1972).

[13]*See* text with note 14, Chapter 7. Also, there is a growing body of litigation pertaining to Internet expression considered inflammatory or threatening. *See infra* text accompanying notes 91–94.

[14]*See* Ronald T. Hyman, *Death Threats by Students: The Law and Its Implications* (Dayton, OH: Education Law Association, 2006).

[15]Lovell v. Poway Unified Sch. Dist., 90 F.3d 367 (9th Cir. 1996). *See also* Demers v. Leominster Sch. Dep't, 263 F. Supp. 2d 195 (D. Mass. 2003) (upholding a lengthy suspension of a student who made a threatening drawing and refused a psychiatric evaluation).

[16]United States v. Dinwiddie, 76 F.3d 913 (8th Cir. 1996).

[17]Jones v. State, 64 S.W.3d 728 (Ark. 2002). *See also* Ponce v. Socorro Indep. Sch. Dist., 508 F.3d 765, 767 (5th Cir. 2007) (holding that a student's notebook, outlining a pseudo-Nazi group's plan to commit a "Columbine shooting," constituted a "terroristic threat" that was not protected by the First Amendment). The court relied on Morse v. Frederick, 127 S. Ct. 2618 (2007), in reasoning that evidence of a disruption is not required when there is a threat of special danger to the safety of students. *See infra* text accompanying note 23.

the writer intended to communicate the threat because he shared the letter with a friend whom he assumed would give it to his former girlfriend.[18]

Utterances can be considered inflammatory, and thus unprotected, even if *not* found to be true threats or fighting words. The Ninth Circuit ruled that a student could be subject to emergency expulsion, with a hearing occurring afterward, for writing a poem about someone who committed multiple murders two years earlier and decided to kill himself for fear of murdering others.[19] The poem was not considered a true threat or to contain fighting words. The Wisconsin Supreme Court also held that school authorities had more than enough reason to suspend a student for his creative writing assignment, describing a student removed from class for being disruptive (as the writer had been) who returned the next day to behead his teacher.[20] But the court found no true threat that would justify prosecution as disorderly conduct. More recently, the Fifth Circuit found no true threat in a student's drawing, featuring violence, obscenities, and racial epithets, that the student's brother brought on campus two years later. Nonetheless, the court held that the principal, who suspended the artist, was entitled to qualified immunity because of the unsettled nature of the law in this regard.[21] Courts generally seem more inclined to uphold school disciplinary action, in contrast to criminal prosecution, for students' alleged threats or other inflammatory expression.

Advocacy of Illegal Activity for Minors. The Supreme Court has long recognized that expression inciting imminent lawless action is outside First Amendment

---

[18]Doe v. Pulaski County Special Sch. Dist., 306 F.3d 616 (8th Cir. 2002). *See also In re* A.S., 626 N.W.2d 712 (Wis. 2001) (finding a student's comments that he intended to kill everyone at his middle school to represent an intent to inflict harm in violation of the state disorderly conduct law).

[19]The school board noted in the student's file that the action was for safety rather than disciplinary reasons, and the student was readmitted to school after three psychiatric visits. LaVine v. Blaine Sch. Dist., 257 F.3d 981 (9th Cir. 2001). *See also* Cuesta v. Sch. Bd., 285 F.3d 962 (11th Cir. 2002) (upholding a principal's compliance with the school's zero tolerance policy by reporting to the police a student's distribution of a threatening pamphlet); Sherrell v. N. Cmty. Sch. Corp., 801 N.E.2d 693 (Ind. Ct. App. 2004) (upholding expulsion of a student for telling friends that he was going to bring his father's gun to school and shoot students, which school authorities determined constituted unlawful intimidation).

[20]*In re* Douglas D., 626 N.W.2d 725 (Wis. 2001).

[21]Porter v. Ascension Parish Sch. Bd., 393 F.3d 608 (5th Cir. 2004). *See also* Latour v. Riverside Beaver Sch. Dist., No. 05-1076, 2005 U.S. Dist. LEXIS 35919 (W.D. Pa. Aug. 24, 2005) (finding no true threat or intended violence in students' rap songs that included some violent imagery); D.G. & C.G. v. Indep. Sch. Dist. No. 11, No. 00-C-0614-E, 2000 U.S. Dist. LEXIS 12197 (N.D. Okla. Aug. 21, 2000) (granting injunction to reinstate a student in her regular high school, since the poem she wrote about killing her teacher, which was left in the classroom, was not a true threat); Shoemaker v. State, 38 S.W.3d 350 (Ark. 2001) (finding a state law unconstitutionally vague that criminalized student conduct or expression abusing or insulting a teacher; a student could not be charged with a misdemeanor for calling her teacher "a bitch" because this utterance did not entail fighting words); State v. McCooey, 802 A.2d 1216 (N.H. 2002) (overturning a disorderly conduct conviction of a student who said he might "shoot up the school" if a teacher did not give him a hug; finding no evidence that the expression caused a school disruption to justify the conviction); *In re* C.C.H., 651 N.W.2d 702 (S.D. 2002) (overturning delinquency order and holding that an objectively reasonable recipient would not view the child's threatening remarks against another student, voiced privately to his teacher, as a serious threat).

protection.[22] In 2007, the Court clarified that this stringent standard does not have to be met in public schools. In its first decision regarding student expression in almost two decades, *Morse v. Frederick,* the Court held that given the special circumstances in public schools, students can be disciplined for expression reasonably viewed as promoting or celebrating illegal drug use; incitement to lawless conduct is not required.[23] *Morse* focused on a banner containing the phrase "BONG HITS 4 JESUS," which Joseph Frederick and some friends unfurled across the street from their school as the Olympic torch relay passed by. The Supreme Court reasoned that the students were under the school's control when they were allowed to cross the street and watch the torch relay because it was a school-authorized event supervised by school personnel. Although Frederick had not yet been on school grounds when he joined his friends across the street, the Court declined to apply legal standards used to assess students' off-campus behavior.

Reversing the Ninth Circuit's conclusion that the school could not "punish and censor non-disruptive, off-campus speech by students during school-authorized activities because the speech promotes a social message contrary to the one favored by the school,"[24] the Supreme Court narrowly upheld disciplinary action against the student for displaying the banner. The majority emphasized the importance of deterring drug use by students and concluded that Frederick's action violated the school board's policy of prohibiting expression advocating use of illegal substances. The Court declared that its earlier *Fraser* decision stands for the proposition that considerations beyond the disruption standard articulated in 1969 are appropriate in assessing student expression in public schools.[25] However, a majority of the justices declined to extend school authorities' discretion to the point that they can curtail any student expression they find "plainly offensive" or at odds with the school's "educational mission," which would allow school officials too much discretion.[26] All justices agreed that students can be disciplined for promoting the

---

[22]Brandenburg v. Ohio, 395 U.S. 444, 449 (1969) (distinguishing "mere advocacy" that is protected expression from unprotected incitement to lawless behavior).

[23]127 S. Ct. 2618 (2007). *See also* McCann v. Ft. Zumwalt Sch. Dist., 50 F. Supp. 2d 918 (E.D. Mo. 1999) (upholding school authorities in prohibiting the marching band's performance of a song they feared would be construed as advocating drug use).

[24]Frederick v. Morse, 439 F.3d 1114, 1118 (9th Cir. 2006).

[25]*Morse,* 127 S. Ct. at 2626-2627. *See* Tinker v. Des Moines Indep. Sch. Dist., 393 U.S. 503 (1969); *infra* text accompanying note 48. Since the legalization of marijuana has been controversial in Alaska, perhaps if the banner had been cast as advocating a change in state law, Frederick would have prevailed. All justices agreed that the principal should not be held liable for violating clearly established law, and Justice Breyer thought the decision should have focused only on this issue. *See id.* at 2639 (Breyer, J., concurring in part and dissenting in part).

[26]*See id.* at 2629. Justices Alito and Kennedy emphasized that this decision is restricted to the promotion of illegal drug use and does not extend to censorship of expression on social or political issues that may be viewed as inconsistent with the school's mission. *Id.* at 2636 (Alito, J., joined by Kennedy, J., concurring).

Barnes & Noble Booksellers #2265
5101 Main Street
Williamsburg, VA 23188
757-564-0687

STR:2265 REG:011 TRN:1554 CSHR:Angie P

Fiji Water 500 ML
9780641531224   T3
(1 @ 1.95)   1.95
Tazo Chai Tall
9780641505973   T2
(1 @ 3.25)   3.25
Tazo Chai Tall
9780641505973   T2
(1 @ 3.25)   3.25
Car Macchiato Tall
9780765547316   T2
(1 @ 3.75)   3.75
I Survived the Joplin Tornado, 2011 (I S
9780545658485   T1
(1 @ 4.99)   4.99
I Survived the Sinking of the Titanic, 1
9780545206945   T1
(1 @ 4.99)   4.99
I Survived the Attacks of September 11,
9780545207003   T1
(1 @ 4.99)   4.99
Scone Cinnamon
9781402826450   T2
(1 @ 2.50)   2.50
Almond Biscotti
9780765551498   T2
(1 @ 1.25)   1.25

Subtotal   30.92
Sales Tax T1 (6.000%)   0.90
Sales Tax T2 (10.000%)   1.40
Sales Tax T3 (2.500%)   0.05
TOTAL   33.27
VISA DEBIT   33.27
Card#: XXXXXXXXXXXXX2075

A MEMBER WOULD HAVE SAVED   3.12

Thanks for shopping at
Barnes & Noble

101.37A   12/06/2015 10:15AM

CUSTOMER COPY

Policy on receipt may appear in two sections.

Return Policy

With a sales receipt or Barnes & Noble.com packing slip, a full refund in the original form of payment will be issued from any Barnes & Noble Booksellers store for returns of undamaged NOOKs, new and unread books, and unopened and undamaged music CDs, DVDs, vinyl records, toys/games and audio books made within 14 days of purchase from a Barnes & Noble Booksellers store or Barnes & Noble.com with the below exceptions:

A store credit for the purchase price will be issued (i) for purchases made by check less than 7 days prior to the date of return, (ii) when a gift receipt is presented within 60 days of purchase, (iii) for textbooks, (iv) when the original tender is PayPal, or (v) for products purchased at Barnes & Noble College bookstores that are listed for sale in the Barnes & Noble Booksellers inventory management system.

Opened music CDs, DVDs, vinyl records, audio books may not be returned, and can be exchanged only for the same title and only if defective. NOOKs purchased from other retailers or sellers are returnable only to the retailer or seller from which they are purchased, pursuant to such retailer's or seller's return policy. Magazines, newspapers, eBooks, digital downloads, and used books are not returnable or exchangeable. Defective NOOKs may be exchanged at the store in accordance with the applicable warranty.

Returns or exchanges will not be permitted (i) after 14 days or without receipt or (ii) for product not carried by Barnes & Noble or Barnes & Noble.com.

Policy on receipt may appear in two sections.

Return Policy

With a sales receipt or Barnes & Noble.com packing slip, a full refund in the original form of payment will be issued from any Barnes & Noble Booksellers store for returns of undamaged NOOKs, new and unread books, and unopened and undamaged music CDs, DVDs, vinyl records, toys/games and audio books made within 14 days of purchase from a Barnes & Noble Booksellers store or Barnes & Noble.com with the below exceptions:

A store credit for the purchase price will be issued (i) for purchases made by check less than 7 days prior to the date of return, (ii) when a gift receipt is presented within 60 days of purchase, (iii) for textbooks, (iv) when the original tender is PayPal, or (v) for products purchased at Barnes & Noble College bookstores that are listed for sale in the Barnes & Noble Booksellers inventory management system.

Opened music CDs, DVDs, vinyl records, audio books may not be returned, and can be exchanged only for the same title and only if defective. NOOKs purchased from other retailers or sellers are returnable only to the retailer or seller from which they are purchased, pursuant to such retailer's or seller's return policy. Magazines, newspapers, eBooks, digital downloads, and used books are not returnable or exchangeable. Defective NOOKs may be exchanged at the store in accordance with the applicable warranty.

Returns or exchanges will not be permitted (i) after 14 days or without receipt or (ii) for product not carried by Barnes & Noble or Barnes & Noble.com.

use of illegal drugs, but they differed regarding whether the banner at issue actually did so.[27]

Commercial Expression

Unlike obscene, lewd, inflammatory, or defamatory expression, commercial speech enjoys some measure of constitutional protection. However, expression with economic motives has not been afforded the same level of First Amendment protection as has speech intended to convey a particular point of view.[28] The Supreme Court has recognized that governmental restrictions on commercial speech do not have to be the least restrictive means to achieve the desired end; rather, there only needs to be a reasonable "fit" between the restrictions and the governmental goal.[29] Courts generally have upheld regulations prohibiting sales and fund-raising activities in public schools as justified to preserve schools for their educational function and to prevent commercial exploitation of students.

Some controversies focus on students' rights *not* to be exposed to commercial expression in public schools, rather than on their rights to engage in commercial activity. For example, a number of school districts nationwide subscribe to Channel One; in return for students' watching a 10-minute news program and two minutes of commercials each day, the schools receive free equipment. Although the judiciary has recognized the legal authority of school boards to enter into contracts for supplementary instructional materials that include commercials,[30] several courts have required school boards to excuse students who are offended by the commercial activities.[31] With an increasing number of companies offering monetary enticements for school boards to air commercials over public address systems and display advertisements on scoreboards,[32] such commercial activities in public schools seem destined to generate additional legal challenges.

---

[27]*See id.* at 2647 (2007) (Stevens, J., joined by Ginsberg & Souter, JJ., dissenting) (arguing that the banner was a nonsensical effort to get on television and promoted nothing).

[28]*See, e.g.*, Bolger v. Youngs Drug Prods. Corp., 463 U.S. 60, 64–75 (1983) (holding that unsolicited mailings concern commercial speech, which is afforded less constitutional protection than other forms of expression).

[29]Bd. of Trs. v. Fox, 492 U.S. 469 (1989).

[30]*See, e.g.*, Wallace v. Knox County Bd. of Educ., No. 92-6195, 1993 U.S. App. LEXIS 20477 (6th Cir. Aug. 10, 1993) (finding no violation of students' rights in the school's broadcast of a news program with commercials, since students could be excused from the broadcasts); Dawson v. E. Side Union High Sch. Dist., 34 Cal. Rptr. 2d 108 (Ct. App. 1994) (holding that school boards have the discretion to permit commercial broadcasting in schools); State v. Whittle Communications, 402 S.E.2d 556 (N.C. 1991) (dismissing complaint that contracts between school districts and private company to air broadcasts at school violated state law).

[31]*See, e.g.*, *Dawson*, 34 Cal. Rptr. 2d 108 (holding that students could not be compelled to observe the programs given their commercial content, but the order that they be given an "opt-out" option was not appropriate without any evidence of coercion).

[32]*See* DiLoreto v. Downey Unified Sch. Dist., 196 F.3d 958 (9th Cir. 1999) (holding that school could exclude religious subjects from advertisements allowed on the fence surrounding school's baseball field, which was a nonpublic forum available only for limited purposes); text accompanying note 57, Chapter 2.

School-Sponsored Expression

In contrast to the categories of unprotected expression, students' airing of political or ideological views in public schools *is* protected by the First Amendment. Since the late 1980s, the Supreme Court has emphasized the distinction between student expression that appears to represent the school and *private* student expression of ideological views that merely occurs at school. The latter commands substantial constitutional protection, but student expression appearing to bear the public school's imprimatur can be restricted to ensure that it is consistent with educational objectives. The Court's expansive interpretation of what constitutes school-sponsored expression has narrowed the circumstances under which students can prevail in First Amendment claims.

Type of Forum.   In Free Speech Clause litigation, an assessment of the type of forum the government has created for expressive activities has been important in determining whether expression can be restricted. The Supreme Court has recognized that public places, such as streets and parks, are traditional public forums for assembly and communication where content-based restrictions cannot be imposed unless justified by a compelling government interest.[33] In contrast, expression can be confined to the governmental purpose of the property in a nonpublic forum, such as a public school. Content-based restrictions are permissible in a nonpublic forum to assure that expression is compatible with the intended governmental purpose, provided that regulations are reasonable and do not entail viewpoint discrimination.

The government, however, can create a limited public forum for expression on public property that otherwise would be considered a nonpublic forum and reserved for its governmental function.[34] For example, a student activities program held after school might be established as a limited forum for student expression. A limited forum can be restricted to a certain class of speakers (e.g., students) and/or to specific categories of expression (e.g., noncommercial speech). Otherwise, expression in a limited forum is subject to the same protections that govern a traditional public forum.

During the 1970s and early 1980s, many courts broadly interpreted the circumstances under which limited forums for student expression were created in public schools. School-sponsored newspapers often were considered such a forum, and accordingly, courts held that articles on controversial subjects such as the Vietnam War, abortion, and birth control could not be barred from these publications.[35] Courts placed the burden on school authorities to justify prior administrative review of the content of both school-sponsored and nonsponsored literature.

[33]Cornelius v. NAACP Legal Def. & Educ. Fund, 473 U.S. 788 (1985); Perry Educ. Ass'n v. Perry Local Educators' Ass'n, 460 U.S. 37 (1983).

[34]*See* Kincaid v. Gibson, 236 F.3d 342 (6th Cir. 2001) (holding that a university's yearbook was created as a limited public forum for student expression; the university's actions in confiscating copies because of objections violated the editors' First Amendment rights).

[35]*See, e.g.,* Gambino v. Fairfax County Sch. Bd., 564 F.2d 157 (4th Cir. 1977) (holding that school-sponsored newspaper was established as a forum for student expression).

Hazelwood *and Its Progeny.* In 1988, the Supreme Court delivered a significant decision, *Hazelwood School District v. Kuhlmeier,* holding that school authorities can censor student expression in school publications and other school-related activities as long as the censorship decisions are based on legitimate pedagogical concerns.[36] At issue in *Hazelwood* was a high school principal's deletion of two pages from the school newspaper because of the content of articles on divorce and teenage pregnancy and fears that individuals could be identified in the articles. The Court ruled that the principal's actions were based on legitimate educational concerns. Rejecting the assertion that the school newspaper had been established as a public forum for student expression, the Court declared that only with school authorities' clear *intent* do school activities become a public forum.[37] The Court drew a distinction between a public school's *toleration* of private student expression, which is constitutionally required under some circumstances, and its *promotion* of student speech that represents the school. Reasoning that student expression appearing to bear the school's imprimatur can be censored, the Court acknowledged school authorities' broad discretion to ensure that such expression occurring in school publications and all school-sponsored activities (including extracurricular) is consistent with educational objectives.[38]

Some lower courts have broadly interpreted student expression that might be perceived as bearing the school's imprimatur. Relying on *Hazelwood,* the Sixth Circuit held that a student could be disqualified from running for student council president because his candidacy speech at a school-sponsored assembly was discourteous. Recognizing that "the universe of legitimate pedagogical concerns is by no means confined to the academic," and includes teaching values such as courtesy and respect for authority, the court emphasized that "limitations on speech . . . unconstitutional outside the schoolhouse are not necessarily unconstitutional within it."[39]

Also echoing the *Hazelwood* rationale, the Ninth Circuit rejected Planned Parenthood's claim that a school district's denial of its request to advertise in school newspapers, yearbooks, and programs for athletic events violated free speech rights, concluding that the district could bar advertisements inconsistent with its educational

---

[36]484 U.S. 260 (1988), *on remand,* 840 F.2d 596 (8th Cir. 1988).

[37]*Id.,* 484 U.S. at 267. Application of *Hazelwood* to state-supported institutions of higher education remains controversial. *See* Hosty v. Carter, 412 F.3d 731 (7th Cir. 2005), *cert. denied,* 546 U.S. 1169 (2006) (finding that the *Hazelwood* framework governs subsidized newspapers in state-supported institutions of higher education).

[38]In response to this decision, several state legislatures have enacted laws granting student editors of school-sponsored papers specific rights in determining the content of their publications. *See, e.g.,* Cal. Ed. Code § 48907 (2007); Colo. Rev. Stat. Ann. § 22-1-120 (2007); Iowa Code § 280.22 (2007); Kan. Stat. Ann. § 72-1506 (2006); Mass. Gen. Laws Ann. ch. 71, § 82 (2007). *See also* Pyle v. Sch. Comm., 667 N.E.2d 869 (Mass. 1996) (finding the state law more protective than the First Amendment in that it allows students to engage in vulgar, private expression in public schools as long as the expression is not disruptive).

[39]Poling v. Murphy, 872 F.2d 757, 761 (6th Cir. 1989) (acknowledging that decisions regarding whether specific comments are rude are "best left to the locally elected school board, not to a distant, life-tenured judiciary").

mission or the "proper function of education."[40] Similarly reflecting the broad discretion granted to school authorities, the Fourth Circuit upheld a high school principal's decision to bar the school's use of the Johnny Reb symbol following complaints that it offended African American students.[41] The Eighth Circuit also relied on *Hazelwood* in upholding a principal's decision to disqualify a student council candidate who handed out condoms with stickers bearing his campaign slogan, noting that *Hazelwood* grants school authorities considerable discretion to control student expression in school-sponsored activities.[42] Finding a school's prohibition on speech threatening violence and the use of firearms to be based on legitimate pedagogical concerns, the Third Circuit upheld suspension of a kindergarten student for saying, "I'm going to shoot you," while playing cops and robbers during recess.[43]

Courts have reasoned that the school has the right to disassociate itself from controversial expression that conflicts with its mission and have considered school-sponsored activities to include student newspapers supported by the public school, extracurricular activities sponsored by the school, school assemblies, and classroom activities. The key consideration is whether the expression is viewed as bearing the school's imprimatur; only under such circumstances is *Hazelwood*'s broad deference to school authorities triggered.

There are limits, however, on school authorities' wide latitude to censor student expression that bears the public school's imprimatur. Blatant viewpoint discrimination, even in a nonpublic forum, abridges the First Amendment.[44] For example, the Ninth Circuit held that a school board violated students' First Amendment rights, because it failed to produce a compelling justification for excluding an anti-draft organization's advertisement from the school newspaper, while allowing military recruitment advertisements.[45] Similarly, the Eleventh Circuit placed the burden on school authorities to justify viewpoint discrimination against a peace activist group that was excluded from the public school's career day and not allowed to display its

[40]Planned Parenthood v. Clark County Sch. Dist., 887 F.2d 935, 942 (9th Cir. 1989) (quoting Burch v. Barker, 861 F.2d 1149, 1158 (9th Cir. 1988)), *rehearing en banc*, 941 F.2d 817 (9th Cir. 1991).

[41]Crosby v. Holsinger, 852 F.2d 801 (4th Cir. 1988) (noting also that the one-day delay in posting students' notices of the upcoming board meeting constituted a minimal impairment of expression rights).

[42]Henerey v. City of St. Charles Sch. Dist., 200 F.3d 1128 (8th Cir. 1999). *See also* Fister v. Minn. New Country Sch., 149 F.3d 1187 (8th Cir. 1998) (upholding the suspension and ultimate expulsion of a student for defying school personnel and repeatedly reposting a letter on the divider around her workspace; the letter offended two classmates and severely affected their schoolwork).

[43]S.G. v. Sayreville Bd. of Educ., 333 F.3d 417 (3d Cir. 2003). *See also* Bannon v. Sch. Dist., 387 F.3d 1208 (2d Cir. 2004) (ruling that school murals were a nonpublic forum reasonably viewed as bearing the school's imprimatur, so religious symbols could be censored based on legitimate pedagogical objectives); text accompanying note 52, Chapter 2.

[44]*See* Bd. of Regents v. Southworth, 529 U.S. 217 (2000) (upholding a university's mandatory student activities fees used to facilitate the free and open exchange of ideas among students as long as the institution operated in a viewpoint neutral manner, but striking down the use of a student referendum to determine what clubs would be subsidized, because the referendum disenfranchised minority viewpoints).

[45]San Diego Comm. Against Registration & the Draft v. Governing Bd., 790 F.2d 1471 (9th Cir. 1986).

literature on school bulletin boards and in counselors' offices, when military recruiters were allowed such access.[46] The court found no compelling justification for censoring specific views that the board found distasteful.

Even if viewpoint discrimination is not involved, censorship actions in a non-public forum still must be based on legitimate pedagogical concerns. A Michigan federal district court found no legitimate pedagogical reason for the removal from the school newspaper of a student's article on a pending lawsuit alleging that school bus diesel fumes constitute a neighborhood nuisance.[47]

Protected Private Expression

Student expression that does not fall within one of the categories of unprotected expression or bear the school's imprimatur is governed by the landmark Supreme Court decision, *Tinker v. Des Moines Independent School District*, rendered in 1969.[48] In *Tinker*, three students were suspended from school for wearing black arm-bands to protest the Vietnam War. Hearing about the planned silent protest, the school principals met and devised a policy forbidding the wearing of armbands at school. School officials did not attempt to prohibit the wearing of all symbols, but instead prohibited one form of expression. Concluding that the students were pun-ished for expression that was not accompanied by any disorder or disturbance, the Supreme Court ruled that "undifferentiated fear or apprehension of disturbance is not enough to overcome the right to freedom of expression."[49] Furthermore, the Court declared that school officials must have "more than a mere desire to avoid the dis-comfort and unpleasantness that always accompany an unpopular viewpoint" in order to justify curtailment of student expression.[50] The Court emphasized that "stu-dents in school as well as out of school are 'persons' under our Constitution. They are possessed of fundamental rights which the state must respect."[51]

In *Tinker*, the Supreme Court echoed statements made in an earlier federal appellate ruling: A student may express opinions on controversial issues in the class-room, cafeteria, playing field, or any other place, as long as the exercise of such rights does not "materially and substantially interfere with the requirements of appropriate discipline in the operation of the school" or collide with the rights of others.[52] The Supreme Court emphasized that educators have the authority and duty to maintain discipline in schools, but they must consider students' constitutional rights as they exert control.

[46]Searcey v. Harris, 888 F.2d 1314 (11th Cir. 1989).

[47]Dean v. Utica Cmty. Schs., 345 F. Supp. 2d 799 (E.D. Mich. 2004) (ruling that the censorship was based on the superintendent's disagreement with the views expressed about the lawsuit against the school district).

[48]393 U.S. 503 (1969).

[49]*Id.* at 508.

[50]*Id.* at 509.

[51]*Id.* at 511.

[52]*Id.* at 509 (quoting Burnside v. Byars, 363 F.2d 744, 749 (5th Cir. 1966)).

Because school authorities can censor school-sponsored student expression for educational reasons,[53] the *Tinker* standard applies *only* to protected expression that does not give the appearance of representing the school (see Figure 4.1). Ironically, since *Hazelwood*, student expression in underground student papers distributed at school enjoys greater constitutional protection than does expression in school-sponsored publications. The former is considered private expression

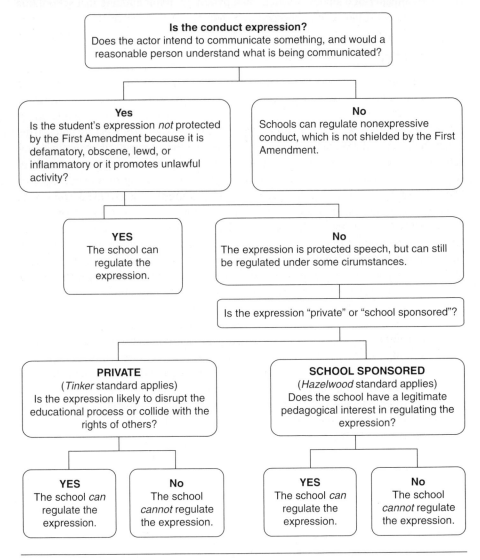

FIGURE 4.1   *Assessing Student Expression Rights*.

Source: Adapted from a figure developed by Amy Steketee, Associate Instructor, Indiana University.

[53]*See supra* text accompanying note 36.

governed by the *Tinker* principle, whereas the latter is subject to censorship under *Hazelwood*. As discussed in Chapter 2, most courts have treated the distribution of religious literature by secondary students like the distribution of other material that is not sponsored by the school.[54]

But even a school-sponsored publication might be considered a forum for student expression under certain circumstances. In a Massachusetts case, school authorities had given students editorial control of school publications, so independent decisions of the students could not be attributed to school officials. In this situation, the student editors of the school newspaper and yearbook rejected advertisements from a parent who was a leading opponent of the district's condom-distribution policy. The First Circuit concluded that school officials, who had recommended that the students publish the ads, could not be held liable for the students' decisions, because the student editors were not state actors.[55]

Prior Restraints.   When determined that protected private expression is at issue, courts then are faced with the difficult task of assessing whether restrictions are justified. Under the *Tinker* principle, private expression can be curtailed if it is likely to disrupt the educational process or intrude on the rights of others. For example, bans on wearing buttons at school have been upheld where linked to an interference with the educational process.[56]

The law clearly allows students to be punished after the fact if they cause a disruption, but school authorities have a greater burden of justification when they impose prior restraints on such expression. The Supreme Court has recognized that "a free society prefers to punish the few who abuse rights of speech after they break the law [rather] than to throttle them and all others beforehand."[57] The imposition of prior restraints on student speech must bear a substantial relationship to an important government interest, and any regulation must contain narrow, objective, and unambiguous criteria for determining what material is prohibited and procedures that allow a speedy determination of whether materials meet those criteria. Recognizing that the Constitution requires a high degree of specificity when imposing restraints on private expression, the Ninth Circuit held that school authorities in a Washington school district could not suspend students for distributing a student paper produced off campus and could not subject the paper's content to prior review. Because "prior restraints are permissible in only the rarest of circumstances," the Ninth Circuit considered the policy subjecting *all* nonschool publications to prior review for the purpose of censorship to be overbroad.[58]

---

[54]*See* text accompanying note 102, Chapter 2. Of course, proselytizing materials in *school-sponsored* publications would be barred by the Establishment Clause.

[55]Yeo v. Town of Lexington, 131 F.3d 241 (1st Cir. 1997).

[56]*See, e.g.,* Guzick v. Drebus, 431 F.2d 594 (6th Cir. 1970); Blackwell v. Issaquena County Bd. of Educ., 363 F.2d 749 (5th Cir. 1966). *But see* Chandler v. McNinnville Sch. Dist., 978 F.2d 524 (9th Cir. 1992); *infra* text accompanying note 69.

[57]Southeastern Promotions v. Conrad, 420 U.S. 546, 559 (1975).

[58]Burch v. Barker, 861 F.2d 1149, 1155 (9th Cir. 1988).

The burden is on school authorities to justify policies requiring administrative approval of unofficial (underground) student publications, but such prior review is not unconstitutional *per se*. The Eighth Circuit rejected a vagueness challenge to a school board's policy requiring administrative review of unofficial student papers distributed at school and barring the distribution of material that advertises something unlawful or is disruptive, obscene, libelous, or pervasively indecent.[59] However, the court invalidated the part of the policy proscribing material that invades others' privacy, reasoning that such expression could not be curtailed unless it would subject the school to a libel suit under state law.

Post-Expression Discipline.   Although prior restraints on private expression may be legally vulnerable, courts are inclined to support disciplinary action and confiscation of materials *after* the expression has occurred, if it is considered unprotected (i.e., comments that are libelous, inflammatory, vulgar, or promote illegal activity) or fosters a disruption of the educational process. As discussed, the Supreme Court in 2007 upheld a high school principal in disciplining a student and confiscating his banner viewed as promoting illegal drug use without evidence that the expression would lead to a disruption.[60] Much earlier, the Fourth Circuit upheld school administrators in impounding copies of a student publication that contained an advertisement for drug paraphernalia and in banning further distribution on school property.[61] The court emphasized that the literature was not subjected to predistribution approval; copies were impounded only after distribution began.

Students also have been disciplined after the fact for distributing material that is abusive toward classmates or teachers. To illustrate, the Eighth Circuit found no impairment of speech rights in requiring a student, who distributed a letter that criticized the girls' varsity basketball coach, to apologize to the coach and teammates as a condition of returning to the team.[62] The student's comments violated

---

[59]Bystrom v. Fridley High Sch. Indep. Sch. Dist. No. 14, 822 F.2d 747 (8th Cir. 1987). Subsequently, disciplinary action was upheld against the students for distributing another unauthorized edition of their underground paper containing material that was disruptive, vulgar, and advocated violence against a teacher. Bystrom v. Fridley High Sch., 686 F. Supp. 1387 (D. Minn. 1987), *aff'd mem.*, 855 F.2d 855 (8th Cir. 1988). *See also* Muller v. Jefferson Lighthouse Sch., 98 F.3d 1530 (7th Cir. 1996) (upholding school district policy requiring copies of nonschool student literature to be given to the principal at least one day before distribution and allowing censorship of material that encourages disruption or illegal acts or is libelous, obscene, or insulting).

[60]Morse v. Frederick, 127 S. Ct. 2618 (2007); *supra* text accompanying note 23.

[61]Williams v. Spencer, 622 F.2d 1200 (4th Cir. 1980) (further holding that the regulation authorizing the principal to halt the distribution of any publication encouraging actions that endanger students' health or safety was not unconstitutionally vague).

[62]Wildman v. Marshalltown Sch. Dist., 249 F.3d 768 (8th Cir. 2001). *See also* Kicklighter v. Evans County Sch. Dist., 968 F. Supp. 712 (S.D. Ga. 1997), *aff'd mem.*, 140 F.3d 1043 (11th Cir. 1998) (finding no impairment of First Amendment rights in requiring a student to apologize to the class for her truculent and disruptive behavior or face a 5-day suspension); Donovan v. Ritchie, 68 F.3d 14 (1st Cir. 1995) (upholding student's 10-day suspension from school and exclusion from various extracurricular activities for distributing an abusive and obscene document about classmates).

provisions of the student conduct handbook and the basketball handbook prohibiting disrespectful and insubordinate behavior. More recently, the Eleventh Circuit found the *Tinker* standard satisfied in that school authorities could forecast a substantial disruption when a student wrote a story about killing a teacher and brought it to school; her suspension was justified because she shared the story with another student.[63]

Students additionally can be disciplined for expression linked to a disruption, such as advocating the destruction of school property in publications they distribute at school.[64] The Seventh Circuit recognized that a "reason to believe" or "reasonable forecast" standard can be applied to punish a student for such expression, even though the anticipated destruction of school property never materializes.[65] In this case, a student was expelled for one year for publishing and distributing at school an article in an underground paper that contained information about how to disable the school's computer system.

Courts have condoned disciplinary action against students who have engaged in walkouts, boycotts, sit-ins, or other protests involving conduct that blocks hallways, damages property, causes students to miss class, or interferes with essential school activities in other ways.[66] The Sixth Circuit held that a petition circulated by four football players, denouncing the head coach, justified their dismissal from the varsity football team. The court reasoned that the petition disrupted the team, and athletes are subject to greater restrictions than applied to the general student body.[67] The Ninth Circuit also ruled that student athletes could be disciplined for refusing to board the team bus and play in a basketball game to protest actions of their coach; their boycott of the game substantially disrupted a school activity.[68] However, this court departed from the Sixth Circuit in finding that the students' petition requesting that the coach resign because of derogatory remarks he made toward players was protected speech. Thus, the Ninth Circuit remanded the case for a determination of whether the students were impermissibly removed from the basketball team in retaliation for their petition. In an earlier Ninth Circuit case, the appeals court overturned the suspension of students for wearing buttons containing the word *scab* in connection with a teachers'

[63]Boim v. Fulton County Sch. Dist., 494 F.3d 978 (11th Cir. 2007). *See also* D.F. v. Bd. of Educ., 386 F. Supp. 2d 119 (E.D.N.Y. 2005) (upholding suspension of student for writing a story portraying sex and violence among named classmates that could materially interfere with the work of the school).

[64]*See, e.g.*, Bd. of Educ. v. Comm'r of Educ., 690 N.E.2d 480 (N.Y. 1997) (upholding suspension of a student for producing a publication that advocated various acts of insubordination including the destruction of school property).

[65]Boucher v. Sch. Bd., 134 F.3d 821, 828 (7th Cir. 1997).

[66]*See, e.g.*, Tate v. Bd. of Educ., 453 F.2d 975 (8th Cir. 1972); Madrid v. Anthony, 510 F. Supp. 2d 425 (S.D. Tex. 2007); Corales v. Bennett, 488 F. Supp. 2d 975 (C.D. Cal. 2007); Walker-Serrano v. Leonard, 168 F. Supp. 2d 332 (M.D. Pa. 2001).

[67]Lowery v. Euverard, 497 F.3d 584 (6th Cir. 2007). *But see* Boyd v. Bd. of Dirs., 612 F. Supp. 86 (E.D. Ark. 1985) (finding that students who walked out of school pep rally to protest the coach's alleged manipulation of the homecoming queen election were engaging in protected expression).

[68]Pinard v. Clatskanie Sch. Dist. 6J, 467 F.3d 755 (9th Cir. 2006).

strike.[69] Recognizing that such expression is governed by *Tinker*, the court held that students could not be disciplined for nondisruptive, private expression that was merely critical of school personnel or policies. However, the court acknowledged that vulgar, lewd, obscene, or plainly offensive buttons could be banned *even if* considered private expression.

Students cannot be disciplined for materials distributed off school grounds unless at a school-sponsored event or the off-campus distribution threatens the educational process. The Second Circuit found that school officials overstepped their authority by disciplining high school students who published a satirical magazine in their homes and sold it at a local store in the absence of evidence that the activity had an adverse impact on the school.[70] The court concluded that to rule otherwise could subject students to school-imposed punishments for such behavior as watching X-rated movies on cable television in their own homes.

Anti-Harassment Policies. A number of school districts have adopted policies prohibiting expression that constitutes verbal or physical harassment based on race, religion, color, national origin, sex, sexual orientation, disability, or other personal characteristics. Until recently, these public school policies have not appeared vulnerable to First Amendment challenges, whereas "hate speech" policies have been struck down in municipalities and public higher education.[71] Public schools have been considered a special environment in terms of government restrictions on private expression, because of their purpose in educating America's youth and inculcating basic values, such as civility and respect for others with different backgrounds and beliefs.[72]

[69]Chandler v. McMinnville Sch. Dist., 978 F.2d 524 (9th Cir. 1992). *See also* Karp v. Becken, 477 F.2d 171 (9th Cir. 1973) (upholding the confiscation of signs that students brought to school for distribution to protest the nonrenewal of a teacher's contract, but invalidating a student's suspension for engaging in this form of pure speech).

[70]Thomas v. Bd. of Educ., 607 F.2d 1043 (2d Cir. 1979). *See also* the discussion of censorship of electronic student expression; *infra* text accompanying note 85.

[71]*Compare* R.A.V. v. City of St. Paul, 505 U.S. 377 (1992) (invalidating under the First Amendment a St. Paul ordinance barring expression that could arouse anger or resentment on the basis of race, color, creed, religion, or gender); Dambrot v. Cent. Mich. Univ., 55 F.3d 1177 (6th Cir. 1995) (striking down the university's policy prohibiting harassing speech as overbroad and vague, but holding that the coach's use of the term *nigger* during locker-room talk was not protected by the First Amendment) *with* Fister v. Minn. New Country Sch., 149 F.3d 1187 (8th Cir. 1998) (upholding school district's policy specifying that fighting, threatening language, other endangerment, or harassment would be grounds for suspension or expulsion); *supra* text accompanying note 42.

[72]*See, e.g.*, Bethel Sch. Dist. No. 403 v. Fraser, 478 U.S. 675 (1986); Charles A. Beard and Mary R. Beard, *New Basic History of the United States* (New York: Doubleday, 1968). School districts' anti-discrimination provisions that conflict with organizations' expression rights also have been controversial. After the Supreme Court upheld the Boy Scouts' constitutional rights to bar homosexuals from being troop leaders, Boy Scouts v. Dale, 530 U.S. 640 (2000), some school districts attempted to deny after-school access to the Boy Scouts to comply with their antidiscrimination policies. *See, e.g.*, Boy Scouts v. Till, 136 F. Supp. 2d 1295 (S.D. Fla. 2001) (finding unconstitutional viewpoint discrimination in the school board's prohibition on the Boy Scouts using school facilities).

A growing body of cases interpreting anti-harassment provisions has focused on students displaying Confederate flags, and some courts have upheld restrictions on such displays. To illustrate, the Tenth Circuit upheld disciplinary action against a Kansas middle school student for drawing a Confederate flag during math class in violation of the school district's anti-harassment policy.[73] The student had been disciplined numerous times during the school year and had been accused of using racial slurs. The court was persuaded that the school district had reason to believe that the display of the Confederate flag might cause a disruption and interfere with the rights of others, as the school district had already experienced some racial incidents related to the Confederate flag. Also, the Eleventh Circuit applied a "flexible reasonableness standard" drawn from *Fraser*, instead of *Tinker*'s disruption standard, to assess a student's display of a small Confederate flag to a group of friends during an outdoor lunch break.[74] Holding that school authorities were not liable for disciplining the student for the display that intruded on the school's legitimate function of inculcating manners and habits of civility, the court observed: "Racist and other hateful views can be expressed in a public forum. But an elementary school under its custodial responsibilities may restrict such speech that could crush a child's sense of self-worth."[75]

The same court found that a school's unwritten policy banning the display of Confederate flags could be justified because there had been race-based fights in the school and the flag can be viewed as an offensive symbol of racism.[76] In addition, the Sixth Circuit upheld a school district's ban on students displaying the Confederate flag, finding the potential for a school disturbance, but acknowledging that school authorities could ban this symbol *without* being able to forecast a school disruption.[77] Other courts, however, have struck down such restrictions on Confederate flag displays in the absence of a link to disruption[78] or if the policies were applied inconsistently.[79]

Several cases have focused on the conflict between expressing religious views and promoting civil expression; these cases are particularly sensitive because they pit

[73]West v. Derby Unified Sch. Dist., 206 F.3d 1358 (10th Cir. 2000). *See also* Governor Wentworth Reg'l Sch. Dist. v. Hendrickson, 421 F. Supp. 2d 410 (D.N.H. 2006) (upholding suspension of a gay student for wearing an arm patch with a swastika and the international "no" symbol superimposed over it, given the friction between gay students and students identifying themselves as "rednecks" and the administrators' need to promote safety), *vacated as moot,* 201 Fed. Appx. 7 (1st Cir. 2007).

[74]Denno v. Sch. Bd., 218 F.3d 1267, 1272 (11th Cir. 2000).

[75]*Id.* at 1273.

[76]Scott v. Sch. Bd., 324 F.3d 1246 (11th Cir. 2003).

[77]D.B. v. Lafon, 217 Fed. Appx. 518 (6th Cir. 2007); *infra* text accompanying note 122.

[78]*See, e.g.,* Bragg v. Swanson, 371 F. Supp. 2d 814 (S.D.W.Va. 2005) (overturning disciplinary action against a student for wearing a T-shirt displaying the Confederate flag in observance of his southern heritage and finding the policy prohibiting displays of the Rebel flag within the category of racist symbols to be overbroad).

[79]*See, e.g.,* Castorina v. Madison County Sch. Bd., 246 F.3d 536 (6th Cir. 2001); *infra* text accompanying note 129.

free speech and free exercise guarantees against the school's authority to instill basic values, including respect for others. The Third Circuit struck down a Pennsylvania school district's anti-harassment policy challenged by plaintiffs who feared reprisals for voicing their religious views about moral issues, including the harmful effects of homosexuality.[80] The court reviewed existing anti-discrimination laws to refute the district court's conclusion that the policy simply curtailed expression already prohibited under such federal and state laws. The court found no evidence that the policy was necessary to advance the recognized compelling government interests in maintaining an orderly school and protecting the rights of others. Concluding that the policy was unconstitutionally overbroad, the court reasoned that the policy went beyond expression that could be curtailed under the *Tinker* disruption standard. Yet, a year later, the same court upheld a school district's anti-harassment policy enacted to respond to incidents of race-based conflicts and narrowly designed to reduce racially divisive expression.[81]

The Ninth Circuit more recently found the second prong of the *Tinker* standard to be controlling when it ruled that a student wearing a T-shirt degrading homosexuality "'collides with the rights of other students' in the most fundamental way."[82] The court reasoned that the school is allowed to prohibit such expression, regardless of the adoption of a valid anti-harassment policy, as long as it can show that the restriction is necessary to prevent the violation of other students' rights *or* a substantial disruption of school activities. The court disagreed with the suggestion that injurious slurs interfering with the rights of others cannot be barred unless they *also* are disruptive, reasoning that the two *Tinker* prongs are independent restrictions. Thus, the court did not find it necessary to address the "substantial disruption" aspect of the *Tinker* standard in upholding the ban on expression denigrating homosexuality.[83] But other courts have applied the *Tinker* disruption standard in ruling that students have a right to express their religious views that denounce

---

[80]Saxe v. State Coll. Area Sch. Dist., 240 F.3d 200 (3d Cir. 2001). *See also* Flaherty v. Keystone Oaks Sch. Dist., 247 F. Supp. 2d 698 (W.D. Pa. 2003) (finding that student handbook policies did not adequately define "abusive," "offensive," "harassment," and "inappropriate," so disciplinary action against a student for postings on a Web site message board could not be based on the vague and overbroad policy).

[81]Sypniewski v. Warren Hills Reg'l Bd. of Educ., 307 F.3d 243 (3d Cir. 2002) (while upholding the policy, the court ordered the phrase banning speech that "creates ill will" to be eliminated as reaching some protected expression). *See infra* text accompanying note 125 for a discussion of the application of the policy.

[82]Harper v. Poway Unified Sch. Dist., 445 F.3d 1166, 1178 (9th Cir. 2006) (quoting Tinker v. Des Moines Indep. Sch. Dist., 393 U.S. 503, 508 (1969)), *cert. granted, judgment vacated, and case remanded to dismiss as moot*, 127 S. Ct. 1484 (2007).

[83]*Harper*, 445 F.3d at 1180 (citing *Saxe*, 240 F.3d at 217). *See also* Zamecnik v. Indian Prairie Sch. Dist., No. 07 C 1586, 2007 U.S. Dist. LEXIS 28172 (N.D. Ill. Apr. 17, 2007) (denying students' request for a preliminary injunction to allow them to wear T-shirts, buttons, or stickers with the phrase "Be Happy, Not Gay" to express their opposition to homosexuality; school authorities have a legitimate pedagogical concern to promote tolerance of differences and to protect students from harassment).

homosexuality.[84] Since the Supreme Court declined to review the merits of the Ninth Circuit case, the collision of religious views and anti-harassment policies seems destined to remain controversial.

Electronic Expression. Another topic generating volatile controversies pertains to students' expression rights involving the Internet. These cases are particularly troublesome because students often prepare and disseminate the materials from their homes, but their expression is immediately available to the entire school population and beyond. Courts have not spoken with a single voice on the First Amendment issues raised in these cases, but most courts have applied the *Tinker* disruption standard in assessing Internet expression.[85] With the increasing amount of material posted on Facebook, MySpace, and other social networking sites, legal activity in this arena is bound to increase.[86]

Students have prevailed in several challenges to disciplinary actions for Web pages they have created at home. For example, a high school senior successfully challenged his suspension for creating a Web site on which he posted mock obituaries of students and allowed visitors to the site to vote on who would "die" next.[87] In granting the injunction, the federal district court noted that the student's Web site was not produced in connection with any class or school activity, and school personnel failed to substantiate that the material threatened or intended harm to anyone. A Michigan federal district court also found an insufficient connection between the disruption of any school activity and a student's Web site called "Satan's Web Page," containing likes and dislikes, including a list of people he wished would die.[88] And a Pennsylvania federal district court invalidated the suspension of a student for sending an e-mail

[84]*See, e.g.,* Nixon v. N. Local Sch. Dist., 383 F. Supp. 2d 965, 971-974 (S.D. Ohio 2005) (rejecting school administrators' assertion that a shirt denigrating homosexuality, Islam, and abortion was "plainly offensive" under *Fraser*; applying *Tinker* instead and finding no disruption or evidence that the expression interfered with the rights of others); K.D. v. Fillmore Cent. Sch. Dist., No. 05-CV-0336(E), 2005 U.S. Dist. LEXIS 33871 (W.D.N.Y. Sept. 2, 2005) (upholding student's right to wear a pro-life T-shirt representing political speech in the absence of creating a substantial disruption among classmates); Chambers v. Babbitt, 145 F. Supp. 2d 1068 (D. Minn. 2001) (granting a temporary order allowing a student to wear a sweatshirt bearing the message "straight pride" in the absence of any disruption). *See also* Hansen v. Ann Arbor Pub. Schs., 293 F. Supp. 2d 780 (E.D. Mich. 2003) (finding viewpoint discrimination against a student when school officials denied her request to participate on a panel and express her views against homosexuality as part of diversity week and when portions of her speech were censored in the school's general assembly on "What Diversity Means to Me").

[85]393 U.S. 503, 508 (1969); *supra* text accompanying note 48.

[86]There are more than 200 social networking sites, and MySpace has approximately 60 million members who share journals, photos, etc. *See* Thomas Wheeler II, "Lessons from the Lord of the Flies: The Responsibility of Schools to Protect Students from Internet Threats and Cyber-Hate Speech," *Education Law Reporter*, vol. 215 (2007), pp. 227–244.

[87]Emmett v. Kent Sch. Dist. No. 415, 92 F. Supp. 2d 1088 (W.D. Wash. 2000). *See also* Beussink v. Woodland R-IV Sch. Dist., 30 F. Supp. 2d 1175 (E.D. Mo. 1998) (ordering a preliminary injunction to block a student's suspension for using his home computer to create a home page criticizing school administrators, given the lack of evidence of interference with school discipline).

[88]Mahaffey v. Aldrich, 236 F. Supp. 2d 779 (E.D. Mich. 2002).

message to friends that included a discourteous and rude "top ten list" about the school's athletic director.[89] The student did not print the list or bring copies to school, although a friend who received his e-mail message did so, and school authorities did not produce evidence linking the message to a disruption of classes or the management of the school. More recently, the same court reasoned that disciplinary action against a student who created on MySpace a parody profile of the school principal was not justified because there was no disruption of the high school's daily operations.[90] However, the school policies requiring students to express their ideas in a respectful manner and to refrain from verbal abuse were not found to be overbroad.

In contrast, the Fifth Circuit upheld a student's conviction under federal law for his Internet communication threatening to shoot and kill students at his high school, finding only general intent required to constitute a threat in violation of the federal prohibition on knowingly and intentionally transmitting in interstate commerce a threat to injure another.[91] Also, the Pennsylvania Supreme Court upheld a student's expulsion because he created a Web site ("Teacher Sux") on his home computer that contained derogatory comments about teachers and administrators and a graphic depiction of the algebra teacher's death. The court reasoned that the off-campus activities substantially disrupted the school, noting that the algebra teacher was so upset by the material that she had to take a leave of absence.[92] Similarly, a Washington federal district court denied a preliminary injunction to a student who was suspended for posting on YouTube a video he had secretly filmed of one of his teachers bending over with a classmate standing behind her making pelvic thrusts in her direction. The court reasoned that disciplinary action was justified by showing that the expression disturbed the work of the school, including "the maintenance of a civil and respectful atmosphere toward teachers and students alike."[93] The Second Circuit also upheld a semester expulsion of a student for displaying in his instant messaging buddy icon a drawing of a pistol firing at a person's head, with the caption "Kill Mr. VenderMolen," his English teacher, finding that the icon, although displayed outside of school, violated school rules and disrupted school operations.[94] In these cases, the key determinant of disciplinary action appears to be whether the material created off campus has a direct and detrimental impact on the school.

Time, Place, and Manner Regulations. Although private expression enjoys greater constitutional protection than does school-sponsored expression, the judiciary consistently has upheld reasonable policies regulating the time, place, and manner of

[89]Killion v. Franklin Reg'l Sch. Dist., 136 F. Supp. 2d 446 (W.D. Pa. 2001).

[90]Layshock v. Hermitage Sch. Dist., 496 F. Supp. 2d 587 (W.D. Pa. 2007).

[91]United States v. Morales, 272 F.3d 284 (5th Cir. 2001) (interpreting 18 U.S.C. § 875(c) (2007) that makes the posting of interstate threats a misdemeanor).

[92]J.S. v. Bethlehem Area Sch. Dist., 807 A.2d 847 (Pa. 2002). *See also* J.S. v. Blue Mt. Sch. Dist., No. 3:07cv585, 2007 U.S. Dist. LEXIS 23406 (M.D. Pa. Mar. 29, 2007) (denying restraining order and temporary injunction to prevent suspension of student who created a fake MySpace for the principal, depicting him as bisexual, because the expression disrupted the school).

[93]Requa v. Kent Sch. Dist. No. 415, 492 F. Supp. 2d 1272, 1280 (W.D. Wash. 2007).

[94]Wisniewski v. Bd. of Educ., 494 F.3d 34 (2d Cir. 2007).

private expression. For example, students can be prohibited from voicing political and ideological views and distributing literature during instructional time. Additionally, school authorities can ban literature distribution near the doors of classrooms while class is in session, near building exits during fire drills, and on stairways when classes are changing, to ensure that the distribution of student publications does not impinge upon other school activities.

Time, place, and manner regulations, however, must be reasonable, content neutral, and uniformly applied to expressive activities. Also, they cannot restrict more speech than necessary to ensure nondisruptive distribution of materials.[95] School officials must provide students with specific guidelines regarding when and where they can express their ideas and distribute materials. Moreover, literature distribution cannot be relegated to remote times or places either inside or outside the school building, and regulations must not inhibit any person's right to accept or reject literature that is distributed in accordance with the rules. Policies governing demonstrations should convey to students that they have the right to gather, distribute petitions, and express their ideas under nondisruptive circumstances.[96] If regulations do not precisely inform demonstrators of what behavior is prohibited, the judiciary may conclude that punishment cannot be imposed.

Future Directions.   It appears likely that courts will continue to be called upon to balance students' rights to express views and receive information with educators' duty to maintain an appropriate educational environment. Since the mid-1980s, the Supreme Court has broadened the category of unprotected student expression to include lewd, vulgar, and indecent expression as well as expression promoting illegal activity and has given school authorities latitude to determine what belongs in these categories (see Figure 4.1). The Supreme Court also has granted school authorities broad discretion to censor student expression that appears to represent the school, which further restricts the application of *Tinker*. Nonetheless, courts continue to rely on the *Tinker* disruption standard in evaluating student political expression as well as nonschool-sponsored underground publications, anti-harassment policies, and postings on personal Web pages.

Student-Initiated Clubs

Free expression and related association rights have arisen in connection with the formation and recognition of student clubs. Freedom of association is not specifically included among First Amendment protections, but the Supreme Court has held that

[95]*See* M.B. v. Liverpool Cent. Sch. Dist., 487 F. Supp. 2d 117 (N.D.N.Y. 2007); text accompanying note 102, Chapter 2.

[96]*See, e.g.*, Orin v. Barclay, 272 F.3d 1207 (9th Cir. 2001) (upholding a community college in granting permits for protests on the condition that students would not create a disturbance or interfere with campus activities, but striking down the condition barring religious activities during protests); Godwin v. E. Baton Rouge Parish Sch. Bd., 408 So. 2d 1214 (La. 1981) (holding that prohibition on carrying signs, placards, or posters in the school board office building is a reasonable restriction on the place and manner of communication).

associational rights are "implicit in the freedoms of speech, assembly, and petition."[97] Public school pupils have not prevailed in asserting that free expression and association rights shield student-initiated social organizations or secret societies with exclusive membership usually determined by a vote of the clubs' members.[98]

In contrast, prohibitions on student-initiated organizations with *open* membership are vulnerable to First Amendment challenge. Even before Congress enacted the Equal Access Act (EAA), it was generally accepted that public school access policies for student meetings must be content neutral and cannot disadvantage selected groups. The EAA, enacted in 1984, stipulates that if federally assisted secondary schools provide a limited open forum for noncurricular student groups to meet during noninstructional time, access cannot be denied based on the religious, political, philosophical, or other content of the groups' meetings.[99] The EAA was championed by the Religious Right, but its protection encompasses far more than student-initiated religious expression.

As discussed in Chapter 2, the Supreme Court in 1990 rejected an Establishment Clause challenge to the EAA in *Board of Education of the Westside Community Schools v. Mergens*.[100] The Court held that if a federally assisted high school allows even one noncurricular group to use school facilities during noninstructional time, the EAA guarantees equal access for other noncurricular student groups. Of course, meetings that threaten a disruption can be barred. Moreover, school authorities can decline to establish a limited forum for student-initiated meetings and thus confine school access to student organizations that are an extension of the curriculum, such as drama groups, language clubs, and athletic teams. A Colorado school district revised its policy to create a two-tiered classification of curricular and noncurricular student organizations, with official recognition still limited to curricular groups. The federal district court reasoned that the EAA does not bar schools from offering curriculum organizations certain privileges as long as all noncurriculum student groups are treated in the same manner.[101]

Controversies have surfaced over what constitutes a curriculum-related group, since the EAA is triggered only if noncurriculum student groups are allowed school access during noninstructional time. Many of these cases have focused on the Gay-Straight Alliance (GSA). For example, after the Salt Lake City School Board implemented a policy denying school access to all noncurriculum student groups, it

[97]Healy v. James, 408 U.S. 169, 181 (1972).

[98]*See* Robinson v. Sacramento Unified Sch. Dist., 53 Cal. Rptr. 781 (Ct. App. 1966); Passel v. Ft. Worth Indep. Sch. Dist., 453 S.W.2d 888 (Tex. Civ. App. 1970).

[99]20 U.S.C. § 4071 (2007). *See* text accompanying note 83, Chapter 2.

[100]496 U.S. 226 (1990) (rejecting the contention that only noncurricular, *advocacy* groups are protected under the EAA). *See also* Student Coal. for Peace v. Lower Merion Sch. Dist., 776 F.2d 431 (3d Cir. 1985), *on remand*, 633 F. Supp. 1040 (E.D. Pa. 1986) (finding that the Student Coalition for Peace had to be granted access to the school's limited forum during noninstructional time to hold its peace exposition and recognizing students' private right to initiate suits to compel EAA compliance).

[101]Palmer High Sch. Gay-Straight Alliance v. Colo. Springs Sch. Dist. No. 11, No. C.A. A.03-M-2535(CBS), 2005 WL 3244049 (D. Colo. Mar. 30, 2005).

rejected the GSA's petition to hold meetings in a public high school. The GSA then asserted that it was related to the curriculum and should be treated like other curriculum-related groups. The federal district court ultimately enjoined school authorities from denying access to a student club designed to address issues related to the school's history and sociology courses, even though the club's major focus was on the rights of gay, lesbian, bisexual, and transgendered (GLBT) persons.[102] Also, a California federal district court ruled that a school board had established a limited forum by allowing some noncurriculum student groups to meet during non-instructional time and thus could not discriminate against the GSA. The board claimed that the club was not protected under the EAA because it was related to the sex education curriculum, but the court held that the board cannot foreclose access to its limited forum "merely by labeling a group curriculum-related."[103] The Eighth Circuit addressed a Minnesota school district's distinction between curricular student groups that were allowed to use the public address system and other forms of communication and noncurricular groups that could not use such communication avenues or participate in fundraising activities or field trips.[104] Concluding that some groups identified as curricular, such as cheerleading and synchronized swimming, were not related to material regularly taught in the curriculum, the court enjoined the district from treating the club, Straights and Gays for Equality, differently from other student groups.

However, departing from the judicial trend, a Texas federal district court upheld school authorities in denying the Gay and Proud (GAP) Youth Group's request to hold meetings and post flyers about their meetings in the school.[105] Although recognizing that the school had established a limited open forum for student clubs to meet, it agreed with school authorities that some of the materials promoted by the GAP Youth on its Web site were inappropriate for minors and conflicted with the board's promotion of its adopted abstinence policy. Thus, the court reasoned that denial of the request was justified by the compelling interest in protecting the well-being of students.[106] In contrast, a Florida federal district court found a substantial likelihood that the GSA would prevail in establishing that it was not a "sex-based club," to which

---

[102]E. High Sch. Prism Club v. Seidel, 95 F. Supp. 2d 1239 (D. Utah 2000). *See also* E. High Gay/Straight Alliance v. Bd. of Educ., 81 F. Supp. 2d 1166 (D. Utah 1999) (finding genuine issues regarding whether the school had an unwritten policy excluding all gay-positive viewpoints from student club meetings); Van Schoick v. Saddleback Valley Unified Sch. Dist., 104 Cal. Rptr. 2d 562 (Ct. App. 2001) (finding triable issues pertaining to whether all clubs meeting at a high school were curriculum related, which would preclude meetings of the Fellowship of Christian Athletes during noninstructional time); text accompanying note 90, Chapter 2.

[103]Colin v. Orange Unified Sch. Dist., 83 F. Supp. 2d 1135, 1146 (C.D. Cal. 2000).

[104]Straights & Gays for Equality (SAGE) v. Osseo Area Schs., 471 F.3d 908 (8th Cir. 2006).

[105]Caudillo v. Lubbock Indep. Sch. Dist., 311 F. Supp. 2d 550 (N.D. Tex. 2004).

[106]*Id.* at 570. The Equal Access Act stipulates that "nothing in this subchapter shall be construed to limit the authority of the school, its agents or employees, to maintain order and discipline on school premises, to protect the well-being of students and faculty, and to assure that attendance of students at meetings is voluntary." 20 U.S.C. § 4071(f) (2007).

student access can be restricted until age 18 under state law, and found no conflict between the club's purpose and the school's abstinence-based policy.[107] Thus, a preliminary injunction was issued so the school district could not deny the GSA access to the forum it provided for student clubs to meet. Even if it were agreed that a secondary school has *not* established a limited forum, it still cannot exert viewpoint discrimination against particular curriculum-related groups.

Student Appearance

Fads and fashions in hairstyles and clothing have regularly evoked litigation as educators have attempted to exert some control over pupil appearance. Courts have been called upon to weigh students' interests in selecting their attire and hairstyle against school authorities' interests in preventing disruptions and promoting school objectives.

Hairstyle

Substantial judicial activity in the 1970s focused on school regulations governing the length of male students' hair. The Supreme Court, however, refused to hear appeals of these cases, and federal circuit courts of appeal reached different conclusions in determining the legality of policies governing student hairstyle. The First, Fourth, Seventh, and Eighth Circuits declared that hairstyle regulations impaired students' First Amendment freedom of symbolic expression, the Fourteenth Amendment right to personal liberty, or the right to privacy included in the Ninth Amendment's unenumerated rights.[108] In contrast, the Third, Fifth, Sixth, Ninth, and Tenth Circuits upheld grooming policies pertaining to pupil hairstyle, finding no constitutional rights at stake.[109]

If school officials have offered health or safety reasons for grooming regulations, such as requiring hair nets, shower caps, and other hair restraints intended to protect students from injury or to promote sanitation, the policies typically have been upheld. Furthermore, restrictions on male students' hairstyles at vocational schools have been upheld to create a positive image for potential employers visiting the school for recruitment purposes. Special grooming regulations have been endorsed as conditions of participation in extracurricular activities for legitimate health or

[107]Gay-Straight Alliance v. Sch. Bd., 483 F. Supp. 2d 1224 (S.D. Fla. 2007).

[108]*See* Massie v. Henry, 455 F.2d 779 (4th Cir. 1972); Bishop v. Colaw, 450 F.2d 1069 (8th Cir. 1971); Richards v. Thurston, 424 F.2d 1281 (1st Cir. 1970); Breen v. Kahl, 419 F.2d 1034 (7th Cir. 1969).

[109]*See* Zeller v. Donegal Sch. Dist., 517 F.2d 600 (3d Cir. 1975), *overruling* Stull v. Sch. Bd. of W. Beaver Jr.–Sr. High Sch., 459 F.2d 339 (3d Cir. 1972); King v. Saddleback Jr. Coll. Dist., 445 F.2d 932 (9th Cir. 1971); Freeman v. Flake, 448 F.2d 258 (10th Cir. 1971); Jackson v. Dorrier, 424 F.2d 213 (6th Cir. 1970); Ferrell v. Dallas Indep. Sch. Dist., 392 F.2d 697 (5th Cir. 1968).

safety reasons, and, in some instances, to enhance the school's image.[110] Of course, students can be disciplined for hairstyles that cause a disruption, such as hair groomed or dyed in a manner that distracts classmates from educational activities.

It appears that different hair length and hairstyle restrictions can be applied to male and female students to reflect community norms or to deter gang activity. In two cases, the Texas Supreme Court rejected claims that restrictions applied only to the length of male students' hair constituted sex discrimination, refusing to use the state constitution to micro-manage public schools.[111] More recently, a Louisiana federal district court upheld a school rule forbidding only male students from wearing braids as justified to promote unity and defer gang activity.[112]

But hairstyle regulations cannot be arbitrary or devoid of an educational rationale. For example, a Texas federal district court ruled that school officials failed to show a valid justification to impair Native American students' protected expression right to wear long hair that posed no disruption.[113]

Attire

Although public school students' hair length has subsided as a major subject of litigation, other appearance fads have become controversial as students have asserted a First Amendment right to express themselves through their attire at school. Some courts have distinguished attire restrictions from hair regulations because clothes, unlike hair length, can be changed after school. Even in situations where students' rights to govern their appearance have been recognized, the judiciary has noted that attire can be regulated if immodest, disruptive, or unsanitary, or if it promotes illegal behavior.

Dress Codes. Under the principle established in *Fraser*, lewd and vulgar expression is outside the protective arm of the First Amendment. Thus, indecent attire can be

[110]*See, e.g.*, Davenport v. Randolph County Bd. of Educ., 730 F.2d 1395 (11th Cir. 1984) (finding neither arbitrary nor unreasonable a coach's requirement that student athletes, as representatives of the school, must be clean shaven); Menora v. Ill. High Sch. Ass'n, 683 F.2d 1030 (7th Cir. 1982) (holding that Jewish basketball players had no First Amendment right to wear yarmulkes fastened by bobby pins in violation of the state high school association rule forbidding players from wearing hats or other headgear during games for safety reasons); Long v. Zopp, 476 F.2d 180 (4th Cir. 1973) (recognizing that legitimate health and safety concerns might justify a restriction on hair length during football season, but finding no justification for denying a letter to a student who violated such a restriction after football season ended).

[111]Bd. of Trs. v. Toungate, 958 S.W.2d 365 (Tex. 1997); Barber v. Colo. Indep. Sch. Dist., 901 S.W.2d 447 (Tex. 1995); *infra* note 116.

[112]Fenceroy v. Morehouse Parish Sch. Bd., No. 05-0480, 2006 U.S. Dist. LEXIS 949 (W.D. La. Jan. 6, 2006). *But see* Cordova v. Chonko, 315 F. Supp. 953 (N.D. Ohio 1970) (holding that long-haired male and female band members must be subject to the same restrictions); Sims v. Colfax Cmty. Sch. Dist., 307 F. Supp. 485 (S.D. Iowa 1970) (ruling in favor of a female student who challenged a school rule prohibiting both males and females from wearing their hair longer than one finger width above the eyebrow).

[113]Ala. & Coushatta Tribes v. Trs., 817 F. Supp. 1319 (E.D. Tex. 1993), *remanded*, 20 F.3d 469 (5th Cir. 1994).

curtailed regardless of whether the attire would meet the *Tinker* test of threatening a disruption. For example, an Idaho federal district court held that a school could prevent a student from wearing a T-shirt that depicted three high school administrators drunk on school grounds, noting that the student had no free expression right to portray administrators in a fashion that would undermine their authority and compromise the school's efforts to educate students about the harmful effects of alcohol.[114] More recently, a Georgia federal district court upheld the suspension of a student who wore a T-shirt with the phrases "kids have civil rights too" and "even adults lie."[115] The court ruled that wearing the shirt was the last incident in a series of disruptions justifying the student's suspension.

Several courts have upheld dress codes that prohibit male students from wearing earrings, rejecting the assertion that jewelry restrictions must be applied equally to male and female students. In an illustrative case, an Illinois federal district court found the school district's ban on male students wearing earrings rationally related to the school's legitimate objective of inhibiting the influence of gangs, as earrings were used to convey gang-related messages.[116] Also, while acknowledging the absence of a gang-related justification, an Indiana appeals court nonetheless upheld a school district's ban on male students wearing earrings in elementary schools as advancing legitimate educational objectives and community values supporting different attire standards for males and females.[117]

In a New Mexico case, the federal district court upheld a student's suspension for wearing "sagging" pants in violation of the school's dress code.[118] Rejecting the student's contention that his attire conveyed an African American cultural message, the court noted that "sagging" pants could as easily be associated with gang affiliation or simply reflect a fashion trend among adolescents. An Illinois federal court found no First Amendment right for gifted students to wear a shirt they had designed for their class shirt. The court reasoned that school authorities had legitimate pedagogical concerns that the shirt, depicting in a satirical manner a physically handicapped child with the word *gifties,* could be viewed as ridiculing students with disabilities and could threaten school discipline.[119] Also, an Ohio federal court upheld the removal of two students from the high school prom for dressing in clothing of the opposite sex, reasoning that the school board's dress regulations were

---

[114]Gano v. Sch. Dist. No. 411, 674 F. Supp. 796 (D. Idaho 1987).

[115]Smith v. Greene County Sch. Dist., 100 F. Supp. 2d 1354 (M.D. Ga. 2000). *See also* Broussard v. Sch. Bd., 801 F. Supp. 1526 (E.D. Va. 1992) (upholding one-day suspension of a student who refused to change her shirt printed with the words "Drugs Suck," because "suck" is offensive and vulgar to many people).

[116]Olesen v. Bd. of Educ., 676 F. Supp. 820 (N.D. Ill. 1987). *See also Barber*, 901 S.W.2d 447 (upholding earring and hair-length restrictions applied only to male students).

[117]Hines v. Caston Sch. Corp, 651 N.E.2d 330 (Ind. Ct. App. 1995).

[118]Bivens *ex rel.* Green v. Albuquerque Pub. Schs., 899 F. Supp. 556 (D.N.M. 1995), *aff'd mem.*, 131 F.3d 151 (10th Cir. 1997).

[119]Brandt v. Bd. of Educ., 326 F. Supp. 2d 916 (N.D. Ill. 2004).

"reasonably related to the valid educational purposes of teaching community values and maintaining school discipline."[120]

In one of the most expansive interpretations of *Fraser,* the Sixth Circuit upheld a school district's decision to prohibit students from wearing Marilyn Manson T-shirts. The appeals court agreed with school authorities that the shirts were offensive, promoted destructive conduct, and were counter to the school's efforts to denounce drugs and promote human dignity and democratic ideals.[121] The court held that under *Fraser,* schools can prohibit student expression that is inconsistent with its basic educational mission even though such speech might be protected by the First Amendment outside the school environment.

In 2007, the Sixth Circuit also broadly interpreted the authority of school personnel when it upheld a school district's ban on students displaying the Confederate flag, finding the potential for disruption and rejecting the students' contention that the ban represented viewpoint discrimination.[122] The school district's dress code among other things prohibits clothing exhibiting references to illegal substances, negative slogans, or vulgarities or causing a disruption. Although the court found "ample reason" for school authorities to anticipate a disruption from students wearing the banned symbol, as noted previously, the court concluded that such a link to a disruption is not required.

Several very restrictive dress codes have received judicial endorsement. The Sixth Circuit upheld a middle school's restrictive dress code as reasonable to create unity and focus attention on learning. The court found no violation of a student's free expression rights, her right to wear clothes of her choice, or her father's right to control his daughter's attire.[123] An Illinois court upheld a restrictive dress code that confined student clothing to all black, all white, or a combination of the two, and prohibited logos, patches, imprinted words, and designs on clothing.[124] Noting the opportunity to opt out of the dress code for religious reasons, the court held that the restriction on student expression in the school's nonpublic forum is justified by pedagogical concerns

[120]Harper v. Edgewood Bd. of Educ., 655 F. Supp. 1353, 1355 (S.D. Ohio 1987).

[121]Boroff v. Van Wert City Bd. of Educ., 220 F.3d 465 (6th Cir. 2000).

[122]D.B. v. Lafon, 217 Fed. Appx. 518 (6th Cir. 2007). *See also* Madrid v. Anthony, 510 F. Supp. 2d 425 (S.D. Tex. 2007) (upholding a ban on students, who were mostly Hispanic, wearing T-shirts with "We Are Not Criminals" to protest pending immigration legislation; school authorities instituted the ban to curb the escalating racial tension in the school that threatened student safety).

[123]Blau v. Ft. Thomas Pub. Sch. Dist., 401 F.3d 381 (6th Cir. 2005). Among other things, the code prohibited revealing or baggy clothing; tops and bottoms that do not overlap; visible body piercing (other than ears); clothing that is distressed or has holes; flip-flop sandals or high platform shoes; pants, shorts, or skirts that are not solid navy, black, khaki, or white; tops with writing on them and logos larger than the size of a quarter except for the school's logo; and tops that are not a solid color. *Id.* at 385–386. *See also* Long v. Bd. of Educ., 121 F. Supp. 2d 621 (W.D. Ky. 2000), *aff'd mem.*, 21 Fed. Appx. 252 (6th Cir. 2001) (upholding a restrictive student dress code devised by a Kentucky school-based council that limits the colors, materials, and type of clothing allowed, and bars logos, shorts, cargo pants, jeans, and other specific items; finding legitimate safety justifications and no intent to suppress free speech); Byars v. City of Waterbury, 795 A.2d 630 (Conn. Super. Ct. 2001) (finding restrictive school dress code rationally related to reducing disruptions and loss of instructional time).

[124]Vines v. Zion Sch. Dist., No. 01 C 7455, 2002 U.S. Dist. LEXIS 382 (N.D. Ill. Jan. 10, 2002).

that include maintaining an orderly environment and inculcating civility and traditional moral, social, and political norms.

However, as with hairstyle regulations, school authorities must have an educational rationale for attire restrictions, such as enhancing learning or preventing class disruptions. The Third Circuit struck down a prohibition on wearing T-shirts with the comedian Jeff Foxworthy's "red-neck sayings," as not sufficiently linked to racial harassment or other disruptive activity.[125] Also, a Texas federal district court found overly broad and vague a dress code prohibiting students from wearing gang-related apparel since the term *gang-related* was ambiguous and not defined. Two students who wore rosaries outside their shirts were advised that they were in violation of the policy, and the court held that wearing rosaries was a well-recognized form of religious expression protected by the First Amendment.[126] A New York federal court denied a school board's request to dismiss a student's claim that her free expression rights were violated by school authorities who said she could not wear a necklace supporting the war in Iraq because it could be viewed as violating the school's policy prohibiting gang-related clothing.[127] A student also prevailed in wearing a T-shirt depicting three black silhouettes holding firearms with "NRA" and "Shooting Sports Camp" superimposed over the silhouettes. School authorities asked the student to change the shirt, contending that it conflicted with the school's mission of deterring violence. Applying *Tinker* instead of *Fraser*, the Fourth Circuit held that the student's free expression rights were overriding because the shirt was not disruptive and did not promote gun use.[128]

In addition, dress codes must not be discriminatorily enforced. The Sixth Circuit ordered a school district to reconsider suspensions of two students who wore T-shirts with a country singer on the front and the Confederate flag on the back and who refused to turn the shirts inside out or to go home and change.[129] School authorities

[125]Sypniewski v. Warren Hills Reg'l Bd. of Educ., 307 F.3d 243 (3d Cir. 2002); *supra* text accompanying note 81.

[126]Chalifoux v. New Caney Indep. Sch. Dist., 976 F. Supp. 659 (S.D. Tex. 1997). *See also* Stephenson v. Davenport Cmty. Sch. Dist., 110 F.3d 1303 (8th Cir. 1997) (finding policy prohibiting gang symbols, which was challenged by a student who was forced to remove a small tattoo of a cross on her hand, to give insufficient notice to students of what is prohibited and to allow school officials unfettered discretion to decide what constitutes banned symbols).

[127]Grzywna v. Schenectady Cent. Sch. Dist., 489 F. Supp. 2d 139 (N.D.N.Y. 2006). *See also* DePinto v. Bayonne Bd. of Educ., 514 F. Supp. 2d 633 (D.N.J. 2007) (enjoining school authorities from prohibiting the wearing of buttons depicting Hitler youth to protest the school's dress code; the buttons, while in poor taste, were not disruptive, vulgar, or sexually charged).

[128]Newsom v. Albemarle County Sch. Bd., 354 F.3d 249 (4th Cir. 2003). *See also* Griggs v. Ft. Wayne Sch. Bd., 359 F. Supp. 2d 731 (N.D. Ind. 2005) (finding no legitimate pedagogical reason to ban a T-shirt with the Marine Creed and a large picture of an M16 rifle, as the shirt did not threaten violence). *But see* Douglass v. Londonderry Sch. Bd., 413 F. Supp. 2d 1 (D.N.H. 2005) (holding that student yearbook editors could refuse to run a senior portrait of a student in trap shooting attire and holding a shotgun; the editors were not acting under color of state law and had offered to publish the picture in the community sports section of the yearbook).

[129]Castorina v. Madison County Sch. Bd., 246 F.3d 536 (6th Cir. 2001). For a discussion of challenges to anti-harassment policies, *see supra* text accompanying note 72.

asserted that the shirts violated the school's dress code prohibiting clothing or emblems that contain slogans or words depicting alcohol or tobacco or have illegal, immoral, or racist implications, but the court found no evidence of racial tension in the school or that the shirt would likely lead to a disruption. There also was evidence that the dress code had been selectively enforced in a viewpoint-specific manner; students had been allowed to wear shirts celebrating Malcolm X. Thus, the court remanded the case to determine if the students' First Amendment rights had been violated.

The Second Circuit relied on *Tinker* in protecting a student's right to wear a shirt expressing political views; the shirt depicted George W. Bush negatively (i.e., calling him "Chicken Hawk in Chief" and linking him to drinking, taking drugs, and being a crook and draft dodger).[130] Reasoning that simply because the expression is in poor taste is not a sufficient reason to curtail students' expression rights, the appeals court concluded that for student expression to be censorable as plainly offensive under *Fraser*, it would need to contain sexual innuendos and/or profanity. Since neither was at issue, the court applied the *Tinker* disruption standard and found that the student wearing the controversial shirt was not linked to a disruption of the educational process.

Student Uniforms. Some student attire controversies since the 1990s have focused on school board policies specifying uniforms for students, and the line is not always clear between restrictive dress codes and student uniforms. Voluntary and mandatory student uniforms are gaining popularity in large-city school districts, including Baltimore, Chicago, Houston, Indianapolis, Los Angeles, Miami, New Orleans, New York City, and Philadelphia. Advocates assert that student uniforms eliminate gang-related attire, reduce violence and socioeconomic distinctions, and improve school climate by placing the emphasis on academics rather than fashion fads.

The Fifth Circuit rejected challenges to uniform policies in Louisiana and Texas school districts. Recognizing that attire can communicate a message entitled to First Amendment protection, the court nonetheless reasoned that the student uniform policies are justified by substantial government interests unrelated to suppressing expression, such as improving achievement, decreasing disciplinary problems, improving safety, decreasing socioeconomic tensions, and increasing attendance. In the Louisiana case, the court rejected the parents' claim that the uniforms posed a financial burden, noting that the uniforms were inexpensive and a donation program was available for those who could not afford them.[131] In the Texas case, the court noted that parents could apply for their children to be exempt from wearing the uniform based on philosophical or religious objections or medical necessity; thus, the court found no violation of parents' religious freedom or their Fourteenth Amendment right to direct the upbringing of their children.[132]

[130]Guiles v. Marineau, 461 F.3d 320, 322 (2d Cir. 2006), *cert. denied,* 127 S. Ct. 3054 (2007).

[131]Canady v. Bossier Parish Sch. Bd., 240 F.3d 437 (5th Cir. 2001).

[132]Littlefield v. Forney Indep. Sch. Dist., 268 F.3d 275 (5th Cir. 2001) (upholding policy requiring students to wear specific types of shirts or blouses of particular colors with blue or khaki pants, shorts, skirts, or jumpers; specifying that clothing be made of specific materials; requiring certain types of shoes; and prohibiting any clothing suggesting gang affiliation).

After the New York City school board adopted a citywide uniform policy for children in elementary schools, a father brought suit claiming that if his child took advantage of the "opt out" provision, the child would "stick out" in violation of the child's rights.[133] But the Second Circuit held that the opt-out provision adequately addressed parents' rights to direct the upbringing of their children. Courts have not been persuaded that any rights are violated because a stigma is associated with exercising the First Amendment right to be exempt from certain requirements. The Third Circuit also rejected parents' request to use the religious exemption for their children to be exempt from the school district's mandatory dress code based on their atheistic beliefs. The court reasoned that the narrow religious exemption allowed for students to exercise their religious convictions without undermining the goals of the uniform policy.[134]

Although federal appellate courts have differed in their interpretations of constitutional protections regarding appearance regulations, school officials would be wise to ensure that they have a legitimate educational justification for any grooming or dress code. Policies designed to protect students' health and safety, reduce violence and discipline problems, and enhance learning usually will be endorsed. Given the current student interest in tattoos, body piercing, and other fashion fads and school authorities' concerns about attire linked to gangs and violence, continued legal controversies over student appearance in public schools seem assured.

Extracurricular Activities

School-sponsored activities that are not part of the regular academic program have generated considerable litigation. Almost every secondary school offers some extracurricular activities, and about 80 percent of high school students participate in at least one activity. In most states, a not-for-profit private organization regulates interscholastic sports and often has jurisdiction over other competitive activities among private and public schools. The Supreme Court ruled in 2001 that where such associations are extensively entwined with state school officials, they are considered state actors.[135] Thus, these private organizations are subject to constitutional restrictions on their activities and can be liable for constitutional violations.

---

[133]Lipsman v. N.Y. City Bd. of Educ., No. 98 Civ. 2008 (SHS), 1999 U.S. Dist. LEXIS 10591, *11 (S.D.N.Y. July 14, 1999), *aff'd*, 13 Fed. Appx. 13 (2d Cir. 2000). *See* also Mitchell v. McCall, 143 So. 2d 629, 632 (Ala. 1962) (finding no impairment of rights because the exempted child appears as a "speckled bird" to classmates; exercising the right to be treated differently is subject to such inconveniences).

[134]Wilkins v. Penns Grove-Carneys Point Reg'l Sch. Dist., 123 Fed. Appx. 493 (3d Cir. 2005). *See also* Jacobs v. Clark County Sch. Dist., 373 F. Supp. 2d 1162 (D. Nev. 2005) (upholding a content-neutral uniform policy, but striking down the provision giving the school district broad discretion to determine whether wearing the uniform violated a student's religious beliefs).

[135]Brentwood Acad. v. Tenn. Secondary Sch. Athletic Ass'n, 531 U.S. 288 (2001). *See also* Tenn. Secondary Sch. Athletic Ass'n v. Brentwood Acad., 127 S. Ct. 2489 (2007); *infra* text accompanying note 139.

It is clear that once a state provides public education, students cannot be denied attendance without due process of law,[136] but this state-created property right to attend school does not extend to extracurricular activities. The prevailing view is that conditions can be attached to extracurricular participation, because such participation is a privilege rather than a right.[137] Even though school authorities may not be required by the Fourteenth Amendment to provide due process when denying students extracurricular participation, a hearing for the students to defend their actions is always advisable. And if school boards have established rules for suspending or expelling students from extracurricular activities, courts will require compliance.[138]

The remainder of this section focuses on various features of extracurricular activities that have generated legal activity. Allegations of discrimination based on disabilities, sex, and marital status in connection with such activities are discussed in Chapters 5 and 6.

Attendance, Training, and Recruitment Regulations

State athletic associations place various restrictions on member public and private schools in terms of recruiting athletes. The Supreme Court ruled in 2007 that the Tennessee Secondary School Athletic Association's enforcement of its anti-recruitment rule against Brentwood Academy, a private school member, does not violate the academy's free expression rights. The Court declared that the anti-recruitment rule strikes "nowhere near the heart of the First Amendment."[139] Recognizing that such associations do not have unlimited authority to condition membership on the relinquishment of constitutional rights, the Court held that they can impose only conditions necessary to manage an efficient and effective high school athletic league.

---

[136]*See* Goss v. Lopez, 419 U.S. 565 (1975); text with note 57, Chapter 7.

[137]*See, e.g.*, James v. Tallahassee High Sch., 104 F.3d 372 (11th Cir. 1996) (finding no property right to participate in extracurricular activities, the court dismissed a cheerleader's challenge to the sponsor's decision to choose head cheerleaders even though the student handbook indicated that the respective squads would select their leaders); Ryan v. Cal. Interscholastic Fed'n, 114 Cal. Rptr. 2d 798 (Ct. App. 2001) (finding participation in interscholastic athletics a privilege in upholding eight-semester rule); Taylor v. Enumclaw Sch. Dist. No. 216, 133 P.3d 492 (Wash. Ct. App. 2006) (holding that a student could be suspended from interscholastic sports for possessing alcohol and tobacco on school grounds; such participation is a privilege not a right). *But see* Butler v. Oak Creek-Franklin Sch. Dist., 172 F. Supp. 2d 1102 (E.D. Wis. 2001) (finding reasonable likelihood that there was a property interest to continue athletic participation, necessitating procedural due process before imposing a one-year suspension on a student's eligibility).

[138]*See, e.g.,* Ferguson v. Phoenix-Talent Sch. Dist. No. 4, 19 P.3d 943 (Or. Ct. App. 2001) (recognizing that disciplinary rules pertaining to extracurricular activities must be uniformly applied, but holding that the rule placing a four-week limit on suspensions from extracurricular participation for drug offenses did not apply to the removal of a student as class president for drug possession).

[139]*Brentwood*, 127 S. Ct. at 2493 (finding also no due process violation as appropriate procedures were followed, and even if there was a closed door meeting, this presented a harmless infringement of due process rights). *See also* NCAA v. Lasege, 53 S.W.3d 77 (Ky. 2001) (holding that high school and collegiate athletic association rules will not be invalidated unless such associations act arbitrarily and capriciously toward student athletes). Courts also have upheld the exclusion of home schooled students from interscholastic teams. *See* text accompanying note 22, Chapter 3.

The Court reasoned that the content-neutral restriction on high schools communicating with middle school students is necessary to protect vulnerable students from schools using undue influence to attract athletes and to foster an appropriate competitive environment. Noting that schools make voluntary decisions to join such associations, the Supreme Court reasoned that those electing to do so must abide by the association's rules.

Schools frequently condition extracurricular participation on students attending practice sessions and games or performances. For example, the Fourth Circuit rejected a parent's challenge to her son's removal from the high school band for missing a required band trip.[140] Courts also have recognized that school officials should be given latitude in establishing training and conduct standards for high school athletes to foster discipline. The judiciary has upheld the suspension of students from interscholastic athletic competition for violating regulations prohibiting smoking and drinking, even if the regulations apply to athletes' off-campus, off-season conduct.[141] In an illustrative case, an Illinois court rejected a student's challenge to his suspension from participating in the entire football season because of a violation of the school's zero-tolerance policy pertaining to alcohol use.[142] In general, courts will not interfere with attendance requirements or training regulations simply because they appear harsh; students voluntarily subject themselves to the regulations as a condition of participation. The judiciary is reluctant to invalidate disciplinary action for rule violations unless the rules are clearly arbitrary, discriminatory, or excessive.

Restrictions on Eligibility

Courts have allowed school authorities flexibility in formulating eligibility rules for extracurricular activities. Schools can impose conditions such as skill prerequisites for athletic teams, academic and leadership criteria for honor societies, and musical proficiency for band and choral groups. Members of athletic teams and other extracurricular groups often are selected through a competitive process, and students have no inherent right to be chosen. Selection can be based on subjective judgments, and as long as fair procedures are uniformly applied without discrimination, courts will not disturb such decisions.[143]

---

[140]Bernstein v. Menard, 728 F.2d 252 (4th Cir. 1984) (holding that the band director's conduct was reasonable; finding the lawsuit frivolous and awarding attorneys' fees to the defendant school district). *See also* Keller v. Gardner Cmty. Consol. Grade Sch. Dist. 72C, 552 F. Supp. 512 (N.D. Ill. 1982) (upholding regulation that students missing a practice session cannot play in the next game).

[141]*See, e.g., Taylor*, 133 P.3d 492.

[142]Jordan v. O'Fallon Twp. High Sch. Dist., 706 N.E.2d 137 (Ill. App. Ct. 1999).

[143]*See, e.g.,* Pfeiffer v. Marion Ctr. Area Sch. Dist., 917 F.2d 779 (3d Cir. 1990) (holding that a pregnant student could be dismissed from the National Honor Society for engaging in premarital sex in violation of the Society's standards); Bull v. Dardanelle Pub. Sch. Dist. No. 15, 745 F. Supp. 1455 (E.D. Ark. 1990) (holding that students have no constitutional right to run for student council; the requirement that teachers approve council candidates was not vague).

One of the most obvious conditions is that students can be required to have physical examinations and be in good physical health to participate on athletic teams. The Supreme Court also has upheld policies requiring student athletes and those participating in other extracurricular activities to submit to random urinalysis as a condition of participation.[144] A New York federal district court found a valid health reason for a school to deny participation on the high school lacrosse team to a student who refused to get a tetanus vaccination.[145] As addressed in Chapter 6, the imposition of additional health restrictions on athletes with disabilities has generated litigation. Given federal and state protections of such children, school authorities would be wise to have evidence of legitimate health or safety risks before excluding specific children with disabilities from athletic teams.[146]

Courts generally approve residency requirements as conditions of interscholastic competition. To prevent schools, including private schools,[147] from recruiting student athletes, most state athletic associations prohibit involvement in interscholastic competition for one year after a change in a student's school without a change in the parents' address. Several federal as well as state courts have ruled that such residency requirements applied to public and private schools are rationally related to legitimate government interests and do not place an impermissible burden on students' rights to travel or on their freedom of family association.[148]

Some courts, however, have ordered exceptions where a student's welfare has necessitated the move. For example, the Seventh Circuit concluded that the state athletic association acted arbitrarily and capriciously when it declared a student ineligible for athletic competition for one year after he moved from his divorced father's home to his mother's home in another district because he was not performing well in school.[149] An Indiana court similarly found that a student qualified for a hardship exception where a change in financial circumstances caused him to transfer from a

[144]Bd. of Educ. v. Earls, 536 U.S. 822 (2002); Vernonia Sch. Dist. 47J v. Acton, 515 U.S. 646 (1995). For a discussion of this topic, *see* text accompanying note 200, Chapter 7.

[145]Hadley v. Rush Henrietta Cent. Sch. Dist., No. 05-CV-6331T, 2007 U.S. Dist. LEXIS 30586 (W.D.N.Y. Apr. 25, 2007).

[146]*See, e.g.*, Doe v. Woodford County Bd. of Educ., 213 F.3d 921 (6th Cir. 2000) (upholding exclusion of a student with hemophilia and hepatitis B from athletic participation that would put him at increased risk of physical injury). *See* text accompanying note 116, Chapter 6.

[147]*See* Zeiler v. Ohio High Sch. Athletic Ass'n, 755 F.2d 934 (6th Cir. 1985) (upholding the association's rule barring from interscholastic competition those students whose parents live in another state as not impairing rights of Michigan residents who attended private high schools in the Toledo area).

[148]*See, e.g.*, Niles v. Univ. Interscholastic League, 715 F.2d 1027 (5th Cir. 1983); *In re* United States *ex rel.* Mo. State High Sch. Activities Ass'n, 682 F.2d 147 (8th Cir. 1982); Parker v. Ariz. Interscholastic Ass'n, 59 P.3d 806 (Ariz. Ct. App. 2002). *See also* Ryan v. Cal. Interscholastic Fed'n, 114 Cal. Rptr. 2d 798 (Ct. App. 2001) (upholding residency requirement for a student transferring from another country).

[149]Crane v. Ind. High Sch. Athletic Ass'n, 975 F.2d 1315 (7th Cir. 1992). *See also* Crocker v. Tenn. Secondary Sch. Athletic Ass'n, 735 F. Supp. 753 (M.D. Tenn. 1990) (holding that a student with learning disabilities who transferred from a private school to a public school to receive special education could not be denied extracurricular participation for one year).

private to a public school.[150] Furthermore, if there are compelling medical reasons necessitating a student's change of residence or the change is necessitated for the student to receive special education services, courts will order exceptions to transfer restrictions. A few courts have even questioned whether such residency requirements for transfer students serve their intended purpose (i.e., deterring the recruitment of high school athletes), and they have recognized the negative consequences for students whose moves are not athletically motivated.[151] Nonetheless, most residency requirements continue to receive judicial endorsement.

Courts also usually uphold age restrictions on extracurricular participation to equalize competitive conditions and protect athletes. In a typical case, the Supreme Court of Oklahoma upheld a rule barring students who reach their nineteenth birthday by September 1 from participating in interscholastic athletics as fair and reasonably related to legitimate state interests. The court agreed with the state defendants that older and more mature athletes could pose a threat to the health and safety of younger students and that the rule eliminated the possibility of redshirting athletes.[152] Similarly, courts usually have endorsed rules limiting athletic eligibility to eight consecutive semesters or four years after completion of the eighth grade.[153] However, several courts have enjoined state athletic associations from enforcing maximum age and eight-semester requirements where the students in question had been required to repeat courses or withdraw from school for a term because of extensive illnesses.[154] Also, as discussed in Chapter 6, the application of such eligibility requirements to students with disabilities has been controversial.[155]

A nationwide trend among school districts is to condition extracurricular participation on satisfactory academic performance. Several states through legislation

---

[150]Ind. High Sch. Athletic Ass'n v. Durham, 748 N.E.2d 404 (Ind. Ct. App. 2001).

[151]*See, e.g.*, Ind. High Sch. Athletic Ass'n v. Carlberg, 661 N.E.2d 833 (Ind. Ct. App. 1996) (enjoining application of transfer rule to student who transferred for academic and financial reasons); Sullivan v. Univ. Interscholastic League, 616 S.W.2d 170 (Tex. 1981) (invalidating transfer rule because it did not provide a means to rebut the presumption of recruiting athletes).

[152]Mahan v. Agee, 652 P.2d 765 (Okla. 1982). *See also* Ark. Activities Ass'n v. Meyer, 805 S.W.2d 58 (Ark. 1991) (finding rational basis for athletic association's age limitation); Thomas v. Greencastle Cmty. Sch. Corp., 603 N.E.2d 190 (Ind. Ct. App. 1992) (finding age restriction on participation neither under nor over inclusive).

[153]*See, e.g.*, Ala. High Sch. Athletic Ass'n v. Medders, 456 So. 2d 284 (Ala. 1984); Grabow v. Mont. High Sch. Ass'n, 59 P.3d 14 (Mont. 2002); J.M., Jr. v. Mont. High Sch. Ass'n, 875 P.2d 1026 (Mont. 1994).

[154]*See, e.g.*, Clay v. Ariz. Interscholastic Ass'n, 779 P.2d 349 (Ariz. 1989) (holding that the interscholastic association had arbitrarily refused to consider an exception to the eight consecutive-semester eligibility rule for a student who was unable to attend school while being rehabilitated for drug use and incarcerated for theft related to his drug problems). *See also* Jordan v. Ind. High Sch. Athletic Ass'n, 813 F. Supp. 1372 (N.D. Ind. 1993), *vacated*, 16 F.3d 785 (7th Cir. 1994) (allowing student to play his senior year because his move from Illinois to Indiana, where he repeated his junior year, was not athletically motivated and he had not been redshirted).

[155]*See, e.g.*, Washington v. Ind. High Sch. Athletic Ass'n, 181 F.3d 840 (7th Cir. 1999) (affirming preliminary injunction for learning-disabled student to receive a waiver from the eight-semester rule to accommodate his disability); text accompanying note 122, Chapter 6.

or administrative rules have adopted statewide "no pass, no play" provisions, and these measures consistently have been upheld as advancing the state's legitimate interest in educational excellence.[156] In an illustrative case, the West Virginia Supreme Court endorsed academic standards for extracurricular participation, holding that the state board of education's rule, requiring students to maintain a 2.0 grade-point average (GPA) to participate, was a legitimate exercise of its supervisory power. Moreover, the court upheld a county school board's regulation that went beyond the state policy by requiring students to maintain a passing grade in all classes as a prerequisite to extracurricular participation.[157] A Kentucky appeals court similarly upheld a school board's policy requiring students to maintain a 2.0 GPA in five of six subjects as a condition of participating in extracurricular activities.[158]

In view of the national concern about achieving educational excellence, school boards and state legislatures are apt to place additional academic conditions on extracurricular participation. Only if academic standards are not uniformly applied are they likely to be invalidated.[159]

Fees for Participation

Some courts have ruled that public schools can condition extracurricular participation on the payment of fees. For example, the Montana and Wisconsin high courts upheld the legality of charging fees for activities that are optional or elective.[160] In upholding fees for playing on interscholastic athletic teams, a Michigan appeals court recognized the availability of a confidential waiver process for students who could not afford the fees. The court noted that no student had been denied participation because of inability to pay, and further declared that interscholastic athletics are not considered an integral, fundamental part of the educational program, which would necessitate providing them at no cost to students.[161]

---

[156]*See, e.g.,* Montana v. Bd. of Trs., 726 P.2d 801 (Mont. 1986); Spring Branch Indep. Sch. Dist. v. Stamos, 695 S.W.2d 556 (Tex. 1985). *But see* Ingram v. Toledo City Sch. Dist., 339 F. Supp. 2d 998 (N.D. Ohio 2004) (ruling that a student with disabilities who failed English was entitled to play football because the school's failure to implement his individualized education program was beyond the student's control).

[157]Truby v. Broadwater, 332 S.E.2d 284 (W. Va. 1985).

[158]Thompson v. Fayette County Pub. Schs., 786 S.W.2d 879 (Ky. Ct. App. 1990).

[159]*See, e.g.,* Fontes v. Irvine Unified Sch. Dist., 30 Cal. Rptr. 2d 521 (Ct. App. 1994) (striking down a policy imposing a higher GPA for eligibility for the pep and cheerleading squads than for interscholastic sports as not rationally related to a realistically conceivable purpose).

[160]*See* Granger v. Cascade County Sch. Dist. No. 1, 499 P.2d 780 (Mont. 1972); Bd. of Educ. v. Sinclair, 222 N.W.2d 143 (Wis. 1974). *See also* Paulson v. Minidoka County Sch. Dist. No. 331, 463 P.2d 935, 938 (Idaho 1970) (finding extracurricular activities to be outside the regular academic courses for which fees could not be charged).

[161]Attorney Gen. v. E. Jackson Pub. Schs., 372 N.W.2d 638 (Mich. Ct. App. 1985).

The Indiana Supreme Court struck down a uniform $20 activities fee for all students, considering it a charge for attending public school, but the court recognized that fees could be assessed for participation in specific extracurricular activities.[162] However, individual state mandates may preclude charging students for extracurricular activities.[163] Given the fiscal constraints faced by school districts, an increasing number of school boards are likely to consider charging such fees, and the legality of these arrangements will depend on judicial interpretations of state law.

Other Conditions

A number of other conditions have been attached to extracurricular participation. Some courts, for example, have upheld limitations on student participation in out-of-school athletic competition as a condition of varsity participation to protect students from overtaxing themselves and to make interscholastic athletics more competitive and fair.[164] Restrictions on the number of team members allowed to participate in championships also have been upheld as rationally related to the legitimate state objectives of reducing costs of play-off contests and promoting fair play in championship games.[165] Additionally, requirements specifying that athletes must have participated in a certain portion of season contests to be eligible for tournament play have been upheld.[166]

Although extracurricular activities continue to generate controversies, typically courts have allowed school authorities discretion in attaching a variety of conditions to student participation. Educators should ensure, however, that all policies pertaining to extracurricular activities are reasonable, clearly stated, related to an educational purpose, publicized to parents and students, and applied without discrimination.

---

[162]Nagy v. Evansville-Vanderburgh Sch. Crop., 844 N.E.2d 481 (Ind. 2006).

[163]*See, e.g.,* Hartzell v. Connell, 679 P.2d 35, 44-45 (Cal. 1984) (finding that extracurricular activities are an integral part of the educational program and thus encompassed within the state constitution's guarantee of a free public education and the state administrative code's stipulation that students shall not be required to pay any fees or deposits).

[164]*See, e.g.,* Burrows v. Ohio High Sch. Athletic Ass'n, 891 F.2d 122 (6th Cir. 1989) (finding prohibition of soccer squad members participating in spring independent soccer if they play fall interscholastic soccer to be rationally related to the association's legitimate interest of promoting fairness in competition); Kite v. Marshall, 661 F.2d 1027 (5th Cir. 1981) (upholding rational basis for interscholastic league's rule restricting participation by students who attended summer camps).

[165]*See, e.g.,* The Fla. High Sch. Activities Ass'n v. Thomas, 434 So. 2d 306 (Fla. 1983). *See also* Graham v. Tenn. Secondary Sch. Athletic Ass'n, 107 F.3d 870 (6th Cir. 1997) (upholding association's "quota rule" that limits the number of students who play varsity sports and receive financial aid to prevent private schools from using aid to recruit athletes).

[166]*See, e.g.,* Pearson v. Ind. High Sch. Athletic Ass'n, No. IP 99 1857-C-T/G, 2000 U.S. Dist. LEXIS 10501 (S.D. Ind. Feb. 22, 2000) (upholding requirement that tennis players participate in a minimum of 50 percent of the season's contests in the number-one doubles position to qualify for the doubles tournament).

Conclusion

Noninstructional issues have generated a substantial amount of school litigation. Many cases have focused on students' First Amendment freedoms of speech and press, but other constitutional rights, such as due process and equal protection guarantees, also have been asserted in challenging restrictions on students' noninstructional activities. In the latter 1960s and early 1970s, the federal judiciary expanded constitutional protections afforded to students in noninstructional matters after the Supreme Court rendered the landmark *Tinker* decision. Yet, the reach of the *Tinker* standard was narrowed somewhat after the Supreme Court ruled in *Fraser* and *Hazelwood* that lewd or vulgar speech and attire are not protected by the First Amendment and that school authorities can censor school-sponsored expression. Although the *Tinker* principle has been revitalized in First Amendment challenges to anti-harassment policies and electronic censorship, the Supreme Court in *Morse* again restricted use of the disruption standard if expression can be viewed as promoting or celebrating illegal activity. *Tinker* has not been overturned, but it governs more limited circumstances than was true in the 1970s. Concerns over student violence coupled with restrictions imposed on expression in response to terrorism have placed new strains on First Amendment freedoms in public schools. Tensions are exacerbated by students' ability to distribute materials to broad audiences over the Internet.

Students do not need to rely solely on constitutional protections, because federal and state laws, most notably the Equal Access Act, also protect students' expression and association rights and afford protections in noninstructional matters. Also, state association rules govern many aspects of extracurricular activities among member schools. Although judicial criteria applied in weighing the competing interests of students and school authorities continue to be refined, the following generalizations characterize the current posture of the courts.

1. Students do not have a First Amendment right to engage in expression that is defamatory, obscene, lewd, or inflammatory or that promotes illegal activity in public schools.
2. School boards can ban commercial solicitation on school premises, but they also have the authority to contract with companies to advertise in public schools unless there is a state prohibition.
3. Student expression that represents the school is subject to restrictions; school authorities have broad discretion to censor such expression, provided the decisions are based on pedagogical concerns and do not entail viewpoint discrimination.
4. Student-initiated expression of ideological views that merely occurs at school (in contrast to representing the school) cannot be curtailed unless a material interference with or substantial disruption of the educational process can reasonably be forecast from the expression.
5. School authorities cannot bar controversial or critical content from student literature that is not school sponsored even though it is distributed at school; policies

requiring prior administrative review of such material must specify the procedures for review and the types of material that are prohibited.

6. School authorities cannot punish students for the content of materials that are published and distributed off school grounds, including material posted from home on the Internet, unless such distribution substantially interferes with the operation of the school.

7. Most courts have justified school districts' anti-harassment policies that prohibit uncivil and disrespectful expression as necessary to promote legitimate school objectives, even though similar policies could not be imposed outside school settings.

8. Anti-harassment provisions cannot be vague or overly broad in restricting protected expression.

9. Any regulation imposing time, place, and manner restrictions on student expression must be specific, publicized to students and parents, and applied without discrimination.

10. Under the Equal Access Act (EAA), if a federally assisted secondary school establishes a limited open forum for student-initiated clubs to meet during noninstructional time, the access policy must be content neutral; however, public schools are not required to create such a forum for noncurriculum student groups to meet.

11. Student and community groups not covered by the EAA have First Amendment expressive association and private speech protections against viewpoint discrimination in terms of public school access.

12. School authorities can restrict student hairstyles and attire that are vulgar, jeopardize health and safety, or threaten to disrupt the educational process; any restrictions must be justified for educational reasons.

13. Restrictive student dress codes and uniforms can be imposed in public schools if justified by legitimate educational objectives, such as reducing violence and improving achievement, and are not designed to suppress expression.

14. Students do not have an inherent right to participate in extracurricular activities.

15. Nonprofit, private associations that regulate interscholastic sports and other competitive activities among private and public schools within states are considered state actors and subject to constitutional restrictions on their actions.

16. School authorities possess considerable latitude in attaching reasonable conditions to extracurricular participation (e.g., skill criteria, attendance and training regulations, residency rules, academic standards, age restrictions, and length of eligibility requirements).

17. Restrictions can be imposed on student participation in extracurricular activities based on legitimate health and safety considerations, and student athletes can be subjected to drug testing.

18. Whether public schools can charge fees for extracurricular participation depends upon judicial interpretation of a state's constitutional and statutory provisions.

5

Student Classifications

It might appear from a literal translation of the word *equality* that once a state establishes an educational system, all students must be treated in the same manner. Courts, however, have recognized that individuals are different and that equal treatment of unequals can have negative consequences. Accordingly, valid classification practices, designed to enhance the educational experiences of children by recognizing their unique needs, generally have been accepted as a legitimate prerogative of educators. While educators' authority to classify students has not been seriously contested, the bases for certain classifications and the procedures used to make distinctions among students have been the focus of substantial litigation. This chapter explores differential treatment of students based on race, native language, ability and achievement, age, and sex.

Legal Context

The Fourteenth Amendment to the United States Constitution states in part that no state shall deny to any person within its jurisdiction equal protection of the laws. This applies to subdivisions of states, including school districts. Given this explicit provision, there has been considerable litigation regarding what constitutes "equal protection." Facial discrimination (e.g., local board policy mandating race-segregated schools) will be examined through one of three prevailing tests: strict, intermediate, or rational basis scrutiny.

Identifying the appropriate standard of review requires a determination of whether a *suspect class* is involved.[1] To date, only alienage, race, and national origin have been identified by the Supreme Court as suspect classes.[2] Any grouping or school

---

[1]Level of scrutiny also is determined by the presence of fundamental or quasi-fundamental rights. Such rights will not be reviewed in this chapter as this discussion focuses on suspect classes.

[2]*See* Graham v. Richardson, 403 U.S. 365 (1971) (alienage); Hunter v. Erickson, 393 U.S. 385 (1969) (race); Korematsu v. United States, 323 U.S. 214 (1944) (national origin).

assignment based on these characteristics would be strictly scrutinized by the courts and upheld only if it advances a compelling government interest and is narrowly tailored. If the challenged classification is sex, intermediate scrutiny is applied.[3] This standard requires governmental actions to be substantially related to advancing significant governmental objectives. Moreover, the classification must be necessary, not merely convenient, and will not be upheld if there are reasonable, less restrictive means of reaching the same goal. Where any other classification or form of discrimination is present (e.g., disability, age), courts apply rational basis scrutiny. All that is required under this level of review is that some rational basis was used to base the state's decision. This is a very low threshold and is generally met with relative ease.

A fourth level of review is applied where acts of the state have the outward appearance of being neutral but in reality have a disproportionate adverse affect on a protected class of persons; when this occurs, the plaintiff must prove that the state intended to discriminate. For example, if standardized test scores provide the basis for assigning students to various programs (e.g., gifted, developmental) and result in disproportionate placement according to race, the plaintiff bears the burden of demonstrating that school personnel intended to discriminate in their selection and use of the tests. This standard is difficult to meet and generally results in a verdict for the state. (See Fourteenth Amendment, Figure 1, in Appendix.)

In addition to those constitutional protections, equal educational opportunities are guaranteed through various federal and state laws. In many instances, the statutes create new substantive rights that are more extensive than constitutional guarantees. Among the more significant federal laws discussed in this chapter are Title VI of the Civil Rights Act of 1964 (barring discrimination on the basis of race, color, or national origin by recipients of federal financial assistance), the Equal Educational Opportunities Act of 1974 (guaranteeing public school students equal educational opportunity without regard to race, color, sex, or national origin), Title IX of the Education Amendments of 1972 (prohibiting sex discrimination in institutions with federally assisted educational programs), and the Age Discrimination Act of 1975 (prohibiting federal aid recipients from discriminating based on age).

Classifications Based on Race

Historically, the most prevalent reason for classifying students according to race has been to establish or perpetuate racially segregated schools. Widespread racial segregation in educational institutions existed in this country from the colonial period well into the twentieth century. Even after the adoption of the Fourteenth Amendment in 1868, most schools remained segregated either by state constitution or statute, local ordinance, district policy or practice, or court interpretation, and were seldom equal. When such practices were challenged, courts generally mandated only that children be provided with access to public education. They did not require equal access to

---

[3]Miss. Univ. for Women v. Hogan, 458 U.S. 718 (1982). Intermediate scrutiny also applies in cases dealing with illegitimacy. *See* Clark v. Jeter, 486 U.S. 456 (1988).

integrated schools or to equal school facilities, the provision of equal curricular or extracurricular opportunities, instruction by equally trained professionals, or instruction of equal duration (i.e., an equivalent school year or school day).

Today, most former *de jure* segregated schools[4] are already, or are in the process of becoming, integrated. In some instances, costs have exceeded $200 million, and court supervision has lasted 20 to 30 years or longer. No other area of school law has involved such volatile debate, obligated such a high percentage of a school district's budget, or resulted in greater political and social turmoil than desegregation.

Most lawsuits challenging school segregation claim a violation of the Fourteenth Amendment. Because race qualifies as a suspect class, the state or local school district must demonstrate a compelling interest in its use of facially discriminatory racial classifications *and* show that its procedures are narrowly tailored if it were to use race as a basis to segregate school children, to deny equal educational opportunity, or to advantage one student over another.

Pre-*Brown* Litigation

The first published school segregation case was *Roberts v. City of Boston* in 1849, 19 years prior to the passage of the Fourteenth Amendment.[5] In that case, the city had established separate primary schools for minority children but had staffed them with teachers receiving the same compensation and having the same qualifications as other teachers in the system. When a minority child was denied admission to the Caucasian school nearest her home due to her race, she filed unsuccessful administrative appeals. The parents contended that (1) the separation of the races was a violation of the state constitution; (2) segregation was illegal, since the school committee did not have the authority to discriminate on the basis of race; (3) segregation inflicted upon minority children a stigma of caste; and (4) a school exclusively devoted to any single racial group was not equal to one where all groups met together.

The parents sought both an injunction to require admission and damages, as permitted under an 1845 state statute when any child was unlawfully excluded from public school instruction. Upholding the school committee, the state supreme court reasoned that the child had not been excluded from all public schools of the city, as two schools reserved exclusively for minority children were open to her. The court asserted that although equality is a broad principle, it did not warrant the conclusion that all individuals have the same legal rights (e.g., men and women, as well as adults and children, possess different powers and rights).

The *Roberts* case set the stage for 105 years of case law that generally supported the concept of separate but equal public schools. Between 1849 and 1868, cases dealt with state laws requiring school attendance, mandating equal protection, or prohibiting discrimination. After 1868 and the passage of the Fourteenth

---

[4]De jure segregated schools are those where the separation of the races was required by law or the result of other action by the state or its agents.

[5]59 Mass. (5 Cush.) 198 (1849).

Amendment, most cases leading up to *Brown v. Board of Education* in 1954 alleged a federal constitutional violation.

Perhaps the most infamous case supporting the "separate but equal" interpretation was *Plessy v. Ferguson* in 1896, in which the Supreme Court upheld racial segregation of passengers in railroad coaches as required by Louisiana law.[6] Violation of the statute resulted in a $25 fine or imprisonment for 20 days. Such a penalty could be imposed against either the individual who attempted to occupy the coach or compartment reserved for members of another race or the officer of any railroad who failed to make the proper assignment. The only identified exemption to this requirement was a nurse who was attending a child of another race. Although "separate but equal" case law and state statutes were common 75 to 100 years before *Plessy*, it nevertheless is *Plessy* that most often is mentioned today when the standard is discussed.

Following *Plessy*, the separate but equal standard thrived.[7] Individuals, groups, and organizations wishing to equalize educational opportunities or to integrate schools made little progress during the nineteenth and early twentieth centuries. Then, in the late 1930s and 1940s courts began looking more closely at "separate" facilities and programs and occasionally concluded that they were not "equal." Several of these cases involved the National Association for the Advancement of Colored People (NAACP) under the leadership of Charles Houston and Thurgood Marshall (a future United States Supreme Court justice).

The approach that Houston and Marshall took was based on the premise that if they could successfully attack the "equal" standard, the "separate" standard would be susceptible to challenge. They also reasoned that the social, political, and judicial climates were such that cases in higher education were more likely to succeed initially than were cases at the PK–12 level. Four key higher education appeals reached the Supreme Court between 1938 and 1950. Houston and/or Marshall were among counsel for the plaintiffs in each. These cases included claims from minority students that there were no separate but equal programs available (two cases), that the separate program was inferior, or that the education received within a previously all-Caucasian institution was unequal due to the student's separation from the rest of the student body.[8] The plaintiffs in each case prevailed.

Given the success of the higher education plaintiffs, the time appeared ripe to attack the PK–12 "separate but equal" standard directly. This occurred in 1954 when the Supreme Court combined cases from four states—Kansas, South Carolina, Virginia, and Delaware.[9] Once again, Marshall served as lead attorney for the plaintiffs.

[6]163 U.S. 537 (1896). *See also,* Bolling v. Sharpe, 347 U.S. 497 (1954) (invalidating school segregation in Washington D.C., under the Fifth Amendments' Due Process Clause because the Fourteenth Amendment does not apply in that jurisdicton).

[7]*See, e.g.,* Gong Lum v. Rice, 275 U.S. 78 (1927).

[8]McLaurin v. Okla. State Regents for Higher Educ., 339 U.S. 637 (1950); Sweatt v. Painter, 339 U.S. 629 (1950); Sipuel v. Bd. of Regents, 332 U.S. 631 (1948) (*per curiam*); Missouri *ex rel.* Gaines v. Canada, 305 U.S. 337 (1938).

[9]Brown v. Bd. of Educ., 98 F. Supp. 797 (D. Kan. 1951); Briggs v. Elliott, 98 F. Supp. 529 (E.D.S.C. 1951), *vacated and remanded,* 342 U.S. 350 (1952), *on remand,* 103 F. Supp. 920 (E.D.S.C. 1952); Davis v. County Sch. Bd., 103 F. Supp. 337 (E.D. Va. 1952); Gebhart v. Belton, 87 A.2d 862, *aff'd,* 91 A.2d 137 (Del. 1952).

Although these cases differed regarding conditions and facts, minority children in each state sought the assistance of the courts under the Fourteenth Amendment to obtain admission to public schools on a nonsegregated basis. In the landmark decision, collectively called *Brown v. Board of Education*, Chief Justice Warren, writing for a unanimous Court, declared education to be "perhaps the most important function of state and local governments"[10] and repudiated the separate but equal doctrine, stipulating that racially segregated public schools were "inherently unequal."[11]

Because of the significant impact of this decision and the difficulty in fashioning an immediate remedy, the Supreme Court delayed an implementation decree for one year, soliciting friend-of-the-court briefs[12] regarding strategies to convert *de jure* segregated dual school districts into integrated unitary districts. Then, in 1955 in *Brown II* the Court concluded that the conversion from dual to unitary must occur "with all deliberate speed,"[13] although it gave little guidance as to what specific time frame was required or to what extent integration was mandated. As a result, states varied widely in their efforts to comply.

De Jure Segregation in the South

Despite the *Brown* mandate to end segregation, during the next decade the Supreme Court was forced to react to a number of blatant violations, such as state officials' efforts to physically block the desegregation of schools in Little Rock,[14] and an attempt to avoid integration by closing public schools in one Virginia county, while maintaining public schools in other counties in the state.[15] The Court also invalidated provisions in Knoxville that allowed students to transfer back to their former schools if, after rezoning, they would be assigned to a school where their race would be in the minority,[16] and found unconstitutional a one-grade-per-year plan[17] that had been adopted in Fort Smith, Arkansas.[18] Such a practice was not an overt violation of *Brown* but certainly represented an effort to strain the "all deliberate speed" mandate.

Even where violations were found, however, many lower courts hesitated to require anything more than the removal of barriers to integration, given the dearth of

[10]347 U.S. 483, 493 (1954) (Brown I).

[11]*Id.* at 495.

[12]Friend-of-the-court (*amicus curiae*) briefs are provided by nonparties to inform or perhaps persuade the court.

[13]Brown v. Bd. of Educ., 349 U.S. 294, 301 (1955) (Brown II).

[14]Cooper v. Aaron, 358 U.S. 1 (1958).

[15]Griffin v. County Sch. Bd., 377 U.S. 218 (1964).

[16]Goss v. Bd. of Educ., 373 U.S. 683 (1963).

[17]A one-grade-per-year plan requires the integration of one grade each fall term until the system is unitary and all grades are integrated.

[18]Rogers v. Paul, 382 U.S. 198 (1965) (*per curiam*).

guidance regarding compliance.[19] Then, in a trilogy of cases in 1968, the Supreme Court announced that school officials in systems that were segregated by law in 1954 had an affirmative duty to take whatever steps were necessary to convert to unitary school systems and to eliminate the effects of past discrimination.[20] Furthermore, the Court declared that desegregation remedies would be evaluated based on their effectiveness in dismantling dual school systems. Thus, the notion of state neutrality was transformed into a requirement of affirmative state action to desegregate; the mere removal of barriers to school integration was not sufficient.

In one of these 1968 cases, *Green v. County School Board*, the Court reviewed a freedom-of-choice plan adopted by a small district in Virginia. The district historically operated only two schools, both kindergarten through twelfth grade: one for African Americans, the other for Caucasians. To eliminate race-based assignments within the district, the local board implemented a plan to allow children to attend the school of their choice. During the three-year period immediately following implementation, no Caucasian children enrolled in the historically African American school, while only a few African American children enrolled in the historically Caucasian school. The district contended that any resulting segregation was due to the choices of individuals, not to government action, and was therefore permissible; the Supreme Court disagreed. The problem with this plan was not that it was unconstitutional per se, but that it simply was not achieving school integration. As a result, the district was ordered to come forward with a new plan that promised "realistically to work and to work now."[21] In addition, the Court ruled that school authorities must eliminate the racial identification of schools in terms of the *composition of the student body, faculty, and staff; transportation; extracurricular activities; and facilities*. These six elements still are used today and are referred to in the aggregate simply as the *Green* criteria.

In 1971, additional direction was provided when the Supreme Court ruled in *Swann v. Charlotte-Mecklenburg Board of Education* that the elimination of invidious racial distinctions may be sufficient in connection with transportation, support personnel, and extracurricular activities, but that more was necessary in terms of constructing facilities and making faculty and student assignments.[22] The Court endorsed the practice of assigning teachers on the basis of race until faculties were integrated and declared that new schools must be located so that the dual school system would not be perpetuated or reestablished.

Correcting racial imbalance among student populations, however, was more difficult. For the vestiges of segregation to be eliminated, the school district had to achieve racial balance in a sufficient number of schools, although every school did

[19]*See, e.g.*, Briggs v. Elliott, 132 F. Supp. 776, 777 (E.D.S.C. 1955) (declaring that the Constitution "does not require integration" but "merely forbids discrimination").

[20]Green v. County Sch. Bd., 391 U.S. 430 (1968); Raney v. Bd. of Educ., 391 U.S. 443 (1968); Monroe v. Bd. of Comm'rs, 391 U.S. 450 (1968).

[21]*Green*, 391 U.S. at 439.

[22]402 U.S. 1 (1971).

not have to reflect the racial composition of the school district as a whole. The presence of a small number of predominantly one-race schools in the district did not necessarily mean that it continued to practice state-imposed segregation, but the burden of proof was placed on school officials to establish that such schools were not the result of present or past discriminatory action. To achieve the desired racial balance, the Court suggested pairing or consolidating schools, altering attendance zones, and using racial quotas, but rejected the practice of assigning students to the schools nearest their homes if it failed to eliminate *de jure* segregation. The Court also endorsed the use of reasonable busing as a means to integrate schools, yet qualified that endorsement by noting that the soundness of any transportation plan must be evaluated based on the time involved, distance traveled, and age of students.

By applying the criteria established in *Green* and *Swann,* substantial desegregation was attained in southern states during the 1970s. Where unconstitutional segregation was found, federal courts exercised broad power in ordering remedies affecting student and staff assignments, curriculum, school construction, personnel practices, and budgetary allocations. Judicial activity was augmented by threats from the former Department of Health, Education, and Welfare to terminate federal funds to school districts not complying with Title VI of the Civil Rights Act of 1964.[23] Title VI, like the Fourteenth Amendment, requires the integration only of *de jure* segregated school districts.

Distinguishing between *De Jure* and *De Facto* Segregation

Since the Supreme Court carefully limited its early decisions to states and school districts with a long history of school segregation by official policy, questions remained regarding what type of evidence—other than explicit legislation requiring school segregation—was necessary to establish unconstitutional *de jure* segregation.[24] That is, what factors would distinguish *de jure* segregation from permissible *de facto* segregation? The answer to this question began to evolve in *Keyes v. School District No. 1, Denver*, in which the Supreme Court in 1973 held that if "no statutory dual system has ever existed, plaintiffs must prove not only that segregated schooling exists but also that it was brought about or maintained by intentional state action."[25] Some federal courts have assumed that a presumption of unlawful purpose can be established if the natural, probable, and foreseeable results of public officials' acts perpetuate segregated conditions,[26] while others have required evidence that policy makers actually harbored a desire to segregate.[27] Although courts vary in the processes they use to

[23]42 U.S.C. §§ 2000d–2000d-7 (2007).

[24]In the 1960s, some courts reasoned that school segregation did not warrant remedial action in school districts where segregation was not imposed by law in 1954. *See, e.g.,* Deal v. Cincinnati Bd. of Educ., 369 F.2d 55 (6th Cir. 1966).

[25]413 U.S. 189, 198 (1973).

[26]*See, e.g.,* Arthur v. Nyquist, 573 F.2d 134 (2d Cir. 1978).

[27]*See, e.g.,* Vill. of Arlington Heights v. Metro. Hous. Dev. Corp., 429 U.S. 252 (1977).

determine whether school districts are guilty of discriminatory intent, they often consider the impact of the disputed governmental act, the history of discriminatory official action, procedural and substantive departures from norms generally followed, and discriminatory statements made publicly or in legislative or administrative sessions. If intent is proven, courts then are responsible for fashioning appropriate remedies.[28]

School districts that either have no history of unlawful segregation or have become unitary while under court supervision will not be responsible for correcting any future racial imbalance they have not created. In 1976, the Supreme Court in *Pasadena City Board of Education v. Spangler* held that the school district, having implemented a student reassignment plan to comply with a court order, did not have an affirmative duty to revise remedial efforts annually when demographic shifts resulted in some schools becoming more than 50 percent minority.[29] The district court had made a lifetime commitment to the "no majority of any minority" rule. The Supreme Court held that although the original lower court decision was justified to correct *de jure* segregation, the continuation of the order exceeded the court's authority once integration goals had been achieved.

More recently, in San Francisco a federal district court refused to extend an expired consent degree created to integrate the public schools in regard to nine racial and ethnic groups.[30] The school district had never been found guilty of *de jure* segregation or in noncompliance with the decree. In rejecting plaintiff's request, the court reasoned that there were no vestiges of prior *de jure* segregation; the district had fulfilled its responsibilities under the decree in good faith; and the prior agreement had proven to be ineffective, if not counterproductive, in achieving diversity.

Fashioning Appropriate Remedies

Because each desegregation case involves a combination of unique circumstances and violations, it is not surprising that each remedy also is unique and at times requires rezoning; the provision of thematic magnet schools; the development of new curricular offerings; the closing, reopening, renovation, or construction of schools; busing; the transfer and/or retraining of current staff; or the hiring of additional staff. Basically, the courts can require nearly anything of districts and states that would result in fulfillment of the primary objective—the integration of public schools. "All deliberate speed" in many instances has taken decades, while cost often seemed irrelevant.

Rezoning and the Closing, Reopening, or Construction of Schools.   Although at times politically unpopular, the rezoning of schools often was the fastest, least

---

[28]*See, e.g.,* Price v. Austin Indep. Sch. Dist., 945 F.2d 1307 (5th Cir. 1991).

[29]427 U.S. 424 (1976). *See also* Holton v. City of Thomasville Sch. Dist., 425 F.3d 1325 (11th Cir. 2005) (concluding that the segregation occurring since acquiring unitary status was caused by demographic changes and not official action; although the school district could voluntarily develop a new desegregation plan, federal law did not require it and courts were without the authority to order it).

[30]San Francisco NAACP v. San Francisco Unified Sch. Dist., 413 F. Supp. 2d 1051 (N.D. Cal. 2005).

expensive, and simplest way to integrate students. Because of a long history of gerrymandering boundary lines with the intent to segregate, many school boundaries during the 1950s and 1960s had little to do with geographic barriers (e.g., rivers, hills); safety issues (e.g., location of busy roads, factories); or the size, location, or dispersion of the student population. As a result, significant integration often has resulted through the simple use of good-faith redistricting and/or, in fairly narrow circumstances, the creation of new or consolidated school districts.[31]

In addition, early in the twentieth century many school districts were able to remain or become segregated by strategically locating new schools; downsizing or closing existing buildings; or operating schools that were overenrolled, often requiring the use of mobile units or temporary classrooms. Just as these methods were used to segregate, they also have been used to integrate. Where there has been a history of *de jure* segregation, it is common to require adjustments in building use and to determine site selection of future schools at least in part on the impact that their locations will have on the effort to integrate.

Busing.   Contributing to the cost and controversy was the use of busing to accomplish integration when other alternatives had not succeeded. Even though busing is admittedly effective at achieving student integration, it also represents a significant expense; is inefficient in the use of student time; and is an unpopular option with many students, parents, taxpayers, and voters of all races. Consequently, several bills to limit the authority of federal courts to order the busing of students have been introduced in Congress. Foremost among these were provisions included in Title IV of the Civil Rights Act of 1964[32] and the Equal Educational Opportunities Act (EEOA) of 1974.[33] Title IV provides technical assistance in the preparation, adoption, and implementation of desegregation plans; gives direction in the operation of training institutes to improve the ability of educators to deal effectively with special education problems occasioned by desegregation; and places limitations on court-ordered busing.

Furthermore, the EEOA prohibits public schools from denying equal educational opportunities to students based on their race, color, sex, or national origin; purports that the neighborhood is the appropriate basis for determining public school assignment; and stipulates that busing may be used only in situations where the intent to segregate is established. The EEOA explicitly forbids deliberate segregation and, where it was formerly practiced, requires educational agencies to remove the vestiges of the dual school system. The discriminatory assignment of faculty and staff and the transfer of students (voluntary or otherwise) from one school to another, when the purpose and effect are to increase segregation, also violate the EEOA.

Moreover, state busing limitation measures have generated litigation. In 1971, the Supreme Court in *North Carolina State Board of Education v. Swann* struck down a state law forbidding the busing of students to create racially balanced

[31]Newburg Area Council v. Bd. of Educ., 510 F.2d 1358 (6th Cir. 1974).

[32]42 U.S.C. §§ 2000c–2000c-9 (2007).

[33]20 U.S.C. § 1701 *et seq.* (2007).

schools. The Court concluded that the provision unconstitutionally restricted the discretion of local school authorities to formulate plans to eliminate dual school systems.[34] Accordingly, busing as an option to achieve integration could not be banned. This option was qualified in 1982, however, when the Court in *Crawford v. Board of Education* upheld a state constitutional amendment in California that permitted busing only when *de jure* segregation was present.[35] Prior to the adoption of the amendment, the state constitution prohibited *de facto* as well as *de jure* school segregation, thus requiring remedial plans to ensure racial balance in all school districts, including those where the separation of the races was caused by something other than official action (e.g., housing patterns, individual freedom of choice). This objective became both expensive and unpopular to the majority of state residents and was eventually discontinued. When the amendment was challenged, the Court concluded that California was legally obligated to integrate only *de jure* segregated school districts.

Programmatic Options. Since the early 1980s, the federal judiciary has become less aggressive in requiring massive student reassignment plans to integrate schools. In the alternative, compensatory education programs, bilingual/bicultural programs, and counseling and career guidance services, among others, have been included in desegregation plans to help overcome the effects of prior racial isolation.[36] Most plans include magnet schools that offered theme-oriented instructional programs or an expanded curriculum in an effort to attract a racially balanced student body and to limit the use of busing.[37] Other plans provide specialized learning centers to improve remediation for underachieving pupils.[38] As with freedom of choice or transfer plans, courts will uphold the use of these program and curricular options to integrate schools, but only if they succeed in achieving the desired level of integration within a reasonable period of time.

Interdistrict Remedies. Another controversial approach to integration has been the use of remedies that cross school district boundaries. Many city school districts experienced both real and percentage increases in minority populations due to a variety of reasons, including "white flight" and "zone jumping."[39] Integration in these areas then becomes problematic, given the presence primarily of one race. As a result, several courts have reasoned that if racial integration in a predominantly one-race district is to be achieved, adjacent districts must be involved in student transfer and busing plans.

---

[34]402 U.S. 43 (1971).

[35]458 U.S. 527 (1982).

[36]*See, e.g.,* Keyes v. Sch. Dist. No. 1, 895 F.2d 659 (10th Cir. 1990); Little Rock Sch. Dist. v. Pulaski County Special Dist., 716 F. Supp. 1162 (E.D. Ark. 1989).

[37]*See, e.g.,* Bradley v. Pinellas County Sch. Bd., 165 F.R.D. 676 (M.D. Fla. 1994).

[38]Tasby v. Black Coal. to Maximize Educ., 771 F.2d 849 (5th Cir. 1985).

[39]Zone jumping occurs when a student transfers from the assigned attendance zone to an adjacent zone. *See, e.g.,* Elston v. Talladega County Bd. of Educ., 997 F.2d 1394 (11th Cir. 1993).

In *Milliken v. Bradley*, the Sixth Circuit had ordered a metropolitan desegregation remedy for Detroit and 53 suburban school districts, reasoning that intentional school segregation implicated the entire metropolitan area. The Supreme Court disagreed in 1974, however, and held that the plaintiffs did not carry their burden of proof in substantiating purposeful discrimination on the part of the suburban districts.[40] Moreover, the Court emphasized that a remedy must not be broader in scope than warranted by the constitutional violation. Since intentional school segregation was proven only in the Detroit system, the case was remanded for the formulation of a remedy within that district.

Three years later, in *Milliken II,* the Court articulated a three-part framework to guide district courts in the exercise of their authority. This framework requires that the nature and scope of the desegregation remedy:

- Be determined by the nature and scope of the constitutional violation,
- Be remedial so as to restore the victims of discriminatory conduct to the position they would have occupied in the absence of such conduct, and
- Take into account the interests of state and local authorities in managing their own affairs.[41]

Accordingly, an interdistrict remedy may include only those districts that were involved in *de jure* segregation; courts are not authorized to include districts that were not segregated or were segregated only due to *de facto* circumstances.[42]

In a 1995 decision involving interdistrict remedies, *Missouri v. Jenkins*, the Supreme Court evaluated Kansas City's 18-year history of desegregation orders. Over this period, the district court ordered approximately $1.5 billion in program improvements, comprehensive magnet schools, transportation, capital improvements, and salary assistance.[43] By 1994, the average annual costs were over $200 million, thereby earning the reputation as the "most ambitious and expensive remedial program in the history of school desegregation."[44] Of particular importance in the Kansas City case were the lower court's orders (1) to further increase the salaries of teachers and staff and (2) to continue to fund a wide variety of expensive programs, many of which were available nowhere else in the state or nation. The district court reasoned that these expenditures were needed if educational opportunities were to be improved to the degree necessary to attract nonminority students (i.e., those either residing outside the district or attending private schools) to the Kansas City public schools.

The Supreme Court disagreed, noting that racial imbalance within a school district, without additional evidence supporting a Fourteenth Amendment violation did

[40]418 U.S. 717 (1974) (Milliken I).

[41]Milliken v. Bradley, 433 U.S. 267, 280–281 (1977) (Milliken II).

[42]*See, e.g.,* Edgerson v. Clinton, 86 F.3d 833 (8th Cir. 1996); Lauderdale County Sch. Dist. v. Enter. Consol. Sch. Dist., 24 F.3d 671 (5th Cir. 1994).

[43]515 U.S. 70 (1995).

[44]*Id.* at 78.

not infringe the Constitution and that the lower court's plan to attract nonresident nonminority students represented an interdistrict remedy and was therefore inappropriate for the court to have ordered. Furthermore, the court's order requiring the continued funding of the costly educational programs clearly exceeded its authority. The district court attempted to justify its decision by noting that student achievement levels still were at or below national norms and that students had not yet reached their maximum potential. The Supreme Court admonished that instead of a "maximum potential" standard, the court should have determined whether the lower achievement of minority students was attributable to prior *de jure* segregation and, if so, whether it had been remedied to the extent practicable. Once this had been accomplished, control of the schools was ordered to be returned to state and local school officials.

Notwithstanding the limitations on courts to order interdistrict remedies, unitary districts have at times voluntarily entered into such agreements. In a South Carolina case, a federal district court addressed the legality of a transfer provision involving a county school district and each of its integrated constituent districts. The districts had agreed to a plan allowing for interdistrict student transfers, assuming that the reasons for the requests were nondiscriminatory. The court acknowledged that local educators were authorized to set transfer policies, but nonetheless identified for the record several specific constitutional bases for transfers (e.g., to receive instruction in courses not available in the home district; to attend school with a sibling in a special program or where the child's parent is a teacher).[45] Also, where interdistrict transfers would result in greater racial balance in a particular school or district, the court encouraged the sending districts to consider that fact in evaluating the student's proposal. On the other hand, if a valid request were denied solely because it had an adverse effect on the desired racial balance, such an act by a unitary district would violate the transferring student's equal protection rights.

Staff Desegregation Remedies. The Supreme Court has emphasized that integration of the school staff is an essential component of an effective desegregation remedy.[46] Staff integration will allow students to be exposed to faculty of their own race as well as to faculty of other races. This often is accomplished through the use of race-based faculty assignment and transfer procedures. However, having a diverse faculty in each school will not be possible if a critical mass of underrepresented faculty has not been hired for the school district as a whole. Although districts may aggressively recruit qualified minority and other faculty, racial preference in hiring will not be permitted unless remedial in nature and court ordered. Where proof of prior discrimination exists, courts then are responsible for preparing a narrowly tailored plan to correct the constitutional violation. To accomplish this task, courts will

[45]United States v. Charleston County Sch. Dist., 960 F.2d 1227 (4th Cir. 1992), *on remand*, 856 F. Supp. 1060, 1063–1065 (D.S.C. 1994).

[46]*See, e.g.*, Swann v. Charlotte-Mecklenburg Bd. of Educ., 402 U.S. 1, 19 (1971); United States v. Montgomery County Bd. of Educ., 395 U.S. 225, 232 (1969). *See also* Lee v. Lee County Bd. of Educ., No. 70-T-845-E, 2002 U.S. Dist. LEXIS 10277 (M.D. Ala., May 29, 2002) (declaring the district unitary except for faculty assignments to two schools).

compare the racial composition of the faculty with that of the qualified relevant labor market, rather than with that of the surrounding community or the student body, in determining the targeted number, percent, or ratio. It is important to note that neither societal discrimination, racial imbalance, nor the desire for role models or diversity will justify imposing racial quotas in employment.

The racial balance of a school faculty also can be affected when it is necessary to downsize the staff. This can occur when either fewer schools are used (e.g., when two *de jure* districts are combined and fewer schools of larger size are operated) or fewer students are educated (e.g., when students move from the district or enroll in private schools). Although there may be exceptional circumstances where preference in hiring is permitted, that is not the case when determining whom to lay off. As a result, the diversity gained through the use of goals, court-ordered quotas, or affirmative action may be lost during a reduction-in-force (RIF) as the consideration of race in identifying the persons to be released is not permitted. The Supreme Court in *Wygant v. Jackson Board of Education* struck down a school district's negotiated agreement that gave preferential protection to minority teachers from layoffs to maintain the percentage of minority teachers employed prior to a RIF.[47] The Court concluded that the practice violated the Fourteenth Amendment and reasoned that the justification for the contested staff reduction policy—the need for minority role models—failed to qualify as a compelling interest and that the preferential layoff procedures were not narrowly tailored. Although *Wygant* did not involve a school district engaged in court-ordered integration, there is no reason to believe that the use of racial preferences would be permitted in such districts. Race-based relief may perhaps help remedy one constitutional violation, but it would create another.

Fiscal Responsibilities.   Numerous school districts have spent over $200 million to integrate their schools. The funds often were used to provide equal educational opportunity for students in existing programs and facilities. At other times, courts have required not only that there be integration, but that districts also construct or renovate facilities; purchase new furnishings, equipment, and technology; improve or expand curricular offerings; establish magnet schools; or increase staff salaries. Related costs almost always exceeded the local district's budget, if not also its tax-generating ability. Nevertheless, courts have shown little sympathy when the lack of sufficient funds has been proposed as a defense for maintaining dual school systems.[48]

Due to the extensive and seemingly endless costs associated with desegregation, balancing school budgets has been challenging. In theory, the solution appears clear: reduce expenditures and increase revenues. In practice, barriers often exist to accomplishing either, such as the inability to further reduce staff, declines in state support during periods of recession, and voter resistance to increased taxes. Among the more viable options to lower expenditures is the closing of schools. This results in lower maintenance and operation costs and the need for fewer faculty and staff. But

[47]476 U.S. 267 (1986).

[48]*See, e.g., In re* Little Rock Sch. Dist., 949 F.2d 253 (8th Cir. 1991).

the option to close schools is available only in those districts where there has been consolidation or where enrollments have declined. If decisions to close schools are motivated by legitimate budgetary or pedagogical concerns and do not adversely affect integration, they will be allowed. In contrast, where desegregation is impeded, school closings will not generally be permitted.

Another approach to balancing the budget is to reduce the number of faculty and staff, even when school closings are not feasible. Given that 85 percent or more of a district's operating budget is typically needed to compensate personnel, engaging in a RIF may at times help balance an otherwise deficit budget. Without consolidation, however, it is unlikely that districts will be able to significantly trim the number of staff, as many already operate with only essential personnel. Moreover, if the number of staff is reduced further, districts in some states will receive less state aid, as it is common for states to penalize districts that operate with too few teachers, counselors, or other support staff. Such a reduction in state dollars would in whole or in part offset any budgetary advantage the district may have experienced as a result of downsizing.

When lowering expenditures is not possible, or the amount of reduction is insufficient to meet budgetary needs, increasing revenues becomes paramount. This may be accomplished by increasing, extending, or creating local taxes. In a significant 1990 decision, *Missouri v. Jenkins*, the Supreme Court held that federal courts may order school districts to impose tax increases to fund desegregation remedies but that courts may not impose such increases directly.[49] However, if the school district is unable to further increase its taxes due to existing state laws, the courts have the limited authority to override such provisions as they apply to a *de jure* district.

In addition, courts at times have held states responsible for all or part of desegregation costs, depending on the extent to which the state was found culpable in causing or perpetuating the segregation.[50] Such was the case in Michigan in 1977 when the Supreme Court in *Milliken v. Bradley* ordered the state to underwrite half of the costs of remedial programs, in-service training, guidance and counseling services, and community relations programs in Detroit because of the role the state played in creating the dual system.[51]

Achieving Unitary Status

Federal courts have found numerous school systems guilty of having engaged in *de jure* segregation and have fashioned a variety of remedies. Some orders required only a few years to demonstrate compliance, while others continue to exist today, even though the original decisions may have been rendered in the 1950s, 1960s, or 1970s. Such lengthy supervision has usurped the traditional roles of trained and

---

[49]495 U.S. 33 (1990).

[50]*See, e.g.,* Jenkins *ex rel.* Agyei v. Missouri, 13 F.3d 1170 (8th Cir. 1994). *But see* DeKalb County Sch. Dist. v. Schrenko, 109 F.3d 680 (11th Cir. 1997) (concluding that the state need not reimburse the school district for costs associated with desegregation-related transportation, majority-to-minority transfer initiatives, and a magnet school program).

[51]433 U.S. 267 (1977) (Milliken II).

licensed school administrators, elected school boards, and state legislatures regarding funding, facilities, personnel, and curriculum. Although federal judges generally lack the knowledge and expertise to properly administer schools or to make curricular or instructional decisions, on occasion they assumed control of these matters and then retained it for decades at a time, even when compliance seemingly had occurred. With key decisions in 1991 and 1992, however, the Supreme Court provided complying districts with a means to an end.

In *Board of Education v. Dowell*, the school district had been operating since 1972 under a court-ordered plan that entailed substantial student busing to achieve integration. Five years after the initial decision, the federal district court ruled that the board had complied with the order in good faith and was entitled to pursue its legitimate policies without further court supervision. At that time, judicial monitoring was removed, but the 1972 decree was not dissolved. Later, after demographic changes led to greater burdens on minority students in continuing the student busing program, the school board in 1984 adopted a neighborhood school assignment policy for kindergarten through grade 4. The new plan was challenged because it would result in about half of the elementary schools becoming 90 percent minority or 90 percent Caucasian. The lower court upheld the plan, but the Tenth Circuit reversed. The appeals court reasoned that the district's circumstances had not changed enough to justify modifying the 1972 decree.[52] The court conjectured that compliance alone could not be the basis for dissolving an injunction and concluded that the school board failed to meet its burden of proof.

On further appeal, the Supreme Court held that the appellate court's standard for dissolving the original decree was too stringent and emphasized that federal supervision of local school systems was intended only as a temporary measure to remedy past discrimination. The Court reasoned that the intent of a desegregation plan is met upon finding—as the district court had done—that the school system was operating in compliance with the Equal Protection Clause and was not likely to return to its former ways. Furthermore, the Court concluded that the federal judiciary should terminate supervision of school districts where school boards have complied with desegregation mandates in good faith and have eliminated vestiges of past discrimination "to the extent practicable."[53] In making this determination, the district court on remand was directed to assess the six factors identified in *Green* (i.e., student, faculty, and staff assignments; transportation; extracurricular activities; and facilities). The lower court also was instructed to reconsider whether current residential segregation in Oklahoma City was the result of private decision making and economics or a vestige of prior school segregation.

Although the *Dowell* decision gave districts hope to eventually end judicial supervision, many districts have had difficulty proving that they were unitary.[54]

---

[52]890 F.2d 1483 (10th Cir. 1989).

[53]Bd. of Educ. v. Dowell, 498 U.S. 237, 249–250 (1991).

[54]*Compare* Lee v. Talladega County Bd. of Educ., 963 F.2d 1426 (11th Cir. 1992) (ending judicial supervision) *with* Lee v. Etowah County Bd. of Educ., 963 F.2d 1416 (11th Cir. 1992) (continuing judicial supervision).

Courts have not agreed on how long a district must be in compliance prior to ending court supervision and whether all *Green* criteria had to be met simultaneously. Then, in 1992 the Supreme Court clarified several related issues in a Georgia case, *Freeman v. Pitts*. In *Freeman*, the Court purported that a district court must relinquish its supervision and control over those aspects of a school system in which there has been compliance with a desegregation decree even if other aspects of the decree have not been met. Through this approach the Court sought to restore to state and local authorities control over public schools at the earliest possible date and noted that "[p]artial relinquishment of judicial control . . . can be an important and significant step in fulfilling the district court's duty to return the operations and control of schools to local authorities."[55] To guide the lower courts in determining whether supervision should be removed, the Court identified three questions:

- Has there been full and satisfactory compliance with the decree in those aspects of the system where supervision is to be withdrawn?
- Is the retention of judicial control necessary or practicable to achieve compliance with the decree in other facets of the school system?
- Has the district demonstrated good faith commitment to the court's entire decree and relevant provisions of federal law?

With this guidance, numerous districts have been able to show that they have achieved a unitary operation. In 2001, the Seventh Circuit released an Illinois school district from an extensive lower court order requiring the expenditure of over $238 million. The schools were found to be desegregated, and although advanced elective courses enrolled proportionately more majority than minority students, there was no proof that such imbalance was caused by discrimination, past or present.[56] Similarly, the Eleventh Circuit supported the position that Hillsborough County, Florida, schools were unitary notwithstanding the current demographic imbalance that the court reasoned could not be assumed to be due to prior *de jure* segregation.[57] Unitary status also was recognized in a number of additional cases, including those from Duval County, Florida; Charlotte-Mecklenburg, North Carolina; Muscogee County, Georgia; Russell County, Alabama; and Auburn, Alabama.[58]

In contrast, the Eighth Circuit refused to release the Little Rock School District, although noting the district's involvement in desegregation since 1956, a highly

---

[55]503 U.S. 467, 489 (1992).

[56]People Who Care v. Rockford Bd. of Educ., 246 F.3d 1073 (7th Cir. 2001).

[57]Manning v. Sch. Bd., 244 F.3d 927 (11th Cir. 2001).

[58]NAACP, Jacksonville Branch v. Duval County Sch., 273 F.3d 960 (11th Cir. 2001); Belk v. Charlotte-Mecklenburg Bd. of Educ., 269 F.3d 305 (4th Cir. 2001); Lockett v. Bd. of Educ., 111 F.3d 839 (11th Cir. 1997); Lee v. Russell County Bd. of Educ., No. 70-T-848-E, 2002 U.S. Dist. LEXIS 4075 (M.D. Ala. Feb. 25, 2002); Lee v. Auburn City Bd. of Educ., No. 70-T-851-E, 2002 U.S. Dist. LEXIS 2527 (M.D. Ala. Feb. 14, 2002). Others, however, were not released from judicial supervision. *See, e.g.*, Jenkins v. Missouri, 216 F.3d 720 (8th Cir. 2000); Liddell v. Special Sch. Louis County, 149 F.3d 862 (8th Cir. 1998); Brown v. Bd. of Educ., 978 F.2d 585 (10th Cir. 1992), *vacated and remanded*, 503 U.S. 978 (1992).

detailed district court order that appeared to go beyond the scope of the voluntary agreement, and the fact that plaintiff failed to show that prior *de jure* segregation was causally linked to the achievement gap between African American and Caucasian students.[59] The court reasoned that continued court supervision was necessary to ensure that the school district complied with the voluntary agreement it had knowingly entered in an effort to address the historically low academic achievement of African American students. The agreement went beyond what the court could order, but nonetheless became a financial obligation (i.e., "a promise made is a debt unpaid").[60]

Postunitary Transfer and School Assignment

Litigation will not end simply because the school district has achieved unitary status and has initially been relieved of judicial control and supervision. Any decision that may even potentially result in racial imbalance, whether *de jure* or *de facto*, is likely to be challenged. Accordingly, the placement of a new school or the creation of a new school district will foreseeably be scrutinized,[61] as will policies regarding school transfer, initial school assignment, open enrollment, or charter schools. However, a transfer policy that results in only an insignificant change in minority-majority enrollment within the district will not typically justify reasserting judicial supervision.[62]

Furthermore, students have challenged school district policies that were designed and administered to maintain the racial balance accomplished through years of court supervision, integrate *de facto* segregated communities, or achieve the goal of a diverse student body. In such instances, students generally were permitted to enroll in schools where their race was a minority or otherwise underrepresented, but not vice versa. Given the use of race, numerous cases have been filed, with courts rendering mixed opinions.[63] Guidance for lower courts began to emerge in 2003 when the Supreme Court, in *Grutter v. Bollinger*,[64] permitted a law school to consider race as one of several factors in determining the composition of its first-year class. In denying the plaintiff's race-based Fourteenth Amendment claim, the Court majority identified a compelling interest (i.e., the benefits derived from a diverse student

[59]Little Rock Sch. Dist. v. N. Little Rock, 451 F.3d 528 (8th Cir. 2006).

[60]*Id.* at 541.

[61]*See, e.g.,* Anderson v. Canton Mun. Separate Sch. Dist., 232 F.3d 450 (5th Cir. 2000); Valley v. United States, 173 F.3d 944 (5th Cir. 1999).

[62]United States v. Texas, 457 F.3d 472 (5th Cir. 2006).

[63]*Compare* Eisenberg v. Montgomery County Pub. Schs., 197 F.3d 123 (4th Cir. 1999) (concluding that a race-based transfer plan used to determine enrollment in a magnet school with an enriched curriculum violated the Fourteenth Amendment even if diversity qualified as a compelling state interest, as the action of the board was not narrowly tailored) *with* Brewer v. W. Irondequoit Cent. Sch. Dist., 212 F.3d 738 (2d Cir. 2000) (concluding that plaintiff had not demonstrated a likelihood of success as the state had a compelling interest in its use of racial classifications to reduce racial isolation and *de facto* segregation).

[64]539 U.S. 306 (2003). Since *Grutter*, Michigan voters amended the state constitution to prohibit the consideration of race in making admissions decisions—Mich. Const. Art. I, § 26. This law has been unsuccessfully challenged. *See* Coal. to Defend Affirmative Action v. Granholm, 473 F.3d 237 (6th Cir. 2006).

body) and reasoned that the school's admission procedures were sufficiently narrowly tailored not to adversely affect the rights of rejected Caucasian applicants.[65]

With *Grutter* as justification, if not incentive, school districts[66] once again are considering race in making placement decisions, but this time with the motive to integrate rather than segregate. Nonetheless, numerous questions remain concerning the legality of such practices. A partial answer was provided in a 2007 Supreme Court decision, *Parents Involved in Community Schools v. Seattle School District No. 1*. The plurality opinion identified an Equal Protection Clause violation where both the Seattle, Washington, and Jefferson County, Kentucky, school districts relied on race to determine school assignment, once residence and availability of space were considered.[67] Seattle had never been found guilty of *de jure* segregation or been subjected to court-ordered desegregation, while Jefferson County had its court order dissolved in 2000 after it had eliminated the vestiges of prior segregation to the greatest extent practicable.

The Court reasoned that each district's diversity plan relied on race in a nonindividualized mechanical way even though other means were available to address integration goals of the *de facto* segregated communities. The plans were neither race neutral nor narrowly tailored. Moreover, they were not designed to result in the achievement of broad-based student diversity, but rather were created to address the racial balancing of whites and nonwhites in Seattle and blacks and "others" in Jefferson County.

Although both of these race-based programs were disallowed, only four justices (Roberts, Alito, Scalia, Thomas) appear to foreclose the use of race in making placement decisions where there has been no proven history of race discrimination. The fifth member of the plurality opinion (Kennedy) and the justices in the minority (Breyer, Ginsburg, Souter, Stevens) are willing to consider a school district's use of race in making student assignments even in *de facto* segregated school districts, assuming such practices address a compelling interest (i.e., diversity) and are narrowly tailored. Accordingly, expect to see continued growth in the number of cases regarding student assignment, as school districts go beyond complying with court-ordered desegregation plans and attempt to identify narrowly tailored means to achieve diversity.

Race as a Factor in Admission to Private Schools

When private schools use race as a factor to determine admission, only Title VI and 42 U.S.C. Section 1981 at the federal level will apply, in addition to any related state

---

[65]For a critical review of this opinion, *see* Stephen B. Thomas, "Grutter v. Bollinger: The Supreme Court Missed a Stitch," *UCEA Review*, vol. XLVI, no. 1 (2004), pp. 14–17.

[66]At the university level since *Grutter, see also* Smith v. Univ. of Wash., 392 F.3d 367 (9th Cir. 2004) (upholding the consideration of race and ethnicity as factors in the university's admissions program).

[67]127 S. Ct. 2738 (2007). This case aggregated the claims from Parents Involved in Cmty. Sch. v. Seattle Sch. Dist., No. 1, 426 F.3d 1162 (9th Cir. 2005) and McFarland v. Jefferson County Pub. Schs., 416 F.3d 513 (6th Cir. 2005).

laws or local ordinances. Title VI forbids race discrimination but applies only to those schools that receive federal financial assistance. On the other hand, Section 1981 prohibits both race and ethnicity discrimination in entering into and fulfilling contracts and requires compliance of all public and private schools, regardless whether they qualify as recipients of federal aid. The seminal case applying this law to a private education setting is *Runyon v. McCrary,* in which the Supreme Court held that Section 1981 was violated when private school administrators rejected all applicants to their school who were not Caucasian.[68] The Court concluded that the practice violated the right to contract due to race, and purported that its ruling violated neither parents' privacy rights nor their freedom of association.

Notwithstanding, the Ninth Circuit in 2006 found no Section 1981 violation where a private school in Hawaii founded by the descendents of King Kamehameha I denied admission to an applicant because he was not of Hawaiian ancestry. In fact, only one non-Hawaiian had previously been admitted, given the highly unusual situation that year where the pool of Hawaiian applicants was one less than the number of available openings.[69] Students were required to pay a modest tuition, thus establishing a contract. In rendering its decision permitting continued use of race in making admission decisions and distinguishing the present case from *Runyon*, the court reasoned that:

- The preference was remedial in nature in that it was targeted to assist native Hawaiian students who were performing less well academically than all other classes of students;
- Non-Hawaiian applicants did not have their rights unnecessarily trammeled or face an absolute bar to their advancement—other schools were available that provided adequate education for non-Hawaiians; and
- The preference was limited—first, when the number of openings exceeds the number of Hawaiian applicants, non-Hawaiians will be admitted; second, the preference will last only long enough to remedy the current educational effects of past, private, and government-sponsored discrimination as well as existing social and economic deprivation.

The next decade should continue to provide ample case law dealing with racial preference. Future cases are likely to be similar to those litigated over the past few years and will continue to identify a new class of victims (i.e., those not Hawaiian, African American, etc., depending on the target of affirmative action).

Race Discrimination and Matriculated Students

Although there are a number of laws that prohibit race discrimination in educational settings, there is no doubt that discrimination continues, although likely to be more subtle and therefore difficult to prove than in prior years. Such discrimination has

[68]427 U.S. 160 (1976).

[69]Doe v. Kamehameha Schs., 470 F.3d 827 (9th Cir. 2006), *cert. dismissed*, 127 S. Ct. 2160 (2007).

been alleged in such areas as the assignment to ability-based courses or programs (e.g., gifted, advanced, developmental);[70] athletic eligibility;[71] racial profiling;[72] academic dismissal from special programs;[73] sexual harassment and molestation;[74] the creation of a hostile environment;[75] and the like.

In an exemplary case, an African American student was denied a temporary restraining order and preliminary injunction stopping school authorities from expelling him for the remainder of the current academic year (it was already May) plus the entire academic year that was to follow. On two separate occasions, the freshman brushed his teacher's buttocks with the back of his hand and made inappropriate sexual comments about her to other students. The district court upheld the punishment, notwithstanding some minor procedural violations, and found no evidence that the student had been discriminated against due to race.[76] The court also noted that the severity of the punishment was not extraordinary given the intimate touching and was necessary to ensure a safe learning environment.

Because claims of race discrimination against matriculated students are seldom litigated today, it is unclear the extent or frequency of violations. Nonetheless, from a school district perspective, it is prudent to establish a written policy prohibiting race and other forms of impermissible discrimination; inform educators and staff of their individual responsibilities; promptly and thoroughly investigate claims of impropriety; conduct fair and impartial hearings; and determine an appropriate response (e.g., suspension of a student, termination of an employee) for those who have engaged in discriminatory behavior.

Classifications Based on Native Language

Among the numerous identifiable "classes" of students in American schools are "linguistic minorities," some of whom have been denied an adequate education due to the failure of the school district to address their language barriers through appropriate instruction. Although programs that are designed to meet the educational needs of

---

[70]*See, e.g.*, Hobson v. Hansen, 269 F. Supp. 401 (D.D.C. 1967), *aff'd sub nom.* Smuck v. Hobson, 408 F.2d 175 (D.C. Cir. 1969).

[71]*See, e.g.*, Allen-Sherrod v. Henry County Sch. Dist., 248 Feb. Appx. 145 (11th Cir. 2007).

[72]*See, e.g.*, Carthans v. Jenkins, No. 04 C 4528, 2005 U.S. Dist. LEXIS 23294 (N.D. Ill. Oct. 6, 2005).

[73]*See, e.g.*, Brewer v. Bd. of Trs. of Univ. of Ill., 479 F.3d 908 (7th Cir. 2007) (finding no discrimination and identifying no comparable student of another race who had ever been retained with a grade point average lower than plaintiff's who did not have extraordinarily compelling circumstances).

[74]Doe v. Smith, 470 F.3d 331 (7th Cir. 2006).

[75]Qualls v. Cunningham, 183 Fed. Appx. 564 (7th Cir. 2006) (finding no support for the claim that school officials had created a racially hostile environment that caused plaintiff to receive poor grades and ultimately resulted in his academic dismissal).

[76]*See, e.g.*, Brown v. Plainfield Cmty. Consol. Dist. 202, 500 F. Supp. 2d 996 (N.D. Ill. 2007).

linguistic minorities are largely financed through state and local funds, the federal government provides modest funding for research regarding how students learn a second language, how to train instructors, and the effectiveness of alternative teaching methodologies and programs.[77] The Office of English Language Acquisition administers the grant programs, provides leadership and technical assistance, coordinates services, promotes best practice, and assesses outcomes. Through efforts such as these, many students today are provided with English language instruction that allows them to benefit from the public school curriculum. However, when access to school is denied or when language barriers are not removed,[78] students often turn to federal courts for protection. The rights of linguistic minorities are protected by the Fourteenth Amendment,[79] Title VI of the Civil Rights Act of 1964, and the Equal Educational Opportunities Act of 1974 (EEOA).

Title VI stipulates that "[n]o person in the United States shall, on the ground of race, color, or national origin, be excluded from participation in, be denied the benefits of, or be subjected to discrimination under any program or activity receiving [f]ederal financial assistance from the Department of Education."[80] Moreover, this statute requires compliance throughout a school district if *any* activity is supported by federal funds (e.g., special education). Discrimination against linguistic minorities is considered a form of national origin discrimination and is therefore prohibited by Title VI.

In addition, the EEOA requires public school systems to develop appropriate programs for limited English proficient (LEP) students.[81] The act mandates in part that "[n]o state shall deny equal educational opportunity to an individual on account of his or her race, color, sex, or national origin, by . . . the failure by an educational agency to take appropriate action to overcome language barriers that impede equal participation by its students in its instructional program."[82] The EEOA does not impose any specific type of instruction or teaching methodology on education agencies but rather requires "appropriate action."[83]

In the only United States Supreme Court decision involving the rights of LEP students, *Lau v. Nichols*, Chinese children asserted that the San Francisco public schools failed to provide for the needs of non-English-speaking students. The

---

[77]20 U.S.C. §§ 3420, 3423d, 6931, 6932 (2007).

[78]Most bilingual and ESL programs are intended to eliminate foreign language barriers. As a result, there have been times when students speaking minority English dialects or American Sign Language have been denied specialized language services. *See, e.g.*, Kielbus v. New York City Bd. of Educ., 140 F. Supp. 2d 284 (E.D.N.Y. 2001) (sign language); Martin Luther King Junior Elementary Sch. Children v. Ann Arbor Sch. Dist. Bd., 473 F. Supp. 1371 (E.D. Mich. 1979) (black English).

[79]*Strict scrutiny* is applied when the acts are facially discriminatory; *intent* is required when the acts are facially neutral (e.g., when tests administered only in English are used to determine enrollment in gifted programs).

[80]42 U.S.C. § 2000d *et seq.* (2007). Regulations may be found at 34 C.F.R. § 100 *et seq.* (2007).

[81]20 U.S.C. § 1701 *et seq.* (2007).

[82]20 U.S.C. § 1703(f) (2007).

[83]*See, e.g.*, Flores v. Arizona, 172 F. Supp. 2d 1225 (D. Ariz. 2000).

Supreme Court agreed with the students and held that the lack of sufficient remedial English instruction violated Title VI. The Court reasoned that equality of treatment was not realized merely by providing students with the same facilities, textbooks, teachers, and curriculum, and that requiring children to acquire English skills on their own before they could hope to make any progress in school made "a mockery of public education."[84] The Court emphasized that "basic English skills are at the very core of what these public schools teach," and, therefore, "students who do not understand English are effectively foreclosed from any meaningful education."[85]

As a rule, courts acknowledge that there are numerous legitimate educational theories and practices that may be used to eliminate language barriers and do not typically require one method over another. In fact, they tend to order the use of bilingual education (often the method preferred by plaintiffs) only when less expensive and less cumbersome options have proven ineffective.[86] In making such determinations, courts will examine the level of resources committed to the various programs, the competency and training of the instructors, the methods of classifying students for instruction, and the procedures for evaluating student progress.

A Colorado federal district court, in assessing compliance of the Denver public schools, concluded that the law does not require a full bilingual education program for every LEP student but does place a duty on the district to take action to eliminate barriers that prevent LEP children from participating in the educational program. Good faith effort is inadequate. What is required, according to the court, is an effort that "will be reasonably effective in producing intended results."[87] Such an effort was not found in the Denver public schools. Although a transitional bilingual program was selected by district personnel, it was not being implemented effectively, primarily due to poor teacher training, selection, and assignment. Accordingly, an EEOA violation was found. Likewise, the Seventh Circuit, in examining Illinois's compliance, argued that "appropriate action" under the law certainly means more than "no action."[88] Once again, the court found that the selection of transitional bilingual education was appropriate, but that it had not been effectively implemented. The court identified both an EEOA violation and a violation of Title VI regulations.

In contrast, a California school district's Spanish bilingual program and three forms of English as a Second Language were judicially endorsed. District teachers were found to be proficient, qualified, and experienced; native-language academic support was available for 38 languages in all subjects; and a cultural enrichment program was operating for kindergarten through grade 3. Plaintiffs claimed a violation of the EEOA and Title VI and requested instruction in the students' native tongue. The court disagreed and found that the program was based on sound theory, implemented

[84]Lau v. Nichols, 414 U.S. 563, 566 (1974).

[85]*Id.*

[86]*See, e.g.*, Guadalupe Org. v. Tempe Elementary Sch. Dist. No. 3, 587 F.2d 1022 (9th Cir. 1978); Castaneda v. Pickard, 648 F.2d 989 (5th Cir. 1981).

[87]Keyes v. Sch. Dist. No. 1, 576 F. Supp. 1503, 1520 (D. Colo. 1983).

[88]Gomez v. Ill. State Bd. of Educ., 811 F.2d 1030, 1043 (7th Cir. 1987).

consistent with that theory, and produced satisfactory results (i.e., area LEP students were learning at rates equal to or higher than their English-speaking counterparts).[89]

California has generated a significant amount of case law involving the instruction of non- and limited-English speaking students. Many suits attack Proposition 227, which requires that all children within public schools be taught English through "sheltered English immersion" (SEI). This approach requires the use of specially designed materials and procedures where "nearly all" classroom instruction is in English. In most instances, the law requires school districts to abandon their use of bilingual education. Notwithstanding the prior use of bilingual programming, immigrant children within the state had experienced a high dropout rate and were low in English literacy. Only those children who already possess good English language skills or those for whom an alternate course of study would be better suited may be excused from the SEI initiative. Even then, 20 or more exempted students per grade level are required before an alternative program such as bilingual education needs to be provided.

To ensure that the SEI approach is used, the state legislature included a *parental enforcement provision* in the law which gives parents the right to sue to receive SEI instruction, as well as for actual damages and attorneys' fees. Any educator who willfully and repeatedly refuses to teach "overwhelmingly" in English may be held personally liable. The state teachers' association attacked this provision as being unconstitutionally vague. But the Ninth Circuit found terms such as "nearly all" and "overwhelmingly" to be no more vague than other descriptive terms used in the writing of statutes and reasoned that such language was likely to chill only a negligible amount of non-English speech, if any.[90]

Another type of national origin/language discrimination was alleged in Kansas where the principal and several teachers prohibited students from speaking Spanish while on school grounds.[91] Following his suspension for speaking Spanish, a student claimed Fourteenth Amendment, Section 1983, and Title VI violations. The court dismissed the Fourteenth Amendment and Section 1983 claims against the school district, as the district could not be vicariously liable under *respondeat superior* because the principal and teachers were not final decision makers—such authority was held by the school board and could not be delegated. Similar claims against individual defendants also were dismissed, as the educators were entitled to qualified immunity. Moreover, the plaintiff failed to establish that there was a clearly established right to speak a foreign language while at a public school. In spite of the above, the court refused to dismiss the plaintiff's Title VI claim, given the disparate impact the practice had on Hispanic students.

In light of the significant growth of Hispanic and other populations immigrating to the United States, expect growth in this area of litigation. Claims of discrimination as well as controversies about appropriate programming should become increasingly common, particularly within southern border states.

[89]Teresa P. v. Berkeley Unified Sch. Dist., 724 F. Supp. 698 (N.D. Cal. 1989).

[90]Cal. Teachers Ass'n v. State Bd. of Educ., 271 F.3d 1141 (9th Cir. 2001).

[91]Rubio v. Turner Unified Sch. Dist. No. 202, 453 F. Supp. 2d 1295 (D. Kan. 2006).

Classifications Based on Ability or Achievement

Courts have generally upheld decisions related to grade placement, denial of promotion, and assignment to instructional groups. Ability grouping purportedly permits more effective and efficient teaching by allowing teachers to concentrate their efforts on students with similar needs. Grouping according to ability or achievement is permissible, although there have been challenges concerning the use of standardized intelligence and achievement tests for determining pupil placements in regular classes and special education programs. These suits have alleged that such tests are racially and culturally biased and that their use to classify or track pupils results in erroneous placements that stigmatize children. Other challenges have arisen regarding the rights of gifted and talented students to an appropriate education.

Tracking Schemes

In the most widely publicized case pertaining to ability grouping, *Hobson v. Hansen*, the use of standardized intelligence test scores to place elementary and secondary students in various ability tracks in Washington, D.C., was attacked as unconstitutional.[92] Plaintiffs contended that some children were incorrectly assigned to lower tracks and had very little chance of advancing to higher ones because of the limited curriculum and lack of remedial instruction. The federal district court examined the test scores used to track students, analyzed the accuracy of the test measurements, and concluded that mistakes often resulted from placing pupils on this basis. For the first time, a federal court evaluated testing methods and held that they discriminated against minority children. In prohibiting the continued use of such test scores, the court emphasized that it was not abolishing the use of tracking systems per se and reasoned that "[w]hat is at issue here is not whether defendants are entitled to provide different kinds of students with different kinds of education."[93] The court noted that classifications reasonably related to educational purposes are constitutionally permissible unless they result in discrimination against identifiable groups of children.

The Fifth Circuit agreed with this latter point in its evaluation of a tracking scheme in Jackson, Mississippi.[94] Although the court had previously struck down the plan given its impact on integration efforts, it later noted that "as a general rule, school systems are free to employ ability grouping, even when such a policy has a segregative effect, so long . . . as such a practice is genuinely motivated by educational concerns and not discriminatory motives."[95]

[92]269 F. Supp. 401 (D.D.C. 1967), *aff'd sub nom.* Smuck v. Hobson, 408 F.2d 175 (D.C. Cir. 1969). Because ability grouping based on various forms of assessment (usually testing) is facially neutral, the appropriate Fourteenth Amendment standard is *intent*. Meeting this standard of review has been difficult, particularly when cases also do not involve *de jure* segregation.

[93]*Hobson*, 269 F. Supp. at 511.

[94]Singleton v. Jackson Mun. Separate Sch. Dist., 419 F.2d 1211 (5th Cir. 1969).

[95]Castaneda v. Pickard, 648 F.2d 989, 996 (5th Cir. 1981).

Based on evidence indicating that ability grouping provided better educational opportunities for African American students, the Eleventh Circuit upheld grouping practices in several Georgia school districts even though they had not achieved desegregated status.[96] Ability grouping allowed resources to be targeted toward low-achieving students and resulted in both gains on statewide tests and the reassignment of many students to higher-level achievement groups. The court further noted that, unlike students in earlier cases, these students had not attended inferior segregated schools. School systems undergoing desegregation may be subjected to closer judicial review when implementing ability grouping, but such plans will be prohibited only if found to be a ploy to resegregate or discriminate.[97]

When children are evaluated and provided with appropriate programs or grouped by ability, it is essential that all testing instruments be reliable, valid, and unbiased to the extent practical and possible. Although a few courts have found some tests to include specific questions that are racially biased[98] or administered in discriminatory ways (e.g., not in the student's native language or other mode of communication), such cases occur far less often today. Test developers have made extensive efforts to improve the reliability and validity of their instruments and to remove known forms of cultural, ethnic, and racial bias. As a result, it is unlikely that a nationally normed and marketed test used to measure ability or aptitude will be found racially biased. Nonetheless, prudent educators should take every precaution to ensure that accurate assessments are employed; only qualified personnel are hired; tests are administered in a nondiscriminatory manner; multiple criteria are used in determining an appropriate track or placement; and test results are used in good faith. Care also should be taken to ensure that teachers do not discriminate against students assigned to lower tracks or develop stereotypes about their abilities or potential.[99]

Gifted and Talented Students

Often overlooked when identifying unique needs and providing appropriate programs are those students labeled as "gifted" or "talented." Included within these populations are students who give evidence of high performance capability in areas such as intellectual, creative, artistic, or leadership capacity, or in specific academic fields. Over the years, the federal government has provided only limited aid for gifted education, and there is no federal statute specifying substantive rights for the gifted as there is for children with disabilities. What funds that have been made available have

---

[96]Ga. State Conference of Branches of NAACP v. Georgia, 775 F.2d 1403 (11th Cir. 1985).

[97]*See, e.g.,* Bester v. Tuscaloosa City Bd. of Educ., 722 F.2d 1514 (11th Cir. 1984). *See also* Holton v. City of Thomasville Sch. Dist., 425 F.3d 1325 (11th Cir. 2005) (remanding with instructions to assess whether the tracking scheme employed by the school district is based on the present results of past segregation or is designed to remedy such results through better educational opportunities).

[98]*See* Larry P. v. Riles, 495 F. Supp. 926 (N.D. Cal. 1979), *aff'd,* 793 F.2d 969 (9th Cir. 1984).

[99]*See, e.g.,* United States v. City of Yonkers, 197 F.3d 41 (2d Cir. 1999).

been used to establish preservice and in-service training for personnel; develop and operate model projects and exemplary programs; strengthen the capability of state educational agencies and institutions of higher education to provide leadership and assistance; provide technical assistance and information dissemination; carry out research; and conduct evaluations.

Given a limited federal role, rights for gifted and talented students are based overwhelmingly on state law or local school board policy. A few states meet the needs of such children in much the same way that the Individuals with Disabilities Education Act addresses the needs of children with disabilities—that is, through an individualized plan of instruction. Other states provide a spattering of programs throughout the state or offer selected accelerated courses. A few states, however, have not even counted the number of gifted students residing within their boundaries, nor have they agreed on definitions for identifying qualified youth; the appropriate instruments or cut-off scores to be used in assessment; the depth, duration, or delivery of an appropriate curriculum; or the procedures to regulate admissions in light of court-ordered integration mandates.[100]

Pennsylvania, one of the leading states in mandating programs for the gifted, includes gifted and talented students under its designation of "exceptional children" who "deviate from the average in physical, mental, emotional or social characteristics to such an extent that they require special educational facilities or services."[101] The Pennsylvania Supreme Court interpreted this law as placing a mandatory obligation on school districts to establish individualized programs for gifted students beyond the general enrichment program.[102] However, the court qualified its interpretation of state statute by observing that the law does not require "exclusive individual programs outside or beyond the district's existing, regular, and special education curricular offerings"[103] and does not impose a duty to maximize a child's potential. Given this precedent, when the parents of a gifted child demanded reimbursement for college tuition, the board was within its authority to deny the request.[104] The board had never agreed to pay for the courses and had provided the student with advanced programming, permission to be away from school during his college courses, and independent study.

[100]*See, e.g.,* Manning v. Sch. Bd., 24 F. Supp. 2d 1277 (M.D. Fla. 1998).

[101]Pa. Stat. Ann. tit. 24 § 13-1371(1) (2007).

[102]Centennial Sch. Dist. v. Commonwealth Dep't of Educ., 539 A.2d 785 (Pa. 1988).

[103]Centennial Sch. Dist., 539 A.2d at 791. *See also* Saucon Valley Sch. Dist. v. Robert O., 785 A.2d 1069 (Pa. Commw. Ct. 2001) (determining that a hearing panel exceeded its authority when it ordered that a gifted student should be placed in the graduating class before his own, given that the district had failed to provide him with accelerated and enriched programming).

[104]New Brighton Area Sch. Dist. v. Matthew Z., 697 A.2d 1056 (Pa. Commw. Ct. 1997). *See also* Brownsville Area Sch. Dist. v. Student X, 729 A.2d 198 (Pa. Commw. Ct. 1999) (determining that college courses and other education beyond the current offerings of the district did not have to be provided to a gifted student).

A similar case was filed in California, where the parents of an "extremely" gifted child under the age of 16 sued the state to require it to pay for their child's postsecondary college education.[105] The parents argued that the state was responsible for providing children with a free public education and that a program should be tailored to meet his special needs, as is done for students with disabilities. A California appeals court disagreed and identified no federal or state law that obligated the state to pay for the college education of its children, even if within compulsory school age.

Parental demands for individualized programming designed to meet their child's special needs also emanated from parents in Connecticut. A gifted student claimed to have the right to individualized education under state statute, given that gifted children were included within the state definition of exceptional children (i.e., those who do not progress effectively in a regular school program without special education). The local school board refused to provide the program and the student filed suit. The Supreme Court of Connecticut disagreed with the student's claim and held that he was not entitled to special education, that the state never intended to extend such a right, and that special education must be provided only for students with disabilities. No equal protection violation was proven because the state's action of serving individuals with disabilities, but not the gifted, met rational basis scrutiny.[106]

Along these same lines, New York law stipulates that school districts *should* develop programs to assist gifted students in achieving their full potential. However, an appellate court found that the use of the word *should* indicated that the development of gifted programs was optional, not mandatory.[107] Consequently, the court held that a district was permitted to serve only a portion of the students identified as gifted and to select those students through a lottery system. Although use of a lottery may seem illogical, it provides an equal opportunity for each qualified youth to participate and does not illegally discriminate.

The procedures used to select students who are to participate in gifted programs continue to be challenged. Criteria such as intelligence, test scores, grade point average, and teacher evaluations are used in the selection process. Although under certain circumstances age may be a permissible criterion for admission (see discussion below), sex and race will seldom be permitted unless court ordered.[108] Even then, the court must determine that procedures are narrowly tailored, with any advantage or preference to last only long enough to address prior discrimination.

---

[105]Levi v. O'Connell, 50 Cal. Rptr. 3d 691 (App. Ct. 2006).

[106]Broadley v. Bd. of Educ., 639 A.2d 502 (Conn. 1994).

[107]Bennett v. City Sch. Dist., 497 N.Y.S.2d 72 (App. Div. 1985).

[108]Rosenfeld v. Montgomery County Pub. Schs., 25 Fed. Appx. 123 (4th Cir. 2001) (affirming dismissal of case as the plaintiff eventually was admitted to the gifted program; the court acknowledged, however, that if different, less stringent selection criteria had been used for minority students, the plaintiff would have had a basis for seeking damages).

Classifications Based on Age

Age is one of the factors most commonly used to classify individuals, not only in schools but also in society. For example, a specified age is used as a prerequisite to obtaining a driver's license, buying alcoholic beverages, viewing certain movies, and receiving federal benefits. The two primary federal grounds used by students when they claim age-based violations are the Fourteenth Amendment[109] and the Age Discrimination Act of 1975,[110] which applies to recipients of federal financial assistance. The Age Discrimination Act is seldom used today, and when a violation is claimed it generally is directed toward a college or university (e.g., a claim that age was used as a basis to deny admission[111]) rather than toward PK–12 schools. The few cases that have been filed against elementary and secondary schools tend to concentrate in the areas of early school admission or eligibility for advanced programs or activities.[112]

Ranges vary, but within most states students must attend school between the ages of 6 and 16 and may attend between 3 and 21. Students below or above state-established age limits have neither a state property right nor a federal constitutional right to public school attendance. Nevertheless, parents have challenged state and local decisions denying admission or services. In a Texas case, a policy was challenged that excluded children under the age of 6 as of September 1 of the current year from admission to the first grade.[113] The plaintiff had completed kindergarten in a private accredited school and had scored well on a standardized test, but was two months too young to qualify. The district had uniformly adhered to the state statute and local policy, refusing all requests for early admission. Noting this uniform application, the Texas Court of Appeals upheld the school district's action.

Similar decisions have been reached by other courts in denying students admission to kindergarten and other programs.[114] Rationales used to justify the consideration of age include the state's right to limit the benefit of public education and related curricular and extracurricular opportunities to children between specific ages, the administrative need to project enrollment, the costs of assessing learning readiness,

---

[109]Under the Fourteenth Amendment, rational basis scrutiny is required in age cases in which the policy or practice is facially discriminatory, and intent must be shown where the act is facially neutral.

[110]42 U.S.C. §§ 6101 *et seq.* (2007).

[111]*See, e.g.*, Homola v. S. Ill. Univ. at Carbondale, Sch. of Law, No. 93-1940, 1993 U.S. App. LEXIS 34465 (7th Cir. Dec. 16, 1993); Giuffria v. La. State Univ., No. 04-458 § "A" (2), 2006 U.S. Dist. LEXIS 1159 (E.D. La. Jan. 9, 2006).

[112]*See, e.g.*, Wieker v. Mesa County Valley Sch. Dist. #51, No. 05-cv-806-WYD-CBS, 2007 U.S. Dist. LEXIS 11956 (D. Col., Feb. 21, 2007) (granting summary judgment to the school district where an athlete claimed she had been dismissed from the team because of her age).

[113]Wright v. Ector County Indep. Sch. Dist., 867 S.W.2d 863 (Tex. Ct. App. 1993). *See also* Morrison v. Chi. Bd. of Educ., 544 N.E.2d 1099 (Ill. App. Ct. 1989) (holding that local board had discretion whether to assess a child to determine readiness to attend kindergarten).

[114]*See, e.g.*, Zweifel v. Joint Dist. No. 1, Belleville, 251 N.W.2d 822 (Wis. 1977); O'Leary v. Wisecup, 364 A.2d 770 (Pa. Commw. Ct. 1976).

the difficulty of meeting a wide range of individual needs, and the desire for children to develop emotionally, socially, and physiologically prior to admission.

In addition to admissions decisions, age also is permissibly used as one of several criteria to determine eligibility for special courses or programs (e.g., college credit courses; gifted programs), selected activities (e.g., interscholastic sports[115]), or specialized services (e.g., those available to children with disabilities). With few exceptions (e.g., when interscholastic sports participation has been written into an overage student's individualized educational program), it is unlikely that schools will be restricted in their uniform application of legitimate age requirements. Where exceptions are made, school personnel must document a legal and permissible basis.

Classifications Based on Sex[116]

Classifications and discriminatory treatment based on sex[117] in public education are as old as public education itself, as the first public schools and colleges primarily served males. When women were eventually allowed to enroll, programs were typically segregated and inferior. Over the years, sex equality in public schools has improved, but at times classifications based on sex have limited both academic as well as extracurricular activities for females. Aggrieved parties often turn to federal courts to vindicate their rights. In most cases, plaintiffs allege a violation of either the Fourteenth Amendment[118] or Title IX of the Education Amendments of 1972.[119] Under Title IX, educational recipients of federal financial assistance are prohibited from discriminating, excluding, or denying benefits because of sex.[120]

In addition, Title IX has been interpreted to prohibit retaliation against both students and staff who themselves are not the target of intentional discrimination but are adversely treated due to their advocacy roles. The Supreme Court addressed this issue in 2005 in *Jackson v. Birmingham Board of Education*, where a teacher/coach was removed from his coaching position, allegedly due to his complaints about the treatment of the girls' basketball team (i.e., not receiving equal funding, equal access

---

[115]*See, e.g.*, Cruz v. Pa. Interscholastic Athletic Ass'n, 157 F. Supp. 2d 485 (E.D. Pa. 2001).

[116]"Sex" generally refers to having male or female reproductive systems, whereas "gender" generally refers to social identity related to one's sex.

[117]This section deals only with discrimination based on sex and does not include cases of alleged discrimination due to being homosexual, transsexual, etc. *See, e.g.*, C.N. v. Wolf, 410 F. Supp. 2d 894 (C.D. Cal. 2005) (same sex privacy); L.W. v. Toms River Reg'l Schs., 886 A.2d 1090 (N.J. Super. Ct. App. Div. 2005) (sexual orientation harassment).

[118]Under the Fourteenth Amendment, *intermediate scrutiny* is applied in sex-based cases where facial discrimination exists, while *intent* is used where facially neutral practices result in alleged discrimination.

[119]20 U.S.C. § 1681 (2007).

[120]If aid is received by any program or activity within the school system, compliance must be demonstrated districtwide. Also, although Title IX does not include a specific statute of limitations, the courts have elected to borrow the relevant limitations period for personal injury. *See, e.g.*, Stanley v. Trs. of Cal. State Univ., 433 F.3d 1129 (9th Cir. 2006) (identifying the appropriate limitations period to be one year).

to equipment and facilities, etc.).[121] The Court reasoned that discriminatory treatment against advocates was impliedly prohibited by Title IX and remanded the case for a determination of whether the coach's advocacy was in fact the motivating factor in his removal.

Interscholastic Sports

Sex discrimination litigation involving interscholastic sports has focused on two primary themes: the integration of single-sex teams and the unequal treatment of males and females. Although courts will issue injunctions to correct discriminatory conduct where it is found, they will not award monetary damages unless the school receives actual notice of the violation and then is shown to be deliberately indifferent to the claim.[122]

Single-Sex Teams.   One of the more controversial issues involving high school athletics is the participation of males and females together in contact sports (i.e., wrestling, rugby, ice hockey, football, basketball, and other sports that involve physical contact). Title IX explicitly permits separation of students by sex within contact sports. However, the Sixth Circuit has interpreted the act to give discretion to individual school districts, rather than athletic associations, to determine whether to allow coeducational participation in contact sports in their efforts to provide equal athletic opportunities for males and females.[123] Nonetheless, most school districts have elected to take the less controversial route and prohibit coeducational participation. When exclusion occurs, plaintiffs have no basis for suit under Title IX against either the school district or the athletic association. The explicit wording of the statute protects the school district, while the athletic association will not qualify as either a direct or indirect recipient of federal financial assistance, thereby exempting it from Title IX requirements.[124] This does not foreclose the athlete's opportunity to participate in coeducational contact sports, however, as suits still may be filed under the Fourteenth Amendment, where intermediate scrutiny is applied, regardless of the sex of the plaintiff.[125]

Although most athletic associations that regulate interscholastic competition are private corporations, the Supreme Court has found that they are entwined with their respective state governments and therefore are involved in state action.[126] As a

---

[121]544 U.S. 167 (2005). *See also* Burch v. Regents of the Univ. of Cal., 433 F. Supp. 2d 1110 (E.D. Cal. 2006) (denying summary judgment where a nonrenewed coach advocated for the rights of female wrestlers and claimed retaliation).

[122]Grandson v. Univ., 272 F.3d 568 (8th Cir. 2001).

[123]Yellow Springs Exempted Vill. Sch. Dist. v. Ohio High Sch. Athletic Ass'n, 647 F.2d 651 (6th Cir. 1981).

[124]*See* NCAA v. Smith, 525 U.S. 459 (1999).

[125]*See, e.g.*, Clark v. Arizona, 695 F.2d 1126 (9th Cir. 1982).

[126]Brentwood Acad. v. Tenn. Secondary Sch. Athletic Ass'n, 531 U.S. 288 (2001). *See* text accompanying note 135, Chapter 4.

result, athletes who are denied coeducational sports opportunities may sue both their public school district and the state athletic association for perceived constitutional violations. The Fourteenth Amendment does not necessarily require integration of contact sports, as it permits separate teams where such teams are found equal. But where separate teams are not available or are found unequal, school districts are required to allow the participation of female athletes on traditionally male teams, including those that involve contact.

A Fourteenth Amendment claim was proffered in a case heard by a federal district court in New York, when it reviewed a female student's request to try out for the junior varsity football squad.[127] The school district was unable to show that its policy of prohibiting mixed competition served an important governmental objective, as is required under intermediate scrutiny. In rejecting the district's assertion that its policy was necessary to ensure the health and safety of female students, the court noted that no female student was given the opportunity to show that she was as fit, or more fit, than the weakest male member of the team.

A Wisconsin federal district court similarly ruled that female students have the constitutional right to compete for positions on traditionally male contact teams, declaring that once a state provides interscholastic competition, such opportunities must be provided to all students on equal terms.[128] The court reasoned that the objective of preventing injury to female athletes was not sufficient to justify the prohibition of coeducational teams in contact sports. If school officials were reluctant to permit sex-integrated play, they had other options available—interscholastic competition in contact sports could be eliminated for all students or separate and equal teams for females could be established. But if comparable sex-segregated programs were provided, female athletes could not assert the right to try out for the male team simply because of its higher level of competition.

Where integration is either permitted or required in a contact sport, each athlete must receive a fair, nondiscriminatory opportunity to participate. In a 1999 case from North Carolina, a female kicker made the football team but was later dropped; she also was given only limited opportunities to participate or to condition. The Fourth Circuit concluded that where integration is permitted it may not be accompanied by sex discrimination; the court then remanded for a determination of whether the restrictions placed on the kicker were sex based.[129]

In addition to the controversies regarding coeducational participation in contact sports, there have been numerous challenges to policies denying integration of males and females in noncontact sports. Females filed the majority of these suits and prevailed in nearly every instance.[130] Title IX regulations explicitly require recipient

[127]Lantz v. Ambach, 620 F. Supp. 663 (S.D.N.Y. 1985). *See also* Adams v. Baker, 919 F. Supp. 1496 (D. Kan. 1996) (upholding female student's right under the Fourteenth Amendment to participate in wrestling).

[128]Leffel v. Wis. Interscholastic Athletic Ass'n, 444 F. Supp. 1117 (E.D. Wis. 1978).

[129]Mercer v. Duke Univ., 190 F.3d 643 (4th Cir. 1999).

[130]*See, e.g.*, Croteau v. Fair, 686 F. Supp. 552 (E.D. Va. 1988); Israel v. W. Va. Secondary Sch. Activities Comm'n, 388 S.E.2d 480 (W. Va. 1989).

districts to allow coeducational participation in those sports that are available only to one sex, presuming that athletic opportunities for that sex have been historically limited. Thus, females tend to succeed in their claims, whereas males tend to fail.[131] As a rule, school districts have been able to show an important governmental interest (e.g., redressing disparate athletic opportunities for females) in support of their decisions to exclude males from participating on teams traditionally reserved for females, while males have had difficulty supporting the claim that their athletic opportunities have been historically limited.

Fewer Sports Opportunities for Females.   Although athletic opportunities for females have significantly increased since passage of Title IX in 1972, equal opportunity has not been achieved within all school districts. State efforts to provide a greater number of opportunities for females have been weakened significantly by public education budgetary problems. Expenditures for special education, literacy, technology, smaller class size, school safety, and the like have been given priority when dividing a shrinking public purse. Given such financial constraints, equality of athletic opportunities for males and females often has been achieved either by reducing the number of sports traditionally available for males,[132] or by lowering the number of participants on boys' teams (e.g., football) to provide generally equal opportunities for males and females.[133] Also, efforts have been made to disguise the existing inequity (e.g., double counting participants in women's indoor and outdoor track, but not double counting men in fall/spring events such as track, golf, and tennis[134]) to avoid taking corrective action.

At times, female athletes have expressed an insufficient interest in a given sport to have it approved by the state athletic association. In a Kentucky case, high school athletes claimed a Title IX violation when the state athletic association refused to approve females' interscholastic fast-pitch softball. The association's decision was based on its policy of not sanctioning a sport unless at least 25 percent of its member institutions demonstrated an interest in participation. Since only 17 percent indicated an interest, approval was denied. In the original hearing on this controversy, the Sixth Circuit had held that the 25 percent requirement did not violate the Equal Protection Clause, as the facially neutral policy was not proven to entail intentional discrimination.[135] The case then was remanded and later appealed. The court again found no

---

[131]*See, e.g.*, Williams v. Sch. Dist., 998 F.2d 168 (3d Cir. 1993); Rowley v. Members of the Bd. of Educ., 863 F.2d 39 (10th Cir. 1988); B.C. v. Bd. of Educ., Cumberland Reg'l Sch. Dist., 531 A.2d 1059 (N.J. Super. Ct. App. Div. 1987).

[132]*See, e.g.*, Chalenor v. Univ. of N.D., 291 F.3d 1042 (8th Cir. 2002); Boulahanis v. Bd. of Regents, 198 F.3d 633 (7th Cir. 1999); Miami Univ. Wrestling Club v. Miami Univ., 195 F. Supp. 2d 1010 (S.D. Ohio 2001).

[133]Neal v. Bd. of Trs., 198 F.3d 763 (9th Cir. 1999).

[134]Miller v. Univ. of Cincinnati, No. 1:05-cv-764, 2007 U.S. Dist. LEXIS 70484 (S.D. Ohio Sept. 21, 2007).

[135]Horner v. Ky. High Sch. Athletic Ass'n, 43 F.3d 265 (6th Cir. 1994).

Title IX violation and further concluded that grouping sports by sex did not violate federal law. Moreover, the court resolved that the plaintiffs did not qualify for attorneys' fees because they did not prevail.[136] Plaintiffs had argued that since fast-pitch softball is now available in the state, they ultimately were the winning party. The court noted, however, that such relief was not court ordered and plaintiffs could not show that they were responsible for the change in state law directing the association to offer the requested sport.

In a higher education case, Brown University responded to budget cuts in 1991 by eliminating two interscholastic teams for men and two for women. At the time of the reductions, only 37 percent of the participants in varsity sports, compared to 48 percent of the institution's students, were women. By 1994, the ratio had not significantly changed. The First Circuit found a Title IX violation, concurring with the Office for Civil Rights' policy interpretation that for schools to be in compliance they should (1) provide interscholastic sports opportunities for both sexes in terms of numbers of participants that are substantially proportionate to the respective enrollments of male and female students, (2) show a history of expanding sports programs for the underrepresented sex, or (3) provide enough opportunities to match the sports interests and abilities of the underrepresented sex.[137] The court rejected the university's unproven assertion that female students were less interested in sports and viewed the comment as being based on a stereotypical view of women.

Modified Sports and Separate Seasons for Females. Among the equity claims initiated by female athletes are those contesting the use of sex-based modifications in sports. Although federal courts historically have permitted different rules for males and females (e.g., split-court rules for women's basketball[138]), differential treatment of male and female athletes cannot be justified by unfounded and unsupported perceptions about either sex regarding strength, endurance, or ability.

Also, maintaining separate playing seasons for female and male teams has been challenged as a violation of the equal protection clauses of both federal and state constitutions. In some instances, separate seasons have been upheld due to a lack of adequate facilities and general comparability of programs;[139] in other instances separate seasons have been found to violate equal protection rights. This was the case in Michigan where the Sixth Circuit upheld a lower court ruling concluding that the difficulty in finding facilities, coaches, and officials did not justify

[136]Horner v. Ky. High Sch. Athletic Ass'n, 206 F.3d 685 (6th Cir. 2000). *See also* Kelley v. Bd. of Trs., 35 F.3d 265 (7th Cir. 1994) (permitting the termination of men's swimming while retaining women's swimming).

[137]Cohen v. Brown Univ., 101 F.3d 155 (1st Cir. 1996). *See also* Pederson v. La. State Univ., 213 F.3d 858 (5th Cir. 2000) (concluding that university had violated Title IX by failing to accommodate the interests and abilities of female athletes).

[138]*Compare* Cape v. Tenn. Secondary Sch. Athletic Ass'n, 563 F.2d 793 (6th Cir. 1977) (permitting the use of split-court rules as they reflected physical differences between males and females) *with* Dodson v. Ark. Activities Ass'n, 468 F. Supp. 394 (E.D. Ark. 1979) (invalidating the use of separate basketball rules for males and females).

[139]*See, e.g.,* Ridgeway v. Mont. High Sch. Ass'n, 749 F. Supp. 1544 (D. Mont. 1990).

the use of separate seasons for males and females where the girls bore the burden of off-season participation.[140] The court opined that if single-sex seasons were in fact necessary, the burden must be shared. For example, the junior varsity teams of both sexes could be placed into the disadvantageous season; as a result, the varsity teams then could compete during the preferred time period. This plan would result in the same utilization of facilities and staff, yet the advantages and disadvantages of off-season play would be equally divided between the sexes.

This position also was subscribed to by the West Virginia high court when it held that the scheduling of the girls' basketball season outside the traditional season violated the state Equal Protection Clause.[141] Such a practice did not serve an important governmental interest and effectively excluded female athletes from interstate competition, disadvantaged them with regard to gaining access to college recruiters, limited their time in the gym to hot summer months, and resulted in reduced interest by the public and the media. The simple solution was to have both teams share facilities and play during the "regular" season when at all possible. When that was not feasible, alternating the season among male and female teams was found permissible, assuming that the burden was shouldered equally by both sexes.

Academic Programs

Allegations of sex bias in public schools have not been confined to athletic programs. Differential treatment of males and females in academic courses and schools also has generated litigation.[142] Because the "separate but equal" principle has been applied in cases alleging a Fourteenth Amendment violation, public school officials are required to show a substantial justification for classifications based on sex that are used to segregate or exclude either males or females in academic programs. In contrast, Title IX excludes elementary and secondary school admission policies from its coverage (i.e., the operation of a single-sex PK–12 school does not violate Title IX).[143] But, a recipient school district cannot use a single-sex admissions policy to deny a student, because of that student's sex, the opportunity to participate in or benefit from its total districtwide curriculum. Accordingly, if a single-sex school operates the only performing arts program in the district, officials are responsible for acquiring comparable programming elsewhere or for admitting the student of the excluded sex. The Department of Education prefers that when such sex-segregated programming is made available, it should be offered in a single-sex program (i.e., similar to the Fourteenth Amendment standard of separate but equal).[144] Legal issues related to single-sex schools, sex-segregated courses and programs, and sex-based admission criteria are reviewed below.

[140]Cmtys. for Equity v. Mich. High Sch. Athletic Ass'n, 459 F.3d 676 (6th Cir. 2006).

[141]State *ex rel.* Lambert v. W. Va. State Bd. of Educ., 447 S.E.2d 901 (W. Va. 1994).

[142]Gossett v. Oklahoma, 245 F.3d 1172 (10th Cir. 2001).

[143]34 C.F.R. § 106.15(d) (2007).

[144]*See* Office for Civil Rights, *Guidelines Regarding Single Sex Classes and Schools, 2005,* available at www.ed.gov/about/offices/list/ocr/t9-guidelines-ss.html.

Single-Sex Schools. The Third Circuit held that the operation of two historically sex-segregated public high schools (one for males, the other for females) in which enrollment is voluntary and educational offerings are essentially equal, is permissible under the Equal Protection Clause, Title IX, and the Equal Educational Opportunities Act of 1974.[145] Noting that Philadelphia's sex-segregated college preparatory schools offered functionally equivalent programs, the court concluded that the separation of the sexes was justified because youth might study more effectively in sex-segregated high schools. The court emphasized that the female plaintiff was not compelled to attend the sex-segregated academic school; she had the option of enrolling in a coeducational school within her attendance zone. Furthermore, the court stated that her petition to attend the male academic high school was based on personal preference rather than on an objective evaluation of the offerings available in the two schools. Subsequently, an equally divided United States Supreme Court affirmed this decision without delivering an opinion.

In contrast, Detroit school officials did not prevail in their attempt to segregate inner-city, African American male students to address more effectively these students' unique educational needs. Three African American male academies (preschool to fifth grade, sixth to eighth grade, and high school) were proposed. The three-year experimental academies were designed to offer an Afrocentric curriculum, emphasize male responsibility, provide mentors, offer Saturday classes and extended classroom hours, and provide individual counseling. No comparable program existed for females, although school authorities indicated that one would be forthcoming. The district court issued a preliminary injunction prohibiting the board from opening the academies, given the likelihood that the practice violated the Equal Protection Clause. Additionally, the court reasoned that failing to provide the injunction could result in irreparable injury to the female students and cause great disruption if the schools were allowed to open and then were forced to close.[146] The court noted that the district failed to show a substantial justification for its actions, as is required under the Fourteenth Amendment for facially discriminatory acts involving sex.

In a higher education case, but one with PK–12 implications, the Supreme Court in 1982 struck down a nursing school's admission policy that restricted admission in degree programs to females without providing comparable opportunities for males.[147] Although the Court acknowledged that sex-based classifications may be justified in limited circumstances when a particular sex has been disproportionately burdened, it rejected the university's contention that its admission policy was necessary to compensate for past discrimination against women. The Court found no evidence that women had ever been denied opportunities in the field of nursing that would justify remedial action by the state. In applying intermediate scrutiny, the Court concluded that the university failed its burden of showing that the facially discriminatory sex

---

[145]Vorchheimer v. Sch. Dist., 532 F.2d 880 (3d Cir. 1976), *aff'd by equally divided court,* 430 U.S. 703 (1977).

[146]Garrett v. Bd. of Educ., 775 F. Supp. 1004 (E.D. Mich. 1991).

[147]Miss. Univ. for Women v. Hogan, 458 U.S. 718 (1982).

classification served an important governmental objective, or that its discriminatory means were substantially related to the achievement of those objectives.

Similarly, the Fourth Circuit addressed male-only admissions policies in Virginia. The court found such a policy at the Virginia Military Institute (VMI) to be in violation of the Equal Protection Clause because there were no comparable opportunities for females.[148] The appellate court held that VMI's claims that its male-only program provided needed diversity in higher education did not justify exclusion of women. The state was given three options: admit women, establish a parallel institution for women, or abandon state support for VMI. The state chose to establish a parallel program for women at Mary Baldwin College, a small private women-only institution; that decision was initially upheld.[149] On appeal in *United States v. Virginia*, however, the Supreme Court reversed the lower courts and held that the state had violated the Fourteenth Amendment by its failure to provide equal opportunities for women in the area of military training.[150] A new program at Mary Baldwin would never be able to approach the success, quality, and prestige associated with that provided at VMI. Also, the Court refuted the reasons given by VMI for its refusal to admit women. The exclusion of women from VMI failed to further the institution's purported purpose of providing diversity in higher education; VMI's distinctive teaching methods and techniques could be used unchanged in many instances or slightly modified in the instruction of women; and privacy issues were resolvable.[151]

Sex-Segregated Courses and Programs. Unequal educational opportunities for males and females will not be permitted by courts. Although most cases challenging the exclusion of one sex from specific curricular offerings have been settled on constitutional grounds, Title IX regulations also prohibit sex-segregated courses such as physical education (although students may be grouped by skill level), vocational education, and music (although requirements based on vocal range that result in disparate impact are permissible), as well as others.[152] There are two exceptions, however, where classes *may be* segregated by sex: (1) physical education classes during participation in contact sports,[153] and (2) portions of classes that deal exclusively with human sexuality.[154]

Sex-Based Admission Criteria. At times, two sets of admission standards have been used, one for males and one for females. Without a substantial justification, this

[148]United States v. Virginia, 976 F.2d 890 (4th Cir. 1992).

[149]United States v. Virginia, 852 F. Supp. 471 (W.D. Va. 1994), *aff'd*, 44 F.3d 1229 (4th Cir. 1995).

[150]518 U.S. 515 (1996).

[151]*See also* Faulkner v. Jones, 51 F.3d 440 (4th Cir. 1995) (admitting a female applicant to an all-male cadet corps as the state was unable to show a substantial justification for the discrimination as is required under the Fourteenth Amendment; and reasoning that establishing a comparable parallel all-female cadet corps would not address the female student's interest in a timely manner).

[152]34 C.F.R. § 106.34(a)(2), (4) (2007); 34 CFR § 106.35 (2007).

[153]34 C.F.R. § 106.34(a)(1) (2007).

[154]34 C.F.R. § 106.34(a)(3) (2007).

facially discriminatory practice will not satisfy constitutional scrutiny or provisions of Title IX.[155] For example, the admission practices of two Boston schools were found to have discriminated against female applicants and were therefore invalidated.[156] Due to the different seating capacities of the two schools, the Latin School for males required a lower score on the entrance examination than did the school for females. Although permitting the operation of sex-segregated schools, the federal district court was unsympathetic to the school's alleged physical plant problems and ruled that the same entrance requirements had to be applied to both sexes. Similarly, the Ninth Circuit concluded that a school district's plan to admit an equal number of male and female students to a high school with an advanced college preparatory curriculum violated equal protection guarantees because it resulted in unequal admission criteria.[157] The court found the district's policy to be an illegitimate means of reaching its goal of balancing the number of male and female students enrolled in the school.

If the district uses reliable, valid, and bias-free forms of assessment to admit students to special programs or to grant awards or scholarships, decisions will be upheld even if a disparate impact occurs. Moreover, it is recommended that multiple forms of assessment be used and that all personnel involved in assessment have appropriate credentials and training.

Sexual Harassment of Students

Title IX and the Fourteenth Amendment also have been applied in sex-based claims of sexual harassment and abuse of students. Note, however, that Title IX does not apply when the harassment is due to sexual preference, transvestism, transsexualism, or other behaviors that are sexual in nature; it applies only when the harassment is due to being male or being female. In an exemplary Tenth Circuit case, Title IX was held not to apply where a male high school football player was hazed by his teammates, taped while nude to a towel rack, and then subjected to viewing by his former girlfriend, who had been invited into the locker room. He reported the incident, resulting in the eventual cancellation of the final game of the season. Following this altercation, he was subjected to great animosity, verbal threats, and harassment from numerous students until he eventually transferred schools. Nonetheless, because the plaintiff was unable to show that his harassment was due to his being male, the Title IX portion of his suit was dismissed.[158]

Historically, charges of sexual harassment against school districts generally were dismissed.[159] But then in 1992 the Supreme Court heard the appeal of a case in which a female student alleged that a coach initiated sexual conversations, engaged

[155] 45 C.F.R. § 86.35(b) (2007).

[156] Bray v. Lee, 337 F. Supp. 934 (D. Mass. 1972).

[157] Berkelman v. S.F. Unified Sch. Dist., 501 F.2d 1264 (9th Cir. 1974).

[158] Seamons v. Snow, 84 F.3d 1226 (10th Cir. 1996).

[159] *See, e.g.*, D.R. v. Middle Bucks Area Vocational Technical Sch., 972 F.2d 1364 (3d Cir. 1992); J.O. v. Alton Cmty. Unit Sch. Dist. 11, 909 F.2d 267 (7th Cir. 1990).

in inappropriate touching, and had coercive intercourse with her on school grounds on several occasions. In this case, *Franklin v. Gwinnett County Public Schools*, the Court held that Title IX prohibited the sexual harassment of students and that damages could be awarded where appropriate.[160] Since *Gwinnett,* numerous other cases with mixed results have been filed by current and former students alleging hostile environment,[161] student-to-student harassment,[162] sexual involvement and abuse of students by school staff,[163] off-campus harassment that resulted in an on-campus hostile environment,[164] harassment by a student teacher,[165] and same sex and opposite sex harassment.[166] With *Gwinnett* as a starting point, two similar but slightly different standards have evolved: one for employee-to-student harassment and the other for student-to-student harassment.

Employee-to-Student Harassment. In 1998, the Supreme Court provided further guidance in *Gebser v. Lago Vista Independent School District* regarding the liability of school districts when students are harassed by school employees.[167] In this case, a high school student and a teacher were involved in a relationship that had not been reported to the administration until the couple was discovered having sex and the teacher was arrested. The district then terminated the teacher's employment and the parents sued under Title IX. On appeal, the Supreme Court held that to be liable the district had to have *actual notice* of the harassment. The Court reasoned that allowing recovery of damages based on either *respondeat superior* or *constructive notice* (i.e., notice that is inferred or implied) would be inconsistent with the objective of the act, as liability would attach even though the district had no actual knowledge of the conduct or an opportunity to take action to end the harassment.[168] Accordingly, for there to be an award of damages, an official who has the authority to address the alleged discrimination must have *actual knowledge* of the inappropriate conduct and then fail

---

[160]503 U.S. 60 (1992).

[161]*See, e.g.,* Jennings v. Univ. of N.C., 444 F.3d 255 (4th Cir. 2006).

[162]*See, e.g.,* Doe v. Dallas Indep. Sch. Dist., No. 3:01-CV-1092-R, 2002 U.S. Dist. LEXIS 13014 (N.D. Tex. July 16, 2002); Rowinsky v. Bryan Indep. Sch. Dist., 80 F.3d 1006 (5th Cir. 1996).

[163]*See, e.g.,* Canutillo Indep. Sch. Dist. v. Leija, 101 F.3d 393 (5th Cir. 1996).

[164]*See, e.g.,* Patricia H. v. Berkeley Unified Sch. Dist., 830 F. Supp. 1288 (N.D. Cal. 1993).

[165]*See, e.g.,* Oona R.-S. v. Santa Rosa City Schs., 890 F. Supp. 1452 (N.D. Cal. 1995).

[166]*See, e.g.,* Shrum v. Kluck, 249 F.3d 773 (8th Cir. 2001) (male-to-male); M.H.D. v. Westminster Schs., 172 F.3d 797 (11th Cir. 1999) (male-to-female); Kinman v. Omaha Pub. Sch. Dist., 171 F.3d 607 (8th Cir. 1999) (female-to-female). *See also* Oncale v. Sundowner Offshore Servs., 523 U.S. 75 (1998) (permitting same-sex sexual harassment cases to be filed under Title VII of the Civil Rights Act of 1964).

[167]524 U.S. 274 (1998).

[168]*See also* Henderson v. Walled Lake Consol. Schs., 469 F.3d 479 (6th Cir. 2006) (observing that even if administrators had notice that a female soccer player was involved in a relationship with her coach, such awareness did not establish notice that the plaintiff, another member of the team, had been exposed to a hostile environment); Baynard v. Malone, 268 F.3d 228 (4th Cir. 2001) (noting that actual notice may be established where an appropriate person is notified that a teacher is abusing a student; the identity of the particular child is unnecessary).

to ameliorate the problem. Moreover, the failure to respond must amount to *deliberate indifference* to the discrimination. In the instant case, the plaintiff did not argue that actual notice had been provided and the district's failure to promulgate a related policy and grievance procedure failed to qualify as deliberate indifference.

In subsequent litigation, courts have assessed who is an "appropriate official" with authority, what constitutes "actual knowledge," and what substantiates "deliberate indifference." *Gebser* did not identify which individuals in the school district must have knowledge. Is this a person who can initiate an investigation, or must the individual possess the power to terminate the suspected abuser?[169] Without deciding whether a principal possesses this authority, several courts have assumed for the purpose of analyzing claims that principals have the power to remedy abuse.[170] The Third Circuit concluded that a principal's knowledge is sufficient, noting that "if a principal is not an 'appropriate person' for purposes of Title IX, a substantial portion of the Supreme Court's analysis in *Gebser* was nothing more than a meaningless discussion."[171] The Fourth Circuit, however, specifically ruled that a principal in Virginia does not possess the requisite power to hire, fire, transfer, or suspend teachers to serve as a proxy for the school district.[172]

Questions also have arisen concerning notice of sexual harassment or abuse. Evidence indicating a potential or theoretical risk has not been equated with actual knowledge. The Third Circuit warned that "a 'possibility' cannot be equated with a 'known act.'"[173] For example, the Eighth Circuit noted that sexual abuse could not be inferred simply because a teacher was spending considerable time with one student or appeared to be showing favoritism.[174] A New York federal district court, however, found that a principal had notice of a teacher's sexual harassment of a student when the student's mother reported his inappropriate sexual comments, touching, and innuendoes.[175]

To counter claims of deliberate indifference, school officials must show that they took action on complaints. For example, a principal who followed up a complaint by asking the counselor to interview the student and the accused teacher as well as other possible witnesses, contacting his supervisor, and taking corrective measures even though it appeared nothing had happened was not responding with

---

[169]*See also* Warren v. Reading Sch. Dist., 278 F.3d 163 (3d. Cir. 2002) (remanding for a determination of who may qualify as an "appropriate person" to receive actual notice under the *Gebser* standard; a criminally prosecuted male teacher was fired due to his sexual involvement with male students).

[170]Davis v. Dekalb County Sch. Dist., 233 F.3d 1367 (11th Cir. 2000); Doe v. Dallas Indep. Sch. Dist., 220 F.3d 380 (5th Cir. 2000); Flores v. Saulpaugh, 115 F. Supp. 319 (N.D.N.Y. 2000).

[171]Warren v. Reading Sch. Dist., 278 F.3d 163, 170 (3d Cir. 2002).

[172]Baynard v. Malone, 268 F.3d 228 (4th Cir. 2001).

[173]Bostic v. Smyrna Sch. Dist., 418 F.3d 355 (3d Cir. 2005). *But see* Jane Doe v. Green, 298 F. Supp. 2d 1025, 1034 (D. Nev. 2004) (stating "a complaint of harassment need not be undisputed or uncorroborated before it can be considered to fairly alert the school district of the potential for sexual harassment").

[174]P.H. v. Sch. Dist., 265 F.3d 653 (8th Cir. 2001).

[175]*Flores*, 115 F. Supp. 319.

indifference.[176] Although these actions did not prevent the teacher from sexually molesting students, the court found the relevant fact to be that the principal did not act with deliberate indifference.

Also of relevance in hostile environment cases where school personnel are allegedly involved is the fact that, at least for younger children, the behavior does not have to be "unwelcome," as in Title VII (Civil Rights Act of 1964) employment cases.[177] The Seventh Circuit reviewed a case where a 21-year-old male kitchen worker had a consensual sexual relationship with a 13-year-old middle school female.[178] The court noted that under Indiana criminal law a person under the age of 16 cannot consent to sexual intercourse and that children may not even understand that they are being harassed. To rule that only behavior that is not unwelcome is actionable would permit violators to take advantage of young, impressionable youth who voluntarily participate in requested conduct. Moreover, if welcomeness were an issue properly before the court, the children bringing the suits would be subject to intense scrutiny regarding their degree of fault.

Student-to-Student Harassment.   Educators must be in control of the school environment, including student conduct, and eliminate known dangers and harassment. Not all harassment will be known, however, and not all behavior that is offensive will be so severe as to violate Title IX. Also, for student-to-student harassment to be actionable the behavior must be unwelcome.

Further clarification regarding liability associated with student-to-student harassment was provided in 1999 when the Supreme Court in *Davis v. Monroe County Board of Education*[179] proposed a two-part test: (1) whether the board acted with deliberate indifference to known acts of harassment;[180] and (2) whether the harassment was so severe, pervasive, and objectively offensive that it effectively barred the victim's access to an educational opportunity or benefit.[181] The Court remanded the case to determine whether these standards were met. The plaintiff's daughter had allegedly been subjected to unwelcome sexual touching and rubbing, as well as sexual talk. On one occasion, the violating student put a doorstop in his pants and acted in a sexually suggestive manner toward the plaintiff. Ultimately, the youth

---

[176]*Davis*, 233 F.3d 1367.

[177]*But see* Escue v. N. Okla. Coll., 450 F.3d 1146 (10th Cir. 2006) (concluding that there was insufficient evidence for a jury to conclude that the professor's conduct was unwelcome or that consent from the college student was not provided).

[178]Mary M. v. N. Lawrence Cmty. Sch. Corp., 131 F.3d 1220 (7th Cir. 1997).

[179]526 U.S. 629 (1999).

[180]*See also* Oden v. N. Marianas Coll., 284 F.3d 1058 (9th Cir. 2002) (concluding that administrative sluggishness did not equate to deliberate indifference in a case in which a student's initial hearing was slightly delayed).

[181]*See also* Bruneau v. S. Kortright Cent. Sch. Dist., 163 F.3d 749 (2d Cir. 1998) (affirming lower court's determination that offensive behavior of male students against a female student did not qualify as harassment or adversely affect her education).

was charged with and pled guilty to sexual battery for his misconduct. The victim and her mother notified several teachers, the coach, and the principal of these incidences. No disciplinary action was ever taken other than to threaten the violating student with possible sanctions.

Neither Eleventh Amendment immunity[182] nor the claim that the violator was engaged in First Amendment protected free speech may be used as defenses to Title IX actions.[183] As a result, damage awards[184] are available from educational institutions receiving federal funds, although not from those persons who were directly responsible for the harassment.[185] "Individuals" are not "recipients" and cannot, therefore, be held liable under this particular law.[186] Whether 42 U.S.C. Section 1983 can be attached to Title IX to increase possible damage awards has not been resoled.[187] However, violators can be sued directly under state tort law for sexual battery or intentional infliction of emotional distress,[188] and criminal charges may be filed against perpetrators where force is used or minors are involved. Moreover, being found guilty of sexual harassment can justify demotion, suspension, or termination, even for tenured educators.

The high volume of sexual harassment litigation will likely continue. Even when administrators deal with claims of sexual harassment in timely and effective ways, parents still may file suit. They will be understandably angry that their child has been subjected to inappropriate behavior and will be looking for someone to blame, if not pay.

Marriage and Pregnancy

Legal principles governing the rights of married and pregnant students have changed dramatically since 1960. The evolution of the law in this area is indicative of the judicial commitment to protect students from unjustified classifications that limit educational opportunities. When public school students are discriminated

[182]*See, e.g.,* Franks v. Ky. Sch. for the Deaf, 142 F.3d 360 (6th Cir. 1998).

[183]*See, e.g.,* Cohen v. San Bernardino Valley Coll., 883 F. Supp. 1407 (C.D. Cal. 1995), *aff'd in part, rev'd in part, remanded,* 92 F.3d 968 (9th Cir. 1996).

[184]*See, e.g.,* Doe v. East Haven Bd. of Educ., 200 Fed. Appx. 46 (2d Cir. 2006) (affirming award of $100,000 to a victim of student-to-student harassment; finding officials deliberately indifferent to the harassment, taunting, and name calling following plaintiff's rape). However, it is unlikely that punitive awards are available under Title IX. *See* Schultzen v. Woodbury Cent. Cmty. Sch. Dist., 187 F. Supp. 2d 1099 (N.D. Iowa 2002).

[185]*See, e.g.,* Hartley v. Parnell, 193 F.3d 1263 (11th Cir. 1999); Floyd v. Waiters, 133 F.3d 786 (11th Cir. 1998).

[186]Floyd, 133 F.3d 786.

[187]*Compare* Doe v. Smith, 470 F.3d 331 (7th Cir. 2006) (dismissing § 1983 claims and determining that Title IX provides adequate statutory recourse for the alleged discrimination) *with* Cmtys. for Equity v. Mich. High Sch. Athletic Ass'n, 459 F.3d 676 (6th Cir. 2006) (concluding that § 1983 and the Fourteenth Amendment may be used to supplement the relief sought under Title IX), *cert. denied,* 127 S. Ct. 1912 (2007).

[188]*See, e.g.,* Johnson v. Elk Lake Sch. Dist., 283 F.3d 138 (3d Cir. 2002).

against because they are married, both the Fourteenth Amendment and Title IX may be violated. Strict scrutiny is used in evaluating claims under the Equal Protection Clause because marriage qualifies as an implied fundamental right.[189] Accordingly, states will have to show a compelling interest in their differential treatment of married students to satisfy the Constitution.

Title IX regulations explicitly prohibit a recipient from applying "any rule concerning a student's actual or potential parental, family, or marital status which treats students differently on the basis of sex."[190] Discrimination based on pregnancy, childbirth, false pregnancy, termination of pregnancy, or recovery therefrom is prohibited. Moreover, student privacy is protected by state and federal privacy laws, including the Fourth Amendment. In an exemplary case, a federal district court held that requiring a student to take a pregnancy test administered in a coercive environment constitutes an unreasonable search and seizure.[191]

Where separate programs for pregnant students are available, the student may volunteer to participate but may not be automatically enrolled or coerced. However, the school district may require the student to obtain a physician's statement attesting that she is physically and emotionally able to continue in general education, assuming that students with other physical or emotional conditions also are required to provide such documentation. Where programs are provided separately, they must be comparable to those offered nonpregnant students.

In Massachusetts, a federal district court held that school authorities could not exclude a pregnant, unmarried student from regular high school classes.[192] School officials had proposed that the pregnant student be allowed to use all school facilities, attend school functions, participate in senior activities, and receive assistance from teachers in continuing her studies. The district stipulated, however, that she was not to attend school during regular school hours. Since there was no evidence of any educational or medical reason for this special treatment, the court held that the pregnant student had a constitutional right to attend classes with other pupils. Similarly, a Texas civil appeals court invalidated a public school rule that prohibited mothers from attending regular classes.[193] The only alternative available to the excluded students was to attend adult education classes, which required students to be at least 21 years old. The court ruled that such a policy violated pregnant students' entitlement to free public schooling. Other courts also have invalidated the exclusion of married students from extracurricular activities, reasoning that such denial results in impermissible discrimination.[194]

---

[189]Loving v. Virginia, 388 U.S. 1, 12 (1967).

[190]34 C.F.R. § 106.40 (2007).

[191]Villanueva v. San Marcos Consol. Indep. Sch. Dist., A-05-CA-455 LY, 2006 U.S. Dist. LEXIS 68280 (W.D. Tex. Sept. 7, 2006).

[192]Ordway v. Hargraves, 323 F. Supp. 1155 (D. Mass. 1971).

[193]Alvin Indep. Sch. Dist. v. Cooper, 404 S.W.2d 76 (Tex. Civ. App. 1966).

[194]See, e.g., Beeson v. Kiowa County Sch. Dist. RE-1, 567 P.2d 801 (Colo. Ct. App. 1977); Bell v. Lone Oak Indep. Sch. Dist., 507 S.W.2d 636, 641–642 (Tex. Civ. App. 1974).

Conclusion

A basic purpose of public education is to prepare students for postsecondary life, regardless of their innate characteristics. Accordingly, courts and legislatures have become increasingly assertive in guaranteeing that students have the chance to realize their capabilities while in school. Arbitrary classification practices that disadvantage certain groups are not tolerated. Conversely, valid classifications, applied in the best interests of students, are generally supported. In exercising professional judgment pertaining to the classification of students, educators should be cognizant of the following generalizations drawn from judicial and legislative mandates.

1. School segregation resulting from state laws or other intentional state action (e.g., gerrymandering school attendance zones) violates the Equal Protection Clause of the Fourteenth Amendment.
2. Where a school district has not achieved unitary status, school officials have an affirmative duty to eliminate the vestiges of past intentional discrimination; under such a duty, official action (or inaction) is assessed in terms of its effect on reducing segregation.
3. Segregatory effect alone does not establish unconstitutional intent; however, the consequences of official actions can be considered in substantiating discriminatory motive.
4. The scope of a desegregation remedy cannot exceed the scope of the constitutional violation.
5. States can, but are not obligated to, go beyond the requirements of the Fourteenth Amendment in remedying school segregation; such additional state mandates can subsequently be repealed without violating the United States Constitution.
6. Interdistrict desegregation remedies cannot be judicially imposed unless there is evidence of intentional discrimination with substantial effect across district lines.
7. School districts cannot plead "lack of funds" as a defense for failing to remedy unconstitutional school segregation; a state can be required to share the costs of remedial plans if it played a role in creating or maintaining the segregated system.
8. Courts can set aside state limitations on local taxing authority and can order school boards to raise sufficient funds to support remedial plans, but courts cannot directly impose tax increases.
9. Judicial supervision can be terminated, in whole or in part, where school districts have complied with desegregation mandates in good faith and have eliminated the vestiges of past discrimination as far as practicable.
10. In determining whether a school district has eliminated the vestiges of school segregation, courts assess racial equality in student, faculty, and staff assignments; transportation; extracurricular activities; and facilities.
11. Once a school district has eliminated the vestiges of its prior discriminatory conduct to the court's satisfaction, future acts must represent purposeful

discrimination to violate the Fourteenth Amendment; school districts are not obligated to continue remedies after unitary status is attained and resegregation occurs through no fault of school officials.

12. The use of race in determining school or program assignment to achieve diversity in student bodies will not be permitted unless shown to be narrowly tailored.

13. Children who are English deficient are entitled to compensatory instruction designed to overcome English language barriers.

14. Students can be classified by age, but such classifications must be substantiated as necessary to advance legitimate educational objectives.

15. Ability-tracking schemes are permissible, but pupil assignments should be based on multiple criteria.

16. Although school districts may operate segregated schools for males and females, they must be substantially equal if they are to be separate.

17. Criteria for admission to selective public programs or schools must be the same for males and females.

18. If a school district establishes an interscholastic athletic program, opportunities must be made available to male and female athletes on an equal basis (i.e., mixed-sex teams or comparable sex-segregated teams).

19. Sexual harassment of students, by either employees or other students, can result in liability against the school district when an official with the authority to correct the situation has received actual notice of the harassment and has failed to correct it or shown deliberate indifference toward the action.

20. Students cannot be disadvantaged based on marital status or pregnancy.

6

Rights of Students with Disabilities

Since children with disabilities represent a vulnerable minority group, their treatment has resulted in considerable judicial and legislative concern. Courts have addressed the constitutional rights of such children to attend school and to be classified accurately and instructed appropriately. Federal and state statutes have further delineated the rights of students with disabilities and have provided funds to assist school districts in meeting their special needs.

Legal Context

The first significant court case to impact children with disabilities dealt with racial segregation rather than special education and was filed under the Fourteenth Amendment to the Constitution rather than a narrowly tailored disability statute. Nevertheless, the Court's 1954 pronouncement in *Brown v. Board of Education* that "education must be made available to all on equal terms"[1] ultimately served as a basis for the admission to public schools of a number of previously limited or excluded populations, including those classified by race, sex, national origin, and disability. Related court cases, lobbying efforts, and changes in state laws eventually helped pave the way for the passage of federal laws specially designed to protect and enhance the rights of individuals with disabilities—the Rehabilitation Act, the Americans with Disabilities Act, and the Individuals with Disabilities Education Act (see Table 6.1).

[1]347 U.S. 483, 493 (1954).

TABLE 6.1   *Applicability of Selected Federal Laws Affecting Students with Disabilities*

Federal Law	Public Recipient Required to Comply	Public Non-Recipient Required to Comply	Private Recipient Required to Comply	Private Non-Recipient Required to Comply
Fourteenth Amendment Equal Protection Clause	yes	yes	no	no—except state athletic ass'ns
Fourteenth Amendment Due Process Clause	yes	yes	no	no—except state athletic ass'ns
42 USC § 1983	yes	yes	no	no—except state athletic ass'ns
Rehabilitation Act § 504	yes	no	yes	no
ADA—Title II	yes	yes	no	no
ADA—Title III	no	no	yes	yes
IDEA	yes, if recipient of IDEA funds	no	no, service contracts do not qualify	no

Rehabilitation Act

Section 504 of the Rehabilitation Act of 1973 applies to both public and private recipients of federal financial assistance and is enforced in large part by the Office for Civil Rights. Section 504 stipulates that otherwise qualified individuals shall not be excluded from participating in, be denied the benefits of, or be subjected to discrimination by recipient programs or activities, if that treatment is due to their respective disabilities.[2] Furthermore, if any program or activity operated by a covered entity (e.g., school district) receives federal funds from the Department of Education, all operations of the recipient must comply with the act's provisions. Compliance requires the recipient to file an *assurance of compliance* (i.e., a written guarantee that it will not discriminate based on disability), remediate violations of the act, correct those circumstances that historically limited the participation of persons with disabilities in the recipient's program, conduct a

---

[2]29 U.S.C. § 794(a) (2007). *See also* Clark v. Banks, 193 Fed. Appx. 510 (6th Cir. 2006) (finding that plaintiff was not denied the right to transfer schools due solely to her disability; her residence and issues related to funding also were considered).

self-evaluation to determine the level of compliance, identify a coordinator, adopt grievance procedures, and provide notice to participants that the recipient's program does not discriminate based on disability.[3]

Under the Rehabilitation Act, an individual with a disability is one who *has a physical or mental impairment*[4] that substantially limits one or more major life activities, *has a record of impairment*, or *is regarded as having an impairment*.[5] These latter two definitions (i.e., "record of" and "regarded as") apply when a person has been subjected to discrimination, such as being terminated as a teacher due to having a record of hospitalization for tuberculosis[6] or excluded from school for being HIV positive.[7] However, only those children who meet the first definition in that they have an impairment that is substantially limiting will be eligible for reasonable accommodations and modifications. Students with only a record of past impairment are not currently in need of accommodation, while students who are only regarded as having an impairment have no actual disability to accommodate.

When assessing whether a person qualifies as disabled and is therefore eligible for services under Section 504, consideration will be given to the results of positive and negative *mitigating or corrective measures*.[8] *Positive results* can be seen when a student with impaired vision has a visual acuity of 20/20 with glasses or contact lenses or when a child with impaired hearing has average hearing with a hearing aid. *Negative results* can be observed when a student is medicated due to a health problem, but as a result has difficulty focusing or staying alert in class. Consideration of such positive and negative factors provides a clearer understanding of whether a limitation qualifies as a disability and provides important information regarding the nature and extent of the impairment.

In addition, the limitation must *substantially limit* a *major life activity*.[9] In making this determination, courts compare the performance difficulties of the student with those of the theoretical "average person" (or in this discussion, "average student") in the general population. To qualify, the student will have to be either incapable of performing the designated activity or significantly restricted; merely functioning below

[3]34 C.F.R. §§ 104.5–104.8 (2007).

[4]34 C.F.R. § 104.3(j)(2(i)) (2007) (defining physical or mental impairments as including "any physiological disorder or condition, cosmetic disfigurement, or anatomical loss affecting one or more of the following body systems: neurological; musculoskeletal; special sense organs; respiratory, including speech organs; cardiovascular; reproductive, digestive, genito-urinary; hemic and lymphatic; skin; and endocrine; or any mental or psychological disorder, such as mental retardation, organic brain syndrome, emotional or mental illness, and specific learning disorders").

[5]34 C.F.R. § 104.3(j)(1) (2007).

[6]Sch. Bd. v. Arline, 480 U.S. 273 (1987) (concluding that a teacher suffering from the contagious disease of tuberculosis qualified as an individual with a disability because she had a record of physical impairment that limited a major life activity—working).

[7]Ray v. Sch. Dist., 666 F. Supp. 1524 (M.D. Fla. 1987).

[8]Sutton v. United Air Lines, 527 U.S. 471 (1999); Murphy v. United Parcel Serv., 527 U.S. 516 (1999).

[9]Major life activities include caring for oneself, performing manual tasks, walking, seeing, hearing, speaking, breathing, learning, working. *See* 34 C.F.R. § 104.3(j)(2)(ii) (2007).

average will be insufficient.[10] This assessment requires a case-by-case evaluation, because impairments will vary in severity, affect people differently, and may or may not be restricting given the nature of the life activity. As a result, some students with physical or mental impairments will be substantially limited and others with the same diagnosis will not, with only the former qualifying as disabled under Section 504. Failure to recognize the fact that Section 504 provides protection only for persons who are disabled, not for those who are merely impaired, can lead to the overclassification of students. This then could result in increased administrative and instructional costs, greater parental expectations for programming, and the increased likelihood of litigation.

When a student's limitation qualifies as a disability, it still is necessary to determine whether he or she is *otherwise qualified*. At the PK–12 level, children qualify if they are of school age, or if they are eligible for services for the disabled under either state law or the Individual with Disabilities Education Act (IDEA).[11] Students who qualify under Section 504, but not under the IDEA (e.g., general education children who are wheelchair confined) need to be provided with accommodation plans that will include individualized aids and services that allow participation in the recipient's program.[12] The programs must be delivered in accessible facilities,[13] and programming must be designed and selected to meet the needs of students with disabilities to the same extent that their nondisabled peers' needs are met. Furthermore, children with disabilities should not be segregated from other children unless in the rare instance appropriate services cannot otherwise be provided in the general education classroom. Where such segregation exists, programs must be comparable in materials, facilities, teacher quality, length of school term, and daily hours of instruction.

When the recipient and the parents disagree on whether an appropriate education has been provided, the parents have the right to review records, participate in an impartial hearing, and be represented by counsel. Section 504 is not specific as to the procedures that must be followed, but it does acknowledge that providing notice and hearing rights comparable to those mandated under the IDEA will suffice.[14] In addition, parents have the right to file a complaint with the Office for Civil Rights within 180 days of the alleged discrimination. Officials are responsible for investigating the claim and for reviewing pertinent practices and policies. Where violations exist, federal regulations support the use of informal negotiations and voluntary action on the

---

[10]*See, e.g.,* Costello v. Mitchell Pub. Sch. Dist. 79, 266 F.3d 916 (8th Cir. 2001); Bercovitch v. Baldwin Sch., 133 F.3d 141 (1st Cir. 1998).

[11]34 C.F.R. § 104.3(I)(2) (2007).

[12]Furthermore, it is the position of the Office for Civil Rights that a student who qualifies under the IDEA is not entitled also to receive a plan formulated consistent with the provisions of § 504. Response to McKethan, 25 IDELR 295 (OCR 1996).

[13]34 C.F.R. § 104.22 (2007). To comply, a recipient need not make each existing facility or every part of a facility accessible, but must operate its programs so that they are accessible to individuals with disabilities. Accessibility can be achieved through redesign of equipment, reassignment of classes to accessible buildings, delivery of services to alternate sites, alteration of existing facilities, and construction of new facilities. A recipient is not required to renovate or construct when other less expensive but effective methods are available.

[14]*See* text accompanying notes 140–154, *infra*.

part of the recipient to gain compliance.[15] If the recipient fails to correct its discriminatory practices, federal funds may be terminated.

There is a private right of action under Section 504, although IDEA exhaustion requirements have to be met if the relief sought also is available under the IDEA. Moreover, where a suit is filed under both the IDEA and Section 504, that portion of the Section 504 claim dealing with the provision of an appropriate program will be dismissed if the IDEA suit is dismissed.[16] Immunity defenses under the Eleventh Amendment are unlikely to be accepted,[17] and attorneys' fees may be awarded to prevailing plaintiffs. In addition, damage awards are available where bad faith or gross misjudgment is supported in cases regarding the failure to provide accommodations and modifications.[18]

Americans with Disabilities Act

In 1990, Congress passed the Americans with Disabilities Act (ADA).[19] Two titles of that act are of particular importance to students with disabilities: Title II applies to public schools and Title III applies to those that are private. Like Section 504, these titles prohibit discrimination against persons (birth to death) who are disabled. Unlike Section 504, the ADA requires compliance of schools that do not receive federal aid and were not heretofore federally regulated. Complaints must be filed with the Department of Justice within 180 days of an alleged violation.

Upon completion of a formal Title II complaint, the department investigates and attempts informal resolution. If a violation is identified, but a settlement is not reached, a letter is sent to the complainant and the school; the letter identifies each violation and proposed remedy, as well as information regarding additional ADA rights. When agreement is reached, the parties are required to sign a written document specifying time lines and any corrective action to be taken for each infraction, and to provide assurance that discrimination will not recur. Where voluntary compliance is not forthcoming, department officials will recommend to the U.S. attorney general that specific actions be taken, such as additional efforts to acquire voluntary compliance or a lawsuit.

The attorney general also is responsible for investigating alleged violations filed against private schools under ADA Title III. If there is reason to believe that an infraction has occurred, the private school can be required to submit to a compliance review. Where a pattern or practice of discrimination exists, or where perceived discrimination is so significant as to represent an issue of general public importance, a civil action may be initiated. Courts are authorized to require private schools to provide auxiliary aids or services; modify policies, practices, procedures, or methods; make facilities readily accessible to and usable by individuals with disabilities; or require other relief as appropriate.

[15]34 C.F.R. § 100.7(c), (d) (2007).
[16]N.L. v. Knox County Schs., 315 F.3d 688 (6th Cir. 2003).
[17]Jim C. v. United States, 235 F.3d 1079 (8th Cir. 2000).
[18]Smith v. Special Sch. Dist. No. 1, 184 F.3d 764 (8th Cir. 1999).
[19]42 U.S.C. §§ 12101–12213 (2007).

Private schools, however, are not required to provide auxiliary aids and services that would either fundamentally alter the nature of the goods, services, facilities, privileges, advantages, or accommodations they provide or that would result in undue burden.[20] Furthermore, even though private schools are expected to remove barriers in existing facilities that restrict or deny access, this mandate is limited to those tasks that are "readily achievable," "easily accomplished," and "without much difficulty or expense."[21]

Individuals with Disabilities Education Act

Two years after the passage of the Rehabilitation Act, and 15 years before the passage of the ADA, Part B of the Education of the Handicapped Act was amended by Public Law 94-142. This law now is known as the Individuals with Disabilities Education Act (IDEA)[22] and is enforced by the Office of Special Education Programs. States, but not local education agencies (e.g., public school districts), have the option of declining IDEA funds, thereby avoiding the myriad compliance requirements. But states still are required to address the needs of students with disabilities as stipulated in Section 504. All states currently participate in the IDEA financial assistance program.

To qualify for services, a child must be mentally retarded, hard of hearing, deaf, speech or language impaired, visually impaired, blind, emotionally disturbed, orthopedically impaired, autistic, other health impaired, learning disabled,[23] or suffer from traumatic brain injury, *and,* as a result, be in need of special education and related services.[24] Accordingly, it is possible to have a disability but not be in need of special education and, therefore, not qualify for services under the IDEA. Although a child must qualify as "disabled" under one or more of the above categories for the state and district to receive federal funding, it is not necessary to label the child to provide an individualized education program.[25] It is important, however, for the child's needs to be correctly identified and for those needs to be properly addressed.

---

[20]28 C.F.R. § 36.303(a) (2007). Undue burden in this context is similar to that under § 504 (but unavailable under the IDEA) and includes both administrative feasibility and cost.

[21]28 C.F.R. § 36.304(a) (2007).

[22]20 U.S.C. § 1400 *et seq.* (2007). Revisions of the IDEA at times are referred to as Public Law 94-142, IDEA '97, or IDEA '04 (also known as the Individuals with Disabilities Education Improvement Act (IDEIA)). The name of the law, however, has not changed in recent years and will be referred to as the Individuals with Disabilities Education Act.

[23]In determining whether a child has a specific learning disability, the district is not required to consider whether a severe discrepancy exists between achievement and ability. *See* 20 U.S.C. § 1414(b)(6)(A) (2007).

[24]20 U.S.C. § 1401(3)(A) (2007). Not all children with special needs will qualify as disabled. *See, e.g.,* Hood v. Encinitas Union Sch. Dist., 486 F.3d 1099 (9th Cir. 2007) (determining that although a student had diagnosed health impairments, she did not require special education and related services; as a result, she was not eligible for IDEA services); Bd. of Educ. v. J.D., No. 99-2180, 2000 U.S. App. LEXIS 26902 (4th Cir. Oct. 26, 2000) (upholding a district court ruling that the drug-using student was socially maladjusted and did not have a qualifying disability).

[25]20 U.S.C. § 1412 (a)(3)(B) (2007). *See also* Cronkite v. Long Beach Unified Sch. Dist., No. 97-55544, 1999 U.S. App. LEXIS 4733 (9th Cir. March 18, 1999) (concluding that the district had provided the student with an appropriate education and that the IDEA does not require the district to use a specific term— e.g., dyslexia—provided the IEP properly identifies and addresses the disability).

Individualized Education Programs

The process of preparing and delivering an appropriate program begins when a child with a disability is identified and ends only when the child withdraws or graduates[26] from school, fails to qualify for services, or reaches the age of 21. To begin this process, the child is identified and evaluated; then an individualized education program (IEP) is written and a placement is prepared.

Initial Identification

Under IDEA's "child find" mandate, states are required to identify, locate, and evaluate all[27] resident children with disabilities (including those who are homeless, limited English proficient, or wards of the state), regardless of the severity of their disability or whether they attend public or private schools.[28] Although federal law requires that children with disabilities be identified, it does not dictate how this is to occur. Nevertheless, courts give deference to districts when their efforts are substantial, in good faith, and ultimately effective.[29] Consequently, state procedures vary widely and include practices such as census taking; community surveys; public awareness activities; referrals by parents, teachers, and medical doctors; and the screening of kindergarten and preschool children.

The screening process may necessitate the use of tests that are administered to all children, not simply those students suspected of having disabilities. Prior to testing, parents must be given notice that identifies the tests to be used and provides a general explanation of their intended purpose. Educators, however, need not acquire consent at this time. When these initial referral and screening efforts have been completed, children potentially in need of special education ideally will be identified and will require additional evaluation.

Evaluation

Next, school districts are responsible for evaluating further those children residing in their respective service areas who may qualify for special education, given referrals or the results of preliminary exams. Although state residency laws vary, generally children who physically live in the district's service area with a custodial

---

[26]T.S. v. Indep. Sch. Dist. No. 54, Stroud, Okla., 265 F.3d 1090 (10th Cir. 2001) (finding the case moot as the student had already graduated—he had filed for a due process hearing the last day of classes his senior year, claiming the district had failed to process his graduation properly; he was not contesting the propriety of graduation, although he did question the services provided).

[27]No child with a disability is to be denied an appropriate program ("zero reject"). *See* 20 U.S.C. § 1412(a)(2) (2007).

[28]20 U.S.C. § 1412(a)(3)(A) (2007); 20 U.S.C. § 1412(a)(10)(A)(ii) (2007).

[29]Doe v. Metro. Nashville Pub. Schs., 9 Fed. Appx. 453 (6th Cir. 2001) (holding that the district had effectively participated in "child-find" given its dissemination of information to schools, day-care centers, nursery schools, hospitals, and medical personnel; public service announcements; participation in PTA meetings; and implementation of an outreach program).

parent,[30] legal guardian, or foster parent; are emancipated minors; or have reached the age of majority and live apart from their parents will qualify as "residents."[31]

Prior to placement of a child with disabilities, the IDEA requires the performance of a multifactored evaluation using a variety of technically sound assessment tools and strategies to gather information related to the child's academic, functional, and developmental abilities. No single criterion or procedure may be used to determine a child's eligibility or placement. Assessments must be validated for the purposes they are used, administered by qualified personnel, selected and employed in ways that neither racially nor culturally discriminate, given in accordance with the producer's instructions, and available in the child's native language or other mode of communication.[32]

Notice must be provided to the parents that the district intends to conduct an evaluation of their child. It must describe any assessments the district proposes to conduct (including each procedure, test, record, or report that will be used), as well as any other information relevant to the matter. Generally, informed parental consent[33] must be acquired prior to personalized testing for either an initial evaluation or reevaluation;[34] but consent is not required for curricular, state, or districtwide assessments.[35] However, if a parent refuses consent for the initial evaluation, or fails to respond to the request to provide consent, the district may undertake due process to authorize an evaluation.[36] If the hearing officer supports the district's request to perform an assessment, or if reassessment is needed to determine the appropriateness of a contested current placement, the parents are required to make the child available.[37]

---

[30]Joshua W. v. U.S.D. 259 Bd. of Educ., No. 98-3248, 2000 U.S. App. LEXIS 8837 (10th Cir. May 2, 2000) (denying reimbursement for tuition paid to a private school and concluding that the child was not entitled to services as neither parent continued to live in the district—staying with his sister did not qualify as a "person acting as a parent" under state law).

[31]*See* text accompanying note 39, Chapter 3.

[32]20 U.S.C. § 1414(b)(2), (3) (2007).

[33]20 U.S.C. § 1414(a)(1)(D)(i)(I) (2007).

[34]*But see* Shelby S. *ex rel.* Kathleen T. v. Conroe Indep. Sch. Dist., 454 F.3d 450 (5th Cir. 2006) (determining that the district was within its right to reevaluate a child, notwithstanding a lack of parental consent, where such reevaluation was critical to the district preparing an appropriate IEP), *cert. denied*, 127 S. Ct. 936 (2007).

[35]In addition to those assessments used to prepare the IEP, included within the IEP, or required in particular courses, students with disabilities are required to participate in *all* state and districtwide assessments, with accommodations and alternate forms of assessment as appropriate. States may elect to provide students with significant cognitive disabilities with alternate assessments keyed to alternate achievement standards. *See* 20 U.S.C. § 1412(a)(16) (2007).

[36]20 U.S.C. § 1414(a)(1)(D)(ii)(I) (2007).

[37]Loren F. v. Atlanta Indep. Sch. Sys., 349 F.3d 1309 (11th Cir. 2003) (observing that the lower court in reaching its decision may consider the delays caused by the parents as well as their failure to make their child available for evaluation); Patricia P. v. Bd. of Educ., 203 F.3d 462 (7th Cir. 2000) (denying reimbursement to parents who failed to cooperate by allowing the district a reasonable opportunity to evaluate their child; the extent of their cooperation had been to allow their child to be tested if Illinois personnel were willing to travel to a unilaterally selected private school in Maine).

When either parental consent is provided or authorization is acquired from a hearing officer, the IEP team and other qualified professionals are responsible for reviewing existing data on the child, including evaluations and information provided by the parents, current classroom-based assessments, and observations by teachers and related services providers.[38] The IEP team then can identify what additional information, if any, is needed. After all relevant input has been aggregated, the team must ascertain whether the child qualifies as disabled and if so whether special education and related services will be required. The team should determine the child's present level of academic achievement and developmental needs, and project whether any additions or modifications to the instruction or services are necessary to enable the child to meet measurable annual goals and to participate, as appropriate, in the general education curriculum.[39]

If parents[40] are dissatisfied with the original evaluation or resulting placement decision, they have the right to request an independent second evaluation. The public school pays for the additional evaluation, unless officials contest the need for reassessment through due process or the evaluation already obtained by the parents does not meet district criteria.[41] Where the district elects to challenge payment for a second evaluation, it must be prepared to demonstrate that all procedures and appropriate professional practices were followed. If the impartial hearing officer rules in favor of the district, and that decision is not appealed, the parents still may acquire a second, independent evaluation but must pay for it. Where additional evaluations are acquired, school personnel are required to consider their results but are not required to follow them.[42]

The 2004 amendments to the IDEA were in part designed to reduce the number of evaluations, the frequency of IEP meetings, and the amount of overall paperwork.[43] Generally, placements must be reviewed annually, or more often as appropriate, and a reevaluation must be performed every three years. However, a reevaluation is not required if the IEP team determines that it is unnecessary, in whole or in part, unless requested by the child's parent. Even when parents make routine requests for reevaluation, they need not be performed more than once per year,

[38]20 U.S.C. § 1414(c)(1)(A) (2007).

[39]20 U.S.C. § 1414(c)(1)(B) (2007).

[40]Note that the IDEA defines parent broadly as a natural, adoptive, or foster parent; a guardian; an individual acting in place of a natural or adoptive parent (e.g., grandparent, stepparent, or other relative); or a surrogate. *See* 20 U.S.C. § 1401(23) (2007).

[41]34 C.F.R. § 300.502(a)(1), (b) (2007). *See also* Evanston Cmty. Consol. Sch. Dist. No. 65 v. Michael M., 356 F.3d 798 (7th Cir. 2004) (denying reimbursement for a second unnecessary evaluation). Moreover, if a hearing officer requests that an evaluation be conducted, the district bears all costs. *See* 34 C.F.R. § 300.502(d) (2007).

[42]34 C.F.R. § 300.502(c)(1) (2007). *See also* T.S. v. Bd. of Educ., 10 F.3d 87 (2d Cir. 1993) (holding that an independent evaluation had been "considered," even though only two members of the placement committee read the report, limited discussion ensued, and a placement contrary to that recommended was selected).

[43]Fifteen states are participating in a pilot program to explore the effectiveness of multiyear IEPs. *See* 20 U.S.C. § 1414(d)(5)(A) (2007).

unless agreed to by the district.[44] Where a reevaluation supports amendment to the IEP, the IDEA permits the district to make the necessary changes, without conducting a full IEP team meeting, if it acquires parental approval.[45]

IEP Team

The school district, through its IEP teams, is responsible for determining whether children qualify under the IDEA for services and, if so, for designing appropriate, least restrictive placements. The team includes:

- The parents or a surrogate,[46]
- Not less than one general and one special education teacher,
- A representative of the local educational agency who is qualified to provide or supervise specially designed instruction and is knowledgeable about the general education curriculum and available resources,
- An individual who can interpret instructional implications of evaluation results,
- Other individuals with special knowledge or expertise, and
- The child, if appropriate.[47]

Some committees consist of 10 or more participants, but all need not be present at every meeting. Excusal is permitted where the parents consent and those members not attending have the opportunity to submit their input in writing prior to the meeting.[48] Failure to acquire written consent, particularly for removal of the general education teacher, has been found so significant as to result in an IDEA violation and an inappropriate placement.[49]

IEP Preparation

The parents must agree to the IEP meeting time and location, and the district must ensure that the parents have the opportunity to participate fully, which may require

---

[44]20 U.S.C. § 1414(a)(2)(B)(i) (2007).

[45]20 U.S.C § 1414(d)(3)(D) (2007).

[46]Where no parent can be identified or located, a surrogate must be appointed within 30 days of the awareness that a surrogate is needed. The surrogate possesses all of the IDEA rights and responsibilities of the parent. The surrogate may not be an employee of the district or have interests that conflict with those of the child and must have the knowledge and skills needed to ensure adequate representation. *See* 20 U.S.C. § 1415(b)(2)(B) (2007).

[47]20 U.S.C. § 1414(d)(1)(B) (2007).

[48]20 U.S.C. § 1414(d)(1)(C) (2007).

[49]M.L. v. Fed. Way Sch. Dist., 394 F.3d 634 (9th Cir. 2004). *But see* Sanford v. Birmingham Pub. Schs., 70 Fed. Appx. 295, 297 (6th Cir. 2003) (finding that the absence of the physician was not fatal to the challenged IEP).

hiring foreign-language translators or sign-language interpreters.[50] Participation may be accomplished through video conferencing and conference calls, if necessary. If no parent is available or willing to attend, school officials should document each effort to encourage parental involvement.

In preparation for the first IEP meeting, the district may elect to prepare a tentative IEP as a basis for discussion. This initial IEP should be presented as a draft and in no way should be represented as final.[51] When agreement is ultimately reached, the IEP should:

- Record the child's present level of academic achievement and functional performance;
- State annual and short-term goals and objectives;
- Note how performance will be measured;
- Identify special education, related services, supplementary aids and services, and transition services (beginning at age 16) to be provided;
- Explain the extent, if any, to which the child will not be included in general education activities;
- Specify any accommodations that will be made in performing state or district assessments (or an explanation of why alternate assessments are necessary);
- Identify the date to initiate services;
- Project the frequency, location, and duration of services; and
- Provide a statement indicating that the student has been familiarized with his IDEA rights and informed that such rights will transfer to him or her at the age of majority[52] (except when the student is found to be incompetent under state law[53]).

Also contributing to the effort to be more cost and time efficient is the provision that requires districts to accept existing IEPs for students who move into the local service area during the school year. The receiving district must provide services comparable to those identified by the former district, whether in state or out of state. This placement should be continued until the district has evaluated the child and developed a new IEP consistent with IDEA procedures.[54]

---

[50]However, this right to participate does not extend to preparatory meetings conducted by the local school district to generate proposals to be discussed with the parents at a later IEP meeting. *In re D.*, 32 IDELR 103 (SEA CT, 2000).

[51]*See, e.g.*, Deal v. Hamilton County Bd. of Educ., 392 F.3d 840 (6th Cir. 2004) (determining that the district violated the IDEA by predetermining the child's placement prior to parental involvement and by failing to involve a general education teacher in several relevant discussions); N.L. v. Knox County Schs., 315 F.3d 688 (6th Cir. 2003) (observing that the IDEA prohibits the district from presenting a completed IEP to the parents at the first meeting or from attempting to force the parents to accept the IEP).

[52]20 U.S.C. § 1414(d)(1)(A) (2007).

[53]20 U.S.C. § 1415(m)(1) (2007).

[54]20 U.S.C. § 1414(d)(2)(C)(i) (2007).

Free Appropriate Public Education

Once the IEP is agreed upon, district personnel must prepare the actual placement and coordinate needed services. Parental consent again is required. Unlike the evaluation phase, however, if the parents refuse the initial placement proposed by the district, educators are not permitted to seek authorization through due process. But if the parents reject a placement, the district is not in violation of the IDEA and is not required to convene an IEP meeting or prepare a placement.[55]

Where consent is provided, all children age 3 through 21 with qualifying disabilities must be provided a free appropriate public education that is made available in the least restrictive environment.[56] The placement must address the unique needs of the child and be delivered by "highly qualified" instructors.[57] Moreover, to qualify as appropriate, the placement must be provided at public expense and under public supervision and direction (even if the school district selects a private school placement); meet the standards of the state educational agency; include an appropriate preschool, elementary school, or secondary school education; and be delivered in conformity with the IEP.[58]

As needed, students also must be provided supplementary aids and services in the general education classroom to enable children with disabilities to be educated with nondisabled children to the maximum extent appropriate;[59] transition services to assist in transitioning from school to postschool activities such as postsecondary education, vocational training, integrated employment, continuing and adult education, adult services, independent living, or community participation;[60] and assistive technology devices and services to enable the child to increase, maintain, or improve functional capabilities.[61] Moreover, special education and related services should be made available as soon as possible following completion of the IEP, although no specific time line is identified in the IDEA.[62] Where services are prepared, they must be provided as close to the child's home as possible, and preferably in the school the child would have attended if not disabled. But it is not realistic to assume that all programs can be made available in every neighborhood school.

---

[55]20 U.S.C. § 1414(a)(1)(D)(ii)(II), (III) (2007).

[56]This is true unless students age 3 to 5 and 18 through 21 are not served within the state. *See* 20 U.S.C. § 1412(a)(1)(B) (2007).

[57]*Highly qualified* is defined in § 9109 of the Elementary and Secondary Education Act of 1965 (20 U.S.C. § 7801 (2007)). *See also* 20 U.S.C. § 1401(10) (2007). However, there is no private right of action if the child is taught by a teacher who is not highly qualified. *See* 20 U.S.C. § 1401(10)(E) (2007).

[58]20 U.S.C. § 1401(9) (2007).

[59]20 U.S.C. § 1401(33) (2007).

[60]20 U.S.C. § 1401(34) (2007).

[61]20 U.S.C. § 1401(1), (2) (2007).

[62]*See, e.g.*, D.D. v. New York City Bd. of Educ., 465 F.3d 503 (2d Cir. 2006).

Even though IEPs must be "appropriate," they need not be "the best" available or represent "optimum" programs that will maximize learning potential.[63] This issue was addressed in 1982 in *Board of Education v. Rowley*,[64] in which parents had requested that the school district provide a sign-language interpreter for their daughter in her academic classes, given her minimal residual hearing. The child's IEP specified a general education first-grade placement with special instruction from a tutor one hour per day and a speech therapist three hours per week, but did not include interpreter services. An interpreter had been provided during a two-week period when she was in kindergarten, but the practice was discontinued based on recommendations by the interpreter and other educators working with the child. Due to this omission, the parents were dissatisfied with the IEP and, after unsuccessful administrative review, filed suit.

On appeal, the Supreme Court rejected the standard proposed by the lower court (i.e., maximization of the potential of children with disabilities commensurate with the opportunity provided to other children[65]) and reasoned that "the intent of the act was more to open the door of public education to [children with disabilities] on appropriate terms than to guarantee any particular level of education once inside."[66] The IDEA was found to guarantee a "basic floor of opportunity,"[67] consisting of access to specialized instruction and related services that are individually designed to provide educational benefit. Applying these principles, the Court held that the plaintiff was receiving an appropriate education in that she was incurring educational benefit from individualized instruction and related services, as evidenced by her better than average performance in class, promotion from grade to grade, and positive interpersonal relationships with educators and peers.

The Court also made clear that lower courts are not to define an appropriate education. Rather, their review is limited to two questions:

- Has the state complied with the procedures identified in the act?
- Is the IEP developed through these procedures reasonably calculated to enable the child to receive educational benefit?[68]

---

[63]*See, e.g.*, D.B. v. Craven County Bd. of Educ., No. 99-1326, 2000 U.S. App. LEXIS 6176 (4th Cir. Apr. 3, 2000) (concluding that the district had provided the plaintiff with a free appropriate public education and that even if his writing skills were not as good as his parents would have liked, the IDEA requires that schools provide educational opportunities, not that they guarantee that every child will attain full potential; the student's poor achievement appeared to be related more to lack of effort and the failure to turn in assignments than to writing skill).

[64]458 U.S. 176 (1982).

[65]483 F. Supp. 528, 534 (S.D.N.Y. 1980).

[66]458 U.S. 176, 192 (1982).

[67]*Id.* at 200.

[68]*Id.* at 207.

Lower courts have interpreted this latter requirement to mandate educational programs that provide more than "trivial advancement."[69]

The two questions posed by the Supreme Court were addressed in an Eleventh Circuit case in which a student with a learning disability had been provided special instruction, classes, and services, including a portable classroom. The student did not make significant progress early in the year, as she was refusing to complete work assignments and had engaged in assaultive behavior. She had threatened other students with a nail, stuck a teacher in the finger, and hit and kicked several staff members. Following these incidents, she called her mother to report that her teachers were trying to "murder" her. She was suspended for seven days for her conduct. Upon her return, the child was even less compliant than before and her mother attended class on a regular basis. The mother helped her daughter complete in-class independent work assignments, was disrespectful to teachers, and took over her daughter's classroom instruction. The mother eventually removed her daughter from school and filed for due process. On appeal, the Eleventh Circuit held that although there were some minor procedural deficiencies, an appropriate program had been provided.[70] The IEP was prepared in a coordinated and collaborative manner and was designed to provide benefit, even if the degree of actual benefit was difficult to assess given the involvement of the mother.

Courts often defer to state and local educators and administrative review officials regarding the nature of IEPs and matters of pedagogy but still will not uphold proposed placements that are found inappropriate and not supported by the data. In such situations, courts have not been reluctant to direct the development of an appropriate public placement, or to approve a private one.[71] For example, the Ninth Circuit concluded that a California school district failed to provide an appropriate education by placing a child with autism in a program for the "communicatively handicapped." The court noted that the program was not individualized, the student's needs were not being met, and the teacher was not trained to work with autistic children.[72] The district was required to reimburse the parents for the costs of an out-of-district placement, including expenses associated with commuting, lodging, and tuition, as well as attorneys' fees.

Least Restrictive Environment

Children with disabilities are to be educated with children who are not disabled to the maximum extent appropriate. Special classes, separate schooling, or other removal of

[69]*See, e.g.*, Ridgewood Bd. of Educ. v. N.E. *ex rel.* M.E., 172 F.3d 238 (3d Cir. 1999).

[70]Sch. Bd. v. K.C., 285 F.3d 977 (11th Cir. 2002).

[71]County Sch. Bd. of Henrico County v. Z.P., 399 F.3d 298, 311 (4th Cir. 2005) (remanding with instructions for the lower court to reexamine the appropriateness of plaintiff's IEP as proposed by the district; the state hearing officer had ruled on behalf of the parents, finding the placement to be inappropriate, but that decision was reversed by the trial court).

[72]Union Sch. Dist. v. Smith, 15 F.3d 1519 (9th Cir. 1994). *But see* M.M. v. Sch. Bd. Miami-Dade County, 437 F.3d 1085 (11th Cir. 2006) (finding that the IDEA does not require that the best program be provided and that the methods employed by the district to address plaintiff's severe bilateral sensorial hearing loss provided an appropriate program).

a child from general education may occur only if the nature or severity of the disability is such that education cannot be achieved satisfactorily.[73] In making least restrictive environment (LRE) decisions, school personnel should determine the types of placements for delivery of the IEP along the continuum of alternative placements and then select the option that is least restrictive. Alternative placements may include:

- A general education classroom with various support services,
- A general classroom with or without itinerant teachers or resource rooms,
- Self-contained special classes,
- Special schools,
- Home instruction, or
- Instruction in hospitals or residential institutions.[74]

Educational and noneducational benefits for each placement should be assessed, including the effect the child with a disability may have on classmates.[75]

General education with supplemental aides and services represents the LRE for most children; for a few, however, the LRE will be in a setting that is more restrictive.[76] The IEP team need not select a placement that is entirely in general education or entirely segregated. In some instances, it is appropriate to deliver the child's program within a range of LRE settings (e.g., a segregated program to assist in the development of lip reading, but a general education setting for other instructional and noninstructional activities).[77] States are responsible for ensuring that teachers and administrators are fully informed about their LRE responsibilities and for providing them with technical assistance and training.[78]

Moreover, children should not be placed experimentally in the general classroom under the guise of full inclusion[79] and then provided appropriate placements

[73]20 U.S.C. § 1412 (a)(5)(A) (2007). *See, e.g.,* L.E. v. Ramsey Bd. of Educ., 435 F.3d 384 (3d Cir. 2006) (upholding lower court determination that the general education classroom, even with supplemental aides and services, could not provide plaintiff with an appropriate education).

[74]34 C.F.R. § 300.115(b) (2007). Also of note is that if the parents elect not to have their child medicated while at school, the student may not be denied an appropriate placement because he is not being medicated. The selection of services and the determination of the least restricted environment may be affected, however. *See* 20 U.S.C. § 1412(a)(25) (2007).

[75]*See, e.g.,* Alex R. v. Forrestville Valley Cmty. Unit Sch. Dist. #221, 375 F.3d 603 (7th Cir. 2004) (upholding lower court determination that consideration of a child's regular outbursts and physical attacks of others in identifying LRE was appropriate).

[76]*See, e.g.,* Beth B. v. Van Clay, 282 F.3d 493 (7th Cir. 2002) (supporting selection of a placement that was more restrictive than general education as the child's academic progress was virtually nonexistent and her developmental progress was limited within general education).

[77]*See, e.g.,* Brillon v. Klein Indep. Sch. Dist., 100 Fed. Appx. 309 (5th Cir. 2004).

[78]34 C.F.R. § 300.119 (2007). *See also* Asbury v. Mo. Dep't of Elementary and Secondary Educ., 248 F.3d 1163 (8th Cir. 2001) (affirming summary judgment for defendant where the plaintiff claimed that the district had failed to properly train its personnel to educate children with autism).

[79]The term *full-inclusion* is used here to refer to placement in general education where the child's educational needs are appropriately addressed through the use of supplemental aides and services.

only after they fail to meet short-term objectives or acquire educational benefit. Inappropriate placements may require the unnecessary expenditure of thousands of dollars, violate the child's right to a free appropriate public education, and most important, delay the provision of truly appropriate and beneficial education.

Private Schools

Many children with disabilities attend private schools. Some are placed in a private program by the public school district, given the availability of an appropriate program. Other children attend private schools due to parental preference, given factors such as the nature of the curriculum, program quality, religious orientation, and convenience.

Public Placement of a Child in a Private School. When a school district cannot effectively address specific individual student needs, where appropriate programs are not available within a child's reasonable commute, or if existing programs are not age appropriate, the IDEA does not necessarily require creation of new programs or schools.[80] In the alternative, placement often may be made in other public schools or in private facilities, including those that are residential. Although the fiscal obligation can be substantial, the school district will be held financially responsible for residential placements that are required to provide an appropriate program. In such instances, the district must cover all nonmedical costs, including room and board. The IDEA's provision for residential care, however, is not intended to compensate for a poor home environment or to serve as a means of delivering social, medical, or incarceration services.[81] Accordingly, if a residential placement is sought by the parents for reasons other than the child's education (e.g., the risk the child poses in the home,[82] the inability to shelter or feed the youth, the student being the target of a parent's abuse), the request may be denied.

When the public school system selects a private placement, a representative of the private school should participate in IEP placement meetings either in person or through a telephone conversation. Subsequent meetings to review and revise the IEP may be initiated and conducted by private school personnel, if approved by district officials. Where this occurs, both the parents and a public school representative must be involved in any decision about the child's IEP, and the district must authorize any change prior to implementation.

It is important to note that private schools are not required to implement special programs or to lower their academic standards to permit placement of children with disabilities.[83] Applicants who cannot participate effectively in the private school's general education curriculum, assuming the availability of "minor adjustments," may be denied admission.

[80]*See* T.R. *ex rel.* N.R. v. Kingwood Twp. Bd. of Educ., 205 F.3d 572 (3d Cir. 2000).

[81]*See, e.g.*, Dale M. v. Bd. of Educ., 237 F.3d 813 (7th Cir. 2001).

[82]*See, e.g.*, Gonzalez v. P.R. Dep't of Educ., 254 F.3d 350 (1st Cir. 2001).

[83]St. Johnsbury Acad. v. D.H., 240 F.3d 163 (2d Cir. 2001).

Parental Placement of a Child in a Private School. In some instances, parents elect to place their children in private schools, either initially[84] or when they perceive public programs to be inappropriate. Parents always have the option of selecting an alternative program, but such placements will be at parental expense unless the parents can show that the public placement is inappropriate and that their selected placement is appropriate.

The Supreme Court addressed this issue in 1985 in *School Committee of Burlington v. Department of Education of Massachusetts*.[85] In that case, a father had disagreed with the school district's proposed educational placement of his child with learning disabilities and, after seeking an independent evaluation from medical experts and initiating the appeals process, enrolled the child in a private school. The Court rejected the school district's argument that a change in placement without district consent waived all rights to reimbursement. In the Court's opinion, denying relief would defeat the IDEA's major objective of providing an appropriate program. When the school district's proposed placement is ultimately found to be inappropriate, reimbursement is considered necessary since the review process can be quite lengthy. The Court reasoned that children should not be educationally disadvantaged by an inappropriate placement and that parents should not be economically penalized for removing their children.

The Supreme Court, however, issued one caveat: parents who unilaterally seek private placements do so at their own financial risk. If the public school placement is found to be proper, reimbursement will be denied, even if the parentally selected program is shown to be appropriate, better, or even cheaper.[86] Furthermore, reimbursement will be denied when both the public and private placements are shown to be inappropriate.[87] Thus, relief can be acquired only if the public placement is inappropriate and the private placement is appropriate.[88]

---

[84]*Compare* Bd. of Educ. of city of New York v. Tom F., 193 Fed. Appx. 26 (2d Cir. 2006) (noting that 20 U.S.C. § 1412(a)(10)(C)(i) did not require reimbursement where children had not previously received special education under public school supervision). *affirmed by an equally divided court*. 128 S. Ct. 1 (2007) with Frank G. v. Bd. of Educ., 459 F.3d 356 (2d Cir. 2006) (concluding that prior receipt of services under public supervision is not necessary to seek reimbursement; all that is required is reasonable notice and the intent to reject the proposed placement), *cert. denied*. 128 S. Ct. 436 (2007).

[85]471 U.S. 359 (1985).

[86]L.T. v. Warwick Sch. Comm., 361 F.3d 80 (1st Cir. 2004) (finding the district proffered placement to be appropriate and noting that the inquiry ends at that point so there is no need to consider whether the program preferred by the parents would be better).

[87]M.S. v. Yonkers Bd. of Educ., 231 F.3d 96 (2d Cir. 2000).

[88]*Compare* Montgomery Twp. Bd. of Educ. v. South Carolina, 135 Fed. Appx. 534 (3d Cir. 2005) (upholding reimbursement for unilaterally selected private education) *and* Knable v. Bexley City Sch. Dist., 238 F.3d 755 (6th Cir. 2001) (providing reimbursement to parents of child with oppositional defiant disorder given the lack of due process provided by the district—a proper IEP meeting was not conducted, so an appropriate IEP was never in place) *with* Houston Indep. Sch. Dist. v. Bobby R., 200 F.3d 341 (5th Cir. 2000) (denying reimbursement for a placement unilaterally selected by the parent given that the district had provided the student with a FAPE that was reasonably calculated to provide educational benefit as evidenced by increased test scores in a range of areas).

A subsequent Supreme Court decision in 1993, *Florence County School District Four v. Carter*, gave additional support to parents seeking reimbursement for private placements.[89] In that case, a child with a learning disability was removed by her parents from what was proved to be an inappropriate public placement and enrolled in an appropriate private program. Controversy developed when the parents sought reimbursement but were denied because the private school was not included on the state-approved list—a list that was not made available to the public, as the district preferred to evaluate each case individually. The Court held that reimbursement could not be denied simply because the school was not state approved. The touchstone was that the public program was inappropriate, while the unilaterally selected program was appropriate. As a result, the reimbursement of reasonable costs was required.

Parental choices are not always found either reasonable or appropriate, however. For example, the Eleventh Circuit upheld a lower court decision denying reimbursement, as the student had been provided an IEP that was reasonably calculated to confer an appropriate education. The requested residential placement was found to be both unnecessary and not least restrictive. The court also rejected the opinion of an expert hired by the parents who had indicated that the family needed someone to take care of their son in their home, because family members had responsibilities other than caretaker and teacher.[90] In another case, the parents sued a school district for failure to provide their child with an appropriate education, notwithstanding the out-of-state placement of the child in a private residential facility and payment for three round-trips home for the child to visit. The parents were demanding that the district pay transportation costs (including airfare for both parents and two siblings), hotel, food, and rental car expenses so they could visit the child. The court acknowledged that the IEP encouraged the development of family relations, but ruled that the district was not required to "foot the bill for family gatherings."[91]

In an effort to limit district liability for private placements unilaterally selected by parents, the IDEA permits reduction or denial of reimbursement if the parents fail to provide public officials with notification of their intent or if a court finds their conduct unreasonable.[92] Proper notification can be accomplished either by discussing the matter with the IEP team during a formal meeting or by providing the district with written notice, including an explanation of the reasons for the decision, at least 10 days prior to the projected removal of the child. At that point, if the

---

[89]510 U.S. 7 (1993).

[90]Devine v. Indian River County Sch. Bd., 249 F.3d 1289 (11th Cir. 2001).

[91]Cohen v. Sch. Bd., 450 So. 2d 1238, 1240 (Fla. Dist. Ct. App. 1984).

[92]*See, e.g.,* Loren F. v. Atlanta Indep. Sch. Sys., 349 F.3d 1309 (11th Cir. 2003) (noting that if the parents are found on remand to have significantly hindered or frustrated IEP development, equitable relief may be denied on that ground alone; also observing that the lower court may consider the delays caused by the parents as well as their failure to make their child available for evaluation); Pollowitz v. Weast, 90 Fed. Appx. 438 (4th Cir. 2001) (determining that reimbursement was unnecessary as the parents failed to provide the district with notice of withdrawal).

district elects to perform additional student evaluations, the parent is required to make the child available.

Services Available in Private Schools.   Students enrolled by their parents in private schools have no individual right to receive special education and related services provided by the school district.[93] Instead, public officials are responsible for meeting with parents and other representatives of the children to decide who is to receive services; what, where, and how services are to be provided; and how services are to be evaluated. In selecting a site for the delivery of services, officials will consider available alternative delivery systems as well as whether provision on campus (e.g., at a religious school) violates state law.[94] If off-campus delivery is selected, eligible children must be transported from the private school to the site and back or to their homes.

Funding for private school services is provided in the IDEA at a per-pupil prorated amount equal to the federal funds spent on IEP services provided to children in the public school district.[95] This amount is modest, however, when compared to the dollars contributed by state and local governments. As a result, services that are made available to children enrolled in private schools will tend to be fewer in number or for shorter time periods than those available to children placed or served by the local school district.[96] When parents with children in private schools have challenged this disparity as a violation of the Equal Protection or Free Exercise Clauses, they have been unsuccessful.[97]

Change of Placement.   Following an appropriate initial placement in a public or private school, adjustments to a child's IEP may be necessary because of the results of an annual review or reevaluation; discontinuation of a school, program, or service; violent or disruptive behavior; or graduation. Before changing a substantive aspect of a student's program, written notice must be given to the parents of their right to review the proposed alteration, and informed consent generally must be provided. However, if the parent does not respond to efforts to communicate, district personnel should document the date and type of each effort and then may proceed to deliver the program as amended.[98] If the parents later contact the district, they may challenge the placement decision through due process.

[93]Foley v. Special Sch. Dist., 153 F.3d 863 (8th Cir. 1998).

[94]W.J.M. *ex rel.* K.D.M. v. Reedsport Sch. Dist., 196 F.3d 1046 (9th Cir. 1999) (upholding an Oregon administrative regulation stipulating that if a district decides to provide services to children in private schools, such appropriate special education and services must be provided in a religiously neutral setting).

[95]20 U.S.C. § 1412(a)(10)(A)(i)(I) (2007).

[96]Jasa v. Millard Pub. Sch. Dist. No. 17, 206 F.3d 813 (8th Cir. 2000) (concluding that the district had provided the child with a FAPE and need not fund the same services in a private school unilaterally selected by the parents).

[97]*See, e.g.,* Gary S. v. Manchester Sch. Dist., 374 F.3d 15 (1st Cir. 2004).

[98]20 U.S.C. § 1414(c)(3) (2007).

Related Services

A free appropriate public education may include related services in addition to special education. Related services are defined as transportation and such developmental, corrective, and other supportive services (including speech pathology and
audiology, psychological services, physical and occupational therapy, recreation,
social work services, early identification and assessment, orientation and mobility
services, school health services, counseling services, medical services for diagnostic
and evaluation purposes, parent counseling and training, school nurse services, and
interpreting services) that are necessary for a child with a disability to benefit from
special education.[99] Services such as physical therapy, occupational therapy, and
speech therapy also may qualify as related services. The areas of transportation, psychological services, and health services are reviewed briefly here.

Transportation

Federal regulations require the provision of transportation as a related service for
qualified children to and from school, within school buildings, and on school
grounds, even if specialized equipment is needed in making programs and activities
accessible. A child qualifies for transportation if it is provided for other children, or if
it is included within an IEP or Section 504 plan. Failure to provide the service to
qualified students has resulted in courts requiring districts to reimburse parents for
transportation costs, time, effort, babysitting services, and interest on their
expenses.[100] Nonetheless, courts also have concluded that where alternative transportation was provided, the district was not required to reimburse parents who
wanted to transport their own child;[101] that a child's hearing impairment did not qualify her for special transportation;[102] and that transportation did not have to be provided following involvement in a privately funded after-school program that was
unrelated to the IEP.[103]

Psychological Services

Psychological services are explicitly identified in federal law as related services to
be included within IEPs where appropriate. Such services include administering and
interpreting psychological and educational tests as well as other assessment procedures; obtaining, integrating, and interpreting information about the child's behavior and condition; consulting with staff in planning IEPs; planning and managing a

[99]20 U.S.C. § 1401(a)(26) (2007).

[100]*See, e.g.*, Hurry v. Jones, 734 F.2d 879 (1st Cir. 1984); Taylor v. Bd. of Educ., 649 F. Supp. 1253 (N.D.N.Y. 1986).

[101]DeLeon v. Susquehanna Cmty. Sch. Dist., 747 F.2d 149 (3d Cir. 1984).

[102]McNair v. Oak Hills Local Sch. Dist., 872 F.2d 153 (6th Cir. 1989).

[103]Roslyn Union Free Sch. Dist. v. Univ. of N.Y., 711 N.Y.S.2d 582 (App. Div. 2000).

program of psychological services; and assisting in the development of positive behavioral intervention strategies.[104] When psychological services are needed to help the child to benefit from instruction and are provided by a psychologist or other qualified individual, the services should be included within the IEP. However, if parents request psychiatric and other medical services,[105] or if psychological services are not required to provide a free appropriate public education (FAPE),[106] such requests may be denied.

Health and Nursing Services

Courts have differentiated between medical and health services. As indicated, the IDEA excludes medical services except for diagnostic and evaluative purposes and defines both medical (i.e., those provided by a licensed physician) and health services (i.e., those provided by a school nurse or other qualified person).

The Supreme Court began its review of school health-care issues in *Irving Independent School District v. Tatro*.[107] In that 1984 case, a child required clean intermittent catheterization every three to four hours. The Court found catheterization to be essential in that it would enable the child to attend school and thereby benefit from instruction, and noted that it could be performed by either a nurse or a trained layperson. Accordingly, the service was not a medical service and could not be excluded from the child's IEP for that reason.

In post-*Tatro* years, the issue of health care has been volatile, given the growing number of medically fragile children now in public schools, the desire of many parents to have their health-impaired child integrated into general education, and the escalating costs of health care. Courts ultimately adopted a "bright-line" test requiring the provision of all health-care services provided by anyone other than a physician, if required to enable the child to attend school and benefit from the IEP.

In 1999, in *Cedar Rapids Community School District v. Garret F.*,[108] a child had a severed spinal column and was paralyzed from the neck down. To remain in school, he required full-time nursing care (e.g., catheterization, suctioning, ambubagging, ventilator assistance, emergency aid). The school district argued that the services collectively should be viewed as medical, even if individually they qualified as health services, and asserted that it would incur an undue financial burden if required to provide the services. The Court acknowledged the legitimate financial concerns of the district, but noted that the law as currently constructed required the court to reject the undue burden claim.[109] Moreover, by applying the bright-line test,

[104]34 C.F.R. § 300.34(c)(10) (2007).

[105]Butler v. Evans, 225 F.3d 887 (7th Cir. 2000).

[106]Nack v. Orange City Sch. Dist., 454 F.3d 604 (6th Cir. 2006).

[107]468 U.S. 883 (1984).

[108]526 U.S. 66 (1999).

[109]Although unavailable under the IDEA, the undue burden defense is available under both § 504 and the ADA.

the Court ruled that any health service a student may need to participate in a school setting[110] had to be provided, regardless of cost or resulting financial impact on the district.

Tangential to this controversy is the issue of who is to pay for required health services. As a rule, services that are included within the IEP are the responsibility of the local school district. However, some financial assistance may be available from Medicaid. Due to a 1988 Supreme Court decision, *Bowen v. Massachusetts*,[111] and an amendment to Title XIX of the Social Security Act (Medicaid),[112] health services included on the state-approved list can no longer be excluded from reimbursement solely because they are provided at school during the school day. Medicaid-eligible individuals include those who are receiving aid to families with dependent children, qualified low-income pregnant women and their children, low-income people age 65 or older, and others who are blind or disabled and are receiving Supplemental Security Income. The use of Medicaid is limited, however, as not all children are Medicaid-eligible and not all health services are included on state-approved lists that vary somewhat by state.

Extended School Year

As noted, federal statutes require that IEPs be both appropriate and designed to provide educational benefit. In meeting these mandates, it may be necessary for a particular child to receive services beyond the traditional nine-month school year. While school districts can prescribe a fixed number of instructional days for students without disabilities, such a determination must be made on an individual basis for children with disabilities. Nonetheless, where extended school year (ESY) services are found "beneficial" or even "maximizing," but are not "essential" to the provision of an appropriate program, they are not required under the IDEA.[113]

Where ESY services are provided, programs will vary widely. Some mandate the extension of the full IEP for one, two, or three additional months; others utilize new or different services; and yet others acquire all or some of the same services, but in different amounts. Furthermore, in fairly narrow circumstances an ESY program may include the delivery of only related services, such as physical therapy during the summer to allow a child to remain sufficiently flexible or mobile to participate within the IEP in the fall. The IEP team is responsible for making

---

[110]Note, however, that some health-care services do not have to be provided when the child is homebound. *See, e.g.*, Daniel O. v. Mo. State Bd. of Educ., No. 99-2792, 2000 U.S. App. LEXIS 7032 (8th Cir. April 19, 2000).

[111]487 U.S. 879 (1988).

[112]42 U.S.C. § 1396 (2007).

[113]Kenton County Sch. Dist., v. Hunt, 384 F.3d 269 (6th Cir. 2004) (remanding and requiring parents to bear the burden of showing that an ESY was needed to avoid something more than adequately recoupable regression and that the current IEP without ESY failed to provide an appropriate program).

individualized decisions regarding eligibility for ESY services and for selecting appropriate services, including their amount and duration.[114]

Eligibility decisions should be made annually during the IEP review and be based on regression-recoupment,[115] individual need, the nature and severity of the disability, self-sufficiency and independence, whether educational benefit can be incurred without such services, whether short-term goals and objectives are being met, and whether progress is being made toward the accomplishment of long-term goals. Receipt of ESY services in previous years, however, is not a factor to consider in making the eligibility decision for the current year.

Participation in Sports

Children with disabilities, like many children without disabilities, often are interested in participating in interscholastic sports. But, the requests of these student-athletes to participate have at times been denied because either they failed to meet eligibility requirements or their participation represented too great a risk to themselves or to others. Although most disputes are based on either the Rehabilitation Act or the Americans with Disabilities Act (ADA), a few cases have been filed under the IDEA.

The IDEA has been involved in two types of sports-related disability cases: (1) where parents wanted to include sports in the IEP; and (2) where the IEP team included sports in the IEP and the state athletic association penalized the school for allowing an ineligible student to participate. Because sports participation is seldom considered essential for students to incur educational benefit, it typically is not included in IEPs.[116] Furthermore, from the school district's perspective, it generally is not prudent to include sports, or any other extracurricular activity, in IEPs. Such a practice establishes an entitlement to team membership (not to participation *per se*, however) and enables sports participation to become a right that can be withdrawn only through due process.

In the second scenario (i.e., where the team is penalized), state athletic associations do not receive IDEA funds or any other type of federal financial assistance and

---

[114]J.H. v. Henrico County Sch. Bd., 395 F.3d 185 (4th Cir. 2005) (remanding with instructions for the lower court to have the hearing officer determine the amount of ESY services necessary for the plaintiff's speech, language, and occupational skills acquired during kindergarten not to be placed in jeopardy).

[115]In this context, *regression* refers to the loss of knowledge, ability, or skill a student may experience during a break in instruction, while *recoupment* refers to the time it takes to regain the knowledge, ability, or skill that was lost once instruction is resumed. *See* Johnson v. Indep. Sch. Dist. No. 4, 921 F.2d 1022 (10th Cir. 1990) (holding that this analysis must include not only retrospective data related to regression but also predictive data).

[116]*But see* Kling v. Mentor Pub. Sch. Dist., 136 F. Supp. 2d 744 (N.D. Ohio 2001) (granting preliminary injunction to require the participation of an overage athlete who was likely to receive educational benefits only with the inclusion of sports on his IEP; this decision was made following a determination of whether the intent of the age policy would be fulfilled notwithstanding the student's involvement).

consequently are not required to comply with either the IDEA or Section 504 (although disability discrimination suits under the ADA are possible). Accordingly, if the IEP team were to include sports in the IEP and thereby allow an otherwise ineligible student to participate in an interscholastic contest, school officials may have created a situation that will result in rules violations and penalties. The Montana Supreme Court "strongly encouraged" educators to be prudent in including sports in IEPs and warned that they might be "making a promise [they] simply cannot keep."[117] Given this situation, the district would have to sue the athletic association (presumably under the Fourteenth Amendment[118]) to terminate whatever remedial actions have been taken against it. In the end, even if the district is to prevail, it will incur substantial expense and have to dedicate considerable personnel time to a problem that could have easily been avoided by not including sports participation in IEPs.

Unlike the IDEA, there are myriad related scenarios and cases regarding athletic participation filed under Section 504 and the ADA. Most claims have alleged discrimination due to facially neutral regulations that disproportionately affect students with disabilities, such as age limitations,[119] grade-point average restrictions,[120] one-year residency and transfer requirements,[121] and eight-semester/four-season limitations.[122]

Historically, all students were required to meet eligibility criteria and were allowed to play only when they were otherwise qualified to participate *and* if they made the team. The courts permitted and often required the uniform application of such rules, but that trend may be changing. A related issue reviewed by the Supreme Court in a professional sport context has application to interscholastic sports. In *PGA Tour v. Martin* in 2001, the Supreme Court supported a professional golfer's request to ride a cart rather than walk the course, as the event rules required.[123] Walking caused him pain that resulted in fatigue and anxiety that could lead to hemorrhaging and the development of blood clots or fractures. The Court reasoned that "shot making" was

---

[117]J.M. v. Mont. High Sch. Ass'n, 875 P.2d 1026, 1032 (Mont. 1994).

[118]Such suits are more likely today given the Supreme Court's ruling in Brentwood Acad. v. Tenn. Secondary Sch. Athletic Ass'n., 531 U.S. 288 (2002), where the state athletic association was declared a state actor, notwithstanding the fact that it was a private corporation.

[119]*See, e.g.*, Sandison v. Mich. High Sch. Athletic Ass'n, 64 F.3d 1026 (6th Cir. 1995); Dennin v. Conn. Interscholastic Athletic Conference, 913 F. Supp. 663 (D. Conn. 1996).

[120]*See, e.g.*, Hoot v. Milan Area Sch., 853 F. Supp. 243 (E.D. Mich. 1994).

[121]*See, e.g.*, Crocker v. Tenn. Secondary Sch. Athletic Ass'n, 980 F.2d 382 (6th Cir. 1992).

[122]*Compare* Washington v. Ind. High Sch. Athletic Ass'n, 181 F.3d 840 (7th Cir. 1999) (determining that a student who had dropped out of school and later reentered and played basketball should not have been declared ineligible under the rule limiting participation during the first eight semesters following commencement of the ninth grade; reasoning that waiver of the rule in this instance involving this student would not represent a fundamental alteration or create an undue financial burden for the association) *with* McPherson v. Mich. High Sch. Athletic Ass'n, 119 F.3d 453 (6th Cir. 1997) (upholding application of an eight-semester rule against a student with ADHD and seizure disorder and concluding that its waiver would represent a fundamental alteration of the sports program and create an immense and undue financial burden for the state association).

[123]532 U.S. 661 (2001).

the essence of golf and that walking was neither an essential attribute nor an indispensable feature of the sport, notwithstanding contradictory testimony from golf legends Arnold Palmer, Jack Nicklaus, and Ken Venturi. This decision will have implications for all sports. It does not require lowering the basket, widening the goal, or bringing in the fences in basketball, soccer, and baseball, respectively, but it does require the evaluation of any rule that disqualifies an otherwise qualified participant with a disability. Review of such rules should reveal whether they are essential features of the sport or are peripheral and therefore subject to alteration or elimination.

Given the Supreme Court majority opinion in *PGA Tour*, state athletic associations need to follow a four-step process in the development and application of their policies and rules:

- Identify those rules that potentially disqualify students with disabilities because of the limitations posed by their disabilities;
- Determine whether each identified rule supports a necessary and valid purpose;
- Assess whether the requested modification or adjustment is reasonable and necessary for the individual to participate in the activity; and
- Ascertain whether provision of the modification or adjustment would fundamentally alter the nature of the competition, adversely affect the demonstrated valid purpose of the rule, or result in an unfair advantage.[124]

Another type of sports-related case involves disqualified athletes with physically limiting conditions who nonetheless are otherwise qualified to participate. In many of these situations, the athlete is willing to assume the risks of participation, sign a waiver of liability if injured in the normal occurrence of the game, and provide affidavits signed by physicians both indicating that participation is safe and identifying any necessary safety wear. Since the mid- to late-1970s, the majority of courts have supported the right of student athletes to participate, even with the absence of organs, limbs, vision, and the like.[125] Recently, however, two courts addressing claims of discrimination filed by college athletes have sided with the educational institutions.[126] Both courts indicated that they were not in a position to determine which "experts" were correct concerning the degree of risk that would be present if the athlete were to participate. Instead, it was their view that deference should be given to the institution's

---

[124]*See, e.g.,* Cruz v. Penn. Interscholastic Athletic Ass'n, 157 F. Supp. 2d 485 (E.D. Pa. 2001) (applying PGA Tour criteria and granting a preliminary injunction where a student with a disability was denied the opportunity to participate in sport due to being overage).

[125]*See, e.g.,* Grube v. Bethlehem Area Sch. Dist., 550 F. Supp. 418 (E.D. Penn. 1982) (loss of kidney).

[126]*See, e.g.,* Knapp v. Northwestern Univ., 101 F.3d 473 (7th Cir. 1996) (determining that participation in basketball could be denied to an athlete who had previously experienced sudden cardiac death but was revived and had an internal cardioverter-defibrillator implanted in his abdomen that was designed to enable his heart to restart if it were to stop again); Pahulu v. Univ. of Kan., 897 F. Supp. 1387 (D. Kan. 1995) (denying right to play football to an athlete who suffered a hit to the head and incurred a markedly stenotic cervical canal resulting in an extremely high risk of permanent severe neurological injury if he were again to engage in contact such as that found in football).

experts as long as their professional judgment was reasonable, rational, and supported by substantial, competent evidence.

Discipline

Students with disabilities are not exempt from reasonable disciplinary measures, although due process exceeding that provided general education students is required at times, and penalties may be limited in type and duration. In 1988, the Supreme Court in *Honig v. Doe* held that an indefinite suspension of two students pending the outcome of expulsion proceedings was a prohibited change in placement and violated the stay-put provision of the IDEA.[127] The state superintendent of public instruction had urged the Supreme Court to recognize a "dangerousness" exception to the stay-put requirement. Notwithstanding, the Court stated that Congress deliberately stripped schools of the unilateral authority to exclude students with disabilities. The history of exclusion of such students prior to passage of the IDEA and the early litigation that guided the development of the law convinced the Court that the conspicuous absence of an emergency exception was intentional.

The Supreme Court, however, emphasized that school officials are not without options when confronted with a dangerous student. They may use a range of normal procedures (e.g., suspension of up to 10 days, detention, time out[128]). In addition, the Court indicated that if other forms of discipline are not successful, and the student already has been suspended for the maximum 10-day period but continues to pose a threat, school officials may seek injunctive relief if the parents refuse to agree to a change in placement.

Among the disciplinary options available to school officials, suspension and expulsion have resulted in considerable judicial action. Each is reviewed here in greater detail.[129]

Suspension

The IDEA allows school officials to consider unique circumstances on a case-by-case basis if there has been a violation of the student conduct code. When officials determine that a *suspension* (i.e., removal of a student from the educational setting for 10 or fewer days) is justified, no procedures beyond those provided general education students are required. The resulting suspension may be either an in-school assignment to a suspension room or out-of-school, requiring complete removal from the school

---

[127]484 U.S. 305 (1988).

[128]Not all assignment to time-out will be found legal, however. *See, e.g.,* Covington v. Knox County Sch. Sys., 205 F.3d 912 (6th Cir. 2000) (observing that plaintiff had been routinely locked in a small time-out room for up to several hours at a time, denied lunch, required to disrobe on one occasion, and forced to remain in the room following urination that resulted when the confinement period was lengthy).

[129]*See* text accompanying notes 27–29, Chapter 7.

setting. Students with disabilities may not generally be suspended for more than 10 consecutive days or receive repetitive brief suspensions that aggregate to more than 10 days during the school year. Successive suspensions exceeding the 10-day limit are possible, but only where they do not represent a pattern of removal and are based on separate incidents of misconduct. In the comparatively exceptional circumstance where removal justifiably exceeds the 10-day limit, services consistent with the IEP must be provided beginning the eleventh day.[130]

The key in determining whether a day of suspension is to apply toward the total is to assess whether the child has been removed from the IEP, not whether the child has received an in-school or out-of-school suspension. If a student is assigned to a time-out room, rather than an in-school suspension room, and instruction and services identified within the IEP continue to be delivered by properly credentialed individuals, it is unlikely that the time removed from the general education classroom will contribute to the 10-day limit. To reduce the likelihood of litigation, however, it is recommended that assignment to time-out be included within the IEPs of students who are likely to require such assignments as a form of behavior modification or intervention. Once the parent has agreed to such a provision, assignment to time-out will be consistent with rather than removal from the IEP.

Expulsion

When violations of the conduct code are excessive or severe, school officials have the authority to approve expulsions. *Expulsion* is the removal of a student for more than 10 consecutive days. When students with disabilities are expelled, a change of placement results, and procedures that exceed those required for general education students are required. In such instances, an expulsion will be justified only if the district has properly implemented the student's IEP and the contested conduct does not have a direct and substantial relationship to the student's disability.[131] When expulsion is supported, the student may be assigned either to a home placement or to an interim alternative educational setting. The student's record may include reference to the student being expelled and the basis for the expulsion. Notwithstanding the above, if the student is to be removed from his or her current placement for more than 10 days, services consistent with the IEP need to be delivered in the new environment that will enable the student to make progress toward achieving identified goals and objectives. These services are required regardless of whether the behavior was disability related.[132] In short, educational services cannot be terminated for children with disabilities for longer than 10 days.

Where there is a determination that the behavior is a manifestation of the student's disability,[133] the IEP team is responsible for conducting a functional behavioral

[130]34 C.F.R. § 300.530(b); 34 C.F.R. § 300.536 (2007).

[131]20 U.S.C. § 1415(k)(1)(E)(i) (2007).

[132]20 U.S.C. § 1415(k)(1)(D) (2007).

[133]*See* Peter S. Latham, Patricia H. Latham, and Myrna R. Mandlawitz, *Special Education Law* (Boston: Pearson, 2008), pp. 76–77.

assessment and for implementing a behavioral intervention plan.[134] Interventions should address the conduct that resulted in the disciplinary action and should be modified when needed. Notwithstanding, assignment to an alternative setting for up to 45 days is permissible under the IDEA, even when the student's behavior is disability related. This may occur only where the student has committed one of the following violations on school grounds or at a school function:

- Carries a weapon;
- Knowingly possesses, uses, sells, or solicits illegal drugs; or
- Inflicts serious bodily injury upon another.[135]

If the parents disagree with a decision to remove their child from school, they may appeal that decision to a hearing officer. Similarly, school officials may appeal when they are concerned that a student's continued presence within the school setting is substantially likely to result in injury to the student or others. The hearing officer has the authority to either return the student to the placement from which he or she was removed or order placement to an interim alternative educational setting. The hearing should occur within 20 school days of the date of request and a decision must be provided within 10 school days after the hearing. During this period, the student remains in the current placement (i.e., the interim alternative setting), unless the removal period has expired, or the parent and district agree otherwise.[136]

Interestingly, even students who are not yet identified as disabled at times may be protected by the IDEA, but only if school officials had "knowledge" that they may be disabled. Knowledge exists where parents express in writing to administrative or supervisory personnel their concern that their child may be in need of special education and related services or request an evaluation. Knowledge also may be established where an educator expresses concern about a student's behavior directly to supervisory personnel. Note, however, that the student is not entitled to IDEA protection in a given disciplinary hearing if:

- Notification of a possible disability occurred following the inappropriate conduct,
- The child was found not to qualify as disabled given the results of an expedited evaluation,
- The parents did not allow the district to conduct the evaluation, or
- The parents previously refused IDEA services.[137]

Where an evaluation is conducted and the student does not qualify as both disabled and in need of special education and related services, instruction during the

[134]20 U.S.C. § 1415(k)(1)(F)(i) (2007). Failure to provide such a plan can result in the denial of FAPE and an IDEA violation. *See* Metro. Bd. of Pub. Educ. v. Bellamy, 116 Fed. Appx. 570 (6th Cir. 2004).

[135]20 U.S.C. § 1415(k)(1)(G) (2007).

[136]20 U.S.C. § 1415(k)(3)(B), (4) (2007).

[137]20 U.S.C. § 1415(k)(5) (2007).

removal period need not be provided, unless available to other general education students who have been removed from school. In contrast, if the student does qualify as disabled, special education and related services consistent with the newly developed IEP need to be provided no later than practical and feasible, and preferably no later than following the tenth day of removal.[138]

It should be recognized that the IDEA does not prohibit personnel from reporting any crime a student may have committed to law enforcement authorities.[139] Law enforcement officials are not bound by the IDEA and may require an unruly or delinquent student to submit to treatment, home detention, or incarceration, in addition to any penalty the district may provide.

Procedural Safeguards

School officials generally make good faith efforts to meet the needs of children with disabilities, yet there will be times when the parents disagree with evaluation, program, or placement decisions. Understandably, many parents seek the best possible education for their children. Alternatively, school districts may offer what parents perceive as only a minimally appropriate program, or even less.[140] Where disagreement persists, the IDEA has provided a variety of means by which parents or districts may seek third-party review.

Parents are entitled to receive a copy of IDEA procedural safeguards at least one time per year in addition to the initial referral or request for evaluation, upon filing of a complaint, or upon request. This could be accomplished in hard copy or over the Internet and must be in the native language of the parents and written in an easily understood manner.[141] These materials will provide the parents with information regarding the entire IEP process, as well as their rights to due process.

Stay-Put Provision

During IDEA administrative appeals, the student is assigned to the then-current educational placement, an interim alternative educational setting (if placed following an appropriate disciplinary hearing), or another placement agreed to by the parents and school officials.[142] This stay-put provision applies in cases where any change of

---

[138]20 U.S.C. § 1415(k)(5)(D)(ii) (2007).

[139]20 U.S.C. §1415(k)(6) (2007).

[140]Everett v. Santa Barbara High Sch. Dist., 28 Fed. Appx. 683 (9th Cir. 2002) (concluding that the district failed to provide the plaintiff with an appropriate program, all parties agreed that the child was improperly assigned to a class for the seriously emotionally disturbed; he was placed in home instruction without an instructor, and only one of the two teachers was properly credentialed).

[141]20 U.S.C. § 1415(d)(1), (2) (2007).

[142]20 U.S.C. § 1415(j) (2007); 20 U.S.C. § 1415(k)(4)(A). At least one court has interpreted this provision to require the continuation of services as specified in an Individualized Family Service Plan as the child transitioned to an IEP at age 3. *See* Pardini v. Allegheny Intermediate Unit, 420 F.3d 181 (3d Cir. 2005).

placement is to occur,[143] including those where the content of the placement remains the same, but the least restrictive environment (LRE) has been altered.[144] If the complaint deals with the initial placement of the child, the general education classroom represents the current placement, although additional services may be agreed to by the parties. Once administrative appeals have been exhausted, the current placement may change, depending on the position taken by the state hearing officer (one-tier state) or state review official (two-tier state). See Figure 6.1 for a comprehensive view of the process.

Informal Meeting

Within 15 days of receiving a complaint, the school district must offer the parents the opportunity to participate in an informal meeting with relevant members of the IEP team to discuss the basis of their complaint. The school's attorney should not participate, unless the parents have their own attorney present. This meeting is not mandatory and can be waived. Conversely, if the parents elect to participate, they may be able to resolve their differences with the district and enter into what the courts will consider to be a legally binding agreement. Either party may elect to rescind this agreement within three business days.[145]

Mediation

Mediation represents a second option; it too is voluntary. The sessions are designed to be nonadversarial and involve only the parents, essential educators, and the mediator. Participation in the process may not be used to deny or delay a parent's right to a due process hearing or other IDEA rights. When parents elect to mediate, sessions must be provided in a timely manner and held in a convenient location; discussions must remain confidential and may not be used as evidence in any subsequent due process hearing or civil proceeding.[146] Even when total agreement is not achieved, mediators often help the parties identify points of agreement and disagreement, clarify available options, and narrow the dispute, thereby reducing the complexity and cost of administrative and judicial proceedings.

The mediator must be impartial and trained in effective mediation techniques. Mediators do not "rule," as would a court, nor do they make IEP decisions—that responsibility remains with the IEP team. The mediator is responsible for conducting the meeting, facilitating discussion, helping the parties make mutually beneficial

[143]However, where a child transitions from an IFSP to an IEP, changing the personnel to provide the services (e.g., tutors) was not found to be a violation of the stay-put provision. *See* Johnson v. Special Educ. Hearing Office, 287 F.3d 1176 (9th Cir. 2002).

[144]Hale v. Poplar Bluff R-1 Sch. Dist., 280 F.3d 831 (8th Cir. 2002) (requiring the provision of compensatory education during the summer as the district had violated the stay-put provision by changing the student's placement from homebound to school without going through due process).

[145]20 U.S.C. § 1415(f)(1)(B) (2007).

[146]20 U.S.C. § 1415(e)(2)(G) (2007).

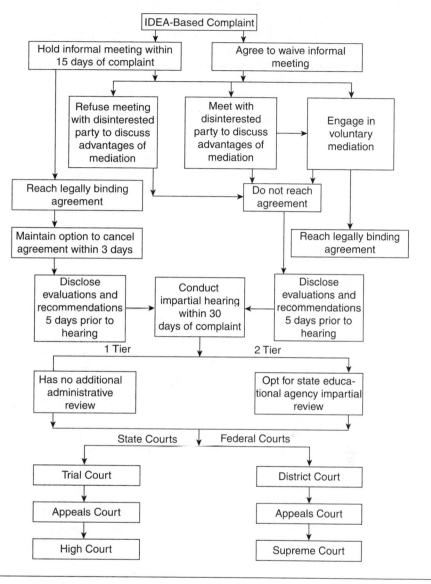

FIGURE 6.1   *IDEA Complaint Procedure*

decisions, and preparing written copies of any agreement the parties may have reached. Unlike settlements generated through the informal meeting, mediation agreements may not be voided within three days and are legally binding on the parties once signed.[147]

[147]*See, e.g.*, Amy S. v. Danbury Local Sch. Dist., 174 Fed. Appx. 896 (6th Cir. 2006).

If the parents are not interested in participating in mediation, the district may request that they discuss the matter with a disinterested third party from a parent training and information center or a community parent resource center. This party will review the advantages of the mediation process. If this effort proves futile, the parents then may proceed to impartial hearing.

Impartial Due Process Hearing

If mediation and the informal meeting are not undertaken or prove unsuccessful, either party may request that an impartial due process hearing be conducted within 30 days of the original complaint. In a one-tier state, the impartial hearing will be conducted by a state official, with no further administrative appeal available. In a two-tier state, the initial hearing is conducted locally by an impartial hearing officer; any resulting decision then may be appealed to a state review official. Although the school district is not responsible for providing the parents with an attorney, it is required to provide a list of sources for them to obtain assistance in understanding their IDEA rights.[148]

If parents elect to initiate the due process procedures, they must notify the district. This notice should include the child's name, address, school of attendance, a description of the problem to be addressed at the hearing, and a proposed resolution.[149] All parties to the initial administrative hearing must disclose to other parties at least five business days prior to a hearing any evaluations, recommendations, and evidence that the party intends to use. If disclosure is not provided, the hearing officer is empowered to prohibit the introduction of the nondisclosed information, unless consent of the receiving party is provided.[150]

The parties may be accompanied and advised by counsel as well as other persons with special knowledge or training relevant to the child; present evidence; and confront, cross-examine, and compel the attendance of witnesses.[151] The burden of persuasion is on the party seeking relief in an administrative hearing.[152] Although this burden could fall upon either the parents or the district, depending on which party seeks to challenge the existing IEP, most cases are filed by parents. Once the proceedings have been completed, the parents may obtain at no cost a written *or* an electronic verbatim record of such hearing, findings of facts, and decisions. Hearing officer opinions must be based only on evidence presented by

---

[148]20 U.S.C. § 1415(c)(1)(D) (2007).

[149]20 U.S.C. § 1415(b)(7) (2007).

[150]20 U.S.C. § 1415(f)(2) (2007).

[151]20 U.S.C. § 1415(h) (2007).

[152]Schaffer v. Weast, 546 U.S. 49 (2005). Prior to this opinion, the Third Circuit had placed the burden on the school district. More recently, the Third Circuit suggested that it might be possible for states to go beyond the IDEA through state statute and put the burden once again on the school district, although it did not indicate why a state would want to do so. *See* L.E. v. Ramsey Bd. of Educ., 435 F.3d 384 (3d Cir. 2006).

the parties and available no later than 45 days following the receipt of a request for a hearing.[153]

State Review

If the impartial hearing is conducted at the local level (signifying a two-tier state), either party aggrieved by the findings and decision may appeal to the state. At the state level, the review official is responsible for ensuring that the hearing officer followed appropriate procedures, impartially reviewed the record in its entirety, and sought additional evidence, if necessary. The review official also may permit the parties the opportunity for oral or written argument. Following the completion of these procedures, the reviewer must make an independent decision and provide the parties with written findings no later than 30 days following the request for review.[154]

Civil Action

Prior to filing an IDEA suit, parents are required to exhaust administrative remedies (i.e., an impartial hearing and state review where appropriate), unless such remedies would prove futile or fail to provide the required relief, or where emergency conditions exist that could result in severe or irreparable harm to the child.[155] Such mandatory administrative remedies cannot be avoided by filing under the Constitution, the Americans with Disabilities Act, the Rehabilitation Act, or other applicable federal law, if the requested relief also is available under the IDEA. The exhaustion requirement helps reduce the caseload for courts, limits expenditures associated with litigation, and ensures that recipients and states have the opportunity to resolve matters in ways that ideally are less adversarial and more child focused than a lawsuit.

Either party to an IEP dispute may bring a civil action in a state trial court or federal district court within 90 days of the hearing officer's decision. When an action is filed, the court receives the records of the administrative proceedings; hears additional evidence at the request of a party; bases its decision on the preponderance of the evidence; and grants such relief as it determines to be appropriate.[156] Courts will

---

[153]34 C.F.R. § 300.515(a) (2007).

[154]34 C.F.R. § 300.515(b) (2007).

[155]Frazier v. Fairhaven Sch. Comm., 276 F.3d 52 (1st Cir. 2002); Rose v. Yeaw, 214 F.3d 206 (1st Cir. 2000). *See also* Blanchard v. Morton Sch. Dist., 420 F.3d 918 (9th Cir. 2005) (concluding that exhaustion is not required where the mother sought damages for her emotional distress allegedly caused by the IEP process); Ortega v. Bibb County Sch. Dist., 397 F.3d 1321 (11th Cir. 2005) (concluding that tort-like damages are not available under the IDEA; the child had collapsed on the playground, dislodged his tracheotomy tube, and died of asphyxiation); McCormick v. Waukegan Sch. Dist., 374 F.3d 564 (7th Cir. 2004) (determining that exhaustion is not required where the relief sought is not available under the IDEA; and opining that tort-like damages are not available under the IDEA).

[156]20 U.S.C. § 1415(i)(2)(B), (C) (2007).

provide "due weight" to the judgment of educators and the rulings of hearing officers and state review officials, assuming of course that their decisions are supported by the evidence and their rulings do not exceed their authority.[157]

Remedies and Attorneys' Fees

In IDEA cases, courts have awarded declaratory relief, injunctive relief, compensatory education,[158] and reimbursement for evaluations, tuition, transportation, and related services.[159] Moreover, most courts have concluded that damage awards are not available under the IDEA, even in conjunction with 42 U.S.C. Section 1983 (i.e., a statute providing the right to sue a state actor for conduct that deprives selected federal rights).[160] The Supreme Court has drawn a sharp distinction between awarding damages and requiring reimbursement; the latter has been viewed simply as the recovery of justified costs that should have been initially incurred by the public school system.[161] Similarly, numerous lower courts have held that awards of compensatory education were necessary where districts failed to provide an appropriate program, committed gross procedural violations that delayed instruction, or prematurely terminated services by offering a diploma.[162] In contrast, the Supreme Court in 2006 held that expert fees, such as those provided an educational consultant, were not

[157]*Compare* Shore Reg'l High Sch. Bd. of Educ. v. P.S., 381 F.3d 194 (3d Cir. 2004) (reversing the lower court and noting that due weight had not been provided an administrative law judge's determinations) *with* Alex R. v. Forrestville Valley Cmty. Unit Sch. Dist. #221, 375 F.3d 603 (7th Cir. 2004) (determining that the hearing officer exceeded her authority when she ordered that every student in the district be exposed to a disability awareness and sensitivity curriculum, even if they never came into contact with the plaintiff); H.W. v. Highland Park Bd. of Educ., 108 Fed. Appx. 731 (3d Cir. 2004) (reversing the lower court and concluding that it had given undue weight to the experts' supporting the parent's preferred all-girl placement rather than focus on whether the public placement was appropriate).

[158]Park v. Anaheim Union High Sch. Dist., 464 F.3d 1025 (9th Cir. 2006) (awarding compensatory damages).

[159]*See, e.g.*, DeKalb County Sch. Dist. v. M.T.V., 164 Fed. Appx. 900 (11th Cir. 2006) (upholding lower court decision requiring the district to reimburse the parents for vision therapy services); Bucks County Dep't of MH/MR v. De Mora, 379 F.3d 61 (3d. Cir. 2004) (providing tuition reimbursement where an appropriate program had not been provided under Part C; a portion of the reimbursement was to compensate a parent for the time spent serving as a Lovaas instructor).

[160]*See, e.g.,* Wolverton v. Doniphan R-1 Sch. Dist., 16 Fed. Appx. 523 (8th Cir. 2001) (determining that the IDEA does not allow the recovery of damages in a case where a student assigned to a classroom for behaviorally disadvantaged students was sprayed with mace by a security guard for behavior that could have been attributed to his mental illness). *See* text accompanying notes 210–221, Chapter 11.

[161]Sch. Comm. of Burlington v. Dep't of Educ. of Mass., 471 U.S. 359 (1985). *See also* Long v. Dawson Springs Indep. Sch. Dist., 197 Fed. Appx. 427 (6th Cir. 2006) (determining that damages are not available under the IDEA or indirectly under § 1983 for IDEA violations).

[162]*See, e.g.*, Reid v. District of Columbia, 401 F.3d 516 (D.C. Cir. 2005) (ordering the provision of compensatory education that would elevate the student to the level he would have reached absent the district's failures, and not permitting IDEA hearing officers to reduce or discontinue compensatory education awards). *But see* G. v. Fort Bragg Dep't Schs., 343 F.3d 295 (4th Cir. 2003) (reversing lower court's denial of compensatory education).

recoverable.[163] The Court reasoned that Congress failed to give states notice that their acceptance of IDEA funds would obligate them to compensate prevailing parties who had been assisted by nonattorney experts.

In addition to the above, attorneys' fees may be available to those who prevail in special education cases.[164] To qualify as a prevailing party, the plaintiff must succeed on a key or primary issue and not simply on a minor, procedural, or tactical matter.[165] Fees are based on the actual time needed to represent the client during both administrative and judicial proceedings, and the hourly rate must be within the range received by attorneys practicing in the community. Fees may be reduced or eliminated where the attorney fails to provide the district with required notice information, time is spent pursuing unsuccessful claims, proceedings are unnecessarily protracted by the plaintiffs, or the relief that is acquired is no greater than that provided in a settlement offer made prior to the proceedings.[166] Moreover, fees need not be paid for time spent at IEP meetings (unless they are held as a result of an administrative hearing or litigation), or to compensate parents who serve as their own attorney.[167] However, and although they will not be compensated, parents who are not attorneys may represent their child in court.[168]

Furthermore, the IDEA permits the school district to recoup its attorneys' fees against plaintiffs or their attorneys if shown to have filed a case for an improper purpose (e.g., to harass), delayed the proceedings, or unnecessarily increased the costs of litigation, or if the case is found frivolous, unreasonable, or without foundation.[169] This provision may in time prove beneficial to districts trying to safeguard their resources, but to date no IDEA case has been found frivolous by a federal appellate court.

---

[163]Arlington Cent. Sch. Dist. v. Murphy, 548 U.S. 291 (2006). *See also* Santy v. Charter Oak Unified Sch. Dist., 220 Fed. Appx. 712 (9th Cir. 2007) (concluding that fees for a nonlawyer expert or consultant are not recoverable under the IDEA); Goldring v. District of Columbia, 416 F.3d 70 (D.C. Cir. 2005) (refusing to require the District of Columbia to pay the prevailing plaintiff's excessive expert witness fees).

[164]P.N. v. Seattle Sch. Dist. No. 1, 474 F.3d 1165 (9th Cir. 2007) (observing that attorneys' fees under the IDEA are available only when either ordered by the court or there has been judicial sanction of a settlement agreement).

[165]*See, e.g.,* Crawford v. San Dieguito Union Sch. Dist., 202 Fed. Appx. 185 (9th Cir. 2006) (granting 40 percent of the requested attorneys' fees as the plaintiff prevailed on only one of several issues); Linda T. v. Rice Lake Area Sch. Dist., 417 F.3d 704 (7th Cir. 2005) (denying attorneys' fees to parents given that their degree of success was "slight" and that they had failed on the most significant item).

[166]Wikol v. Birmingham Pub. Schs., 360 F.3d 604 (6th Cir. 2004) (remanding with instructions to determine whether that which was received by the plaintiffs was any greater than that offered prior to litigation).

[167]20 U.S.C. § 1415(i)(3)(D) (2007). *See also* Van Duyn v. Baker Sch. Dist. 5J, 481 F.3d 770 (9th Cir. 2007) (awarding attorneys' fees for counsel other than plaintiff's attorney-mother for work performed during the administrative hearing where plaintiff partially prevailed); Woodside v. Sch. Dist. of Phila., 248 F.3d 129 (3d Cir. 2001) (concluding that a parent-attorney cannot receive attorneys' fees for work representing his child in proceedings under the IDEA).

[168]Winkelman v. Parma City Sch. Dist., 127 S. Ct. 1994 (2007).

[169]20 U.S.C. § 1414(i)(3)(B) (2007). *See also* Holmes v. Millcreek Twp. Sch. Dist., 205 F.3d 583 (3d Cir. 2000) (reducing attorneys' fees to one-fourth the original requested amount; the attorney did not prevail on the primary claim, litigation was needlessly protracted, the hourly rate did not reflect experience, and the number of hours billed was excessive).

Conclusion

Several of the more significant points regarding disability law are summarized briefly here.

1. All impairments do not necessarily qualify as disabilities requiring accommodation.
2. Under Section 504 of the Rehabilitation Act and the Americans with Disabilities Act, the appropriate standard for whether an impairment is substantially limiting is to compare one's performance with that of the average person in the general population; mitigating or corrective measures must be considered in determining whether a student qualifies as disabled.
3. The local school district is responsible for identifying all children with disabilities who live within its service area.
4. Children with disabilities are entitled to a free appropriate public education in the least restrictive environment.
5. Assessments are to be administered by properly trained personnel; instruments must be validated for their intended purpose and administered in the child's native language or other mode of communication.
6. An appropriate program for a child with a disability must be specially designed to meet his or her unique needs and provide meaningful access to an individualized education program that confers some educational benefit; the best program or one that maximizes the child's potential is not required.
7. Under the IDEA, an individualized education program (including goals and objectives, specification of the services to be provided, and an education plan) must be developed for each eligible child; under Section 504, an accommodation plan must be developed and implemented.
8. School district placements may be in either public or private (including religious) schools that are capable of providing the student with an appropriate education.
9. Due process procedures must be followed in identifying, evaluating, or changing the educational placement of children with disabilities.
10. Parents may recover tuition and other costs for a unilateral private placement only if the private placement is determined to be appropriate and the placement proposed or provided by the local school district is found to be inappropriate.
11. Related services necessary to support the specially designed instruction for children with disabilities are required regardless of cost; school districts are not obligated to provide medical services, but they must provide health services, if needed for the child to attend school and benefit from instruction.
12. School districts may not impose arbitrary limits on the number of school days for children with disabilities because certain children may require an extended school year in order to receive "some educational benefit."
13. Students with physical impairments may be denied the opportunity to participate in interscholastic sports if school officials, after consultation with medical experts, determine that it is not safe for the student-athlete to participate on the school's team.

14. During administrative or judicial proceedings regarding a free appropriate public education, the student should remain in the then-current educational placement.
15. Students with disabilities may be suspended for up to 10 days during one school year using the same hearing procedures used with other students.
16. Students with disabilities may be expelled only if (1) currently receiving an appropriate education and (2) the misbehavior is not related to their disability; even then, services consistent with the IEP must be provided.
17. When time-out has been incorporated into a student's IEP, the time that a student is assigned to time-out will not count toward the 10-day limit on suspensions.
18. Students with disabilities who are involved with drugs, carry weapons, or commit serious bodily injury may be placed in an interim alternative educational setting for up to 45 school days, even if the behavior is disability related.

7

Student Discipline

Student misconduct continues to be one of the most persistent and troublesome problems confronting educators. Public concern has focused on school disciplinary problems, particularly those involving use of illicit drugs, alcohol abuse,[1] and violence. In response, schools have directed more efforts toward violence prevention strategies including not only stringent security measures but also modification of the curricula to strengthen students' social skills and the training of teachers and administrators to monitor the school climate. States and local school districts also have enacted restrictive laws or policies that call for zero tolerance of weapons, drugs, and violence on campus. The efficacy of legislating tougher approaches to create safe schools, however, has evoked volatile debates.[2] This chapter does not address the merits of these measures; rather, it examines the range of strategies employed by educators to maintain a safe and secure learning environment from a legal perspective. The analyses focus on the development of conduct regulations, the imposition of sanctions for noncompliance, and the procedures required in the administration of student punishments.

The law clearly authorizes the state and its agencies to establish and enforce reasonable conduct codes to protect the rights of students and school districts and to ensure that school environments are conducive to learning. Historically, courts exercised limited review of student disciplinary regulations, and pupils seldom were successful in challenging policies governing their behavior. In 1923, the Arkansas Supreme Court upheld the expulsion of a student who wore talcum powder on her

---

[1]In March 2007, the U.S. Surgeon General's Office issued its first "call to action" to stop underage drinking, which poses a significant threat to the health and safety of the nation's youth. Kenneth Moritsugu, "The Surgeon General's Call to Action to Prevent and Reduce Underage Drinking" (press conference, March 6, 2007), available at www.surgeongeneral.gov/topics/underagedrinking/moritsugu.html. A national survey reported 11 million underage drinkers in 2005; about 7.2 million were binge drinkers. Substance Abuse and Mental Health Services Administration, *Results from the 2005 National Survey on Drug Use and Health: National Findings* (Rockville, MD: U.S. Department of Health and Human Services, 2006).

[2]Robert C. Johnston, "Federal Data Highlight Disparities in Discipline," *Education Week* (June 21, 2000), p. 3; Advancement Project, *Education on Lockdown: The Schoolhouse to Jailhouse Track* (Washington, D.C.: Author, March 2005).

face in violation of a school rule forbidding pupils to wear transparent hosiery, low-necked dresses, face paint, or cosmetics.[3] In another early case, the Michigan Supreme Court endorsed the suspension of a female high school student for smoking and riding in a car with a young man.[4] In these and similar cases, courts were reluctant to interfere with the judgment of school officials because public education was considered to be a privilege bestowed by the state.

A quantum leap occurred from this early judicial posture to the active protection of students' rights in the late 1960s and early 1970s,[5] but judicial developments have not eroded educators' rights or their responsibilities.[6] The Seventh Circuit noted that the United States Supreme Court "has repeatedly emphasized the need for affirming the comprehensive authority of the states and of school officials, consistent with fundamental constitutional safeguards, to prescribe and control conduct in the schools."[7] Reasonable disciplinary regulations, even those impairing students' protected liberties, have been upheld if justified by a legitimate educational interest.

Educators have not only the authority but also the duty to maintain discipline in public schools. Although rules made at any level (e.g., classroom, building, school board) cannot conflict with higher authorities (e.g., constitutional and statutory provisions), building administrators and teachers retain substantial latitude in establishing and enforcing conduct codes that are necessary for instructional activities to take place. In the subsequent sections of this chapter, educators' prerogatives and students' rights are explored in connection with conduct regulations, expulsions and suspensions, corporal punishment, academic sanctions, and search and seizure.

Conduct Regulations

School boards are granted considerable latitude in establishing and interpreting their own disciplinary rules and regulations.[8] The Supreme Court has held that the interpretation of a school regulation resides with the body that adopted it and is charged with its enforcement.[9] Disciplinary policies, however, have been struck down if unconstitutionally vague. Policies prohibiting improper conduct and behavior inimical to the best interests of the school have been invalidated because they have not

[3]Pugsley v. Sellmeyer, 250 S.W. 538 (Ark. 1923). *See* Jones v. Day, 89 So. 906 (Miss. 1921).

[4]Tanton v. McKenney, 197 N.W. 510 (Mich. 1924).

[5]*See, e.g.*, Tinker v. Des Moines Indep. Sch. Dist., 393 U.S. 503 (1969); text accompanying note 48, Chapter 4.

[6]*See* Hazelwood Sch. Dist. v. Kuhlmeier, 484 U.S. 260 (1988); Bethel Sch. Dist. No. 403 v. Fraser, 478 U.S. 675 (1986); New Jersey v. T.L.O., 469 U.S. 325 (1985).

[7]Boucher v. Sch. Bd., 134 F.3d 821, 827 (7th Cir. 1998).

[8]Price v. New York City Bd. of Educ., no. 109703/06 (N.Y. Sup. Ct. May 7, 2007) (holding that a ban on possession of cell phones had a rational basis).

[9]*See* Bd. of Educ. v. McCluskey, 458 U.S. 966 (1982); Wood v. Strickland, 420 U.S. 308 (1975).

specified the precise nature of the impermissible conduct.[10] Although policies should be precise, courts have recognized that disciplinary regulations do not have to satisfy the stringent criteria or level of specificity required in criminal statutes.[11] The Eighth Circuit noted that the determining factor is whether a regulation's wording is precise enough to notify an individual that specific behavior is clearly unacceptable.[12]

In addition to reviewing the validity of the conduct regulation on which a specific punishment is based, courts evaluate the nature and extent of the penalty imposed in relation to the gravity of the offense. Courts also consider the age, sex, mental condition, and past behavior of the student in deciding whether a given punishment is appropriate. The judiciary has sanctioned punishments such as the denial of privileges, suspension, expulsion, corporal punishment, and detention after school. Any of these punishments, however, could be considered unreasonable under a specific set of circumstances. Consequently, courts study each unique factual situation; they do not evaluate the validity of student punishments in the abstract.

Litigation challenging disciplinary practices often has focused on the procedures followed in administering punishments rather than on the substance of disciplinary rules or the nature of the sanctions imposed. Implicit in all judicial declarations regarding school discipline is the notion that severe penalties require more formal procedures, whereas minor punishments necessitate only minimal due process. Nonetheless, any disciplinary action should be accompanied by some procedure to ensure the rudiments of fundamental fairness and to prevent mistakes in the disciplinary process. The Fifth Circuit noted, "The quantum and quality of procedural due process to be afforded a student varies with the seriousness of the punishment to be imposed."[13]

The judiciary has recognized that punishment for student conduct off school grounds must be supported by evidence that the behavior has a detrimental impact on

---

[10]*See, e.g.*, Flaherty v. Keystone Oaks Sch. Dist., 247 F. Supp. 2d 698 (W.D. Pa. 2003) (ruling that handbook policies were overbroad and vague in violation of student's First Amendment rights); Killion v. Franklin Reg'l Sch. Dist., 136 F. Supp. 2d 446, 459 (W.D. Pa. 2001) (finding school district's retaliatory policy against verbal or other abuse of teachers unconstitutionally vague— "devoid of any detail"). *But see* Fuller v. Decatur Pub. Sch. Bd. of Educ., 252 F.3d 662 (7th Cir. 2001) (concluding that a prohibition of gang-like behavior was not overly vague when the students' conduct clearly violated the regulation).

[11]*See* Bethel Sch. Dist. No. 403 v. Fraser, 478 U.S. 675 (1986); Layshock *ex rel.* Layshock v. Hermitage Sch. Dist., 496 F. Supp. 2d 587 (W.D. Pa. 2007); text accompanying note 10, Chapter 4.

[12]Woodis v. Westark Cmty. Coll., 160 F.3d 435 (8th Cir. 1998). *See also* West v. Derby Unified Sch. Dist., 206 F.3d 1358 (10th Cir. 2000) (holding that the student knew the school harassment and intimidation policy clearly prohibited him from drawing a Confederate flag); Hammock v. Keys, 93 F. Supp. 2d 1222 (S.D. Ala. 2000) (finding that a school board regulation regarding discipline for drug possession was not impermissibly vague when applied to a student who was expelled after marijuana residue was found in her car); Schmader v. Warren County Sch. Dist., 808 A.2d 596, 600 (Pa. Commw. Ct. 2002) (ruling that the "Miscellaneous Inappropriate Behavior" section of the school district's disciplinary code was not unconstitutionally vague as applied to a third grade student's failure to report a planned assault on another student; language that referred to "behavior that may be harmful to others" gave clear notice to the student that he had a duty to report his classmate's threat).

[13]Pervis v. LaMarque Indep. Dist., 466 F.2d 1054, 1057 (5th Cir. 1972).

other pupils, teachers, or school activities.[14] This has become a much more contentious area with students' increased use of the Internet at home. Personal Web sites and use of social networks such as MySpace and Facebook raise difficult First Amendment issues for school officials attempting to discipline students for off-campus conduct.[15] In an early case, the Connecticut Supreme Court held that school officials could regulate student conduct outside school hours and off school property if such conduct affected the management of the school.[16] This basic principle still guides courts as they assess disciplinary actions. Accordingly, courts have upheld sanctions imposed on students for engaging in assault or criminal acts off school grounds;[17] compiling a list of other students noting derogatory characteristics;[18] making threatening, harassing remarks on a Web site created at home;[19] writing a threatening letter over the summer break to a former girl friend;[20] and shooting a student in the back with a BB gun near a school bus stop.[21] Courts, however, have prohibited school authorities from punishing students for misbehavior off school grounds if pupils had not been informed that such conduct would result in sanctions,[22] if the conduct could not be considered a true threat (i.e., threatening speech not intentionally communicated in the school setting),[23] or if the misbehavior had no direct relationship to the welfare of the school.[24]

[14]For a synthesis of applicable case law on conduct off school grounds, *see* Perry A. Zirkel, "Disciplining Students for Off-Campus Misconduct," *Education Law Reporter*, vol. 163 (2002), pp. 551–553. *See also* D.O.F. v. Lewisburg Area Sch. Dist., 868 A.2d 28 (Pa. Commw. Ct. 2004) (ruling that a student who smoked marijuana on school grounds at 10:30 p.m., an hour and a half after a school event, could not be expelled because he was not "under the Board's supervision at the time of the incident").

[15]*See* "School Safey," *NSBA Legal Clips* (August 24, 2006), reporting a national poll indicating that more than 13 million students, age 6 to 17, have been "cyber-bullied" through Web pages, text messages, e-mails, or cell phones. *See also* Alan Gomez, "Students, Officials Locking Horns over Blogs," *U.S.A. Today* (October 26, 2006) (noting that some districts are adopting policies that warn students they can be disciplined for comments online). *See also* text accompanying note 85, Chapter 4.

[16]O'Rourke v. Walker, 102 Conn. 130 (1925). *See also* Collins v. Prince William County Sch. Bd., 142 Fed. Appx. 144 (4th Cir. 2005) (upholding student's expulsion for making and using explosive devices off campus; incident created substantial disruption in school operations with media and other attention).

[17]Pollnow v. Glennon, 757 F.2d 496 (2d Cir. 1985); Nicholas v. Sch. Comm. 587 N.E.2d 211 (Mass. 1992).

[18]Donovan v. Ritchie, 68 F.3d 14 (1st Cir. 1995).

[19]J.S. v. Bethlehem Area Sch. Dist., 807 A.2d 847 (Pa. 2002). *See also* text accompanying note 85, Chapter 4. *But see* Beussink v. Woodland R-IV Sch. Dist., 30 F. Supp. 2d 1175 (E.D. Mo. 1998) (concluding that a Web site created off campus did not materially and substantially interfere with the educational process).

[20]Doe v. Pulaski County Special Sch. Dist., 306 F.3d 616 (8th Cir. 2002). The junior high school student did not send the letter, but its contents were communicated to the former girlfriend by another student who read the letter.

[21]S.K. and Z.K. v. Anoka-Hennepin Indep. Sch. Dist. No. 11, 399 F. Supp. 2d 963 (D. Minn. 2005).

[22]Galveston Indep. Sch. Dist. v. Boothe, 590 S.W.2d 553 (Tex. Civ. App. 1979). *But see* Howard v. Colonial, 621 A.2d 362 (Del. Super. Ct. 1992) (holding that school board's determination that a 17-year-old drug dealer posed a potential harm to the safety and welfare of students was not arbitrary or capricious in spite of the fact that the student discipline code did not prohibit drug dealing off school grounds).

[23]Porter v. Ascension Parish Sch. Bd., 393 F.3d 608 (5th Cir. 2004).

[24]*See, e.g.*, Killion v. Franklin Reg'l Sch. Dist., 136 F. Supp. 2d 446 (W.D. Pa. 2001); Klein v. Smith, 635 F. Supp. 1440 (D. Me. 1986); M.T. v. Sch. Bd., 779 So. 2d 328 (Fla. Dist. Ct. App. 1999).

School personnel must be careful not to place unnecessary constraints on student behavior. In developing disciplinary policies, all possible means of achieving the desired outcomes should be explored, and means that are least restrictive of students' personal freedoms should be selected. Once it is determined that a specific conduct regulation is necessary, the rule should be clearly written so that it is not open to multiple interpretations. Each regulation should include the rationale for enacting the rule as well as the penalties for infractions. Considerable discretion exists in determining that certain actions deserve harsher penalties (i.e., imposing a more severe punishment for the sale of drugs as opposed to the possession or use of drugs). To ensure that students are knowledgeable of the conduct rules, it is advisable to require students to sign a form indicating that they have read the conduct regulations.[25] With such documentation, pupils would be unable to plead ignorance of the rules as a defense for their misconduct.

In general, educators would be wise to adhere to the following guidelines:[26]

- Rules must have an explicit purpose and be clearly written to accomplish that purpose.
- Any conduct regulation adopted should be necessary in order to carry out the school's educational mission; rules should not be designed merely to satisfy the preferences of school board members, administrators, or teachers.
- Rules should be publicized to students and their parents.
- Rules should be specific and clearly stated so that students know what behaviors are expected and what behaviors are prohibited.
- Student handbooks that incorporate references to specific state laws also should include the law or paraphrase the statutory language.
- Regulations should not impair constitutionally protected rights unless there is an overriding public interest, such as a threat to the safety of others.
- A rule should not be "ex post facto"; it should not be adopted to prevent a specific activity that school officials know is being planned or has already occurred.
- Regulations should be consistently enforced and uniformly applied to all students without discrimination.
- Punishments should be appropriate to the offense, taking into consideration the child's age, sex, disability, and past behavior.
- Some procedural safeguards should accompany the administration of all punishments; the formality of the procedures should be in accord with the severity of the punishment.
- A process for periodic review of the student handbook should be established that involves students and school staff members in the revisions and refinement.

[25]An Alabama federal district court found students' claim that they were not knowledgeable of the school rule against fighting to be frivolous. The court expressed doubt that any student in the United States is not aware that fighting is a serious infraction. Craig v. Selma City Sch. Bd., 801 F. Supp. 585 (S.D. Ala. 1992).

[26]*See* Thomas Baker, "Construing the Scope of Student Conduct Codes," *Education Law Reporter*, vol. 174 (2003), pp. 555–588, for an extensive discussion of the development of conduct codes.

In designing and enforcing pupil conduct codes, it is important that school personnel bear in mind the distinction between students' substantive and procedural rights. If a disciplinary regulation or the administration of punishment violates substantive rights (e.g., restricts protected speech), the regulation cannot be enforced nor the punishment imposed. When only procedural rights are impaired, however, the punishment eventually can be administered if determined at an appropriate hearing that the punishment is warranted.

Expulsions and Suspensions

Expulsions and suspensions are among the most widely used disciplinary measures. Courts uniformly have upheld educators' authority to use such measures as punishments, but due process is required to ensure that students are afforded fair and impartial treatment. Although most states have recognized that students have a property right to an education, this right may be taken away for violations of school rules. This section focuses on disciplinary action in which students are removed from the regular instructional program; suspensions and expulsions from extracurricular activities are addressed in Chapter 4.

Expulsions

State laws and school board regulations are usually quite specific regarding the grounds for expulsions—that is, the removal of students from school for a lengthy period of time (usually in excess of 10 days). Such grounds are not limited to occurrences during school hours and can include infractions on school property immediately before or after school or at any time the school is being used for a school-related activity. Expulsions also can result from infractions occurring en route to or from school or during school functions held off school premises. Although specific grounds vary from state to state, infractions typically considered legitimate grounds for expulsion include violence, stealing or vandalizing school or private property, causing or attempting to cause physical injury to others, possessing a weapon, possessing or using drugs or alcohol, and engaging in criminal activity or other behavior forbidden by state laws.

Procedural Requirements. State statutes specify procedures for expulsion and length limitations. Except for the possession of weapons, a student generally cannot be expelled beyond the end of the current academic year unless the expulsion takes place near the close of the term.[27] A teacher or administrator may initiate expulsion proceedings, but usually only the school board can expel a student. Prior to expulsion, students must be provided procedural protections guaranteed by the United States Constitution; however, school officials can remove students immediately if

[27]*See, e.g.*, S. Gibson Sch. Bd. v. Sollman, 768 N.E.2d 437 (Ind. 2002).

they pose a danger or threat to themselves or others.[28] No duty exists to provide an educational alternative for a properly expelled student unless the school board policies or state mandates specify that alternative programs must be provided or the student is receiving special education services.[29]

Although the details of required procedures must be gleaned from state statutes and school board regulations, courts have held that students facing expulsion from public school are guaranteed at least minimum due process under the Fourteenth Amendment.[30] It is advisable to provide the following safeguards:

- Written notice of the charges;[31] the intention to expel; the place, time, and circumstances of the hearing; and sufficient time for a defense to be prepared,[32]
- A full and fair hearing before an impartial adjudicator,
- The right to legal counsel or some other adult representation,[33]
- The right to be fully apprised of the proof or evidence,[34]
- The opportunity to present witnesses or evidence,[35]
- The opportunity to cross-examine opposing witnesses,[36] and
- Some type of written record demonstrating that the decision was based on the evidence presented at the hearing.[37]

[28]*See, e.g.*, Lavine v. Blaine Sch. Dist., 257 F.3d 981 (9th Cir. 2001).

[29]*See* Gun-Free Schools Act, 20 U.S.C. § 7151 (2007) (allowing school officials to place students expelled for gun possession in alternative instructional programs). *See also* text accompanying notes 127–139, Chapter 6, for a discussion of the expulsion of children with disabilities.

[30]Courts have cautioned that expulsion hearings do not have to conform to the judicial requirements of a trial. *See, e.g.*, Linwood v. Bd. of Educ. 463 F.2d 763 (7th Cir. 1972). *See also* Trujillo v. Taos Mun. Schs., 91 F. 3d 160 (10th Cir. 1997) (concluding that school officials were not required to provide a second hearing to a student who had been permanently expelled).

[31]*See, e.g.*, Adrovet v. Brunswick City Sch. Dist., 735 N.E.2d 995 (Ohio C.P. 1999) (holding that the statute required written notice to the student, not the parent; the court relied on the express wording of the statute). *But see* Watson v. Beckel, 242 F.3d 1237 (10th Cir. 2001) (concluding that failure to specify charges in a written notice did not deny due process when the student had constructive notice—clearly knew the allegations under investigation).

[32]*See, e.g.*, Brian A. v. Stroudsburg Area Sch. Dist., 141 F. Supp. 2d 502 (M.D. Pa. 2001) (ruling that a five-day notice was adequate when the student and parent had been aware of the pending expulsion for weeks).

[33]*See, e.g., In re* Roberts, 563 S.E.2d 37 (N.C. Ct. App. 2002) (finding the school board's denial of student's request to be represented by counsel when faced with expulsion violated his due process rights). Several courts have recognized students' right to seek advice of legal counsel but have not held that a right exists for students' attorneys to participate in a disciplinary proceeding in the role of trial counsel. *See, e.g.*, Osteen v. Henley, 13 F.3d 221 (7th Cir. 1993); Newsome v. Batavia Local Sch. Dist., 842 F.2d 920 (6th Cir. 1988).

[34]*See, e.g.*, Ruef v. Jordan, 605 N.Y.S.2d 530 (App. Div. 1993).

[35]*See, e.g.*, Fuller v. Decatur Pub. Sch. Bd. of Educ., 251 F.3d 662 (7th Cir. 2001).

[36]*See, e.g.*, Dillon v. Pulaski County Special Sch. Dist., 594 F.2d 699 (8th Cir. 1979); *In re* E.J.W., 632 N.W.2d 775 (Minn. Ct. App. 2001). *But see Newsome*, 842 F.2d 920 (holding that denial of cross-examination to protect anonymity of student drug informants did not violate due process rights); Brewer v. Austin Indep. Sch. Dist., 779 F.2d 260 (5th Cir. 1985) (holding that names of witnesses could be withheld to prevent retaliation).

[37]*See, e.g.*, Hass v. W. Shore Sch. Dist., 915 A.2d 1254 (Pa. Commw. Ct. 2007).

Students and parents cannot claim denial of due process rights if they waive the right to a hearing.[38] Also, a student who declines to attend a scheduled expulsion hearing waives the right to present his case.[39]

Procedural safeguards required, however, may vary depending on the circumstances of a particular situation. In a Mississippi case, a student and his parents claimed that prior to an expulsion hearing they should have been given a list of the witnesses and a summary of their testimony.[40] Recognizing that such procedural protections generally should be afforded prior to a long-term expulsion, the Fifth Circuit nonetheless held that they were not requisite in this case. The parents had been fully apprised of the charges, the facts supporting the charges, and the nature of the hearing. Consequently, the court concluded that the student suffered no material prejudice from the school board's failure to supply a list of witnesses; the witnesses provided no surprises or interference with the student's ability to present his case. In a later case involving expulsion for possession of drugs, the same court found no impairment of a student's rights when he was denied an opportunity to confront and rebut witnesses who accused him of selling drugs.[41] The names of student witnesses had been withheld to prevent retaliation against them.

Similarly, the Sixth Circuit noted that it is critical to protect the anonymity of students who "blow the whistle" on classmates involved in serious offenses such as drug dealing.[42] Although the right to cross-examine witnesses did not constitute a denial of due process in this case, the court held that the student's procedural rights were violated because the superintendent disclosed evidence in the school board's closed deliberations that was not introduced during the open hearing. Given this violation, the appellate court remanded the case to determine if the student was entitled to injunctive and compensatory relief.

State laws and school board policies often provide students facing expulsion with more elaborate procedural safeguards than the constitutional protections noted

[38]Porter v. Ascension Parish Sch. Bd., 393 F.3d 608 (5th Cir. 2004) (concluding that when a student admits his guilt the need for a hearing to determine guilt is significantly lessened).

[39]Remer v. Burlington Area Sch. Dist., 286 F.3d 1007 (7th Cir. 2002).

[40]Keough v. Tate County Bd. of Educ., 748 F.2d 1077 (5th Cir. 1984). *See also* Covington County v. G.W., 767 So. 2d 187 (Miss. 2000) (ruling that school officials' failure to provide a list of witnesses did not violate a student's due process rights).

[41]*Brewer*, 779 F.2d 260. *See also* Nash v. Auburn Univ., 812 F.2d 655 (11th Cir. 1987) (holding that where basic fairness is provided in a disciplinary case, cross-examination of witnesses and a full adversarial proceeding are not required); Brown v. Plainfield Community Consol. Dist. 202, 522 F. Supp. 21068 (N.D. Ill. 2007) (ruling that a student expelled for inappropriately touching a teacher did not possess a constitutional due process right to cross-examine student witnesses in his hearing); Bogle-Assegai v. Bloomfield Bd. of Educ., 467 F. Supp. 2d 236 (D. Conn. 2006) (ruling that student statements were admissible even though students were not present at the hearing for cross-examination).

[42]Newsome v. Batavia Local Sch. Dist., 842 F.2d 920 (6th Cir. 1988). *See also* Granowitz v. Redlands Unified Sch. Dist., 105 Cal. App. 4th 349 (Ct. App. 2003) (finding that student was not entitled to know the names of accusers in a case involving sexual misconduct); Scanlon v. Las Cruces Pub. Schs., 172 P.3d 185 (N.M. Ct. App. 2007) (ruling that a student's procedural due process rights were not violated when school officials did not disclose the names of student informants who reported that the student had marijuana in his car).

earlier. Once such expulsion procedures are established, courts will require that they be followed.[43] Under Ohio law, a student's expulsion hearing two weeks after he received the notice was found to violate a statutory requirement that hearings be held no later than five school days after notification.[44] A Washington appellate court held that a student's due process rights were violated when he was not allowed to question witnesses at his expulsion hearing;[45] Washington law specifically provides students the right to confront witnesses.

Expulsions often are challenged as excessive for certain offenses. Unless actions are arbitrary, capricious, or oppressive, school officials have broad discretionary powers in establishing disciplinary penalties. An Illinois student, expelled for the remainder of the school year for possession of caffeine pills, challenged the punishment as too harsh for a first offense.[46] The trial court agreed that the punishment far outweighed the crime, but the appellate court found the action reasonable and justified in light of the dangers posed by unauthorized drugs in the schools. A Pennsylvania federal district court noted that a rational relationship should exist between a student's punishment and offense. Such a relationship was found when a student was permanently expelled for leaving behind in a classroom a written note that claimed there was a bomb in the school.[47]

Students also have challenged expulsions as violating their substantive due process rights. In these instances, school officials have provided full procedural due process, but students allege that the government has deprived them of rights (i.e., school attendance) without reasonable justification. It is often referred to as government abuse of power that "shocks the conscience."[48] The Seventh Circuit ruled that a student's substantive due process rights were not violated when he was expelled for public indecency and possession of pornography when a fellow student jokingly took pictures of him and several classmates in the shower after a wrestling match. Later, the student was given the negatives, which the wrestling coach confiscated. The court said the educators' actions in expelling the student simply did not rise to the level of a constitutional violation. The court reasoned that even though officials overreacted

---

[43]The failure to enact required state rules or to follow them, however, would violate state law rather than the Federal Constitution. *See* White v. Salisbury Twp. Sch. Dist., 588 F. Supp. 608 (E.D. Pa. 1984). *See* Vann *ex rel.* Vann v. Stewart, 445 F. Supp. 2d 882 (E.D. Tenn. 2006); Rogers v. Gooding Pub. Joint Sch. Dist., 20 P.3d 16 (Idaho 2001).

[44]Kresser v. Sandusky Bd. of Educ., 748 N.E.2d 620 (Ohio Ct. App. 2001).

[45]Stone v. Prosser Consol. Sch. Dist. No. 116, 971 P.2d 125 (Wash. Ct. App. 1999). *See also In re* Expulsion of E.J.W., 632 N.W.2d 775 (Minn. Ct. App. 2001) (finding violation of state law when a student accused of involvement in a bomb threat was not given the witnesses' names nor provided an opportunity to confront and cross-examine them).

[46]Wilson v. Cmty. Unit Sch. Dist., 451 N.E.2d 939 (Ill. App. Ct. 1983). *But see* McEntire v. Brevard County Sch. Bd., 471 So. 2d 1287 (Fla. Dist. Ct. App. 1985) (overturning expulsion of student for selling caffeine pills because evidence did not support that the student represented the pills as speed; school board policy prohibited the selling of counterfeit pills only if represented as speed).

[47]Brian A. v. Stroudsburg Area Sch. Dist., 141 F. Supp. 2d 502 (M.D. Pa. 2001).

[48]*See infra* text accompanying notes 81–92.

and used questionable judgment, their actions did not elevate the expulsion to a constitutional matter.[49]

Zero-Tolerance Policies. The concern about school safety led to specific federal and state laws directed at the discipline of students who bring weapons onto school campuses. Under the Gun-Free Schools Act of 1994 requirements, all states have enacted legislation requiring at least a one-year expulsion for students who bring firearms to school.[50] In expanding the scope of the law, states have added to the list of prohibitions by including weapons such as knives, explosive devices, hand chains, and other offensive weapons as well as drugs and violent acts. The federal law also requires state provisions to permit the local school superintendent to modify the expulsion requirement on a case-by-case basis.[51]

Severe criticism has been directed at zero-tolerance policies when school officials fail to exercise discretion and flexibility. The American Bar Association and others have called for an end to such policies that require automatic penalties without assessing the circumstances.[52] A Virginia case underscores the harsh consequences when students encounter inflexible policies. In this case, a 13-year-old student, attempting to save a suicidal friend's life, took the friend's binder containing a knife and placed it in his own locker. Upon hearing about the knife, the assistant principal asked him to retrieve it from his locker. Although the assistant principal felt that the student was acting in the best interest of his friend and at no time posed a threat to anyone, he was expelled from school for four months. The Fourth Circuit, in upholding the expulsion, noted its harshness but found no violation of the student's due process rights. In a concurring opinion, one justice commented: "The panic over school violence and the intent to stop it has caused school officials to jettison the common sense idea that a person's punishment should fit his crime in favor of a single harsh punishment, namely, mandatory school suspension."[53]

---

[49]Tun v. Whitticker, 398 F.3d 899 (7th Cir. 2005).

[50]20 U.S.C. § 7151 (2007). Additionally, most states have enacted gun-free or weapons-free school zone laws restricting possession of firearms in or near schools.

[51]*See* Lyons v. Penn Hills Sch. Dist., 723 A.2d 1073 (Pa. Commw. Ct. 1999) (concluding that the school board exceeded its authority in adopting a zero-tolerance policy for weapons possession that failed to provide the superintendent with discretion to modify mandatory expulsion on a case-by-case basis as required by state law). *See also* Rouleau v. Williamstown Sch. Bd., 892 A.2d 223 (Vt. 2005) (ruling that superintendent's modification of the expulsion requirement because of a student's limited involvement in bringing a pellet gun to campus did not prevent the board barring his participation in cocurricular and other school functions for the remainder of the year).

[52]Report to the ABA House of Delegates, February 19, 2001, American Bar Association, Chicago, IL.

[53]Ratner v. Loudoun County Pub. Schs., 16 Fed. Appx. 140, 143 (4th Cir. 2001). *See also* Vann *ex rel.* Vann v. Stewart, 445 F. Supp. 2d 882 (E.D. Tenn. 2006) (finding a one-year expulsion for the possession of a pocketknife bore a rational relationship to student's offense; school officials were not required to consider modifying the punishment); S. Gibson Sch. Bd. v. Sollman, 768 N.E.2d 437 (Ind. 2002) (ruling that the judiciary's role is to determine whether a school board acted arbitrarily or capriciously and not to assess the harshness of zero-tolerance policies).

Invoking mandatory expulsion policies may implicate constitutional rights if administrators fail to take into consideration the individual student's history and the circumstances surrounding the conduct. The Sixth Circuit noted that expelling a student for weapons possession when the student did not know that the weapon was in his car could not survive a due process challenge.[54] The Tenth Circuit, however, ruled that a one-year removal from school did not violate a student's substantive due process rights when the student "should have known" that a weapon was in his car; the court said the student did not "unknowingly" bring the weapon to school because it was visible in the front console to anyone standing outside the car.[55] In general, courts have been reluctant to impose the knowing possession standard that would require the determination of a student's intent.[56]

Suspensions

Suspensions are frequently used to punish students for violating school rules and standards of behavior when the infractions are not of sufficient magnitude to warrant expulsion. Suspensions include the short-term denial of school attendance as well as the denial of participation in regular courses and activities (in-school suspension). Most legal controversies have focused on out-of-school suspensions, but it is advisable to apply the same legal principles to any disciplinary action that separates the student from the regular instructional program even for a short period of time.

Procedural Requirements. Historically, state laws and judicial decisions differed widely in identifying and interpreting procedural safeguards for suspensions. In 1975, however, the Supreme Court provided substantial clarification regarding the constitutional rights of students confronting short-term suspensions. The Court majority in *Goss v. Lopez* held that minimum due process must be provided before a student is suspended for even a brief period of time.[57] Recognizing that a student's state-created property right to an education is protected by the Fourteenth Amendment, the Court ruled that such a right cannot be impaired unless the student is

---

[54]Seal v. Morgan, 229 F.3d 567 (6th Cir. 2000). *See also* Colvin v. Lowndes County, Miss. Sch. Dist., 114 F. Supp. 2d 504 (N.D. Miss. 1999) (holding that expulsion under the school board's zero-tolerance policy violated due process rights where the school board did not consider facts and circumstances of the student's case).

[55]Butler v. Rio Rancho Pub. Sch. Bd. of Educ., 341 F.3d 1197, 1201 (10th Cir. 2003).

[56]*See In re* B.N.S., 641 S.E.2d 411 (N.C. Ct. App. 2007) (noting that North Carolina's weapons law does not require a showing of criminal intent; mere possession of a pocketknife justified adjudication of the student as delinquent); Bundick v. Bay City Indep. Sch. Dist., 140 F. Supp. 2d 735, 740 (S.D. Tex. 2001) (holding that knowledge "can be imputed from the fact of possession").

[57]419 U.S. 565 (1975). Individuals posing a danger or threat may be removed immediately with notice and a hearing following as soon as possible. *See, e.g.*, Willis v. Anderson Cmty. Sch. Corp., 158 F.3d 415 (7th Cir. 1998); C.B. v. Driscoll, 82 F.3d 383 (11th Cir. 1996).

afforded notice of the charges and an opportunity to refute them.[58] The Supreme Court also emphasized that suspensions implicate students' constitutionally protected liberty interests because of the potentially damaging effects that the disciplinary process can have on a student's reputation and permanent record.

The *Goss* majority strongly suggested that its holding applied to all short-term suspensions, including those of only one class period. Consequently, many school boards have instituted policies that require informal procedures for every brief suspension and more formal procedures for longer suspensions. In the absence of greater specificity in state statutes or administrative regulations, students have a constitutional right to the following protections prior to suspension:

- Oral or written notification of the nature of the violation and the intended punishment,
- An opportunity to refute the charges before an objective decision maker (such a discussion may immediately follow the alleged rule infraction[59]), and
- An explanation of the evidence on which the disciplinarian is relying.

The requirement of an impartial decision maker does not infer that an administrator or teacher who is familiar with the facts cannot serve in this capacity. The decision maker simply must judge the situation fairly and on the basis of valid evidence.[60]

The Supreme Court's *Goss* decision established the rudimentary procedural requirements for short-term suspensions, but students continue to seek expansion of their procedural rights. The Supreme Court specifically noted that such formal procedures as the right to secure counsel, to confront and cross-examine witnesses, and to call witnesses are not constitutionally required. The Court reiterated this stance in a later case by noting that a two-day suspension "does not rise to the level of a penal sanction calling for the full panoply of procedural due process protections applicable to a criminal prosecution."[61] Decisions by lower state and federal courts indicate a reluctance to impose these additional requirements unless mandated by state law. In a Maine case, a student claimed a violation of procedural due process because the school administrator denied him permission to leave during

[58]*See* Meyer v. Austin Indep. Sch. Dist., 167 F.3d 887 (5th Cir. 1999) (noting that school officials' speaking with a student's parents does not necessarily provide a meaningful opportunity for the student to be heard). *But see* Achman v. Chi. Lakes Indep. Sch. Dist., 45 F. Supp. 2d 664 (D. Minn. 1999) (finding that parents' exclusion of their son from a suspension hearing did not deny him an opportunity to be heard, specifically when the principal had witnessed the misconduct).

[59]*See, e.g.*, Maimonis v. Urbanski, 143 Fed. Appx. 699 (7th Cir. 2005); Shuman v. Penn Manor Sch. Dist., 422 F.3d 141 (3d Cir. 2005); Williams *ex rel.* Allen v. Cambridge Bd. of Educ., 370 F.3d 630 (6th Cir. 2004).

[60]*See* Riggan v. Midland Indep. Sch. Dist., 86 F. Supp. 2d 647 (W.D. Tex. 2000) (finding that the principal was not an unbiased decision maker when he also was the aggrieved party); Rigau v. Dist. Sch. Bd., 961 So. 2d 382 (Fla. Dist. Ct. App. 2007) (concluding that the findings in a suspension order did not support the charge that a student was under the influence of alcohol).

[61]Bethel Sch. Dist. No. 403 v. Fraser, 478 U.S. 675, 686 (1986). *See* Maimonis v. Urbanski, 143 Fed. Appx. 699 (7th Cir. 2005); Covington County v. G.W., 767 So. 2d 187 (Miss. 2000).

questioning and failed to advise him of his right to remain silent or to have his parents present during the interrogation.[62] The court rejected all claims, noting that there was no legal authority to substantiate any of the asserted rights. The court reasoned that to rule otherwise would, in fact, contradict the informal procedures outlined in *Goss* allowing for immediate questioning and disciplinary action. Also relying on *Goss*, the Third Circuit ruled that the suspension of a 5-year-old kindergartener for telling his friends, "I'm going to shoot you" while playing a game of cops and robbers satisfied required informal procedures even though the parents contended that they should have been present to help him understand the process.[63]

Although the Supreme Court in *Goss* recognized the possibility of "unusual situations" that would require more formal procedures than those outlined, little guidance was given as to what these circumstances might be. The only suggestion offered in *Goss* was that a disciplinarian should adopt more extensive procedures in instances involving factual disputes "and arguments about cause and effect."[64] Courts have declined to expand on this brief listing. The Sixth Circuit rejected a student's contention that drug charges constituted such an "unusual situation" because of the stigmatizing effect on his reputation. The court did not believe that an eighth grade student suspended for 10 days for possessing a substance that resembled an illegal drug was "forever faced with a tarnished reputation and restricted employment opportunities."[65] Similarly, more extensive procedures were found unnecessary when a student was barred from interscholastic athletics and other activities in addition to a 10-day suspension.[66]

---

[62]Boynton v. Casey, 543 F. Supp. 995 (D. Me. 1982). The "right to remain silent" also has been advanced in other cases, with students arguing that school disciplinary proceedings should be governed by the principle established by the Supreme Court in Miranda v. Arizona, 384 U.S. 436 (1966) (holding that persons subjected to custodial interrogation must be advised of their right to remain silent, that any statement made may be used against them, and that they have the right to legal counsel). Courts have readily dismissed these claims, finding that discussions with school administrators are noncustodial. Clearly, in the *Miranda* decision, the Supreme Court was interpreting an individual's Fifth Amendment right against self-incrimination when first subjected to police questioning in connection with criminal charges. *See, e.g.,* Cason v. Cook, 810 F.2d 188 (8th Cir. 1987); Pollnow v. Glennon, 757 F.2d 496 (2d Cir. 1985); People v. Pankhurst, 848 N.E.2d 628 (Ill. App. Ct. 2006); J.D. v. Commonwealth, 591 S.E.2d 721 (Va. Ct. App. 2004). *But see In re* R.H., 791 A.2d 331 (Pa. 2002) (holding that school police officers were required to give a student *Miranda* warnings prior to interrogation, since they exercised the same powers as municipal police and the interrogation led to charges by the police, not punishment by school officials).

[63]S.G. *ex rel.* A.G. v. Sayreville Bd. of Educ., 333 F.3d 417 (3d Cir. 2003). *See also In re* Andre M., 88 P.3d 552 (Ariz. 2004) (finding that a 16-year-old student's rights were violated when police interrogated him at school and refused to permit his parent to be present).

[64]Goss v. Lopez, 419 U.S. 565, 583–584 (1975).

[65]Paredes v. Curtis, 864 F.2d 426, 429 (6th Cir. 1988).

[66]Palmer v. Merluzzi, 868 F.2d 90 (3d Cir. 1989). *See also* Donovan v. Ritchie, 68 F.3d 14 (1st Cir. 1995) (ruling that a bar to interscholastic athletics and other activities in addition to a 10-day suspension did not necessitate the provision of more formal procedures); Taylor v. Enumclaw Sch. Dist., 133 P.3d 492 (Wash. Ct. App. 2006) (ruling that *Goss* requirements were adequate for both an academic and athletic suspension).

Students also have asserted that suspensions involving loss of course credit or occurring during exam periods require greater due process than outlined in *Goss*. The Fifth Circuit, however, did not find persuasive the argument that the loss incurred for a 10-day suspension during final examinations required more than a mere give-and-take discussion between the principal and the student. In refusing to require more formal proceedings, the court noted that *Goss* makes no distinction as to when a short-term suspension occurs, and a contrary ruling would "significantly undermine, if not nullify, its definitive holding."[67] Similarly, the Seventh Circuit rejected a student's claim that additional procedures were required because a suspension occurred at the end of the school year and precluded the student from taking his final exams and graduating.[68]

Courts have continued to resist attempts to elaborate or formalize the minimal due process requirements outlined in *Goss* for short-term suspensions. As the Supreme Court noted, "Further formalizing the suspension process and escalating its formality and adversary nature may not only make it too costly as a regular discipline tool but also destroy its effectiveness as part of the teaching process."[69]

In-School Suspensions. In-school suspensions may be equivalent to an out-of-school suspension, thereby necessitating minimal due process procedures. A Mississippi federal district court noted that whether procedural due process is required depends on the extent to which the student is deprived of instruction or the opportunity to learn.[70] The physical presence of a student at school does not conclusively relieve school officials of their duty to provide due process for disciplinary measures that exclude a student from the learning process. However, a Tennessee federal district court found that a student's placement in a classroom "time-out box" did not require due process because he continued to work on class assignments and could hear and see the teacher from the confined area.[71] The court emphasized that teachers must be free to administer minor forms of classroom discipline such as time-out, denial of privileges, and special assignments. Similarly, the Sixth Circuit held that a one-day suspension in which a student completed school work and was counted as in attendance did not implicate a property interest in educational benefits or a liberty interest in reputation; it was simply too *de minimis*.[72]

[67]Keough v. Tate County Bd. of Educ., 748 F.2d 1077, 1081 (5th Cir. 1984).

[68]Lamb v. Panhandle Comm. Unit Sch. Dist. No. 2, 826 F.2d 526 (7th Cir. 1987).

[69]Goss v. Lopez, 419 U.S. 565, 583 (1975). *See* Hammock v. Keys, 93 F. Supp. 2d 1222 (S.D. Ala. 2000) (finding that informal give and take immediately following search of the student's car satisfied due process requirements prior to suspension).

[70]Cole v. Newton Special Mun. Separate Sch. Dist., 676 F. Supp. 749 (S.D. Miss. 1987), *aff'd*, 853 F.2d 924 (5th Cir. 1988).

[71]Dickens v. Johnson County Bd. of Educ., 661 F. Supp. 155 (E.D. Tenn. 1987). *See also* Rasmus v. Arizona, 939 F. Supp. 709 (D. Ariz. 1996) (holding that denying a student the ability to work on class assignments during a 10-minute time-out was *de minimis* and did not violate a property right).

[72]Laney v. Farley, 501 F.3d 577 (6th Cir. 2007).

Disciplinary Transfers to Alternative Educational Placements. Closely related to suspensions are *involuntary transfers* of students to alternative educational placements for disciplinary reasons. Such transfers generally do not involve denial of public education, but they might implicate protected liberty or property interests.[73] Legal challenges to the use of disciplinary transfers have addressed primarily the adequacy of the procedures followed. Recognizing that students do not have an inherent right to attend a given school, some courts nonetheless have held that pupils facing involuntary reassignment are entitled to minimal due process if such transfers are occasioned by misbehavior.[74]

A Pennsylvania federal district court also ruled that "lateral transfers" for disciplinary reasons affected personal liberty and property interests of sufficient magnitude to require procedural due process. Even though such transfers involved comparable schools, the court reasoned that a disciplinary transfer carried with it a stigma and thus implicated a protected liberty right. Noting that a transfer of a student "during a school year from a familiar school to a strange and possibly more distant school would be a terrifying experience for many children of normal sensibilities," the court concluded that such transfers were more drastic punishments than suspensions, and thus necessitated due process.[75] As to the nature of the procedures required, the court held that the student and parents must be given notice of the proposed transfer, and that a prompt informal hearing before the school principal must be provided. The court stipulated that if parents were still dissatisfied with the arrangement after the informal meeting, they had the right to contest the transfer recommendation at a more formal hearing.

The Fifth Circuit, however, declined to find a federally protected property or liberty interest when a student arrested for aggravated assault was reassigned to an alternative education program under a Texas statute. According to the court, the student was not denied, even temporarily, a public education. In dismissing the case, the court did note that to ensure fairness, the state and local school districts should provide students and parents an opportunity to explain why a disciplinary transfer may not be warranted; however, failure to do so does not infringe constitutional rights.[76] In a South Carolina case, the state high court ruled that the state law governing the

---

[73]Courts also have held that students do not have an inherent entitlement to specific aspects of a public education program. For example, the Rhode Island federal district court ruled that a student was not deprived of an education because he was removed from a science class the last five weeks of the school year and received individual instruction from a former science teacher. Casey v. Newport Sch. Comm., 13 F. Supp. 2d 242 (D.R.I. 1998).

[74]*See, e.g.*, McCall v. Bossier Parish Sch. Bd., 785 So. 2d 57 (La. Ct. App. 2001). *But see* Martinez v. Sch. Dist. No. 60, 852 P.2d 1275 (Colo. Ct. App. 1992) (rejecting students' argument that a disciplinary transfer for 90 days required a hearing because education was not interrupted).

[75]Everett v. Marcase, 426 F. Supp. 397, 400 (E.D. Pa. 1977). *See also* Riggan v. Midland Indep. Sch. Dist., 86 F. Supp. 2d 647 (W.D. Tex. 2000) (holding that extensive punishment—including a five-day assignment to an alternative school, a three-day suspension, exclusion from graduation, and two letters of apology—implicated property interests requiring at least minimum due process protections).

[76]Nevares v. San Marcos Consol. Indep. Sch. Dist., 111 F.3d 25 (5th Cir. 1997). *See* Ponce v. Socorro Indep. Sch. Dist., 508 F. 3d 765 (5th Cir. 2007).

transfer of students to an alternative school does not provide for an appeal beyond the school board.[77] Only the expulsion of a student can be appealed to a court.

Anti-Bullying Laws.   Numerous studies document the pervasiveness of bullying behavior and its detrimental impact on students' learning and mental health. Since 2000, more than 20 states have enacted anti-bullying legislation because of concerns about connections between school violence and bullying. Like the mandate under the federal zero-tolerance law, these state laws require local school districts to include an anti-bullying policy in their discipline codes. Most of the state laws provide a broad definition of what constitutes bullying behavior. The laws refer to intentional, aggressive behavior, repeated over time, that involves an imbalance of power and strength. Typically, proscribed verbal or written behavior includes name-calling, teasing, intimidation, ridicule, humiliation, physical acts, and taunts.[78]

State laws cap usually do not identify the specific penalties for bullying behavior, leaving local schools significant discretion. Oregon law is typical, requiring that policies include consequences for bullying behavior, but it also goes further than some states by specifying that remedial measures should be taken with the students who bully.[79] Although not addressing initial consequences, Georgia law specifies student assignment to an alternative school after three bullying offenses.[80]

School personnel have always had the authority to discipline students for bullying behavior. The new laws, however, formalize the responsibility for disrupting and deterring bullying behavior. Since the anti-bullying state laws are relatively new, case law is quite limited in interpreting students' rights and school districts' liability.[81] Nonetheless, in developing and administering anti-bullying policies, school officials must take into consideration students' procedural due process rights. Policies imposing short-term suspensions must comply at least with the minimum requirements of *Goss*;[82] more extensive disciplinary measures for bullying behavior will necessitate formal hearings.

Fundamental fairness requires at least minimal due process procedures when students are denied school attendance or removed from the regular instructional program. Severity of the separation dictates the amount of process due under the United States Constitution and state laws. Permanent expulsion from school triggers the most extensive process, whereas minor infractions may involve a brief give and take

---

[77]David v. Sch. Dist., 647 S.E.2d 219 (S.C. 2007).

[78]*See, e.g.*, Ind. Code Ann. § 20-33-8-0.2 (2007) (defining bullying as "overt, repeated acts or gestures, including (1) verbal or written communications transmitted; (2) physical acts committed; or (3) any other behaviors committed by a student or group of students against another student with the intent to harass, ridicule, humiliate, intimidate, or harm the other student").

[79]Or. Rev. Stat. §339.356(1) (2007).

[80]Ga. Code Ann. § 20-2-751.4(b) (2007).

[81]In addition to state laws, victims of bullying may rely on federal civil rights laws if they are in a protected class (i.e., race, sex, national origin, or religion) or seek a remedy for negligence against the aggressor and the school district under state tort law. *See* text accompanying note 73, Chapter 13 (tort law).

[82]*See supra* text accompanying notes 56–73.

between school officials and students. Simply providing students the opportunity to be heard can preserve trust in the school system.

Corporal Punishment

Although many states permit educators to administer corporal punishment, increasingly states are banning the practice either by law or state regulation. In 1971, only one state prohibited corporal punishment; today, more than half proscribe its use.[83] Generally, where state law permits corporal punishment, courts have upheld its reasonable administration and have placed the burden on the aggrieved students to prove otherwise. In evaluating the reasonableness of a teacher's actions in a given situation, courts have assessed the child's age, maturity, and past behavior; the nature of the offense; the instrument used; any evidence of lasting harm to the child; and the motivation of the person inflicting the punishment. This section provides an overview of the constitutional and state law issues raised in the administration of corporal punishment.

Constitutional Issues

In 1977, the Supreme Court addressed the constitutionality of corporal punishment that resulted in the severe injury of two students. The Court held in *Ingraham v. Wright* that the use of corporal punishment in public schools does not violate either the Eighth Amendment's prohibition against the government's infliction of cruel and unusual punishment or the Fourteenth Amendment's procedural due process guarantees.[84] While recognizing that corporal punishment implicates students' constitutionally protected liberty interests, the Court emphasized that state remedies are available, such as assault and battery suits, if students are excessively or arbitrarily punished by school personnel. In essence, the Court majority concluded that state courts under provisions of state laws should handle cases dealing with corporal punishment. The majority distinguished corporal punishment from a suspension by noting that the denial of school attendance is a more severe penalty that deprives students of a property right and thus necessitates procedural safeguards. Furthermore, the majority reasoned that the purpose of corporal punishment would be diluted if elaborate procedures had to be followed prior to its use.[85]

---

[83]*See Global Initiative to End All Corporal Punishment of Children*, available at www.endcorporalpunishment .org/pages/frame.html, for the status of corporal punishment laws in each state and country in the world. The American Academy of Pediatrics has recommended that corporal punishment be abolished in all states because of its detrimental affect on students' self-image and achievement as well as possible contribution to disruptive and violent behavior. American Academy of Pediatrics, "Corporal Punishment in Schools," *Pediatrics*, vol. 106 (Aug. 2000), p. 343; reaffirming 2000 statement, *Pediatrics*, vol. 118 (Sept. 2006), p. 1266.

[84]430 U.S. 651 (1977).

[85]The Court noted that procedures outlined earlier by a federal district court, although desirable, were not required under the United States Constitution. *See* Baker v. Owen, 395 F. Supp. 294 (M.D.N.C. 1975), *aff'd*, 430 U.S. 651 (1977).

The Supreme Court's ruling in *Ingraham*, however, does not foreclose a successful constitutional challenge to the use of *unreasonable* corporal punishment. Some federal appellate courts have held that students' substantive due process right to be free of brutal and egregious threats to bodily security might be impaired by the use of shockingly, excessive corporal punishment.[86] The Fourth Circuit concluded that although *Ingraham* bars federal litigation on procedural due process issues, excessive or cruel corporal punishment may violate students' substantive due process rights, which protect individuals from arbitrary and unreasonable governmental action. According to the appellate court, the standard for determining if such a violation has occurred is "whether the force applied caused injury so severe, was so disproportionate to the need presented, and was so inspired by malice or sadism rather than a merely careless or unwise excess of zeal that it amounted to a brutal and inhumane abuse of official power literally shocking to the conscience."[87] Clearly, student challenges to the reasonable use of ordinary corporal punishment are precluded by this standard.

Substantive due process claims generally are evaluated by examining the need for administering corporal punishment, the relationship between the need and the amount of punishment administered, whether force was applied to maintain or restore discipline or used maliciously with the intent of causing harm, and the extent of a student's injury.[88] The Fifth and Seventh Circuits, disagreeing with the stance of the majority of the appellate courts, concluded that constitutional claims cannot be raised if states prohibit unreasonable student discipline and provide adequate post-punishment civil or criminal remedies for abuse.[89]

---

[86]Johnson v. Newburgh Enlarged Sch. Dist., 239 F.3d 246 (2d Cir. 2001); Neal v. Fulton County Bd. of Educ., 229 F.3d 1069 (11th Cir. 2000); P.B. v. Koch, 96 F.3d 1298 (9th Cir. 1996); Metzger v. Osbeck, 841 F.2d 518 (3d Cir. 1988); Wise v. Pea Ridge Sch. Dist., 855 F.2d 560 (8th Cir. 1988); Garcia v. Miera, 817 F.2d 650 (10th Cir. 1987); Webb v. McCullough, 828 F.2d 1151 (6th Cir. 1987); Hall v. Tawney, 621 F.2d 607 (4th Cir. 1980). *But see supra* text accompanying note 84.

[87]*Hall*, 621 F.2d at 613. *See also* Kirkland *ex rel.* Jones v. Greene County Bd. of Educ., 347 F.3d 903 (11th Cir. 2003) (ruling that a principal could not argue that a student's right to be free from arbitrary and excessive force was not clearly established law; thus, the principal was not entitled to qualified immunity for the alleged violation of a student's substantive due process rights).

[88]*See, e.g., Neal*, 229 F.3d 1069; *Wise*, 855 F.2d 560. More recently, some courts have moved away from substantive due process for analyzing claims of excessive force in Section 1983 actions to the constitutional protections of the Fourth Amendment. The Ninth Circuit noted that the specific constitutional provisions of the Fourth Amendment "provide more guidance to judicial decisionmakers than the more open-ended concept of substantive due process." Doe *ex rel.* Doe v. Hawaii Dep't of Educ., 334 F.3d 906, 908 (9th Cir. 2003). *See also* Preschooler II v. Clark County Sch. Bd. of Trs., 479 F.3d 1175 (9th Cir. 2007) (finding that a teacher's excessive physical force in disciplining a seriously disabled 4-year-old child was not reasonable under the Fourth Amendment). *But see* Flores v. Sch. Bd. of DeSoto Parish, 116 Fed Appx. 504 (5th Cir. 2004) (ruling that permitting excessive force claims to be considered under the Fourth Amendment would undermine the court's [Fifth Circuit] prohibition against substantive due process claims where state law remedies exist).

[89]Moore v. Willis Indep. Sch. Dist., 233 F.3d 871 (5th Cir. 2000); Wallace v. Batavia Sch. Dist. 101, 68 F.3d 1010 (7th Cir. 1995).

Courts allowing substantive due process claims have found the threshold for recovery for the violation of a student's rights to be high. Minor pain, embarrassment, and hurt feelings do not rise to this level; actions must literally be "shocking to the conscience."[90] Actions courts have found not to rise to this level include requiring a 10-year-old boy to clean out a stopped-up toilet with his bare hands,[91] a push to a student's shoulder causing her to fall against a door jam,[92] and the piercing of a student's upper arm with a straight pin.[93] In contrast, the Tenth Circuit ruled that substantive due process rights were implicated where a 9-year-old girl was paddled with a split paddle while she was held upside down by another teacher, resulting in severe bruises, cuts, and permanent scarring.[94] Similarly, other conscience-shocking behavior involved a coach knocking a student's eye out of the socket with a metal weight lock[95] and a teacher physically restraining a student until he lost consciousness and fell to the floor, suffering significant injuries.[96] The Fourth Circuit found that a student's substantive due process rights were implicated when a wrestling coach "initiated and encouraged" wrestling team members to repeatedly beat the student.[97]

State Law

Although the Supreme Court has ruled that the United States Constitution does not prohibit corporal punishment in public schools, its use may conflict with state law provisions or local administrative regulations. As noted, the majority of states now prohibit corporal punishment,[98] and others have established procedures or

[90]*Wise*, 855 F.2d at 564. *See Garcia*, 817 F.2d 650; Woodard v. Los Fresnos Indep. Sch. Dist., 732 F.2d 1243 (5th Cir. 1984). *See also* Golden v. Anders, 324 F.3d 650 (8th Cir. 2003) (finding that a principal's forceful restraint of a sixth grade student who was violently kicking a vending machine was not conscience shocking, since the principal did not maliciously and sadistically injure the student); Daniels v. Lutz, 407 F. Supp. 2d 1038, 1045 (E.D. Ark. 2005) (ruling that a teacher's conduct is not conscience shocking "unless he maliciously and sadistically injures a student").

[91]Harris v. Robinson, 273 F.3d 927 (10th Cir. 2001).

[92]Gottlieb v. Laurel Highlands Sch. Dist., 272 F.3d 168 (3d Cir. 2001). *See also* Thomas v. Bd. of Educ. of W. Greene Sch. Dist., 467 F. Supp 2d 483 (W.D. Pa. 2006) (finding that a teacher's forceful punch, with closed fist, to a student's chest did not rise to a substantive due process violation).

[93]Brooks v. Sch. Bd., 569 F. Supp. 1534 (E.D. Va. 1983). *See also* Smith v. Half Hollow Hills Cent. Sch. Dist., 298 F.3d 168 (2d Cir. 2002) (concluding that a single slap did not violate student's substantive due process rights but refusing to rule that a single slap could never be sufficiently brutal to invoke due process protections); Lilliard v. Shelby County Bd. of Educ., 76 F.3d 716 (6th Cir. 1996) (holding that a single slap did not rise to the level of a constitutional violation).

[94]Garcia v. Miera, 817 F.2d 650 (10th Cir. 1987).

[95]Neal v. Fulton County Bd. of Educ., 229 F.3d 1069 (11th Cir. 2000).

[96]Metzger v. Osbeck, 841 F.2d 518 (3d Cir. 1988). *See also* Ellis *ex rel.* Pendergrass v. Cleveland Mun. Sch. Dist., 455 F.3d 690 (6th Cir. 2006) (concluding that a substitute teacher slamming an elementary student's head into a chalkboard, throwing her to the floor, and choking her violated the student's substantive due process rights).

[97]Meeker v. Edmundson, 415 F.3d 317 (4th Cir. 2005).

[98]*See supra* text accompanying note 78.

conditions for its use. Teachers can be disciplined or discharged for violating these state and local provisions regulating corporal punishment. Courts have upheld dismissals based on insubordination for failure to comply with reasonable school board requirements in administering corporal punishment. Teachers also have been dismissed under the statutory grounds of "cruelty" for improper use of physical force with students. In Illinois, a tenured teacher was dismissed on this ground for using a cattle prod in punishing students.[99] Other disciplinary measures also may be taken against teachers. A Nebraska teacher who "tapped" a student on the head was suspended without pay for 30 days under a state law that prohibits the use of corporal punishment.[100]

Beyond statutory or board restrictions, other legal means exist to challenge the use of unreasonable corporal punishment in public schools. Teachers can be charged with criminal assault and battery, which might result in fines and imprisonment. Civil assault and battery suits for monetary damages can be initiated against school personnel.

When corporal punishment is allowed, educators should use caution in administering it, since improper administration can result in dismissal, monetary damages, and even imprisonment. Corporal punishment should never be administered with malice, and the use of excessive force should be avoided. Teachers would be wise to keep a record of incidents involving corporal punishment and to adhere to minimum procedural safeguards, such as notifying students of behavior that will result in a paddling, asking another staff member to witness the act, and providing parents on request written reasons for the punishment. Moreover, teachers should become familiar with relevant state laws and school board policies before attempting to use corporal punishment in their classrooms.

Academic Sanctions

It is indisputable that school authorities have the right to use academic sanctions for poor academic performance. Consistently, courts have been reluctant to substitute their own judgment for that of educators in assessing students' academic accomplishments. Failing grades, denial of credit, academic probation, retention, and expulsion from particular programs have been upheld as legitimate means of dealing with poor academic performance. The Supreme Court stated:

> When judges are asked to review the substance of a genuinely academic decision, . . . they should show great respect for the faculty's professional judgment. Plainly, they may not override it unless it is such a substantial departure from accepted academic norms as to demonstrate that the person or committee responsible did not actually exercise professional judgment.[101]

[99]Rolando v. Sch. Dirs. 358 N.E.2d 945 (Ill. App. Ct. 1976).

[100]Daily v. Bd. of Educ., 588 N.W.2d 813 (Neb. 1999).

[101]Regents of Univ. of Mich. v. Ewing, 474 U.S. 214, 225 (1985).

Courts usually have granted broad discretionary powers to school personnel in establishing academic standards,[102] but there has been less agreement regarding the use of grade reductions or academic sanctions as punishments for student absences and misbehavior. More complex legal issues are raised when academic penalties are imposed for nonacademic reasons.

Absences

Excessive student absenteeism remains a growing concern and has led many school boards to impose academic sanctions for absences. These practices have generated legal challenges related to students' substantive due process rights. To meet the due process requirements, however, the sanction must be reasonable—that is, rationally related to a valid educational purpose. Since students must attend class to benefit from the educational program, most courts have found that academic penalties for absenteeism serve a valid educational goal.

In an Illinois case, a student claimed that a school regulation stipulating that grades would be lowered one letter grade per class for an unexcused absence impaired protected rights.[103] In defending the rule, school officials asserted that it was the most appropriate punishment for the serious problem of truancy. They argued that students could not perform satisfactorily in their class work if they were absent, since grades reflected class participation in addition to other standards of performance. The appeals court was not persuaded by the student's argument that grades should reflect only scholastic achievement, and therefore concluded that the regulation was reasonable.

The Supreme Court of Connecticut upheld a schoolwide policy that provided for a five-point reduction in course grades for each unapproved absence and that denied course credit for such absences in excess of 24. The court drew a sharp distinction between academic and disciplinary sanctions, noting that the school board's policy was academic, rather than disciplinary, in intent and effect. Specifically, the court found that a board's determination that grades should reflect more than examinations and papers "constitutes an academic judgment about academic requirements."[104] The Supreme Court of Missouri drew a similar distinction between academic and disciplinary sanctions but concluded that a school district's policy providing for loss of credit for previously earned academic work was punishment for unsatisfactory attendance rather than deductions for academic performance. Therefore, the court ruled that the student was entitled to a due process hearing prior to imposition of the penalty.[105]

Some courts have upheld even those policies that do not differentiate between excused and unexcused absences in imposing academic penalties. For example, the Supreme Court of Arkansas upheld a board policy that disallowed course credit and

---

[102]Bd. of Curators v. Horowitz, 435 U.S. 78 (1978).

[103]Knight v. Bd. of Educ., 348 N.E.2d 299 (Ill. App. Ct. 1976).

[104]Campbell v. Bd. of Educ., 475 A.2d 289, 294 (Conn. 1984).

[105]State v. McHenry, 915 S.W.2d 325 (Mo. 1995).

permitted expulsion of students who accumulated more than 12 absences per semester.[106] The court, in refusing to substitute its judgment for the school board's, concluded that under state law, this action was within the board's power to make reasonable rules and regulations for the administration of the schools. A Michigan appellate court upheld a school board's authority to require students with more than three days of excused absences to attend after-school study sessions or have their letter grades reduced.[107] Similarly, a New York appellate court found that a policy denying course credit for absences in excess of nine classes for semester courses and 18 absences for full-year courses was rational; students were permitted and encouraged to make up the classes before they exceeded the limit.[108]

To ensure procedural fairness, however, students must be informed that absences will result in academic penalties. In a Missouri case, a student received a failing grade for half of a semester in a music course for missing the last two performances of the semester.[109] The court upheld the grade reduction because students were informed the first day of class that attendance at all performances was required to complete the course and that unexcused absences would result in a failing grade. Where grade reductions are part of academic evaluations, courts generally do not require additional procedural safeguards beyond notice. An Indiana appellate court found that sufficient procedural protections were provided to a student who was removed from a geometry class under the school's chronic tardiness policy when he had received a prior warning from the teacher, a detention for absences, and a conference with his parents and teacher.[110]

Given the serious truancy problem confronting many school districts, it seems likely that school officials will continue to consider the imposition of academic sanctions. The legality of such policies will depend primarily on judicial interpretation of applicable state law.

Misconduct

Academic sanctions imposed for student misconduct also have been challenged. It is generally accepted that students can be denied credit for work missed while suspended from school. In fact, if students could make up such work without penalty, a suspension might be viewed as a vacation rather than a punishment. More controversy has surrounded policies that impose an additional grade reduction for suspension days, and courts have not agreed regarding the legality of this practice.

For example, a Kentucky appeals court voided a regulation whereby grades were reduced because of unexcused absences resulting from student suspensions.[111]

[106]Williams v. Bd. of Educ., 626 S.W.2d 361 (Ark. 1982).

[107]Slocum v. Holton Bd. of Educ., 429 N.W.2d 607 (Mich. Ct. App. 1988).

[108]Bitting v. Lee, 564 N.Y.S.2d 791 (App. Div. 1990).

[109]R.J.J. *ex rel.* Johnson v. Shineman, 658 S.W.2d 910 (Mo. Ct. App. 1983).

[110]M.S. v. Eagle-Union Cmty. Sch. Corp., 717 N.E.2d 1255 (Ind. Ct. App. 1999).

[111]Dorsey v. Bale, 521 S.W.2d 76 (Ky. Ct. App. 1975).

The school board policy stated that work missed because of unexcused absences could not be made up, and that five points would be deducted for every unexcused absence from each class during the grading period. The court held that the use of suspensions or expulsions for misconduct was permissible, but the additional lowering of grades as a punitive measure was not. A Pennsylvania court also agreed with this reasoning and found grade reductions for suspensions to be beyond a school board's authority.[112] In the court's opinion, it was a clear misrepresentation of students' scholastic achievement; the penalty went beyond the five-day suspension and downgraded achievement for a full grading period. The Mississippi Supreme Court, relying on a state law mandating the maintenance of alternative schools for suspended students, concluded that students attending these schools are not absent from school.[113] Under this law, a school board cannot count suspension days as unexcused for grading purposes unless the student fails to attend the alternative school.

In contrast, the Supreme Court of Indiana upheld the denial of course credit for a high school junior expelled three days before the end of a semester after the discovery of a small amount of marijuana in his truck. The court noted that although state law did not mandate loss of credit, the board could impose such a penalty.[114] A Texas appellate court upheld a school system's right to lower course grades for suspension days imposed for misconduct in addition to giving zeros on graded class work during the suspension.[115] Relying on a state attorney general's opinion approving grade reductions, the court found the pivotal question to be whether the board had actually adopted a policy that would authorize grade reductions. According to the court, oral announcements in school assemblies explaining grade penalties constituted a valid policy. Moreover, the court noted that the grade reduction did not impair constitutionally protected property or liberty rights.

Similar to some corporal punishment claims, students have asserted that drastic academic sanctions for disciplinary incidents violate their substantive due process rights.[116] The Seventh Circuit determined that the removal of two students from a band class for playing two unauthorized music pieces at a school concert did not meet the required constitutional threshold.[117] Exclusion of the students from the class resulted in a grade of F for the term and prevented one of the students from graduating with honors. The court said that although the school might have overreacted, its

[112]Katzman v. Cumberland Valley Sch. Dist., 479 A.2d 671 (Pa. Commw. Ct. 1984). *See also In re* Angela, 340 S.E.2d 544 (S.C. 1986) (ruling that under state law, suspension absences could not be counted as unexcused for determining delinquency).

[113]Bd. of Trs. v. T.H., 681 So. 2d 110 (Miss. 1996).

[114]S. Gibson Sch. Bd. v. Sollman, 768 N.E.2d 437 (Ind. 2002).

[115]New Braunfels Indep. Sch. Dist. v. Armke, 658 S.W.2d 330 (Tex. Civ. App. 1983).

[116]*See supra* text accompanying notes 81–84, for a discussion of substantive due process rights.

[117]Dunn v. Fairfield Cmty. High Sch. Dist., 158 F.3d 962 (7th Cir. 1998). *See also* Zellman v. Indep. Sch. Dist. No. 2758, 594 N.W.2d 216 (Minn. Ct. App. 1999) (holding that a zero grade for plagiarizing a history project did not involve a protected property or liberty interest).

action was certainly not an extraordinary departure from established norms to substantiate a constitutional violation.

Generally, courts have ruled that academic course credit or high school diplomas cannot be withheld solely for disciplinary reasons. As early as 1921, the Supreme Court of Iowa held that students who had completed all academic requirements had the right to receive a high school diploma even though they refused to wear graduation caps during the ceremony.[118] The court ruled that the school board was obligated to issue a diploma to a pupil who had satisfactorily completed the prescribed course of study and who was otherwise qualified to graduate from high school. More recently, a Pennsylvania court held that a student who completed all coursework and final exams while expulsion proceedings were pending could not be denied a diploma, because state law specifies that a diploma must be issued once all requirements are met.[119]

Courts have issued conflicting decisions regarding the legality of denying a student the right to participate in graduation ceremonies as a disciplinary measure. A New York appeals court held that a student could not be denied such participation on disciplinary grounds unless conduct was related to a threatened disruption of the graduation ceremony,[120] whereas a North Carolina federal district court held that a student could be denied the privilege of participating in the graduation ceremony as a penalty for misconduct.[121] In the latter case, the federal court concluded that the student was not deprived of any property right, since he received his high school diploma even though he was not allowed to take part in the ceremony. A Pennsylvania appellate court reversed a trial court order permitting a student to participate in the graduation ceremony after he was suspended for violating the district's alcohol policy.[122] The appeals court found no arbitrary, capricious, or prejudicial actions on the part of the school board to justify judicial interference with the school's decision.

Although the use of academic sanctions for student misconduct and truancy is prevalent, students will likely continue to challenge such practices. To ensure fairness, any regulation stipulating that grades will be lowered for nonacademic reasons should be reasonable, related to absences from class, and serve a legitimate school purpose. Furthermore, students must be informed of these rules through the school's official student handbook or similar means.

---

[118]Valentine v. Indep. Sch. Dist. 183 N.W. 434 (Iowa 1921).

[119]Ream v. Centennial Sch. Dist., 765 A.2d 1195 (Pa. Commw. Ct. 2001); 24 Pa. Stat. Ann. § 16-1613 (2007).

[120]Ladson v. Bd. of Educ., 323 N.Y.S.2d 545 (App. Div. 1971).

[121]Fowler v. Williamson, 448 F. Supp. 497 (W.D.N.C. 1978). *See also* Reese v. Jefferson Sch. Dist. No. 14J, 208 F.3d 736 (9th Cir. 2000) (holding that exclusion of four female students from a graduation ceremony for throwing water balloons at boys in the boys' restroom did not violate the Equal Protection Clause when the school did not punish the boys for alleged misconduct that had not been reported before the incident); Nieshe v. Concrete Sch. Dist., 127 P.3d 713 (Wash. Ct. App. 2005) (concluding that participation in a graduation ceremony did not constitute a liberty or property interest).

[122]Flynn-Scarcella v. Pocono Mountain Sch. Dist., 745 A.2d 117 (Pa. Commw. Ct. 2000).

Search and Seizure

Search and seizure cases involving public schools have increased in recent years, with the majority resulting from the confiscation of either illegal drugs or weapons. Students have asserted that warrantless searches conducted by school officials impair their rights under the Fourth Amendment of the Constitution. Through an extensive line of decisions, the Supreme Court has affirmed that the basic purpose of the Fourth Amendment is to "safeguard the privacy and security of individuals against arbitrary invasions by governmental officials."[123] This amendment protects individuals against unreasonable searches by requiring state agents to obtain a warrant based on probable cause prior to conducting a search. Under the *probable cause standard*, a governmental official must have reasonable grounds of suspicion, supported by sufficient evidence, to cause a cautious person to believe that the suspected individual is guilty of the alleged offense and that the search will produce evidence of the crime committed. Governmental officials violating Fourth Amendment rights may be subject to criminal or civil liability, but the most important remedy for the aggrieved individual is the exclusionary rule.[124] This rule renders evidence of an illegal search inadmissible in criminal prosecutions.[125] Also, under the "fruit of the poisonous tree" doctrine, additional evidence obtained later, resulting from the events set in motion by the illegal search, may be excluded.

Significant Fourth Amendment questions have been raised in the public school setting. Since Fourth Amendment protections apply only to searches conducted by agents of the state, a fundamental issue in education cases is whether school authorities function as private individuals or as state agents. Although most courts had found the Fourth Amendment applicable to public schools, it was not until 1985, in *New Jersey v. T.L.O.*, that the Supreme Court finally held that the amendment's prohibition of unreasonable searches applies to school authorities.[126] The Court concluded that school officials are state agents, and all governmental actions—not merely those of law-enforcement officers—come within the constraints of the Fourth Amendment.

Although finding the Fourth Amendment applicable, the Court in *T.L.O.* concluded that educators' substantial interest in maintaining discipline required "easing" the warrant and probable cause requirements imposed on police officers. The Court reasoned that "requiring a teacher to obtain a warrant before searching a child suspected of an infraction of school rules (or of the criminal law) would unduly interfere with the maintenance of the swift and informal disciplinary procedures needed in the schools."[127] In modifying the level of suspicion required to conduct a search, the Court found the public interest was best served in the school setting with a standard less than

[123]Camara v. Mun. Ct. of S.F., 387 U.S. 523, 528 (1967).

[124]*See* Mapp v. Ohio, 367 U.S. 643 (1961).

[125]Evidence seized by a private person, however, is admissible since the exclusionary rule does not apply. *See, e.g.*, People v. Stewart, 313 N.Y.S.2d 253 (1970).

[126]469 U.S. 325 (1985).

[127]*Id.* at 340.

probable cause. Accordingly, the Court held that the legality of a search should depend "simply on the reasonableness, under all the circumstances, of the search."[128]

The Court in *T.L.O.* advanced two tests for determining reasonableness. First, is the search justified at its inception? That is, are there "reasonable grounds for suspecting that the search will turn up evidence that the student has violated or is violating either the law or the rules of the school?"[129] Second, is the scope of the search reasonable? In the Court's words, are "the measures adopted reasonably related to the objectives of the search and not excessively intrusive in light of the age and sex of the student and the nature of the infraction?"[130]

The "reasonableness" standard allows courts substantial latitude in interpreting Fourth Amendment rights. Among the factors that courts have considered in assessing reasonable grounds for a search are the child's age, history, and record in the school; prevalence and seriousness of the problem in the school to which the search is directed; exigency to make the search without delay and further investigation; probative value and reliability of the information used as a justification for the search; school officials' experience with the student and with the type of problem to which the search is directed; and the type of search.[131] Clearly, reasonable suspicion requires more than a hunch, good intentions, or good faith. The Supreme Court, in upholding an exception to the warrant requirement for a "stop and frisk" search for weapons by police officers, concluded that to justify the intrusion, the police officer must be able to point to *specific and articulable facts.*[132] In recognizing an exception for school searches, it appears that, at a minimum, the judiciary will require searches of students to be supported by objective facts.[133]

Informants often play an important role in establishing the "specific and articulable facts" necessary to justify a search. Reliability of informants can be assumed unless school officials have reason to doubt the motives of the reporting student, teacher, parent, citizen, or anonymous caller.[134] The amount of detail given by an informant adds to the veracity of the report— that is, identifying a student by name, what the student is wearing, and the specific contraband and where it is located will help support a decision to search.[135] Additionally, even with limited information, the

---

[128]*Id.* at 341.

[129]*Id.* at 342.

[130]*Id.*

[131]*See, e.g.,* Vernonia Sch. Dist. 47J v. Acton, 515 U.S. 646 (1995); *T.L.O.,* 469 U.S. 325; Cornfield v. Consol. High Sch. Dist. No. 230, 991 F.2d 1316 (7th Cir. 1993); *In re* Angelia D.B., 564 N.W.2d 682 (Wis. 1997).

[132]Terry v. Ohio, 392 U.S. 1, 21 (1968).

[133]*See, e.g., Cornfield,* 991 F.2d 1316; People v. Taylor, 625 N.E.2d 785 (Ill. App. Ct. 1993); State v. Finch, 925 P.2d 913 (Or. Ct. App. 1996).

[134]*See* C.B. v. Driscoll, 82 F.3d 383 (11th Cir. 1996); *In re* L.A., 21 P.3d 952 (Kan. 2001) (finding that a student's tip to the Crime Stoppers organizer established reasonable suspicion). The Supreme Court in *T.L.O.* noted that because the expectation of privacy is diminished in school settings, officials do not have to show the reliability level required of police officers. For a discussion of the higher standards for law enforcement, *see* Florida v. J.L., 529 U.S. 266 (2000).

[135]*See, e.g.,* Wofford v. Evans, 390 F.3d 318 (4th Cir. 2004); S.D. v. State, 650 So. 2d 198 (Fla. Dist. Ct. App. 1995).

level of danger presented by an informant's tip may require an immediate response. A California appellate court commented that "the gravity of the danger posed by possession of a firearm or other weapon on campus was great compared to the relatively minor intrusion involved in investigating" the accused students.[136]

A further requirement of reasonableness is individualized suspicion. The Supreme Court in *T.L.O.* did not address individualized suspicion, but the Court did state that "exceptions to the requirement of individualized suspicion are generally appropriate only where the privacy interests implicated by a search are minimal and where 'other safeguards' are available 'to assure that the individual's reasonable expectation of privacy is not subject to the discretion of the official in the field.'"[137] In the absence of exigency requiring an immediate search, courts have been reluctant to support personal searches lacking individualized suspicion.[138]

In assessing the constitutionality of searches in public schools, two questions are central: (1) What constitutes a search? (2) What types of searches are reasonable? What constitutes a search must be appraised in the context of the Supreme Court's statement that "the Fourth Amendment protects people, not places. What a person knowingly exposes to the public, even in his own home or office, is not a subject of Fourth Amendment protection. But what he seeks to preserve as private, even in an area accessible to the public, may be constitutionally protected."[139] According to the Court's rulings, essential considerations in determining whether an action is a search are an individual's reasonable expectation of privacy (reasonable in the sense that society is prepared to recognize the privacy)[140] and the extent of governmental intrusion.[141]

The reasonableness of a specific type of search must be evaluated in terms of all the circumstances surrounding the search.[142] This would include variables such as who initiated the search, who conducted the search, need for the search, purpose of the search, information or factors prompting the search, what or who was searched, and use of the evidence.

An individual may waive entitlement to Fourth Amendment protection by consenting to a search or volunteering requested evidence. The consent, however, is valid only if voluntarily given in the absence of coercion. Serious questions arise as to whether a student's consent is actually voluntary. Did the student have a free choice? Was the student aware of his or her Fourth Amendment rights? A Texas federal district court reasoned that the very nature of the school setting diminishes the presumption of consent.[143] Students are accustomed to receiving and following orders of

[136]*In re* Alexander B., 270 Cal. Rptr. 342, 344 (Ct. App. 1990).

[137]New Jersey v. T.L.O., 469 U.S. 325, 342 n.8 (1985).

[138]*See, e.g.,* Bell v. Marseilles Elementary Sch., 160 F. Supp. 2d 883 (N.D. Ill. 2001); Kennedy v. Dexter Consol. Schs., 10 P.3d 115 (N.M. 2000).

[139]Katz v. United States, 389 U.S. 347, 351–352 (1967).

[140]*Id.* at 361 (Harlan, J., concurring).

[141]United States v. Chadwick, 433 U.S. 1, 7 (1977).

[142]Terry v. Ohio, 392 U.S. 1, 9 (1968). *See also* State v. Drake, 662 A.2d 265 (N.H. 1995).

[143]Jones v. Latexo Indep. Sch. Dist., 499 F. Supp. 223 (E.D. Tex. 1980).

school officials; refusal to obey a request is considered insubordination. In this case, the threat to call the students' parents and the police if they did not cooperate further substantiated a coercive atmosphere. In another case, the Sixth Circuit stated that there is "a presumption against the waiver of constitutional rights," placing the burden on school officials to show that students knowingly and intelligently waived their Fourth Amendment rights.[144] Although some courts have found student consent valid,[145] the inherent pitfalls of pursuing such a search in the absence of reasonable suspicion must be duly considered.

In the following sections, various types of school search are examined as to reasonableness. Figure 7.1 shows that as the invasiveness of the search increases, the degree of suspicion required to search also rises.

Lockers

In concluding that students have some legitimate expectation of privacy in their lockers, the Mississippi high court relied on the United States Supreme Court's statement that "schoolchildren may find it necessary to carry with them a variety of legitimate, noncontraband items, and there is no reason to conclude that they have necessarily

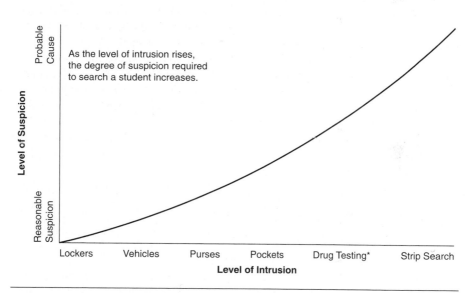

FIGURE 7.1 *Degree of Suspicion Required to Conduct Student Searches*

*Under school district drug-testing policies, athletes and students participating in extracurricular activities can be subjected to suspicionless drug tests.

[144]Tarter v. Raybuck, 742 F.2d 977, 980 (6th Cir. 1984).

[145]*See, e.g.*, Rone v. Daviess County Bd. of Educ., 655 S.W.2d 28 (Ky. Ct. App. 1983); Commonwealth v. Carey, 554 N.E.2d 1199 (Mass. 1990).

waived all rights to privacy in such items merely by bringing them onto school grounds."[146] Courts, however, have singled out school lockers as generating a lower expectation of privacy, frequently distinguishing locker searches on the basis that a locker is school property, and students do not retain exclusive possession, particularly when they have signed a form acknowledging that the locker is school property and subject to inspection. Under the view of joint control, school officials have been allowed to inspect lockers or even to consent to searches by law-enforcement officers.[147]

A Kansas case illustrates the general judicial view toward locker searches. The Supreme Court of Kansas held that the right of inspection is inherent in the authority granted to school officials to manage schools.[148] The court maintained that it is a proper function of school personnel to inspect the lockers under their control and to prevent the use of lockers in illicit ways or for illegal purposes. The Tenth Circuit also concluded "school authorities have, on behalf of the public, an interest in these lockers and a duty to police the school, particularly where possible serious violations of the criminal laws exist."[149] An important point in both of these cases, however, is that school officials retained a list of the combinations and had occasionally inspected the lockers. These points have been emphasized in other cases to support the nonexclusive nature of lockers.[150]

Applying the *T.L.O.* standard for reasonableness, the Supreme Court of Mississippi concluded that a student informant's tip indicating another student had a gun on the school premises reasonably suggested that school officials "search out the truth of the matter."[151] Similarly, a California appellate court reasoned that an anonymous parent informant reporting that a student had been seen at an evening school event with a gun substantiated reasonable suspicion to inspect the student's locker several days later.[152] The court commented that the locker search represented minimal intrusion in the context of the threat firearms pose to the safety of all students. The Massachusetts high court also concluded that a student eyewitness to an attempted sale of marijuana not only provided reasonable suspicion but probable cause to search the suspected student's locker.[153]

---

[146]*In re* S.C., 583 So. 2d 188 (Miss. 1991) (quoting New Jersey v. T.L.O., 469 U.S. 325, 339 (1985)).

[147]*But see infra* text accompanying notes 202–213, for cases addressing the involvement of law enforcement personnel.

[148]State v. Stein, 456 P.2d 1, 2 (Kan. 1969).

[149]Zamora v. Pomeroy, 639 F.2d 662, 670 (10th Cir. 1981).

[150]*See, e.g., In re* Patrick Y., 746 A.2d 405 (Md. 2000); Commonwealth v. Cass, 709 A.2d 350 (Pa. 1998); *In re* Isiah B., 500 N.W.2d 637 (Wis. 1993). *See also In re* S.C., 583 So. 2d 188 (holding that the existence of a master key did not lower the expectation of privacy, but that a policy of regularly inspecting the students' lockers might have that effect).

[151]*In re* S.C., 583 So. 2d at 192. *See also In re* Juvenile, 931 A.2d 1229 (N.H. 2007) (finding student reports to a teacher that the accused juvenile possessed a "large pot pipe" justified an assistant principal's search of the juvenile's locker).

[152]*In re* Joseph G., 38 Cal. Rptr. 2d 902 (Ct. App. 1995).

[153]Commonwealth v. Snyder, 597 N.E.2d 1363 (Mass. 1992).

Most student conduct codes and some state laws specify guidelines for locker searches. These codes or laws may establish that reasonable suspicion is required prior to conducting a search. In a Pennsylvania case, the state supreme court relied on the *T.L.O.* decision and the student code in establishing a legitimate expectation of privacy in lockers. The code specified: "Prior to a locker search a student shall be notified and given an opportunity to be present. However, where school authorities have a *reasonable suspicion* a locker contains materials that pose a threat to the health, welfare, and safety of students in the school, students' lockers may be searched without prior warning [emphasis added]."[154] Although the court held that students possessed a reasonable expectation of privacy in their lockers, it was minimal. In balancing students' privacy interests and school officials' concerns, the court found the schoolwide blanket search reasonable based on the heightened awareness of drug activity that permeated the entire school and the compelling concern about drug use.

Due to incidents of school violence in recent years, some states have enacted broad laws eliminating any presumption of privacy in school lockers. For example, a Michigan law states: "A pupil who uses a locker that is the property of a school district . . . is presumed to have no expectation of privacy in that locker or that locker's content."[155] Furthermore, school officials can search the lockers at any time and can request the assistance of the local law-enforcement agency.

Search of Personal Possessions: Purses, Book Bags, and Other Property

Students have a greater expectation of privacy in their personal property or effects than in their school lockers. In the Supreme Court's *T.L.O.* decision, a teacher had reported that a student was smoking in the restroom. Upon questioning by the assistant principal, the student denied smoking and, in fact, denied that she even smoked. The assistant principal then opened the student's purse, seeking evidence to substantiate that she did smoke. In the process of removing a package of cigarettes, he spotted rolling papers and subsequently found marijuana and other evidence implicating her in drug dealing. Using the "reasonable suspicion" test, the Supreme Court found that the search in *T.L.O.* was reasonable. The school official had a basis for suspecting that the student had cigarettes in her purse. Although possession was not a violation

[154]Commonwealth v. Cass, 709 A.2d 350, 353 (Pa. 1998). *See also Snyder*, 597 N.E.2d 1363 (finding expectation of privacy of lockers based on the student handbook). *But see In re Patrick Y.*, 746 A.2d 405 (holding that a local policy specifying probable cause to search lockers did not establish a reasonable expectation of privacy because state law provided that lockers were school property and could be searched without even reasonable suspicion).

[155]MCLS § 380.1306 (2007). *See also* Ohio Rev. Code § 3313.20 (2007) (specifying that a locker can be searched when reasonable suspicion exists that it contains evidence of the violation of a school rule or the law, or can be subject to random search if the board of education posts notice in a conspicuous place in each school building to that affect). An Ohio appellate court concluded that this aspect of the law violates the Ohio and federal constitutions. *In re* Adam, 697 N.E.2d 1100 (Ohio Ct. App. 1997).

of a school rule, it was not irrelevant; discovery of cigarettes provided evidence to corroborate that she had been smoking and challenged her credibility. No direct evidence existed that the student's purse contained cigarettes, but, based on a teacher's report that the student had been smoking, it was logical to suspect that she might have cigarettes in her purse. Characterizing this as a "commonsense" conclusion, the Court noted that "the requirement of reasonable suspicion is not a requirement of absolute certainty: 'sufficient probability, not certainty, is the touchstone of reasonableness under the Fourth Amendment.'"[156]

Other courts have noted that searches of students' personal possessions—such as wallets, purses, and book bags—do violate students' subjective expectations of privacy and, as such, require individualized suspicion that a violation of a law or school rule has occurred.[157] The Fourth Circuit found that a Little Rock school district policy permitting school officials to conduct full-scale, random, periodic inspections of students' book bags and other personal possessions without any individualized suspicion constituted a major invasion of students' expectation of privacy.[158] The court held that school officials could not argue that under the policy students waived their privacy rights when they brought their possessions onto school property. Finding lack of individualized suspicion, the Supreme Court of California declined to uphold the search of a student's calculator case in the absence of articulable facts to support the search.[159] The vice principal's search was based on the student's tardiness for class, his "furtive gestures" to hide the calculator, and his comment that the principal needed a warrant. These actions alone did not point to the possible violation of any specific rule or law.

On the other hand, the New York high court concluded that a security officer's investigation of a student's book bag was reasonable based on hearing an "unusual metallic thud" when the student tossed the bag on a metal shelf. Following the sound, the security officer ran his fingers over the outside of the book bag and detected the outline of a gun. The court noted that the sound alone was insufficient to justify searching the bag, but the discovery of the presence of a gun-like shape established reasonable suspicion to open the bag.[160]

[156]New Jersey v. T.L.O., 469 U.S. 325, 346 (1985).

[157]*See* Bravo v. Hsu, 404 F. Supp. 2d 1195 (C.D. Cal. 2005).

[158]Doe v. Little Rock Sch. Dist., 380 F.3d 349 (4th Cir. 2004). *But see* H.Y. *ex rel.* K.Y. v. Russell County Bd. of Educ., 490 F. Supp. 2d 1174 (M.D. Ala. 2007) (holding that the classroom search of students' book bags and personal possessions for missing money was justified even though individualized suspicion did not exist; school officials had an important interest in promoting order and discipline).

[159]*In re* William G., 709 P.2d 1287 (Cal. 1985). *But see* People v. Dilworth, 661 N.E.2d 310 (Ill. 1996) (upholding the search of a student's flashlight based on a report that he was selling drugs).

[160]*In re* Gregory M., 627 N.E.2d 500 (N.Y. 1993). *See also* DesRoches v. Caprio, 156 F.3d 571 (4th Cir. 1998) (concluding that the student had a legitimate expectation of privacy in his backpack, necessitating individualized suspicion to search); S.A. v. State, 654 N.E.2d 791 (Ind. Ct. App. 1995) (finding that the search of a book bag was justified by an informant's tip related to a stolen book of school locker combinations); *In re* Murray, 525 S.E.2d 496 (N.C. Ct. App. 2000) (holding that a tip from a student established reasonable suspicion to search a book bag).

In a Massachusetts case, the state high court assessed whether a student had a legitimate expectation of privacy in his handwriting.[161] The charges against the student grew out of several incidents of graffiti on school property containing obscenities and racial slurs, some directed toward one teacher. Because prior occurrences made the student a potential suspect, several of his homework assignments, along with two other students' papers, were analyzed to determine if they matched the graffiti. Based on a match with the student's writing, he was charged with malicious destruction of property and violation of the targeted teacher's civil rights. The court refused to suppress the handwriting analyses and samples, finding that it was reasonable for school authorities to suspect the student and that the inspection of the papers involved minimal intrusion.

A student's car, like other personal possessions, may be searched if reasonable suspicion can be established. A Texas federal district court, however, declined to uphold a general dragnet search of a school parking lot.[162] The school's interest in the contents of the cars was viewed as minimal, since students did not have access to their cars during the school day. Furthermore, the search was indiscriminate, lacking any evidence of individualized suspicion. In contrast, a Florida district court upheld the search of a student's car after a school aide observed in plain view a water pipe, commonly used to smoke marijuana.[163] The aide regularly patrolled the school parking lot to ensure enforcement of school regulations and to supervise students during their lunch break. In the court's opinion, patrolling the lot fell within the school's duty to maintain order and discipline and did not constitute a search.

Personal Search of a Student

Warrantless searches of a student's person raise significant legal questions. Unlike locker searches, it cannot be asserted that there is a lower expectation of privacy. Students have a legitimate expectation of privacy in the contents of their pockets and their person. The Fifth Circuit noted that "the Fourth Amendment applies with its fullest vigor against any intrusion on the human body."[164] In personal searches, not only is it necessary to have reasonable cause to search, but also the search itself must be reasonable. Reasonableness is assessed in terms of the specific facts and circumstances of a case.

---

[161]Commonweatlh v. Buccella, 751 N.E.2d 373 (Mass. 2001). *See also* Klump v. Nazareth Area Sch. Dist., 425 F. Supp. 2d 622 (E.D. Pa. 2006) (finding that a student stated a cause of action when school officials used his seized cell phone to call other students in his directory, check his messages, and hold an instant messaging conversation without identifying themselves).

[162]Jones v. Latexo Indep. Sch. Dist., 499 F. Supp. 223 (E.D. Tex. 1980).

[163]State v. D.T.W., 425 So. 2d 1383 (Fla. Civ. App. 1983). *See also* Covington County v. G.W., 767 So. 2d 187 (Miss. 2000) (holding that a report of a student drinking beer in the school parking lot justified search of his truck; no warrant was required).

[164]Horton v. Goose Creek Indep. Sch. Dist., 690 F.2d 470, 478 (5th Cir. 1982).

Search of Students' Clothing.   A New Mexico appellate court found the search of a student's pockets reasonable under the *T.L.O.* standard.[165] In this case, an assistant principal and a police officer assigned full time to the school asked a student to empty his pockets based on his evasive behavior, smell of burnt marijuana, and a large bulge in his right pocket. When the student refused to remove his hand from his pocket, the school official felt that the incident had become a safety issue. She then asked the resource officer to search the student. The officer removed the student's hand from his right pocket and reached in and pulled out a .38 caliber handgun. The court held that the search was justified on the basis of suspicious behavior and that the scope of the search was not excessive or intrusive. Similarly, the Alabama Supreme Court found the search of two fifth grade students for the alleged theft of nine dollars reasonable based on the fact that they had been alone in the classroom at the time the money disappeared.[166] In finding this to be a very limited search, the court concluded that it was reasonable for the teacher to suspect the two students and that a search would turn up evidence of the theft.

The Washington appellate court, however, declined to support the search of a student's pockets because he was in the school parking lot during the school day, a violation of the closed campus policy. The court emphasized that "there must be a nexus between the item sought and the infraction under investigation."[167] In the absence of other suspicious factors about the student, violation of the school's closed campus rule did not justify the automatic search that led to the discovery of marijuana.

Strip Searches.   Although personal searches are permitted, strip searches usually cannot be justified on the basis of reasonable suspicion. The Second Circuit noted that "as the intrusiveness of the search intensifies, the standard of Fourth Amendment 'reasonableness' approaches probable cause, even in the school context."[168] The Seventh Circuit, in a strongly worded statement, proclaimed in an Indiana case: "It does not require a constitutional scholar to conclude that a nude search of a thirteen-year-old

[165]*In re* Josue T., 989 P.2d 431 (N.M. Ct. App. 1999). *See also* Greenleaf v. Cote, 77 F. Supp. 2d 168 (D. Me. 1999) (holding that information from student informant justified personal search of student for evidence of beer drinking); D.L. v. State, 877 N.E.2d 500 (Ind. Ct. App. 2007) (finding that a pat-down search of a student that produced drugs was justified at its inception because the student was discovered in the hallway without identification or a pass during a nonpassing time); Wilcher v. State, 876 S.W.2d 466 (Tex. Ct. App. 1994) (concluding that reasonable suspicion existed to search a student who was not in class based on information that he possessed a gun).

[166]Wynn v. Bd. of Educ., 508 So. 2d 1170 (Ala. 1987). *See also* Bridgman v. New Trier High Sch. Dist. No. 203, 128 F.3d 1146 (7th Cir. 1997) (holding that a student's unruly behavior, bloodshot eyes, and dilated pupils established reasonable suspicion to conduct search); D.B. v. State, 728 N.E.2d 179 (Ind. Ct. App. 2000) (finding that the smell of cigarette smoke coming from a bathroom stall and the student's unresponsiveness to questioning justified search).

[167]State v. B.A.S., 13 P.3d 244, 246 (Wash. Ct. App. 2000). *See also* D.I.R. v. State, 683 N.E.2d 251 (Ind. Ct. App. 1997) (concluding that the search of a student's pocket because she arrived late to school was not justified); Commonwealth v. Damian D., 752 N.E.2d 679 (Mass. 2001) (finding that a student's truancy did not establish reasonable suspicion to support school officials' search).

[168]M.M. v. Anker, 607 F.2d 588, 589 (2d Cir. 1979).

child is an invasion of constitutional rights of some magnitude. More than that: it is a violation of any known principle of human decency."[169]

The Ninth Circuit found a pat-down search and subsequent strip search to be unlawful.[170] Such an invasion of privacy could not be justified on the basis that a bus driver saw the student exchange "what appeared to be money" for an unidentified object. Similarly, the West Virginia high court found the strip search of a 14-year-old eighth-grader suspected of stealing $100 excessively intrusive, and thus unreasonable in scope.[171] The court concluded that unless exigent circumstances necessitate an immediate search to protect the safety of other students, a warrantless strip search is impermissible. In another strip search to locate stolen money, an Illinois federal district court found the lack of individualized suspicion and the level of intrusion pivotal in holding a search of 30 students unconstitutional.[172]

More recently, the Second Circuit emphasized the high level of suspicion required for a strip search.[173] According to the court, the quality and quantity of evidence prior to the search is pivotal in determining the reasonableness of the search. In this case, the court examined four factors and found each insufficient. A student's tip about another student's possession of drugs alone did not justify a search without further investigation to corroborate the information. The suspected student's past disciplinary problems, unrelated to drug use, were not a significant factor to initiate a highly intrusive search. Furthermore, the student's denial of the accusation in a "suspicious" manner without any substantive details of behavior did not supply justification. Neither did discovery of cigarettes in the student's purse justify the decision to conduct a strip search. Since the court ruled the search unconstitutional at its inception, the court did not review the reasonableness of the scope of the search.

A few strip searches have been upheld with sufficient evidence of individualized suspicion, specifically related to drug use. The Ninth Circuit upheld the strip search of a female middle school student suspected of possessing prescription drugs.[174] Among the significant facts establishing reasonable suspicion were a face-to-face student informant who had been given pills by the suspected student and corroboration from another student who also had received pills and still had pills in her possession. Although the court recognized that the scope of this search was personally intrusive, it was held to be reasonable, considering the small size of

[169]Doe v. Renfrow, 631 F.2d 91, 92–93 (7th Cir. 1980).

[170]Bilbrey v. Brown, 738 F.2d 1462 (9th Cir. 1984).

[171]State *ex rel.* Galford v. Mark Anthony B., 433 S.E.2d 41 (W. Va. 1993). *See also* Fewless v. Bd. of Educ., 208 F. Supp. 2d 806 (W.D. Mich. 2002) (ruling that a strip search of a 14-year-old student based on the report of two hostile classmates did not constitute reasonable suspicion to justify the search); Konop v. Northwestern Sch. Dist., 26 F. Supp. 2d 1189 (D.S.D. 1998) (holding that the strip search of eighth grade girls was unreasonable and violated clearly established law); Kennedy v. Dexter Consol. Schs., 10 P.3d 115 (N.M. 2000) (concluding that the strip search of two high school students without individualized suspicion to find a missing ring violated clearly established law).

[172]Bell v. Marseilles Elementary Sch., 160 F. Supp. 2d 883 (N.D. Ill. 2001).

[173]Phaneuf v. Frailin, 448 F.3d 591 (2d Cir. 2006).

[174]Redding v. Safford Unified Sch. Dist., 504 F.3d 828 (9th Cir. 2007).

the contraband that could have been hidden easily on her body. Similarly, the Seventh Circuit found that substantial evidence existed to search a high school student with an "unusual bulge" in his sweatpants.[175] Acknowledging that the potential impact of a strip search is substantial, the court, however, emphasized that with the administrators' suspicion that the student was "crotching drugs," a strip search was the least intrusive way to proceed. Both circuit courts considered the nature of the contraband sought and the likelihood of it being hidden on the body in determining that the scope of the searches was reasonable.

Although most courts have found strip searches unreasonable in the absence of individualized suspicion, many have not found that the law is clearly enough established to deny qualified immunity to school officials conducting the unconstitutional searches. The Supreme Court in 2002 ruled that the state of the law at the time of an individual's action must give "fair and clear warning" that specific rights have been established.[176] The Eleventh Circuit held that "clearly established" rights are determined by looking to decisions of the Supreme Court, its own circuit's decisions, and the decisions of the highest court of the state where the case was initiated.[177] Similarly, the Sixth Circuit found the strip search of 25 high school students for several hundred dollars unreasonable but granted teachers qualified immunity because case law did not clearly establish that the search was impermissible at the time it was conducted.[178] As courts continue to rule that strip searches are unconstitutional, it will be more difficult for educators to argue that the law is not clearly established regarding the unlawfulness of strip searches of students.[179]

Courts have not prohibited strip searches of students, but enough caveats exist to alert school officials of the inherent risks of such intrusive personal searches. The judicial trend indicates that reasonable suspicion alone may be inadequate to justify most strip searches; rather, the required standard approaches probable cause necessitating specific evidence linked to an individual student. Except for emergency situations posing immediate danger to the safety of students, few circumstances appear to necessitate such intrusions.

Seizure of Students.   Courts have examined claims that detentions by school officials constitute an unlawful seizure of a student. A seizure occurs when individuals

[175]Cornfield v. Consol. High Sch. Dist. No. 230, 991 F.2d 1316 (7th Cir. 1993). *See also* Jenkins v. Talladega City Bd. of Educ., 115 F.3d 821 (11th Cir. 1997) (holding that a teacher and a principal had qualified immunity in conducting a strip search of three second grade students in 1992 to find a missing $7.00 because of the lack of settled legal authority at that time).

[176]Hope v. Pelzer, 536 U.S. 730 (2002).

[177]Thomas v. Roberts, 323 F.3d 950 (11th Cir. 2003).

[178]Beard v. Whitmore Lake Sch. Dist., 402 F.3d 598 (6th Cir. 2005). *See also* Beard v. Whitmore Lake Sch. Dist., 244 Fed. Appx. 607 (6th Cir. 2007) (concluding that school officials were not liable under § 1983 for conducting the strip searches because no evidence existed to show that they were deliberately indifferent to high school students' rights nor did a pattern or practice of conducting unconstitutional searches exist).

[179]*Id.*; *Thomas*, 323 F.3d 950; Carlson *ex rel.* Stuczynski v. Bremen High Sch. Dist., 423 F. Supp. 2d 823 (N.D. Ill. 2006); Watkins v. Millennium Sch., 290 F. Supp. 2d 890 (S.D. Ohio 2003).

feel they are not free to leave, such as students detained by school administrators for questioning. As in the cases involving searches, courts examine school officials' actions to determine if a seizure or detainment of a student is reasonable—that is, justified at its inception and not excessively intrusive in light of the student's age and sex and the specific infraction. The Third Circuit found the "seizure" of a student for approximately four hours while school officials investigated a claim of sexual harassment to be reasonable in light of the serious nature of the accusation against the student.[180] A California district court concluded that the detention of an eighth grade student in the principal's office for three hours was justified to prevent classroom disruptions, to discipline the student, and to prevent her from using drugs or giving them to others.[181]

A teacher's momentary physical restraint of students, however, has typically not been considered a "seizure" under the Fourth Amendment. Citing the special nature of the school environment, courts have ruled that physical restraint in disciplinary situations in the school environment does not involve the deprivation of liberty the Fourth Amendment prohibits.[182] Thus, a teacher who physically grasps a student by the shoulders and escorts him out of the classroom has not violated the student's Fourth Amendment right to be free from an unreasonable seizure.

Metal Detectors

With the increased concern about the high rate of violence in schools, metal detectors have become more commonplace as school officials seek to maintain a safe educational environment. Moreover, the use of metal detectors is no longer limited to secondary schools. In 2000, the Chicago chief education officer approved metal detectors for all the district's 489 elementary school.[183] Although metal detectors have become standard equipment in airports and many public buildings, their use does constitute a search for Fourth Amendment purposes. Such public searches have been found to be reasonable in balancing the threat of violence against the minimally intrusive nature of the search. As challenges have been raised about the use of metal detectors in schools, similar reasoning is applied.

The Pennsylvania high court upheld a general, uniform search of all students for weapons as they entered the high school building; each student's personal belongings were searched, and then a security officer scanned each student with a metal detector.[184] Individualized suspicion was not required in light of the high rate of violence in the

---

[180]Shuman v. Penn Manor Sch. Dist., 422 F.3d 141 (3d Cir. 2005). *See also* Wofford v. Evans, 390 F.3d 318 (4th Cir. 2004) (finding that school officials seized student but did not have to notify parents prior to detaining the student for questioning); Doe *ex rel.* Doe v. Hawaii Dep't. of Educ., 334 F.3d 906 (9th Cir. 2003) (ruling that the taping of a student to a tree for five minutes was a seizure).

[181]Bravo *ex rel.* Ramirez v. Hsu, 404 F. Supp. 1195 (C.D. Cal. 2005).

[182]*See* Flores v. Sch. Bd. of DeSoto Parish, 116 Fed. Appx. 504 (5th Cir. 2004); Gottlieb v. Laurel Highlands Sch. Dist., 272 F.3d 168 (3d Cir. 2001).

[183]Jessica Portner, "Girl's Slaying Elicits Calls for Metal Detectors," *Education Week* (March 15, 2000), p. 3.

[184]*In re* F.B., 726 A.2d 361 (Pa. 1999).

school district. The court concluded that the search involved a greater intrusion on students' privacy interests than the search of a locker, but still found it to be a minimal intrusion. Similarly, the Eighth Circuit found a search of all male students from grades 6 to 12 for dangerous weapons to be minimally intrusive based on reasonable suspicion that weapons had been brought to school that day.[185] Students were scanned with a metal detector after they removed their shoes and the contents of their pockets. If the metal detector sounded, a subsequent pat-down search was conducted.

An Illinois appellate court assessed the reasonableness of the use of metal detectors from the perspective of schools' "special needs."[186] In the first year of using the detectors, Chicago school officials confiscated over 300 weapons (including 15 guns) from the high schools. With continued use of these devices, they showed a reduction of about 85 percent in weapons confiscated. The court, in concluding that individualized suspicion was not required to use metal detectors, noted that the purpose of the screening was to ensure a safe school environment for all students, not to secure evidence of a crime.

In each of the cases litigated, courts pointed to the violent context that led school officials to use metal detectors and the minimally intrusive nature of these devices. With increasing use, it can be expected that courts will continue to review the constitutional issues raised by metal detectors in school searches.

Drug-Detecting Canines

The use of drug-detecting dogs in searches raises a number of controversial questions regarding Fourth Amendment rights. Does a dog sniffing students constitute a search? Must reasonable suspicion exist to justify the use of dogs? Does the alert of a dog establish reasonable suspicion? A few courts have addressed these issues.

The Tenth Circuit upheld the use of trained police dogs in the sniffing of lockers but did not directly address the constitutional issues presented by the canine searches. Rather, the court discussed generally the school administrator's duty to inspect, even to the point that an inspection may violate Fourth Amendment rights. Under this broad grant of authority, the alert of a dog three times at a locker established reasonable suspicion to conduct a search.[187]

The Fifth Circuit, on the other hand, confronted the question of whether sniffing by a dog is a search in terms of an individual's reasonable expectation of privacy.[188] The appellate court noted that most courts, including the United States

---

[185]Thompson v. Carthage Sch. Dist., 87 F.3d 979 (8th Cir. 1996).

[186]People v. Pruitt, 662 N.E.2d 540 (Ill. App. Ct. 1996). *See also In re* Latasha, 70 Cal. Rptr. 2d 886 (Ct. App. 1998) (holding that "special needs" administrative searches without individualized suspicion, such as use of metal detectors, involve minimal intrusion).

[187]Zamora v. Pomeroy, 639 F.2d 662, 670 (10th Cir. 1981). *See also* Bundick v. Bay City Indep. Sch. Dist., 40 F. Supp. 2d 735 (S.D. Tex. 2001) (finding that the alert of a trained and certified dog provided sufficient cause to search a student's truck without a warrant).

[188]Horton v. Goose Creek Indep. Sch. Dist., 690 F.2d 470 (5th Cir. 1982). *See* Jennings v. Joshua Indep. Sch. Dist., 877 F.2d 313 (5th Cir. 1989); Jones v. Latexo Indep. Sch. Dist., 499 F. Supp. 223 (E.D. Tex. 1980).

Supreme Court, have held that a law-enforcement agent's use of canines for sniffing objects does not constitute a search.[189] Specifically, the court referenced cases involving checked luggage, shipped packages, public lockers, and cars on public streets. According to the court, a reasonable expectation of privacy does not extend to the airspace surrounding these objects. The court maintained that what has evolved is a doctrine of "public smell," equivalent to the "plain view" theory (that is, an object in plain view can be seized under certain circumstances). This point was illustrated by the example of a police officer detecting the odor of marijuana from an object or property. No search is involved because the odor is considered to be in public view and thus unprotected.

From this line of reasoning, the Fifth Circuit noted that the use of canines has been viewed as merely enhancing the ability to detect an odor, as the use of a flashlight improves vision. Accordingly, the court concluded that sniffing of student lockers and cars in public view was not a search, and therefore the Fourth Amendment did not apply. Although permitting the use of dogs to detect drugs, the court held that reasonable suspicion is required for a further search of a locker or car by school officials, and that such suspicion can be established only on showing that the dogs are reasonably reliable in detecting the actual presence of contraband.[190]

In most instances, judicial support for the use of dogs has been limited to the sniffing of objects. The Seventh Circuit, however, concluded that the presence of dogs in a classroom was not a search.[191] In this well-publicized Indiana case, school officials with the assistance of police officers conducted a schoolwide inspection for drugs in which trained dogs were brought into each classroom for approximately five minutes. When a dog alerted beside a student, school officials requested that the student remove the contents of his or her pockets or purse. A continued alert by the dog resulted in a strip search. The appellate court, in weighing the minimal intrusion of the dogs against the school's desire to eliminate a significant drug problem, concluded that sniffing of the students by the dogs did not constitute a search invoking Fourth Amendment protections. Search of pockets and purses, however, did involve an invasion of privacy but was justified because the dog's alert constituted reasonable cause to believe that the student possessed drugs. However, as discussed previously, the court drew the line at conducting a strip search based on a dog's alert.

---

[189]The Supreme Court concluded that the brief detention of a passenger's luggage at an airport for the purpose of subjecting it to a "sniff" test by a trained narcotics detection dog did not constitute a search under the Fourth Amendment. Use of canines was characterized as unique, involving a very limited investigation and minimal disclosure. United States v. Place, 462 U.S. 696 (1983). *See also Horton*, 690 F.2d at 477, for citations to other law enforcement cases.

[190]Subsequently, in denying a rehearing, the court clarified the issue of the dogs' reliability. According to the court, a school district does not have to establish with "reasonable certainty that contraband is present . . . or even that there is probable cause to believe that contraband will be found." Rather, there must be some evidence to indicate that the dogs' performance is reliable enough to give rise to a reasonable suspicion. *Horton*, 693 F.2d at 525. *See also* Commonwealth v. Cass, 709 A.2d 350 (Pa. 1998) (holding canine sniff is not a search under the Fourth Amendment).

[191]Doe v. Renfrow, 631 F.2d 91 (7th Cir. 1980).

In contrast to the reasoning of the Seventh Circuit, a Texas federal district court concluded that the use of dogs in a blanket "sniffing" (or inspection) of students did constitute a search. The court noted that drug-detecting dogs posed a greater intrusion on personal privacy than electronic surveillance devices, which have not required individualized suspicion. According to the court, "The dog's inspection was virtually equivalent to a physical entry into the students' pockets and personal possessions."[192] In finding the dog's sniffing to be a search, the court further held that for school authorities to use dogs in a search, they must have prior individualized suspicion that a student possesses contraband that will disrupt the educational process.[193] In essence, a dog alert cannot be used to establish such suspicion.

Similarly, the Fifth Circuit held that sniffing of students by dogs significantly intrudes on an individual's privacy, thereby constituting a search.[194] Although recognizing that the sniffing of a person is a search, the court did not prohibit such searches but held that their intrusiveness must be weighed against the school's need to conduct the search. The court concluded that even with a significant need to search, individualized suspicion is required prior to the use of dogs because of the degree of intrusion on personal dignity and security. The Ninth Circuit concurred, noting that the significant intrusion on a student's expectation of privacy posed by dogs requires individualized suspicion.[195]

Given the scope of the drug problem in public schools, it seems likely that school districts will continue to consider the use of drug-detecting canine units. Until the Supreme Court addresses whether such a practice constitutes a search in schools (requiring individualized suspicion) or whether a dog alert can establish reasonable grounds for a personal search, different interpretations among lower courts seem destined to persist.

Drug Testing

In an effort to control drug use among students,[196] some districts have considered schoolwide drug-testing programs. Such programs raise serious questions about

---

[192]*Jones*, 499 F. Supp. at 233.

[193]*Id. See also* Kuehn v. Renton Sch. Dist. No. 403, 694 P.2d 1078, 1081 (Wash. 1985), in which the state high court declared: "The Fourth Amendment demands more than a generalized probability; it requires that the suspicion be particularized with respect to each individual searched."

[194]*Horton*, 690 F.2d 470.

[195]B.C. v. Plumas Unified Sch. Dist., 192 F.3d 1260 (9th Cir. 1999).

[196]The National Center on Addiction and Substance Abuse in its annual back-to-school survey of 12- to 17-year-olds in 2007 reported that 80 percent of high school students and 44 percent of middle school students would return that fall to schools where drugs were used, kept, or sold. This is a substantial increase from its findings in 2002 (increase of 39 percent for high school students and 63 percent for middle school). National Center on Addiction and Substance Abuse, *National Survey of American Attitudes on Substance Abuse XII: Teens and Parents* (NY: Columbia University, 2007), available at http://casacolumbia.org.

students' privacy rights. In 1989, the Supreme Court held that urinalysis, the most frequently used means for drug testing, is a search under the Fourth Amendment.[197] Although the Court upheld the testing of government employees for drug use in two separate decisions, the holdings were narrowly drawn and based on a compelling governmental interest. In one case, the Court upheld the testing of railroad employees who are involved in certain types of accidents, emphasizing the highly regulated nature of the industry and the need to ensure the safety of the public.[198] In the second case, drug testing of customs employees seeking promotion to positions involving the interdiction of illegal drugs or requiring the use of firearms was justified based on safety and security concerns.[199] Individualized suspicion was not a precondition for conducting the urinalysis in these cases, but the narrow circumstances justifying the testing programs minimized the discretion of supervisors and the potential for arbitrariness.

The Supreme Court has rendered two decisions regarding the drug testing of students. In 1995, the Court in *Vernonia School District 47J v. Acton* upheld a school district's drug policy authorizing random urinalysis drug testing of students participating in athletic programs.[200] Emphasizing the district's "custodial and tutelary" responsibility for children, the Court recognized that school personnel can exercise a degree of supervision and control over children that would not be permitted over adults. This relationship was held to be pivotal in assessing the reasonableness of the district's drug policy—a policy undertaken "in furtherance of the government's responsibilities, under a public school system, as guardian and tutor of children entrusted to its care."[201] Addressing students' legitimate privacy expectations, the Court noted that the lower privacy expectations within the school environment are reduced even further when a student elects to participate in sports. In concluding that students had a decreased expectation of privacy, the Court specifically identified the communal undress in locker rooms and showers and the highly regulated nature of athletics, involving physical examinations, conduct rules related to training and dress, and minimum grade point averages.

In examining the intrusiveness of the search, the Supreme Court found that the manner in which the urine samples were collected and monitored was not overly intrusive. Also, the Court stressed that the urinalysis report—which could reveal significant information about one's body, including not only drug use but various medical conditions—was disclosed only to a limited number of individuals and was not reported to law-enforcement authorities. Furthermore, the Court emphasized that the search was directed narrowly at athletes, a group in which drug use had been high and the risk for harm to themselves and others was significant.

---

[197]Skinner v. Ry. Labor Executives' Ass'n, 489 U.S. 602 (1989); Nat'l Treasury Employees Union v. Von Raab, 489 U.S. 656 (1989). *See also* Juran v. Independence, Or. Sch. Dist., 898 F. Supp. 728 (D. Or. 1995) (finding that breathalyzer tests also implicate Fourth Amendment protections).

[198]*Skinner*, 489 U.S. 602.

[199]*Nat'l Treasury Employees Union*, 489 U.S. 656.

[200]515 U.S. 646 (1995).

[201]*Id.* at 665.

In 2002, the Supreme Court in *Board of Education v. Earls* again reviewed a drug-testing policy but one that applied to students in all extracurricular activities, including athletics.[202] The policy required students to take a drug test prior to participation, to submit to random drug testing while involved in the activity, and to agree to be tested at any time when reasonable suspicion existed. Acknowledging that athletes' lower expectation of privacy was noted in *Vernonia*, the Court emphasized that the critical element in upholding the earlier policy was the school context. In sustaining the drug-testing policy in *Earls*, the Court reasoned that the collection procedures, like *Vernonia*, were minimally intrusive, information was kept in confidential files with limited access, and test results were not given to law-enforcement authorities. Based on these factors, the Court concluded that the drug-testing policy was not a significant invasion of students' privacy rights. Although the students had argued that no pervasive drug problem existed to justify an intrusive measure like drug testing, the Court responded that it had never required such evidence before allowing the government to conduct suspicionless drug testing. Moreover, in light of the widespread use of drugs nationally and some evidence of increased use in this school, the Court found it "entirely reasonable" to enact this particular drug-testing policy.

Similar drug tests of students have been upheld under state constitutions. For example, the Supreme Court of Indiana, adhering to reasoning analogous to the Supreme Court's decision in *Earls*, found a school's policy of random drug testing of students participating in athletics, extracurricular, and cocurricular activities permissible under state law.[203] Moreover, the court indicated that the fact the test was preventive and rehabilitative rather than punitive was an important factor under the Indiana Constitution.

Although it is clear that specific subgroups of students, such as athletes and participants in extracurricular activities, can be subjected to drug testing, courts have not permitted blanket testing of all students.[204] A Texas federal district court did not find exigent circumstances or other demonstrated compelling interests to justify a mandatory testing program of all students in grades 6 through 12.[205] Accordingly, the federal court held the program unreasonable and unconstitutional under the Fourth Amendment. The Seventh Circuit rejected a school district's policy requiring drug and alcohol testing of all students suspended for three or more days for violating any school rule.[206]

---

[202]536 U.S. 822 (2002).

[203]Linke v. Northwestern Sch. Corp., 763 N.E.2d 972 (Ind. 2002).

[204]With the vast majority of students participating in extracurricular activities, school districts appear to be moving toward testing all students. It should be noted, however, that any student may be tested when individualized suspicion exists. *See* Dominic J. v. Wyo. Valley W. High Sch., 362 F. Supp. 2d 560 (M.D. Pa. 2005).

[205]Tannahill *ex rel.* Tannahill v. Lockney Indep. Sch. Dist., 133 F. Supp. 2d 919 (N.D. Tex. 2001).

[206]Willis v. Anderson Cmty. Sch., 158 F.3d 415 (7th Cir. 1998). *See also* Joy v. Penn-Harris-Madison Sch. Corp., 212 F.3d 1052 (7th Cir. 2000) (upholding random drug and alcohol testing of students involved in extracurricular activities and students driving to school; court rejected testing students for nicotine to determine tobacco use); Penn-Harris-Madison Sch. Corp. v. Joy, 768 N.E.2d 940 (Ind. Ct. App. 2002) (finding, under state constitution, drug and alcohol testing permissible for students participating in extracurricular activities and students driving to school; nicotine testing violated students' liberty interests).

In this case, the student was suspended for fighting, and upon his return to school was informed that he was required to submit to a test for drug and alcohol use. When the student refused, school officials suspended him again; refusal to take the test was treated as admission of unlawful drug use. In ruling that the policy violated the Fourth Amendment, the court did not find a connection between fighting and use of drugs. Furthermore, the suspension procedures in Indiana require school officials to meet with students prior to suspension. At the initial suspension for fighting or any other infraction, it is possible to determine if individualized suspicion exists at that time to support testing a particular student for drugs or alcohol.

Although blanket or random drug testing of all students is not likely to withstand judicial challenge, many schools subject students to urinalysis based on individualized suspicion, and such practices have not been invalidated by courts. Any drug-testing program, however, must be carefully constructed to avoid impairing students' Fourth Amendment privacy rights. The policy must be clearly developed, specifically identifying reasons for testing. Data collection procedures must be precise and well defined. Students and parents should be informed of the policy, and it is advisable to request students' consent prior to testing. However, neither student nor parental consent is required to conform to Fourth Amendment requirements.[207] If the test indicates drug use, the student must be given an opportunity to explain the results. Providing for the rehabilitation of the student rather than punishment strengthens the policy.

Police Involvement

A "reasonable suspicion" or a "reasonable cause to believe" standard is invoked in assessing the legality of school searches, but a higher standard may be required when police officers are involved. The nature and extent of such involvement are important considerations in determining whether a search is reasonable. If the police role is one of finding evidence of a crime, probable cause would be required.[208] Whereas early decisions generally supported police participation in searches initiated and conducted by school officials, more recently courts have tended to draw a distinction between searches with and without police assistance.[209]

The more stringent judicial posture is represented in an Illinois decision in which a school principal received a call that led him to suspect that three girls possessed illegal drugs.[210] On the superintendent's advice, the principal called the police

[207]*See* Hedges v. Musco, 204 F.3d 109 (3d Cir. 2000); Gutin v. Washington Township Bd. of Educ., 467 F. Supp. 2d 414 (D.N.J. 2006).

[208]*See, e.g.,* Picha v. Wielgos, 410 F. Supp. 1214 (N.D. Ill. 1976); State v. K.L.M., 628 S.E.2d 651 (Ga. Ct. App. 2006).

[209]However, searches by trained police officers employed by, or assigned to, a school district generally are governed by the *T.L.O.* reasonable suspicion standard rather than the probable cause standard. *See, e.g.,* State v. Serna, 860 P.2d 1320 (Ariz. Ct. App. 1993); S.A. v. State, 654 N.E.2d 791 (Ind. Ct. App. 1995); *In re* Angelia D.B., 564 N.W.2d 682 (Wis. 1997).

[210]*Picha*, 410 F. Supp. 1214. *See also* People v. Pankhurst, 848 N.E.2d 628 (Ill. App. Ct. 2006).

to assist in the investigation. After the police arrived, the school nurse and the school psychologist searched each girl; however, no drugs were discovered. Subsequently, the students filed suit alleging that their civil rights had been violated. The court found that the police were not called merely to assist in maintaining school discipline but to search for evidence of a crime. Under the circumstances, the court concluded that the students had a constitutional right not to be searched unless the police had a warrant based on probable cause.

In contrast, the same Illinois court held that a police officer's involvement in persuading a student to relinquish the contents of his pockets did not violate Fourth Amendment rights under the *T.L.O.* standard.[211] The police officer's role was quite limited in this case. He was in the school building on another matter, and his role in the search was restricted simply to asking the student to empty his pockets. There was no police involvement in the investigation that led to detaining the student, nor was the evidence used for criminal prosecution. Furthermore, the facts did not indicate that the school and the police officer were attempting to avoid the warrant and probable cause requirements.

Similarly, the Eighth Circuit held that the assistance of a police officer assigned as a liaison officer in a high school did not subject a search for stolen property to the Fourth Amendment's probable cause standard.[212] Relying on *T.L.O.*, the court found no evidence that the search activities were at the behest of a police official. Rather, the vice principal had initiated and conducted the investigation with limited assistance from the police officer. Although the police officer had participated in a pat-down search, it occurred only after the vice principal had discovered evidence of drug-related activity in a student's purse. The court found this search by a school official working in conjunction with a police officer to be permissible. Other courts have recognized the special role of school liaison or resource officers, noting that the "reasonable under the circumstances" standard applies when officers are working with school officials to maintain a safe school environment.[213] In an Eleventh Circuit case, the court ruled that the actions of a deputy sheriff (assigned as a school resource officer) were not reasonable when he handcuffed a compliant 9-year-old girl solely to punish her for being disrespectful to a coach. The student was not viewed as a threat to the coach or anyone else. The court commented that any reasonable officer of the law would have known that this action was unreasonable.[214]

---

[211]Martens v. Dist. No. 220, 620 F. Supp. 29 (N.D. Ill. 1985). *See also* Commonwealth v. Carey, 554 N.E.2d 1199 (Mass. 1990).

[212]Cason v. Cook 810 F.2d 188 (8th Cir. 1987). *See also* Shade v. City of Farmington, 309 F.3d 1054 (8th Cir. 2002) (holding a police officer's search of a student at the request of school officials permissible even though it occurred en route to a body shop class away from school grounds).

[213]*See, e.g.*, Wilson *ex rel.* Adams v. Cahokia Sch. Dist., 470 F. Supp. 2d 897 (S.D. Ill. 2007); *In re* Randy G., 28 P.3d 239 (Cal. 2001). *In re* Josue T., 989 P.2d 431 (N.M. Ct. App. 1999). *But see* Commonwealth v. Williams, 749 A.2d 957 (Pa. Super. Ct. 2000) (holding that school district police officers did not have authority to search a student's car parked off school property).

[214]Gray *ex rel.* Alexander v. Bostic, 458 F.3d 1295 (11th Cir. 2006), *Cert. denied*, 127 S. Ct. 2428(2007) (ruled that deputy sheriff was not entitled to qualified immunity because he should have known that action was unreasonable).

In a number of decisions applying the reasonable suspicion standard to school searches, courts have specifically noted or implied that this lower standard is not applicable if law-enforcement officials are involved. A Florida district court stated, "The reasonable suspicion standard does not apply in cases involving a search directed or participated in by a police officer."[215] Similarly, a Kentucky appellate court found the lower standard appropriate for searches in school settings in the absence of police participation.[216]

In a Fifth Circuit case, students claimed violation of their constitutional rights when police officers called them out of class for questioning about a rumored after-school fight that was going to occur later that day.[217] Reviewing the case in the context of the special needs of the school environment, the court found the temporary "seizure" reasonable and constitutional. Recognizing that students can be detained and questioned about school discipline issues by school officials, the court concluded that the police officers did no more than the school officials could have done themselves to deter the fight. Similarly, the Fourth Circuit upheld the use of police when school officials received reliable information that a 10-year-old girl had brought a gun to school. With police officers' expertise in locating hidden weapons, the court found school officials' action appropriate in requesting assistance to preserve the safety of students and staff.[218]

Troubling questions, however, are raised when the fruits of warrantless searches result in the criminal prosecution of students.[219] Classifying searches on the basis of who conducts the search and for what purpose is inadequate. Searches cannot be discreetly classified as either administrative (school related) or criminal. A search may be clearly criminal when the purpose is to find evidence of a crime, thereby necessitating probable cause prior to the search. But administrative searches undertaken strictly for disciplinary or safety purposes may result in prosecution of students if evidence of a crime is uncovered and reported to the police. In fact, school

---

[215]State v. D.T.W., 425 So. 2d 1838, 1385 (Fla. Civ. App. 1983). *See also In re* A.J.M., 617 So. 2d 1137 (Fla. Dist. Ct. App. 1993).

[216]Rone v. Daviess County Bd. of Educ., 655 S.W.2d 28 (Ky. Ct. App. 1983). *See also* D.R.C. v. State, 646 P.2d 252 (Alaska Ct. App. 1982) (recognizing the implicit assumption that police involvement would require probable cause).

[217]Milligan v. City of Slidell, 226 F.3d 652 (5th Cir. 2000). *See also* Douglas v. Beaver County Sch. Dist. Bd., 82 Fed. Appx. 200 (10th Cir. 2003) (ruling that principal acquiescing to police request to briefly interview a student did not violate a clearly established right a reasonable person would have known); Burreson v. Barneveld Sch. Dist., 434 F. Supp. 2d 588 (W.D. Wis. 2006) (concluding that the principal directing a student to his office to be interviewed by police for a nonschool matter did not violate the Fourth Amendment). *But see In re* R.H., 791 A.2d 331 (Pa. 2002) (holding that school officers were authorized to exercise the same powers as municipal police on school property and thus required to provide a student *Miranda* warnings prior to an interrogation that led to criminal charges).

[218]Wofford v. Evans, 390 F.3d 318 (4th Cir. 2004). *See also* Pace v. Talley, 206 Fed. Appx. 388 (5th Cir. 2006) (finding that school officials' report to police of student's misconduct prior to talking with the student did not violate any established constitutional rights).

[219]Even if evidence is declared inadmissible in criminal proceedings, it still can be used by school personnel in a suspension or expulsion hearing.

authorities have a duty to alert the police if evidence of a crime is discovered, even though the search was initiated for school purposes.

Although many legal issues involving search and seizure in schools still are controversial, school personnel can generally protect themselves by adhering to a few basic guidelines. First, students and parents should be informed at the beginning of the school term of the procedures for conducting locker and personal searches. Second, any personal search conducted should be based on "reasonable suspicion" that the student possesses contraband that may be disruptive to the educational process. Third, the authorized person conducting a search should have another staff member present who can verify the procedures used in the search. Furthermore, school personnel should refrain from using strip searches or mass searches of groups of students. And, finally, if police officials initiate a search in the school, either with or without the school's involvement, it is advisable to ensure that they first obtain a search warrant.

Remedies for Unlawful Disciplinary Actions

Several remedies are available to students who are unlawfully disciplined by school authorities. When physical punishment is involved, students can seek damages through assault and battery suits against those who inflicted the harm.[220] For unwarranted suspensions or expulsions, students are entitled to reinstatement without penalty to grades and to have their school records expunged of any reference to the illegal disciplinary action.[221] Remedies for violation of procedural due process rights may include reversal of a school board's decision rather than remand for further proceedings.[222] If academic penalties are unlawfully imposed, grades must be restored and transcripts altered accordingly.[223] For unconstitutional searches, illegally seized evidence may be suppressed, school records may be expunged, and damages may be awarded if the unlawful search results in substantial injury to the student.[224] Courts also may award court costs when students successfully challenge disciplinary actions.

The Supreme Court has held that school officials can be sued for monetary damages in state courts as well as in federal courts under 42 U.S.C. Section 1983 if they arbitrarily violate students' federally protected rights in disciplinary

---

[220]*See* Ingraham v. Wright, 430 U.S. 651 (1977).

[221]*See, e.g.*, John A. v. San Bernardino City Unified Sch. Dist., 654 P.2d 242 (Cal. 1982); McEntire v. Brevard County Sch. Bd., 471 So. 2d 1287 (Fla. Civ. App. 1985); Ruef v. Jordan, 605 N.Y.S.2d 530 (App. Div. 1993).

[222]*See, e.g.*, *In re* Roberts, 563 S.E.2d 37 (N.C. Ct. App. 2002).

[223]*See, e.g.,* Shuman v. Cumberland Valley Sch. Dist. Bd. of Dirs., 536 A.2d 490 (Pa. Commw. Ct. 1988); Katzman v. Cumberland Valley Sch. Dist., 479 A.2d 671 (Pa. Commw. Ct. 1984).

[224]*See, e.g.*, Anable v. Ford, 663 F. Supp. 149 (W.D. Ark. 1985); Commonwealth v. Cass, 666 A.2d 313 (Pa. Super. Ct. 1995); Coronada v. State, 835 S.W.2d 636 (Tex. Crim. App. 1992).

proceedings.[225] In *Wood v. Strickland*, the Court declared that ignorance of the law is not a valid defense to shield school officials from liability if they should have known that their actions would impair students' clearly established federal rights.[226] Under *Wood*, a showing of malice is not always required to prove that the actions of school officials were taken in bad faith, but a mere mistake in carrying out duties does not render school authorities liable. The Court also recognized in *Wood* that educators are not charged with predicting the future direction of constitutional law. Other courts have reiterated school officials' potential liability in connection with student disciplinary proceedings, but to date, students have not been as successful as teachers in obtaining monetary awards for constitutional violations. Courts have been reluctant to delineate students' "clearly established" rights, the impairment of which would warrant compensatory damages.

In 1978, the Supreme Court placed restrictions on the amount of damages that could be awarded to students in instances involving the impairment of procedural due process rights. In *Carey v. Piphus*, the Court declared that students who were suspended without a hearing, but were not otherwise injured, could recover only nominal damages (not to exceed one dollar).[227] This case involved two Chicago students who had been suspended without hearings for allegedly violating school regulations. They brought suit against the school district, claiming an abridgment of their constitutional rights. The Supreme Court ruled that substantial damages could be recovered only if the suspensions were unjustified. Accordingly, the case was remanded for the district court to determine whether the students would have been suspended if correct procedures had been followed.

This decision may appear to have strengthened the position of school boards in exercising discretion in disciplinary proceedings, but the Supreme Court indicated that students might be entitled to substantial damages if suspensions are proven to be unwarranted. To illustrate, an Arkansas federal district court assessed punitive damages against a high school coach for intentionally impairing students' free speech rights in a disciplinary action.[228] Students also have received damages when subjected to unlawful searches. For example, the Seventh Circuit assessed damages against school officials for an intrusive body search.[229] The New Mexico Supreme Court affirmed substantial compensatory and punitive damages to two

---

[225]Howlett v. Rose, 496 U.S. 356 (1990), *on remand*, 571 So. 2d 29 (Fla. Dist. Ct. App. 1990); Wood v. Strickland, 420 U.S. 308 (1975). 42 U.S.C. § 1983 provides a damages remedy for deprivations of federally protected rights under color of state law. *See also* Logiodice v. Trs., 296 F.3d 22 (1st Cir. 2002) (holding that a private school receiving tuition payments for high school students from several public school districts was not a state actor requiring it to provide a student procedural due process prior to suspension); text accompanying note 185, Chapter 11.

[226]420 U.S. 308 (1975).

[227]435 U.S. 247 (1978).

[228]Boyd v. Bd. of Dirs., 612 F. Supp. 86 (E.D. Ark. 1985).

[229]Doe v. Renfrow, 631 F.2d 91 (7th Cir. 1980).

high school students subjected to an unconstitutional strip search.[230] In addition to damages, students also may be awarded attorneys' fees.

Educators should take every precaution to afford fair and impartial treatment to students. School personnel would be wise to provide at least an informal hearing if in doubt as to whether a particular situation necessitates due process. Liability never results from the provision of too much due process, but damages can be assessed if violations of procedural rights result in unjustified suspensions, expulsions, or other disciplinary actions. Although constitutional and statutory due process requirements do not mandate that a specific procedure be followed in every situation, courts will carefully study the record to ensure that any procedural deficiencies do not impede the student's efforts to present a full defense.

Also, school authorities should ensure that constraints placed on student conduct are necessary for the proper functioning of the school. Educators have considerable latitude in controlling student behavior to maintain an appropriate educational environment and should not feel that the judiciary has curtailed their authority to discipline students. As noted in *Goss*, courts "have imposed requirements which are, if anything, less than a fair-minded principal would impose."[231]

Conclusion

In 1969, Justice Black noted, "school discipline, like parental discipline, is an integral and important part of training our children to be good citizens—to be better citizens."[232] Accordingly, school personnel have been empowered with the authority and duty to regulate pupil behavior in order to protect the interests of the student body and the school. Reasonable sanctions can be imposed if students do not adhere to legitimate conduct regulations. Courts, however, will intervene if disciplinary procedures are arbitrary or impair students' protected rights. Although the law pertaining to certain aspects of student discipline remains in a state of flux, judicial decisions support the following generalizations.

1. School authorities must be able to substantiate that any disciplinary regulation enacted is reasonable and necessary for the management of the school or for the welfare of pupils and school employees.
2. All regulations should be stated in precise terms and disseminated to students and parents.
3. Punishments for rule infractions should be appropriate for the offense and the characteristics of the offender (e.g., age, mental condition, and prior behavior).
4. Some type of procedural due process should be afforded to students prior to the imposition of punishments. For minor penalties, an informal hearing suffices;

---

[230]Kennedy v. Dexter Consol. Schs., 10 P.3d 115 (N.M. 2000).

[231]Goss v. Lopez, 419 U.S. 565, 583 (1975).

[232]Tinker v. Des Moines Indep. Sch. Dist., 393 U.S. 503, 524 (1969) (Black, J., dissenting).

for serious punishments, more formal procedures are required (e.g., notification of parents, representation by counsel, opportunity to cross-examine witnesses).

5. Students can be punished for misbehavior occurring off school grounds if the conduct directly relates to the welfare of the school.

6. Suspensions and expulsions are legitimate punishments if accompanied by appropriate procedural safeguards and not arbitrarily imposed.

7. The transfer of students to different classes, programs, or schools for disciplinary reasons should be accompanied by procedural due process.

8. If not prohibited by state law or school board policy, reasonable corporal punishment can be used as a disciplinary technique.

9. Use of excessive force in administering corporal punishment that rises to the level of shocking the conscience may violate a student's substantive due process rights.

10. Academic sanctions for nonacademic reasons should be reasonable, related to absences from class, and serve a legitimate school purpose.

11. School personnel have broad latitude in searching school lockers, especially under school policies that inform students that lockers are subject to periodic inspections.

12. Educators can search students' personal effects on reasonable suspicion that the students possess contraband that is either illegal or in violation of school policy.

13. Strip searches should be avoided unless evidence substantiates that there is probable cause to search or an emergency exists.

14. General scanning of students with metal detectors is only minimally intrusive on students' Fourth Amendment rights when weighed against school officials' interest in providing a safe school environment.

15. The use of canines to sniff objects is generally not viewed as a search, but courts are not in agreement regarding whether their use with students is a search that would require individualized suspicion.

16. Students who voluntarily elect to participate in athletics and extracurricular activities may be subjected to random drug testing; others are required to submit to urinalysis based on individualized suspicion.

17. When law-enforcement officials are involved in the search of a student to secure evidence of a crime, it is advisable to secure a search warrant.

18. If students are unlawfully punished, they are entitled to be restored (without penalty) to their status prior to the imposition of the punishment and to have their records expunged of any reference to the illegal punishment.

19. School officials can be held liable for compensatory damages if unlawful punishments result in substantial injury to students (e.g., unwarranted suspensions from school); however, only nominal damages, not to exceed one dollar, can be assessed against school officials for the abridgment of students' procedural rights (e.g., the denial of an adequate hearing).

8

Terms and Conditions of Employment

Maintenance of a uniform system of public schools is one of the preeminent functions of the state, with the responsibility for the governance of education being vested with the legislature. The judiciary has clearly recognized the plenary power of the legislature in establishing, conducting, and regulating all public education functions. The legislature, through statutory law, establishes the boundaries within which educational systems operate; however, the actual administration of school systems is delegated to state boards of education, state departments of education, and local boards of education. These agencies enact rules and regulations pursuant to legislative policy for the operation of public schools.

While state statutes and regulations are prominent in defining school personnel's employment rights, they cannot be viewed independently of state and federal constitutional provisions, civil rights laws, and negotiated agreements between school boards and teacher unions. These provisions may restrict or modify options available under the state school code. For example, the authority to transfer teachers may be vested in the school board, but the board cannot use this power to discipline a teacher for exercising protected constitutional rights. The board's discretion may be further limited if it has agreed in the master contract with the teachers' union to follow certain procedures prior to transferring an employee.

Among the areas affected by state statutory and regulatory provisions are the terms and conditions of educators' employment. With the intense public pressure to improve students' academic performance to meet annual yearly progress (AYP) under the No Child Left Behind (NCLB) Act, most states have enacted education reform legislation demanding greater accountability from public schools.[1] These efforts have had an impact not only on the curriculum and operation of schools but also on expectations for educators. NCLB demands that students be taught only by

---

[1]20 U.S.C. § 6301 *et seq.* (2007).

highly qualified educators in core subjects in each elementary and secondary school in all districts. At a minimum, highly qualified teachers hold a bachelor's degree, possess full state certification or licensure, and have demonstrated competence in their subject areas. Local school boards must ensure that these new demands are met, and courts have recognized the boards' expansive authority to fulfill these responsibilities. This chapter presents an overview of state requirements pertaining to licensure, employment, contracts, tenure, and related conditions of employment. Also, two topics of increasing interest to educators, using copyrighted materials and reporting child abuse, are addressed. Specific job requirements that implicate constitutional rights or anti-discrimination mandates are addressed in subsequent chapters.

Licensure or Certification

To qualify for a teaching position in public schools, prospective teachers must acquire a valid license or certificate. Licenses are issued according to each state's statutory provisions. States have not only the right but also the duty to establish minimum qualifications and to ensure that teachers meet these standards. Although the responsibility for licensing resides with legislatures, administration of the process has been delegated to state boards of education and departments of education. In addition to state licensure, many teachers seek National Board Certification, involving an intensive assessment of teaching knowledge and skills by the National Board for Professional Teaching Standards. States and local school districts often provide financial support for teachers seeking this designation and also may provide annual stipends for National Board Certified Teachers.[2]

Licenses are granted primarily on the basis of professional preparation. In most states, educational requirements include a college degree, with minimum credit hours or courses in various curricular areas. Other prerequisites to certification may include a minimum age, U.S. citizenship, signing of a loyalty oath, and passage of an academic examination. Additionally, an applicant for certification may be required to have "good moral character." The definition of what constitutes good character often is elusive, with a number of factors entering into the determination.[3] Courts generally will not rule on the wisdom of a certifying agency's assessment of character; they will intervene only if statutory or constitutional rights are abridged.

Certification of teachers by examination was common prior to the expansion of teacher education programs in colleges and universities. Then, for many years, only a few southern states required passage of an exam. With the emphasis on improving the quality of teachers and the strong movement toward standards-based licensure, most states now require some type of standardized test or performance-based assessment

---

[2]*See* National Board for Professional Teaching Standards, available at www.nbpts.org/resources/state_local_information, for state and local information regarding each state.

[3]*See* Arrocha v. Bd. of Educ., 712 N.E.2d 669 (N.Y. 1999) (concluding that an individual's conviction for selling cocaine affected his ability to serve as a role model for high school students).

for teacher education programs, initial license, and license renewal.[4] If a state establishes a test or assessment process as an essential eligibility requirement, it can deny a license to individuals who do not pass.[5] Many states using standardized tests employ the National Teachers Examination. The United States Supreme Court has upheld its use even though the test has been shown to disproportionately disqualify minority applicants.[6] Constitutional and statutory challenges to employment tests are discussed in Chapter 10.

Signing a loyalty oath may be a condition of obtaining a teaching certificate, but such oaths cannot be used to restrict association rights guaranteed under the United States Constitution. The Supreme Court has invalidated oaths that require teacher applicants to swear that they are not members of subversive organizations;[7] however, teachers can be required to sign an oath pledging faithful performance of duties and support for the Federal Constitution and an individual state's constitution.[8] According to the Supreme Court, these oaths must be narrowly limited to affirmation of support for the government and a pledge not to act forcibly to overthrow the government.[9] Following the September 11, 2001, terrorist attacks, many states began enforcing the signing of existing loyalty oaths for public employment or enacted new laws. For example, Ohio's PATRIOT Act requires applicants for public employment to swear they are not terrorists and have no involvement with terrorist groups; refusal to sign the oath can result in exclusion from employment consideration.[10] A number of these new loyalty oaths may be challenged as too broad under the Supreme Court's earlier rulings.

As a condition of licensure, a teacher may be required to be a citizen of the United States. In 1979, the Supreme Court addressed whether such a New York statutory requirement violated the Equal Protection Clause of the Fourteenth Amendment.[11]

---

[4]Most states have set up professional standards boards to govern and regulate standards-based criteria and assessment for licenses. The principal purpose of these boards, whose membership is composed primarily of teachers, is to address issues of educator preparation, licensure, and relicensure.

[5]*See, e.g.*, Ass'n of Mexican-Am. Educators v. California, 231 F.3d 572 (9th Cir. 2000); Feldman v. Bd. of Educ., 686 N.Y.S.2d 842 (App. Div. 1999); Dauer v. Dep't of Educ., 874 A.2d 159 (Pa. Commw. Ct. 2005). *See also* Nunez v. Simms, 341 F.3d 385 (5th Cir. 2003) (ruling that a teacher working under a temporary permit could not be continued after her third year of employment when she failed to pass the state examination); Mass. Fed'n of Teachers v. Bd. of Educ., 767 N.E.2d 549 (Mass. 2002) (finding the imposition of a math assessment test for recertification of teachers in certain schools to be within the state board's authority)

[6]United States v. South Carolina, 445 F. Supp. 1094 (D.S.C. 1977), *aff'd sub nom.* Nat'l Educ. Ass'n v. South Carolina, 434 U.S. 1026 (1978). *See also* Gulino v. N.Y. State Educ. Dep't, 460 F.3d 361 (2d Cir. 2006) (vacating and remanding for a determination of whether state's examination is job related), *petition for cert. filed*, 76 U.S.L.W. 3082 (U.S. Aug. 27, 2007); text accompanying note 33, Chapter 10. In challenges alleging discrimination, consent decrees between states and plaintiffs have contained agreements for the development of tests that reduce the discriminatory impact on minority candidates. *See, e.g.,* Allen v. Ala. State Bd. of Educ., 164 F.3d 1347 (11th Cir. 1999), *on remand*, 190 F.R.D. 602 (M.D. Ala. 2000).

[7]Keyishian v. Bd. of Regents, 385 U.S. 589 (1967).

[8]Ohlson v. Phillips, 397 U.S. 317 (1970).

[9]Cole v. Richardson, 405 U.S. 676 (1972); Connell v. Higginbotham, 403 U.S. 207 (1971).

[10]Ohio Rev. Code 119 § 2909.34 (2007).

[11]Ambach v. Norwick, 441 U.S. 68 (1979).

Under the New York education laws, a teacher who is eligible for citizenship but refuses to apply for naturalization cannot be certified. Although the Supreme Court has placed restrictions on the states' ability to exclude aliens from governmental employment, it also has recognized that certain functions are "so bound up with the operation of the state as a governmental entity as to permit the exclusion from those functions of all persons who have not become part of the process of self-government."[12] Applying this principle, the Court held that teaching is an integral "governmental function"; thus, a state must show only a rational relationship between a citizenship requirement and a legitimate state interest. The Court concluded that New York's interest in furthering its educational goals justified the citizenship mandate for teachers. More recently, a Georgia federal district court, in issuing a permanent injunction against applying a citizenship requirement law, distinguished New York's citizenship licensure requirement from a Georgia statute banning aliens from all public employment. Because the law swept broadly across all government jobs rather than being narrowly drawn, the law failed to advance a compelling state interest.[13]

Some litigation has focused on legislative efforts to alter certification standards by imposing new or additional requirements as prerequisites to recertification. The Supreme Court of Texas held that teachers possessing life certificates could be required to pass an examination as a condition of continued employment.[14] Since the certificate was found to be a "license" rather than a "contract," the court held that new conditions for retention of the certificate could be imposed. The Supreme Court of Connecticut, even though recognizing teaching certificates as contracts, still upheld the state's authority to replace permanent certificates with 5-year certificates renewable upon the completion of continuing education requirements.[15] Holding that this change was constitutionally acceptable, the court found only a minimal impairment of contractual rights, which could be justified by the state's significant interest in improving public education. Under statutory law, however, the Supreme Court of Rhode Island found that the State Board of Regents for Elementary and Secondary Education could not revoke valid 5-year certificates for teachers' failure to meet new agency requirements.[16] Since state law provided that certificates were valid for a specified period of time and could be revoked only for cause, teachers could not be required to meet a state agency's new requirements until their certificates expired.

Licenses are issued for designated periods of time under various classifications such as emergency, temporary, provisional, professional, and permanent. Renewing or upgrading a license may require additional university course work, other continuing education activities, or passage of an examination. Licenses also specify professional position (e.g., teacher, administrator, librarian), subject areas (e.g., history,

---

[12]*Id*. at 73–74.

[13]Chang v. Glynn County Sch. Dist., 457 F. Supp. 2d 1378 (S.D. Ga. 2006) (enjoining school district from discharging two resident alien teachers certified under Georgia law).

[14]State v. Project Principle, 724 S.W.2d 387 (Tex. 1987).

[15]Conn. Educ. Ass'n v. Tirozzi, 554 A.2d 1065 (Conn. 1989).

[16]Reback v. R.I. Bd. of Regents for Elementary and Secondary Educ., 560 A.2d 357 (R.I. 1989).

English, math), and grade levels (e.g., elementary, high school). Where license subject areas have been established, a teacher must possess a valid license to teach a specific subject. A school district's failure to employ licensed teachers may result in the loss of state accreditation and financial support.

A certificate or license indicates only that a teacher has satisfied minimum state requirements; no absolute right exists to acquire a position. It does not entitle an individual to employment in a particular district or guarantee employment in the state, nor does it prevent a local school board from attaching additional prerequisites for employment. For example, an Iowa appellate court upheld a local school board's authority to require physical education teachers to complete training in cardiopulmonary resuscitation and water-safety instruction.[17] If a local board imposes additional standards, however, the requirements must be uniformly applied.

Teaching credentials must be in proper order to ensure full employment rights.[18] Under most state laws, teachers must file their certificates with the district of employment.[19] Failure to renew a certificate prior to expiration or to meet educational requirements necessary to maintain or acquire a higher grade certification can result in loss of employment. Without proper certification, a teaching contract is unenforceable.[20]

The state is empowered not only to certify teachers but also to suspend[21] or revoke certification. Although a local board may initiate charges against a teacher, only the state can alter the status of a teacher's certificate. Revocation is a harsh penalty, generally foreclosing future employment as a teacher. As such, it must be based on statutory cause with full procedural rights provided to the teacher.[22] The most frequently cited grounds for revoking certification are immorality, incompetency, contract violation, and neglect of duty. Examples of actions justifying

---

[17]Pleasant Valley Educ. Ass'n v. Pleasant Valley Cmty. Sch. Dist., 449 N.W.2d 894 (Iowa Ct. App. 1989).

[18]*See* Keatley v. Mercer County Bd. of Educ., 490 S.E.2d 306 (W. Va. 1997) (ruling that an applicant who does not physically possess a certificate can be hired if all requirements will have been met for certification at the time of appointment).

[19]*See* Lucio v. Sch. Bd., 574 N.W.2d 737 (Minn. Ct. App. 1998) (ruling that the school district has a duty to determine the licensure status of teachers).

[20]*See* Maasjo v. McLaughlin Sch. Dist., 489 N.W.2d 618 (S.D. 1992) (holding that a school board could terminate a superintendent because he lacked proper administrative endorsement). *See also* Rettie, v. Unified Sch. Dist., 167 P.3d 810 (Kan. Ct. App. 2007) (ruling that even though failure to maintain a valid certificate is grounds for termination, a teacher still has the right to a termination hearing under Kansas law); Giedra v. Mt. Adams Sch. Dist., 110 P.3d 232 (Wash. Ct. App. 2005) (ruling that teachers who failed to renew their certificates in a timely manner were entitled to a hearing prior to termination of their contracts; teachers had been denied an opportunity to explain the circumstances affecting their discharge).

[21]*See* Prof'l Standards Comm'n v. Denham, 556 S.E.2d 920 (Ga. Ct. App. 2001) (upholding suspension of license for six months for improperly coaching students for a standardized test).

[22]*See, e.g.,* Gee v. Prof'l Practices Comm'n, 491 S.E. 2d 375 (Ga. 1997); Bowalick v. Commonwealth, 840 A.2d 519 (Pa. Commw. Ct. 2004). *See also* text accompanying notes 53–95, Chapter 11, for details of procedural due process.

revocation include misrepresenting experience and credentials in a job application and altering one's certificate (immorality),[23] theft of drugs and money (conduct unbecoming a teacher),[24] assault on a minor female (lack of good moral character),[25] and harassment of other teachers, removal of confidential files, and inappropriate discussion of sex life (unprofessional conduct).[26]

When revocation or suspension of a certificate is being considered, assessment of a teacher's competency encompasses not only classroom performance but also actions outside the school setting that may impair the teacher's effectiveness.[27] A Florida appellate court ruled that the state's Education Practices Commission did not violate a teacher's rights in permanently revoking her certificate for sending sexually explicit material over the Internet to her seventh grade middle school students.[28] In an Arizona case, the appellate court upheld license revocation of a teacher who had been in numerous altercations with neighbors and had been charged on several occasions with disorderly conduct and criminal damage. His tendency to act with violence and aggression was deemed to affect his fitness to teach.[29] The Supreme Court of Kansas concluded that an act of burglary was sufficiently related to a teacher's fitness to teach to warrant suspension of the certificate for such a crime.[30] Courts will not overturn the judgment of state boards regarding an educator's fitness to teach unless evidence clearly establishes that the decision is unreasonable or unlawful.[31]

---

[23]Nanko v. Dep't of Educ., 663 A.2d 312 (Pa. Commw. Ct. 1995). *See also* Patterson v. Superintendent of Pub. Instruction, 887 P.2d 411 (Wash. Ct. App. 1995) (supporting six-month suspension of certificate for falsifying and omitting information from application).

[24]Crumpler v. State Bd. of Educ., 594 N.E.2d 1071 (Ohio Ct. App. 1991).

[25]*In re* Appeal of Morrill, 765 A.2d 699 (N.H. 2001). *See also* Boguslawski v. Dep't of Educ., 837 A.2d 614 (Pa. Commw. Ct. 2003) (finding that a teacher's improper touching of fourth grade male students supported revocation for immorality and intemperance).

[26]Bills v. Ariz. State Bd. of Educ., 819 P.2d 952 (Ariz. Ct. App. 1991). *See also* Knight v. Winn, 910 So. 2d 310 (Fla. Dist. Ct. App. 2005) (finding revocation of certificate appropriate for abusive comments to students and threats made in a letter of resignation); Prof'l Standards Comm'n v. Valentine, 603 S.E.2d 792 (Ga. Ct. App. 2004) (upholding a six-month suspension of teacher's license for verbal altercations on school grounds; teacher was being monitored by the commission because of an earlier DUI arrest).

[27]*See, e.g.*, Winters v. Ariz. Bd. of Educ., 83 P.3d 1114 (Ariz. Ct. App. 2004). *See also* Prof'l Standards Comm'n v. Peterson, 643 S.E.2d 899 (Ga. Ct. App. 2007) (determining that failure of two teachers to supervise underage drinking at a party in their home did not justify a short suspension of certificates; it did not affect their effectiveness in the classroom).

[28]Wax v. Horne, 844 So. 2d 797 (Fla. Dist. Ct. App. 2003).

[29]*Winters*, 83 P.3d 1114.

[30]Hainline v. Bond, 824 P.2d 959 (Kan. 1992).

[31]*See* Brehe v. Mo. Dep't of Elementary & Secondary Educ., 213 S.W.3d 720, 723 (Mo. Ct. App. 2007) (finding that pleading guilty to a second-degree child endangerment charge did not substantiate a "crime involving moral turpitude" under state law to justify suspension of license); Epstein v. Benson, 618 N.W.2d 224 (Wis. Ct. App. 2000) (concluding that carrying a concealed weapon is a crime but did not constitute immoral conduct to justify revocation of teaching certificate).

Employment by Local School Boards

As noted, a certificate or license does not guarantee employment in a state; it attests only that educators have met minimum state requirements. The decision to employ a certified teacher or administrator is among the discretionary powers of local school boards.[32] While such powers are broad, school board actions may not be arbitrary, capricious, or violate an individual's statutory or constitutional rights.[33] Furthermore, boards must comply with mandated statutory procedures as well as locally adopted procedures.[34] Employment decisions also must be neutral as to race, religion, national origin, and sex.[35] Unless protected individual rights are abridged, courts will not review the wisdom of a local school board's judgment in employment decisions made in good faith.

The responsibility for hiring teachers and administrators is vested in the school board as a collective body and cannot be delegated to the superintendent or board members individually.[36] In most states, binding employment agreements between a teacher or an administrator and the school board must be approved at legally scheduled board meetings. A number of state laws specify that the superintendent must make employment recommendations to the board; however, the board is not compelled to follow these recommendations unless mandated to do so by law.

School boards possess extensive authority in establishing job requirements and conditions of employment for school personnel. The following sections examine the school board's power to impose specific conditions on employment and to assign personnel.

Employment Requirements

The state's establishment of minimum certification standards for educators does not preclude the local school board from requiring higher professional or academic standards as long as they are applied in a uniform and nondiscriminatory

---

[32]*See* Carter County Bd. of Educ. v. Carter County Educ. Ass'n, 56 S.W.3d 1 (Tenn. Ct. App. 1996) (holding that selection of principals is a discretionary right of the school board; appointment is not subject to collective bargaining). In some instances, this discretionary power may be vested in local school-based councils. For example, under the Chicago School Reform Act, 105 ILCS § 5/34-2.2(c) (2007), the local school council is authorized to appoint a principal without school board approval. Under Kentucky's Education Reform Act, KRS § 160.345(2)(h) (2007), superintendents must forward all principal applicants who meet statutory requirements to the site-based school council, not simply the ones the superintendent recommends and supports, Young v. Hammond, 139 S.W.3d 895 (Ky. 2004). Massachusetts's Education Reform Act, Mass. Gen. Laws ch. 71, § 59B (2007), lodges the responsibility for hiring and firing of teachers and other building personnel with school principals under the supervision of the superintendent.

[33]*See generally* Chapter 9 for a discussion of teachers' constitutional rights.

[34]*See, e.g.*, Swanson v. Bd. of Educ., 600 S.E.2d 299 (W. Va. 2004).

[35]*See generally* Chapter 10 for a discussion of discriminatory employment practices. Under limited circumstances, sex may be a *bona fide* occupational qualification (e.g., supervision of the girls' locker room).

[36]*See, e.g.*, Watson v. N. Panola Sch. Dist., 188 Fed. Appx. 291 (5th Cir. 2006).

manner.[37] For example, school boards often establish continuing education requirements for teachers, and a board's right to dismiss teachers for failing to satisfy such requirements has been upheld by the Supreme Court.[38] The Court concluded that school officials merely had to establish that the requirement was rationally related to a legitimate state objective, which in this case was to provide competent, well-trained teachers.

School boards can adopt reasonable health and physical requirements for school personnel. Courts have recognized that such standards are necessary to safeguard the health and welfare of students and other employees. The First Circuit held that a school board could compel an administrator to submit to a psychiatric examination as a condition of continued employment because a reasonable basis existed for the board members to believe that the administrator might jeopardize the safety of students.[39] Similarly, the Sixth Circuit ruled that a school board could justifiably order a teacher to submit to mental and physical examinations when his aberrant behavior affected job performance.[40]

Health and physical requirements imposed on school personnel, however, must not be applied in an arbitrary manner. The Second Circuit found a New York school board's actions arbitrary and unreasonable when it insisted that a female teacher on extended sick leave submit to an exam by the district's male physician rather than a female physician (to be selected by the board).[41] In a more recent Second Circuit case, the court held that it was reasonable to request that a teacher undergo a psychiatric examination prior to returning to work after an extended sick leave, but the demand to release the teacher's medical records to the examining physician as well as the school board was arbitrary.[42] School officials were not competent to assess the records, thus the request served no legitimate purpose. School board standards for physical fitness also must be rationally related to ability to perform teaching duties. Additionally, regulations must not contravene various state and federal laws designed to protect the rights of persons with disabilities.[43]

---

[37]*See, e.g.*, Dennery v. Bd. of Educ., 622 A.2d 858 (N.J. 1993). *See also* Bd. of Educ. v. Scott, 617 S.E.2d 478 (W. Va. 2005) (ruling that the school board could expand qualifications for an aide position to include licensure as a practical nurse).

[38]Harrah Indep. Sch. Dist. v. Martin, 440 U.S. 194 (1979) (upholding a policy requiring teachers to earn an additional five semester hours of college credit every three years while employed).

[39]Daury v. Smith, 842 F.2d 9 (1st Cir. 1988).

[40]Sullivan v. River Valley Sch. Dist., 197 F.3d 804 (6th Cir. 1999). *See also* Moore v. Bd. of Educ., 134 F.3d 781 (6th Cir. 1998) (upholding a finding of insubordination for refusing to submit to mental and physical examinations); Gardner v. Niskayuna Cent. Sch. Dist., 839 N.Y.S.2d 317 (App. Div. 2007) (finding that a school board is charged with determining that teachers are fit to teach; thereby, teachers may be required to submit to physical or mental exams).

[41]Gargiul v. Tompkins, 704 F.2d 661 (2d Cir. 1983), *vacated and remanded*, 465 U.S. 1016 (1984).

[42]O'Connor v. Pierson, 426 F.3d 187 (2d Cir. 2005). *But see* Appel v. Spiridon, 463 F. Supp. 2d 255, 266 (D. Conn. 2006) (concluding that the university's demand for a faculty member to be subjected to an involuntary psychiatric examination when such a requirement had never been imposed on similarly situated faculty members appeared to be "an arbitrary and irrational measure").

[43]*See* Chapter 10 for a discussion of discrimination based on disabilities.

Under state laws, most school boards are required to conduct criminal records checks of all employees prior to employment. The screening process may require individuals to consent to fingerprinting. Concern for students' safety also has led some school districts to require teacher applicants to submit to drug testing. The Sixth Circuit upheld such testing, noting that teachers occupy safety-sensitive positions in a highly regulated environment with diminished privacy expectations.[44]

School boards may require school personnel to live within the school district as a condition of employment. Typically, residency requirements have been imposed in urban communities and encompass all city employees including educators. Proponents contend that the policy builds stronger community relationships and stabilizes the city tax base. Such requirements, however, have been challenged as impairing equal protection rights under the United States Constitution by interfering with interstate and intrastate travel on equal terms. The Supreme Court has upheld a municipal regulation requiring all employees hired after a specified date in Philadelphia to be residents of the city.[45] Those already employed were not required to alter their residence. A fire department employee who was terminated when he moved to New Jersey challenged the requirement as unconstitutionally interfering with interstate travel. In upholding the regulation, the Court distinguished a requirement of residency of a given duration prior to employment (which violates the right to interstate travel) from a continuing residency requirement applied after employment. The Court concluded that a continuing residency requirement, if "appropriately defined and uniformly applied," does not violate an individual's constitutional rights.[46] Lower courts have applied similar reasoning in upholding residency requirements for public educators.[47] Although residency requirements after employment do not violate the Constitution, they may be impermissible under state law.[48]

Unlike residency requirements, school board policies requiring employees to send their children to public schools have been declared unconstitutional. Parents have a constitutionally protected right to direct the upbringing of their children that cannot be restricted without a compelling state interest. The Eleventh Circuit Appellate Court held that a school board policy requiring employees to enroll their children in public schools could not be justified to promote an integrated public school system

---

[44]Knox County Educ. Ass'n v. Knox County Bd. of Educ., 158 F.3d 361 (6th Cir. 1998). For further discussion of Fourth Amendment rights of employees, *see* text accompanying note 170, Chapter 9.

[45]McCarthy v. Phila. Civil Serv. Comm'n, 424 U.S. 645 (1976).

[46]*Id*. at 647. In several later cases, the Supreme Court reiterated that policies requiring residence prior to employment for conferring certain benefits or employment preference violate the Equal Protection Clause and the constitutional right to travel. *See* Attorney Gen. of N.Y. v. Soto-Lopez, 476 U.S. 898 (1986); Hooper v. Bernalillo County Assessor, 472 U.S. 612 (1985); Zobel v. Williams, 457 U.S. 55 (1982).

[47]*See, e.g.*, Wardwell v. Bd. of Educ., 529 F.2d 625 (6th Cir. 1976); Providence Teachers' Union Local 958 v. City Council, 888 A.2d 948 (R.I. 2005).

[48]*See, e.g.*, Ind. Code Ann. § 20-28-10-13 (2007); Mass. Gen. Laws ch. 71 § 38 (2007). As urban school systems face difficulty in recruiting teachers, some (e.g., Philadelphia, Pittsburgh, and Providence) have abolished their residency requirements. *See* Jeff Archer, "City Districts Lifting Rules on Residency," *Education Week* (January 16, 2002), pp. 1, 13.

and good relationships among teachers when weighed against the right of parents to direct the education of their children.[49]

Assignment of Personnel and Duties

The authority to assign teachers to schools within a district resides with the board of education.[50] As with employment in general, these decisions must not be arbitrary or made in bad faith or in retaliation for the exercise of protected rights. Within the limits of certification, a teacher can be assigned to teach in any school at any grade level.[51] Assignments designated in the teacher's contract, however, cannot be changed during a contractual period without the teacher's consent.[52] That is, a board cannot reassign a teacher to a first grade class if the contract specifies a fifth grade assignment. If the contract designates only a teaching assignment within the district, the assignment still must be in the teacher's area of certification. Also, objective, nondiscriminatory standards must be used in any employment or assignment decision. Assignments to achieve racial balance may be permitted in school districts under court order because they have not eliminated the effects of school segregation. Any racial classification, however, must be temporary and necessary to eradicate the effects of prior discrimination.[53]

School boards retain the authority to assign or transfer teachers, but such decisions often are challenged as demotions requiring procedural due process. Depending on statutory law, factors considered in determining whether a reassignment is a demotion may include reduction in salary, responsibility, and stature of position.[54] A Pennsylvania teacher contested a transfer from a ninth to a sixth grade class as a

---

[49]Stough v. Crenshaw County Bd. of Educ., 744 F.2d 1479 (11th Cir. 1984). *See* Barrett v. Steubenville City Schs, 388 F.3d 967 (6th Cir. 2004); Peterson v. Minidoka County Sch. Dist. No. 331, 118 F.3d 1351 (9th Cir. 1997); Curlee v. Fyfe, 902 F.2d 401 (5th Cir. 1990).

[50]*See, e.g.*, Thomas v. Smith, 897 F.2d 154 (5th Cir. 1989); Sekor v. Bd. of Educ., 689 A.2d 1112 (Conn. 1997). *See also* Lazuk v. Denver Sch. Dist. No. 1, 22 P.3d 548 (Colo. Ct. App. 2000) (ruling that state law permitted a school board to delegate the power to transfer a teacher; state statute limited the transfer to positions in which the teacher is qualified to teach).

[51]*See, e.g.*, Gordon v. Nicoletti, 84 F. Supp. 2d 304 (D. Conn. 2000); Wells v. Del Norte Sch. Dist. C-7, 753 P.2d 770 (Colo. Ct. App. 1987). *See also* Hinckley v. Sch. Bd. of Indep. Sch. Dist. No. 2167, 678 N.W.2d 485 (Minn. Ct. App. 2004) (determining that school board is not required to change job duties to realign positions when individual does not hold valid license).

[52]The collective bargaining agreement also may limit a school board's discretion in transferring teachers. *See, e.g.*, Leary v. Daeschner, 228 F.3d 729 (6th Cir. 2000).

[53]*See, e.g.*, Wygant v. Jackson Bd. of Educ., 476 U.S. 267 (1986).

[54]*See* Manila Sch. Dist. No. 15 v. White, 992 S.W.2d 125 (Ark. 1999) (ruling that the elimination of a teacher's coaching duties and assigning him as a director/teacher of an alternative school was nonrenewal of contract, not reassignment); Hamilton v. Telfair County Sch. Dist., 455 S.E.2d 23 (Ga. 1995) (holding that one must show an adverse effect on salary, responsibility, and prestige); Ranta v. Eaton Rapids Sch. Bd., 721 N.W.2d 806 (Mich. Ct. App. 2006) (finding that board's cap on contribution to health insurance premiums did not constitute a demotion as defined by the Teacher Tenure Act; with salary increase, teachers did not receive less compensation).

demotion. The court, noting the equivalency of the positions, stated, "There is no less importance, dignity, responsibility, authority, prestige, or compensation in the elementary grades than in secondary."[55] The reassignment of an Ohio classroom teacher as a permanent substitute or floating teacher, however, was found to be a demotion in violation of the state tenure law.[56] The court recognized the pervasive authority of the superintendent and board to make teaching assignments, but noted that other statutory provisions, such as the state tenure law, may limit this power. This reduction in status without notice and a hearing was found to deprive the teacher of due process guarantees.

Administrative reassignments frequently are challenged as demotions because of reductions in salary, responsibility, and status of the position. Again, as in the assignment of teachers, statutory law defines an individual employee's rights.[57] The South Carolina appellate court concluded that the reassignment of an assistant superintendent to a principal position was within the school board's discretion when it did not involve a reduction in salary or violate the district's regulations.[58] Similarly, the Seventh Circuit found that the reassignment of a principal to a central office position did not involve an economic loss requiring an opportunity for a hearing.[59] A Wisconsin principal was not removed from her position, but the school board reassigned many of her duties and responsibilities. She resigned her position and claimed that violation of her property interests in the position precipitated the resignation. The Seventh Circuit concluded that under Wisconsin law no right existed to performing specific duties as a principal.[60] A reassignment from an administrative to a teaching position because of financial constraints or good faith reorganization is not a demotion requiring due process unless procedural protections are specified in state law.

A transfer may violate federal rights even if it is not considered a demotion under state law. The Eleventh Circuit noted that a transfer might establish an adverse employment action if it involves a reduction in pay, prestige, or responsibility. Under Georgia law an individual must show a loss of all three to suffer a demotion. In remanding a case for trial under federal law, the appellate court noted that a female principal had presented sufficient evidence for a jury to conclude that she had suffered an adverse employment action when transferred to another administrative position.[61]

---

[55]*In re* Santee, 156 A.2d 830, 832 (Pa. 1959).

[56]Mroczek v. Bd. of Educ., 400 N.E.2d 1362 (Ohio C.P. 1979).

[57]School boards can exercise significant discretion in the transfer of administrators as long as their decisions are not arbitrary or capricious, or in violation of protected constitutional rights. *See* Finch v. Fort Bend Indep. Sch. Dist., 333 F.3d 555 (5th Cir. 2003).

[58]Barr v. Bd. of Trs., 462 S.E.2d 316 (S.C. Ct. App. 1995). *See also* Johnson v. Spartanburg County Sch. Dist. No. 7, 444 S.E.2d 501 (S.C. 1994) (holding that the transfer of an assistant principal to a teaching position at a lower salary violated procedural protections of state law).

[59]Bordelon v. Chi. Sch. Reform Bd. of Trs., 233 F.3d 524 (7th Cir. 2000).

[60]Ulichny v. Merton Cmty. Sch. Dist., 249 F.3d 686 (7th Cir. 2001).

[61]Hinson v. Clinch County, Ga. Bd. of Educ., 231 F.3d 821 (11th Cir. 2000). *See* Kodl v. Bd. of Educ., 490 F.3d 558 (7th Cir. 2007) (finding that an older middle school teacher's transfer to an elementary school did not violate any federal rights).

Statutory procedures and agency regulations established for transferring or demoting employees must be strictly followed. For example, under a West Virginia State Board of Education policy, school boards cannot initiate a disciplinary transfer unless there has been a prior evaluation informing the individual that specific conduct can result in a transfer.[62] Furthermore, there must be an opportunity for employees to improve their performance. Under Pennsylvania law, demotions related to declining enrollment involve a realignment of staff, and to assure proper realignment of positions, procedural protections are required.[63]

The assignment of noninstructional duties often is defined in a teacher's contract or the master contract negotiated between the school board and the teachers' union. In the absence of such specification, it is generally held that school officials can make reasonable and appropriate assignments.[64] Courts usually restrict assignments to activities that are an integral part of the school program and, in some situations, to duties related to the employee's teaching responsibilities.[65] A New Jersey appellate court stated that the reasonableness of an assignment should be evaluated in terms of time involvement, teachers' interests and abilities, benefits to students, and the professional nature of the duty.[66] Refusal to accept reasonable assigned duties can result in dismissal.[67]

Contracts

The employment contract defines the rights and responsibilities of the teacher and the school board in the employment relationship. The general principles of contract law apply to this contractual relationship. Like all other legal contracts, it must contain the basic elements of (1) offer and acceptance, (2) competent parties, (3) consideration, (4) legal subject matter, and (5) proper form.[68] Beyond these basic elements, it also must meet the requirements specified in state law and administrative regulations.

[62]Hosaflook v. Nestor, 346 S.E.2d 798 (W. Va. 1986).

[63]Fry v. Commonwealth, 485 A.2d 508 (Pa. Commw. Ct. 1984).

[64]*See* Lewis v. Bd. of Educ., 537 N.E.2d 435 (Ill. App. Ct. 1989) (holding that assignments cannot be unreasonable, onerous, or burdensome); Pleasant Valley Educ. Ass'n v. Pleasant Valley Cmty. Sch. Dist., 449 N.W.2d 894 (Iowa Ct. App. 1989) (finding that school boards have extensive authority in assigning personnel). *See also* Griffin-Spalding County Sch. Sys., 451 S.E.2d 480 (Ga. Ct. App. 1994) (concluding that a state statute prohibiting the assignment of instructional, administrative, and supervisory responsibilities during teachers' duty-free lunch period did conflict with a principal's decision to require teachers to remain on campus during lunch).

[65]*See* Wolf v. Cuyahoga Falls City Sch. Dist., 556 N.E.2d 511 (Ohio 1990) (holding that supervision of the student newspaper was related to teaching journalism, but supplemental contract was required for the newspaper sponsor because other teachers who performed similar class-related duties were paid).

[66]Bd. of Educ. v. Asbury Park Educ. Ass'n, 368 A.2d 396 (N.J. Super. Ct. Ch. Div. 1976).

[67]*See* Jones v. Ala. State Tenure Comm'n, 408 So. 2d 145 (Ala. 1981) (holding that counselor's refusal to supervise students before school hours could result in dismissal).

[68]For a discussion of contract elements, *see* Kern Alexander and M. David Alexander, *American Public School Law*, 6th ed. (Belmont, CA: West/Thomson Learning, 2005).

The authority to contract with teachers is an exclusive right of the board. The school board's offer of a position to a teacher, including (1) designated salary, (2) specified period of time, and (3) identified duties and responsibilities, creates a binding contract when accepted by the teacher. In most states, only the board can make an offer, and this action must be approved by a majority of the board members in a properly called meeting. In a Washington case, the coordinator of special services extended a teacher an offer of employment at the beginning of the school year, pending a check of references from past employers. The recommendations were negative, and the teacher was not recommended to the board even though she had been teaching for several weeks. The state appellate court held that no enforceable contract existed; under state law, hiring authority resides with the board.[69]

School boards also can enforce the performance of a valid teacher's contract. Most state statutes specify a deadline for resignation of teaching positions for the next school year (e.g., July 1). Such provisions reduce disruptions in the opening of the school year. Resignation can occur after the statutory deadline if the school board agrees. If the board declines to accept a resignation, however, the contract is enforceable and the teacher's license can be suspended for the year.[70]

Contracts can be invalidated because of lack of competent parties. To form a valid, binding contract, both parties must have the legal capacity to enter into an agreement. The school board has been recognized as a legally competent party with the capacity to contract. A teacher who lacks certification or is under the statutorily required age for certification is not considered a competent party for contractual purposes. Consequently, a contract made with such an individual is not enforceable.[71]

Consideration is another essential element of a valid contract. Consideration is something of value that one party pays in return for the other party's performance. Teachers' monetary compensation is established in the salary schedule adopted by the school board or negotiated between the school board and teachers' association.[72] The contract also must involve a legal subject matter and follow the proper form required by law. Most states prescribe that a teacher's contract must be in writing to

---

[69]McCormick v. Lake Wash. Sch. Dist., 992 P.2d 511 (Wash. Ct. App. 2000). *See also* Branch v. Greene County Bd. of Educ., 533 So. 2d 248 (Ala. Civ. App. 1988) (holding that superintendent's promise of a contract made without concurrence of school board does not create a contract); Brown v. Caldwell Sch. Dist. No. 132, 898 P.2d 43 (Idaho 1995) (holding that assistant superintendent's offer of employment to a teacher could not bind school board).

[70]*See, e.g.*, Bd. of Educ. v. State Teachers Certification Bd., 842 N.E.2d 1230 (Ill. App. Ct. 2006); Bolyard v. Bd. of Educ., 589 S.E.2d 523 (W. Va. 2003).

[71]*See, e.g.*, Nunez v. Simms, 341 F.3d 385 (5th Cir. 2003); Springer v. Bullitt County Bd. of Educ., 196 S.W.3d 528 (Ky. Ct. App. 2006).

[72]*See* Sherwood Nat'l Educ. Ass'n v. Sherwood-Cass R-VIII Sch. Dist., 168 S.W.3d 456 (Mo. Ct. App. 2005) (finding the payment of commitment fees to teachers to return signed contracts early, agreeing to work two years in the district, to be "off salary schedule" and thus invalid); Davis v. Greenwood Sch. Dist., 620 S.E.2d 65 (S.C. 2005) (holding that the reduction of a 10 percent incentive annual payment to teachers for acquiring national board certification to a $3,000 flat rate per year did not violate teachers' contracts and was within the board's discretion to manage the district's finances).

be enforceable,[73] but if there is no statutory specification, an oral agreement is legally binding on both parties.

In addition to employment rights derived from the teaching contract, other rights accrue from collective bargaining agreements in effect at the time of employment. Statutory provisions and school board rules and regulations also may be considered part of the terms and conditions of the contract.[74] If not included directly, the provisions existing at the time of the contract may be implied. Moreover, the contract cannot be used as a means of waiving teachers' statutory or constitutional rights.[75]

Term and Tenure Contracts

Two basic types of employment contracts are issued to teachers: term contracts and tenure contracts. Term contracts are valid for a fixed period of time (e.g., one or two years). At the end of the contract period, renewal is at the discretion of the school board; nonrenewal requires no explanation unless mandated by statute. Generally, a school board is required only to provide notice prior to the expiration of the contract that employment will not be renewed. Tenure contracts, created through state legislative action, ensure teachers that employment will be terminated only for adequate cause and that procedural due process will be provided.[76] After the award of tenure or during a term contract, school boards cannot unilaterally abrogate teachers' contracts. At a minimum, the teacher must be provided with notice of the dismissal charges and a hearing.[77]

Since tenure contracts involve statutory rights, specific procedures and protections vary among the states. Consequently, judicial interpretations in one state provide little guidance in understanding another state's law. Most tenure statutes specify requirements and procedures for obtaining tenure and identify causes and procedures for dismissing a tenured teacher. In interpreting tenure laws, courts have attempted to

---

[73]*See, e.g.,* Jones v. Houston Indep. Sch. Dist., 805 F. Supp. 476 (S.D. Tex. 1991), *aff'd,* 979 F.2d 1004 (5th Cir. 1992); Bradley v. W. Sioux Cmty. Sch. Bd. of Educ., 510 N.W.2d 881 (Iowa 1994); Bd. of Educ. v. Jones, 823 S.W.2d 457 (Ky. 1992).

[74]*See, e.g.,* Stone v. Mayflower Sch. Dist., 894 S.W.2d 881 (Ark. 1995), Mifflinburg Area Educ. Ass'n v. Mifflinburg Area Sch. Dist., 724 A.2d 339 (Pa. 1999).

[75]*See* Denuis v. Dunlap, 209 F.3d 944 (7th Cir. 2000) (holding that the teacher was not required to relinquish constitutional privacy rights regarding medical or financial records for an employment background check); Parker v. Indep. Sch. Dist. No. I-003 Okmulgee County, Okla., 82 F.3d 952 (10th Cir. 1996) (ruling that a school board could not evade procedural protections of the Oklahoma Teacher Due Process Act by having a teacher sign a contract permitting summary removal as a teacher if her supplemental coaching position was terminated).

[76]*See, e.g.,* Scobey Sch. Dist. v. Radakovich, 135 P.3d 778 (Mont. 2006); Weston v. Indep. Sch. Dist. No. 35,170 P.3d 539 (Okla. 2007).

[77]Tenure laws provide teachers employment security; they protect educators from political reprisal and prevent dismissals without cause. *See* Cimochowshi v. Hartford Pub. Schs., 802 A.2d 800 (Conn. 2002); Palmer v. La. State Bd. of Elementary and Secondary Educ., 842 So. 2d 363 (La. 2003); Wirt v. Parker Sch. Dist., 689 N.W.2d 901 (S.D. 2004); Hicks v. Gayville-Volin Sch. Dist., 668 N.W.2d 69 (S.D. 2003). *See also* text accompanying note 53, Chapter 11, for discussion of procedural due process requirements.

protect teachers' rights while simultaneously preserving school officials' flexibility in personnel management.

    Prior to a school board's awarding a tenure contract to a teacher, most states require a probationary period of approximately three years to assess a teacher's ability and competence. During this probationary period, teachers receive term contracts, and there is no guarantee of employment beyond each contract. Tenure statutes generally require regular and continuous service to complete the probationary period. For example, the Supreme Court of Virginia held that the tenure law providing for a "probationary term of service of three years" required three consecutive years of employment immediately prior to the award of tenure. Interpreting this mandate, the court concluded that lapses in an appointment in which a teacher worked over a period of seven years did not qualify her for tenure.[78] Similarly, the Alaska Supreme Court found part-time employment totaling two years did not meet state statutory requirement of employment "continuously for two full school years."[79]

    The authority to grant a tenure contract is a discretionary power of the local school board that cannot be delegated. Although the school board confers tenure, it cannot alter the tenure terms established by the legislature; the legislature determines the basis for tenure, eligibility requirements, and the procedures for acquiring tenure status.[80] Thus, if a statute requires a probationary period, this term of service must be completed prior to the school board awarding tenure. When teachers meet the statutory requirements, the school board cannot refuse to carry out its obligation to award tenure, nor can the board require new teachers to waive tenure rights as a precondition to employment. Moreover, a board may be compelled to award tenure if a teacher completes the statutory requirements and the school board does not take action to grant or deny tenure.[81] Unless specified in statute, however, tenure is not transferable from one school district to another.[82] This ensures that school officials are provided an opportunity to evaluate teachers before granting tenure.

    A tenure contract provides a certain amount of job security, but it does not guarantee permanent employment, nor does it convey the right to teach in a

---

[78]Corns v. Russell County Va. Sch. Bd., 52 F.3d 56 (4th Cir. 1995), *certifying question to* 454 S.E.2d 728, 732 (Va. 1995).

[79]Fairbanks N. Star Borough Sch. Dist. v. NEA-Alaska, 817 P.2d 923, 925 (Alaska 1991).

[80]*See, e.g.,* State *ex rel.* Cohn v. Shaker Heights City Sch. Dist., 678 N.E.2d 1385 (Ohio 1997); Scheer v. Indep. Sch. Dist. No. I-26, 948 P.2d 275 (Okla. 1997).

[81]*See, e.g.,* Speichler v. Bd. of Coop. Educ. Servs., 681 N.E.2d 366 (N.Y. 1997). *But see* Bowden v. Memphis Bd. of Educ., 29 S.W.3d 462 (Tenn. 2000) (ruling that a teacher did not acquire tenure upon reappointment after the probationary period when the superintendent failed to provide statutory notice to the school board that the teacher was eligible for tenure).

[82]*See, e.g.,* Washington v. Indep. Sch. Dist., 590 N.W.2d 655 (Minn. Ct. App. 1999). *See also* Nelson v. Bd. of Educ., 689 A.2d 1342 (N.J. 1997) (holding that tenure is earned in a specific position listed in state law only if the individual has served in that capacity; tenure as a supervisor did not extend to tenure as a principal or other administrative position).

particular school, grade, or subject area. Teachers may be reassigned to positions for which they are certified as well as dismissed for the causes specified in the tenure law.[83]

In establishing tenure, a legislature may create a contractual relationship that cannot be altered without violating constitutional guarantees. The Federal Constitution, Article I, Section 10, provides that the obligation of a contract cannot be impaired. The Supreme Court found such a contractual relationship in the 1927 Indiana Teacher Tenure Act, which prevented the state legislature from subsequently depriving teachers of rights conveyed under the act.[84] A statutory relationship that does not have the elements of a contract, however, can be altered or repealed at the legislature's discretion.[85] Some state tenure laws are clearly noncontractual, containing provisos that the law may be altered, while other state laws are silent on revisions. The Seventh Circuit noted there is a general presumption that statutes do not create contract rights. Relying on this presumption, the appellate court held that there was no impairment of the state's contractual obligations when principals' tenure was repealed in the Chicago School Reform Act.[86] If a tenure law is asserted to be contractual, the language of the act is critical in the judiciary's interpretation of legislative intent.

A number of states limit the award of tenure to teaching positions, thereby excluding administrative, supervisory, and staff positions. Where tenure is available for administrative positions, probationary service and other specified statutory terms must be met. Although tenure as a teacher usually does not imply tenure as an administrator, most courts have concluded that continued service as a certified professional employee, albeit as an administrator, does not alter tenure rights acquired as a teacher.[87] The Supreme Court of Wyoming noted, "It is desirable—and even important—to have people with extensive classroom teaching experience in administrative positions. It would be difficult to fill administrative positions with experienced teachers if the teachers would have to give up tenure upon accepting administrative roles."[88]

[83]*See* Chapter 11 for an extended discussion of termination of employment.

[84]Indiana *ex rel.* Anderson v. Brand, 303 U.S. 95 (1938). Under such legislation, the status of teachers who have received tenure cannot be altered, but the legislature is not prohibited from changing the law for future employees.

[85]*See* State v. Project Principle, 724 S.W.2d 387 (Tex. 1987) (holding that teaching certificate was a license rather than a contract and thus could be subject to future restrictions by the state).

[86]Pittman v. Chi. Bd. of Educ., 64 F.3d 1098 (7th Cir. 1995). Although a Tennessee appellate court was not examining the contractual nature of the Private Tenure Act that conferred tenure upon principals in the Knox County School System, the court found that the Education Improvement Act repealed the principals' tenure, Knox County Educ. Ass'n v. Knox County Bd. of Educ., 60 S.W.3d 65 (Tenn. Ct. App. 2001).

[87]*See, e.g.,* Downing v. City of Lowell, 741 N.E.2d 469 (Mass. App. Ct. 2001); E. Canton Educ. Ass'n v. McIntosh, 709 N.W.2d 468 (Ohio 1999).

[88]Spurlock v. Bd. of Trs., 699 P.2d 270, 272 (Wyo. 1985).

Supplemental Contracts

School boards can enter into supplement contracts with teachers for duties beyond the regular teaching assignments. As with teaching contracts, authority to employ resides with the school board.[89] Generally, these are limited contracts specifying the additional duties, compensation, and time period and can be terminated at their completion without violating a teacher's due process rights.[90] Extra duties often relate to coaching, department chair duties, supervision of student activities or clubs, and extended school year assignments.

Although supplemental service contracts are usually considered outside the scope of tenure protections, coaches, in particular, have asserted that supplemental contracts are an integral part of the teaching position and thereby must be afforded the procedural and substantive protections of state tenure laws. Several courts have noted that tenure rights apply only to employment in certified areas and that the lack of certification requirements for coaches in a state negates tenure claims for such positions.[91] The Supreme Court of Iowa, however, held that even a requirement that coaches must be certified did not confer teachers' tenure rights on coaching positions.[92] In this case, the coaching assignment was found to be clearly an extra duty, requiring a separate contract and compensation based on an extra-duty pay scale.

Other courts also have distinguished coaching and various extra duties from teaching responsibilities based on the extracurricular nature of the assignment and supplemental compensation.[93] In denying the claim of a 10-year veteran baseball coach, the Ninth Circuit held that the coach did not have a protected interest in his coaching position since California law specified that extra-duty assignments could be terminated by the school board at any time.[94] When both classroom teaching and

[89]*See, e.g.*, Gilmore v. Bonner County Sch. Dist. No. 82, 971 P.2d 323 (Idaho 1999). *See also* Hanlon v. Logan County Bd. of Educ., 496 S.E.2d 447 (W. Va. 1997) (holding that a school board can enter into extracurricular assignment contracts with individuals who are not employed in the school system).

[90]*See, e.g.*, Norlin v. Bd. of Trs., 107 P.3d 445 (Kan. Ct. App. 2004).

[91]*See, e.g.*, Smith v. Bd. of Educ., 708 F.2d 258 (7th Cir. 1983); Coles v. Glenburn Pub. Sch. Dist. 26, 436 N.W.2d 262 (N.D. 1989); Lawrence County Educ. Ass'n v. Lawrence County Bd. of Educ., 2007 WL 4442736 (Tenn. 2007).

[92]Slockett v. Iowa Valley Cmty. Sch. Dist., 359 N.W.2d 446 (Iowa 1984). *But see* Reid v. Huron Bd. of Educ., 449 N.W.2d 240 (S.D. 1989) (ruling that the position of head coach came under the continuing contract law since state administrative rules defined certification requirements for the job).

[93]*See, e.g.*, Lancaster v. Indep. Sch. Dist. No. 5, 149 F.3d 1228 (10th Cir. 1998); Sch. Comm. of Natick v. Educ. Ass'n of Natick, 666 N.E.2d 486 (Mass. 1996). *But see* Smith v. Bd. of Educ., 341 S.E.2d 685 (W. Va. 1985) (finding that failure of a school board to renew a coaching contract was considered a transfer, which under state law required procedural due process).

[94]Lagos v. Modesto City Schs. Dist., 843 F.2d 347 (9th Cir. 1988). *But see* Kingsford v. Salt Lake City Sch. Dist., 247 F.3d 1123 (10th Cir. 2001) (remanding to determine if school officials created an "implied-in-fact" promise that coaches would only be terminated for cause; case prompted state legislature to amend law to specify that extra-duty assignments are limited contracts). *See also* text accompanying note 53, Chapter 11, for a discussion of procedural due process protections.

extra-duty assignments are covered in the same contract, however, protected property interests may be created. Accordingly, the teacher would be entitled to due process prior to the termination of the extra-duty assignment.[95]

Because coaching assignments generally require execution of a supplemental contract, a teacher can usually resign a coaching position and maintain the primary teaching position.[96] School boards having difficulty in filling coaching positions, however, may tender an offer to teach on the condition that an individual assume certain coaching responsibilities. If a single teaching and coaching contract is found to be indivisible, a teacher cannot unilaterally resign the coaching duties without relinquishing the teaching position.[97] Individual state laws must be consulted to determine the status of such contracts.

Where teaching and coaching positions are combined, a qualified teaching applicant who cannot assume the coaching duties may be rejected. This practice, however, may be vulnerable to legal challenge if certain classes of applicants, such as women, are excluded from consideration. In an Arizona case, female plaintiffs successfully established that a school district was liable for sex discrimination by coupling a high school biology teaching position with a football coaching position. The school board was unable to demonstrate a business necessity for the practice that resulted in female applicants for the teaching position being eliminated from consideration.[98]

Domestic Partner Benefits

Increasingly, legal challenges are being brought to secure health, retirement, and other benefits for domestic partners of gay, lesbian, bisexual, and transgendered employees. Rights may exist under state constitutional and statutory provisions or institutional policies. Only Vermont and Connecticut have sanctioned same-sex civil unions by law, and the Massachusetts high court has held that denial of civil marriage to same-sex couples violates the state constitution.[99] Several other states—California, Hawaii, Maine, and New Jersey—have enacted domestic partnership laws. Rights under these laws, however, vary significantly, being only symbolic in some instances

[95]*See, e.g.*, Farner v. Idaho Falls Sch. Dist. No. 91, 17 P.3d 281 (Idaho 2000).

[96]*See, e.g.*, Lewis v. Bd. of Educ., 537 N.E.2d 435 (Ill. App. Ct. 1989), Hachiya v. Bd. of Educ., 750 P.2d 383 (Kan. 1988). *See also* Parker v. Indep. Sch. Dist. No. I-003, 82 F.3d 952 (10th Cir. 1996) (holding that the school board could not circumvent the teacher's entitlement to procedural due process with the termination of her teaching position by having the teacher sign a contract that specified she would not be reemployed as a teacher if her coaching contract was not renewed; court emphasized that the school board could not amend or repeal statutory rights).

[97]*See, e.g.*, Smith v. Petal Sch. Dist., 956 So. 2d 273 (Miss. Ct. App. 2006), *Cert. denied*, 957 So. zd 1004 (Miss. 2007).

[98]Civil Rights Div. v. Amphitheater Unified Sch. Dist. No. 10, 706 P.2d 745 (Ariz. Ct. App. 1985).

[99]Goodridge v. Dep't of Pub. Health, 798 N.E.2d 941 (Mass. 2003). *See also* Varnum v. Brien, case no. CV5965 (Iowa Dist. Ct. August 30, 2007) (ruling that it is unconstitutional under the Iowa Constitution for the state to deny same-sex couples the right to marry), *appeal pending.*

and in others conferring full rights and benefits.[100] In reviewing claims for benefits, some courts have held that the denial of benefits discriminates on the basis of marital status or that unmarried partners have been treated differently by benefits policies and denial is unrelated to any legitimate governmental interest.[101]

Yet, other courts have firmly upheld the denial of benefits, finding no discrimination.[102] With the federal Defense of Marriage Act (DOMA) and subsequent adoption of mini-DOMAs in 42 states, employees will continue to face significant challenges in achieving equality of benefits for their domestic partners.[103] For example, in 2007 the Michigan Court of Appeals interpreted the state's constitutional marriage amendment as precluding employers from providing same-sex domestic partner benefits. The court ruled that the law, which provides that "the union of one man and one woman in marriage shall be the only agreement recognized as a marriage or similar union for any purpose," blocks the recognition of domestic partnership agreements because it is a status *similar* to marriage.[104] If other state courts follow the Michigan reasoning, the state DOMAs will render many existing domestic partnership programs invalid.

Leaves of Absence

Contracts may specify various types of leaves of absence. Within the parameters of state law, school boards have discretion in establishing requirements for these leaves. A school board may place restrictions on when teachers can take personal leave, for example, such as mandating no leaves on the day before or after a holiday, or no more than two consecutive days of personal leave.[105] This topic often is the subject of

[100]*See* Janice McClendon "A Small Step Forward in the Last Civil Rights Battle: Extending Benefits under Federally Regulated Benefit Plans to Same-Sex Couples," *New Mexico Law Review,* vol. 36 (Winter 2006), pp. 99–123.

[101]*See, e.g.,* Univ. of Alaska v. Tumeo, 933 P.2d 1147 (Alaska 1998); Snetsinger v. Mont. Univ. Sys., 104 P.3d 445 (Mont. 2004); Tanner v. Or. Health Scis. Univ., 971 P.2d 435 (Or. Ct. App. 1998); Baker v. State, 744 A.2d 864 (Vt. 1999). *See also* Devlin v. City of Phil., 862 A.2d 1234 (Pa. 2004) (holding that city did not exceed it authority in extending benefits to life partners of its employees); Pritchard v. Madison Metro. Sch. Dist., 625 N.W.2d 613 (Wis. Ct. App. 2001) (denying plaintiffs' challenge that the school system was in violation of state law by providing insurance coverage for unmarried partners of a school district employee).

[102]*See* Rutgers Council of AAUP Chapters v. Rutgers State Univ., 689 A.2d 828 (N.J. Super. Ct. App. Div. 1997); Funderburke v. Uniondale Union Free Sch. Dist. No. 15, 660 N.Y.S.2d 659 (Sup. Ct. 1997). *See also* Donna Euben, *Domestic Partnership Benefits on Campus: A Litigation Update* (Washington, D.C.: American Association of University Professors, 2002).

[103]McClendon, *Supra* note 100, p. 101. *See also* Defense of Marriage Act, 1 U.S.C. § 7 (2007); 28 U.S.C. § 1738C (2007). Congress passed the DOMA in reaction to growing concern about states recognizing same-sex marriages. Under the federal law, marriage is defined as a union between a man and a woman. Furthermore, the act states that individual states are not required to recognize same-sex marriages sanctioned by other states.

[104]Nat'l Pride at Work v. Gov. of Mich., 732 N.W.2d 139, 143 (Mich. Ct. App. 2007), *appeal granted*, 731 N.W. 2d 405 (Mich. 2007).

[105]*See, e.g.,* Amaral-Whittenberg v. Alanis, 123 S.W.3d 714 (Tex. App. 2003).

collective negotiations, with leave provisions specified in bargained agreements. School boards, however, cannot negotiate leave policies that impair rights guaranteed by the United States Constitution and various federal and state anti-discrimination laws.[106] Similarly, where state law confers specific rights, local boards do not have the discretion to deny or alter these rights. Generally, statutes identify employees' rights related to various kinds of leaves such as sick leave, personal leave, pregnancy or child-care leave, sabbatical leave, disability leave, and military leave. State laws pertaining to leaves of absence usually specify eligibility for benefits, minimum days that must be provided, whether leave must be granted with or without pay, and restrictions that may be imposed by local school boards. If a teacher meets all statutory and procedural requirements for a specific leave, a school board cannot deny the request.

Personnel Evaluations

To ensure a quality teaching staff, many states have enacted laws requiring periodic appraisal of teaching performance. Beyond the purposes of faculty improvement and remediation, results of evaluations may be used in a variety of employment decisions including retention, tenure, dismissal, promotion, salary, reassignment, and reduction in force. When adverse personnel decisions are based on evaluations, legal concerns of procedural fairness arise. Were established state and local procedures followed? Did school officials employ equitable standards? Was sufficient evidence collected to support the staffing decision? Were evaluations conducted in a uniform and consistent manner?

School systems have broad discretionary powers to establish teacher performance criteria, but state statutes may impose specific evaluation requirements. More than half of the states have enacted laws governing teacher evaluation.[107] Content and requirements vary substantially across states, with some states merely mandating the establishment of an appraisal system and others specifying procedures and criteria to be employed. Iowa law notes only that the local board must establish an evaluation system.[108] California, on the other hand, specifies the intent of evaluations, areas to be assessed, frequency of evaluations, notice to employees of deficiencies, and an opportunity to improve performance.[109] Florida requires the superintendent of schools to establish criteria and procedures for appraisal, including evaluation at least once a year, a written record of assessment, prior notice to teachers of criteria and procedures, and a meeting with the evaluator to discuss the results of the evaluation.[110]

[106]Charges of discrimination in connection with leave policies pertaining to pregnancy-related absences and the observance of religious holidays are discussed in Chapter 10.

[107]Perry A. Zirkel, *The Law of Teacher Evaluation* (Bloomington, IN: Phi Delta Kappa, 1996).

[108]Iowa Code Ann. § 279.14 (2007). *See also* Ark. Code Ann. § 6-17-1504 (2007).

[109]Cal. Code Ann. §§ 44660–44665 (2007). *See also* Chi. Bd. of Educ. v. Smith, 664 N.E.2d 113 (Ill. App. Ct. 1996).

[110]Fla. Stat. § 231.29 (2007).

Although a few evaluation systems are established at the state level, state laws usually require local officials to develop evaluation criteria, often in conjunction with teachers or other professionals.[111] Unless prohibited as managerial policy, it also may be negotiable with the teachers' union.[112]

When evaluation procedures are identified in statutes, board policies, or employment contracts, courts generally require strict compliance with these provisions. A Washington appellate court required the reinstatement of a principal because the school board had not adopted evaluation criteria and procedures as required by law.[113] The court noted that in the absence of evaluation criteria the principal would serve at the whim of the superintendent and would be deprived of guidelines to improve his performance. Under the Ohio statutory evaluation requirement for nontenured teachers, failure to comply with the twice-yearly evaluation mandate resulted in the reinstatement of a nontenured teacher.[114] The West Virginia Supreme Court held that a school system could not transfer an individual because the decision was not based on performance evaluations as required by state board policy.[115]

Where school boards have been attentive to evaluation requirements, courts have upheld challenged employment decisions.[116] A California appellate court found that a teacher's dismissal comported with state evaluation requirements because he received periodic appraisals noting specific instances of unsatisfactory performance.[117] The evaluation reports informed the teacher of the system's expectations, his specific teaching weaknesses, and actions needed to correct deficiencies. An Iowa court found a school district's policy requiring a formal evaluation every three years for nonprobationary teachers to be adequate under a statutory requirement that "the board shall establish evaluation criteria and shall implement evaluation procedures."[118] The court denied a teacher's claim that the law required an additional evaluation whenever termination of employment was contemplated. According to the Supreme Court of South Dakota, violation of an evaluation

---

[111]*See, e.g.*, Ariz. Rev. Stat. Ann. § 15-537 (2007); Conn. Gen. Stat. Ann. § 10-151b (2007) Or. Rev. Stat. Ann. § 342.850 (2007).

[112]*See, e.g., In re* Pittsfield Sch. Dist., 744 A.2d 594 (N.H. 1999). *See also* text accompanying notes 52–54, Chapter 12.

[113]Hyde v. Wellpinit Sch. Dist. 49, 611 P.2d 1388 (Wash. Ct. App. 1980).

[114]Snyder v. Mendon-Union Local Sch. Dist. Bd. of Educ., 661 N.E.2d 717 (Ohio 1996). *See also* McComb v. Gahana-Jefferson City Sch. Dist. Bd. of Educ., 720 N.E.2d 984 (Ohio Ct. App. 1998) (concluding that prior to nonrenewal, the teacher was provided specific recommendations for improvement in evaluations as required by state law).

[115]Holland v. Bd. of Educ., 327 S.E.2d 155 (W. Va. 1985).

[116]*See, e.g.*, Tippecanoe Educ. Ass'n v. Tippecanoe Sch. Corp., 700 N.E.2d 241 (Ind. Ct. App. 1998); Thomas v. Bd. of Educ., 643 N.E.2d 132 (Ohio 1994).

[117]Perez v. Comm'n on Prof'l Competence, 197 Cal. Rptr. 390 (Ct. App. 1983). *See also* Hoffner v. Bismarck Pub. Sch. Dist., 589 N.W.2d 195 (N.D. 1999) (concluding that a principal's nonrenewal complied with the statute requiring that reasons be drawn from findings arising from written evaluations).

[118]Johnson v. Bd. of Educ., 353 N.W.2d 883, 887 (Iowa Ct. App. 1984).

procedure *per se* does not require reinstatement of a teacher.[119] Reinstatement is justified only if the violation substantially interfered with a teacher's ability to improve deficiencies.

Courts are reluctant to interject their judgment into the teacher evaluation process. Judicial review generally is limited to the procedural issues of fairness and reasonableness. Several principles emerge from case law to guide educators in developing equitable systems: standards for assessing teaching adequacy must be defined and communicated to teachers; criteria must be applied uniformly and consistently; an opportunity and direction for improvement must be provided; and procedures specified in state laws and school board policies must be followed.

Personnel Records

Because multiple statutes in each state (as well as employment contracts) govern school records, it is difficult to generalize as to the specific nature of teachers' privacy rights regarding personnel files. State privacy laws that place restrictions on maintenance and access to the records typically protect personnel information. Among other provisions, these laws usually require school boards to maintain only necessary and relevant information, provide individual employees access to their files,[120] inform employees of the various uses of the files, and establish a procedure for challenging the accuracy of information. Collective bargaining contracts may impose additional and more stringent requirements regarding access and dissemination of personnel information.[121]

A central issue in the confidentiality of personnel files is whether the information constitutes a public record that must be reasonably accessible to the general public. Public record, freedom of information, or right-to-know laws that grant broad access to school records may directly conflict with privacy laws, requiring courts to balance the interests of the teacher, the school officials, and the public. The specific provisions of state laws determine the level of confidentiality granted

---

[119]Schaub v. Chamberlain Bd. of Educ., 339 N.W.2d 307 (S.D. 1983). It must be emphasized that failure to follow established evaluation procedures does not necessarily result in a denial of constitutional due process rights in termination actions if the minimum notice, specification of charges, and opportunity for a hearing are provided. *See, e.g.,* Goodrich v. Newport News Sch. Bd., 743 F.2d 225 (4th Cir. 1984); Farmer v. Kelleys Island Bd. of Educ., 638 N.E.2d 79 (Ohio 1994). *See also* text accompanying note 53, Chapter 11.

[120]*See* Cook v. Lisbon Sch. Comm., 682 A.2d 672 (Me. 1996) (holding that the school committee must produce documents requested by the employee within statutory time period of five working days; providing the material months after the request was made is inadequate); Boor v. McKenzie County Pub. Sch. Dist. No. 1, 560 N.W.2d 213 (N.D. 1997) (concluding that a principal's notations of complaints in his desk journal against a teacher did not violate state law prohibiting a secret personnel file when he had promptly brought the complaints to the teacher's attention).

[121]*But see* Bradley v. Bd. of Educ., 565 N.W.2d 650 (Mich. 1997) (holding that the board could not bargain away the requirements of the state Freedom of Information Act).

personnel records.[122] The federal Freedom of Information Act (FOIA),[123] which serves as a model for many state FOIAs, often is used by courts in interpreting state provisions. Unlike the federal law, however, many states do not exempt personnel records. In the absence of a specific exemption, most courts have concluded that any doubt as to the appropriateness of disclosure should be decided in favor of public disclosure.[124] The Supreme Court of Michigan held that teachers' personnel files are open to the public because they are not specifically exempt by law.[125] The Supreme Court of Washington noted that the public disclosure act mandated disclosure of information that is of legitimate public concern.[126] As such, the state superintendent of public instruction was required to provide a newspaper publisher records specifying the reasons for teacher certificate revocations. The Supreme Court of Connecticut interpreted the state Freedom of Information Act exemption, prohibiting the release of information that would constitute an "invasion of personal privacy," to include employees' evaluations[127] but not their sick-leave records.[128] In the termination of a teacher for conducting pornographic Internet searches on his work computer, the Supreme Court of Wisconsin held that a memorandum and CD created from a

[122]*See* Wakefield Teachers Ass'n v. Sch. Comm., 731 N.E.2d 63 (Mass. 2000) (concluding that a disciplinary report is personal information that is exempt under the public records law). *See also* Gutman v. Bd. of Educ., 2007 WL 4438938 (N.Y App. Div. 2007) (holding that a disciplinary reprimand could not be placed in teachers' personnel files without due process as mandated by state law); Bangor Area Educ. Ass'n, 720 A.2d 198 (Pa. Commw. Ct. 1998) (confirming that teachers' personnel files are not public records); Abbott v. N.E. Indep. Sch. Dist., 212 S.W.3d 364, 367 (Tex. App. 2006) (concluding that a principal's memorandum to a teacher about complaints and providing her directions for improvement was "a document evaluating the performance of a teacher" and thus exempt from release under the state's public information act).

[123]5 U.S.C. § 552 (2007).

[124]*See, e.g.*, Kirwan v. The Diamondback, 721 A.2d 196 (Md. 1998); Brouillet v. Cowles Pub. Co., 791 P.2d 526 (Wash. 1990); Wis. Newspress v. Sch. Dist., 546 N.W.2d 143 (Wis. 1996).

[125]Bradley v. Bd. of Educ., 565 N.W.2d 650 (Mich. 1997).

[126]*Brouillet*, 791 P.2d 526. *See also* S. Bend Tribune v. S. Bend Cmty. Sch. Corp., 740 N.E.2d 937 (Ind. Ct. App. 2000) (holding that a public agency must disclose designated personnel information for present or former employees but not information pertaining to applicants for positions); Cypress Media v. Hazleton Area Sch. Dist., 708 A.2d 866 (Pa. Commw. Ct. 1998) (finding that applications for employment are not public records).

[127]Chairman v. Freedom of Info. Comm'n, 585 A.2d 96 (Conn. 1991). *But see* DeMichele v. Greenburgh Cent. Sch. Dist. No. 7, 167 F.3d 784 (2d Cir. 1999) (noting that under New York law the disposition of misconduct charges is not exempt private information); Carpenter v. Freedom of Info. Comm'n, 755 A.2d 364 (Conn. App. Ct. 2000) (ruling that a record of personal misconduct was not a record of teaching performance or evaluation exempt under state law); Linzmeyer v. Forcey, 646 N.W.2d 811 (Wis. 2002) (finding that the open records law applies to the report of a police investigation; the police had investigated a high school teacher for allegedly engaging in inappropriate conduct with female students).

[128]Perkins v. Freedom of Info. Comm'n, 635 A.2d 783 (Conn. 1993). *But see* Brogan v. Sch. Comm. of Westport, 516 N.E.2d 159 (Mass. 1987) (holding that individual absentee records noting dates and generic types of absences were not records of a "personal nature" exempt from the Public Records Law). *See also* Scottsdale Unified Sch. Dist. No. 48 v. KPNX Broad. Co., 955 P.2d 534 (Ariz. 1998) (finding that the public availability of teachers' birth dates did not negate teachers' legitimate expectation of privacy).

forensic analysis of the teacher's computer were "records" subject to release under the state's Open Records Law after the school district completed its investigation.[129] Generally, information that must be maintained by law is a public record (i.e., personal directory information, salary, employment contracts, leave records, and teaching license) and must be released.

Educators have not been successful in asserting that privacy interests in personnel records are protected under either the Family Educational Rights and Privacy Act of 1974 (FERPA) or the United States Constitution. FERPA has been found to apply only to students and their educational records, not to employees' personnel records.[130] Similarly, employees' claims that their constitutional privacy rights bar disclosure of their personnel records have been unsuccessful. In a case in which a teacher's college transcript was sought by a third party under the Texas Open Records Act, the Fifth Circuit ruled that even if a teacher had a recognizable privacy interest in her transcript, that interest "is significantly outweighed by the public's interest in evaluating the competence of its school teachers."[131]

Access to personnel files also has been controversial in situations involving allegations of employment discrimination.[132] Personnel files must be relinquished if subpoenaed by a court. The Equal Employment Opportunity Commission (EEOC) also is authorized to subpoena relevant personnel files to enable the commission to investigate thoroughly allegations that a particular individual has been the victim of discriminatory treatment. Holding that confidential peer review materials used in university promotion and tenure decisions were not protected from disclosure to the EEOC, the Supreme Court ruled that under the provisions of Title VII of the Civil Rights Act of 1964 the commission must only show relevance, not special reasons or justifications, in demanding specific records. Regarding access to peer review materials, the Court noted that "if there is a 'smoking gun' to be

---

[129]Zellner v. Cedarburg Sch. Dist., 731 N.W.2d 240 (Wis. 2007). *See also* Navarre v. S. Wash. County Schs., 652 N.W 2d 9 (Minn. 2002) (finding that the release of information about a disciplinary matter before final disposition violated the counselor's rights under state law protecting private personnel data); Williams v. Bd. of Educ., 747 A.2d 809 (N.J. Super. Ct. App. Div. 2000) (holding that tenure charge documents are a public record).

[130]*See, e.g.*, Klein Indep. Sch. Dist. v. Mattox, 830 F.2d 576 (5th Cir. 1987); Brouillet v. Cowles Publ'g Co., 791 P.2d 526 (Wash. 1990). *See* Cypress Media v. Hazelton Area Sch. Dist., 708 A.2d 866 (Pa. Commw. Ct. 1998) (concluding that release of college transcripts of *applicants* for teaching positions would violate FERPA).

[131]*Klein*, 830 F.2d at 580. *See also* Hovet v. Hebron Pub. Sch. Dist., 419 N.W.2d 189 (N.D. 1988).

[132]Federal Procedural Rules, approved by the Supreme Court in April 2006 and effective December 1, 2006, require employers to be more aware about the storage of electronic information. When school officials are involved in the discovery phase of litigation, they must be able to produce e-mail, instant messages, and other digital communications created in their system. The rules send a clear message that digital and electronic communications must be preserved as other documents are preserved. *See* Corey Murray, "High Court: Don't Delete That E-Mail," *eSchool News online* (January 1, 2007), available at http://eschoolnews.org/news/showstory.cfm?ArticleID=6748.

found that demonstrates discrimination in tenure decisions, it is likely to be tucked away in peer review files."[133]

With respect to the maintenance of records, information clearly cannot be placed in personnel files in retaliation for the exercise of constitutional rights. Courts have ordered letters of reprimand expunged from files when they have been predicated on protected speech and association activities. Reprimands, while not a direct prohibition on protected activities, may present a constitutional violation because of their potentially chilling effect on the exercise of constitutional rights.[134]

Other Employment Issues

In addition to the terms and conditions of employment already discussed, other reasonable requirements can be attached to public employment as long as civil rights laws are respected and constitutional rights are not impaired without a compelling governmental justification. Public educators are expected to comply with such reasonable requirements as a condition of maintaining their jobs. Some requirements, such as those pertaining to the instructional program and prohibitions against proselytizing students, are discussed in other chapters. Requirements pertaining to two topics have received substantial attention since the 1980s and warrant discussion here—using copyrighted materials and reporting child abuse/harassment.

Using Copyrighted Materials

Educators' extensive use of published materials and various other media in the classroom raises issues relating to the federal copyright law. As a condition of employment, educators are expected to comply with restrictions on the use of copyrighted materials. Although the law grants the owner of a copyright exclusive control over the protected material, courts since the 1800s have recognized exceptions to this control under the doctrine of "fair use." The fair use doctrine cannot be precisely defined, but judiciary frequently has described it as the "privilege in others than the owner of the copyright to use the copyrighted material in a reasonable manner without his consent, notwithstanding the monopoly granted to the owner."[135]

---

[133]Univ. of Pa. v. EEOC, 493 U.S. 182, 193 (1990). *See* Univ. of Pittsburgh v. Dep't of Labor and Indus., 896 A.2d 683 (Pa. Commw. Ct. 2006) (ruling under the state's Personnel Files Act that a faculty member did not have the right to inspect external letters written for his promotion file; letters were considered references rather than personnel evaluations that would have been open to inspection).

[134]*See* Aebisher v. Ryan, 622 F.2d 651 (2d Cir. 1980) (concluding that a letter of reprimand for speaking to the press about violence in the school implicated protected speech); Columbus Educ. Ass'n v. Columbus City Sch. Dist., 623 F.2d 1155 (6th Cir. 1980) (holding that a letter of reprimand issued to a union representative for zealous advocacy of a fellow teacher violated the First Amendment); Swilley v. Alexander, 629 F.2d 1018 (5th Cir. 1980) (ruling that a union president's press release was protected conduct and letter of reprimand implicated liberty interests).

[135]Marcus v. Rowley, 695 F.2d 1171, 1174 (9th Cir. 1983).

Congress incorporated the judicially created fair use concept into the 1976 revisions of the Copyright Act.[136] In identifying the purposes of the fair use exception, Congress specifically noted teaching. The exception provides needed flexibility for teachers but by no interpretation grants them exemption from copyright infringement. The law stipulates four factors to assess whether the use of specific material constitutes fair use or an infringement:

> (1) the purpose and character of the use, including whether such use is of a commercial nature or is for non-profit educational purposes; (2) the nature of the copyrighted work; (3) the amount and substantiality of the portion used in relation to the copyrighted work as a whole; and (4) the effect of the use upon the potential market for or value of the copyrighted work.[137]

To clarify fair use pertaining to photocopying from books and periodicals, the House of Representatives and Senate conferees incorporated into their report a set of classroom guidelines developed by a group representing educators, authors, and publishers. These guidelines are only part of the legislative history of the act and do not have the force of law, but they have been widely used as persuasive authority in assessing the legality of reproducing printed materials in the educational environment. The guidelines permit making single copies of copyrighted material for teaching or research but are quite restrictive on the use of multiple copies. To use multiple copies of a work, the tests of brevity, spontaneity, and cumulative effect must be met. Brevity is precisely defined according to type of publication. For example, reproduction of a poem cannot exceed 250 words; copying from longer works cannot exceed 1,000 words or 10 percent of the work (whichever is less); only one chart or drawing can be reproduced from a book or an article. Spontaneity requires that the copying be initiated by the individual teacher (not an administrator or supervisor) and that it occur in such a manner that does not reasonably permit a timely request for permission. Cumulative effect restricts use of the copies to one course; limits material reproduced from the same author, book, and journal during the term; and sets a limit of nine instances of multiple copying for each course during one class term. Furthermore, the guidelines do not permit copying to substitute for anthologies or collective works or to replace consumable materials such as workbooks.

Publishers have taken legal action to ensure compliance with these guidelines. The Sixth Circuit held that Michigan Document Services, Inc., a commercial copy shop, violated the fair use doctrine in the reproduction of course packets for faculty at the University of Michigan. Three publishers (Macmillan, Princeton University Press, and St. Martin's Press) challenged the duplication of copyrighted material for

---

[136] 17 U.S.C. § 101 *et seq.* (2007). A Wisconsin teacher raised a novel "fair use" claim when he argued that his school district could not release to a newspaper a compact disc containing pornographic images he had downloaded from the Internet because the images were copyrighted works, thereby not a public record under the state's Open Records Law. The state high court ruled that the images were a public record because they could be accessed free of charge via the Internet, and the school district would not profit from distribution of the images. Zellner v. Cedarburg Sch. Dist., 731 N.W.2d 240 (Wis. 2007).

[137] 17 U.S.C. § 107 (2007).

commercial sale by a for-profit corporation. The copy shop owner argued that such reproduction of multiple copies for classroom use is a recognized statutory exemption. The appellate court disagreed, reasoning that the sale of multiple copies for commercial, rather than educational purposes, destroyed the publishers' potential licensing revenue from photocopying. Furthermore, course packets contained creative material and involved substantial portions of the copyrighted publications (as much as 30 percent for one work).[138] This ruling does not prevent faculty use of course packets or anthologies in the classroom, but it does require permission from publishers and the possible payment of fees prior to photocopying.

The fair use doctrine and congressional guidelines have been strictly construed in educational settings. Even though the materials reproduced meet the first factor in determining fair use—educational purpose—the remaining factors also must be met. The Ninth Circuit held that a teacher's use of a copyrighted booklet to make a learning activity packet abridged the copyright law.[139] The court concluded that fair use was not met in this case because the learning packet was used for the same purpose as the protected booklet, the nature of the work reproduced was a "creative" effort rather than "information," and one-half of the packet was verbatim copy of the copyrighted material. Furthermore, the copying was found to violate the guideline of spontaneity in that it was reproduced several times over two school years. It is important to note that the appeals court did not find the absence of personal profit on the part of the teacher to lessen the violation.

Although not using the material for teaching purposes, a Chicago teacher and editor of a newspaper called *Substance* published copyrighted tests used to assess educational levels of Chicago public high school freshmen and sophomores. He published entire copies of a number of the subject area tests along with his criticism of the tests. The tests were clearly marked with the copyright notice and included a warning that the material could not be duplicated. The Chicago school board sued, claiming infringement of its copyright. An Illinois federal district court ruled that the teacher did not possess a First Amendment right to publish the copyrighted tests; the Copyright Act limits First Amendment freedoms.[140] Furthermore, the publication of the material did not fall within the "fair use" guidelines.

Rapid developments in instructional technology pose a new set of legal questions regarding use of videotapes, DVDs and computer software. Recognizing the need for guidance related to recording material, Congress issued guidelines for educational use in 1981.[141] These guidelines specify that recording must be made at the request of the teacher. The material recorded must be used for relevant classroom

[138]Princeton Univ. Press v. Mich. Document Servs., 99 F.3d 1381 (6th Cir. 1996). *See also* Basic Books v. Kinko's Graphics Corp., 758 F. Supp. 1522 (S.D.N.Y. 1991) (concluding that the photocopying of copyrighted works for course packets violated fair use; awarding eight publishers $510,000 in damages).

[139]Marcus v. Rowley, 695 F.2d 1171 (9th Cir. 1983).

[140]Chi. Sch. Reform Bd. v. Substance, Inc., 79 F. Supp. 2d 919 (N.D. Ill. 1999).

[141]"Guidelines for Off-the-Air Recording of Broadcast Programming for Educational Purposes," Cong. Rec. § E4751, October 14, 1981.

activities only once within the first 10 days of recording. Additional use is limited to instructional reinforcement or evaluation purposes. After 45 calendar days, the tape or DVD must be erased. A New York federal district court held that a school system violated the fair use standards by extensive off-the-air taping and replaying of entire television programs.[142] The recording interfered with the producers' ability to market the tapes and films. In a subsequent appeal, the school system sought permission for temporary taping; however, because of the availability of these programs for rental or lease, even temporary recording and use was held to violate fair use by interfering with the marketability of the films.[143]

Recording television broadcasts on home recorders for later classroom use may constitute copyright infringement if off-the-air taping guidelines are not followed. Under the legal principles advanced by the Supreme Court in *Sony Corporation v. Universal City Studios*, "even copying for noncommercial purposes may impair the copyright holder's ability to obtain the rewards that Congress intended him to have."[144] In this case, the Court found that personal video recording for the purpose of "time shifting" for the viewer's convenience was a legitimate, unobjectionable purpose, posing minimal harm to marketability. Home recording for broader viewing by students in the classroom, however, would be beyond the purposes envisioned by the Court in *Sony* and would necessitate careful adherence to the guidelines for limited use discussed above.

Under 1980 amendments to the copyright law, software was included as protected intellectual property.[145] Established copyright principles provide guidance in analyzing fair use. It is clear from the amended law that only one duplicate or backup copy can be made of the master computer program by the owner. This is to ensure a working copy of the program if the master copy is damaged. Application of the fair use exception does not alter this restriction for educators. While duplicating multiple copies would be clearly for educational purposes, other factors of fair use would be violated: the software is readily accessible for purchase (not impossible to obtain), programs can only be duplicated in their entirety, and copying substantially reduces the potential market.

In spite of the amendments, publishers continue to be concerned about illegal copying of computer software in the school environment. Limited school budgets and high costs have led to abuse of copyrighted software. In 1999, the Los Angeles Board of Education settled what might be the worst case of software piracy discovered in public schools.[146] An investigation by a group of software companies discovered more than 1,400 copies of software, such as Microsoft Word and Adobe Photoshop, allegedly being used without authorization. The school district denied the violation but settled to avoid the costs of a trial.

[142]Encyclopedia Britannica Educ. Corp. v. Crooks, 542 F. Supp. 1156 (W.D.N.Y. 1982).

[143]Encyclopedia Britannica Educ. Corp. v. Crooks, 558 F. Supp. 1247 (W.D.N.Y. 1983).

[144]464 U.S. 417, 450 (1984).

[145]17 U.S.C. § 117 (2007).

[146]"L.A. School Board Settles Software Copyright Suit," *School Law News*, vol. 27 (March 5, 1999), p. 2. The case was settled for $300,000 plus an additional $1.5 million for a task force to monitor software usage over a three-year period.

A question not answered by the copyright law but plaguing schools is the legality of multiple use of a master program. That is, can a program be loaded in a number of computers in a laboratory for simultaneous use, or can a program be modified for use in a network of microcomputers? Again, application of the fair use concept would indicate that multiple use is impermissible. The most significant factor is that the market for the educational software would be greatly diminished. A number of students using the master program one at a time (serial use), however, would appear not to violate the copyright law. To acquire broad use of particular software, school systems must either purchase multiple copies or negotiate site license agreements with the publishers.

As schools are developing their capacity to take advantage of the Internet, copyright law also is evolving. Congress amended the law in 1998, passing the Digital Millennium Copyright Act.[147] The "White Paper" produced by President Clinton's Working Group on Intellectual Property Issues identified numerous and complex issues that influenced the amended law.[148] Questions were raised about what constitutes distribution (traditionally interpreted as a hard copy being transferred to another individual as opposed to transmission over data lines) and publication (current definition limits protection to physical copies). The amended law reinforces that an individual's copyright is secured when the work is created and "fixed in any tangible medium of expression."[149] Even though critics find many ambiguities in the law, they agree that it includes a clear commitment to extending "fair use" to digital technology for educators.

In 2002, greater clarity was provided for educators regarding the use of digital media in distance education with the enactment of the Technology, Education, and Copyright Harmonization (TEACH) Act (included in the 21st Century Department of Justice Appropriations Authorization Act, H.R. 2215).[150] The act gives accredited nonprofit educational institutions more flexibility in using the Internet to distribute copyrighted materials in distance education programs. Basically, the act allows copyrighted materials to be used in distance education courses in the same way they can be used in regular classrooms. Previously, the law did not permit two-way transmission of copyrighted materials and prevented sharing of materials through digital transmissions.

Litigation clearly indicates that material published and distributed on the Internet will be fully protected by the basic principles of copyright law. For example, in 2001 the Ninth Circuit imposed an injunction against Napster Corporation and its distribution of a file-sharing program that allowed individuals to download music files.[151] More recently, the Supreme Court found that two

---

[147]17 U.S.C. § 1201 ct seq. (2007).

[148]Bruce A. Lehman, Chair, Working Group on Intellectual Property Rights, "Report on Intellectual Property and the National Information Infrastructure" (Washington, D.C.: Information Infrastructure Task Force, 1995).

[149]17 U.S.C. § 102 (2007).

[150]17 U.S.C. §110 (2007). *See also* Constance Hawke, "The P2P File Sharing Controversy: Should Colleges Be Involved?" *Education Law Reporter*, vol. 184 (2004), pp. 681–691.

[151]A&M Records v. Napster, 239 F.3d 1004 (9th Cir. 2001).

software companies, presenting themselves as "alternatives" to Napster, infringed the copyright of songwriters, music publishers, and motion picture studios who had brought suit to prevent unauthorized use of their protected property. Like Napster, the challenged software companies distributed free software products that allowed individuals to share electronic files through peer-to-peer networks. The Supreme Court specifically held that "one who distributes a device with the object of promoting its use to infringe copyright, as shown by clear expression or other affirmative steps taken to foster infringement, is liable for the resulting acts of infringement by third parties."[152] Although the file-sharing software had some lawful uses, its primary purpose and use was to share copyrighted files. That rendered the software companies culpable.

Extraordinary technological advances have given teachers and their school systems the means to access a wide range of instructional materials and products, but the federal copyright law that restricts unauthorized reproduction protects many of them. Because violation of the law can result in school district and educator liability, school boards should adopt policies or guidelines to prohibit infringement and to alert individuals of practices that violate protected materials.[153]

Reporting Suspected Child Abuse

Child abuse and neglect are recognized as national problems, with reported cases remaining at a high level.[154] Because the majority of these children are school age, educators are in a unique role to detect signs of potential abuse. States, recognizing the daily contact teachers have with students, have imposed certain *duties* for reporting suspected abuse.

All states have enacted laws identifying teachers among the professionals required to report signs of child abuse. Most state laws impose criminal liability for failure to report. Penalties may include fines ranging from $500 to $5,000, prison terms up to one year, or both. Civil suits also may be initiated against teachers for

---

[152]Metro-Goldwyn-Mayer Studios Inc. v. Grokster, Ltd., 545 U.S. 913, 919 (2005). The lower courts had ruled that the software companies could not be held liable for unlawful use of the file-sharing programs. The Supreme Court remanded the case to the district court for trial.

[153]*See* 17 U.S.C. § 511(a) (2007). In response to several appellate court decisions holding that under the Eleventh Amendment states and their agents were not subject to suit in federal courts for the infringement of copyrights, Congress amended the copyright law (Copyright Remedy Clarification) specifically abrogating immunity. *See also* BV Eng'g v. Univ. of Cal., L.A., 858 F.2d 1394 (9th Cir. 1988); Richard Anderson Photography v. Brown, 852 F.2d 114 (4th Cir. 1988).

[154]In 2005, 3.3 million referrals (involving approximately 6 million children) were made to child protection agencies, and almost 900,000 children were found to be victims of abuse. U.S. Department of Health and Human Services, Administration for Children and Families, *Child Maltreatment 2005* (Washington, D.C.: U.S. Government Printing Office, 2007). Over half of the reports were made by professionals, including educators, police, lawyers, and social services staff. *See also* Charol Shakeshaft, *Educator Sexual Misconduct: A Synthesis of Existing Literature* (Washington, D.C.: U.S. Office of Education, 2004). This report is a national study of child abuse in schools conducted under the requirements of § 5414 of the Elementary and Secondary Education Act of 1965, amended by No Child Left Behind Act of 2001, 20 U.S.C. § 6301 *Ct seq*; (2007).

negligence in failing to make such reports.[155] Additionally, school systems may impose disciplinary measures against a teacher who does not follow the mandates of the law. The Seventh Circuit upheld the suspension and demotion of a teacher-psychologist for not promptly reporting suspected abuse.[156] The court rejected the teacher's claim to a federal right of confidentiality, noting the state's compelling interest to protect children from mistreatment.

Although specific aspects of the laws may vary from one state to another, definitions of abuse and neglect often are based on the federal Child Abuse Prevention and Treatment Act (CAPTA) of 1974, which provides funds to identify, treat, and prevent abuse. CAPTA identifies child abuse and neglect as:

> the physical or mental injury, sexual abuse or exploitation, negligent treatment, or maltreatment of a child under the age of eighteen, or the age specified by the child protection law of the state in question, by a person who is responsible for the child's welfare under the circumstances which indicate that the child's health or welfare is harmed or threatened thereby.[157]

Several common elements are found in state child abuse statutes. The laws mandate that certain professionals such as doctors, nurses, and educators report suspected abuse. Statutes do not require that reporters have absolute knowledge, but rather "reasonable cause to believe" or "reason to believe" that a child has been abused or neglected.[158] Once abuse is suspected, the report must be made immediately to the designated child protection agency, department of welfare, or law enforcement unit as specified in state law. All states grant immunity from civil and criminal liability to individuals if reports are made in good faith.[159]

School districts often establish reporting procedures that require teachers to report suspected abuse to the school principal or school social worker. However, if statutory provisions specify that teachers must promptly report suspected abuse to another agency or law enforcement, teachers are not relieved of their individual obligation to report to state authorities. Furthermore, the Kentucky Supreme Court

---

[155]The Ohio Supreme Court ruled that a school system and its employees did not have sovereign immunity for damages when state law expressly imposed liability for failure to report suspected abuse. Campbell v. Burton, 750 N.E.2d 539 (Ohio 2001). In a subsequent ruling, the Ohio high court held that a school board may be held liable if it fails to file a sexual abuse report and the suspected teacher later abuses another student. Yates v. Mansfield Bd. of Educ., 808 N.E.2d 861 (Ohio 2004). *See also* Chapter 13 for discussion of the elements of negligence.

[156]Pesce v. J. Sterling Morton High Sch. Dist. 201, 830 F.2d 789 (7th Cir. 1987). *See also* State v. Grover, 437 N.W.2d 60 (Minn. 1989) (finding the principal criminally negligent for failure to report child abuse by a teacher).

[157]42 U.S.C. § 5101 (2007).

[158]*See, e.g.*, Kimberly S.M. v. Bradford Cent. Sch., 649 N.Y.S.2d 588 (App. Div. 1996). *See also* Hughes v. Stanley County Sch. Dist., 638 N.W.2d 50 (S.D. 2001) (finding that the school board lacked evidence to support its allegation that a teacher failed to report suspected abuse).

[159]*See, e.g.*, Landstrom v. Ill. Dep't of Children and Family Servs., 892 F.2d 670 (7th Cir. 1990); Liedtke v. Carrington, 763 N.E.2d 213 (Ohio Ct. App. 2001).

held that reporting to a supervisor then imposes a burden on the supervisor to make a separate report.[160] Some state laws do relieve teachers of the obligation to report if someone else has already reported or will be reporting the incident. But teachers should always follow up to ensure the report was made to the appropriate agency.

State laws are explicit on reporting requirements for suspected child abuse, but it is difficult to prove that a teacher had sufficient knowledge of abuse to trigger legal liability for failure to report. Therefore, it is desirable for school officials to establish policies and procedures to encourage effective reporting. The pervasiveness of the problem and concern about the lack of reporting by teachers also indicate a need for in-service programs to assist teachers in recognizing signs of abuse and neglect in children.

Recent litigation has not involved so much the failure of teachers to report but rather allegations that educators are the abusers. These cases have received substantial publicity and raised questions regarding the duties of teachers, administrators, and school boards to report suspicions of abuse and to prevent such abuse by employees from occurring in the school setting.

Litigation has addressed whether a school district's failure to protect students from suspected abuse by school employees violates students' constitutional or statutory rights.[161] Damages can be sought under the Civil Rights Act of 1871, 42 U.S.C. Section 1983, if a claimant has been deprived of a federally protected right by an individual acting under official state policy or custom.[162] Although the Supreme Court did not find a violation of a federal right in a case involving a social worker's failure to intervene when she knew a child was being severely beaten by his father (a private individual), abuse in the school setting involves actions by public employees.[163] The Third Circuit recognized a clearly established constitutional right to bodily security—to be free from sexual abuse—and found that school districts may violate this right by maintaining a policy, practice, or custom reflecting "deliberate indifference" to this right. The court concluded that the student's evidence showing that school officials' actions in discouraging and minimizing reports of sexual misconduct by teachers and failing to take action on complaints may have established a custom or practice in violation of Section 1983.[164] If school officials do not have knowledge of abuse or act with indifference to complaints, liability will not be assessed.[165]

---

[160]Commonwealth v. Allen, 980 S.W.2d 278 (Ky. 1998). *See also* Barber v. State, 592 So. 2d 330 (Fla. Dist. Ct. App. 1992) (noting that requiring multiple reports of the same incident of abuse demonstrates the gravity of the situation).

[161]*See* Doe v. Gooden, 214 F.3d 952 (8th Cir. 2000) (ruling that failure to report suspected abuse as required by state law does not establish unconstitutional misconduct); Abeyta v. Chama Valley Indep. Sch. Dist., 77 F.3d 1253 (10th Cir. 1996) (holding that sex-specific verbal abuse by a teacher does not give rise to a constitutional violation; calling a student a prostitute is a substantial abuse of authority but not a violation of substantive due process rights).

[162]*See* text accompanying note 107, Chapter 11.

[163]DeShaney v. Winnebago County Dep't of Soc. Servs., 489 U.S. 189 (1989).

[164]Stoneking v. Bradford Area Sch. Dist., 882 F.2d 720 (3d Cir. 1989). For a definition of the "deliberate indifference" standard, *see* City of Canton, Ohio v. Harris, 489 U.S. 378 (1989).

[165]*See, e.g.*, P.H. v. Sch. Dist., 265 F.3d 653 (8th Cir. 2001); Canutillo Indep. Sch. Dist. v. Leija, 101 F.3d 393 (5th Cir. 1996); Gates v. Unified Sch. Dist. No. 449, 996 F.2d 1035 (10th Cir. 1993).

To impose liability on school districts under Section 1983, students must show that the district maintained a "policy" or "custom" that deprived the students of their protected federal rights. The Eleventh Circuit did not find that a policy or custom existed when school officials consistently followed up on every complaint against a teacher. Evidence in the case did not show deliberate indifference, which could have been used to establish a "custom."[166] However, in denying summary judgment in a Section 1983 suit, the Sixth Circuit concluded that a "custom" of inaction had been established when school officials repeatedly ignored and covered up a teacher's misconduct over a lengthy period of time.[167] With the pattern of complaints and inappropriate behavior, the school district was on notice that the teacher posed a threat to the welfare of students; the unreasonable responses showed deliberate indifference.

With the judicial recognition that sexual abuse by school employees can result in school district liability, school boards are developing and implementing policies for handling child abuse complaints and protecting teachers and other school employees from becoming the targets of false child abuse charges. It is becoming increasingly common for school boards to prohibit physical contact between teachers and students in the absence of another adult and to place restrictions on private meetings between students and teachers before or after school. Employees can face disciplinary action for failing to comply with such directives,[168] even if they are not found guilty of actual child abuse.

Conclusion

Except for certain limitations imposed by constitutional provisions and federal civil rights laws, state statutes govern educators' employment. The state prescribes general requirements for certification, contracts, tenure, and employment. Local school boards must follow state mandates and, in addition, may impose other requirements. In general, the following terms and conditions govern teacher employment.

1. The state establishes minimum qualifications for certification, which may include professional preparation, a minimum age, U.S. citizenship, good moral character, signing a loyalty oath, and passing an academic examination.
2. A teacher must acquire a valid certificate to teach in public schools.
3. Certification does not assure employment in a state.
4. Certification may be revoked for cause, generally identified in state law.
5. School boards are vested with the power to appoint teachers and to establish professional and academic employment standards above the state minimums.

---

[166]Sauls v. Pierce County Sch. Dist., 399 F.3d 1279 (11th Cir. 2005). *See also* Kline *ex rel.* Arndt v. Mansfield, 454 F. Supp. 2d 258 (E.D. Pa. 2006) *judgment aff'd*, 2007 WL 4171108 (3d Cir. 2007).

[167]Doe v. Warren Consol. Schs., 93 Fed. Appx. 812 (6th Cir. 2004).

[168]See *In re* Binghamton City Sch. Dist., 823 N.Y.S.2d 231 (App. Div. 2006).

6. Courts generally have upheld school board residency requirements, reasonable health and physical standards, and background checks prior to employment if formulated on a reasonable basis.

7. A teacher may be assigned or transferred to any school or grade at the board's discretion, as long as the assignment is within the teacher's certification area and not circumscribed by contract terms.

8. School officials can make reasonable and appropriate extracurricular assignments.

9. Teacher contracts must satisfy the general principles of contract law as well as conform to any additional specifications contained in state law.

10. Tenure is a statutory right ensuring that dismissal is based on adequate cause and accompanied by procedural due process.

11. Tenure must be conferred in accordance with statutory provisions.

12. Supplemental contracts for extra-duty assignments are generally outside the scope of tenure laws.

13. A school board's broad authority to determine teacher performance standards may be restricted by state-imposed evaluation requirements.

14. Maintenance, access, and dissemination of personnel information must conform to state law and contractual agreements.

15. Personnel records can be subpoenaed to assess discrimination charges.

16. Educators must comply with the federal copyright law; copyrighted materials may be used for instructional purposes without the publisher's permission if "fair use" guidelines are followed.

17. All states have laws requiring teachers to report suspected child abuse and granting immunity from liability if reports are made in good faith.

18. School districts will be held liable for teacher harassment or abuse of students if someone in a position of authority to take corrective measures has actual knowledge of the abuse and responds with deliberate indifference.

9

Teachers' Substantive Constitutional Rights

Although statutory law is prominent in defining specific terms and conditions of employment, substantive rights also are conferred on public employees by the Federal Constitution. These rights cannot be abridged by state or school board action without an overriding governmental interest, nor can employment be conditioned on their relinquishment. The exercise of these protected rights often results in conflicts between school officials and teachers which require judicial resolution.

This chapter presents an overview of the scope of teachers' constitutional rights as defined by the judiciary in connection with free expression, academic freedom, freedom of association, freedom of choice in appearance, and privacy rights. Some of the cases do not involve school situations, but the legal principles apply to all public employees. Constitutional rights pertaining to equal protection, due process, and religious guarantees as well as remedies available to aggrieved employees are discussed in other chapters.

Freedom of Expression

Until the mid-twentieth century, it was generally accepted that public school teachers could be dismissed or disciplined for expressing views considered objectionable by the school board. The private-sector practice of firing such employees was assumed to apply to public employment as well. Although it is now clearly established that freedom of expression is not forfeited by accepting public school employment, courts have acknowledged that this right must be weighed against the school district's interest in maintaining an effective and efficient school system. In this section, the evolution of legal principles and their application to specific school situations are reviewed.

Legal Principles

Similar to student free speech cases, an initial determination must be made regarding whether the public employee's claim involves expression *at all*. Expressive conduct is protected by the First Amendment, but the Supreme Court has emphasized that not all conduct is considered speech. An action constitutes expression for First Amendment purposes only if it attempts "to convey a particularized message" that will likely be understood by those receiving the message.[1]

In the landmark 1968 decision, *Pickering v. Board of Education*, the Supreme Court recognized that teachers have a First Amendment right to air their views on matters of public concern.[2] Pickering wrote a letter to a local newspaper, criticizing the school board's fiscal policies, especially the allocation of funds between the education and athletic programs. The school board dismissed Pickering because of the letter, which included false statements allegedly damaging the reputations of school board members and district administrators, and the Illinois courts upheld his dismissal.

Reversing the state courts, the Supreme Court first identified expression pertaining to matters of public concern as constitutionally protected and reasoned that the funding and allocation issues raised by Pickering were clearly questions of public interest requiring free and open debate. The Court then applied a balancing test, weighing the teacher's interest in expressing his views on public issues against the school board's interest in providing educational services. The Court recognized that the school board would prevail if Pickering's exercise of protected expression jeopardized his classroom performance, relationships with his immediate supervisor or coworkers, or school operations. Concluding that Pickering's letter did not have a detrimental effect in any of these areas, the Court found no justification for limiting his contribution to public debate. Indeed, the Court noted that a teacher's role provides a special vantage point from which to formulate "informed and definite opinions" on the allocation of school district funds, thus making it essential for teachers to be able to speak about public issues without fear of reprisal, unless the false statements are "knowingly or recklessly" made.[3]

Since *Pickering*, teachers have frequently challenged dismissals or other disciplinary actions on grounds that their exercise of protected expression elicited adverse employment consequences. In 1977, the Supreme Court in *Mt. Healthy City School*

[1] Texas v. Johnson, 491 U.S. 397, 404 (1989). *See also* United States v. O'Brien, 391 U.S. 367, 376 (1968). Conduct that does not possess sufficient communicative elements is not shielded by the First Amendment. *See, e.g.*, Montanye v. Wissahickon Sch. Dist., 218 Fed. Appx. 126 (3d Cir. 2007) (finding a teacher's actions in scheduling a student's therapy sessions, transporting the student to those sessions, and attending some of the sessions did not involve intent to convey any message deserving First Amendment protection).

[2] 391 U.S. 563 (1968). *See also* Givhan v. W. Line Consol. Sch. Dist., 439 U.S. 410 (1979) (concluding that as long as the expression pertains to matters of public concern, rather than personal grievances, statements made in private or through a public medium are constitutionally protected; the forum where the expression occurs does not determine whether it is of public or private interest).

[3] *Pickering*, 391 U.S. at 572, 574. *See also* Bd. of County Comm'rs v. Umbehr, 518 U.S. 668 (1996) (holding that independent contractors are considered the same as public employees in weighing the government's interests against the contractors' free speech interests under the *Pickering* balancing test).

District v. Doyle established the principle that a public educator can be disciplined or dismissed if sufficient cause exists *independent* of the exercise of protected speech. In this case, a school board voted not to renew the contract of a nontenured teacher who had made a telephone call to a local radio station to comment on a proposed teacher grooming code. The teacher had been involved in several previous incidents, but in not renewing his contract the board cited "lack of tact in handling professional matters" with reference only to the radio call and obscene gestures made to several female students.[4] The lower courts ruled in favor of the teacher, but the Supreme Court reversed and remanded the case. The Court held that on remand the burden of proof is on the employee to show that the speech was constitutionally protected and was a substantial or motivating factor in the school board's adverse action. Once established, the burden then shifts to the school board to show by a preponderance of evidence that it would have reached the same decision in the absence of the teacher's exercise of protected speech. The Supreme Court reasoned that protected expression should not place a public employee in a better or worse position with regard to continued employment. On remand, the board established that there were sufficient grounds other than the radio station call to justify the teacher's nonrenewal.[5]

In a significant 1983 decision, *Connick v. Myers*, the Supreme Court's interpretation of the *Pickering* balancing test narrowed the circumstances under which public employees can prevail in free expression cases.[6] Of particular importance was the Court's conclusion that the *form* and *context* as well as the content of the expression should be considered in assessing whether it relates to matters of public concern or to personal grievances that are not protected by the First Amendment. Thus, the Court indicated that the factors applied under the *Pickering* balancing test to determine whether speech negatively affects governmental interests can be considered in the *initial* assessment of whether the expression informs public debate. If the expression is simply a personal grievance, the constitutional analysis ends.

In *Connick*, an assistant district attorney was dissatisfied with her proposed transfer and circulated to coworkers a questionnaire concerning office operations and morale, level of confidence in supervisors, and pressure to work in political campaigns. She was subsequently terminated and challenged the action as violating her First Amendment rights. Reversing the lower courts, the Supreme Court ruled that the questionnaire related primarily to a personal employment grievance rather than matters of public interest. Only one question (regarding pressure to participate in political campaigns) was found to involve a public issue. Weighing various factors— the importance of close working relationships to fulfill public responsibilities, the employee's attempt to solicit a vote of no confidence in the district attorney, distribution of the questionnaire during office hours, the district attorney's conclusion that his office operations were endangered, and the questionnaire's limited connection to a

[4]429 U.S. 274, 282 (1977).

[5]Doyle v. Mt. Healthy City Sch. Dist., 670 F.2d 59 (6th Cir. 1982).

[6]461 U.S. 138 (1983).

public concern—the Court concluded that the employee's dismissal did not offend the First Amendment.

In 1994, the Supreme Court again addressed the scope of public employees' free speech rights in *Waters v. Churchill.*[7] Churchill, a nurse at a public hospital, was discharged for making critical comments about hospital operations to a coworker during a break. The comments were overheard by other coworkers, and although there was dispute about the exact nature of the comments, Churchill's supervisors maintained that the expression disrupted the work environment. Reversing the Seventh Circuit's decision, the Supreme Court plurality categorized Churchill's expression about the hospital's training policy and its impact on patient care as criticisms of her employer rather than comments on matters of public concern. The plurality further concluded that as long as the employer conducted an investigation and acted in good faith, it could discharge an employee for remarks it *believed* were made, regardless of what was actually said. In short, a government employer can reach its factual conclusions without being held to the evidentiary rules that courts must follow.

In 2006, the Supreme rendered *Garcetti v. Ceballos*, adding another threshold question in assessing constitutional protection of public employees' expression and making it even more difficult for public employees to prevail in claims that their expression rights have been abridged (see Figure 9.1).[8] The Court established a bright-line rule that expression pursuant to official job responsibilities is not protected. Thus, whether the employee is speaking as a private citizen or as an employee is the first consideration, because if speaking as an employee, there is no further constitutional assessment.

In *Garcetti*, the Supreme Court ruled five-to-four that the district attorney's office did not impair the free speech rights of Ceballos, an assistant district attorney, by allegedly retaliating against him for writing a memorandum indicating that the arresting deputy sheriff may have lied in the search warrant affidavit in a criminal case. Ceballos informed the defense counsel of his belief that the affidavit included false statements, and the defense subpoenaed Ceballos to testify at the hearing in which the warrant was unsuccessfully challenged. Ceballos alleged that he subsequently was mistreated by superiors, denied a promotion, given an undesirable transfer, and retaliated against in other ways.

The Ninth Circuit ruled in favor of Ceballos, but the Supreme Court reversed, reasoning that Ceballos was speaking about a task he was paid to perform and concluding that "when public employees make statements pursuant to their official duties, . . . the Constitution does not insulate their communications from employer discipline."[9] Whereas the Ninth Circuit placed its emphasis on whether the expression was of public or private concern, the Supreme Court majority placed its emphasis on

[7]511 U.S. 661 (1994). *See also* Rankin v. McPherson, 483 U.S. 378, 380 (1987) (assessing the content, form, and context of a public employee's pejorative statement to a coworker following the assassination attempt on President Reagan and finding no basis for the employee's dismissal in the absence of the expression interfering with job performance).
[8]126 S. Ct. 1951 (2006).
[9]*Id.* at 1960.

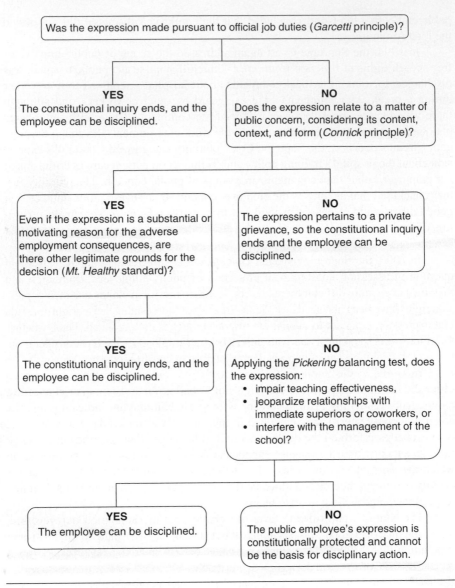

FIGURE 9.1   *Analyzing Public Educators' Expression Rights*

whether the public employee was speaking as a citizen or in the context of job duties. The Court majority reiterated that the forum where the comments were made—inside the workplace—was not the central consideration, but rather the controlling factor was whether the expression occurred as part of official responsibilities.[10]

---

[10]*Id.* at 1959–1961. But the Court specifically left open whether its analysis would apply to speech related to instruction. *Id.* at 1962, *infra* text accompanying note 67.

Application of the Legal Principles

For almost 15 years following *Pickering*, lower courts broadly interpreted what constitutes expression relating to matters of public concern that is entitled to constitutional protection. During the 1970s and early 1980s, for example, courts relied on the *Pickering* balancing test in upholding public school teachers' rights to express their views on matters of public interest, such as wearing black arm bands as a symbolic protest against the Vietnam War,[11] making public comments favoring a collective bargaining contract,[12] and criticizing the instructional program and other school policies.[13]

Since the early 1980s, however, courts have seemed increasingly inclined to view teachers' and other public employees' expression as relating to *private* employment disputes, rather than to matters of public concern. Many courts relied on *Connick*[14] in broadly interpreting what falls in the category of unprotected private grievances. To illustrate, courts considered the following expression to be unprotected: discussing salaries during a lunch break;[15] filing a grievance about being assigned a job-sharing teaching position,[16] accusing the superintendent of inciting student disturbances;[17] sending sarcastic, critical memoranda to school officials;[18] protesting unfavorable performance evaluations;[19] criticizing harassment and oppression at the high school in a faculty newsletter;[20] commenting about students' test scores after being instructed by the superintendent not to speak publicly on this

[11]*See* James v. Bd. of Educ., 461 F.2d 566 (2d Cir. 1972).

[12]*See* McGill v. Bd. of Educ., 602 F.2d 774 (7th Cir. 1979).

[13]*See* Lemons v. Morgan, 629 F.2d 1389 (8th Cir. 1980); Bernasconi v. Tempe Elementary Sch. Dist. No. 3, 548 F.2d 857 (9th Cir. 1977).

[14]461 U.S. 138 (1983).

[15]Koehn v. Indian Hills Cmty. Coll., 371 F.3d 394 (8th Cir. 2004).

[16]Renfroe v. Kirkpatrick, 722 F.2d 714 (11th Cir. 1984). *See also* Ferrara v. Mills, 781 F.2d 1508 (11th Cir. 1986) (holding that complaints about a policy allowing students to select their subjects and teachers and about the hiring of coaches to teach social studies did not implicate public concerns).

[17]Stevenson v. Lower Marion County Sch. Dist. No. 3, 327 S.E.2d 656 (S.C. 1985). *See also* Ifill v. District of Columbia, 665 A.2d 185 (D.C. 1995) (holding that an employee's communication with school officials regarding dissatisfaction with the work environment dealt with a private grievance).

[18]Hesse v. Bd. of Educ., 848 F.2d 748 (7th Cir. 1988). *See also* Mitchell v. Hillsborough County, 468 F.3d 1276 (11th Cir. 2006) (finding that a public employee's vulgar and tasteless comments about a female commissioner did not pertain to a public concern and could be the basis for dismissal).

[19]Day v. S. Park Indep. Sch. Dist., 768 F.2d 696 (5th Cir. 1985). *See also* Roberts v. Van Buren Pub. Schs., 773 F.2d 949 (8th Cir. 1985) (holding that a grievance expressing elementary teachers' dissatisfaction with the way parental complaints concerning a field trip had been handled pertained more to the teacher/principal relationship than to a public concern).

[20]Sanguigni v. Pittsburgh Bd. of Educ., 968 F.2d 393 (3d Cir.1992). *See also* Patterson v. Masem, 774 F.2d 251 (8th Cir. 1985) (holding that denial of a promotion to a supervisory role was not impermissible retaliation for the teacher recommending that an allegedly racially offensive play not be performed).

topic;[21] and filing a grievance with the teachers' union about the individual's performance rating.[22]

Some courts, however, applied the public/private distinction and found specific expression to pertain to matters of public concern and warrant constitutional protection.[23] Prior to the Supreme Court's 2006 decision in *Garcetti v. Ceballos*,[24] courts often afforded First Amendment protection to public educators who blew the whistle on unlawful or unethical school practices, even though such expression pertained to their job responsibilities. For example, federal appellate courts considered the following to be protected expression: a former assistant principal's complaints about a suspected cheating scheme involving student achievement tests,[25] a special education teacher's assertions that the adapted physical education program violated federal law,[26] and a school nurse's criticisms of immunization practices, the heavy nursing caseload, and student safety.[27] Federal appeals courts also ruled that the following expression could not be the basis for dismissal or other disciplinary action against public educators: criticizing a cutback in the district's high school reading program and filing several grievances with the teachers' union,[28] protesting the school board's decision to cancel an art program serving predominantly minority children,[29] writing

---

[21]Partee v. Metro. Sch. Dist., 954 F.2d 454 (7th Cir. 1992).

[22]Griffin v. Thomas, 929 F.2d 1210 (7th Cir. 1991). For an analysis of pre-*Garcetti* Free Speech Clause cases involving teachers that narrowly define what constitutes "matters of public concern," *see* Karen C. Daly, "Balancing Act: Teachers' Classroom Speech and the First Amendment," *Journal of Law & Education*, vol. 30 (2001), pp. 1–62.

[23]The Sixth Circuit in 2001 declared that "the key question is not whether a person is speaking in his role as an employee or a citizen, but whether the employee's speech in fact touches on matters of public concern." Cockrel v. Shelby County Sch. Dist., 270 F.3d 1036, 1052 (6th Cir. 2001) (citing Connick v. Myers, 461 U.S. 138, 148–149 (1983)); *infra* text accompanying note 66.

[24]126 S. Ct. 1951 (2006); *supra* text accompanying note 8.

[25]Canary v. Osborn, 211 F.3d 324 (6th Cir. 2000). *See also* Taylor v. Chief of Police, 338 F.3d 639 (6th Cir. 2003) (finding officers' report written in the course of their employment to be protected speech because it was intended to communicate potential wrongdoing of a fellow officer, which was a matter of public concern); Delgado v. Jones, 282 F.3d 511 (7th Cir. 2002) (holding that a public employee was retaliated against in violation of the First Amendment for a memorandum alleging criminal activities involving a close relative of an elected official).

[26]Settlegoode v. Portland Pub. Schs., 371 F.3d 503 (9th Cir. 2004) (denying defendants' request for qualified immunity, entitling the teacher to the full jury award, including punitive damages, assessed against the school administrators for the violation of her constitutional rights).

[27]Stever v. Indep. Sch. Dist. No. 625, 943 F.2d 845 (8th Cir. 1991). *See also* McGreevy v. Stroup, 413 F.3d 359 (3d Cir. 2005) (finding that a school nurse's low ratings were in retaliation for speaking out on behalf of two students with disabilities and objecting to pesticide spraying by an unlicensed person).

[28]Fishman v. Clancy, 763 F.2d 485 (1st Cir. 1985). *See also* Cox v. Dardanelle Pub. Sch. Dist., 790 F.2d 668 (8th Cir. 1986) (finding a First Amendment violation in the nonrenewal of a teacher's contract for criticizing the principal's administrative style).

[29]Tompkins v. Vickers, 26 F.3d 603 (5th Cir. 1994). *See also* Kennedy v. Tangipahoa Parish Library Bd., 224 F.3d 359 (5th Cir. 2000) (ruling that a public library employee was unconstitutionally demoted and then terminated because of expressing apprehension about employee safety following the workplace rape of a coworker).

to the state department of education about the district's delay in implementing programs for children with disabilities,[30] and criticizing the school district's method of disciplining students.[31] In a case rendered shortly before *Garcetti*, the Second Circuit ruled that a high school athletic director's critical statements about hazing on the football team pertained to a public concern and could not be the basis for abolishing the athletic director's position.[32] In all of these cases, the expression at issue related to the employee's job, and none of the judicial rulings found the expression unprotected because it occurred pursuant to work responsibilities. However, the continued vitality of these rulings under the *Garcetti* precedent is uncertain.

    Garcetti calls into question the public/private distinction as the guiding consideration and has added another initial consideration in deciding whether a public employee's expression will evoke the *Pickering* balancing test (see Figure 9.1). If the expression is made pursuant to official job responsibilities, it is not protected, and it is thus unnecessary to establish that the expression pertains to a private grievance or has a negative impact on agency operations. The content of the expression appeared to be the crucial consideration prior to the *Garcetti* ruling, but the role of the speaker now seems to trump the content.[33] The broad protection once given to public educators' expression under *Pickering* now is available only if the expression (1) does not occur pursuant to official duties, (2) relates to a public concern (considering its context and form as well as its content), and (3) is the motivating factor in the adverse employment action. *Pickering* has not been overturned, but far fewer circumstances trigger its balancing test.

    In post-*Garcetti* decisions, courts have tended to focus on whether the expression was pursuant to job responsibilities in rejecting First Amendment claims. Whistle-blowers have not been as successful in securing legal redress for retaliation

---

[30]Southside Pub. Schs. v. Hill, 827 F.2d 270 (8th Cir. 1987). *See also* Herts v. Smith, 345 F.3d 581 (8th Cir. 2003) (ruling that a school superintendent's contract was unconstitutionally not renewed due to his testimony in a desegregation case involving the district).

[31]Rankin v. Indep. Sch. Dist. No. 1-3, 876 F.2d 838 (10th Cir. 1989). *See also* Cook v. Gwinnett County Sch. Dist., 414 F.3d 1313 (11th Cir. 2005) (finding that a school bus driver's free speech interest in raising safety concerns outweighed the scant evidence that the employee's expression impeded workplace efficiency).

[32]Cioffi v. Averill Park Cent. Sch. Dist., 444 F.3d 158 (2d Cir. 2006), *cert. denied,* 127 S. Ct. 382 (2006) (while vacating summary judgment for the school district and board, the court granted summary judgment for the board president and superintendent on immunity grounds).

[33]Even prior to *Garcetti,* courts recognized that public employees in policy-making roles relinquished some free speech rights because of the impact of their expression on agency operations. *See, e.g.,* Sharp v. Lindsey, 285 F.3d 479 (6th Cir. 2002) (finding that a tension-free superintendent/principal relationship justified reassigning a principal to a teaching role after a public disagreement regarding the district's new dress code); Vargas-Harrison v. Racine Unified Sch. Dist., 272 F.3d 964 (7th Cir. 2001) (upholding demotion of a principal, who occupied a policy-making role, for expression critical of superiors' policies); Pahmeier v. Marion Cmty. Schs., No. 1:04-CV-365-TS, 2006 U.S. Dist. LEXIS 24048 (N.D. Ind. Mar. 17, 2006) (holding that a high school principal's wearing a red sweatshirt in solidarity with teachers at a public meeting to protest closing her school was not protected expression, since the principal occupied a policy-making role).

as they were prior to *Garcetti*. For example, the Fifth Circuit held that an athletic director who wrote a letter to the school's office manager about appropriations for athletic activities was speaking pursuant to his official duties and could not claim retaliation for being removed from the athletic director position and for his contract not being renewed.[34] The Eleventh Circuit similarly found that a teacher's questions about the fairness of cheerleading tryouts pertained to her duties as a cheerleading sponsor and were not protected expression relating to educational quality issues as she claimed.[35] The Tenth Circuit also ruled that a superintendent's comments about the Head Start program and possible violations of federal law were not protected as they were made in the course of her job duties,[36] and a Delaware federal district court ruled that a school psychologist's complaints about the school's noncompliance with the Individuals with Disabilities Education Act pertained to his job assignment and were not protected by the First Amendment.[37]

     Even where whistle-blowing is not at issue, public school personnel often have not prevailed in their recent free speech claims because courts have concluded that the expression at issue was pursuant to official job duties. To Illustrate, the Eleventh Circuit rejected a terminated principal's claim that the Florida school board violated his First Amendment speech and association rights and his right to petition the government for redress of grievances.[38] He claimed that he was unconstitutionally terminated in retaliation for urging his teachers to support conversion of their school to a charter school. Noting that *Garcetti* shifted the threshold question from whether the employee is speaking on a matter of public concern to whether the employee is speaking as a private citizen, the Eleventh Circuit concluded that the principal was speaking in his professional role in seeking charter school status. Thus, his expression was not protected and could be the basis for dismissal. The court further found

---

[34]Williams v. Dallas Indep. Sch. Dist., 480 F.3d 689 (5th Cir. 2007).

[35]Gilder-Lucas v. Elmore County Bd. of Educ., 186 Fed. Appx. 885 (11th Cir. 2006). *See also* Posey v. Lake Pend Oreille Sch. Dist. No. 84, No. CV05-272-N-EJL, 2007 U.S. Dist. LEXIS 7829 (D. Idaho Feb. 2, 2007) (holding that a school district parking lot attendant's complaints about safety issues were pursuant to his job so he could not allege that his position was eliminated in retaliation for his expression); Cole v. Anne Arundel County Bd. of Educ., No. CCB-05-1579, 2006 U.S. Dist. LEXIS 89426 (D. Md. Nov. 30, 2006) (holding that a school bus driver who complained about bus safety was speaking pursuant to her official duties and could not claim retaliation for the expression).

[36]Casey v. W. Las Vegas Indep. Sch. Dist., 473 F.3d 1323 (10th Cir. 2007) (holding, however, that her comments about the New Mexico Open Meetings Act were outside the scope of her job, so her claim of retaliation for those comments may be legally viable).

[37]Houlihan v. Sussex Technical Sch. Dist., 461 F. Supp. 2d 252 (D. Del. 2006) (holding, however, that the school psychologist stated a valid cause of action for retaliation under the federal Rehabilitation Act, so the school district's motion to dismiss her claim under this law was denied). *See also* Pagani v. Meriden Bd. of Educ., No. 3:05-CV-01115 (JCH), 2006 U.S. Dist. LEXIS 92267 (D. Conn. Dec. 19, 2006) (finding a teacher's report to the Department of Children and Families, that a substitute teacher showed nude photos of himself with female students, was made under the auspices of official responsibilities; the teacher could not claim retaliation for making the report after superiors advised him not to contact the agency).

[38]D'Angelo v. Sch. Bd., 497 F.3d 1203 (11th Cir. 2007).

no evidence that the school board violated the principal's rights to association or to petition the government.

Some employees, however, have succeeded in their expression claims in post-*Garcetti* cases. For example, the Sixth Circuit ruled in favor of a superintendent who claimed that he was not named Director of Schools when the superintendent position was abolished because he expressed his view that associating with homosexuals is not immoral or improper, which the court considered a matter of public concern. The court reasoned that board members were not entitled to qualified immunity because the superintendent's expression rights were clearly established.[39] A North Carolina federal district court also found a principal's expressed concerns that a new school district policy would hurt overall student test scores of her elementary school to be a public issue, which could not be the basis for offering her a two-year instead of the promised four-year contract.[40] But the court noted that the record was not sufficiently developed regarding whether the expression was made pursuant to her official duties. A Delaware federal district court concluded that a teacher's journal documenting his co-teacher's tardiness and other unprofessional conduct was not written pursuant to official duties because he was not hired to evaluate other teachers and evaluation of teacher performance is a matter of public concern. Thus, his refusal to reveal to the principal the name of the person who instructed him to keep the journal could not be the basis for retaliation, including not renewing his contract.[41]

Even if protected speech is involved, courts have relied on *Mt. Healthy* to uphold terminations or transfers where other legitimate reasons justify the personnel actions. In an illustrative case, a principal who gave a speech at a public hearing expressing opposition to closing a school was demoted to a teaching position. He claimed retaliation for his protected expression, but a Kentucky federal court found no evidence that the speech was the motivating factor in the demotion.[42] The Seventh Circuit also rejected a teacher's challenge to disciplinary action for her critical comments pertaining to the need for additional textbooks at her school. The court ruled that the teacher failed to prove that her speech was a substantial or motivating factor

[39]Scarbrough v. Morgan County Bd. of Educ., 470 F.3d 250 (6th Cir. 2006).

[40]Locklear v. Person County of Educ., No. 1:05CV00255, 2006 U.S. Dist. LEXIS 42203 (M.D.N.C. June 22, 2006). *See also* Barclay v. Michalsky, 451 F. Supp. 2d 386 (D. Conn. 2006) (finding factual issues regarding whether a public employee's expression on public concerns regarding poor practices at a mental health hospital were made in the context of her job responsibilities to preclude summary judgment based on *Garcetti*).

[41]Wilcoxon v. Red Clay Consol. Sch. Dist., 437 F. Supp. 2d 235 (D. Del. 2006). *See also* McGuire v. Warren, 207 Fed. Appx. 34 (2d Cir. 2006), *on remand,* 490 F. Supp. 2d 331 (S.D.N.Y. 2007) (allowing the public employee to amend her complaint to establish that termination of her contract to provide student services was in retaliation for protected speech pertaining to criticism of the school district's services for special needs children).

[42]Painter v. Campbell County Bd. of Educ., 417 F. Supp. 2d 854 (E.D. Ky. 2006). *See also* Phelps v. Fullenwider, 126 Fed. Appx. 381 (9th Cir. 2005) (rejecting claim that protected speech was the motivating reason for a school employee's dismissal; finding that parental complaints of inappropriate behavior with students justified the personnel decision); Flath v. Garrison Pub. Sch. Dist., 82 F.3d 244 (8th Cir. 1996) (holding that a teacher who failed to show her nonrenewal was substantially motivated by her criticism of the principal).

in the disciplinary action, given the well-documented incidents of the teacher's misconduct or insubordination.[43] The Tenth Circuit similarly found that a director of bilingual education could not establish that speaking about the program's noncompliance with state guidelines and writing a letter to the editor of the local newspaper were the motivating factors in her termination and held instead that poor job performance justified the action.[44]

School authorities cannot rely on *Mt. Healthy* to justify termination or other disciplinary action if the school officials' stated reasons for personnel decisions are merely a pretext to restrict protected expression. For example, the Seventh Circuit held that a counselor, allegedly dismissed for 14 incidents of insubordination and unprofessional misconduct, was actually fired in retaliation for writing articles for the local paper, commenting to the media about violations of the open-meetings law by the school board, and engaging in other protected expression.[45]

Once determined that expression is protected, the employee then has the burden of demonstrating that it was a key factor in the dismissal or disciplinary decision. Even if established that expression on matters of public concern was the sole basis for adverse action, the public employer still may prevail under the *Pickering* balancing test by showing that its interests in protecting the public agency outweigh the individual's free speech rights.[46]

Prior Restraint and Channel Rules

Although *reprisals* for expression have been the focus of most litigation, courts also have addressed *prior restraints* on public employees' expression and restrictions on the channels through which views may be aired. The judiciary has been more reluctant to condone such prior restraints on expression than it has to uphold disciplinary action after the expression has occurred. A central consideration is whether the prior restraint is content based, triggering strict judicial scrutiny, or whether it is content neutral, thus receiving a "less rigorous examination."[47]

For example, the Tenth Circuit struck down a portion of an Oklahoma law authorizing the termination of teachers for "advocating . . . public or private homosexual

---

[43]Smith v. Dunn, 368 F.3d 705 (7th Cir. 2004). *See also* Love v. Chi. Bd. of Educ., 241 F.3d 564 (7th Cir. 2001) (finding teachers' dismissal was based on poor performance rather than criticism of a specific academic program and of the principal's interactions with teachers).

[44]Deschenie v. Bd. of Educ., 473 F.3d 1271 (10th Cir. 2007) (holding that the time between the expression and termination was too attenuated to show a causal connection).

[45]Dishnow v. Sch. Dist. of Rib Lake, 77 F.3d 194 (7th Cir. 1996).

[46]*See* Fales v. Garst, 235 F.3d 1122 (8th Cir. 2001) (finding teachers' interests in speaking about incidents with special education students was outweighed by school district's interest in efficiently administering the middle school, given the upheaval caused by the expression); Mataraza v. Newburgh Enlarged City Sch. Dist., 294 F. Supp. 2d 483 (S.D.N.Y. 2003) (applying the *Pickering* balancing test and upholding denial of promotion to an assistant principal whose criticisms of the district's curriculum alignment efforts would disrupt implementation of the initiative).

[47]Eclipse Enter. v. Gulotta, 134 F.3d 63, 66 (2d Cir. 1997).

activity in a manner that creates a substantial risk that such conduct will come to the attention of school children or school employees."[48] The appellate court held that such restrictions on teachers' expression could not be imposed unless shown to be necessary to prevent a disruption of school activities. The Supreme Court divided evenly in this case, thereby affirming the appellate court's ruling without setting a national precedent.

The Fifth Circuit also invalidated a school board policy requiring prior approval of all political, sectarian, or special interest materials distributed in the schools. The board had invoked the policy to prevent distribution of documents that were critical of a proposed teacher competency testing program. The court reasoned that school authorities cannot allow only one side to promote its position, noting that literature written by the school board supporting the program had been distributed in the schools. The court emphasized that the policies were not invalidated simply because they required prior approval; rather, the policies were unconstitutional because they did not "furnish sufficient guidance" to prohibit school administrators from exercising "unbridled discretion" in curtailing communication within the schools.[49]

Whether the school has created a forum for expression is important in controversies pertaining to the use of internal communication channels. In a significant 1983 decision, *Perry Education Association v. Perry Local Educators' Association*, the Supreme Court ruled that a school district is not constitutionally obligated to allow a rival teachers' union access to school mailboxes although the exclusive bargaining agent is granted such access. Holding that a public school's internal mail system is not a public forum for expression, the Court declared that "the state may reserve the forum for its intended purposes, communicative or otherwise, as long as the regulation on speech is reasonable and not an effort to suppress expression merely because public officials oppose the speaker's view."[50] The Court determined that alternative communication channels were available to the rival union.

Subsequently, the Supreme Court affirmed the Fifth Circuit's conclusion that a Texas school district had not created a public forum in either its schools or school mail facilities; therefore, the district could deny school access during school hours to representatives of teachers' organizations and could bar their use of the school mail system.[51] However, the Fifth Circuit found a First Amendment violation in school

---

[48]Nat'l Gay Task Force v. Bd. of Educ., 729 F.2d 1270, 1274 (10th Cir. 1984), *aff'd by an equally divided Court*, 470 U.S. 903 (1985).

[49]Hall v. Bd. of Sch. Comm'rs, 681 F.2d 965, 969 (5th Cir. 1982).

[50]460 U.S. 37, 46 (1983). *See* text with note 90, Chapter 12.

[51]Tex. State Teachers Ass'n v. Garland Indep. Sch. Dist., 777 F.2d 1046 (5th Cir. 1985), *aff'd mem.*, 479 U.S. 801 (1986) (holding that the school's selective visitation policy, under which certain groups of educators and representatives of textbook companies and civic and charitable groups were allowed to meet with teachers during school hours, did not create a public forum). *See also* text accompanying note 92, Chapter 12. *See also* Fla. Family Ass'n v. Sch. Bd., 494 F. Supp. 2d 1311 (M.D. Fla. 2007) (holding that the school board did not deprive family organization of its First Amendment rights by blocking its mass e-mail campaign criticizing the board's removal of religious holidays from the school calendar).

policies that denied teachers the right to discuss employee organizations during non-class time or to use school mail facilities for communications including *any* mention of such organizations.

The same court more recently reiterated that a state university's internal mail system is not a public forum and thus declined to interfere with an institution's decision to use e-mail spam guards and to cancel e-mail accounts of adjuncts during semesters they are not teaching.[52] In addition, the Fourth Circuit upheld restrictions on state employees' use of computers owned or leased by the state to access to sexually explicit materials over the Internet.[53] Also, the Seventh Circuit concluded that a part-time university employee could be required to remove a quotation she affixed to work-related e-mail messages, because the employer considered a word in the quotation to be vulgar. The court found a minimal burden on the employee's expression rights and an overriding interest in restricting inappropriate language in the workplace.[54]

Under certain circumstances, a school's mail system might be considered a public forum if school officials have designated it as such. Applying the principle articulated in *Perry*, the Fifth Circuit reasoned that a school was not obligated to open its internal mail system to the general public, but since the school had designated its mail system as a forum for all employee organizations, it could not selectively deny access to some groups.[55] The court also found the school district's guidelines, requiring prior clearance of material distributed through the mail system, to be unconstitutionally vague.

Policies limiting teachers' access to the school board also have generated legal disputes, and several courts have struck down policies prohibiting individual teachers from communicating directly with the board. In 1976, the Supreme Court held that a nonunion teacher has a free speech right to comment on a bargaining issue at a public school board meeting.[56] Subsequently, the Ninth Circuit awarded a teacher-coach damages for his suspension as a coach, which occurred because he did not advise the superintendent before writing a letter to school board members about an issue of public concern.[57] Similarly, the Seventh Circuit struck down a

---

[52]Faculty Rights Coal. v. Shahrokhi, 204 Fed. Appx. 416 (5th Cir. 2006). *See also* Educ. Minn. Lakeville v. Indep. Sch. Dist. No. 194, 341 F. Supp. 2d 1070 (D. Minn. 2004) (rejecting unions' argument that the school district's policy prohibiting the use of internal communication channels to distribute literature endorsing political candidates violated the First Amendment).

[53]Urofsky v. Gilmore, 216 F.3d 401 (4th Cir. 2000). *See also* Herbert v. Wash. St. Pub. Disclosure Comm'n, 148 P.3d 1102 (Wash. Ct. App. 2006) (finding that teachers violated state law by using school mail and e-mail, nonpublic forums, to collect signatures on petitions for ballot measures).

[54]Pichelmann v. Madsen, 31 Fed. Appx. 322 (7th Cir. 2002).

[55]Ysleta Fed'n of Teachers v. Ysleta Indep. Sch. Dist., 720 F.2d 1429 (5th Cir. 1983) (holding further that the school board had not yet produced evidence of a compelling interest for limiting employee organizations to one distribution of recruitment literature per year through the school mail system).

[56]City of Madison, Joint Sch. Dist. No. 8 v. Wis. Employment Relations Comm'n, 429 U.S. 167 (1976). *See* text accompanying note 98, Chapter 12.

[57]Anderson v. Cent. Point Sch. Dist. No. 6, 746 F.2d 505 (9th Cir. 1984).

policy requiring that all communication to the school board be directed through the superintendent and ordered a reprimand for violating the policy to be removed from a teacher's personnel file.[58]

Although prior restraints on teachers' free speech rights are vulnerable to legal attack, courts have upheld reasonable time, place, and manner regulations. Such restrictions must not be based on the content of the speech, and they must serve significant governmental interests and leave alternative communication channels open.[59] In general, time, place, and manner restrictions will be upheld if justified to prevent a disruption of the educational environment and if other avenues are available for employees to express their views.

Expressing Personal Views in the Classroom

Traditionally, it has been assumed that restrictions can be placed on teachers expressing their personal views in the classroom. Because of the captive student audience, teachers cannot use their classrooms—a nonpublic forum—to proselytize children. Since 1988, many courts have applied *Hazelwood v. Kuhlmeier* to assess the constitutionality of teachers' classroom expression of personal opinions,[60] holding that such expression could be curtailed for legitimate pedagogical reasons, an easy standard for school districts to satisfy. For example, the First Circuit held that a teacher's discussion of aborting fetuses with Down syndrome could be censored, noting that the school board may limit a teacher's classroom expression in the interest of promoting educational goals.[61] The Tenth Circuit relied on *Kuhlmeier* in upholding disciplinary action against a teacher who made comments during class about rumors that two students had engaged in sexual intercourse on the school tennis court during lunch hour, reasoning that the ninth grade government class was not a public forum.[62] Also, a Missouri federal district court upheld termination of a teacher for making disparaging classroom comments about

---

[58]Knapp v. Whitaker, 757 F.2d 827 (7th Cir. 1985), *appeal dismissed*, 474 U.S. 803 (1985). *See also* Unified Sch. Dist. No. 503 v. McKinney, 689 P.2d 860 (Kan. 1984) (finding school board guilty of unconstitutional prior restraint for forbidding teachers from speaking at school board meetings or holding press conferences in school buildings).

[59]*See, e.g.,* Godwin v. E. Baton Rouge Parish Sch. Bd., 408 So. 2d 1214 (La. 1981), *appeal dismissed*, 459 U.S. 807 (1982) (finding a ban on handheld signs in the school board offices to serve the legitimate governmental interest of ensuring that school board meetings were conducted in an orderly fashion). *See also* Partee v. Metro. Sch. Dist., 954 F.2d 454 (7th Cir. 1992); *supra* text accompanying note 21.

[60]484 U.S. 260 (1988). *See* text accompanying note 36, Chapter 4.

[61]Ward v. Hickey, 996 F.2d 448 (1st Cir. 1993).

[62]Miles v. Denver Pub. Schs., 944 F.2d 773 (10th Cir. 1991). *See also* Abeyta v. Chama Valley Indep. Sch. Dist. No. 19, 77 F.3d 1253 (10th Cir. 1996) (recognizing that while a teacher calling a student a prostitute in class would be an abuse of authority under state law, such action would not give rise to a federal claim for damages for violating substantive due process rights).

interracial relationships, finding no protected expression and noting that the teacher was aware of the district's anti-harassment policy.[63]

In several cases, public school teachers have not prevailed in their efforts to express their views in materials posted in their classrooms or on the adjacent hall walls. To illustrate, school authorities were upheld in censoring material a teacher posted outside his classroom that denounced homosexuality and extolled traditional family values to offset the school district's materials recognizing Gay and Lesbian Awareness Month.[64] Reasoning that the teacher was speaking for the school, the Ninth Circuit concluded that teachers are not entitled to express views in the classroom that are counter to the adopted curriculum. The Fourth Circuit also upheld a school board's instructions for a teacher to remove religious materials from bulletin boards in his classroom. The court concluded that the items removed (e.g., poster of George Washington praying, an article outlining religious differences among presidential candidates) were curricular in nature and constituted school-sponsored speech, so their removal did not implicate the First Amendment.[65]

The Sixth Circuit seemed to depart from the prevailing trend when it upheld a teacher's right to invite a guest speaker (actor Woody Harrelson) and present information on the industrial and environmental benefits of hemp to her fifth grade class. Even though the teacher was speaking as an employee, the court concluded that the content of her speech involved political and social concerns in the community.[66] Thus, the court found genuine issues of material fact regarding whether the school district's proffered grounds for terminating the teacher based on insubordination, conduct unbecoming a teacher, and other grounds were a pretext for the dismissal based on protected expression. The court recognized that the school district's interest in efficient and harmonious school operations did not outweigh the teacher's interests in speaking to her students about an issue of substantial concern in the state.

It is unclear how the *Garcetti* ruling will affect litigation pertaining to classroom expression. Indeed, the *Garcetti* majority emphasized that "we need not, and for that reason do not, decide whether the analysis we conduct today would apply in

---

[63]Loeffelman v. Bd. of Educ., 134 S.W.3d 637 (Mo. Ct. App. 2004). *But see* Scruggs v. Keen, 900 F. Supp. 821 (W.D. Va. 1995) (holding that a teacher's comments on interracial dating made in response to students' questions during study hall pertained to a public concern; the school district's request for summary judgment was denied because of questions regarding whether the teacher's contract was not renewed to sweep the incident under the rug or if it was based on evidence that her comments included racial slurs).

[64]Downs v. L.A. Unified Sch. Dist., 228 F.3d 1003 (9th Cir. 2000). *See also* Newton v. Slye, 116 F. Supp. 2d 677 (W.D. Va. 2000) (finding no First Amendment right for a teacher to post outside his classroom door the American Library Association's pamphlet listing banned books, which the principal and superintendent felt potentially compromised the school's family life education program and other initiatives).

[65]Lee v. York County Sch. Div., 484 F.3d 687 (4th Cir. 2007), *cert. denied*, 128 S. Ct. 387 (2007).

[66]Cockrel v. Shelby County Sch. Dist., 270 F.3d 1036 (6th Cir. 2001). *But see* Debro v. San Leandro Unified Sch. Dist., No. C-99-0676 VRW, 2001 U.S. Dist. LEXIS 17388 (N.D. Cal. Oct. 11, 2001) (holding that a teacher had no First Amendment right to depart from classroom instruction to discuss tolerance toward homosexuals, even though it is an issue of public interest).

the same manner to a case involving speech related to scholarship or teaching."[67] Thus, some ambiguity remains regarding whether courts will continue to apply *Hazelwood* or will rely on *Garcetti* in assessing teachers' expression pursuant to their instructional duties.

At least one federal appellate court has relied on *Garcetti* in this regard. The Seventh Circuit recently ruled that classroom expression clearly is part of public educators' official duties and can be censored to protect the captive student audience.[68] Accordingly, the court ruled that the teacher's expression of negative views about the war in Iraq during a current events session was not constitutionally protected. The court reasoned that *Garcetti* directly applied in this case because the teacher's current event lesson was an assigned classroom task.

Also, a few lower courts have addressed classroom expression issues. For example, a teacher in Michigan alleged that he was retaliated against after he wore a T-shirt to school that contained a printed message about the teachers' union not being under contract. The federal district court held that the T-shirt worn in his classes caused or had the potential to cause disharmony in the workplace. Although recognizing that the issue of labor negotiations touches on a matter of public concern, the court found the school district's interest in ensuring a professional workplace outweighed the teacher's rights in this instance. The court noted that under *Garcetti*, "government employers, like private employers, need a significant degree of control over their employees' words and actions; without it, there would be little chance for the efficient provision of public services."[69]

In a New York case, a teacher claimed that she was forced to resign after she refused to take down a picture of George Bush. The teacher displayed the picture during an election year and discussed her support for the incumbent. The school district argued that it had no knowledge of the teacher's political activities and requested that she either remove the picture or display one of John Kerry to appear balanced. The federal district court denied the district's summary judgment motion because issues of fact existed including the applicability of *Garcetti* in this instance.[70] Whether courts apply *Garcetti* or *Hazelwood* may have little practical significance, because teachers' classroom expression has always been subject to restrictions to protect students from proselytization.

[67]Garcetti v. Ceballos, 126 S. Ct. 1951, 1962 (2006).

[68]Mayer v. Monroe County Cmty. Sch. Corp., 474 F.3d 477 (7th Cir. 2007), *cert. denied,* 128 S. Ct. 160 (2007). *See also* Calef v. Budden, 361 F. Supp. 2d 493 (D.S.C. 2005) (upholding a school board in declining to use a substitute teacher who had worn an anti-war button to school and criticized U.S. involvement in Iraq and Panama to impressionable middle school students, which jeopardized her teaching effectiveness).

[69]Montle v. Westwood Heights Sch. Dist., 437 F. Supp. 2d 652, 654 (E.D. Mich. 2006).

[70]Caruso v. Massapequa Union Free Sch. Dist., 478 F. Supp. 2d 377 (E.D.N.Y. 2007).

Academic Freedom

From its origin in German universities, the concept of academic freedom historically was applied to postsecondary education and embodied the principle that faculty members should be free from governmental controls in conducting research and imparting knowledge to students. The concept has undergone substantial change in U.S. universities, where faculty members have claimed a First Amendment right to academic freedom in research and teaching, as well as in activities away from the classroom.

Public school teachers have asserted a similar right to academic freedom, but courts have not extended the broad protections found in higher education to public elementary and secondary schools.[71] Teachers possess judicially recognized academic interests, but courts have refrained from establishing precise legal principles in this domain. Rather, controversies have been resolved on a case-by-case basis, involving a delicate balancing of teachers' interests in academic freedom against school boards' interests in assuring an appropriate instructional program and efficient school operations.

Controversies pertaining to censorship of public school courses and materials are addressed in Chapters 2 and 3; this section concentrates specifically on public educators' academic freedom within the classroom setting. Can a teacher determine the most appropriate materials for classroom use? Is a teacher free to determine teaching methodologies? What topics or issues can a teacher discuss in a course?

Course Content

Public school teachers in elementary and secondary schools have never possessed the legal authority to determine the content of the instructional program. As discussed in Chapter 3, state legislatures have plenary power to set the public school curriculum, and they usually grant local school boards considerable authority to establish programs of study and prescribe course content, including the scope and sequence of materials. Several courts have declared that school boards are not legally obligated to accept teachers' curricular recommendations in the absence of a board policy to that effect. In an early case, the Tenth Circuit recognized the school board's authority to determine the curriculum and rejected the notion that teachers "have an unlimited liberty as to structure and content of the courses."[72] Subsequently, the Fifth Circuit

---

[71]Although generally agreed that professors in higher education have more academic freedom than public school teachers, limits can be placed on classroom activities in postsecondary institutions. *See, e.g.,* Edwards v. Cal. Univ. of Pa., 156 F.3d 488 (3d Cir. 1998) (upholding suspension of a tenured university professor for departing from the approved course syllabus and injecting religious teaching in his educational media course).

[72]Adams v. Campbell County Sch. Dist., 511 F.2d 1242, 1247 (10th Cir. 1975). *See also* Cary v. Bd. of Educ., 598 F.2d 535, 543 (10th Cir. 1979) (upholding the school board's right to prescribe the primary textbooks used in the curriculum, even though the decision is influenced by the personal views of board members).

recognized that teachers cannot assert a First Amendment right to substitute their own supplemental reading list for the officially adopted list without securing administrative approval.[73]

The Fourth Circuit held that a high school teacher did not have complete discretion to select the plays performed by her students at state competitions.[74] Because of parental complaints, the principal ordered certain material to be deleted from a play pertaining to a dysfunctional, single-parent family. Finding production of the play to be part of the curriculum, the court recognized that school officials have legitimate pedagogical interests in regulating the content of the curriculum.

Teachers are not permitted to ignore or omit prescribed course content under the guise of academic freedom. To illustrate, the Seventh Circuit upheld a school board's dismissal of a kindergarten teacher who refused to teach patriotic topics for religious reasons.[75] Similarly, other courts have upheld school board requirements for conformity in content and pedagogy. The Third Circuit held that a teacher could not assert a First Amendment right to disregard school board instructions and continue using a classroom management technique, Learnball, that gave students responsibility for establishing class rules and grading procedures.[76] The Colorado Supreme Court also upheld a policy requiring administrative review of "controversial learning resources," noting the district's legitimate pedagogical interest in shaping its secondary school curriculum.[77] Likewise recognizing that states control the curriculum, the Ninth Circuit rejected a vagueness challenge to California legislation holding teachers personally liable for damages if they willfully refuse to teach predominantly in English.[78] The Supreme Court of Alaska also endorsed a school board's rule requiring the superintendent's approval of supplementary materials used

---

[73]Kirkland v. Northside Indep. Sch. Dist., 890 F.2d 794 (5th Cir. 1989). *See also* Webster v. New Lenox Sch. Dist. No. 122, 917 F.2d 1004 (7th Cir. 1990) (rejecting a teacher's claim that he had a First Amendment right to determine the content of his social studies courses; the board's prohibition on religious advocacy, including the teaching of creation science, was upheld); text accompanying note 136, Chapter 2.

[74]Boring v. Buncombe County Bd. of Educ., 136 F.3d 364 (4th Cir. 1998) (rejecting the teacher's challenge to her transfer based on personal conflicts precipitated by her failure to follow the school system's policy regarding controversial materials).

[75]Palmer v. Bd. of Educ., 603 F.2d 1271 (7th Cir. 1979). *See also* Roberts v. Madigan, 921 F.2d 1047 (10th Cir. 1990) (holding that requiring a teacher to remove religiously oriented books from his classroom library and refrain from silently reading his Bible during class did not impair his academic freedom); text accompanying note 62, Chapter 2.

[76]Murray v. Pittsburgh Bd. of Educ., 919 F. Supp. 838 (W.D. Pa. 1996), *aff'd mem.*, 141 F.3d 1154 (3d Cir. 1998).

[77]Bd. of Educ. v. Wilder, 960 P.2d 695, 702 (Colo. 1998) (upholding termination of a teacher for showing his high school class portions of a movie that included nudity, profanity, and graphic violence; also rejecting the teacher's due process claim since sufficient notice of the policy had been provided). *See infra* text accompanying note 87.

[78]Cal. Teachers Ass'n v. State Bd. of Educ., 271 F.3d 1141 (9th Cir. 2001) (noting that it would almost always be clear to teachers when they were dispensing the *instructional curriculum*, which triggers the English language restriction).

in the classroom and rejected a teacher's asserted right to disregard this rule in selecting materials to teach about homosexual rights in a unit on American minorities.[79]

But educators are not legally vulnerable when they are teaching the prescribed curriculum, even though it might be criticized by school patrons.[80] For example, the Sixth Circuit ruled in favor of a teacher who was teaching a life science course in conformance with the school board's directives, finding that community protests did not justify school authorities placing restrictions on his course content. After declining to alter his course, the teacher was suspended and told that he would be terminated after he refused to accept a letter of reprimand. Noting that the films and text used by the teacher had been approved by the school board and used for several years, the court found the teacher's classroom behavior appropriate and consistent with the course objectives.[81] More recently, after a Maine teacher received several complaints about his curriculum from members of a Christian church, the school board ordered the teacher to refrain from teaching certain social science subjects pertaining to prehistoric times and Greek, Roman, and Asian history. The teacher challenged the board's action, and the district court denied the board's request for summary judgment, reasoning that the teacher was threatened with termination for teaching "non-Christian" ancient history. The court emphasized that classrooms cannot be used to promote Christian ideology.[82]

Teaching Strategies

State laws and school board policies establish the basic contours of the curriculum, but teachers retain some discretion in choosing *strategies* to convey prescribed content. However, if the school board has required or prohibited a particular strategy, a teacher cannot assert a right to disregard such directives.[83] In reviewing school board

---

[79]Fisher v. Fairbanks N. Star Borough Sch. Dist., 704 P.2d 213 (Alaska 1985) (finding that the issue was not whether the materials selected by the teacher were appropriate, but rather the school board's authority to make such a determination). *See also* Sch. Admin. Dist. No. 58 v. Mt. Abram Teachers Ass'n, 704 A.2d 349 (Me. 1997) (finding educational policy decisions about selection of novels for the tenth grade curriculum to be within the school board's authority and not subject to grievance and arbitration procedures under the collective bargaining agreement).

[80]It should also be noted that school counselors may discuss controversial issues in confidence with counselees and provide information as well as referrals. For example, counselors can provide factual information on the legal status of abortions, but they cannot urge or coerce students to have an abortion. *See* Arnold v. Bd. of Educ., 880 F.2d 305 (11th Cir. 1989), *on remand*, 754 F. Supp. 853 (S.D. Ala. 1990).

[81]Stachura v. Truszkowski, 763 F.2d 211 (6th Cir. 1985), *rev'd and remanded* (regarding award of compensatory damages) *sub nom.* Stachura v. Memphis Cmty. Sch. Dist., 477 U.S. 299 (1986).

[82]Cole v. Me. Sch. Admin. Dist. No. 1, 350 F. Supp. 2d 143 (D. Me. 2004).

[83]*See, e.g.,* Greenshields v. Indep. Sch. Dist. I-1016, 174 Fed. Appx. 426 (10th Cir. 2006) (holding that a teacher did not argue a First Amendment right to refuse to use an inquiry-based approach employing learning modules to teach science, so the court could not assess the alleged retaliation against her for critical letters she wrote to school administrators about this instructional approach); Millikan v. Bd. of Dirs., 611 P.2d 414 (Wash. 1980) (upholding school board's prohibiting two teachers from team teaching a history course because requiring teachers to cover course content in a conventional manner does not violate their academic freedom).

restrictions on teachers' classroom activities, the judiciary considers a number of factors, such as whether teachers have been provided adequate notice that use of specific teaching methodologies or materials will result in disciplinary action, the relevance of the method to the course of study, the threat of disruption posed by the method, and the impact of the strategy on community norms.

Adequate Notice. Courts in general have recognized teachers' discretion to select appropriate teaching methods that serve a demonstrated educational purpose. If a particular method is supported by professional educators, the teacher has no reason to anticipate that its use might result in disciplinary action unless there is a regulation forbidding the method. This procedural right of notice that specific methods are prohibited often is the decisive factor in academic freedom cases.

Failure to provide notice was questioned in an early case in which a teacher was dismissed for using a slang term for sexual intercourse in a high school discussion of taboo words. The First Circuit ordered the teacher's reinstatement because there was no regulation prohibiting this teaching method.[84] In contrast, the First Circuit found no First Amendment violation in a teacher's suspension for handing a document to a student that contained indecent content. The court noted that the Massachusetts law permitting termination for "conduct unbecoming a teacher" furnishes sufficient notice that indecent speech directed toward students is impermissible.[85] Courts addressing the procedural due process issue have indicated that while teachers enjoy some measure of discretion, the school board can restrict use of specific methods if proper notice is given.

Relevancy. A primary consideration in reviewing the legitimacy of classroom activities is whether instructional strategies are related to course objectives. In the absence of such a relationship, the teacher's behavior is not constitutionally protected. Relevancy applies not only to objectives but also to the age and maturity of the students; a controversial topic appropriate for high school students would not necessarily be suitable for elementary and middle school pupils. Even though a certain method may be considered relevant, if it lacks the general support of the teaching profession, a school board still may prevail in barring its use.

In an early case, the Seventh Circuit upheld dismissal of teachers for distributing without explanation a brochure on the pleasures of drug use and sex to an eighth grade class; the brochure was unrelated to class activities and lacked a legitimate educational purpose.[86] Relevance to course objectives also has been found lacking in

---

[84]Mailloux v. Kiley, 448 F.2d 1242 (1st Cir. 1971) (acknowledging, however, that such language lacks professional support and could be the basis for dismissal if proper notice had been given). *See also* Cohen v. San Bernardino Valley Coll., 92 F.3d 968 (9th Cir. 1996) (overturning disciplinary action against a university professor for making comments on pornography and other sexually oriented topics in his English class, because the institution's sexual harassment policy was too vague to provide notice that such discussions were prohibited).

[85]Conward v. Cambridge Sch. Comm., 171 F.3d 12 (1st Cir. 1999).

[86]Brubaker v. Bd. of Educ., 502 F.2d 973 (7th Cir. 1974).

several cases in which teachers have shown R-rated movies to public school students.[87] Similarly, the Eighth Circuit upheld termination of a teacher who willfully violated board policy by permitting her students to use profanity in their creative writing assignments.[88] The Second Circuit also held that college administrators could claim qualified immunity because they did not violate clearly established law in dismissing an instructor for lack of relevance in a classroom exercise in which students uttered sexually profane comments in a word association exercise.[89]

However, teachers cannot be forced to discontinue instructionally relevant activities solely because of parental displeasure. The Fifth Circuit ruled that a teacher's use of a simulation to teach about post–Civil War U.S. history was related to legitimate educational objectives and therefore could not be the basis for dismissal.[90] More recently, the Seventh Circuit ruled that a teacher's use of three well-respected novels and a movie adaptation of *Romeo and Juliet* was relevant to course objectives. The court reasoned that the teacher deserved her day in court to substantiate that she received negative job evaluations due to community criticism over her discussion of the main themes from these assigned works.[91]

Threat of Disruption.   Among the factors that courts examine in assessing restrictions on classroom instruction is whether the activities pose a threat of disruption to the operation of the school. An Oregon federal district court found a school board's policy of banning all political speakers from the high school unreasonable on several grounds, including the fact that no disruptions had occurred or could be anticipated from political discussions.[92] The ban was imposed after some patrons protested a civics teacher's decision to invite a Communist speaker to address her class as part of a series of presentations representing different political viewpoints. In a case discussed previously, the Fifth Circuit concluded that numerous complaints from

[87]*See, e.g.*, Fowler v. Bd. of Educ., 819 F.2d 657 (6th Cir. 1987); Roberts v. Rapides Parish Sch. Bd., 617 So. 2d 187 (La. Ct. App. 1993). *See also* Silano v. Sag Harbor Union Free Sch. Dist., 42 F.3d 719 (2d Cir. 1994) (upholding censure of guest lecturer for showing film clips of bare-chested women during a lecture on the scientific phenomenon of persistence of vision). *But see* West v. Tangipahoa Parish Sch. Bd., 615 So. 2d 979 (La. Ct. App. 1993) (overturning dismissal of a teacher with an excellent record for showing two R-rated movies to students).

[88]Lacks v. Ferguson Reorganized Sch. Dist. R-2, 147 F.3d 718 (8th Cir. 1998). *See also* Oleske v. Hilliard City Sch. Dist., 764 N.E.2d 1110 (Ohio Ct. App. 2001) (upholding dismissal of a teacher who told dirty jokes to middle school students and referred to another teacher by a derogatory name).

[89]Vega v. Miller, 273 F.3d 460 (2d Cir. 2001) (noting that while the exercise itself may have a legitimate pedagogical purpose, the instructor let its use get out of hand).

[90]Kingsville Indep. Sch. Dist. v. Cooper, 611 F.2d 1109 (5th Cir. 1980). *See also* Hardy v. Jefferson Cmty. Coll., 260 F.3d 671 (6th Cir. 2001) (holding that faculty member's use of "nigger" and "bitch" in a classroom discussion examining the impact of disparaging words was germane to the subject matter and protected by the First Amendment); Hosford v. Sch. Comm. of Sandwich, 659 N.E.2d 1178 (Mass. 1996) (overturning suspension of a teacher for her brief, pedagogically valid discussion of vulgar words).

[91]Evans-Marshall v. Bd. of Educ., 428 F.3d 223 (6th Cir. 2005).

[92]Wilson v. Chancellor, 418 F. Supp. 1358 (D. Or. 1976).

parents and students about use of a simulation to teach history did not constitute a sufficient disruption to destroy the teacher's effectiveness in the classroom. The court stated that the "test is not whether substantial disruption occurs but whether such disruption overbalances the teacher's usefulness as an instructor."[93]

However, an Illinois federal district court recognized that a school board does not necessarily have to show that instructional materials actually caused a disruption to justify nonrenewal of a teacher's contract. Materials may be considered inappropriate for classroom use, such as films with vulgarity and sexually explicit scenes, even though students "quietly acquiesce" to their use.[94] Also, the Supreme Court of Maine held that a school board's decision to cancel a "Tolerance Day" program did not impair First Amendment rights as the decision was based on a legitimate concern for safety, order, and security due to bomb threats that had been received.[95]

Community Standards.   Courts have been protective of school boards' authority to design the curriculum to reflect community values. The Seventh Circuit recognized that school board members represent the community, which "has a legitimate, even a vital and compelling interest in the 'choice of and adherence to a suitable curriculum for the benefit of our young citizens.' "[96] Other courts similarly have acknowledged that community standards can be considered in determining the appropriateness of teaching materials and methods; school boards are empowered to establish the curriculum to transmit community values and to dismiss teachers who repeatedly offend community mores. For example, a New York appeals court held that a teacher who defied warnings that use of certain materials and sexual words in classroom discussions offended community mores had no First Amendment grounds to challenge his reprimand.[97]

Yet, the judiciary also has recognized that school boards cannot suppress legitimate instructional activities that conform to the adopted curriculum, especially if only selected viewpoints on a topic are suppressed.[98] To illustrate, the Eighth Circuit found sufficient evidence that a teacher's contract was not renewed for her alleged promotion of New Age doctrine by sending a letter and a "magic" rock home with her second-graders at the end of the school term.[99] The letter accompanying the rock indicated that if the students rub the magic rock and think good things about

---

[93]*Kingsville Indep. Sch. Dist.*, 611 F.2d at 1113.

[94]Krizek v. Bd. of Educ., 713 F. Supp. 1131, 1140–1141 (N.D. Ill. 1989) (noting further that the severity of the action against the teacher also must be considered in assessing the legitimacy of the board's sanctions).

[95]Solmitz v. Me. Sch. Admin. Dist. No. 59, 495 A.2d 812 (Me. 1985).

[96]Zykan v. Warsaw Cmty. Sch. Corp., 631 F.2d 1300, 1304 (7th Cir. 1980) (quoting Palmer v. Bd. of Educ., 603 F.2d 1271, 1274 (7th Cir. 1979)).

[97]*In re* Arbitration Between Bernstein and Norwich City Sch. Dist., 726 N.Y.S.2d 474 (App. Div. 2001).

[98]*See* Stachura v. Truszkowski, 763 F.2d 211 (6th Cir. 1985), *rev'd and remanded* (regarding award of compensatory damages) *sub nom.* Stachura v. Memphis Cmty. Sch. Dist., 477 U.S. 299 (1986); *supra* text accompanying note 81.

[99]Cowan v. Strafford R-VI Sch. Dist., 140 F.3d 1153 (8th Cir. 1998).

themselves, they can do whatever they set their minds to do. Finding the personnel action impermissible, the teacher was awarded two years of pay, but the court did not order reinstatement because of the damaged relationship between the teacher and school principal.

Given the school board's legitimate interest in advancing community mores, the judiciary has considered community standards in evaluating challenges to various teaching methods. Yet, if a particular strategy is instructionally relevant and supported by the profession, it likely will survive judicial review even though it might disturb some school patrons.

Freedom of Association

Although freedom of association is not specifically addressed in the First Amendment, the Supreme Court has recognized that associational rights are "implicit in the freedoms of speech, assembly, and petition."[100] The Court has consistently declared that infringements on the right to associate for expressive purposes can be justified only by a compelling governmental interest, unrelated to suppressing ideas, that cannot be achieved through less-restrictive means.[101] Accordingly, public educators cannot be disciplined for forming or joining political, labor, religious, or social organizations. Limitations, however, may be placed on associational activities that disrupt school operations or interfere with teachers' professional duties.[102] This section presents an overview of teachers' associational rights in connection with political affiliations and activities. Public educators' rights in connection with labor unions are addressed in Chapter 12.

Political Affiliations

States have made frequent attempts to prohibit or limit teachers' affiliations with subversive political organizations. These restrictions have been imposed to protect public schools from treasonable and seditious acts. In early cases, the Supreme Court held that associational rights could be restricted when a public employee was fully knowledgeable of an organization's subversive purpose,[103] but in the mid-1960s this stance was rejected. Although teachers can be required to affirm their support of the federal and state constitutions,[104] the Supreme Court has invalidated loyalty oaths

---

[100]Healy v. James, 408 U.S. 169, 181 (1972).

[101]*See, e.g.,* NAACP v. Button, 371 U.S. 415 (1963).

[102]*See* Klug v. Chi. Sch. Reform Bd. of Trs., 197 F.3d 853 (7th Cir. 1999) (finding no violation of associational rights in an employee's transfer from a high school dean of students to an elementary school teaching position to neutralize bickering factions at the high school).

[103]*See* Adler v. Bd. of Educ., 342 U.S. 485 (1952).

[104]*See* Cole v. Richardson, 405 U.S. 676 (1972); Connell v. Higginbotham, 403 U.S. 207 (1971). Employees also can be required to pledge that they will oppose the overthrow of the government and that they will fulfill their job responsibilities. *See* text accompanying note 8, Chapter 8.

requiring individuals to deny membership in subversive organizations, such as the Communist Party, as unduly vague or imposing sanctions for guilt by association.[105] The Supreme Court has firmly established that mere membership in such an organization, without the specific intent to further its unlawful aims, cannot disqualify an individual for public school employment.[106] Thus, state statutes barring members of subversive or controversial organizations from public employment are clearly unconstitutional.[107] Neither can a school system impose restrictions, directly or indirectly, on teachers' memberships or their lawful activities in certain organizations. As with protected speech, dismissal of a teacher will not be supported if the motivating factor behind the decision is the teacher's exercise of associational rights.

Governmental action need not proscribe organizational membership to impair freedom of association. Courts will invalidate challenged laws that *inhibit* the free exercise of constitutional guarantees unless the state can show that such measures are substantially related to a compelling governmental interest. The Supreme Court overturned an Arkansas law that required all teachers to submit annually a list of every organization they had joined or regularly supported during the prior five years as constituting "comprehensive interference with associational freedom."[108] Similarly, the Fifth Circuit struck down a Texas statute that allowed county judges to compel certain organizations engaged in activities designed to disrupt public schools to disclose their membership lists.[109] As in the Arkansas case, this law also swept too broadly by exposing to public recrimination those members who did not participate in disruptive activities.

The First Amendment, however, does not preclude school administrators from questioning teachers about associational activities that may adversely affect teaching. In *Beilan v. Board of Public Education*, the Supreme Court held that questions regarding a teacher's activities in the Communist Party were relevant to an assessment of his fitness to serve as a classroom teacher, and that refusal to answer the superintendent's inquiries could result in dismissal.[110] Although organizational membership *per se* is protected, a teacher must respond to queries about associational activities that are related to competence to teach.

Conditioning public employment on partisan political affiliation also has been controversial. Historically, public employment was characterized by the patronage system; when the controlling political party changed, non–civil service employees belonging to the defeated party lost their jobs. In 1976, the Supreme Court ruled that the

---

[105]*See, e.g.*, Keyishian v. Bd. of Regents, 385 U.S. 589, 606–607 (1967); Elfbrandt v. Russell, 384 U.S. 11, 19 (1966); text accompanying note 7, Chapter 8.

[106]*Keyishian*, 385 U.S. at 606–607.

[107]*See, e.g.*, NAACP v. Alabama *ex rel.* Patterson, 357 U.S. 449 (1958). *See also In re* Bay Area Citizens Against Lawsuit Abuse, 982 S.W.2d 371, 376 (Tex. 1998) (quoting *NAACP*, 357 U.S. at 460–461) (recognizing that "curtailing the freedom of association is subject to the closest scrutiny," regardless of the beliefs sought to be advanced by the association).

[108]Shelton v. Tucker, 364 U.S. 479, 490 (1960).

[109]Familias Unidas v. Briscoe, 619 F.2d 391 (5th Cir. 1980).

[110]357 U.S. 399 (1958).

patronage system in an Illinois sheriff's office placed a severe restriction on political association and belief.[111] The constant threat of replacing nonpolicy-making individuals, who cannot undermine policies of the new administration, was considered detrimental to governmental effectiveness and efficiency. In 1980, the Supreme Court reiterated that the democratic process would be preserved by limiting patronage dismissals to policy-making positions.[112]

A decade later the Court extended the principle established in the political firing cases to all aspects of public employment, ruling that party affiliation cannot influence promotion, transfer, recall, and other decisions pertaining to employees who do not establish policies.[113] The Sixth Circuit subsequently recognized four categories of positions that can be conditioned on political affiliation: (1) those named in law as having discretionary authority in carrying out policy, (2) those to which a considerable amount of discretionary authority has been delegated by persons in category one, (3) those who spend a significant portion of time advising position holders in category 1 or 2, or (4) those positions filled to balance political party representation.[114]

Despite being insulated from partisan politics by state law, in some instances public educators have asserted that employment decisions have been based on party affiliation. In such cases, the burden has been placed on the school employee to demonstrate that protected political affiliation was the motivating factor in the board's employment decision. If an employee satisfies this burden, then the board must demonstrate by a preponderance of evidence that it would have reached the same decision in the absence of the political association. In an illustrative case, the First Circuit ordered reinstatement of a school superintendent because evidence supported that her political party affiliation was the motivating factor in the decision to demote her.[115] Also, the Sixth Circuit denied summary judgment to a Kentucky school board that had demoted an administrator who supported the superintendent's opponents. The court noted that the role of grants department director was not a policy-making position and did not involve sensitive or confidential duties or control lines of communication between the superintendent and the public, so the board could not substantiate a policy-making need for her demotion to a classroom teacher.[116]

---

[111]Elrod v. Burns, 427 U.S. 347 (1976).

[112]Branti v. Finkel, 445 U.S. 507 (1980).

[113]Rutan v. Republican Party, 497 U.S. 62 (1990). *See also* Armour v. County of Beaver, 271 F.3d 417 (3d Cir. 2001) (holding that access to confidential information alone was insufficient to establish that political affiliation was an appropriate job requirement for a secretary to the county commissioner).

[114]McCloud v. Testa, 97 F.3d 1536, 1557 (6th Cir. 1996).

[115]Estrada-Izquierdo v. Aponte-Roque, 850 F.2d 10 (1st Cir. 1988). *See also* Piazza v. Aponte-Roque, 909 F.2d 35 (1st Cir. 1990) (finding that nonrenewal of contracts of teachers' aides because of their political party affiliation impaired associational rights); Burris v. Willis Indep. Sch. Dist., 713 F.2d 1087 (5th Cir. 1983) (holding that nonrenewal of an administrator's contract was predicated on his association with previous "old line" board members and thereby violated his associational rights).

[116]Justice v. Pike County Bd. of Educ., 348 F.3d 554 (6th Cir. 2003). *But see* Rivera-Torres v. Rey-Hernandez, 352 F. Supp. 2d 152 (D.P.R. 2004) (rejecting claim by former employees of the Department of Education that their one-year contracts were not renewed because they were politcally affiliated with the prior administration; they lacked a property interest in their contracts beyond the current year).

Political Activity

Teachers, like all citizens, are guaranteed the right to participate in the political process. Often, however, active participation has prompted school officials to place limitations on the exercise of this right, raising difficult legal questions. Can teachers run for political offices? What types of political activities are permitted in the school setting? Can certain political activities outside the school be restricted?

Campaigning for Issues and Candidates.   First Amendment association and free speech rights have been invoked to protect public educators in expressing political views and campaigning for candidates.[117] Even though such political activity is constitutionally protected, restrictions can be placed on educators' activities in the school setting. Making campaign speeches in the classroom is clearly prohibited; teachers cannot take advantage of their position of authority with an impressionable captive audience to impose their political views.[118] However, if campaign issues are related to the class topic, a teacher can present election issues and candidates in a nonpartisan manner.

In general, political activity that would cause divisiveness within the school district also can be restricted. A California appeals court concluded that teachers could be prohibited from wearing union buttons while delivering instruction because the buttons fell within the definition of "political activity" under state law.[119] The Kentucky Supreme Court addressed a statutory prohibition on school employees taking part in the management or activities of any school board campaign. Although finding the word *activities* too vague to describe the prohibited involvement, the court upheld the constitutionality of the prohibition on school employees taking part

---

[117]Expression and association rights were at issue in two recent Supreme Court decisions addressing federal campaign reforms that place limitations on corporations using general treasury funds to pay for "electioneering communication" within 30 days of a federal primary election or 60 days of a federal general election, Bipartisan Campaign Reform Act of 2002, 2 U.S.C. § 441b(b)(2)(2007). *See* FEC v. Wis. Right to Life, 127 S. Ct. 2652 (2007) (holding that corporate or union ads, which are not express advocacy or its functional equivalent, cannot be curtailed without a compelling interest to justify the burden on expression, such as the ads explicitly urging a vote for or against a specific candidate), which largely negates the Court's holding four years earlier in McConnell v. FEC, 540 U.S. 93 (2003) (upholding the federal restrictions on express advocacy as encompassing ads that purport to educate voters about issues but are really aimed at candidates). *See also* Pocatello Educ. Ass'n v. Heideman, 504 F.3d 1053 (9th Cir. 2007) (striking down a ban on public employee payroll deductions for political activities as violating the First Amendment; finding no compelling justification for the content-based law).

[118]*See* Mayer v. Monroe County Cmty. Sch. Corp., 474 F.3d 477 (7th Cir. 2007), *cert. denied,* 128 S. Ct. 160 (2007); *supra* text accompanying note 68.

[119]Turlock Joint Elementary Sch. Dist. v. Pub. Employment Relations Bd., 5 Cal. Rptr. 3d 308 (Ct. App. 2003) (unpublished decision). *See also* Cal. Teachers Ass'n v. San Diego Unified Sch. Dist., 53 Cal. Rptr. 2d 474 (Ct. App. 1996) (holding that a school district could prevent its employees from wearing political buttons in instructional settings, although it could not restrict such expression outside the presence of students); Green Twp. Educ. Ass'n v. Rowe, 746 A.2d 499 (N.J. Super. Ct. App. Div. 2000) (upholding restriction on political activity in front of students, including wearing buttons, but finding overbroad a restriction on employees campaigning outside the presence of students on school property).

in the *management* of school board campaigns as reasonable to advance the state's compelling interest in running school districts efficiently.[120]

Courts have tended to reject restrictions affecting teachers' political activities *outside* the school. Public employees are constitutionally protected from retaliation for participation in political affairs at the local, state, and federal levels. For example, the Sixth Circuit held that the coordinator of gifted education, which was not a policy-making position, could not be reassigned for the exercise of constitutionally protected political expression and association in connection with actively supporting an unsuccessful candidate for school superintendent.[121] The appeals court rejected the contention that political loyalty was essential in carrying out the coordinator's role. Other courts have overturned dismissals, transfers, or demotions predicated on the support or nonsupport of particular candidates in school board elections where protected political activity was a motivating or substantial factor in the adverse employment action against nonpolicy-making employees, and the political activities did not interfere with school operations.[122]

The Federal Constitution protects the right of political party members to champion candidates for government office, but public employees who occupy policy-making positions may be vulnerable to dismissal or other disciplinary action for their political activities. The Fifth Circuit held that a Texas superintendent's free speech and political association rights were not violated when he was relieved of his duties by school board members against whom he had actively campaigned.[123] The court reasoned that the superintendent's political activities precluded an effective working relationship with the new school board. Also, the Fourth Circuit found no First Amendment impairment in demoting a community/schools coordinator with policy-making and public relations responsibilities after she campaigned for an unsuccessful school board candidate and openly criticized board members and school policies.[124]

---

[120]State Bd. for Elementary and Secondary Educ. v. Howard, 834 S.W.2d 657 (Ky. 1992). *See also* Castle v. Colonial Sch. Dist., 933 F. Supp. 458 (E.D. Pa. 1996) (finding that a prohibition on school employees engaging in political activities on school district property violated First Amendment rights of off-duty employees to solicit votes at official polling places on school grounds).

[121]Hager v. Pike County Bd. of Educ., 286 F.3d 366 (6th Cir. 2002).

[122]*See, e.g.*, Kercado-Melendez v. Aponte-Roque, 829 F.2d 255 (1st Cir. 1987) (holding that dismissal of school superintendent and revocation of her teaching license when new political party took office violated First Amendment rights; awarding injunctive relief, back pay, and damages for the unconstitutional dismissal based on political affiliation); Banks v. Burkich, 788 F.2d 1161 (6th Cir. 1986) (ordering reinstatement of a school truant officer who had been demoted for lack of funding but was not rehired when funds became available, for political reasons). *But see* Simmons v. Chi. Bd. of Educ., 289 F.3d 488 (7th Cir. 2002) (ruling that a school district employee was demoted for disobeying his supervisor's instructions and micromanaging his office rather than for his unsuccessful campaign for an alderman seat prior to being hired as treasurer of the Chicago Board of Education); Beattie v. Madison County Sch. Dist., 254 F.3d 595 (5th Cir. 2001) (finding insufficient causal link between employee's termination and her support for the incumbent superintendent candidate).

[123]Kinsey v. Salado Indep. Sch. Dist., 950 F.2d 988 (5th Cir. 1992).

[124]Dabbs v. Amos, 70 F.3d 1261 (4th Cir. 1995) (unpublished decision).

Holding Public Office.   Certain categories of public employees have been prevented from running for political office. In 1973, the Supreme Court upheld a federal law (the Hatch Act) that prevents *federal* employees from holding formal positions in political parties, playing substantial roles in partisan campaigns, and running for partisan office.[125] The Court recognized that legitimate reasons exist for restricting political activities of public employees, such as the need to ensure impartial and effective government, to remove employees from political pressure, and to prevent employee selection based on political factors. In a companion case, the Court upheld an Oklahoma law forbidding classified civil servants from running for paid political offices.[126] Lower courts similarly have endorsed certain restrictions on state and municipal employees running for elective office, such as forbidding municipal employees from holding elective office in the city or town where employed.[127]

Laws or policies prohibiting *all* public employees from running for *any* political office have been struck down as overly broad.[128] And several courts have held that public educators, unlike public employees who are directly involved in the operation of governmental agencies, have the right to run for and hold public office. The Utah Supreme Court, for example, ruled that public school teachers and administrators were not disqualified from serving in the state legislature.[129] A New Mexico appeals court also ruled that service in the legislature by a teacher and administrator would not violate the constitutional separation of powers provision,[130] and the Ohio Supreme Court upheld a public school principal's right to serve as a county commissioner.[131]

Of course, restrictions can be imposed that are necessary to protect the integrity of the educational system. Courts have recognized that certain offices are incompatible with public school employment, especially if they involve an employer/employee relationship. Common law has established that such incompatibility exists when a teacher seeks a position on the school board where employed,[132] but a teacher would not be prevented from serving on the school board of another school district.[133]

---

[125]U.S. Civil Serv. Comm'n v. Nat'l Ass'n of Letter Carriers, 413 U.S. 548 (1973). *See* 5 U.S.C. § 7324 (2007).

[126]Broadrick v. Oklahoma, 413 U.S. 601 (1973).

[127]*See, e.g.*, Fletcher v. Marino, 882 F.2d 605 (2d Cir. 1989); Cranston Teachers Alliance v. Miele, 495 A.2d 233 (R.I. 1985); Acevedo v. City of N. Pole, 672 P.2d 130 (Alaska 1983).

[128]*See, e.g., Cranston Teachers Alliance*, 495 A.2d 233; Minielly v. State, 411 P.2d 69 (Or. 1966).

[129]Jenkins v. Bishop, 589 P.2d 770 (Utah 1978) (*per curiam*).

[130]Stratton v. Roswell Indep. Schs., 806 P.2d 1085 (N.M. Ct. App. 1991).

[131]State *ex rel.* Gretick v. Jeffrey, 465 N.E.2d 412 (Ohio 1984).

[132]*See, e.g.,* Unified Sch. Dist. No. 501 v. Baker, 6 P.3d 848 (Kan. 2000) (invalidating election of teacher to school board where state legislature had not negated the common law doctrine of job incompatibility by authorizing the holding of dual offices); West v. Jones, 323 S.E.2d 96 (Va. 1984) (disqualifying city council member, who also was employed as a public school principal, from voting on appointments to the school board); Thomas v. Dremmel, 868 P.2d 263 (Wyo. 1994) (holding that school maintenance worker could not also serve as an elected member of the district's board of trustees).

[133]*See* La Bosco v. Dunn, 502 N.Y.S.2d 200 (App. Div. 1986).

Public educators can be required to take a leave of absence before running for a public office, if campaigning would interfere with their job responsibilities. But some leave requirements have been judicially struck down where there has been insufficient justification for the policies. A Kentucky appellate court overturned a school board regulation requiring all employees who were political candidates to take a one-month leave of absence prior to the election as violating associational and expression rights; no evidence indicated that the political activities would hinder job performance.[134]

The Supreme Court also affirmed a lower court's decision striking down a Georgia school board's policy requiring any school employee who became a candidate for public office to take a leave of absence without pay for the duration of the candidacy. Finding this policy to be a violation of the federal Voting Rights Act, the Court recognized that it created a substantial economic deterrent to seeking elective public office and was potentially discriminatory since it was adopted after an African American employee announced his candidacy for the state legislature.[135] However, the Supreme Court subsequently upheld the school board's revised policy, which denied special leaves of absence for political purpose.[136] The modified policy was considered a legitimate reaffirmation of the board's authority to require employees to fulfill their contracts.

Although school boards must respect employees' associational rights, they are obligated to ensure that the political activities of public school personnel do not adversely affect the school. Disciplinary actions can be imposed if educators neglect instructional duties to campaign for issues or candidates, use the classroom as a political forum, or disrupt school operations because of their political activities. But school boards must be certain that constraints imposed on employees' freedom of association are not based on mere disagreement with the political orientation of the activities. Personnel actions must be justified as necessary to protect the interests of students and the school.

Personal Appearance

Historically, school boards often imposed rigid grooming restrictions on teachers. In the 1970s, such attempts to regulate teachers' appearance generated considerable litigation, as did grooming standards for students.[137] Controversies have subsided somewhat,

[134]Allen v. Bd. of Educ., 584 S.W.2d 408 (Ky. Ct. App. 1979).

[135]Dougherty County Bd. of Educ. v. White, 439 U.S. 32 (1978).

[136]White v. Dougherty County Bd. of Educ., 579 F. Supp. 1480 (M.D. Ga. 1984), *aff'd mem.*, 470 U.S. 1067 (1985).

[137]For a discussion of restrictions on student appearance, *see* text accompanying note 108, Chapter 4. For a discussion of employees' wearing religious attire in public schools, *see* text accompanying note 113, Chapter 10.

but constraints on school employees' appearance continue to be challenged.[138] School boards have defended their efforts to regulate teacher appearance on the perceived need to provide appropriate role models, set a proper tone in the classroom, and enforce similar appearance and dress codes for students. Teachers have contested these requirements as abridgments of their constitutionally protected privacy, liberty, and free expression rights.

Most courts since the mid-1970s have supported school officials in imposing reasonable grooming and dress restrictions on teachers.[139] The Supreme Court provided some clarification of public employers' authority regarding regulation of employee appearance in a 1976 decision upholding a hair-grooming regulation for police officers. The Court placed the burden on the individual to demonstrate the lack of a rational connection between the regulation and a legitimate public purpose.[140]

The Supreme Court's justification for upholding the grooming regulation for police officers has been followed by lower courts assessing dress and appearance restrictions for teachers. For example, the Second Circuit upheld a Connecticut school board's requirement that all male teachers wear a tie as a rational means to promote respect for authority, traditional values, and classroom discipline.[141] Because of the uniquely influential role of teachers, the court noted that they may be subjected to restrictions in their professional lives that otherwise would not be acceptable. Applying similar reasoning, the First Circuit upheld a school board's dismissal of a teacher for wearing short skirts,[142] and a Connecticut federal court ruled that a school board did not violate a teacher's rights by instructing her to cover the message on her T-shirt, "Jesus 2000-J2K," or change into another top.[143]

Restrictions will not be upheld, however, if found to be arbitrary, discriminatory, or unrelated to a legitimate governmental concern. To illustrate, the Seventh Circuit overturned a school bus driver's suspension after he violated a regulation prohibiting school bus drivers from wearing mustaches.[144] Finding no valid purpose

[138]*See* Polk County Bd. of Educ. v. Polk County Educ. Ass'n, 139 S.W.3d 304 (Tenn. Ct. App. 2004) (holding that the adoption of an employee dress code may be a management prerogative, but its enforcement must be bargained with the teachers' association).

[139]Finding prohibitions on teachers' wearing beards to be a minor deprivation of protected rights and to advance legitimate school board interests in instilling discipline and compelling uniformity, *see, e.g.*, Domico v. Rapides Parish Sch. Bd., 675 F.2d 100 (5th Cir. 1982); Ball v. Bd. of Trs., 584 F.2d 684 (5th Cir. 1978).

[140]Kelley v. Johnson, 425 U.S. 238 (1976).

[141]E. Hartford Educ. Ass'n v. Bd. of Educ., 562 F.2d 838 (2d Cir. 1977).

[142]Tardif v. Quinn, 545 F.2d 761 (1st Cir. 1976). *See also* Zalewska v. County of Sullivan, 180 F. Supp. 2d 486 (S.D.N.Y. 2002) (upholding uniform policy for school district's van drivers to project a professional appearance and ensure safety of vans with chair lifts; the policy's incidental restrictions on expression were minimal).

[143]Downing v. W. Haven Bd. of Educ., 162 F. Supp. 2d 19 (D. Conn. 2001).

[144]Pence v. Rosenquist, 573 F.2d 395 (7th Cir. 1978). *See also* Nichol v. Arin Intermediate Unit 28, 268 F. Supp. 2d 536 (W.D. Pa. 2003) (upholding an instructional assistant's right to wear a small cross and reasoning that the state's religious garb statute was overtly adverse to religion because it singled out and punished only religious, and not secular, symbolic expression).

for the policy, the court noted that its irrationality was exemplified by the fact that the bus driver also was a full-time teacher but was not suspended from his teaching position.

Courts generally acknowledge that the right to govern personal appearance is a protected interest, but it has not been declared a fundamental right requiring heightened judicial scrutiny. Accordingly, school officials can regulate employees' appearance for legitimate reasons as long as the rules are not arbitrary or discriminatory.

Constitutional Privacy Rights

Public employees have asserted the right to be free from unwarranted governmental intrusions in their personal activities.[145] Although the Federal Constitution does not explicitly enumerate personal privacy rights, the Supreme Court has recognized that certain *implied* fundamental rights warrant constitutional protection because of their close relationship to explicit constitutional guarantees. Protected privacy rights have been interpreted as encompassing personal choices in matters such as marriage, contraception, sexual relations, procreation, family relationships, and child rearing.[146] Employment decisions cannot be based on relinquishing such rights without a compelling justification. Litigation covered in this section focuses on constitutional privacy claims initiated under the Fourth Amendment (protection against unreasonable searches and seizures), the Ninth Amendment (personal privacy as an unenumerated right reserved to the people), and the Fourteenth Amendment (equal protection rights and protection against state action impairing personal liberties without due process of law).

In some instances, public employees have asserted that governmental action has impaired their privacy right to intimate association related to creating and maintaining a family. To assess such claims, courts must weigh the employee's rights against the government's interests in promoting efficient public services.[147] For example, public educators cannot be deprived of their jobs because of the politics or other activities of their partners or spouses. Recognizing a classified employee's First Amendment right

---

[145]Most states have laws giving employees access to their personnel files and safeguarding the confidentiality of the records. *See* text accompanying note 120, Chapter 8.

[146]*See* Lawrence v. Texas, 539 U.S. 558 (2003); Loving v. Virginia, 388 U.S. 1 (1967); Griswold v. Connecticut, 381 U.S. 479 (1965); Skinner v. Oklahoma, 316 U.S. 535 (1942); Pierce v. Soc'y of Sisters, 268 U.S. 510 (1925). The Supreme Court in 1973 ruled that the decision to have an abortion also was among these protected privacy rights, Roe v. Wade, 410 U.S. 113 (1973), but the Court recently has allowed states to place some restrictions (e.g., 24-hour waiting period, informed consent, parental consent) on the individual's discretion to have an abortion. And in 2007, the Court upheld a federal prohibition on performing partial-birth abortions, *see* Gonzales v. Carhart, 127 S. Ct. 1610 (2007).

[147]*See, e.g.,* Kelly v. City of Meriden, 120 F. Supp. 2d 191 (D. Conn. 2000) (upholding dismissal of a school social worker who was living with the noncustodial father of children to whom she had provided social services; the city director believed the employee may have violated the ethics code, discredited the agency, and hindered other school social workers in performing their work).

to associate with her husband who disagreed with policies of the school system, the Sixth Circuit found an inference that the superintendent's nonrenewal recommendation was impermissibly based on the employee's marital relationship.[148] Also, a federal court held that a nontenured teacher, who received excellent ratings until subpoenaed at school to testify against her live-in fiancé in a child abuse case, could claim that her contract nonrenewal violated intimate associational rights.[149]

However, public educators cannot assert an associational or privacy right to disregard anti-nepotism policies that prohibit teachers from reporting to their spouses or working in the same building as their spouses. The Sixth Circuit reasoned that such an anti-nepotism policy did not interfere with the fundamental right to marry, because the policy affected working conditions, not the marriage itself.[150] The fact that such policies do not apply to employees who are cohabiting or dating has not nullified anti-nepotism provisions.

The Fifth Circuit recognized that a teacher's interest in breast-feeding her child at school during noninstructional time was sufficiently close to fundamental rights regarding family relationships and child rearing to trigger constitutional protection.[151] The court acknowledged, however, that trial courts must determine whether school boards' interests in avoiding disruption of the educational process, ensuring that teachers perform their duties without distraction, and avoiding liability for potential injuries are sufficiently compelling to justify restrictions imposed on teachers' fundamental privacy interests. The Second Circuit also upheld a teacher's privacy claim in her refusal to submit to a physical examination by the school district's male physician and found support for the unreasonableness of the board's action because the teacher offered to go at her own expense to any female physician the board selected.[152]

Courts in some cases have concluded that governmental interests in ensuring the welfare of students override teachers' privacy interests. For example, teachers cannot

---

[148]Adkins v. Bd. of Educ., 982 F.2d 952 (6th Cir. 1993).

[149]LaSota v. Town of Topsfield, 979 F. Supp. 45 (D. Mass. 1997). *See also* Trujillo v. Bd. of Educ., 212 Fed. Appx. 760 (10th Cir. 2007) (remanding a high school instructor's retaliation claim for supporting his wife's discrimination complaint that resulted from her failure to be hired in a supervisory role; further fact-finding was needed to determine whether the instructor spoke pursuant to his official duties). *But see* Finnegan v. Bd. of Educ., 30 F.3d 273 (2d Cir. 1994) (finding inadequate evidence that a probationary teacher was removed from a coaching position and denied tenure because he married a former member of his volleyball team shortly after she graduated).

[150]Montgomery v. Carr, 101 F.3d 1117 (6th Cir. 1996). *See also* Williams v. Augusta County Sch. Bd., 445 S.E.2d 118 (Va. 1994) (finding that a teacher was ineligible to be rehired by a school board that her brother-in-law chaired).

[151]Dike v. Sch. Bd., 650 F.2d 783 (5th Cir. 1981). *See also* Appel v. Spiridon, 463 F. Supp. 2d 255 (D. Conn. 2006) (awarding preliminary injunction to restrain a university from requiring a professor to undergo a mental health evaluation; no other faculty members had been subjected to such involuntary psychiatric examinations as a condition of maintaining their positions when questions were raised about their professional conduct).

[152]Gargiul v. Tompkins, 704 F.2d 661 (2d Cir. 1983), *vacated and remanded,* 465 U.S. 1016 (1984).

claim privacy rights to have sexual relationships with students or perhaps even former students who have recently graduated.[153] Also, the Second Circuit ruled that a school board did not violate a tenured teacher's privacy rights by not allowing her to return from an extended medical absence unless she provided medical records from the physician and submitted to a physical examination by the school board doctor.[154] Likewise, the First Circuit held that a principal's constitutional privacy rights were not impaired when he was required to undergo a psychiatric examination before returning to work, as there was reason to believe that the welfare of students might be jeopardized.[155]

Teachers have not succeeded in asserting that observations by superiors and other strategies used to assess teaching competence violate protected privacy rights. For example, a Texas appeals court upheld the school in videotaping a teacher's performance for evaluative purposes, concluding that teachers' privacy rights do not shield them from legitimate performance evaluations.[156] More recently, the Supreme Court of Wisconsin held that a teacher's privacy rights did not outweigh the public's interest in knowing about the teacher's conduct in allegedly conducting Internet searches on his school computer to locate material containing pornographic images.[157]

Search and Seizure

Public educators, like all citizens, are shielded by the Fourth Amendment against unreasonable governmental invasions of their person and property. This amendment requires police officers and other state agents to secure a search warrant (based on probable cause that evidence of a crime will be found) before conducting personal searches. The Supreme Court has not addressed teachers' rights in connection with searches initiated by public school authorities, but it has upheld warrantless personal searches of students based on *reasonable suspicion* that contraband detrimental to the educational process is concealed.[158]

---

[153]*See* Flaskamp v. Dearborn Pub. Schs., 385 F.3d 935 (6th Cir. 2004) (upholding suspension and denial of tenure to a teacher who had an intimate relationship with a former student; the school board could prohibit such activity within a year or two of graduation, given the importance of deterring student/teacher sexual relationships); Berkovsky v. State, 209 S.W. 3d 252 (Tex. App. 2006) (finding that the statute prohibiting improper sexual relationships between educators and students did not implicate a fundamental constitutional right and was not facially overbroad; the statute did not interfere with privacy rights of an educator who had a consensual sexual relationship with an 18-year-old student in violation of the law).

[154]Strong v. Bd. of Educ., 902 F.2d 208 (2d Cir. 1990).

[155]Daury v. Smith, 842 F.2d 9 (1st Cir. 1988). *But see Appel*, 463 F. Supp. 2d 255; *supra* text accompanying note 151.

[156]Roberts v. Houston Indep. Sch. Dist., 788 S.W.2d 107 (Tex. App. 1990). *See also* Brannen v. Bd. of Educ., 761 N.E.2d 84 (Ohio Ct. App. 2001) (holding that use of surveillance cameras to videotape custodians in their break room to identify unauthorized breaks was not an unlawful search).

[157]Zellner v. Cedarburg Sch. Dist., 731 N.W.2d 240 (Wis. 2007). *See also* Urofsky v. Gilmore, 216 F.3d 401 (4th Cir. 2000); *supra* text accompanying note 53.

[158]New Jersey v. T.L.O., 469 U.S. 325 (1985). *See* text accompanying note 128, Chapter 7, for a discussion of the reasonable suspicion standard.

The Supreme Court also has upheld a warrantless search by state hospital supervisors of an employee physician's office in which items seized were used in administrative proceedings resulting in his dismissal for improprieties in managing the residency program.[159] The Court's conclusion that both the basis for the search and the scope of the intrusion were reasonable has implications for searches of other public workers by their employers. Acknowledging that public employees have a reasonable expectation of privacy in their desks and files, the Supreme Court nonetheless concluded that a warrant is not required for work-related searches that are necessary to carry out the business of the agency.

The judiciary has recognized that the reasonableness of a job-related search or seizure by a supervisor in public schools rests on whether educational interests outweigh the individual employee's expectation of privacy.[160] The Fourth Amendment prohibits *arbitrary* invasions of teachers' personal effects by school officials, but in some situations the school's interests are overriding.[161] To illustrate, the Second Circuit upheld the search of a teacher's classroom after he had been suspended for alleged sexual harassment of a student and was provided two opportunities to remove personal items from the classroom.[162] The court further held that the teacher had no valid claim to materials he had prepared in the course of his employment.

Public school employees' Fourth Amendment rights also have been asserted in connection with drug-screening programs. School boards can require employees to have physical examinations as a condition of employment, but mandatory screening for drugs has been challenged as impairing privacy rights. Teachers in a New York school district secured a restraining order prohibiting the school board from forcing probationary teachers to submit urine samples for purposes of determining whether they were using controlled substances.[163] Since there was no *individualized suspicion* of wrongdoing, the drug-testing program was found to violate the teachers' privacy rights. A Georgia federal district court also struck down a statewide drug-testing law that would have required all new state employees and veteran employees transferring to another school district or state agency to submit to urinalysis screening.[164] The

---

[159]O'Connor v. Ortega, 480 U.S. 709 (1987).

[160]*See, e.g.,* Gillard v. Schmidt, 579 F.2d 825 (3d Cir. 1978) (invalidating search of school counselor's desk by a school board member, because the search was politically motivated and lacked sufficient work-related justification).

[161]*See, e.g.,* Alinovi v. Worcester Sch. Comm., 777 F.2d 776 (1st Cir. 1985) (finding that a teacher had no expectation of privacy in withholding from the school administration a paper she had written—and shared with others—about a child with disabilities in her class).

[162]Shaul v. Cherry Valley-Springfield Cent. Sch. Dist., 363 F.3d 177 (2d Cir. 2004). *See also* Soderstrand v. Oklahoma *ex rel.* Bd. of Regents, 463 F. Supp. 2d 1308 (W.D. Okla. 2006) (upholding university authorities in seizing a laptop computer from an employee's desk during an investigation of workplace misconduct involving child pornography).

[163]Patchogue-Medford Congress of Teachers v. Bd. of Educ., 510 N.E.2d 325 (N.Y. 1987).

[164]Ga. Ass'n of Educators v. Harris, 749 F. Supp. 1110 (N.D. Ga. 1990). *See also* Chandler v. Miller, 520 U.S. 305 (1997) (striking down a Georgia law requiring candidates for state office to pass a drug test; finding no special need based on public safety to override the individual's privacy interests); Glover v. E. Neb. Cmty. Office of Retardation, 867 F.2d 461 (8th Cir. 1989) (finding county health agency's policy requiring mandatory screening of employees for hepatitis B and AIDS unreasonable under the Fourth Amendment).

court reasoned that the general interest in maintaining a drug-free workplace was not a compelling governmental interest to justify testing *all* job applicants.

In contrast to *blanket* testing, support for *limited* drug-testing of public employees can be found in two Supreme Court decisions outside the school domain that upheld mandatory drug testing of railroad employees involved in accidents[165] and customs employees who carry firearms or are involved in the interdiction of illegal drugs.[166] The Court found that the safety and security interests served by the programs outweighed employees' privacy concerns. In several rulings, the District of Columbia Circuit subsequently upheld random urinalysis testing of federal employees in safety-sensitive or security-sensitive roles, including Department of Education employees.[167] The same court upheld the District of Columbia Public Schools' policy requiring all employees whose duties affect child safety, such as bus attendants, to submit to a drug test as part of routine medical examinations.[168] The Fifth Circuit also upheld drug testing of school employees in safety-sensitive positions, including the school custodian, whose performance of maintenance duties affects almost 900 students.[169]

What constitutes safety-sensitive roles in the school context, however, remains unclear. Some courts now seem more inclined than they were in the past to interpret expansively the positions in this category. The Sixth Circuit upheld a school district's policy requiring suspicionless drug testing for all individuals who apply for, transfer to, or are promoted to safety-sensitive positions, including teachers who are entrusted with the care of children and are on the "frontline" of school security.[170] Furthermore, the court upheld drug testing of any individual for whom there was reasonable suspicion of drug possession or use, but it remanded the case for additional factual inquiry regarding the provision calling for alcohol testing of all employees.[171] A Kentucky federal district court subsequently upheld random, suspicionless drug testing of a school district's employees in safety-sensitive roles, including teachers, as justified to comply with the Drug-Free Workplace Act of 1988, designed to ensure that

---

[165]Skinner v. Ry. Labor Executives' Ass'n, 489 U.S. 602 (1989). In this case, the Court also upheld alcohol testing of employees.

[166]Nat'l Treasury Employees Union v. Von Raab, 489 U.S. 656 (1989).

[167]*See, e.g.*, Stigile v. Clinton, 110 F.3d 801 (D.C. Cir. 1997); Am. Fed'n of Gov't Employees, AFL-CIO v. Sanders, 926 F.2d 1215 (D.C. Cir. 1991) (unpublished decision); Nat'l Treasury Employees Union v. Yeutter, 918 F.2d 968 (D.C. Cir. 1990).

[168]Jones v. McKenzie, 833 F.2d 335 (D.C. Cir. 1987), *vacated and remanded sub nom.* Jenkins v. Jones, 490 U.S. 1001 (1989), *on remand*, 878 F.2d 1476 (D.C. Cir. 1989).

[169]Aubrey v. Sch. Bd., 148 F.3d 559 (5th Cir. 1998). *See also* English v. Talladega County Bd. of Educ., 938 F. Supp. 775 (N.D. Ala. 1996) (upholding random drug testing of school bus mechanics).

[170]Knox County Educ. Ass'n v. Knox. County Bd. of Educ., 158 F.3d 361, 375 (6th Cir. 1998).

[171]*Id.* at 386 (remanding this issue for the district court to determine whether the low level of alcohol impairment identified, .02, was reasonably related to the purpose of the testing program). In 2007, the Hawaii State Teachers Association approved a collective bargaining agreement stipulating that all public school teachers will be subject to random as well as suspicion-based drug and alcohol testing, but the American Civil Liberties Union is challenging the provision's legality. *See* National School Boards Association, "Employment & Labor," *Legal Clips* (October 11, 2007), p. 3.

recipients of federal grant funds maintain a drug-free work environment.[172] But the Fifth Circuit struck down policies in two Louisiana school districts that required employees injured in the course of employment to submit to urinalysis, finding an insufficient nexus between such injuries and drug use.[173]

Of course, employees, like students, can be subjected to alcohol and drug testing where there is reasonable suspicion that the individual is under the influence of those substances. Employees can be dismissed for refusing to submit to such a test,[174] but in some instances, reasonable suspicion has not been established to justify targeting particular individuals.[175] The law is still evolving regarding what constitutes individualized suspicion of drug use and the circumstances under which certain public employees can be subjected to urinalysis without such suspicion.

Lifestyle Controversies

Although regulations are far less restrictive today than in the early 1900s, when some school districts prohibited female teachers from marrying or even dating, school boards still attempt to proscribe aspects of teachers' personal lives that are inimical to community values. School officials have defended some behavior constraints on the grounds that teachers serve as exemplars for students and therefore should conform to community norms to ensure an appropriate educational environment. The Supreme Court has acknowledged that a "teacher serves as a role model for . . . students, exerting a subtle but important influence over their perceptions and values."[176] Recognizing that teachers are held to a higher standard of conduct than general citizens, the judiciary has upheld dismissals for behavior that jeopardizes student welfare, even if it takes place during the summer break.[177]

In recent years, teachers frequently have challenged school officials' authority to place restrictions on their personal lifestyles. Although the right to such personal freedom is not an enumerated constitutional guarantee, it is a right implied in the concept of personal liberty embodied in the Fourteenth Amendment. Constitutional protection

[172]Crager v. Bd. of Educ., 313 F. Supp. 2d 690 (E.D. Ky. 2004) (citing 41 U.S.C. § 702 (2007)). This law stipulates that federal grant and contract recipients cannot receive federal funds unless they implement policies to ensure that workplaces are free from the illegal use, possession, or distribution of controlled substances and establish drug-free awareness programs to inform employees about the policies, the dangers of drug abuse, penalties for drug use violations, and employee assistance available.

[173]United Teachers v. Orleans Parish Sch. Bd., 142 F.3d 853 (5th Cir. 1998).

[174]*See, e.g.*, Hearn v. Bd. of Pub. Educ., 191 F.3d 1329 (11th Cir. 1999) (upholding termination of a teacher who refused to undergo urinalysis after a drug-detecting dog identified marijuana in her car).

[175]*See, e.g.*, Warren v. Bd. of Educ., 200 F. Supp. 2d 1053 (E.D. Mo. 2001) (finding genuine issues as to whether the teacher's behavior suggested drug use and whether she consented to the drug test); Best v. Dep't of Health & Human Servs., 563 S.E.2d 573 (N.C. Ct. App. 2002) (overturning public employees' dismissals for refusal to submit to a drug test in the absence of reasonable cause for a public employer to believe they were using a controlled substance).

[176]Ambach v. Norwick, 441 U.S. 68, 78-79 (1979).

[177]*See, e.g.*, Bd. of Educ. v. Wood, 717 S.W.2d 837 (Ky. 1986).

afforded to teachers' privacy rights is determined not only by the *location* of the conduct, but also by the *nature* of the activity. The judiciary has attempted to balance teachers' privacy rights against the school board's legitimate interests in safeguarding the welfare of students and the effective management of the school. Sanctions cannot be imposed solely because school officials disapprove of teachers' personal and private conduct, but restrictions can be placed on unconventional behavior that is detrimental to job performance or harmful to students. Educators can be terminated based on evidence that would not be sufficient to support criminal charges,[178] but they cannot be dismissed for unsubstantiated rumors about their activities.[179]

The precise contours of public educators' constitutional privacy rights have not been clearly delineated; constitutional claims involving pregnancies out of wedlock, unconventional living arrangements, homosexuality, and other alleged sexual improprieties usually have been decided on a case-by-case basis. Since many of these cases also are discussed in Chapter 11 in connection with dismissals based on charges of immorality, the following discussion is confined to an overview of the constitutional issues.

Recognizing that decisions pertaining to marriage and parenthood involve constitutionally protected privacy rights, courts have been reluctant to support dismissal actions based on teachers' unwed, pregnant status in the absence of evidence that the condition impairs fitness to teach. In a typical case, the Fifth Circuit invalidated a Mississippi school district's rule prohibiting the employment of unwed parents in order to promote a "properly moral scholastic environment," reasoning that the policy violated equal protection and due process rights by equating birth of an illegitimate child with immoral conduct.[180] Compelled leaves of absence for pregnant, unmarried employees similarly have been invalidated as violating constitutional privacy rights.[181]

Most courts have reasoned that public employees, including educators, have a protected privacy right to engage in consenting sexual relationships out of wedlock, and that such relationships cannot be the basis for dismissal unless teaching effectiveness is impaired. For example, the Sixth Circuit ruled that a school board's nonrenewal of a nontenured teacher because of her involvement in a divorce abridged constitutional privacy rights,[182] and a Florida appeals court overturned a school

[178]*See, e.g.*, Montefusco v. Nassau County, 39 F. Supp. 2d 231 (E.D.N.Y. 1999) (holding that although the criminal investigation did not result in criminal charges, the school board could suspend the teacher with pay and remove extracurricular assignments for his possession of candid pictures of teenagers taken at the teacher's home).

[179]*See, e.g.*, Peaster Indep. Sch. Dist. v. Glodfelty, 63 S.W.3d 1 (Tex. App. 2001) (holding that widespread gossip triggered by unproven allegations of sexual misconduct could not be the basis for not renewing teachers' contracts).

[180]Andrews v. Drew Mun. Separate Sch. Dist., 507 F.2d 611, 614 (5th Cir. 1975).

[181]*See* Ponton v. Newport News Sch. Bd., 632 F. Supp. 1056 (E.D. Va. 1986).

[182]Littlejohn v. Rose, 768 F.2d 765 (6th Cir. 1985). *See also* Bertolini v. Whitehall City Sch. Dist., 744 N.E.2d 1245 (Ohio Ct. App. 2000), text accompanying note 113, Chapter 11.

board's termination of an unmarried teacher for lacking good moral character because at times she spent the night with an unmarried man.[183]

Some courts, however, have upheld dismissals or other disciplinary actions based on public employees' lifestyles that involve adulterous or other unconventional sexual relationships or activities that allegedly impaired job performance. To illustrate, the U.S. Supreme Court upheld dismissal of a police officer for selling videotapes of himself stripping off a police uniform and masturbating.[184] The Court rejected the officer's assertion that his off-duty conduct was constitutionally protected expression unrelated to his employment. A New York federal court also upheld termination of a teacher for actively participating in a group supporting consensual sexual activity between men and boys, reasoning that his activities in this organization were likely to impair teaching effectiveness and disrupt the school.[185]

Whether employment decisions can be based on a teacher's sexual orientation has been controversial, and the scope of constitutional protections afforded to gay, lesbian, bisexual, and transgendered (GLBT) educators continues to evolve. Among factors courts consider are the nature of the conduct (public or private), the notoriety it generates, and its impact on teaching effectiveness.

The law is clear that educators can be dismissed on the grounds of immorality for engaging in public sexual activity, whether the acts are heterosexual or homosexual in nature.[186] The Tenth Circuit upheld an Oklahoma statute permitting a teacher to be discharged for engaging in public homosexual activity, finding that this provision was neither vague nor a violation of equal protection rights.[187] However, as discussed previously, the court struck down the portion of the law authorizing the dismissal or nonrenewal of teachers for *advocating* public or private homosexuality as overbroad in restricting teachers' free speech rights.

In 2003, the Supreme Court delivered a significant decision, *Lawrence v. Texas,* in which it recognized a privacy right for consenting adults of the same sex to have sexual relations in the privacy of their homes by striking down a Texas law imposing criminal penalties for such conduct.[188] This ruling overturned a 1986 Supreme Court decision in which the Court upheld a Georgia law attaching criminal penalties to public *or private* consensual sodomy.[189] The Court in *Lawrence* emphasized that private,

---

[183]Sherburne v. Sch. Bd., 455 So. 2d 1057 (Fla. Dist. Ct. App. 1984).

[184]City of San Diego v. Roe, 543 U.S. 77 (2004) (finding no protected expression involved). *See also* City of Sherman v. Henry, 928 S.W.2d 464 (Tex. 1996) (finding no fundamental right to engage in adultery, so a patrolman's constitutional privacy rights were not violated when he was denied a promotion based on his affair with a fellow officer's wife).

[185]Melzer v. Bd. of Educ., 196 F. Supp. 2d 229 (E.D.N.Y. 2002).

[186]*See, e.g.*, Morgan v. State Bd. of Educ., 2002 Ohio 2738 (Ct. App. 2002) (upholding revocation of teaching certificate for disorderly conduct conviction stemming from his participation in public sex acts).

[187]Nat'l Gay Task Force v. Bd. of Educ., 729 F.2d 1270 (10th Cir. 1984), *aff'd by an equally divided court*, 470 U.S. 903 (1985). *See supra* text accompanying note 48.

[188]539 U.S. 558 (2003).

[189]Bowers v. Hardwick, 478 U.S. 186 (1986).

consensual sexual behavior in one's home is constitutionally protected and cannot be the basis for criminal action.

In addition to asserting protected privacy rights, some GLBT employees have claimed discrimination under the Equal Protection Clause of the Fourteenth Amendment. Discrimination in employment is discussed in detail in Chapter 10, so equal protection claims pertaining to GLBT educators are reviewed only briefly here. To substantiate an Equal Protection Clause violation, a teacher must prove that sexual orientation was the motivating factor in the adverse employment action and that there was no rational basis for the differential treatment.[190]

Dismissals of public educators based solely on sexual orientation, in the absence of criminal charges, have generated a range of judicial interpretations. During the 1970s and 1980s, a few courts permitted school districts to dismiss GLBT teachers or reassign them to nonteaching roles even when there was no link to teaching effectiveness.[191] The Sixth Circuit upheld a school district in not renewing a guidance counselor's contract after she revealed her sexual orientation and that of two students to other school employees. Rejecting the claim that the nonrenewal impaired free speech rights, the court held that her statements regarding her sexual orientation were not matters of public concern.[192] Subsequently, the Tenth Circuit, even though recognizing that refusal to hire a teacher on the basis of perceived homosexual tendencies was arbitrary and capricious, nonetheless held that the law was not clearly established in this regard in 1988 and thus granted the principal immunity for his role in the personnel decision based on sexual orientation.[193]

More recent litigation reflects the current judicial posture, requiring evidence that one's sexual orientation and private sexual behavior have a negative impact on teaching effectiveness before disciplinary action can be imposed. To illustrate, a Utah federal court overturned the school district's removal of a girls' volleyball coach, finding no job-related basis for the coach's removal based solely on the community's negative response to her sexual orientation. The court also noted that the school

---

[190]*See* Romer v. Evans, 517 U.S. 620 (1996) (invalidating an amendment to the Colorado Constitution that prohibited all legislative, executive, or judicial action designed to protect gay individuals).

[191]*See, e.g.*, Burton v. Cascade Sch. Dist., 512 F.2d 850 (9th Cir. 1975); Acanfora v. Bd. of Educ., 491 F.2d 498 (4th Cir. 1974); Gaylord v. Tacoma Sch. Dist. No. 10, 559 P.2d 1340 (Wash. 1977). *But see* Bd. of Educ. v. Jack M., 566 P.2d 602 (Cal. 1977); Morrison v. State Bd. of Educ., 461 P.2d 375 (Cal. 1969) (requiring evidence of impaired teaching effectiveness to discharge teachers for private homosexuality); text accompanying note 115, Chapter 11.

[192]Rowland v. Mad River Local Sch. Dist., 730 F.2d 444 (6th Cir. 1984) (rejecting also the Fourteenth Amendment equal protection claim because the counselor was not treated differently from other similarly situated employees facing nonrenewal of their contracts).

[193]Jantz v. Muci, 976 F.2d 623, 629 (10th Cir. 1992) (recognizing also that under Kansas law the authority to hire rests with school boards, not with principals, and finding no evidence of a delegation of such discretionary authority). *See also* Snyder v. Jefferson County Sch. Dist. R-1, 842 P.2d 624 (Colo. 1992) (terminating a teacher who let his teaching certificate expire while on leave to have gender reassignment surgery).

district could not instruct the coach to avoid mentioning her sexual orientation and ordered the coach to be reinstated and paid damages.[194] An Ohio federal district court similarly awarded a teacher reinstatement, back pay, and damages after finding that his contract was not renewed because of his sexual orientation rather than for his teaching deficiencies as the school board had asserted.[195]

A New Jersey teacher prevailed in his claim that he was harassed by teachers and students because he was gay, and that his resulting anxiety attacks forced him to take a leave of absence, after which his contract was not renewed.[196] A New York federal district court also held that a teacher stated a valid claim, precluding summary judgment, that a school district violated her Fourteenth Amendment equal protection rights when it failed to discipline students who harassed the teacher because she was a lesbian and treated her differently from other similarly situated non-GLBT teachers.[197] However, the Seventh Circuit held that a school had not violated a teacher's equal protection rights in connection with parental and student harassment of the teacher based on sexual orientation, because school officials took some action to respond to the teacher's complaints of harassment and treated the allegations as they would treat harassment complaints filed by other teachers.[198]

In recent cases, courts generally have not been convinced that teachers become poor role models simply because of their alternative lifestyles. The case law suggests that there has been a shift from condoning dismissals for merely being GLBT to requiring evidence that an individual's sexual orientation has an adverse impact on job performance. Recent decisions suggest that it would be difficult to produce a rational basis for terminating or in other ways treating GLBT teachers differently from other educators.

Conclusion

Although public educators do not shed their constitutional rights as a condition of public employment, under certain circumstances restrictions on these freedoms are justified by overriding governmental interests. Constitutional protections afforded to

---

[194]Weaver v. Nebo Sch. Dist., 29 F. Supp. 2d 1279 (D. Utah 1998).

[195]Glover v. Williamsburg Local Sch. Dist., 20 F. Supp. 2d 1160 (S.D. Ohio 1998).

[196]Curcio v. Collingswood Bd. of Educ., No. 04-5100 (JBS), 2006 U.S. Dist. LEXIS 46648 (D.N.J. June 28, 2006). *See also* Murray v. Oceanside Unified Sch. Dist., 95 Cal. Rptr. 2d 28 (Ct. App. 2000) (ruling in favor of an award-winning biology teacher who used the California nondiscrimination law to challenge years of harassment by colleagues based on her sexual orientation).

[197]Lovell v. Comsewogue Sch. Dist., 214 F. Supp. 2d 319 (E.D.N.Y. 2002).

[198]Schroeder v. Hamilton Sch. Dist., 282 F.3d 946 (7th Cir. 2002).

educators continue to be delineated by the judiciary; the following generalizations reflect the status of the law in the substantive areas discussed in this chapter.

1. When speaking as citizens, public educators have a First Amendment right to express their views on issues of public concern; dismissal or other retaliatory personnel action, such as transfers, demotions, or written reprimands, cannot be predicated solely on protected speech.
2. Public employees' expression pursuant to official job responsibilities is not constitutionally protected.
3. Expression pertaining to personal employment disputes, attacks on supervisors, or speech intended to disrupt the school is not constitutionally protected.
4. If a public employer acts in good faith, conducts a reasonable investigation, and concludes from the evidence that the employee's offensive comments are unprotected, the employee can be dismissed for the expression.
5. The exercise of protected speech will not invalidate a dismissal action if the school board can show by a preponderance of evidence that it would have reached the same decision had the protected speech not occurred.
6. Even if expression made as a citizen on public issues is the sole basis for adverse employment action, the school board still might prevail under the *Pickering* balancing test if established that its interests in providing effective and efficient educational services outweigh the individual's free expression rights.
7. A school's internal mail system is not a traditional open forum for expression, and unless designated as such, access to the mail system can be restricted to business relating to the school's educational function as long as restrictions are not viewpoint based.
8. Reasonable time, place, and manner restrictions can be imposed on educators' expression, but arbitrary prior restraints on the content and channel of communication violate the First Amendment.
9. Public school teachers do not have the right to determine the content of the instructional program, but they do have some latitude in selecting appropriate strategies to convey the prescribed content.
10. In evaluating the appropriateness of teaching materials and strategies, courts consider relevance to course objectives, threat of disruption, age and maturity of students, and community standards.
11. Public employees cannot be retaliated against because of their membership in labor unions, political groups, or organizations with unlawful purposes.
12. A public educator's participation in political activities outside the classroom cannot be the basis for adverse employment decisions, unless the employee has policy-making responsibilities and such participation would jeopardize relationships at work.
13. State laws can impose restrictions on the types of elected offices that public educators can hold (e.g., two incompatible positions cannot be held).
14. Public employees can be required to take temporary leave from their positions to campaign for political office if established that campaign demands would interfere with professional responsibilities.

15. School officials can impose reasonable restrictions on educators' personal appearance if there is a rational basis for such regulations.
16. Public educators' desks and files at school can be searched based on reasonable suspicion that the search is necessary for educational reasons.
17. Public educators can be subjected to urinalysis with reasonable suspicion of drug use; employees in safety-sensitive roles can be subjected to blanket or random drug testing.
18. Public educators enjoy protected privacy rights in their personal lifestyles; however, adverse employment consequences may be justified if their private lives have a detrimental effect on job performance.
19. In general, school districts cannot disadvantage employees based on their sexual orientation unless an employee's conduct has a negative impact on teaching effectiveness or other job duties.

10

Discrimination in Employment

All persons and groups are potential victims of discrimination in employment. People of color and women claim discrimination in traditionally segregated job categories, whereas Caucasians and males claim that affirmative action has denied them the right to compete on equal grounds. The young argue that the old already hold the good jobs and that entry is nearly impossible, and the old contend that they often are let go when "downsizing" occurs and that reemployment at the same level and salary is unlikely. Religious minorities might not be allowed to dress the way they please or may be denied leave for religious observance, and religious majorities (particularly in private schools) have concerns about governmental intrusion into their homogeneous work environments. Likewise, persons with disabilities often complain that they are not given the opportunity to show what they can do, whereas employers often contend that the costs of accommodating those with disabilities could be significant and never ending. Given these diverse interests, it is not surprising that literally hundreds of employment discrimination suits are filed each year.

Legal Context

Most, but not all, forms of employment discrimination violate either federal or state law. Foremost among these mandates are the Fourteenth Amendment to the United States Constitution and Title VII of the Civil Rights Act of 1964; both are discussed here, given their broad application. Other more narrowly tailored statutes are reviewed in the respective sections addressing discrimination based on race and national origin, sex, sexual orientation, religion, age, and disability.

Fourteenth Amendment

The Fourteenth Amendment to the United States Constitution mandates that no state shall deny to any person within its jurisdiction equal protection of the laws. This applies to subdivisions of the state, including public school districts. Under the Equal Protection Clause, if a government policy or law facially discriminates in employment, one of three forms of scrutiny will be used to determine its constitutionality: *strict, intermediate,* or *rational basis* (see Figure 1A appendix).

    Facial discrimination (e.g., the posting of an elementary school principal's position stipulating that it has been reserved for a female applicant) indicates that the school district intended to discriminate. Where facial discrimination exists, the government employer bears the burden of justifying its policies, practices, or acts. The degree of difficulty in carrying that burden is in part determined by the level of scrutiny applied by courts. As discussed in Chapter 5, a policy or practice that discriminates based on race, national origin, or alienage is *strictly scrutinized* and can be justified only if narrowly tailored and supported by a compelling state interest.[1] When a plaintiff claims discrimination based on sex or illegitimacy, *intermediate scrutiny* is used, requiring the classification to serve important governmental objectives and the discriminatory acts to be substantially related to the achievement of those objectives.[2] And, finally, *rational-basis scrutiny* is applied when any other plaintiff class is involved (e.g., classes based on religion, age, sexual orientation, disability).[3] This level of scrutiny requires only that the justification not be arbitrary, capricious, or without foundation.

    Whereas intent to discriminate is apparent with facial discrimination, some policies or practices are facially neutral but result in a disproportionate impact on a protected group (e.g., use of a standardized test in hiring that results in disparate impact based on race). Unlike Title VII (discussed below), to establish a constitutional violation the employee must prove that the employer intended to discriminate. To substantiate discriminatory *intent*, the court will examine criteria such as the pattern of discriminatory impact; the historical background of the act, policy, or practice that supports a discriminatory motive; the specific sequence of events leading up to the allegedly unconstitutional behavior; and departures from normal procedures.[4] Although disproportionate impact is not irrelevant in these cases, it is not "the sole touchstone of invidious discrimination forbidden by the Constitution,"[5] and without more does not prove a Fourteenth Amendment violation.

Title VII

Title VII is enforced by the Equal Employment Opportunity Commission (EEOC) and prohibits employers with 15 or more employees from discriminating on the basis

[1]*See, e.g.*, Graham v. Richardson, 403 U.S. 365 (1971) (alienage); Hunter v. Erickson, 393 U.S. 385 (1969) (race); Korematsu v. United States, 323 U.S. 214 (1944) (nationality).

[2]Clark v. Jeter, 486 U.S. 456 (1988) (illegitimacy); Miss. Univ. for Women v. Hogan, 458 U.S. 718 (1982) (sex).

[3]*See, e.g.*, Johnson v. Univ. of Iowa, 431 F.3d 325 (8th Cir. 2005) (concluding that rational-basis scrutiny is all that is required where adoptive parents were permitted leave time, but natural fathers were not; the court noted that rational basis was met, as adoptive parents do not have insurance to offset costs associated with adoption and may be required to take time off work to perform necessary paperwork).

[4]Vill. of Arlington Heights v. Metro. Hous. Dev. Corp., 429 U.S. 252, 265–268 (1977).

[5]Washington v. Davis, 426 U.S. 229, 242 (1976).

of race, color, religion, sex, or national origin and covers hiring, promotion, and compensation practices as well as fringe benefits and other terms and conditions of employment.[6] However, protection against discriminatory employment practices is not absolute for individuals within these classifications since both Congress and courts have identified exceptions. In creating and amending Title VII over the years, Congress has expressly permitted employers to facially discriminate based on religion, sex, or national origin (but not on race or color) if they can show the existence of a *bona fide occupational qualification* (BFOQ) that is reasonably necessary to the normal operation of their particular enterprise. Additionally, courts have specified that employers may use facially neutral employment practices that result in disparate impact on a protected class, but only if a *business necessity* is identified in the use of that practice and there are no less discriminatory ways of meeting that need.

Qualifying as an Employer.   Title VII applies to employers with 15 or more employees who work 20 or more weeks during the calendar year. Although this requirement is seemingly simple, its application has been complex. The Supreme Court resolved some of the issues in *Walters v. Metropolitan Educational Enterprises,*[7] in which it adopted the "payroll method" to assess employment status. All that is necessary under this approach is to determine when the employee began employment and when he or she left (if at all). The person is counted as an employee for each working day after being hired and before leaving. If 15 or more workers are on the payroll for 20 or more weeks during the year (or the preceding year), then the employer is covered by Title VII. It is not relevant whether the employee worked partial days, every other day, or was on call, leave, or vacation. However, employees who begin or depart in the middle of a week do not count toward the total for that particular week.[8]

Disparate Treatment and Impact.   When evaluating Title VII claims, courts have developed two legal theories: disparate treatment and disparate impact. *Disparate treatment* is applied when the individual claims less favorable treatment when compared to other applicants or employees. D*isparate impact* is used when an employer's ostensibly neutral practice has a discriminatory impact on the class the claimant represents. Additionally, it is possible for an employee to file a Title VII complaint based on retaliation.[9]

---

[6]42 U.S.C. § 2000e *et seq.* (2007).

[7]519 U.S. 202 (1997).

[8]Although *Walters* is a Title VII retaliation case, the definition established by the Court has been applied to cases under the Americans with Disabilities Act (ADA), given the similarity of the two statutes. *See, e.g.,* Owens v. S. Devel. Council, 59 F. Supp. 2d 1210 (M.D. Ala. 1999). Also, the EEOC has adopted that approach under the Age Discrimination in Employment Act of 1967, 29 U.S.C. § 630(b) (2007). This law is applicable to employers with 20 or more employees. Moreover, the Department of Labor requires use of the payroll method under the Family Medical Leave Act of 1993, 29 U.S.C. § 2611(4)(A)(i) (2007), although the number of employees required for compliance under that law is 50.

[9]*See, e.g.,* Cole v. Del. Technical and Cmty. Coll., 459 F. Supp. 2d 296 (D. Del. 2006).

In proving disparate treatment, plaintiffs may use direct or circumstantial evidence. *Direct evidence* is rarely available and results only when the employer has provided a written or spoken statement that:

- Is clear,
- Comes from an individual involved in making employment decisions,
- Refers specifically to the individual denied the employment opportunity, and
- Is expressed close in time to when the employment decision was made.[10]

Examples include an employer denying an employee a requested raise because he was "just a white guy,"[11] and a supervisor who fired an older female employee with the stated desire to replace her with "a young chippie" with large breasts.[12]

Notwithstanding the above, plaintiffs usually do not have direct evidence of discrimination so they often rely on circumstantial evidence[13] to substantiate that they received less favorable treatment and that such conduct, if otherwise unexplained, is "more likely than not based on the consideration of impermissible factors."[14] To support a circumstantial claim, the plaintiff must show that he or she:

- Was a member of a protected class;
- Applied for and was qualified for the job; and
- Was denied the position, while the employer continued to seek applicants with the plaintiff's qualifications.

These criteria were articulated by the Supreme Court in 1973 in *McDonnell Douglas Corporation v. Green*[15] and, with some modification, are applied beyond claims of hiring discrimination to alleged disparate treatment in areas such as promotion, termination, and tenure.

If the claim is supported, the burden shifts to the employer to state a reason for its action that does not violate Title VII. Such a reason may be either objective (e.g., a higher level degree), subjective (e.g., stronger interpersonal skills), or a combination.

---

[10]David J. Walsh, *Employment Law for Human Resource Practice,* 2d ed. (Mason, OH: Thomson Southwestern, 2006), p. 69.

[11]Gagnon v. Sprint Corp., 284 F.3d 839, 846 (8th Cir. 2002).

[12]Glanzman v. Metro. Mgt. Corp., 391 F.3d 506, 510 (3d Cir. 2004).

[13]*See, e.g.*, Walker v. Bd. of Regents of Univ. of Wis. Sys., 410 F.3d 387 (7th Cir. 2005) (identifying several types of circumstantial evidence: timing of events; ambiguous statements, oral or written; behavior or comments directed at other employees in the protected group; treatment provided similarly situated employees; more favorable treatment provided a person not within the employee's protected class; whether the employer's proffered reason for the difference is unworthy of belief; and any other evidence from which an inference of discriminatory intent might be drawn).

[14]Furnco Constr. Corp. v. Waters, 438 U.S. 567, 577 (1978). *See also* Glover v. Bd. of Educ. of Rockford Pub. Schs., 187 Fed. Appx. 614 (7th Cir. 2006) (finding no evidence that supported the use of a discriminatory motive on the part of the employer).

[15]411 U.S. 792, 802 (1973).

If the employer is unable to produce a nondiscriminatory reason for the action, a directed verdict for the plaintiff would be granted. But given the ease of presenting a nondiscriminatory reason, employers in nearly every instance provide a response. After the employer provides a rebuttal, the plaintiff then has the additional burden of proving by a preponderance of the evidence not only that the proffered reason was false but also that it served as a pretext for prohibited intentional discrimination.[16] In most instances of alleged discrimination, the plaintiff is unable to show that the employer's purported nondiscriminatory basis was pretextual. When that occurs, it is common for the defendant to request summary judgment in an effort to end the litigation. Summary judgment will be issued only if the evidence shows that there remains no genuine issue of material fact and that the moving party is entitled to judgment as a matter of law.

Other times, the case may be presented before a jury, which then is responsible for determining whether the law has been violated and, if so, the appropriate level of damages. Following a jury decision, an unsatisfied party may file a motion asking for *judgment as a matter of law*. In a Seventh Circuit case, a former vice chancellor sued her institution alleging sex discrimination, among other constitutional and statutory claims.[17] The jury was not persuaded by plaintiff's evidence supporting race discrimination and an infringement of free speech rights, but was satisfied that she had proven her employer had discriminated against her due to sex. The university then filed for a judgment as a matter of law, which was granted by the district court and affirmed by the Seventh Circuit. To grant such a request, the court must be persuaded that no reasonable jury could have ruled in favor of the plaintiff, given the evidence adduced at trial. The court was satisfied that the adverse employment decision was based on plaintiff's intimidating and unsupportive management style resulting in low staff morale, refusal to investigate staff concerns, and insubordination. The occasional, if not rare, sexist comment made within the organization (e.g., that she needed to "hang on to her girdle"[18]) was insufficient to support a Title VII violation.[19]

In contrast to disparate treatment claims, to prove disparate impact the plaintiff is not initially required to support discriminatory intent but must establish that an

---

[16]*See, e.g.,* St. Mary's Honor Ctr. v. Hicks, 509 U.S. 502, 514-515 (1993). *See also* Riley v. Birmingham Bd. of Educ., 154 Fed. Appx. 114 (11th Cir. 2005) (determining that the Caucasian plaintiff failed to show that race was a factor in his demotion and his failure to be selected for the head coaching position; testimony that the African American principal, who had hired African Americans for several positions, had stated "we have to take care of our own," was found insufficient to show pretext); Sarmiento v. Queens Coll., 153 Fed. Appx. 21 (2d Cir. 2005) (finding that a rejected applicant for a teaching position failed to support either race discrimination or retaliation; noting that although at least one of the defendants confirmed animosity toward the plaintiff, there was no proof that such animosity was due to race).

[17]Walker v. Bd. of Regents of Univ. of Wis. Sys., 410 F.3d 387 (7th Cir. 2005).

[18]*Id.* at 390.

[19]*But see* Waite v. Bd. of Trs. of Ill. Cmty. Coll. Dist. No. 508, 408 F.3d 339 (7th Cir. 2005) (finding one statement by one employee that the Jamaican plaintiff had a "plantation mentality" sufficient for a jury to find discriminatory intent, even though the person uttering the phrase was not a decision maker in the plaintiff's suspension).

employer's facially neutral practice had a disproportionate impact on the plaintiff's protected class. This generally is accomplished through the use of statistics. Once this type of *prima facie* case is established, the employer then must show that the challenged policies or practices (or its employment practices in the aggregate) are job related and justified by a business necessity. Accordingly, an employer's nondiscriminatory reason for the act is insufficient to rebut a *prima facie* case of discriminatory impact. Moreover, although difficult to do, even if a business necessity is identified, a plaintiff still may prevail by showing that the employer's facially neutral practice had a discriminatory purpose.

The Supreme Court has recognized, however, that mere awareness of a policy's adverse impact on a protected class does not constitute proof of unlawful motive; a discriminatory purpose "implies that the decisionmaker . . . selected or reaffirmed a particular course of action at least in part 'because of,' not merely 'in spite of,' its adverse effects upon an identifiable group."[20] Nonetheless, foreseeably discriminatory consequences can be considered by courts in assessing intent, although more will be needed to substantiate unlawful motive. Furthermore, the employee may prevail if it is shown that the employer refused to adopt an alternative policy identified by the employee that realistically would have met the employer's business needs without resulting in disparate impact.

Retaliation. By the time a complaint is filed with the EEOC or a state or federal court, the working relationship between the employer and the employee is strained, sometimes beyond repair. In response to filing, an employee may not be terminated, demoted, or harassed, but less extreme acts such as rudeness or "the cold shoulder" will not typically violate Title VII.[21] Where actionable behavior occurs, the employee may file a second claim alleging retaliation. To support this type of case, the employee is required to show that he or she participated in statutorily protected activity (i.e., the filing of a complaint or suit), that an adverse employment action was taken by the employer, and that a causal connection existed between the protected activity and the adverse action.[22] If the employee can show that filing the complaint was the basis for the adverse employment decision, even if the original complaint of discrimination fails, the court will provide appropriate relief.[23] It also is critical to show that the retaliatory action followed soon after engagement in the protected activity. Furthermore, showing that the administrator responsible for the adverse action knew of the filing of the original complaint is essential to showing that he or she retaliated in response to that filing.[24]

---

[20]Personnel Adm'r of Mass. v. Feeney, 442 U.S. 256, 279 (1979).

[21]Walsh, *supra* note 10, p. 90.

[22]*See, e.g.*, Valdes v. Union City Bd. of Educ., 186 Fed. Appx. 319 (3d Cir. July 21, 2006).

[23]*See, e.g.*, Nye v. Roberts, 145 Fed. Appx. 1 (4th Cir. 2005) (concluding that a letter of reprimand chastising the plaintiff for filing a complaint of sexual harassment may allow a jury to find that the school district had retaliated against the plaintiff).

[24]*See, e.g.*, Boynton v. W. Wyo. Cmty. Coll., 157 Fed. Appx. 33 (10th Cir. 2005).

Relief.   If it is proven that the employee was a victim of prohibited discrimination, courts have the authority to require a *make-whole remedy* where the person is placed in the same position he or she otherwise would have been, absent discriminatory activity. In meeting this objective, courts may provide injunctive and declaratory relief; require that a person be reinstated, hired, tenured, or promoted; direct the payment of back pay, interest on back pay, or front pay;[25] assign retroactive seniority; and provide attorneys' fees and court costs. Requiring the employer to apologize for the discrimination appears to go beyond the court's authority, however.[26] In cases in which intentional discrimination is proven, a court also may provide compensatory and punitive damages. But, an employer may not be held liable for the discriminatory acts of its managerial staff when their decisions are contrary to the employer's good faith efforts to comply with Title VII.[27]

Race and National-Origin Discrimination

Race and national-origin discrimination in employment continue in spite of nearly 140 years of protective statutes and constitutional amendments. For most of that period, however, the relief received by plaintiffs was typically limited to a make-whole remedy and seldom penalized the employer sufficiently to discourage future discrimination. Due to changes in statutes and case law, it now is possible for successful plaintiffs to receive substantial monetary awards well beyond a make-whole remedy. Race and national origin lawsuits are filed under the Fourteenth Amendment,[28] Title VII, and 42 U.S.C. Section 1981.

Section 1981 originally was Section 1 of the Civil Rights Act of 1866. At one time, this statute prohibited only race discrimination in making and enforcing contracts, but now Section 1981 applies when either race or ethnicity discrimination is alleged in making, performing, modifying, and terminating contracts, as well as in the enjoyment of all benefits, privileges, terms, and conditions of the contractual relationship.[29]

---

[25]For example, if a teacher were denied a principalship due to race, the court may direct the district to hire the teacher for the next available position. If the principalship line provided greater compensation than did the teacher line, the court could require that the difference in salary be awarded to the teacher up to the time of promotion. That portion of the salary paid in the future is termed *front pay*, while that portion due for the period between the failure to hire and the court's ruling is termed *back pay*.

[26]Woodruff v. Ohman, 29 Fed. Appx. 337 (6th Cir. 2002).

[27]Kolstad v. Am. Dental Ass'n, 527 U.S. 526 (1999).

[28]The Fourteenth Amendment requires the application of strict scrutiny in cases in which race or national-origin discrimination is facial and proof of intent where the alleged discrimination is facially neutral. Moreover, the Fifth Amendment has an express Due Process Clause and an implied Equal Protection Clause. It is used when a violation is claimed within the District of Columbia, because the Fourteenth Amendment limits only state action. *See, e.g.*, Washington v. Davis, 426 U.S. 229 (1976).

[29]*See, e.g.*, Amini v. Oberlin Coll., 440 F.3d 350 (6th Cir. 2006).

Hiring and Promotion Practices

Unless a school district is under a narrowly tailored court order to correct prior proven acts of race discrimination, it may not advantage or disadvantage an applicant or employee because of that individual's race. When unsuccessful candidates believe that race played a role in the decision-making process, they will generally allege disparate treatment, requiring the heightened proof of discriminatory intent. In attempting to support such a claim, many plaintiffs have difficulty overcoming employers' purported nondiscriminatory reasons for their decisions.[30] For example, in an Eleventh Circuit case, an African American failed to support his claim that the university's proffered reasons for not selecting him (i.e., that he had little experience and performed poorly during the interview) were pretextual, notwithstanding the fact that a person of a different race ultimately was hired.[31] The court also acknowledged the importance of subjective evaluations in the employment process to assess qualities such as attitude and enthusiasm, and approved the use of such measures, unless applied in a discriminatory manner.

At other times, plaintiffs are able to show that no legitimate bases supported the employer's decision and that the selection was based on impermissible factors. In a Second Circuit case dealing with national-origin discrimination, the plaintiff was a Caucasian American of Eastern European origin who had applied for the director position of a Spanish language program.[32] An American male of Hispanic descent ultimately was appointed to the position, satisfying a university affirmative action policy that encouraged the hiring of women and racial minorities. Purportedly, the same standards were to be used to evaluate the applicants once a diversified pool of candidates was identified. Nonetheless, the Caucasian plaintiff was able to show that he was the only finalist who possessed a doctorate; that neither of the other finalists had published as extensively or had as much college teaching; that he had experience in running the program (i.e., during an interim appointment for which he received glowing commendations); that the university had deviated from established procedures; and that he was the only finalist who could teach Portuguese, a requirement for the position. The court concluded that ample evidence was presented to permit a reasonable fact finder to conclude that the university's employment decision was more likely than not due to impermissible discrimination based on national origin.

---

[30]*See, e.g.,* Barber v. Univ. of Med. and Dentistry of N.J., 118 Fed. Appx. 588 (3d Cir. 2004); Mosby v. Norwalk Bd. of Educ., 4 Fed. Appx. 15 (2d Cir. 2001).

[31]Goodman v. Georgia Southwestern State Univ., 147 Fed. Appx. 888 (11th Cir. 2005). *But see* Taylor v. Bd. of Educ., 240 Fed. Appx. 717 (6th Cir. 2007) (reversing summary judgment for the board; noting that questions remained as to whether the African American plaintiffs were better qualified than the Caucasian counselors who were selected). *See also* Hammons v. George C. Wallace State Cmty. Coll., 174 Fed. Appx. 459 (11th Cir. 2006) (finding that plaintiff was unable to show she was replaced by someone of another race or that the two persons allegedly better treated were similarly situated; concluding that plaintiff failed to show that her nonrenewal was based on race, rather than poor supervisory and interaction skills). Note, however, that it is not always dispositive of a discrimination claim when the successful applicant and the plaintiff are of the same class. The selected candidate may have been chosen only after the employer learned that a suit had been filed. *See, e.g.,* Lowry v. Bedford County Sch. Bd., No. 98-1165, 1999 U.S. App. LEXIS 16770 (4th Cir. July 19, 1999).

[32]Stern v. Trs. of Columbia Univ., 131 F.3d 305 (2d Cir. 1997).

Testing.   Among the more controversial objective measures used in hiring and promotion (e.g., degree level, a specified number of years' experience) is the use of standardized test scores. The EEOC requires employers to conduct validity studies for tests used in making employment decisions if they result in adverse impact on a protected class. *Adverse impact* exists when:

- One group succeeds at a rate that is less than four-fifths, or 80 percent, of that achieved by the group with the highest passing rate (e.g., adverse impact results if 90 percent of Caucasians pass a test, but fewer than 72 percent of African Americans do so) *or*
- For small populations, the difference in scores between the two groups is statistically significant.

For tests with a disparate impact to be used, they must be reliable and valid, and they must qualify as a business necessity.[33] Also, tests may be administered to applicants for positions other than those for which the tests have been validated, but only if there are no significant differences in the skills, knowledge, and abilities required by the jobs.[34] Tests may not be discriminatorily administered, nor may their results be discriminatorily used. Moreover, employers may not use different cut-off scores for different racial groups or adjust scores based on race.

Notwithstanding the restrictions posed above, many employers both small and large feel that the use of tests is so important to the accomplishment of organizational goals that they feel compelled to use them. For example, it has been held that a state has the right to require its current and future teachers to demonstrate their general literacy as well as their content knowledge. In *United States v. South Carolina*, the Supreme Court affirmed a lower court's conclusion that South Carolina's use of the National Teachers Examination (NTE) for teacher certification and salary purposes satisfied the Equal Protection Clause.[35] The federal district court had held that the test was valid, since it measured knowledge of course content in teacher preparation courses, and that it was not administered with an intent to discriminate against minority applicants for teacher certification. The court also found sufficient evidence to establish a relationship between the use of the test scores in determining the placement of teachers on the salary scale and legitimate employment objectives, such as encouraging teachers to upgrade their skills. The option proposed by the plaintiffs (i.e., graduation from an approved teacher preparation program) was rejected by the court as incapable of assuring minimally competent teachers because of the wide range in university admission requirements, academic standards, and grading practices.

---

[33]Griggs v. Duke Power Co., 401 U.S. 424, 432 (1971) (holding that a private company's use of both a high school diploma requirement and a test of general intelligence as prerequisites to initial employment and a condition of transfer violated Title VII; neither requirement was shown to be related to successful job performance, and both operated to disqualify minority applicants at a higher rate than those who were Caucasian).

[34]Albemarle Paper Co. v. Moody, 422 U.S. 405, 432 (1975).

[35]445 F. Supp. 1094 (D.S.C. 1977), *aff'd sub nom.* Nat'l Educ. Ass'n v. South Carolina, 434 U.S. 1026 (1978).

It is likely that states, districts, and teacher-training institutions will continue to use tests as a requirement for admission to training programs; a prerequisite to licensure; and a basis for graduation, hiring, and promotion. To avoid discriminatory actions, test performance should not be the sole criterion for making personnel decisions. Also, even when multiple criteria are used, each criterion must be validated if it results in disproportionate impact, or if it is part of a process that in the aggregate results in disproportionate impact.[36]

Adverse Decisions

Employers cannot dismiss, decline to renew, or demote employees on the basis of race or national origin.[37] In 1993, the Supreme Court rendered a significant decision in a race-based termination case, *St. Mary's Honor Center v. Hicks*,[38] in which a minority employee of a halfway house was demoted and eventually fired. In response to plaintiff's *prima facie* case,[39] the employer argued that the suspension, letter of reprimand, and demotion were necessary because of the employee's poor supervision of his subordinates, his failure to conduct a proper investigation of a brawl between inmates, and the use of threatening words with his immediate superior. Given this response, the burden shifted back to the employee to show both that the proffered reasons were not to be believed *and* that the true basis for the termination was race.

The district court had determined that the employer's reasons were untrue, noting that the plaintiff was the only supervisor disciplined for violations committed by his subordinates and that similar, and at times more severe, violations by others were either treated more leniently or disregarded. The district court noted, and the Supreme Court agreed, however, that even though the employee was able to show that the purported reasons were false, he failed to show that race was a factor in his termination. Because the plaintiff was unable to meet his entire burden of persuasion, he could not prove a Title VII violation.[40]

[36]Connecticut v. Teal, 457 U.S. 440 (1982).

[37]*See, e.g.,* Seagrave v. Dean, 908 So. 2d 41 (1st Cir. 2005); Juniel v. Park Forest–Chi. Heights, Ill., Sch. Dist., 46 Fed. Appx. 853 (7th Cir. 2002). Title VII also prohibits race-motivated harassment in the workplace. *But see* Sallis v. Univ. of Minn., 408 F.3d 470 (8th Cir. 2005) (concluding that rude and insensitive racial remarks that were infrequently used did not create a hostile work environment).

[38]509 U.S. 502 (1993).

[39]That is, the plaintiff was African American, qualified for the position, demoted, and later discharged, and the position remained open until ultimately filled by a Caucasian.

[40]*See also* Keri v. Bd. of Trs. of Purdue Univ., 458 F.3d 620 (7th Cir. 2006) (determining that professor failed to demonstrate that the university's stated reasons—student complaints—for his dismissal were a pretext for discrimination); Bickerstaff v. Vassar Coll., 160 Fed. Appx. 61 (2d Cir. 2005) (concluding that plaintiff failed to support her claims of race discrimination, retaliation, and hostile work environment; noting that (1) plaintiff's limited annual pay increases were due to poor teaching evaluations, (2) changes to her office space were in response to her unwillingness to relocate with the rest of her program, (3) she was not selected as director because the members of the steering committee did not support her, and (4) she was not given a joint appointment, given that the additional departments did not want her in their respective programs).

Likewise, in an Eleventh Circuit case, an African American school district employee responsible for electric motor repair was terminated when the district learned of his conviction for child molestation and multiple counts of assault and battery. A Caucasian employee with a 1977 molestation conviction had not been terminated. Initially, the jury awarded the plaintiff approximately $140,000, which he appealed as the amount did not include a compensatory award. The school district also appealed, claiming that it had the right to terminate the employment of child molesters. In its defense, the district explained that the Caucasian employee was not terminated when the incident occurred 24 years earlier due to an agreement that was entered into with the state attorney's office and the local superintendent. The appeals court concluded that the frequency (four), recency (one case was still pending), and violent nature (use of a machete) of the plaintiff's crimes were the bases for his termination and not his race.[41] Similar decisions have been reached by other courts when adverse decisions were based on legitimate nonpretextual factors such as neglect of duty, incompetence, punctuality, insubordination, falsification of records, theft, threatening students, stalking and rape, and the like.[42]

In some cases, plaintiffs even have difficulty in showing that the conduct of their respective employers qualified as adverse actions (e.g., change of school, grade level, teaching assignment[43]). The Eleventh Circuit upheld summary judgment in a race discrimination case.[44] The African American plaintiff had been given poor performance evaluations by a relatively new principal as well as an independent observer. However, her nonrenewal notice was not delivered in a timely manner. As a result, she was offered a contract, but elected to decline it. The court reasoned that because a new contract had been proffered, plaintiff failed to show that she was subjected to an adverse employment act. The threat of nonrenewal and close supervision were insufficient to qualify as adverse acts.

Affirmative Action

Affirmative action has been defined as "steps taken to remedy the grossly disparate staffing and recruitment patterns that are the present consequences of past discrimination and to prevent the occurrence of employment discrimination in the future."[45] Correcting such imbalances requires the employer to engage in activities such as expanding its training programs, becoming actively involved in recruitment, eliminating invalid

---

[41]Silvera v. Orange County Sch. Bd., 244 F.3d 1253 (11th Cir. 2001). *See also* Conward v. Cambridge Sch. Comm., 171 F.3d 12 (1st Cir. 1999) (upholding termination of a teacher for unbecoming conduct when he handed a female student a document with the title "Application for a Piece of Ass" and observing that plaintiff failed to show that his treatment was race related).

[42]*See, e.g.,* Shaw v. Monroe, 20 Fed. Appx. 563 (7th Cir. 2001) (stalking and rape); Clearwater v. Indep. Sch. Dist. No. 166, 231 F.3d 1122 (8th Cir. 2000) (tardiness); Jones v. Sch. Dist., 198 F.3d 403 (3d Cir. 1999) (threatening students).

[43]*See, e.g.,* Pipkin v. Bridgeport Bd. of Educ., 159 Fed. Appx. 259 (2d Cir. 2005).

[44]Christian v. Cartersville City Schs., 167 Fed. Appx. 89 (11th Cir. 2006).

[45]United States Commission on Civil Rights, *Statement of Affirmative Action for Equal Employment Opportunities* (Washington, D.C.: U.S. Commission on Civil Rights, 1973).

selection criteria that result in disparate impact, and modifying collective bargaining agreements that impermissibly restrict the promotion and retention of minorities. Courts will uphold most strategies that the EEOC identifies as affirmative action under both Title VII (for which the EEOC has regulatory authority) and the Fourteenth Amendment (for which the EEOC does not have regulatory authority). However, courts will prohibit the use of affirmative action plans that provide a discriminatory "preference" rather than an "equal opportunity. "

In 1989, the Supreme Court began to question a variety of public-sector practices that provided racial preferences.[46] In the aggregate, these cases applied strict scrutiny to race-based affirmative action programs operated by federal, state, and local levels of government; discredited societal discrimination as a justification for such programs; required showing specific discriminatory action to impose a race-based remedy; and allowed only narrowly tailored plans that would further a compelling interest. Given this precedent, existing public-sector affirmative action plans that provide racial preferences without a proven history of discrimination or are based only on underrepresentation are likely to be found unconstitutional.

In addition to affirmative action in hiring and promotion, there also have been efforts to protect the diversity gained through court order and voluntary affirmative action by providing a preference in organization downsizing. When a reduction in school staff is necessary due to financial exigency, declining enrollment, or a change in education priorities, it generally is based, at least in part, on tenure and seniority within teaching areas. Accordingly, it is important for all employees to be in their rightful place on the seniority list. To obtain their rightful place, employees have been awarded varying levels of retroactive seniority (i.e., time between rejection of the application due to impermissible discrimination and court-ordered initial employment), in addition to those years they have accrued while actually on the job.[47]

In some cases, employers have proposed the modification of seniority systems to give an overall preference to all minorities regarding eligibility for promotion and other job benefits or in protection from a reduction-in-force (RIF). Such affirmative action plans are similar to awards of retroactive seniority, but in contrast to seniority adjustments for individual discrimination victims, class remedies benefit class members who may not have been the victim of prior acts of discrimination. Courts will prohibit such practices, even if the employer is found guilty of a pattern or practice of racial discrimination.[48] The appropriate form of relief is to award competitive seniority to individual victims to restore them to their rightful place. Moreover, courts may not disregard a seniority system in fashioning a class remedy.

In 1986, the Supreme Court reviewed a case involving a voluntary affirmative action plan that included a layoff quota, *Wygant v. Jackson Board of Education*.[49] In that case, the Court struck down a school district's collective bargaining agreement that

---

[46]*See, e.g.,* Adarand Constructors v. Pena, 515 U.S. 200 (1995); Northeastern Fla. Chapter of the Associated Gen. Contractors of Am. v. City of Jacksonville, 508 U.S. 656 (1993); Martin v. Wilks, 490 U.S. 755 (1989).

[47]*See, e.g.*, Franks v. Bowman Trans. Co., 424 U.S. 747 (1976).

[48]Firefighters Local Union No. 1784 v. Stotts, 467 U.S. 561 (1984).

[49]476 U.S. 267 (1986). *See also* text accompanying note 6, Chapter 12.

protected minority teachers from layoffs to preserve the percentage of minority person-nel employed prior to the RIF. The Court reasoned that the quota system, which resulted in the release of some Caucasian teachers with greater seniority than some of the minority teachers who were retained, violated the Equal Protection Clause. Societal discrimination alone was not sufficient to justify the class preference. Recognizing that racial classifications in employment must be justified by a compelling governmental interest and that means must be narrowly tailored to accomplish that purpose, the Court concluded that the layoff provision in question did not satisfy either of these conditions. Additionally, the Court further rejected the lower courts' reliance on the "role model" theory tying the percentage of minority teachers to the percentage of minority students, noting that the proper comparison for determining employment discrimination is between the racial composition of the teaching staff and the qualified relevant labor market.[50] The Court was concerned that the use of the role model theory would allow school boards to go far beyond legitimate remedial purposes.

Case law involving affirmative action and racial preference may increase given the Supreme Court's decision in *Grutter v. University of Michigan*[51] and the desire of many educational entities to increase the diversity of their instructional and adminis-trative staff. At this time, however, it is questionable whether the compelling interest identified in *Grutter* (i.e., the benefits derived from a diverse student body) will expand to include employees and whether the justices' five-to-four decision will effectively negate years of Supreme Court precedent prohibiting the explicit use of race without showing prior institutional discrimination. Even then, the district's affir-mative action plan would have to be narrowly tailored.

In a case from the Seventh Circuit, a white female college instructor was not selected for a full-time teaching position.[52] The selected candidate was an African American male who had been evaluated second lowest of all finalists; moreover, he had not been a finalist until an administrator placed him within the group to be inter-viewed. Standard procedures were not followed and there were numerous examples of suspicious timing, ambiguous statements, and questionable practices. The college defended its position by noting that *Grutter* permitted such race-conscious decision making. Nonetheless, the Third Circuit concluded that the plaintiff provided signifi-cant evidence of both race and sex discrimination and remanded the case.[53]

---

[50]*Id.* at 275–276.

[51]539 U.S. 306 (2003).

[52]Rudin v. Lincoln Land Cmty. Coll., 420 F.3d 712 (7th Cir. 2005).

[53]*See also* Taxman v. Bd. of Educ., 91 F.3d 1547 (3d Cir. 1996) (concluding that an affirmative action plan preferring minority teachers over equally qualified nonminority teachers violated Title VII; and finding that the plan had been adopted to promote racial diversity rather than to remedy prior race discrimination by the district, provided preference of "unlimited duration," imposed job loss on tenured nonminority employees, and unnecessarily trammeled the interests of nonminority employees). *But see* Petit v. City of Chi., 352 F.3d 1111 (7th Cir. 2003) (upholding an affirmative action plan as consistent with *Grutter* and requiring raw score adjustments for race and ethnicity for promotion of patrol officers; reasoning that the "standardization" of the scores should not be seen as an arbitrary advantage given to the minority officers, but rather as eliminating the advantage that Caucasian officers had on the test).

Sex Discrimination

Prior to 1963, there were no federal statutes prohibiting discrimination based on sex. Women were commonly denied employment if a qualified male applicant was in the pool, were offered less money for the same or similar job, or were expected to do work that would not have been asked of a man. Today, most forms of sex discrimination are prohibited, including those associated with hiring, promotion, and virtually all terms and conditions of employment. The Fourteenth Amendment,[54] Title VII of the Civil Rights Act of 1964, and other federal and state laws have played significant roles in allowing victims of sex discrimination to vindicate their rights in court. Note, however, that laws prohibiting sex discrimination do not apply in cases in which the discrimination is due either to being transsexual, homosexual, or transvestite, or to qualifying in other "sex" categories. For example, in a Fifth Circuit case, the plaintiff claimed that although he was better qualified, he was not selected for a technology position, in large part due to the successful female candidate having an affair with a high-ranking university administrator.[55] In finding no Title VII violation, the Fifth Circuit noted that the law prohibited sex discrimination (i.e., due to being male or female), not paramour favoritism. Such a basis, although perhaps unfair, results in discrimination against both males and females who were not paramours and, accordingly, is not centered on plaintiff's sex.

Hiring and Promotion Practices

Sex discrimination is facial when an employer openly seeks a person of a particular sex (e.g., the posting of a position for a female guidance counselor). It becomes illegal discrimination when being male or female is unrelated to meeting job requirements (e.g., hiring only males as basketball coaches). At other times, employment practices are facially neutral (e.g., requiring head coaching experience in football in order to qualify as athletic director), but nevertheless result in nearly the same level of exclusion as when the discrimination is facial. When this occurs, an action will be upheld only if found to qualify as a business necessity and other less discriminatory options do not meet the needs of the organization.

Where applicants or employees have been treated unfairly solely because of their sex, plaintiffs typically file a Title VII suit alleging disparate treatment. The standards for a sex-based *prima facie* case are similar to those used for race. Also, assuming that a claim is supported, the employer then must identify a basis other than sex for its decision, such as showing that the successful applicant was equally or better qualified or that the plaintiff was unqualified.[56] Where a nondiscriminatory basis

---

[54]The Fourteenth Amendment requires the application of intermediate scrutiny in cases in which sex discrimination is facial and proof of intent in cases in which the alleged discrimination is facially neutral. *See* Hundertmark v. Florida, 205 F.3d 1272 (11th Cir. 2000) (applying intermediate scrutiny).

[55]Wilson v. Delta State Univ., 143 Fed. Appx. 611 (5th Cir. 2005).

[56]*See, e.g.*, Straughter v. Vicksburg Warren Sch. Dist., 152 Fed. Appx. 407 (5th Cir. 2005).

has been identified, applicants still may obtain relief if the reasons are shown to be pretextual.[57] For example, rejected applicants could likely prevail where employers base their decisions on stereotypic attitudes about the capabilities of the applicant's sex; where job advertisements include phrases, *prefer male* or *prefer female*; or where job descriptions are specifically drafted to exclude qualified applicants of a particular sex.

One of the most significant cases involving sex-based discrimination in promotion was *Texas Department of Community Affairs v. Burdine*, a 1981 Supreme Court decision.[58] In this case, a female accounting clerk was denied promotion and later was terminated along with two other employees, although two males were retained. In response to the female's *prima facie* case, the public employer claimed that the three terminated employees did not work well together and that the male who was promoted to the position sought by the female employee was subjectively better qualified, although he had been her subordinate prior to the promotion. In rendering its decision, the Court emphasized that Title VII does not require the hiring or promotion of equally qualified women or the restructuring of employment practices to maximize the number of underrepresented employees. Instead, the employer has the discretion to choose among equally qualified candidates as long as the decision is not based on unlawful criteria. In this case, the female employee failed to show pretext, resulting in a decision for the employer.

In contrast, the Eighth Circuit found that a female teacher who was passed over eight times for promotion to an administrative position was the victim of intentional sex discrimination.[59] The court had concerns regarding how the superintendent assessed the leadership abilities of male and female applicants as well as his statement that he was "leery" about assigning a female as principal of a junior high school. The applicant was able to show that both sex (the need for male disciplinarians) and race (the need for minority role models) were considered in selecting Caucasian and African American males to fill the positions.[60]

In addition, it is important that employers follow established procedures and use published criteria as the bases for identifying the successful candidate. In a Third Circuit case, the search committee used an unpublished criterion in selecting the plaintiff for a community college position.[61] An unsuccessful male applicant complained that

---

[57]*See, e.g.,* Goodwin v. Bd. of Trs. Univ. of Ill., 442 F.3d 611 (7th Cir. 2006) (concluding in a sex-and race-discrimination case that plaintiff provided indirect proof that her demotion was pretexual—coworkers had seen an image of three 1,000-pound scantily clad women on her computer screen, but she neither invited them to see the picture nor turned her computer in such a way that they would be involuntarily exposed and possibly offended).

[58]450 U.S. 248 (1981).

[59]Willis v. Watson Chapel Sch. Dist., 899 F.2d 745 (8th Cir. 1990), *on remand*, 749 F. Supp. 923 (E.D. Ark. 1990).

[60]*But see* Gore v. Ind. Univ., 416 F.3d 590 (7th Cir. 2005) (concluding that plaintiff failed to show he was discriminated against due to his sex when a university committee made up of three men and two women failed to hire him as a lecturer; in fact, one of the individuals ultimately hired was male).

[61]Morrissey v. Luzerne County Cmty. Coll., 117 Fed. Appx. 809 (3d Cir. 2004).

"interpersonal skill" was not mentioned in the job description or in the vacancy announcement. The president of the institution proposed that although he felt that the committee had selected the best-qualified person from the pool of applicants, a new search should be conducted, given the prior failure to base the selection on published criteria. Accordingly, a new search was performed, but a candidate not in the first pool was selected who had better overall experience and preparation. The court determined that (1) it was within the discretionary authority of the president, as set forth in the college's hiring procedures, to void the first search and to conduct a second; and (2) the second posting resulted in the hiring of the best-qualified candidate.[62] The plaintiff (i.e., the female applicant who was originally selected) failed to show both that the president's proffered reason for the second search (i.e., procedural error) was so plainly wrong that it could not have been the true reason *and* that the president intended to discriminate based on sex and age.

Not all sex-based distinctions are prohibited as Title VII explicitly allows for a *bona fide occupational qualification* (BFOQ) exception. For a BFOQ to be upheld, it needs to be narrowly defined and applied only when necessary to achieve the employer's objectives. There have been few school-based BFOQ cases, since the vast majority of jobs in education can be performed by either males or females. The only readily identifiable BFOQ in education would be the hiring of a female to supervise the girls' locker room and the hiring of a male to supervise the boys' locker room.

Moreover, where sex does not qualify as a BFOQ, a position may not be left vacant when qualified persons of the nonpreferred sex are available in the labor pool. In such a case, the Seventh Circuit concluded that a reasonable jury had sufficient data to conclude that the plaintiff, a male, was discriminated against solely because of sex when the dean refused to accept his nomination for a position that the dean hoped would be filled by a female.[63] The dean based his decision on the need to meet the affirmative action target for his college. The target was established to create a diversified staff, not to eradicate the consequences of prior discrimination.

Compensation Practices

Claims of sex-based compensation discrimination involving comparative entry salaries, raises, supplemental or overtime opportunities, or other perquisites and benefits are not uncommon within business and industry, and even occur at times in higher education. However, because most PK–12 salary decisions are based on objective criteria such as seniority and degree level, the number of public school cases has been small. In addition to the occasional claim from teachers, staff, and administrators, there have been challenges to the use of facially neutral salary adjustments, such

---

[62]*See also* Mella v. Mapleton Pub. Schs., 152 Fed. Appx. 717 (10th Cir. 2005) (finding that plaintiff failed to show pretext in the district's failure to promote her to manager of technology; and noting that the panel making the decision found two other applicants to be better qualified).

[63]Hill v. Ross, 183 F.3d 586 (7th Cir. 1999).

as "head of household" or "principal wage earner" allowances. These practices have been invalidated if not shown to be job related.[64]

The Fourteenth Amendment, Title VII, and the Equal Pay Act (EPA) of 1963 may be used where plaintiffs claim that their salaries are based in whole or in part on sex. The EPA applies only when the dispute involves sex-based wage discrimination claims of unequal pay for equal work.[65] As a result, the act does not apply when race-based or age-based salary differences are challenged, or when the work is unequal.[66] The plaintiff need not prove that the employer intended to discriminate, as with Title VII disputes; proof that the compensation is different and not based on factors other than sex will suffice. Furthermore, the law prohibits the lowering of the salaries for the higher paid group and therefore requires the salaries for the lower paid group to be raised. It is important to note that relief under the EPA is not barred by Eleventh Amendment immunity.[67]

Because the EPA is limited to controversies dealing with equal work, its application is restricted to those circumstances where there are male and female employees performing substantially the same work but for different pay. Accordingly, if there are no male secretaries for a salary comparison, there can be no EPA violation, regardless of how abysmal the salaries of female secretaries may be. In determining whether the jobs in question are equal, courts look at more than position titles and will examine the comparative skills, effort, responsibilities, and working conditions associated with each job and the nature of required tasks. If the jobs are found substantially equal but with unequal pay, the employer then must show that the different salaries were based on seniority, merit, quantity or quality of production, or any factor other than sex.[68] Where the employer purports to be using a merit system, it should be uniformly applied and be based on established criteria.[69]

Sex-based wage discrimination claims, however, are not confined exclusively to violations of the EPA; they also may be filed under Title VII.[70] As with race-based cases, intent will have to be proven in a disparate treatment case, whereas salary differences will have to be significant for plaintiffs to prevail in a disparate impact case.[71] When statistics are used to substantiate a claim, identifiable variables that affect salary must be included (e.g., seniority, degree level, merit, administrative assignments, supplemental duties). The Fourth Circuit ruled in favor of male faculty

---

[64]*See, e.g.,* EEOC v. Fremont Christian Sch., 781 F.2d 1362 (9th Cir. 1986).

[65]29 U.S.C. § 206(d) (2007). *See also* Ghirardo v. Univ. of So. Cal., 156 Fed. Appx. 914 (9th Cir. 2005) (finding no EPA violation when plaintiff failed to show her total compensation or annual raises were due to her sex; rather, her total salary was comparable to males and recent raises were minor due to her undisputed failure to attend retreats, refusal to meet with the dean, and other instances of recalcitrance).

[66]*See, e.g.,* Vasquez v. El Paso County Cmty. Coll., 177 Fed. Appx. 422 (5th Cir. 2006).

[67]*See, e.g.,* Siler-Khodr v. Univ. of Tex. Health Sci. Ctr., 261 F.3d 542 (5th Cir. 2001).

[68]*See, e.g.,* Wollenburg v. Comtech Mfg. Co., 201 F.3d 973 (7th Cir. 2000).

[69]*See, e.g.,* Port Auth. v. Ryduchowski, 530 U.S. 1276 (2000).

[70]*See, e.g.,* Farrell v. Butler Univ., 421 F.3d 609 (7th Cir. 2005).

[71]*See, e.g.,* Chance v. Rice Univ., 989 F.2d 179 (5th Cir. 1993).

members who claimed Title VII and EPA violations when their university voluntarily increased the salaries of female faculty, allegedly to eliminate salary inequities.[72] The study did not include performance criteria used for merit, consider the impact of prior administrative experience on salary, or provide any type of adjustment for career interruptions when measuring academic experience.

Termination, Nonrenewal, and Denial of Tenure

Title VII prohibits arbitrary removal of employees and the denial of tenure if based on sex, or other prohibited basis.[73] In disparate treatment cases, the employee is required to prove that the employer elected to terminate or not renew the employee's contract due to sex rather than job performance, inappropriate conduct, interpersonal relationships, financial exigency, or other just cause. As in most cases where proof of intent is required, employees alleging sex discrimination often have difficulty supporting their claims, even if true. Occasionally, however, corroborating evidence will be inadvertently provided by officials responsible for making personnel decisions.

In a Tenth Circuit decision, a female former principal was "bumped" by an associate superintendent, who assumed her position as well as his own. The district initially proposed that the RIF was necessary due to financial exigency but later claimed that the female principal had continuing difficulty with her faculty, which allegedly was the basis for her contract not being renewed. The appeals court found the evidence to be contradictory, including the superintendent's annual evaluation of the principal in which she received high marks for establishing and maintaining staff cooperation and creating an environment conducive to learning. Given such discrepancies, the appeals court reversed the lower court's grant of summary judgment for the school district.[74]

In contrast, in a Third Circuit case, a female served as an athletic administrator, program head, and professor.[75] She worked for the college for approximately 10 years, but eventually was terminated. She alleged that her removal was due to her support of equity in sports for women. Nonetheless, the Third Circuit determined that the administration provided sufficient documentation showing that the plaintiff had alienated others in her leadership role, and that her ineffective interpersonal skills created poor relations and low morale within her unit.

When making tenure decisions, it is important to follow all published and agreed-upon procedures, to meet all time restrictions, and to provide all internal appeals. Where facial discrimination does not exist, most plaintiffs will attempt to show that persons of the opposite sex were treated differently (i.e., required to meet

[72]Smith v. Va. Commonwealth Univ., 84 F.3d 672 (4th Cir. 1996).

[73]Weinstock v. Columbia Univ., 224 F.3d 33 (2d Cir. 2000). Moreover, Title VII also prohibits behaviors that would result in the constructive discharge of employees. *See, e.g.*, Palomo v. Trs. of Columbia Univ., 170 Fed. Appx. 194 (2d Cir. 2006).

[74]Cole v. Ruidoso Mun. Sch., 43 F.3d 1373 (10th Cir. 1994).

[75]Atkinson v. LaFayette Coll., 460 F.3d 447 (3d Cir. 2006).

different standards; assessed differently in meeting the same standards). The problem with this approach is that it often is difficult to identify a comparable party or to challenge subjective judgments regarding performance or potential.

Sexual Harassment

Sexual harassment generally refers to repeated and unwelcome sexual advances, sexually suggestive comments, or sexually demeaning gestures or acts. Both men and women have been victims of sexual harassment from persons of the opposite or same sex.[76] The harasser may be a supervisor, an agent of the employer, a coworker, a nonemployee, or even a student. Critical to a successful claim is proof that the harassment is indeed based on sex, rather than sexual preference, being transsexual, transvestism, or another factor. For example, in an Eleventh Circuit case, a male teacher and female teacher had a consensual relationship that the male eventually ended. The female then began making threatening overtures toward the wife and son of her former lover, resulting in the wife acquiring a restraining order. As the teachers taught at the same school, the female also sought to embarrass her male colleague in front of other staff and students whenever possible. After unsuccessful administrative claims, the male teacher filed suit, claiming hostile environment harassment. The Eleventh Circuit disagreed and determined that the female teacher had targeted the male teacher because he ended their relationship and not because he was male.[77]

There are two types of harassment cognizable under Title VII:[78] *quid pro quo* and hostile environment. Each is reviewed briefly here.

Quid Pro Quo. *Quid pro quo* harassment literally means giving something for something. To establish a *prima facie* case of *quid pro quo* harassment against an employer, the employee must show that he or she was subjected to unwelcome sexual harassment in the form of sexual advances and requests for sexual favors, that the harassment was based on the person's sex (i.e., being male or female), and that submission to the unwelcome advances was an express or implied condition for either favorable actions or avoidance of adverse actions by the employer. Although only a preponderance of evidence is required in such cases, acquiring the necessary 51 percent can be difficult, particularly given that the violator is unlikely to provide corroborating testimony. Also, the alleged behavior usually takes place behind closed doors so as to limit the opportunity for others to observe the conduct. If the employee succeeds, however, the law imposes strict liability on the employer, given the harasser's authority to alter the terms and conditions of employment.[79]

[76]*See, e.g.*, Oncale v. Sundowner Offshore Servs., 523 U.S. 75 (1998).

[77]Succar v. Dade County Sch. Bd., 229 F.3d 1343 (11th Cir. 2000).

[78]In addition to filing a Title VII claim, plaintiffs may file charges under state employment law or state tort law. Tort claims may include intentional infliction of emotional distress, assault and battery, invasion of privacy, and defamation.

[79]*See, e.g.*, Highlander v. K.F.C. Nat'l Mgmt. Co., 805 F.2d 644, 648 (6th Cir. 1986).

Hostile Environment. In *Meritor Savings Bank v. Vinson,* the Supreme Court in 1986 recognized for the first time that a Title VII violation can be predicated on harassment that creates a hostile or offensive working environment in addition to harassment that involves conditioning employment benefits on sexual favors.[80] To prevail under this theory, the plaintiff must show that the environment in fact is hostile; it needs to be severe or pervasive.[81] Conduct unreasonably interfering with an individual's work performance or creating an intimidating, hostile, or offensive working environment is actionable. Courts generally consider whether the victim:

- Solicited or initiated the conduct,
- Considered the conduct undesirable and offensive,
- Contributed to creating the environment, and
- Informed the harasser that the unwelcome conduct was offensive

Although the Supreme Court provided significant guidance in the *Meritor* case, it left unanswered questions regarding the need to prove psychological injury, particularly in the absence of tangible job losses. The Supreme Court addressed this issue in 1993 in *Harris v. Forklift Systems.*[82] A female executive was regularly exposed to hostile and abusive conduct by the company's president. Among the president's controversial behaviors was his request of female staff to get coins from his front pants pocket or for them to retrieve coins that he had tossed on the floor. Following the president's comment that the plaintiff must have promised sex to a customer to have acquired a lucrative contract, she quit her job and eventually sued. The lower court held that a reasonable victim would have found the president's conduct offensive but that it was not so egregious as to interfere with her work performance or to cause injury; this opinion was affirmed by the Sixth Circuit.

In a rare unanimous decision, the Supreme Court reversed and identified what it perceived to be a middle path between finding any conduct that is merely offensive to violate Title VII and requiring the conduct to cause a diagnosed psychological injury. The Court held that Title VII is violated if the environment would reasonably be perceived as hostile and abusive and that psychological injury need not be proven. The Court suggested the following criteria in assessing whether an environment is in fact hostile:

- The frequency and severity of the discriminatory conduct;
- Whether the behavior is physically threatening or humiliating, or merely an offensive utterance; and
- Whether the conduct unreasonably interferes with an employee's work performance.

[80]477 U.S. 57 (1986).

[81]*See, e.g.,* Haugerud v. Amery Sch. Dist., 259 F.3d 678 (7th Cir. 2001). *But see* Whittaker v. N. Ill. Univ., 424 F.3d 640 (7th Cir. 2005) (concluding that offensive comments that were not made in plaintiff's presence and were unknown to her until after her employment did not contribute to the creation of a hostile environment), *cert. denied,* 126 S. Ct. 2986 (2006).

[82]510 U.S. 17 (1993).

Employer liability in hostile environment claims is more difficult to establish than in *quid pro quo* claims, but it may be easier to substantiate in light of more recent rulings. In *Burlington Industries v. Ellerth*[83] and *Faragher v. City of Boca Raton*,[84] the Supreme Court in 1998 proclaimed that an employer is subject to vicarious liability for the acts of its supervisors with immediate authority over an alleged victim. However, the employer may raise an affirmative defense to liability if the employee suffered no tangible employment loss. Such a defense requires that the employer exercise reasonable care to prevent or promptly correct harassing behavior *and* that the employee failed to take advantage of preventive and corrective opportunities provided by the employer. Accordingly, to guard against liability, school districts should:

- Prepare and disseminate sexual harassment policies;
- Provide appropriate in-service training;
- Establish appropriate grievance procedures, including at least two avenues for reporting in case one avenue is blocked by the harasser or supportive colleague;
- Select both male and female disinterested investigators;
- Take claims seriously and investigate promptly;
- Take corrective action in a timely manner; and
- Maintain thorough records of all claims and activities.

Pregnancy Discrimination

Under the Pregnancy Discrimination Act (PDA),[85] an amendment to Title VII enacted in 1978, employers may not discriminate based on pregnancy, childbirth, or related medical conditions.[86] As such, pregnancy may not be used as a basis for refusing to hire an otherwise qualified applicant; denying disability, medical, or other benefits; or terminating or nonrenewing employment. To succeed, the plaintiff must show that the employer knew she was pregnant prior to the adverse action and that pregnancy, rather than some other factor, was the basis of an adverse decision. In 1999, the Sixth Circuit remanded a case to determine whether the private religious school terminated the employment of a teacher due to having engaged in premarital sex (in violation of religious tenants) or to becoming pregnant. The court determined that termination for having engaged in sex was a permissible basis for the adverse employment decision, but that termination could not be based on pregnancy.[87]

---

[83]524 U.S. 742 (1998).

[84]524 U.S. 775 (1998).

[85]42 U.S.C. § 2000e(k) (2007).

[86]The PDA was passed in response to two Supreme Court decisions in which the denial of benefits for pregnancy-related conditions was found not to violate either Title VII or the Fourteenth Amendment. *See,* Gen. Elec. Co. v. Gilbert, 429 U.S. 125 (1976); Geduldig v. Aiello, 417 U.S. 484 (1974).

[87]Cline v. Catholic Diocese, 206 F.3d 651 (6th Cir. 1999). *See also* Parker-Bigback v. St. Labre Sch., 7 P.3d 361 (Mont. 2000) (holding that Title VII did not prohibit a religious school from terminating a teacher's employment for living with a man out of wedlock; noting that her employment contract stipulated that she would conduct her private life consistent with church doctrine).

Before passage of the PDA, the Fourth Circuit relied on the Fourteenth Amendment in striking down a school board's practice of not renewing teachers' contracts where a foreseeable period of absence could be predicted for the ensuing year.[88] The policy had been applied only to pregnant employees, thus imposing a disproportionate burden on female teachers. The Supreme Court also has held that women of child-bearing age cannot be denied equal access to what the employer perceives as "high risk" forms of employment, if they are otherwise qualified for the jobs (e.g., janitorial jobs requiring the use of strong chemicals).[89]

If an employer requires a doctor's statement for other conditions, it also may require one for pregnancy prior to granting leave or paying benefits. And, if employees are unable to perform their jobs due to pregnancy, the employer is required to treat them the same as any other temporarily disabled person. Possible forms of accommodation may be to modify tasks, alternate assignments, or provide disability leave (with or without pay). If a pregnant employee takes a leave of absence, her position must be held open the same length of time that it would be if she were sick or disabled. Moreover, maternity leave cannot be considered an interruption in employment for the purposes of accumulating credit toward tenure or seniority if employees retain seniority rights when on leave for other disabilities.[90]

Mandatory pregnancy leave policies requiring teachers to take a leave of absence prior to the birth of their children and specifying a return date also violate the Due Process Clause by creating an *irrebuttable presumption* that all pregnant teachers are physically incompetent as of a specified date.[91] School boards, however, may establish maternity leave policies that are justified by a business necessity, such as the requirement that the employee notify the administration of her intended departure and return dates, assuming this is required for other forms of extended personal leave. The business necessity of such a policy is to allow for planning and staffing in the employee's absence.

Although employers may not treat pregnant employees less favorably, they may grant special leave and other benefits that are unavailable to nonpregnant persons. As indicated by the Ninth Circuit, the PDA was intended "to construct a floor beneath which pregnancy disability benefits may not drop" rather than "a ceiling above which they may not rise."[92] However, supplemental benefits that go beyond those made available to other employees may have additional restrictions and limitations. For example, the Seventh Circuit determined that a school district's maternity leave procedures may be more restrictive than the procedures for other forms of leave and still not violate the PDA.[93] The appeals court concluded that the school board treated pregnant

[88]Mitchell v. Bd. of Trs., 599 F.2d 582 (4th Cir. 1979).

[89]Int'l Union, United Auto., Aerospace, & Agric. Implement Workers of Am. v. Johnson Controls, 499 U.S. 187 (1991).

[90]Nashville Gas Co. v. Satty, 434 U.S. 136 (1977).

[91]Cleveland Bd. of Educ. v. LaFleur, 414 U.S. 632 (1974).

[92]Cal. Fed. Savings & Loan Ass'n v. Guerra, 758 F.2d 390, 396 (9th Cir. 1985), *aff'd*, 479 U.S. 272 (1987).

[93]United States v. Bd. of Educ., 983 F.2d 790 (7th Cir. 1993).

and nonpregnant teachers the same with regard to other forms of leave, plus gave pregnant teachers a further option of using maternity leave with some restrictions.

Notwithstanding the fact that special benefits may be available only to pregnant employees, the Third Circuit invalidated a leave policy that permitted female employees, but not male employees, to use up to one year of combined sick leave and unpaid leave for child rearing.[94] Noting that the leave was not tied to any continuing disability related to pregnancy or childbirth, the court held that denial of a year of unpaid leave for child rearing to a male teacher constituted sex discrimination under Title VII.

Retirement Benefits

Although the longevity figures for men and women have narrowed over the past 35 years, it remains true that women on average live longer than men. In fact, in 2003 women had a projected life expectancy that was 5.3 years longer than men, although that number had been on the decline since 1970, when it peaked at 7.6 years.[95] Recognition of female longevity historically resulted in differential treatment of women with respect to retirement benefits, since employers either required women to make a higher contribution or awarded them lower annual benefits upon retirement. But in 1978 the Supreme Court rejected the use of sex-segregated actuarial tables in retirement benefits programs. The Court invalidated a retirement program requiring women to make a higher contribution to receive equal benefits on retirement, noting that sex was the only factor considered in predicting life expectancy.[96] Similarly, in 1983 the Court prohibited the state of Arizona from administering a deferred compensation program by contracting with insurance companies that used sex-segregated actuarial tables to determine benefits.[97] In the latter case, female employees received lower monthly annuity payments than did males who contributed the same amount.

Sexual-Preference Discrimination

When public employees are discriminated against due to sexual preference in hiring, promotion, termination, or any other term or condition of employment, they may file suit under the Fourteenth Amendment.[98] Both public- and private-sector employees also may base related complaints on state statutes and local ordinances, where they exist.

---

[94]Schafer v. Bd. of Pub. Educ., 903 F.2d 243 (3d Cir. 1990).

[95]E. Arias, "United States Life Tables, 2003," *National Vital Statistics Reports,* vol. 54, no.14 (2006), available at www.cdc.gov/nchs/data/nvsr/nvsr54/nvsr54_14.pdf.

[96]City of L.A. Dep't of Water & Power v. Manhart, 435 U.S. 702 (1978).

[97]Ariz. Governing Comm. for Tax Deferred Annuity & Deferred Comp. Plans v. Norris, 463 U.S. 1073 (1983).

[98]Under the Fourteenth Amendment, rational-basis scrutiny is applied in sexual-preference cases when facial discrimination is supported, whereas discriminatory intent must be proven when the discrimination is facially neutral.

Access to Benefits

The amount of salary or level of benefits a school district provides its employees may not be determined by an employee's sexual orientation. However, unless restricted by state law or local ordinance, school districts may limit the availability of family benefits to legal spouses and dependents. Because only heterosexual marriages are recognized across all states, benefits such as retirement, death, health care, eye care, and dental are not generally available to same-sex partners or the children of same-sex partners, unless the children have been legally adopted by the employee.[99] This position was fortified by the passage of the Defense of Marriage Act in 1996.[100] That statute gives states the option of refusing to extend marriage benefits to same-sex partners who were legally married in another state, territory, or country. Nonetheless, some states, locales, and employers—through their constitutions, statutes, ordinances, policies, or common law—have elected to permit same-sex partners to receive benefits.[101]

Harassment

The harassment of employees based on sexual preference also may violate state and local laws as well as the Fourteenth Amendment. Meeting the required intent standard may be difficult, however, in situations where school district employees are not directly responsible for the harassment. The Seventh Circuit was confronted with a case where a former teacher claimed that the school district failed to take reasonable measures to prevent students, parents, and colleagues from harassing him due to his sexual preference.[102] The plaintiff demanded that the district engage in systemwide sensitivity training to condemn discrimination against homosexuals, given that a related memorandum and the disciplining of a few violating students had proved ineffectual. The principal suggested that the plaintiff try to ignore students' behavior, as getting them to stop would be difficult, if not impossible. The teacher sued under the Fourteenth Amendment but was unable to prove either that the district demonstrated the intent to discriminate or was deliberately indifferent to his treatment by students. District personnel were found to have made legitimate efforts to reduce or eliminate the harassment.

Adverse Employment Decisions

Terminating or not renewing employment of a public employee solely due to sexual preference is unlikely to meet even rational-basis scrutiny. However, if a homosexual employee were to engage in a pedophilic relationship, were sexually involved with

[99]Rutgers Council of AAUP Chapters v. Rutgers, 689 A.2d 828 (N.J. Superior Ct., App. Div. 1997).

[100]28 U.S.C. § 1738C (2007). *See* text accompanying note 99, Chapter 8.

[101]Tanner v. Or. Health Scis. Univ., 971 P.2d 435 (Or. Ct. App. 1998).

[102]Schroeder v. Hamilton Sch. Dist., 282 F.3d 946 (7th Cir. 2002).

students, or participated in public acts of indecency, appropriate adverse actions would be justified on grounds of immorality.[103] Of course, such reasons provide bases for terminating heterosexuals as well. In an illustrative case, a first-year teacher's contract was not renewed allegedly due to his inability to manage student behavior effectively and to deficiencies in his teaching skills. The court found these reasons to be pretextual given that a fellow teacher with lower evaluations was retained. Board members provided conflicting testimony on several matters, and plaintiff's negative evaluations followed a classroom visit by his partner, which had resulted in rumors and false accusations of hand-holding. The court identified an equal protection violation and awarded compensatory damages as well as damages for emotional distress.[104]

As noted, a private-sector plaintiff must seek protection under either state law or local ordinance and must show that sexual orientation was in fact the basis of the adverse action to substantiate a valid discrimination claim. Such state and local provisions may not violate federal constitutional rights in their application, however. In *Boy Scouts of America v. Dale*, the Supreme Court in 2000 found that the New Jersey public accommodation law, previously interpreted to require the Boy Scouts to admit a homosexual assistant scoutmaster to its ranks, violated the private nonprofit organization's expressive association rights.[105] The Court observed that plaintiff's openness about his own sexual preference and advocacy of related rights operated against those expressed by the Scouts and that to require the Scouts to retain the plaintiff would significantly burden the organization in its effort to oppose homosexual conduct.[106]

Religion Discrimination

The United States is now more culturally and religiously diverse than at any time in its history. When discrimination occurs, or an employer fails to provide reasonable accommodations, First and Fourteenth Amendment[107] claims have been filed as well as those under Title VII.

The first issue in such cases is whether the discrimination is based on sincerely held religious beliefs. A person's religion does not have to be organized, recognized,

---

[103]*See* text accompanying notes 114–117, Chapter 11.

[104]Glover v. Williamsburg Local Sch. Dist., 20 F. Supp. 2d 1160 (S.D. Ohio 1998).

[105]530 U.S. 640 (2000).

[106]*See also* Hall v. Baptist Mem. Health Care Corp., 215 F.3d 618 (6th Cir. 2000) (finding no Title VII religion violation when a religious employer terminated a student services specialist based on her expressed views and sexual preference).

[107]If an employee claims an Equal Protection Clause violation due to religion-based facial discrimination by government, either strict scrutiny or rational-basis scrutiny could apply, depending on the form of the discrimination. When the government infringes upon the employee's First Amendment right to exercise religious beliefs (a fundamental right), strict scrutiny is applied. On the other hand, if the employee is a victim of discrimination based on religion, rational-basis scrutiny is applied. Intent must be proven in cases involving facially neutral discrimination. *See* Chapter 2 for a discussion of the First Amendment religion clauses as applied to schools.

or well known. Curiously, even opposition to abortion, the draft, and nuclear power have qualified as "religious" beliefs,[108] although a belief in veganism has not.[109] Nonetheless, employers generally should accept an employee's representation of a sincerely held belief, at least for accommodation purposes.[110] Where the employee suffers an adverse employment outcome due to religion, the employer then must show either that an accommodation was offered, but not taken, or that no reasonable accommodation existed that would not result in hardship.

Hiring and Promotion Practices

Private religious organizations are exempt from First and Fourteenth Amendment claims and in large part from the religious restrictions imposed by Title VII.[111] As a result, they are not generally prohibited from establishing religion as a *bona fide occupational qualification* (BFOQ) (e.g., when a Methodist theological seminary requires that its instructors be Methodists) or from making employment decisions that are consistent with the tenants of their particular faith.

   In contrast, religion will never qualify as a BFOQ in public education, and public employers may not inquire as to an applicant's religious beliefs, use the interview process as an opportunity to indoctrinate, or require prospective employees to profess a belief in a particular faith or in God.[112] A person's religious affiliation or practice, if any, should not be considered in making an employment decision.

Accommodation

Recommended forms of religious accommodation include activities such as accepting voluntary substitutions and assignment exchanges, using a flexible schedule, and modifying job assignments. Tests, interviews, and other selection procedures should not be scheduled at times when an applicant cannot attend for religious reasons. However, if requested accommodations would compromise the constitutional, statutory, or contractual rights of others (e.g., interfere with a *bona fide* seniority system) or result in undue hardship, Title VII does not require the employer to make the accommodation. Undue hardship results when extensive changes are required in business practices or when the costs of religious accommodations are more than minimal. Some of

---

[108]Wilson v. U.S. W. Communications, 58 F.3d 1337 (8th Cir. 1995); Am. Postal Workers Union v. Postmaster Gen., 781 F.2d 772 (9th Cir. 1986); Best v. Cal. Apprenticeship Council, 207 Cal. Rptr. 863 (Ct. App. 1984).

[109]Veganism is a philosophy and lifestyle that avoids using animals and animal products for food, clothing, and other purposes. *See* Friedman v. S. Cal. Permanente Med. Group, 125 Cal. Rptr. 2d 663 (Ct. App. 2002).

[110]*But see* Bushhouse v. Local Union 2209, 164 F. Supp. 2d 1066 (N.D. Ind. 2001) (concluding that there was no Title VII violation when a union sought to verify the religious beliefs of an employee who did not want to pay dues based on those beliefs).

[111]42 U.S.C. § 2000e-1(a) (2007).

[112]Torcaso v. Watkins, 367 U.S. 488 (1961).

the more often litigated controversies regarding religious accommodation in public education involve dress codes, personal leave, and job assignments.

Attire Restrictions.   As a general rule, public school district restrictions on the wearing of religious apparel, even if also purportedly cultural, will be upheld where young and impressionable students would perceive the garment as religious.[113] In an illustrative case, the Third Circuit held that a district's refusal to accommodate a Muslim substitute teacher who sought to wear religious attire in the public school classroom did not violate Title VII.[114] The district's action was pursuant to a state statute that regarded the wearing of religious clothing as a significant threat to the maintenance of a religiously neutral public school system. Similar decisions have been reached by a federal court in Mississippi when it upheld the termination of a teacher aide who refused to comply with the school's dress code proscribing religious attire,[115] and by the Oregon Supreme Court when it upheld a statutory prohibition on religious attire in public schools as applied to a female Sikh who dressed in white clothes and turban.[116]

Personal Leave.   Although most public school calendars allow time off for Christmas and Easter to coincide with semester and spring breaks, holy days of religions other than Christianity are not so routinely accommodated. But, when a school district serves a significant number of students or employs a large number of teachers or staff of another religion, it is not uncommon for schools to be closed on several of the more significant days of worship for that religion as well. The "secular purpose" of such an act is the need to operate the school efficiently. If schools were to remain open when many people were absent, administrators would be required to hire numerous substitutes, and teachers would have to prepare a burdensome level of make-up work. When districts elect to remain open in spite of the absence of a large number of students or teachers, substitute teachers often are instructed not to present new material in order to reduce the need to provide repetitive lessons.

Although the aforementioned approach may provide satisfactory results when attempting to accommodate one or two faiths, it is unrealistic to assume that public schools will be closed for the holy days of every religion. Alternatively, school districts often provide a variety of accommodations to avoid unduly burdening the religious beliefs of their employees (e.g., use of personal leave days, flexible schedules), depending upon the nature of their employment.

Modest requests for religious absences are typically met, but others may result in hardship both for the district as well as for students. School officials often have difficulty in determining appropriate limits and procedures. Some guidance is found in a significant 1977 case, *Trans World Airlines v. Hardison*, in which a member of the

---

[113]*See also* text accompanying note 99, Chapter 2.

[114]United States v. Bd. of Educ., 911 F.2d 882 (3d Cir. 1990).

[115]McGlothin v. Jackson Mun. Separate Sch. Dist., 829 F. Supp. 853 (S.D. Miss. 1992).

[116]Cooper v. Eugene Sch. Dist. No. 4J, 723 P.2d 298 (Or. 1986).

Worldwide Church of God challenged his dismissal for refusing to work on Saturdays in contravention of his religious beliefs.[117] The employer asserted that the plaintiff could not be accommodated because shift assignments were based on seniority in conformance with the collective bargaining agreement. Evidence also showed that supervisors had taken appropriate steps in meeting with the plaintiff and in attempting to find other employees to exchange shifts. The Supreme Court found no Title VII violation and reasoned that an employer was not required to bear more than minimal costs in making religious accommodations or to disregard a *bona fide* seniority system in the absence of proof of intentional discrimination.[118]

Where leave has been provided, some employees have been satisfied when allowed to have the day off without adverse impact; others have requested that leave be accompanied with full or partial pay. In *Ansonia Board of Education v. Philbrook*, a teacher asserted that the negotiated agreement violated Title VII by permitting employees to use only three days of paid leave for religious purposes, whereas three additional days of paid personal business leave could be used for specified secular activities.[119] The plaintiff proposed either permitting the use of the paid personal business leave days for religious observances or allowing employees to receive full pay and cover the costs of substitute teachers for each additional day missed for religious reasons. The Supreme Court, in upholding the agreement, held that the employer was not required to show that each of plaintiff's proposed alternatives would result in undue hardship, and noted that the employer could satisfy Title VII by offering a reasonable accommodation, which may or may not be the one the employee preferred.

It is important to note that religious leave need not be paid, unless compensation is provided for other forms of leave.[120] In a Tenth Circuit case, the court rejected a teacher's claim that the school district's leave policy violated Title VII and burdened his free exercise of religion because he occasionally had to take unpaid leave to observe Jewish holidays.[121] The policy allowed teachers two days of paid leave that could be used for religious purposes. The court concluded that the availability of unpaid leave for additional religious observances constituted a reasonable accommodation under Title VII and did not place a substantial burden on free exercise rights.

---

[117]432 U.S. 63 (1977).

[118]*Compare* Graff v. Henderson, 30 Fed. Appx. 809 (10th Cir. 2002) (finding no Title VII violation where a member of the Worldwide Church of God was denied employment when he indicated that he would be unable to work between sundown Friday and sundown Saturday as required for the job; noting that undue hardship would result if the employer were required to make such a dramatic change in its work schedule or to permit the applicant to transfer to another job in violation of the collective bargaining agreement and its mandatory use of seniority) *with* Abramson v. William Paterson Coll., 260 F.3d 265 (3d Cir. 2001) (reversing summary judgment where an Orthodox Jew professor claimed religion discrimination and retaliation when she refused to work on holidays and the Sabbath).

[119]757 F.2d 476 (2d Cir. 1985), *aff'd*, 479 U.S. 60 (1986).

[120]*Id.* at 71.

[121]Pinsker v. Joint Dist. No. 28J, 735 F.2d 388 (10th Cir. 1984).

Job Assignments and Responsibilities. If an employee is hired to perform a certain job, he or she must be willing and able to perform all of the essential functions of the job. In a somewhat unusual case, an interpreter for the hearing impaired refused to translate or sign any cursing or bad language and used her religious beliefs as a basis for the refusal.[122] Given her willing violation of district policy and administrative directives, her contract was terminated. The Missouri appeals court upheld her termination under state law and concluded that the teacher could not have been accommodated without compromising the educational entitlements of her students and that requiring a literal translation of classroom dialogue was not unreasonable.

Likewise, the Third Circuit found that a university hospital had reasonably accommodated a nurse who had refused to participate in abortions, given her Pentecostal religious beliefs.[123] She had been permitted to trade assignments with other nurses, unless an emergency existed. When she failed to treat pregnant patients when they were experiencing life-threatening situations, the hospital gave her the option of transferring to a comparable job where her beliefs would not conflict with essential job requirements, but the nurse refused. The court upheld her subsequent termination and indicated that the public trust requires public-health-care practitioners to provide treatment in the time of emergency.

Adverse Employment Decisions

Employees at times have claimed religious discrimination when they have been transferred, demoted, nonrenewed, terminated, or denied tenure.[124] As with other claims of employment discrimination, the burden is on the plaintiff to prove that the adverse action was motivated by an impermissible reason—in this case, the employee's religious beliefs, practices, or affiliation. Plaintiffs experience difficulty in winning such cases, as employers typically can identify one or more legitimate bases for the adverse action (e.g., lack of commitment,[125] excessive absenteeism[126]). In a private-sector employment case reviewed by the Ninth Circuit, a former employee claimed religious discrimination when terminated.[127] To support its slogan that "diversity is

---

[122]Sedalia # 200 Sch. Dist. v. Mo. Comm'n on Human Rights, 843 S.W.2d 928 (Mo. Ct. App. 1992).

[123]Shelton v. Univ. of Med. & Dentistry, 223 F.3d 220 (3d Cir. 2000). *See also* Bruff v. N. Miss. Health Servs., 244 F.3d 495 (5th Cir. 2001) (upholding termination of a Christian counselor who refused to work with homosexuals or persons living together outside of marriage).

[124]*See, e.g.*, Habib v. Nations Bank, 279 F.3d 563 (8th Cir. 2001) (upholding termination of employee for insubordination when she refused to bring a doctor's statement supporting her need to leave work; she had claimed that the real reason for her firing was her need to pray five times per day, lasting five to 15 minutes each time).

[125]*See, e.g.*, Lee v. Wise County Sch. Bd., No. 97-1471, 1998 U.S. App. LEXIS 367 (4th Cir. Jan. 12, 1998).

[126]*See, e.g.*, Rosenbaum v. Bd. of Trs. of Montgomery Cmty. Coll., No. 98-1773, 1999 U.S. App. LEXIS 4744 (4th Cir. March 19, 1999).

[127]Peterson v. Hewlett-Packard Co., 358 F.3d 599 (9th Cir. 2004).

our strength," the employer displayed diversity posters, including those regarding gays. The plaintiff believed that homosexual activity violated the Bible and began posting within his cubicle large typeface passages from the Bible that could be interpreted to condemn homosexuality. After he refused to remove the postings unless his employer removed its diversity displays regarding gays, he was terminated for insubordination. The court reasoned that plaintiff failed to support his claim of discrimination and that to permit him to maintain his postings, as a religious accommodation, would result in undue hardship on the employer as the material was demeaning and degrading to members of the work force.

The Third Circuit reviewed a case in which a Catholic school teacher signed a pro-choice advertisement in the local newspaper and was terminated.[128] She filed suit, alleging that the severity of her penalty was due to being female; that males who had engaged in other forms of expression were not as harshly treated; and that Title VII protects any employee who contemplates or has an abortion, or supports the right of others to do so. The court avoided having to decide this matter, however, by ruling that the religion clauses of the First Amendment barred the court from determining whether plaintiff's conduct was any more or less violative of church doctrine than was other conduct exhibited by two male employees. The court emphasized, however, that although Congress intended to exempt religious employers from Title VII provisions prohibiting religion discrimination, they still are required to comply with remaining portions of the law, including those prohibiting sex discrimination, unless differential treatment of men and women is dictated by religious tenets.

Age Discrimination

Unlike other characteristics that generate charges of discrimination, age is unique in that everyone is subject to the aging process and eventually will fall within the age-protected category. The mean age of the U.S. population has climbed steadily in recent years, and this phenomenon has been accompanied by an increase in judicial activity pertaining to age discrimination by persons over age 40. In fact, the median age advanced 8.3 years between 1970 (28.1) and 2005 (36.4).[129] There is no reason to believe that the median age will not continue to grow, given continued advancements in health care. Over time, this trend will result in a significant portion of the population that will be age protected in employment and eligible for a range of public services, Medicaid, and eventually retirement. Age discrimination employment claims

---

[128]Curay-Cramer v. Ursuline Acad. of Wilmington, 450 F.3d 130 (3d Cir. 2006).

[129]U.S. Census Bureau, *2005 American Community Survey, Median Age of the Total Population: 2005* (Washington D.C.: U.S. Government Printing Office, 2005), available at http://factfinder.census.gov/servlet/GRTTable?_bm=y&-_box_head_nbr=R0101&-ds_name=ACS_2005_EST_G00_&-format=US-30; U.S. Census Bureau, *Census 2000 Special Reports, Demographic Trends in the 20th Century* (Washington D.C.: U.S. Government Printing Office, 2002), available at www.census.gov/prod/2002pubs/ censr-4.pdf.

may be filed under the Equal Protection Clause (any age),[130] the Age Discrimination in Employment Act (ADEA) of 1967 (over age 40),[131] and state statutes. The Equal Employment Opportunity Commission (EEOC) is responsible for the enforcement of the ADEA.

The purpose of the ADEA is to promote the employment of older persons based on their ability, to prohibit arbitrary age discrimination in employment, and to find ways of addressing problems arising from the impact of age on employment. The ADEA specifically stipulates that "it shall be unlawful for an employer . . . to fail or refuse to hire or to discharge any individual or otherwise discriminate . . . with respect to his compensation, terms, conditions, or privileges of employment, because of such individual's age."[132] However, if the employment decision is based on any reasonable factor other than age (e.g., merit, seniority, vesting in a retirement plan), even though correlated with or associated with age, there is no violation of the ADEA. This standard requires less than is mandated under Title VII (i.e., intent in treatment cases; proof that the practice, policy, or requirement was job related and consistent with business necessity in impact cases). Moreover, if a reasonable factor is identified, the employer avoids liability even if other factors with less discriminatory impact are available and not used. Also, for a violation to be substantiated, age must play a role in the decision-making process *and* have a determinative influence on the outcome.[133]

The ADEA applies to most employers that have 20 or more employees for 20 or more weeks in the current or preceding calendar year. Where violations of the ADEA are found, courts may provide for injunctive relief; compel employment, reinstatement, or promotion; and provide back pay (including interest), liquidated damages, and attorneys' fees. Punitive damages, however, are not available.[134]

Future application of the ADEA in public school cases may be limited at times, however, because the Supreme Court in *Kimel v. Florida Board of Regents* held that Eleventh Amendment immunity may be claimed as a defense where money damages to be paid out of the state treasury are sought in federal court.[135] Accordingly, immunity may be claimed where state laws consider school districts to be "arms of the state" rather than political subdivisions. But even where Eleventh Amendment is used as a defense, plaintiffs can sue under comparable state statutes to vindicate their rights.[136]

---

[130]Facially discriminatory procedures and practices that classify individuals on the basis of age can satisfy the Equal Protection Clause if they are rationally related to a legitimate governmental objective, whereas facially neutral criteria may be successfully challenged only with proof of discriminatory intent. *See, e.g.,* Gregory v. Ashcroft, 501 U.S. 452 (1991).

[131]29 U.S.C. § 621 *et seq.* (2007).

[132]29 U.S.C. § 623(a)(1) (2007).

[133]*See, e.g.,* Hazen Paper Co. v. Biggins, 507 U.S. 604, 617 (1993).

[134]29 U.S.C. § 626(b) (2007).

[135]528 U.S. 62 (2000). *See, e.g.,* Thompson v. Conn. State Univ., 466 F. Supp. 2d 444 (D. Conn. 2006) (dismissing age and race claims by a former employee who claimed discrimination when not informed about a part-time position).

[136]*See* text accompanying note 203, Chapter 11.

Hiring and Promotion Practices

As indicated, under the ADEA, except in those circumstances where age qualifies as a *bona fide occupational qualification* (BFOQ), selection among applicants for hiring or promotion may be based on any factor other than age. Although a BFOQ defense in an educational setting is unlikely in cases involving staff, teachers, or administrators, claims could conceivably be made for school bus drivers and pilots.[137] Where a BFOQ is applied, the employer carries the burden of persuasion to demonstrate that there is reasonable cause to believe that all, or substantially all, applicants beyond a certain age would be unable to perform a job safely and efficiently.

As with Title VII cases, courts will permit plaintiffs in ADEA cases to provide either direct evidence of discrimination or meet *McDonnell Douglas* criteria.[138] In a Sixth Circuit case, a part-time substitute teacher was denied several full-time positions.[139] At trial, the plaintiff met the requirements for a *prima facie* case, while the board proffered the archetypical response (i.e., better-qualified candidates were hired[140]). It then became the plaintiff's responsibility to show that the board's purported reasons were unworthy of credence and a pretext to age discrimination.[141] This proved difficult, as there were over 2,000 applicants, and 41 percent of those hired were over age 20. Under such circumstances, it would be exceedingly difficult to show that were it not for the consideration of age, the plaintiff would have been among those selected. Accordingly, when the plaintiff was unable to fulfill his entire burden, the board's motion for summary judgment was granted.

In the effort to show pretext, a plaintiff need not discredit each and every proffered reason for the rejection, but must cast substantial doubt on many, if not most, of the purported bases so that a fact-finder then could rationally disbelieve the remaining reasons given the employer's loss of credibility.[142] In an illustrative Second Circuit case, a less-experienced, unqualified, younger teacher was selected over the plaintiff.[143] The district purported that the selected applicant performed better during

---

[137]*See, e.g.,* Childers v. Morgan County Bd. of Educ., 817 F.2d 1556 (llth Cir. 1987).

[138]*See supra* text accompanying note 15.

[139]Wooden v. Bd. of Educ., 931 F.2d 376 (6th Cir. 1991).

[140]*But see* Patrick v. Ridge, 394 F.3d 311, 316 (5th Cir. 2004) (noting that when an allegedly better-qualified candidate is selected, it is important that such person actually be in the pool of candidates when the plaintiff is rejected).

[141]*See also* Stone v. Bd. of Educ. of Saranac Cent. Sch. Dist., 153 Fed. Appx. 44 (2d Cir. 2005) (determining that age was not the basis of plaintiff's denial of employment and concluding that she did not interview well and was unfamiliar with newer teaching methods); Herbick v. Salem City Sch. Dist., 151 Fed. Appx. 463 (6th Cir. 2005) (concluding that plaintiff failed to show pretext in her age discrimination claim—the district had elected to combine two part-time teaching positions to create one full-time position, rather than continue to rehire plaintiff on one-year contracts following her retirement); Carter v. George Washington Univ., 387 F.3d 872 (D.C. Cir. 2004) (concluding that plaintiff failed to show that a reasonable jury could infer that the employer's claim that she interviewed poorly was pretextual).

[142]*See, e.g.,* Narin v. Lower Merion Sch. Dist., 206 F.3d 323 (3d Cir. 2000).

[143]Byrnie v. Town of Cromwell, Bd. of Educ., 243 F.3d 93 (2d Cir. 2001).

the interview and was chosen largely on that basis. In ruling that pretext had been shown, the court noted that the successful candidate did not possess the specified degree and had submitted an incomplete file; that the employer had made misleading statements and destroyed relevant evidence; and that the plaintiff possessed superior credentials, except perhaps as to the interview. The fact that the previously selected applicant also was over the age of 40 was irrelevant; what mattered was that she was substantially younger (i.e., age 42) than the plaintiff (age 64).[144]

Compensation and Benefits

Few public school employees have alleged age-based salary discrimination. In large part, this is due to the fact that teachers and staff primarily are paid on salary schedules based on seniority and degree level. As employees become older, they concomitantly gain seniority and receive a higher scheduled salary. Consequently, claims of age-based salary discrimination are less likely to occur within public schools, except possibly for administrators and noncertified staff. Where age discrimination is alleged, the burden of proof remains with the employee to prove that age—rather than performance, longevity, or other factors—was used to determine the level of compensation. Claims of both disparate treatment and disparate impact may be filed. In a seminal case in 2005, *Smith v. City of Jackson*, the Supreme Court examined a claim by police and public safety officers that raises were less generous to officers over age 40 than to those who were younger.[145] The city had elected to increase the salaries of beginning and lower echelon employees in order to bring their salary levels in line with comparable positions available in the area. Officials asserted that this was necessary to attract new employees and to retain those who were recently hired. Individuals with greater than five years tenure and working in higher-level positions received smaller raises than did the targeted employees. The Court found the city's decision to base the level of raise on position qualified as a "reasonable factor other than age" and thus did not identify an ADEA violation.[146]

In addition to the prohibition on age-based compensation discrimination, school districts may not spend less on the benefits package of older employees than on those who are younger. The cost of the benefits package must be the same, even though the benefits derived from an equal expenditure may represent a lower level of benefits for an older worker (e.g., health and life insurance benefits for older workers at times are less, unless a higher premium is paid).[147]

---

[144]*See also* Brennan v. Metro. Opera Ass'n, 192 F.3d 310 (2d Cir. 1999) (noting that the fact that the replacement is substantially younger than the plaintiff is a more valuable indicator of age discrimination than whether the replacement was over age 40).

[145]544 U.S. 228 (2005).

[146]*Id.* at 242. Note also that the business necessity test was not used. Among other inquiries, this test asks whether there are other ways for the employer to achieve a goal that does not result in disparate impact on a protected class. In this case, the chosen method of determining salary level did not have to be the best method, or even one that resulted in less disparate impact. It simply had to qualify as reasonable.

[147]29 C.F.R. § 1625.10(a)(1) (2007).

Adverse Employment Actions

Courts often are asked to determine whether an employee's age was used as a basis to terminate, nonrenew, downsize, fail to rehire following a layoff, demote, or transfer an employee.[148] However, as in most other discrimination cases, every action by an employer that the employee perceives as "adverse" might not qualify as such under law. For example, in a Sixth Circuit case, a university professor had his laboratory space reduced, was required to submit grant proposals for internal review, and had his graduate research assistant removed during one summer.[149] Nonetheless, he failed to show that any of these actions qualified as "adverse," as the employer was able to show that the professor failed to generate sufficient revenue to support the space and graduate assistant and that this failure was due to plaintiff's poor grant preparation. The court made clear that mere inconvenience or an alteration of job responsibilities will not be enough to constitute adverse action. In contrast, where a challenged act qualifies as adverse, a plaintiff must show that the reason submitted by the employer is false *and* that age was used as the basis for the adverse action.[150]

Termination, Nonrenewal, Reduction-in-Force. The termination of at-will employees[151] is comparatively simple, as are the removal of nontenured teachers and the elimination of unnecessary teaching and administrative positions, assuming strict adherence to approved policy. In contrast, to terminate tenured employees, as well as those working within a long-term contract, a "for cause" hearing will be required to permit the school district to show why the removal of the employee is necessary.[152] Although many factors may be considered in making such decisions (e.g., morality, efficiency), the employee's age may not be used, unless age qualifies as a BFOQ. In a 2000 Supreme Court case, *Reeves v. Sanderson Plumbing Products*, a 57-year-old former employee was terminated and replaced with a person in his thirties.[153] In remanding and ruling that the company was not entitled to summary judgment, the Court noted that the plaintiff was able to establish a *prima facie* case, create a jury issue concerning the falsity of the employer's basis for the action, and introduce additional evidence showing that the director was motivated by age-related animus.

---

[148]*See, e.g.*, Prater v. Joliet Jr. Coll., 148 Fed. Appx. 550 (7th Cir. 2005) (determining that a dismissed employee who had claimed age discrimination had been terminated due to reduced grant funding and his refusal to transition to new employment).

[149]Mitchell v. Vanderbilt Univ., 389 F.3d 177 (6th Cir. 2004).

[150]*See, e.g.*, Ware v. Howard Univ., 816 F. Supp. 737 (D.D.C. 1993). *But see* Rowe v. Marley Co., 233 F.3d 825 (4th Cir. 2000) (noting that plaintiff failed to show that former employer's reasons for downsizing were pretextual).

[151]At-will employees have no contract or job expectation and may leave or be terminated at any time.

[152]*See also* text accompanying notes 5–6, Chapter 11.

[153]530 U.S. 133 (2000).

In comparison, summary judgment was awarded in an Eleventh Circuit case in which a teacher failed to support her claim of age discrimination, among others, when she was not offered a fifth one-year contract or tenure.[154] The plaintiff failed to provide documentation regarding the age of those selected, other than her general claim that they were younger, and stated in her own deposition that she had no personal knowledge that hiring decisions were made on the basis of age.[155] As a result, the lower court ruling on behalf of the school district was affirmed.

Transfer.   To establish an ADEA claim, when an employee is subjected to an involuntary transfer, he or she will be required to show that such reassignment was based on age and that the new position was materially less prestigious, less suited to current skills and expertise, or less conducive to career advancement. The fact that the employee preferred one position over another does not establish an ADEA violation. Most courts have ruled for school districts when transfers have been challenged, as they seldom view a change of school or a change of grade level to represent a materially significant disadvantage or to be tantamount to a demotion.[156]

Retaliation

Additionally, as with cases filed under Title VII, employers under the ADEA may not retaliate against employees when they file complaints or suits.[157] A plaintiff need not establish the validity of the original complaint in order to succeed in a case claiming retaliation, but it would be helpful to show that the person responsible for the adverse decisions at least knew of the prior charges of discrimination. Furthermore, the plaintiff shoulders the burden to show that the adverse action was an act of retaliation, and not otherwise justified due to incompetence, insubordination, immorality, or the like.[158]

Retirement

Given that the mandatory retirement of school employees has been eliminated, districts have attempted to entice older employees to retire through attractive retirement benefits packages. Under the ADEA, employers can follow the terms of a *bona fide* retirement plan as long as the plan is not a subterfuge to evade the purposes of the

---

[154]Bartes v. Sch. Bd. of Alachua County, No. 04-15459, 2005 U.S. App. LEXIS 23386 (11th Cir. Oct. 26, 2005).

[155]In addition to termination and nonrenewal cases, at times employees allege that they were constructively discharged due to their age. To succeed, the employee must show that the conditions created by the employer were such that a reasonable person similarly situated would find the work intolerable and that the employer acted with the intent of forcing the employee to quit. *See, e.g.*, Dirusso v. Aspen Sch. Dist. No. 1, 123 Fed. Appx. 826 (10th Cir. 2004).

[156]*See, e.g.*, Galabya v. New York City Bd. of Educ., 202 F.3d 636 (2d Cir. 2000).

[157]*See, e.g.*, Passer v. Am. Chem. Soc'y, 935 F.2d 322 (D.C. Cir. 1991).

[158]*See, e.g.*, Horwitz v. Bd. of Educ., 260 F.3d 602 (7th Cir. 2001).

act.[159] Also, employers may not reduce annual benefits or cease the accrual of benefits after employees attain a certain age as an inducement for them to retire.[160] In a Seventh Circuit case, a school district had offered early retirement to teachers age 58 to 61. The longer teachers waited to retire after their fifty-eighth birthday, the less they received in total dollars as a retirement incentive. The court found the practice to facially discriminate based on age in violation of the ADEA.[161]

There also can be legal problems when an employee is terminated prior to becoming eligible for full retirement benefits (i.e., prior to becoming vested). In a 1993 Supreme Court decision, *Hazen Paper Co. v. Biggins*, the plaintiff was fired at age 62, only a few weeks before completing 10 years of service and being vested in his pension plan.[162] Two issues before the Supreme Court were whether the employer's interference with the vesting of pension benefits violated the ADEA *and* whether the standard for liquidated damages[163] applied to informal age-based decisions by employers in addition to those that were based on formal policies that facially discriminate based on age.

In a unanimous opinion, the Court vacated and remanded the lower court decision for a determination of whether the jury had sufficient evidence to find an ADEA violation. The Court made it clear, however, that disparate treatment is not supported when the factor motivating the employer is something other than the employee's age, even if it is correlated with age (e.g., vesting or pension status).[164] Because age and years of service are distinctly different factors, an employer may take one into account, yet ignore the other. Where violations are found and liquidated damages are sought, the Supreme Court iterated that the plaintiff bears the burden to show that the act was willful in that the employer knew or showed reckless disregard for whether its conduct would violate the ADEA.[165]

Although it is difficult to prevail in an age-discrimination claim, expect the number of cases to remain high as the "baby boomers" become sexagenarians over the next decade. Some will be denied employment, promotion, or vesting, whereas others may be disappointed in their retirement packages. Plaintiffs will allege age discrimination, but in most instances, that claim will be successfully rebutted by employers.

---

[159]*See, e.g.,* United Air Lines v. McMann, 434 U.S. 192 (1977).

[160]29 U.S.C. § 623(i)(1) (2007).

[161]Solon v. Gary Cmty. Sch. Corp., 180 F.3d 844 (7th Cir. 1999).

[162]507 U.S. 604 (1993).

[163]For a discussion of liquidated damages, *see* Trans World Airlines v. Thurston, 469 U.S. 111, 126 (1985).

[164]In *dicta*, the Court observed that an employer could be in violation of § 510 of the Employee Retirement Income Security Act, 29 U.S.C. §§ 1001 to 1461 (2007), if it were to fire employees in order to prevent them from vesting in the retirement program.

[165]In so stating, the Court was critical of lower courts for developing alternative standards for liquidated damages (i.e., that the conduct of the employer must be outrageous, that the evidence be direct rather than circumstantial, and that age be the predominant factor rather than simply a determinative one).

Disability Discrimination

Prior to 1973, federal claims regarding disability discrimination in employment were filed under the Equal Protection Clause.[166] The Fourteenth Amendment is now less often used due to the applicability of two federal statutes: the Rehabilitation Act of 1973 (particularly Section 504[167]), which applies to recipients of federal financial assistance, and Title I of the Americans with Disabilities Act of 1990 (ADA),[168] which applies to most employers with 15 or more employees. These statutes require nondiscrimination against the disabled involving any term, condition, or privilege of employment. When education employers are involved, Section 504 complaints are submitted to the Office for Civil Rights within the Department of Education.[169] In comparison, the Equal Employment Opportunity Commission, the Department of Justice, and private litigants have enforcement rights under the ADA.

The issue of whether Eleventh Amendment immunity may be claimed specifically in Title I, ADA suits was addressed by the Supreme Court in 2001 in *Board of Trustees of the University of Alabama v. Garrett*.[170] In that case, two state employees (a nurse and a prison guard) with disabilities sued the state for monetary damages when their respective employers allegedly discriminated against them. After undergoing a lumpectomy, radiation treatment, and chemotherapy, the nurse returned to work but was forced to resign from her director position; she then applied for and received a lower-paying position as a manager. In contrast, the guard claimed that he had been denied necessary work accommodations (i.e., transfer to a daytime shift and reduced exposure to carbon monoxide and cigarette smoke), given his chronic asthma and sleep apnea.

The primary issue on appeal to the Supreme Court was whether under Title I of the ADA, a federal court could award monetary damages to be paid by a state employer or, in the alternative, whether the Eleventh Amendment prohibited such relief. The Court found that the award violated the Constitution and that there was no proven history or pattern of employment discrimination by the state against the disabled. As with other federal claims discussed in this chapter, whether the *Garrett* decision will restrict ADA suits against school districts will depend on whether courts view them as subdivisions of the state, for which

---

[166]The Fourteenth Amendment requires the application of rational-basis scrutiny in cases where disability discrimination is facial and proof of intent where the alleged discrimination is facially neutral.

[167]29 U.S.C. § 794 (2007).

[168]42 U.S.C. § 12101 *et seq.* (2007).

[169]Complaint forms must be filed in a timely manner and signed by the plaintiff. *See* Fry v. Muscogee County Sch. Dist., 150 Fed. Appx. 980 (11th Cir. 2005) (concluding that plaintiff with morbid obesity failed to sign and thereby verify her ADA complaint—her attorney had signed it for her, but later failed to acquire her signature or properly amend the claim).

[170]531 U.S. 356 (2001).

immunity is not available, or as state agencies or arms of the state, for which immunity is available.[171]

Notwithstanding the fact that the Eleventh Amendment may prohibit awards of monetary damages within a few jurisdictions, do not assume that persons who have been subjected to disability discrimination in employment are powerless to vindicate their rights. The ADA, Title I, still prescribes standards that are applicable to state employers. These standards could be enforced by the United States in federal judicial actions for monetary damages and by employees in actions seeking injunctive relief. Furthermore, many state disability laws provide identical or at least similar coverage to that mandated by the ADA and permit monetary damages under certain circumstances. Furthermore, because all (or nearly all) public schools are recipients of federal financial assistance, they must meet substantially similar obligations under the Rehabilitation Act—a law that at times permits the awarding of money damages.

Qualifying as Disabled

When cases are filed, courts often are asked to resolve questions regarding whether the plaintiff is in fact disabled and, if so, what accommodations are required. A person qualifies as disabled under Section 504 and the ADA if he or she:

- Has a physical or mental impairment that substantially limits one or more major life activities,
- Has a record of impairment,[172] or
- Is regarded as having an impairment.[173]

However, more is required than simple knowledge of a condition that is physically or mentally limiting for the plaintiff to establish that the employer regarded the employee as having an impairment.[174] Additionally, suggesting that an employee see a psychologist before returning to work does not establish the fact that the employer regarded the employee as a person with a mental disability.[175]

---

[171]*See, e.g.*, Mt. Healthy City Sch. Dist. v. Doyle, 429 U.S. 274 (1977) (concluding in a First Amendment suit that the school district was not entitled to assert Eleventh Amendment immunity since under state law the board was more like a county or a city, rather than an arm of the state). *See also* text accompanying notes 203–209, Chapter 11.

[172]For example, when a person is discriminatorily treated because of having a history of hospitalization due to tuberculosis, alcoholism, or drug addiction, the person would qualify for protection as he is viewed as "having a record of impairment."

[173]For example, when a person is discriminatorily treated because of being HIV positive, but does not have AIDS or any type of current physical impairment limiting a major life activity, the person would qualify for protection as he is "regarded as having an impairment."

[174]*See, e.g.*, Amadio v. Ford Motor Co., 238 F.3d 919 (7th Cir. 2001).

[175]*See, e.g.*, Sullivan v. River Valley Sch. Dist., 197 F.3d 804 (6th Cir. 1999).

Although federal regulations define physical or mental impairment broadly,[176] persons who currently are involved in the use of illegal drugs,[177] are unable to perform the duties of the job due to alcohol, have a contagious disease,[178] or otherwise represent a direct threat to the safety[179] or health of themselves or others do not qualify as disabled.[180] If the individual is disqualified due to health issues, the decision needs to be based on current medical evidence, and not on stereotypes or fears. Likewise, persons claiming discrimination due to transvestism, transsexualism, pedophilia, exhibitionism, voyeurism, gender identity disorders not resulting from physical impairments, other sexual behavior disorders, compulsive gambling, kleptomania, pyromania, and psychoactive substance use disorders resulting from current illegal drug use are not protected by either the ADA or Section 504.

Qualifying as *disabled* requires a two-step process: identifying a physical or mental impairment *and* determining whether the impairment *substantially limits* a *major life activity*.[181] The EEOC identifies several major life activities (i.e., walking, seeing, hearing, speaking, breathing, learning, and working) in its guidelines for the ADA[182] and others in related manuals (i.e., caring for oneself, sitting, standing, lifting, concentrating, thinking, and interacting with others),[183] while the Supreme Court has expanded the list also to include both reproduction and performing manual tasks.[184]

In assessing whether an applicant or employee is disabled, the Supreme Court in 1999 also required that mitigating and corrective measures (both positive and negative[185]) be considered.[186] Not all impairments limit major life activity (e.g., a hearing-impaired employee may have average or near-average hearing due to the use

---

[176]34 C.F.R. § 104.3(j)(2)(i) (2007).

[177]*See, e.g.,* Shafer v. Preston Mem. Hosp. Corp., 107 F.3d 274 (4th Cir. 1997) (permitting termination of a nurse for stealing drugs and determining that she was a "current" user, although not caught taking drugs the day of her termination).

[178]Although being HIV positive does not typically make an employee unqualified for employment, it may within medical and other fields when a direct threat results. *See* "California: Sex Film Industry Lifts Moratorium," *New York Times* (May 13, 2004), p. A-17 (observing a direct threat among HIV-positive actors in the porn industry).

[179]*See, e.g.,* Reed v. LePage Bakeries, 244 F.3d 254 (1st Cir. 2001).

[180]*See, e.g.,* Chevron, U.S.A., Inc. v. Echazabal, 536 U.S. 73 (2002).

[181]*See, e.g.,* Hinojosa v. Jostens Inc., 128 Fed. Appx. 364 (5th Cir. 2005).

[182]29 C.F.R. §1630.2(i) (2007).

[183]*Technical Assistance Manual on the Employment Provisions (Title I) of the Americans with Disabilities Act* (January 1992), pp. II-3; *Enforcement Guidance on the Americans with Disabilities Act and Psychiatric Disabilities*, No. 915.002 (March 25, 1997), pp. 6–7.

[184]Bragdon v. Abbott, 524 U.S. 624 (1998) (reproduction); Toyota Motor Mfg. v. Williams, 534 U.S. 184 (2002) (manual tasks).

[185]For example, corrected vision through use of contact lenses is a positive mitigating measure; side effects of medication represent a negative one. *See, e.g.,* Ozlowski v. Henderson, 237 F.3d 837 (7th Cir. 2001).

[186]*See, e.g.,* Sutton v. United Airlines, 527 U.S. 471 (1999); Murphy v. United Parcel Serv., 527 U.S. 516 (1999).

of a hearing aid). Performance is substantially limited when an employee is unable to perform, or is significantly restricted in performing, a major life activity that can be accomplished by the average person in the general population. The nature, severity, duration, and long-term impact of the impairment are considered when determining whether a condition is substantially limiting.[187] Also, an impairment that is substantially limiting for one person may not be for another. To qualify it must prevent or restrict an individual from performing tasks that are of central importance to most people's daily lives. If the life activity claimed is working, impairments are not substantially limiting unless they restrict the ability to perform a broad range of jobs and not just a single or specialized job.[188] In such cases, courts will consider the geographic area to which the plaintiff has reasonable access and the nature of the job from which the individual was disqualified, as well as other jobs that require similar training, knowledge, ability, or skill.[189]

In 2002, the Supreme Court reviewed a claim by an assembly line worker in *Toyota Motor Manufacturing v. Williams*. She asserted that her employer failed to accommodate her bilateral carpal tunnel syndrome, which seemed to be exacerbated by the use of pneumatic tools, repetitive motion, and lifting any significant weight.[190] The Court reasoned that to be substantially limiting, a permanent or long-term impairment must prevent or severely restrict the individual from doing activities that are of central importance to most people's daily lives. This will require a case-by-case analysis, as symptoms vary widely for most impairments. Accordingly, the Court ruled that in qualifying the plaintiff as disabled, the lower court should not have relied on her inability to perform the difficult manual tasks in her specialized assembly line job, but rather should have considered whether she could brush her teeth, bathe, and perform household chores, as these were the activities that were necessary to daily living.

Some of the more unusual, but unsuccessful, attempts to claim protection based on disability involved a left-handed mail carrier, an acrophobic utility systems repairer, an overweight flight attendant, a person with a test-taking phobia, and a teacher with alleged emotional ailments caused by the need to adjust to a new instructional method.[191] In a case heard by the Maine Supreme Court, a teacher purported to have a compulsive sexual addiction that caused him to harass students and seek out the services of prostitutes. He contended that his behavior was a manifestation of his disability and that his rights under the ADA and Section 504,

---

[187]29 C.F.R. § 1630.2(j)(1), (2) (2007).

[188]*See, e.g.*, Samuels v. Kansas City Mo. Sch. Dist., 437 F.3d 797 (8th Cir. 2006).

[189]29 C.F.R. § 1630.2(j)(2), (3) (2007).

[190]534 U.S. 184 (2002).

[191]Pandazides v. Va. Bd. of Educ., 946 F.2d 345 (4th Cir. 1991), *on remand*, 804 F. Supp. 794 (E.D. Va. 1992) (test anxiety); Beauford v. Father Flanagan's Boys' Home, 831 F.2d 768 (8th Cir. 1987) (difficulty adjusting to precision teaching system); Forrisi v. Bowen, 794 F.2d 931 (4th Cir. 1986) (acrophobia); de la Torres v. Bolger, 781 F.2d 1134 (5th Cir. 1986) (left-handedness); Tudyman v. United Airlines, 608 F. Supp. 739 (D.C. Cal. 1984) (weight).

among others, were violated when he was fired. The court disagreed, however, and upheld his termination.[192]

Otherwise Qualified

If a person qualifies as disabled, it then must be determined whether he or she is "otherwise qualified." To be an otherwise qualified individual with a disability, the applicant or employee must be able to perform the essential functions of the job in spite of the disability, although reasonable accommodation at times may be necessary. Generally, employers should not impose a blanket exclusion of persons with particular disabilities, but rather should provide individual review of each person. Only in rare instances will a particular disability disqualify an applicant (e.g., where federal or state law establishes health or ability requirements for particular types of employment).

In identifying the essential functions of the job, courts will give consideration to what the employer perceives to be essential. As long as each identified requirement for employment is either training related (for initial employment) or job related, the employer should not have difficulty in substantiating its claim of business necessity. For example, being on time to work and being at work on a regular daily basis can qualify as a business necessity for most positions in education as well as elsewhere. Employees often have claimed that their respective disabilities were the basis for their lateness or nonarrival. Although this may have been true, courts generally have not found such employees to be otherwise qualified.[193] In 1994, an instructor with an autoimmune system disorder claimed disability discrimination when she was fired for not meeting the attendance requirements of the job. In ruling for the employer, the Fourth Circuit held that the employer was not required to restructure the entire work schedule to accommodate the employee in her efforts to deal with her own needs as well as those of her son, who also was disabled.[194]

Nevertheless, the burden will be on the district to show that the absences are excessive, that the requested accommodations are unreasonable, or that undue hardship would result if the employee were reinstated. In *School Board of Nassau County, Florida v. Arline*, a teacher had three relapses of tuberculosis over a two-year period for which leave was given and was terminated prior to returning to work following the third leave.[195] The Supreme Court held that the teacher qualified as disabled under Section 504 due to her record of physical impairment and hospitalization, but remanded the case for the district court to determine whether risks of infection to others precluded her from being otherwise qualified and whether her condition could be reasonably accommodated without an undue burden on the district. Following remand, the teacher was found to be otherwise qualified, since she posed little risk of infecting others, and was ordered reinstated with back pay.

---

[192]Winston v. Me. Technical Coll. Sys., 631 A.2d 70 (Me. 1993).

[193]*See, e.g.*, Carr v. Reno, 23 F.3d 525 (D.C. Cir. 1994); Walders v. Garrett, 956 F.2d 1163 (4th Cir. 1992).

[194]Tyndall v. Nat'l Educ. Ctrs., 31 F.3d 209 (4th Cir. 1994).

[195]480 U.S. 273 (1987), *on remand*, 692 F. Supp. 1286 (M.D. Fla. 1988).

Reasonable Accommodation

Persons with disabilities must be able to perform all of the essential functions of the position, either with accommodation or without. Employers are responsible for providing reasonable accommodations, such as making necessary facilities accessible and usable, restructuring work schedules, acquiring or modifying equipment, and providing readers or interpreters.[196] Also, when not restricted by bargaining rights or other entitlements, transfer within the organization may qualify as a reasonable accommodation.[197] However, federal law does not require the employer to bump a current employee to allow a person with a disability to fill the position, to fill a vacant position it did not intend to fill, to violate seniority rights, to refrain from disciplining an employee for misconduct, to eliminate essential functions of the job, or to create a new unnecessary position.[198] Moreover, an employer need not transfer the employee to a better position, or select a less-qualified or unqualified applicant solely because of disability.[199] Such forms of accommodation may be theoretically possible but would result in undue hardship to the employer and discriminate against other employees. Courts determine whether undue hardship results after a review of the size of the program and its budget, the number of employees, the type of facilities and operation, and the nature and cost of accommodation. Because there is no fixed formula for calculations, courts have differed markedly in identifying what they consider reasonable.

In selecting reasonable accommodations, the employer should engage in an ongoing *interactive process* with the employee with a disability and consult state and federal agencies when needed.[200] Employees often are a good source for identifying accommodations that will assist them in meeting the essential functions of the job. Note, however, that the employee does not select the accommodations. The employer has the right to select among effective reasonable accommodations. To facilitate the process, it is helpful for the employer to have policies identifying the steps taken in (1) establishing an interactive process with the employee with a disability; (2) requesting reasonable accommodations; and (3) determining those accommodations to be provided.

If the employee remains dissatisfied, the employer should have an internal procedure for appeal. Following this appeal, if the employee is still dissatisfied, a formal complaint may be filed with the appropriate federal or state agency given the nature of the claim. Critical to a successful claim would be proving that the employer was aware of the employee's disability[201] and that a reasonable accommodation exists that

---

[196]*But see* Vollmert v. Wis. Dep't of Trans., 197 F.3d 293 (7th Cir. 1999) (finding that the employer failed to accommodate a staff member with dyslexia and learning disabilities when it transferred her to a position with fewer opportunities for promotion; that the transfer was inappropriate because reasonable accommodations had not been provided for the previous job).

[197]*See, e.g.*, Smith v. Midland Brake, 180 F.3d 1154 (10th Cir. 1999) (*en banc*).

[198]*See, e.g.*, Ozlowski v. Henderson, 237 F.3d 837 (7th Cir. 2001).

[199]*See, e.g.*, EEOC v. Humiston-Keeling, 227 F.3d 1024 (7th Cir. 2000).

[200]*See, e.g.*, Cutrera v. Bd. of Supervisors of La. State Univ., 429 F.3d 108 (5th Cir. 2005).

[201]*See, e.g.*, Whitney v. Bd. of Educ., 292 F.3d 1280 (10th Cir. 2002).

would enable the employee to fulfill job requirements.[202] In a Sixth Circuit case, an HIV-positive surgical technician was laid off once it was determined that patients would be at risk during surgery if the infected technician were to participate. In addition to preparing and handling surgical instruments, he at times was required to put his hands in an incision to make room for the surgeon to work or to provide visibility. In the process, he would have regular exposure to blood and possibly incur needle pricks or even cuts. In the alternative, the medical center offered him a position as cart instrument coordinator, an accommodation that would allow him to remain employed. The plaintiff refused this proposal and was terminated. In upholding the granting of summary judgment for the employer, the court held that no reasonable accommodation would eliminate the direct threat the plaintiff posed and that he therefore was not otherwise qualified for the former position.[203]

Termination and Nonrenewal

There are more individuals with disabilities in the workplace today than ever before with many achieving leadership positions. Not all persons with disabilities have fared well, however, as some have not been selected for initial employment, not granted tenure, not been promoted, not paid fairly, arbitrarily discharged, or forced to resign or retire.[204] At times, such adverse decisions were due to inadequate qualifications or skills, better-qualified applicants, poor job performance, posing a risk, or criminal wrongdoing.[205] At other times, the employee's disability was found to be the basis for the adverse decision, or the environment had become so hostile that the employee's decision to quit qualified as being constructively discharged.[206]

To support a disparate treatment adverse action claim, employees must show that (1) they have a disability that substantially limits a major life activity as compared to the average person in the population; (2) they were the target of an action that qualified as adverse; and (3) the adverse action was due to being disabled. In a First Circuit case, a recovering drug addict employed as a nurse failed in her claim that she had incurred disparate treatment. The First Circuit concluded that she was justifiably terminated for excessive violation of protocols in regard to drug dispersement. On one occasion, she denied asking a new nurse to administer a drug she had prepared as such conduct is in direct violation of policy. However, she later equivocated and ultimately

---

[202]*But see* Merrell v. ICEE-USA Corp., No. 99-4173, 2000 U.S. App. LEXIS 33327 (10th Cir. Dec. 19, 2000) (finding no reasonable accommodation that would allow a man who stocked carbonated beverage machines to meet essential job functions).

[203]Estate of Mauro v. Borgess Med. Ctr., 137 F.3d 398 (6th Cir. 1998).

[204]*See, e.g.*, Cigan v. Chippewa Falls Sch. Dist., 388 F.3d 331 (7th Cir. 2004).

[205]*See, e.g.*, Haulbrook v. Michelin N. Am., 252 F.3d 696 (4th Cir. 2001); Borgialli v. Thunder Basin Coal Co., 235 F.3d 1284 (10th Cir. 2000).

[206]*See, e.g.*, Spells v. Cuyahoga Cmty. Coll., 889 F. Supp. 1023 (N.D. Ohio 1994), *aff'd without published opinion*, 51 F.3d 273 (6th Cir. 1995).

admitted to the violation but only after the administering nurse forthrightly acknowledged her own violation.[207]

Similarly, a former Kentucky teacher claimed that her termination allegedly due to conduct unbecoming was actually based on disability. In her defense, she argued that the alleged questionable behaviors were symptomatic of a head injury she suffered 13 years earlier in a bicycle accident and that she had not committed most of the violations claimed by the board—threatening students and making inappropriate comments about students and their families. In support of her termination, the court noted that she already had been found guilty in criminal court for nine counts of "terroristic threatening" against students. Her conduct, even if disability related, rendered her unqualified to continue as an educator.[208]

There should continue to be ample case law dealing with termination and other claims filed by employees with disabilities. Such claims are likely to focus on the ADA rather than Section 504, given its broader application. Expect school officials to continue to struggle in their efforts to provide effective, cost-efficient accommodations, but also expect generally good-faith efforts as educators attempt to comply with federal and state disability laws.

Conclusion

Federal law requires that employment decisions be based on qualifications, performance, merit, seniority, and the like, rather than factors such as race, national origin, sex, sexual orientation, religion, age, or disability. Statutes vary considerably, however, as to what they require. Moreover, federal regulations are extensive, complex, and at times confounding. As a result, courts differ in applying the law. Even though many questions remain, the following generalizations reflect the current status of the law.

1. The United States Constitution and various civil rights laws protect employees from discrimination in employment based on race, national origin, sex, sexual orientation, religion, age, and disability.
2. For Fourteenth Amendment facial discrimination cases, race and national-origin discrimination claims require the application of strict scrutiny; sex and illegitimacy discrimination receive intermediate scrutiny; and all other employment classifications need to be justified by any rational basis.
3. For Fourteenth Amendment facially neutral cases, regardless of the type of classification involved, the plaintiff is required to show that the employer intended to discriminate.
4. Race may never qualify as a *bona fide* occupational qualification, although sex, religion, national origin, and age may be used under narrowly tailored conditions.

[207]Griel v. Franklin Med. Ctr., 234 F.3d 731 (1st Cir. 2000).

[208]Macy v. Hopkins County Sch. Bd. of Educ., 484 F.3d 357 (6th Cir. 2007).

5. Adverse impact of a facially neutral employment practice on a protected group does not establish a constitutional violation, but such impact can violate Title VII if the employer is unable to show that the challenged practice serves a business necessity.

6. A reliable and valid standardized test can be used to screen job applicants, even though it has a disproportionate impact on a protected class, as long as the test is used to advance legitimate job objectives.

7. In Title VII disparate treatment cases, plaintiffs initially must establish a *prima facie* case of discrimination; then the employer has the opportunity to rebut the inference of discrimination by articulating a legitimate nondiscriminatory basis for the practice. To prevail, the plaintiff then must prove that the proffered reasons were not to be believed and a pretext for discrimination.

8. Public employers may not engage in affirmative action plans involving preferences in hiring and promotion unless a court has determined that the institution has been involved in specific prior acts of discrimination and the affirmative action plan is narrowly tailored to attain a work force reflecting the qualified relevant labor market.

9. Under narrowly tailored circumstances, courts may order hiring and promotion preferences to remedy prior acts of intentional employment discrimination but may not impose layoff quotas.

10. Pregnancy-related conditions cannot be treated less favorably than other temporary disabilities in medical and disability insurance plans or leave policies.

11. Employees cannot be required to take maternity leave at a specified date during pregnancy unless the policy is justified as a business necessity.

12. Employers cannot make a distinction between men and women in retirement contributions and benefits.

13. Employees can gain relief under Title VII for sexual harassment that results in the loss of tangible benefits or creates a hostile working environment.

14. Title VII provides remedies for sex discrimination in compensation that extends beyond the Equal Pay Act guarantee of equal pay for equal work.

15. Persons who are victims of sexual preference discrimination may file suit under the Fourteenth Amendment (public sector) or under applicable state laws or local ordinances, where they exist (public and private sectors).

16. School boards can establish *bona fide* retirement benefits programs, but the Age Discrimination in Employment Act (ADEA) precludes mandatory retirement based on age.

17. For a violation to be substantiated under the ADEA, age must play a role in the decision-making process *and* have a determinative influence on the outcome.

18. Employers must make reasonable accommodations to enable employees to practice their religious beliefs; however, Title VII does not require accommodations that result in undue hardship to the employer.

19. An otherwise qualified individual cannot be excluded from employment solely on the basis of a disability, and employers are required to provide reasonable accommodations for employees with disabilities.

11

Termination of Employment

State laws delineate the authority of school boards in terminating school personnel. Generally, these laws specify the causes for which a teacher may be terminated and the procedures that must be followed. The school board's right to determine the fitness of teachers is well established; in fact, courts have declared that school boards have a duty as well as a right to make such determinations. According to the United States Supreme Court:

> A teacher works in a sensitive area in a schoolroom. There he shapes the attitude of young minds towards the society in which they live. In this, the state has a vital concern. It must preserve the integrity of the schools. That the school authorities have *the right and the duty to screen* the officials, teachers, and employees as to their fitness to maintain the integrity of the schools as a part of ordered society, cannot be doubted.[1] (emphasis added)

This chapter addresses the procedures that must be followed in the termination of a teacher's employment and the grounds for dismissal. The first section provides an overview of due process in connection with nonrenewal and dismissal. Since due process is required only if a teacher is able to establish that a constitutionally protected property or liberty interest is at stake, the dimensions of teachers' property and liberty rights are explored in the context of employment termination. In the next section, specific procedural requirements are identified and discussed. A survey of judicial interpretations of state laws regarding causes for dismissal is presented in the third section. The concluding section provides an overview of remedies available to teachers for violation of their protected rights.

---

[1] Adler v. Bd. of Educ., 342 U.S. 485, 493 (1952).

Procedural Due Process in General

Basic due process rights are embodied in the Fourteenth Amendment, which guarantees that no state shall "deprive any person of life, liberty, or property without due
process of law."[2] Due process safeguards apply not only in judicial proceedings but
also to acts of governmental agencies such as school boards. As discussed in Chapter
1, constitutional due process entails *substantive* protections against arbitrary governmental action and *procedural* protections when the government threatens an individual's life, liberty, or property interests. Most teacher termination cases have focused
on procedural due process requirements.

The individual and governmental interests at stake and applicable state laws
influence the nature of procedural due process required. Courts have established that
a teacher's interest in public employment may entail significant "property" and "liberty" rights necessitating due process prior to employment termination. A *property
interest* is a "legitimate claim of entitlement" to continued employment that is created by state law.[3] The granting of tenure conveys such a property right to a teacher.
Also, a contract establishes a property right to employment within its stated terms.[4] A
property interest in continued employment, however, does not mean that an individual cannot be terminated; it simply means that an employer must follow the requirements of due process and substantiate cause.

The judiciary has recognized that Fourteenth Amendment *liberty rights*
encompass fundamental constitutional guarantees, such as freedom of speech. Procedural due process always is required when a termination implicates such fundamental
liberties. A liberty interest also is involved when termination creates a stigma or damages an individual's reputation in a manner that forecloses future employment opportunities. If protected liberty or property interests are implicated, the Fourteenth
Amendment entitles the teacher to at least notice the reasons for the school board's
action and an opportunity for a hearing.

Employment terminations are classified as either dismissals or nonrenewals. The
distinction between the two has significant implications for teachers' procedural rights.
In this section, the procedural safeguards that must be provided the tenured teacher and
the nontenured teacher are distinguished. Specific attention is given to the conditions

---

[2] As noted in Chapter 1, the Fourteenth Amendment restricts state, in contrast to private, action. The
Supreme Court has recognized that mere regulation by the state will be insufficient to evoke constitutional
protections in private school personnel matters. The Court rejected a suit for damages against a private
school for alleged unconstitutional dismissals, reasoning that there was no "symbiotic relationship"
between the private school and the state. Rendell Baker v. Kohn, 457 U.S. 830 (1982). *See also* Logiodice
v. Trs., 296 F.3d 22 (1st Cir. 2002) (ruling that payment of tuition for public school students to attend private school did not involve state action that would require the school to provide a student procedural due
process prior to suspension).

[3] *See* Bd. of Regents v. Roth, 408 U.S. 564 (1972).

[4] *See, e.g.*, Coggin v. Longview Indep. Sch. Dist., 337 F.3d 459 (5th Cir.). *See also* Watson v. N. Panola Sch.
Dist., 188 Fed. Appx. 291 (5th Cir. 2006) (ruling that principal's oral job offer to teacher did not constitute
a contract without school board approval; teacher could not allege deprivation of a property right).

that may give rise to a nontenured teacher acquiring a protected liberty or property interest in employment, thereby establishing a claim to procedural due process.

Dismissal

The term *dismissal* refers to the termination for cause of any tenured teacher or a probationary teacher within the contract period. Both tenure statutes[5] and employment contracts[6] establish a property interest entitling teachers to full procedural protection. Beyond the basic constitutional requirements of appropriate notice and an opportunity to be heard, state laws and school board policies often contain detailed procedures that must be followed. Failure to provide these additional procedures, however, results in a violation of state law, rather than constitutional law. Statutory procedures vary as to specificity, with some states enumerating detailed steps and others identifying only broad parameters. In addition to complying with state law, a school district must abide by its own procedures, even if they exceed state law. For example, if school board policy provides for a preliminary notice of teaching inadequacies and an opportunity to correct remediable deficiencies prior to dismissal, the board must follow these steps.

A critical element in dismissal actions is a showing of justifiable cause for termination of employment. If causes are identified in state law, a school board must base dismissal on those grounds. Failure to relate the charges to statutory grounds can invalidate the termination decision. Because statutes typically list broad causes—such as incompetency, insubordination, immorality, unprofessional conduct, and neglect of duty—notice of discharge must indicate specific conduct substantiating the legal charges. Procedural safeguards ensure not only that a teacher is informed of the specific reasons and grounds for dismissal, but also that the school board bases its decision on evidence substantiating those grounds. Detailed aspects of procedural due process requirements and dismissal for cause are addressed in subsequent sections of this chapter.

Nonrenewal

Unless specified in state law, procedural protections are not accorded the probationary teacher when the employment contract is not renewed.[7] At the end of the contract period, employment can be terminated for any or no reason, as long as the reason is

---

[5]If a statute conferring specific property rights (e.g., tenure) is rescinded or amended to eliminate those rights, individuals are not entitled to procedural due process related to that deprivation; statutory benefits can be revoked without due process unless the change impairs contractual rights. *See, e.g.,* Indiana *ex rel.* Anderson v. Brand, 303 U.S. 95 (1938); Pittman v. Chi. Bd. of Educ., 64 F.3d 1098 (7th Cir. 1995). However, school boards generally cannot amend, repeal, or circumvent statutory rights (e.g., entitlement to procedural due process) through the employment contract. *See, e.g.,* Parker v. Indep. Sch. Dist. No. I-003 Okmulgee County, Okla., 82 F.3d 952 (10th Cir. 1996).

[6]*See, e.g.,* Gibson v. Caruthersville Sch. Dist. No. 8, 336 F.3d 768 (8th Cir. 2003).

[7]*See, e.g.,* Lighton v. Univ. of Utah, 209 F.3d 1213 (10th Cir. 2000); Provoda v. Maxwell, 808 P.2d 28 (N.M. 1991); Tucker v. Bd. of Educ., 624 N.E.2d 643 (N.Y. 1993).

not constitutionally impermissible (e.g., denial of protected speech) and satisfies state law.[8] The most common statutory requirement is notification of nonrenewal on or before a specified date prior to the expiration of the contract. Courts strictly construe the timeliness of nonrenewal notices. When a statute designates a deadline for nonrenewal, a school board must notify a teacher on or before the established date. The fact that the school board has set in motion notification (e.g., mailed the notice) generally does not satisfy the statutory requirement; the teacher's actual receipt of the notice is required. A teacher, however, cannot avoid or deliberately thwart delivery of notice and then claim insufficiency of notice. Failure of school officials to observe the notice deadline may result in a teacher's reinstatement for an additional year or even the granting of tenure in some jurisdictions.[9]

   In the nonrenewal of teachers' contracts, some states require a written statement of reasons and may even provide an opportunity for a hearing at the teacher's request.[10] Unlike evidentiary hearings for dismissal of a teacher, the school board is not required to show cause for nonrenewal;[11] a teacher is simply provided the reasons underlying the nonrenewal and an opportunity to address the school board. When a school board is required to provide reasons, broad general statements, such as "the school district's interest would be best served," "the district can find a better teacher," or "the term contract has expired," will not suffice. The Arkansas high court noted that state law requires boards to give "simple but complete reasons."[12] The Mississippi high court emphasized that although a school board must show that "demonstrable

[8]*See, e.g.*, Grossman v. S. Shore Pub. Sch. Dist., 507 F.3d 1097 (7th Cir. 2007) (ruling that a school district's decision to not renew a guidance counselor's contract because of conduct in praying with students, promoting abstinence, and condemning contraception did not violate her First Amendment rights); Back v. Hastings on Hudson Union Free Sch. Dist., 365 F.3d 107 (2d Cir. 2004) (denying summary judgment to defendants when evidence proffered indicated that school psychologist's denial of tenure was based on gender stereotyping); Flaskamp v. Dearborn Pub. Schs., 385 F.3d 935 (6th Cir. 2004) (ruling that denial of tenure did not abridge privacy rights of teacher who was not candid in answering principal's questions about a relationship with a former student which appeared to have begun prior to graduation). *See also* Chapter 9 for a discussion of teachers' constitutional rights.

[9]*See, e.g.*, Kiel v. Green Local Sch. Dist. Bd. of Educ., 630 N.E.2d 716 (Ohio 1994). *See also* Brunecz v. City of Dunkirk Bd. of Educ., 804 N.Y.S.2d 203 (App. Div. 2005) (declining to award tenure when a notice of nonrenewal was too ambiguous to satisfy the state notice requirements; the teacher received one day's pay for each day that adequate notice was late).

[10]*See, e.g.*, Kidd v. Bd. of Educ., 29 S.W.3d 374 (Ky. Ct. App. 2000) (remanding case to determine if the reasons offered for nonrenewal were true; if not, decision would be voided); Palmer v. La. State Bd. of Elementary and Secondary Educ., 842 So. 2d 363, 371 (La. 2003) (ruling that state law required notice of nonrenewal to include "valid reasons" from the superintendent); Milliken-Dees v. Salem City Sch. Dist. Bd. of Educ., 855 N.E.2d 932 (Ohio Ct. App. 2006) (determining that a nonrenewal notice indicating the school district was facing a deficit failed to inform teachers why each one was selected for nonrenewal); Naylor v. Cardinal Local Sch. Dist. Bd. of Educ., 630 N.E.2d 725 (Ohio 1994) (holding that a "hearing" under Ohio law is more than an informal session with the school board; it includes the right to present evidence, confront and examine witnesses, and review both parties' arguments).

[11]*See, e.g.*, Flath v. Garrison Pub. Sch. Dist. No. 51, 82 F.3d 244 (8th Cir. 1996); Brown v. Reg'l Sch. Dist. 13, 328 F. Supp. 2d 289 (D. Conn. 2004).

[12]Hamilton v. Pulaski County Special Sch. Dist., 900 S.W.2d 205 (Ark. 1995).

reason" exists for a nonrenewal decision, the burden of proof remains with the teacher to prove that the board had no basis for the decision not to renew.[13] Where state law establishes specific requirements and procedures for nonrenewal, failure to abide by these provisions may invalidate a school board's decision. Failure to follow the prescribed statutory procedures for evaluating nontenured teachers in Ohio can result in reversal of a nonrenewal decision with reinstatement for an additional year.[14] Furthermore, a school board must not only follow state law but also must comply substantially with its own nonrenewal procedures.

Although state laws may not provide the probationary teacher with specific procedural protections, a teacher's interest in continued public employment may be constitutionally protected if a liberty or property right guaranteed by the Fourteenth Amendment has been abridged. Infringement of these interests entitles a probationary teacher to due process rights similar to the rights of tenured teachers. These rights are delineated next.

Establishing Protected Property and Liberty Interests

The United States Supreme Court addressed the scope of protected interests encompassed by the Fourteenth Amendment in two significant decisions in 1972: *Board of Regents v. Roth*[15] and *Perry v. Sindermann.*[16] These decisions addressed whether the infringement of a liberty or property interest entitles a probationary teacher to due process rights similar to the rights of tenured teachers. The cases involved faculty members at the postsecondary level, but the rulings are equally applicable to public elementary and secondary school teachers.

In *Roth*, the question presented to the Court was whether a nontenured teacher had a constitutional right to a statement of reasons and a hearing prior to nonreappointment. Roth was hired on a one-year contract, and the university elected not to rehire him for a second year. Since Roth did not have tenure, there was no entitlement under Wisconsin law to an explanation of charges or a hearing; the university simply did not reemploy him for the succeeding year. Roth challenged the nonrenewal, alleging that failure to provide notice of reasons and an opportunity for a hearing impaired his due process rights.

The Supreme Court held that nonrenewal did not require procedural protection unless impairment of a protected liberty or property interest could be shown. To establish infringement of a liberty interest, the Court held that the teacher must show that the employer's action (1) resulted in damage to his or her reputation and standing in the community or (2) imposed a stigma that foreclosed other employment opportunities. The evidence presented by Roth indicated that there was no such damage to his

---

[13]Buck v. Lowndes County Sch. Dist., 761 So. 2d 144 (Miss. 2000).

[14]Snyder v. Mendon-Union Dist. Bd. of Educ., 661 N.E.2d 717 (Ohio 1996).

[15]408 U.S. 564 (1972).

[16]408 U.S. 593 (1972).

reputation or future employment. Accordingly, the Court concluded, "It stretches the concept too far to suggest that a person is deprived of 'liberty' when he simply is not rehired in one job but remains as free as before to seek another."[17]

The Court also rejected Roth's claim that he had a protected property interest to continued employment. In order to establish a valid property right, the Court held that an individual must have more than an "abstract need or desire" for a position; there must be a "legitimate claim of entitlement."[18] The federal Constitution does not define property interests; rather, state laws or employment contracts secure specific benefits. An abstract desire or unilateral expectation of continued employment alone does not constitute a property right. The terms of Roth's one-year appointment and the state law precluded any claim of entitlement.

On the same day it rendered the *Roth* decision, the Supreme Court in the *Sindermann* case explained the circumstances that might create a legitimate expectation of reemployment for a nontenured teacher.[19] Sindermann was a nontenured faculty member in his fourth year of teaching when he was notified, without a statement of reasons or an opportunity for a hearing, that his contract would not be renewed. He challenged the lack of procedural due process, alleging that nonrenewal deprived him of a property interest protected by the Fourteenth Amendment and violated his First Amendment right to freedom of speech.

In advancing a protected property right, Sindermann claimed that the college, which lacked a formal tenure system, had created an informal, or *de facto*, tenure system through various practices and policies. Specifically, Sindermann cited a provision in the faculty guide: "The College wishes the faculty member to feel that he has permanent tenure as long as his teaching services are satisfactory."[20] The Supreme Court found that Sindermann's claim, unlike Roth's, may have been based on a legitimate expectation of reemployment promulgated by the college. According to the Court, the lack of a formal tenure system did not foreclose the possibility of an institution fostering entitlement to a position through its personnel policies.

In assessing Sindermann's free speech claim, the Supreme Court confirmed that a teacher's lack of tenure does not void a claim that nonrenewal was based on the exercise of constitutionally protected conduct. Procedural due process must be afforded when a substantive constitutional right is violated. In a later case, however, the Supreme Court held that if a constitutional right is implicated in a nonrenewal, the teacher bears the burden of showing that the protected conduct was a substantial or motivating factor in the school board's decision.[21] The establishment of this inference of a constitutional violation then shifts the burden to the school board to show

---

[17]*Roth,* 408 U.S. at 575.

[18]*Id.* at 577.

[19]408 U.S. 593 (1972).

[20]*Id.* at 600.

[21]Mt. Healthy City Sch. Dist. Bd. of Educ. v. Doyle, 429 U.S. 274 (1977). *See* text accompanying note 4, Chapter 9, for a discussion of the First Amendment issue in this case.

by a preponderance of evidence that it would have reached the same decision in the absence of the protected activity.

The *Roth* and *Sindermann* cases are the legal precedents for assessing the procedural rights of nontenured teachers. To summarize, the Supreme Court held that a nontenured teacher does not have a constitutionally protected property right to employment requiring procedural due process before denial of reappointment. Certain actions of the school board, however, may create conditions entitling the teacher to notice and a hearing similar to the tenured teacher. Such actions would include:

- Nonrenewal decisions damaging an individual's reputation and integrity;
- Nonrenewal decisions foreclosing other employment opportunities;
- Policies and practices creating a valid claim to reemployment; and
- Nonrenewal decisions violating fundamental constitutional guarantees.

Since the Supreme Court has held that impairment of a teacher's property or liberty interests triggers procedural protections, the question arises concerning what constitutes a violation of these interests. Courts have purposely avoided precisely defining the concepts of liberty and property, preferring to allow experience and time to shape their meanings.[22] Since 1972, the Supreme Court and federal appellate courts have rendered a number of decisions that provide some guidance in understanding these concepts.

Property Interest.   In general, a nontenured employee does not have a property claim to reappointment unless state or local governmental action has clearly established such a right.[23] A federal district court, however, found that a Delaware school board created a reasonable expectation of reemployment, requiring procedural protection, when it advised a principal that his contract would be renewed if his performance were satisfactory.[24] The court concluded that the principal was justified in believing that he would be reappointed after receiving a satisfactory rating. Similarly, the Seventh Circuit found that a promise of two years of employment to a coach/athletic director established a legitimate expectation of continued employment.[25] To persuade the athletic director to

---

[22]*See Roth*, 408 U.S. at 572.

[23]*See, e.g.*, Coreia v. Schuylkill County Area Vocational-Technical School Auth., 241 Fed. Appx. 47 (3d Cir. 2007); Kyle v. Morton High Sch., 144 F.3d 448 (7th Cir. 1998); Goudeau v. Indep. Sch. Dist. No. 37, 823 F.2d 1429 (10th Cir. 1987). *See also* Nunez v. Simms, 341 F.3d 385 (5th Cir. 2003) (holding that when a teacher working under a three-year temporary permit failed to acquire standard certification her employment contract was void; no right to due process existed). *But see* Giedra v. Mt. Adams Sch. Dist., 110 P.3d 232 (Wash. Ct. App. 2005) (ruling that two certificated teachers who allowed their certificates to expire were entitled to a hearing; teachers had an expectation of continued employment and could raise arguments that affected the termination decision).

[24]Schreffler v. Bd. of Educ., 506 F. Supp. 1300 (D. Del. 1981).

[25]Vail v. Bd. of Educ., 706 F.2d 1435 (7th Cir. 1983), *aff'd by an equally divided court,* 466 U.S. 377 (1984). *But see* Thomas v. Bd. of Exam'rs, Chi. Pub. Schs., 866 F.2d 225 (7th Cir. 1988) (finding that entitlement to consideration for a promotion does not constitute a property right).

accept the position, the board had assured him that his one-year contract would be extended for a second year. Based on such an implied contract, the court found that unilateral termination of the contract after one year violated his due process rights. In contrast, the Seventh Circuit concluded that a nontenured teacher could not assert a property interest in continued employment based on a principal's positive mid-year evaluation indicating that the teacher's contract would be renewed.[26]

Protected property interests are not created by mere longevity in employment. Both the Fourth and Tenth Circuits found that issuing an employee a series of annual contracts did not constitute a valid claim to continued employment in the absence of a guarantee in state law, local policy, or an employment contract.[27] Similarly, a statute or collective bargaining agreement providing a teacher, upon request, a hearing and statement of reasons for nonrenewal does not confer a property interest in employment requiring legally sufficient cause for termination.[28] Such a provision simply gives the teacher an opportunity to present reasons why the contract should be renewed.[29]

Although a contract establishes a property interest within the contract terms, due process generally is not required in transferring or reassigning a teacher or administrator unless an identifiable economic impact can be shown. For example, a Chicago principal who was reassigned to the central office was not entitled to a hearing since he continued to receive his regular salary and benefits; deprivations related to professional satisfaction and reputation did not constitute actionable injuries.[30] In contrast, the Sixth Circuit reasoned that a collective bargaining agreement specifying that teachers may not be transferred except for "good cause" and "extenuating circumstances" established a property interest in a particular position in a specific school.[31]

As noted, property rights are created by state laws or contracts but also may emanate from policies, regulations, or ordinances made by a governmental employer pursuant to statutory rule-making authority. Such policies or regulations must create an expectation of employment and impose a binding obligation on the employer in order to create a property interest in continued employment. The sufficiency of the claim, however, must be interpreted in light of state law, irrespective of the claim's

---

[26]Halfhill v. Northeast Sch. Corp., 472 F.3d 496 (7th Cir. 2006). Following the evaluation, the teacher demonstrated a lack of professionalism in handling several incidents with students.

[27]Martin v. Unified Sch. Dist. No. 434, 728 F.2d 453 (10th Cir. 1984); Robertson v. Rogers, 679 F.2d 1090 (4th Cir. 1982).

[28]See, e.g., Perkins v. Bd. of Dirs., 686 F.2d 49 (1st Cir. 1982); Schaub v. Chamberlain Bd. of Educ., 339 N.W.2d 307 (S.D. 1983).

[29]See, e.g., Schaub, 339 N.W.2d 307 (holding that a hearing may be available to a nontenured teacher, but the board is not required to speak, produce evidence, or even answer questions at the hearing).

[30]Bordelon v. Chi. Sch. Reform Bd. of Trs., 233 F.3d 524 (7th Cir. 2000). See also Howard v. Columbia Pub. Sch. Dist., 363 F.3d 797 (8th Cir. 2004) (holding that principal's contract did not specify employment in a particular school); Ulichny v. Merton Cmty. Sch. Dist., 249 F.3d 686 (7th Cir. 2001) (finding that the reduction of a principal's duties and responsibilities did not impair property rights).

[31]Leary v. Daeschner, 228 F.3d 729 (6th Cir. 2000).

origin. In some instances, reference to state law can narrowly restrict or limit alleged property interests. For example, the United States Supreme Court, in construing a North Carolina employee's property rights, relied on the state supreme court's opinion that "an enforceable expectation of continued public employment in that state can exist only if the employer by *statute* or *contract* has actually granted some form of guarantee"[32] (emphasis added). Although, in this case, a city ordinance gave rise to an expectancy of reemployment after the successful completion of a six-month probationary period, the Court reasoned that, in the absence of a statutory or contractual obligation, the employee worked at the will and pleasure of the city. To establish a property right, then, it is necessary to prove not only that the employer's actions create an expectation of employment but also that state law does not limit the claim.

Liberty Interest. As noted previously, liberty interests encompass fundamental constitutional guarantees such as freedom of expression and privacy rights. If governmental action in the nonrenewal of employment threatens the exercise of these fundamental liberties, procedural due process must be afforded. Most nonrenewals, however, do not overtly implicate fundamental rights, and thus the burden is on the aggrieved employee to prove that the proffered reason is pretextual to mask impermissible grounds. Teachers' substantive constitutional rights are discussed at length in Chapter 9.

A liberty interest also may be implicated if the nonrenewal of employment damages an individual's reputation. The Supreme Court established in *Roth* that damage to a teacher's reputation and future employability could infringe Fourteenth Amendment liberty rights. In subsequent decisions, the Court identified prerequisite conditions for establishing that a constitutionally impermissible stigma has been imposed. According to the Court, procedural protections must be afforded only if stigma or damaging statements are related to loss of employment, publicly disclosed, alleged to be false,[33] and virtually foreclose opportunities for future employment.[34]

Under this "stigma-plus" test, governmental action damaging a teacher's reputation, standing alone, is insufficient to invoke the Fourteenth Amendment's procedural safeguards.[35] As such, a teacher who has been defamed by reassignment, transfer, suspension, or loss of a promotion cannot claim violation of a liberty interest.[36] The Fifth Circuit noted that the internal transfer of an employee, unless it is regarded essentially

---

[32]Bishop v. Wood, 426 U.S. 341, 345 (1976).

[33]*See* O'Connor v. Pierson, 426 F.3d 187 (2d Cir. 2005).

[34]*See* Codd v. Velger, 429 U.S. 624 (1977); Bishop v. Wood, 426 U.S. 341 (1976); Paul v. Davis, 424 U.S. 693 (1976).

[35]State constitutions, however, may provide greater protection of due process rights encompassing damage to reputation alone. *See, e.g.*, Kadetsky v. Egg Harbor Twp. Bd. of Educ., 82 F. Supp. 2d 327 (D.N.J. 2000).

[36]*See, e.g.*, Brown v. Simmons, 478 F.3d 922 (8th Cir. 2007); Ulichny v. Merton Cmty. Sch. Dist., 249 F.3d 686 (7th Cir. 2001). *But see* Winegar v. Des Moines Indep. Cmty. Sch. Dist., 20 F.3d 895 (8th Cir. 1994) (holding that disciplinary transfer to another school because of the physical abuse of a student involved a significant liberty interest necessitating an opportunity to be heard).

as a loss of employment, does not provide the loss of a tangible interest necessary to give rise to a liberty interest.[37] Similarly, the nonrenewal of coaching contracts does not involve a liberty interest when individuals retain their teaching positions.[38] Although many of these employment actions may stigmatize and affect a teacher's reputation, they do not constitute a deprivation of liberty in the absence of loss of employment. Furthermore, to sustain a stigmatization claim, an individual must show that a request was made for a name-clearing hearing and that the request was denied.[39]

The primary issue in these terminations is determining what charges stigmatize an individual. Nonrenewal alone is insufficient. As the Ninth Circuit noted, "Nearly any reason assigned for dismissal is likely to be to some extent a negative reflection on an individual's ability, temperament, or character," but circumstances giving rise to a liberty interest are narrow.[40] Not every comment or accusation by school officials that affects one's reputation is actionable under the Fourteenth Amendment.[41] Charges must be serious implications against character, such as immorality and dishonesty, to create a stigma of constitutional magnitude that virtually forecloses other employment. According to the Fifth Circuit, a charge must give rise to "a 'badge of infamy,' public scorn, or the like."[42] Such a liberty violation was clearly illustrated by the termination of a life-science teacher after public attacks on his teaching of human reproduction.[43] In this case, the appellate court found that the teacher was subjected to extensive, embarrassing publicity in the local, national, and even international media (e.g., being referred to as a sex maniac); incurred substantial personal harassment; and suffered permanent damage to his professional career. Termination of a New York probationary teacher implicated a liberty interest when her professional integrity and reputation were impugned by allegations that she helped students cheat on standardized tests, urged other teachers to cheat, and tried to assault another teacher who refused to participate in the scheme.[44] Allegations such as these represent

---

[37]Moore v. Otero, 557 F.2d 435, 438 (5th Cir. 1977).

[38]*See, e.g.,* Lancaster v. Indep. Sch. Dist. No. 5, 149 F.3d 1228 (10th Cir. 1998); Lagos v. Modesto City Schs. Dist., 843 F.2d 347 (9th Cir. 1988).

[39]*See, e.g.,* Puchalski v. Sch. Dist. of Springfield, 161 F. Supp. 2d 395 (E.D. Pa. 2001). *See also* Segal v. City of N.Y., 459 F.3d 207 (2d Cir. 2006) (ruling that the availability of adequate process, even if not used by teacher, defeats claim).

[40]Gray v. Union County Intermediate Educ. Dist., 520 F.2d 803, 806 (9th Cir. 1975). *See also* Beischel v. Stone Bank Sch. Dist., 362 F.3d 430 (7th Cir. 2004); Howard v. Columbia Pub. Sch. Dist., 363 F.3d 797 (8th Cir. 2004).

[41]*See, e.g.,* Ulichny v. Merton Cmty. Sch. Dist., 249 F.3d 686 (7th Cir. 2001); Merkle v. Upper Dublin Sch. Dist., 211 F.3d 782 (3d Cir. 2000). *See also* Santiago v. Fajardo, 70 F. Supp. 2d 72 (D.P.R. 1999) (holding that defamation alone does not violate an individual's liberty interest).

[42]Ball v. Bd. of Trs., 584 F.2d 684, 685 (5th Cir. 1978). *See also* Burke v. Chi. Sch. Reform Bd. of Trs., 169 F. Supp. 2d 843 (N.D. Ill. 2001).

[43]Stachura v. Memphis Cmty. Sch. Dist., 763 F.2d 211 (6th Cir. 1985), *rev'd on damages issue,* 477 U.S. 299 (1986).

[44]Rivera v. Cmty. Sch. Dist. Nine, 145 F. Supp. 2d 302 (S.D.N.Y. 2001).

serious accusations that damage an educator's standing and pose significant threats to future employability.[45]

Among other accusations that courts have found to necessitate a hearing are a serious drinking problem, emotional instability, mental illness, immoral conduct, accusation of child molestation, and extensive professional inadequacies.[46] Reasons held to pose no threat to a liberty interest include job-related comments such as personality differences and difficulty in working with others, hostility toward authority, incompetence, aggressive behavior, ineffective leadership, and nonperformance.[47] Charges relating to job performance may have an impact on future employment but do not create a stigma of constitutional magnitude.

Liberty interests are not implicated unless damaging reasons are publicly communicated in the process of denying employment.[48] The primary purpose of a hearing is to enable individuals to clear their names. Without public knowledge of the reasons for nonreappointment, such a hearing is not required. Furthermore, a protected liberty interest generally is affected only if the *school board publicizes* the stigmatizing reasons, rather than an individual, media, or another source. Accordingly, statements that are disclosed in a public meeting requested by the teacher or made by the teacher to the media or others do not require a name-clearing hearing.[49] Likewise, rumors or hearsay remarks surfacing as a result of nonrenewal do not impair liberty interests. The First Circuit noted, "in terms of likely stigmatizing effect, there is a world of difference between official charges (such as excessive drinking) made publicly and a campus rumor based upon hearsay."[50] Even when a school board publicly announces stigmatizing reasons for its action, there must be a factual dispute regarding the truth of the allegations for a hearing to be required. If a teacher

---

[45]*See, e.g.*, McPherson v. N.Y. City Dep't of Educ., 457 F.3d 211 (2d Cir. 2006) (finding that a teacher's placement on the school board's Ineligible/Inquiry List, which indicates removal for cause, did not specify reasons to justify a due process claim); Townsend v. Vallas, 256 F.3d 661 (7th Cir. 2001) (ruling against a teacher's claim when he did not demonstrate unemployability; he continued to hold a previous part-time job and had not applied for positions in other districts).

[46]*See, e.g.*, Donato v. Plainview-Old Bethpage Cent. Sch. Dist., 96 F.3d 623 (2d Cir. 1996); Vanelli v. Reynolds Sch. Dist. No. 7, 667 F.2d 773 (9th Cir. 1982); Carroll v. Robinson, 874 P.2d 1010 (Ariz. Ct. App. 1994).

[47]*See, e.g.*, Lybrook v. Members of Farmington Mun. Schs. Bd., 232 F.3d 1334 (10th Cir. 2000); Hayes v. Phoenix-Talent Sch. Dist. No. 4, 893 F.2d 235 (9th Cir. 1990); Robertson v. Rogers, 679 F.2d 1090 (4th Cir. 1982); Gilder-Lucas v. Elmore County Bd. of Educ., 186 Fed. Appx. 885, (11th Cir. 2006).

[48]*See, e.g.*, Vega v. Miller, 273 F.3d 460 (2d Cir. 2001); McCullough v. Wyandanch Union Free Sch. Dist., 187 F.3d 272 (2d Cir. 1999); Strasburger v. Bd. of Educ., 143 F.3d 351 (7th Cir. 1998). *See also* Segal v. City of N.Y., 459 F.3d 207 (2d Cir. 2006) (holding that placement of damaging statements in a teacher's personnel file can meet the public disclosure aspect of a stigma-plus claim; future employers may have access to the file). *But see* Burton v. Town of Littleton, 426 F.3d 9 (1st Cir. 2005) (declaring that superintendent sending letter of employee's termination to state commissioner of education did not constitute public dissemination).

[49]*See, e.g.*, Schul v. Sherard, 102 F. Supp. 2d 877 (S.D. Ohio 2000).

[50]Beitzell v. Jeffrey, 643 F.2d 870, 879 (1st Cir. 1981).

does not challenge the truth of the statements, a name-clearing hearing serves no purpose.[51] A teacher, however, is not required to establish that the statements are false to be entitled to a hearing; that is the purpose of the hearing.[52]

Procedural Requirements in Discharge Proceedings

Since termination of a tenured teacher or a nontenured teacher during the contract period requires procedural due process, the central question becomes, *what process is due*? Courts have noted that no fixed set of procedures applies under all circumstances. Rather, due process entails a balancing of the individual and governmental interests affected in each situation. According to the Supreme Court, a determination of the specific aspects of due process requires consideration of

> first, the private interest that will be affected by the official action; second, the risk of an erroneous deprivation of such interest through the procedures used, and the probable value, if any, of additional or substitute procedural safeguards; and finally, the government's interest, including the function involved and the fiscal and administrative burdens that the additional or substitute procedural requirement would entail.[53]

Application of these standards would require only minimum procedures in suspending a student but a more extensive, formal process in dismissing a teacher.

The Fourteenth Amendment requires at least that dismissal proceedings be based on established rules or standards. Specific procedures will depend on state law, school board regulations, and collective bargaining agreements,[54] but they cannot drop below constitutional minimums. For example, a statute requiring tenured teachers to pay half the cost of a hearing that constitutionally must be provided by the school board violates federal rights.[55] In assessing the adequacy of procedural safeguards, the judiciary looks for the provision of certain basic elements to meet constitutional guarantees. At the same time, courts will not find a deprivation of procedural due process rights, if educators do not avail themselves of the available safeguards.[56]

---

[51]*See, e.g.,* Codd v. Velger, 429 U.S. 624 (1977); Coleman v. Reed, 147 F.3d 751 (8th Cir. 1998); *Strasburger*, 143 F.3d 351.

[52]*See, e.g.,* O'Neill v. City of Auburn, 23 F.3d 685 (2d Cir. 1994).

[53]Mathews v. Eldridge, 424 U.S. 319, 335 (1976).

[54]*See, e.g.,* Hanover Sch. Dist. No 28 v. Barbour, 171 P.3d 223 (Colo. 2007); Bd. of Educ. v. Ward, 974 P.2d 824 (Utah 1999).

[55]*See* Rankin v. Indep. Sch. Dist. No. I-3, Noble County, Okla., 876 F.2d 838 (10th Cir. 1989). *See also* Cal. Teachers Ass'n v. State, 975 P.2d 622, 643 (Cal. 1999) (concluding that imposing half the cost of an administrative law judge "chills the exercise of the right to a hearing and vigorous advocacy on behalf of the teacher").

[56]*See, e.g.,* Segal v. City of N.Y., 459 F.3d 207 (2d Cir. 2006); Christensen v. Kingston Sch. Comm., 360 F. Supp. 2d 212 (D. Mass. 2005).

Courts generally have held that a teacher facing a severe loss such as termination must be afforded procedures encompassing the following elements:[57]

- Notification of charges,
- Opportunity for a hearing,
- Adequate time to prepare a rebuttal to the charges,
- Access to evidence and names of witnesses,
- Hearing before an impartial tribunal,
- Representation by legal counsel,
- Opportunity to present evidence and witnesses,
- Opportunity to cross-examine adverse witnesses,
- Decision based on evidence and findings of the hearing,
- Transcript or record of the hearing, and
- Opportunity to appeal an adverse decision

Beyond these constitutional considerations, courts also strictly enforce any additional procedural protections conferred by state laws and local policies.[58] Examples of such requirements might be providing detailed performance evaluations prior to termination, notifying teachers of weaknesses, and allowing an opportunity for improvement before dismissal. Although failure to comply with these stipulations may invalidate the school board's action under state law, federal due process rights *per se* are not violated if minimal constitutional procedures are provided.[59]

Except in limited circumstances, individuals are required to exhaust administrative procedures, or the grievance procedures specified in the collective bargaining agreement, prior to seeking judicial review. Pursuing an administrative hearing promotes resolution of a controversy at the agency level. Furthermore, if the issue is ultimately submitted for judicial review, the court has the benefit of the agency's findings and conclusions. Exhaustion is not required, however, if administrative review would be futile or inadequate. For example, the Connecticut Supreme Court reasoned that seeking an administrative remedy would have been futile for a principal who had been constructively discharged (forced to resign by the superintendent). Since the principal had not been discharged on statutory grounds, an administrative hearing could not grant the relief sought by the principal.[60]

---

[57]This chapter focuses on procedural protections required in teacher terminations. It should be noted, however, that other school board decisions (e.g., transfers, demotions, or mandatory leaves) may impose similar constraints on decision making.

[58]*See, e.g.,* Spainhour v. Dover Pub. Sch. Dist., 958 S.W.2d 528 (Ark. 1998); Barnes v. Spearfish Sch. Dist. No. 40-2, 725 N.W.2d 226 (S.D. 2006).

[59]*See, e.g.,* Osteen v. Henley, 13 F.3d 221 (7th Cir. 1993); Ray v. Birmingham City Bd. of Educ., 845 F.2d 281 (11th Cir. 1988). *But see* Levitt v. Univ. of Tex. at El Paso, 759 F.2d 1224 (5th Cir. 1985) (holding that under certain circumstances, a constitutional deprivation might occur when an omission of state or local procedures results in a denial of the minimal constitutional procedures).

[60]Mendillo v. Bd. of Educ., 717 A.2d 1177 (Conn. 1998).

Various elements of due process proceedings may be contested as inadequate. Questions arise regarding the sufficiency of notice, impartiality of the board members, and placement of the burden of proof. The aspects of procedural due process that courts frequently scrutinize in assessing the fundamental fairness of school board actions are examined next.

Notice

In general, a constitutionally adequate notice is timely, informs the teacher of specific charges, and allows the teacher sufficient time to prepare a response.[61] Beyond the constitutional guarantees, state laws and regulations as well as school board policies usually impose very specific requirements relating to form, timeliness, and content of notice.[62] In legal challenges, the adequacy of a notice is assessed in terms of whether it meets constitutional as well as other requirements. Failure to comply substantially with mandated requisites will void school board action.

The form or substance of notice is usually stipulated in statutes. In determining appropriateness of notice, courts generally have held that substantial compliance with form requirements (as opposed to strict compliance required for notice deadlines) is sufficient. Under this standard, the decisive factor is whether the notice adequately informs the teacher of the pending action rather than the actual form of the notice. For example, if a statute requires notification by certified mail and the notice is mailed by registered mail or is personally delivered, it substantially complies with the state requirement. However, oral notification will not suffice if the law requires written notification. If the form of the notice is not specified in statute, any timely notice that informs a teacher is adequate.

Although form and timeliness are important concerns in issuing a notice, the primary consideration is the statement of reasons for an action. With termination of a teacher's contract, school boards must bring specific charges against the teacher, including not only the factual basis for the charges but also the names of accusers.[63] State laws may impose further specifications, such as North Dakota's requirement that reasons for termination in the notice must be based on issues raised in prior

---

[61]*See, e.g.*, Farley v. Bd. of Educ., 365 S.E.2d 816 (W. Va. 1988) (finding that notice of termination received by teachers one to two days prior to the hearing date set by the school board was not a "meaningful notice" to prepare for a hearing).

[62]*See, e.g.*, Hoschler v. Sacramento City Unified Sch. Dist., 57 Cal. Rptr. 3d 115 (Ct. App. 2007) (concluding that a statute silent on the method of delivery required personal delivery rather than certified mail); Clark County Sch. Dist. v. Riley, 14 P.3d 22 (Nev. 2000) (finding that only four days' notice with no mention of the right to a hearing violated a statute requiring 15 days' notice and the right to a hearing); Morrison v. Bd. of Educ., 47 P.3d 888 (Okla. Civ. App. 2002) (ruling that notice did not conform to statutory requirements; notice was sent by the superintendent rather than the school board and it was received on April 10 rather than *prior to* that date).

[63]*See, e.g.*, Martin v. Sch. Dist. No. 394, 393 F. Supp. 2d 1028 (D. Idaho 2005); Simmons v. New Pub. Sch. Dist. No. Eight, 574 N.W.2d 561 (N.D. 1998). *But see* Johanson v. Bd. of Educ., 589 N.W.2d 815 (Neb. 1999) (holding that due process did not require a school district to provide a summary of the nature of the testimony of each witness).

written evaluations.[64] If the state law identifies grounds for dismissal, charges also must be based on the statutory causes. But a teacher cannot be forced to defend against vague and indefinite charges that simply restate the statutory categories, such as incompetency or neglect of duty. Notice must include specific accusations to allow the teacher to prepare a proper defense. Furthermore, only charges identified in the notice can form the basis for dismissal. The Sixth Circuit found an Ohio school board's termination deficient when it listed three specific charges that were not mentioned in the superintendent's notice for the preliminary hearing, thereby resulting in the teacher not having an opportunity to respond to the charges prior to termination.[65]

Hearing

In addition to notice, some type of hearing is required before an employer makes the initial termination decision; posttermination hearings do not satisfy federal constitutional due process requirements. In a significant 1985 decision, *Cleveland Board of Education v. Loudermill,* the United States Supreme Court recognized the necessity for some kind of a pretermination hearing. Although the Court emphasized that a full evidentiary hearing to resolve the propriety of the discharge is not required, an initial hearing must be provided to serve as a check against wrong decisions.[66] This would entail determining if there are reasonable grounds to believe that the charges are true and that they support the dismissal. Essentially, in such a pretermination hearing, an employee is entitled to notice of the charges and evidence as well as an opportunity to respond, orally or in writing, as to why the proposed action should not be taken. If only the minimal pretermination procedures outlined by the Supreme Court are provided, a full evidentiary posttermination hearing is required.[67] Even extenuating circumstances involving severe disruption to the educational process cannot justify the

[64]Hoffner v. Bismarck Pub. Sch. Dist., 589 N.W.2d 195 (N.D. 1999). *See also* Boss v. Fillmore Sch. Dist. No. 19, 559 N.W.2d 448 (Neb. 1997) (ruling that prior to termination of a superintendent's contract, mandated statutory evaluations must be completed with an opportunity to correct noted deficiencies).

[65]McDaniel v. Princeton City Sch. Dist. Bd. of Educ., 45 Fed. Appx. 328 (6th Cir. 2002).

[66]470 U.S. 532 (1985). *See, e.g.,* Belas v. Juniata County Sch. Dist., 202 Fed. Appx. 585 (3d Cir. 2006); Jefferson v. Jefferson County Pub. Sch. Sys., 360 F.3d 583 (6th Cir. 2004); Finch v. Fort Bend Indep. Sch. Dist., 333 F.3d 555 (5th Cir. 2003).

[67]*See* also, Curtis v. Montgomery County Pub. Schs., 242 Fed. Appx. 109 (4th Cir. 2007) (concluding that the predismissal process provided a teacher, including notice that he was being investigated regarding serious allegations and placed on suspension, satisfied pretermination rights); Rodriguez v. Ysleta Indep. Sch. Dist., 217 Fed. Appx. 294 (5th Cir. 2007) (finding adequate due process when a teacher was provided a pretermination hearing and an opportunity for three additional posttermination hearings under Texas law); Qualls v. Cook, 245 Fed. Appx. 624 (9th Cir. 2007) (finding that limited due process rights existed when a principal was placed on nondisciplinary administrative leave with pay; the principal's minimal property interest rights were not violated by the lack of presuspension hearing when school official provided written notice and a postsuspension hearing); Vukadinovich v. Bd. of Sch. Trs., 978 F.2d 403 (7th Cir. 1992) (holding that a discharged teacher is not entitled to a postdeprivation hearing in addition to a full predeprivation hearing).

omission of a preliminary determination. Under emergency conditions, however, teachers can be suspended with pay pending a termination hearing.[68]

Courts have not prescribed in detail the procedures to be followed in administrative hearings. Basically, the fundamental constitutional requirement is fair play—that is, an opportunity to be heard at a meaningful time and in a meaningful manner. Beyond this general requirement, the specific aspects of a hearing are influenced by the circumstances of the case, with the potential for grievous losses necessitating more extensive safeguards. According to the Missouri Supreme Court, a hearing generally should include a meaningful opportunity to be heard, to state one's position, to present witnesses, and to cross-examine witnesses; the accused also has the right to counsel and access to written reports in advance of the hearing.[69] Implicit in these rudimentary requirements are the assumptions that the hearing will be conducted by an impartial decision maker and will result in a decision based on the evidence presented. This section examines issues that may arise in adversarial hearings before the school board.

Adequate Notice of Hearing.   As noted, due process rights afford an individual the opportunity to be heard at a meaningful time. This implies sufficient time between notice of the hearing and the scheduled meeting. Unless state law designates a time period, the school board can establish a reasonable date for the hearing, taking into consideration the specific facts and circumstances. In a termination action, the school board would be expected to provide ample time for the teacher to prepare a defense; however, the teacher bears the burden of requesting additional time if the length of notice is insufficient to prepare an adequate response. A notice as short as two days was upheld as satisfying due process requirements where the teacher participated in the hearing and did not object to the time or request a postponement.[70] Similarly, a one-day notice was found constitutionally sufficient when the teacher did not attend the meeting to raise objections.[71] A teacher who participates fully in the hearing process or waives the right to a hearing by failure to attend cannot later assert "lack of adequate time" to invalidate the due process proceedings.

---

[68]*But see* Gilbert v. Homar, 520 U.S. 924 (1997) (ruling that a temporary suspension without pay of an employee charged with a felony does not require a pretermination hearing when an employee occupies a position of great public trust); Jerrytone v. Musto, 167 Fed. Appx. 295 (3d Cir. 2006) (ruling that a pretermination hearing was not required prior to a teacher's suspension without pay when criminal charges were filed against him); Mustafa v. Clark County Sch. Dist., 157 F.3d 1169 (9th Cir. 1998) (finding that a teacher who was suspended without pay for alleged sexual misconduct was not entitled to a hearing prior to suspension when he was promptly provided a hearing five days after the suspension).

[69]Valter v. Orchard Farm Sch. Dist., 541 S.W.2d 550 (Mo. 1976). *See also* McClure v. Indep. Sch. Dist. No. 16, 228 F.3d 1205 (10th Cir. 2000) (holding that a teacher was deprived of due process rights when she was not allowed to cross-examine witnesses who provided testimony by affidavit at a termination hearing); Elmore v. Plainview-Old Bethpage Cent., 708 N.Y.S.2d 713 (App. Div. 2000) (concluding that a teacher's due process rights were violated when the hearing officer forbid him to consult with his attorney during breaks in cross-examination).

[70]Ahern v. Bd. of Educ., 456 F.2d 399 (8th Cir. 1972).

[71]Birdwell v. Hazelwood Sch. Dist., 491 F.2d 490 (8th Cir. 1974).

Waiver of Hearing. Although a hearing is an essential element of due process, a teacher can waive this right by failing to request a hearing, refusing to attend it, or walking out of the hearing.[72] Voluntary resignation of a position also waives an individual's entitlement to a hearing.[73] In some states, a hearing before the school board may be waived by an employee's election of an alternative hearing procedure, such as a grievance mechanism or an impartial referee. For example, the Third Circuit held that an employee's choice of either a hearing before the school board or arbitration under the collective bargaining agreement met the constitutional requirements of due process; the school board was not required to provide the individual a hearing in addition to the arbitration proceeding.[74] Similarly, an Ohio federal district court ruled that a teacher who selected a hearing before an impartial referee was not entitled to be heard by the school board prior to its decision on the referee's report.[75]

Impartial Hearing. A central question raised regarding hearings is the school board's impartiality as a hearing body. This issue arises because school boards often perform multiple functions in a hearing; they may investigate the allegations against a teacher, initiate the proceedings, and render the final judgment. Teachers have contended that such expansive involvement violates their right to an unbiased decision maker. Rejecting the idea that combining the adjudicative and investigative functions violates due process rights, courts generally have determined that prior knowledge of the facts does not disqualify school board members.[76] In addition, the fact that the board makes the initial decision to terminate employment does not render subsequent review impermissibly biased. Neither is a hearing prejudiced by a limited, preliminary inquiry to determine if there is a basis for terminating a teacher. Since hearings are costly and time consuming, such a preliminary investigation may save time as well as potential embarrassment.

In *Hortonville Joint School District No. 1 v. Hortonville Education Association,* the United States Supreme Court firmly established that the school board is a proper

[72]*See, e.g.,* Conrad v. Cambridge Sch. Comm., 171 F.3d 12 (1st Cir. 1999); Boner v. Eminence R-1 Sch. Dist., 55 F.3d 1339 (8th Cir. 1995). *See also* McKnight v. Sch. Dist. of Phila.,171 F. Supp. 2d 446 (E.D. Pa. 2001), *aff'd,* 64 Fed. Appx 851 (3d Cir. 2003) (holding that a teacher's right to hearing was not violated when he attended but refused to participate; the school board needed only to provide an opportunity for a hearing). *But see* Baird v. Bd. of Educ. for Warren Cmty. Unit Sch. Dist. No. 205, 389 F.3d 685 (7th Cir. 2004) (finding that superintendent did not waive his rights when he attended his pretermination hearing only to request his right to full procedural due process).

[73]*See, e.g.,* Kirkland v. St. Vrain Valley Sch. Dist. No. RE1J, 464 F.3d 1182 (10th Cir. 2006). *See also* Cross v. Monett R-I Bd. of Educ., 431 F.3d 606 (8th Cir. 2005) (ruling that counselor was not entitled to a hearing when she initiated retirement by submitting a letter of intent to retire).

[74]Pederson v. S. Williamsport Area Sch. Dist., 677 F.2d 312 (3d Cir. 1982).

[75]Jones v. Morris, 541 F. Supp. 11 (S.D. Ohio 1981), *aff'd,* 455 U.S. 1009 (1982).

[76]*See, e.g.,* Withrow v. Larkin, 421 U.S. 35 (1975). *See also* Yukadinovich v. Bd. of Sch. Trs., 278 F.3d 693 (7th Cir. 2002) (concluding that a teacher did not establish bias in a termination hearing held in front of the school board that he had publicly criticized); Moore v. Bd. of Educ., 134 F.3d 781 (6th Cir. 1998) (finding that a superintendent's dual roles as presiding officer at the hearing and investigator did not deprive a teacher of due process).

review body to conduct dismissal hearings.[77] The Court held that a school board's involvement in collective negotiations did not disqualify it as an impartial hearing board in the subsequent dismissal of striking teachers. The Court noted that "a showing that the Board was 'involved' in the events preceding this decision, in light of the important interest in leaving with the board the power given by the state legislature, is not enough to overcome the presumption of honesty and integrity in policymakers with decision-making power."[78]

Although the school board is the proper hearing body, bias on the part of the board or its members is constitutionally unacceptable. A teacher challenging the impartiality of the board has the burden of proving actual, not merely potential, bias. This requires the teacher to show more than board members' predecision involvement or prior knowledge of the issues.[79] A high probability of bias, however, can be shown if a board member has a personal interest in the outcome of the hearing or has suffered personal abuse or criticism from a teacher.

Several cases illustrate instances of unacceptable bias. For example, the Alabama Supreme Court invalidated a teacher termination hearing for "intolerably high bias" created by a school board member's son testifying against the teacher; the son had been the target of alleged personal abuse by the teacher.[80] The Tenth Circuit also ruled that bias was shown in the termination of a superintendent because one of the board members had campaigned to remove the superintendent from his position, and two other board members had made unfavorable statements to the effect that the superintendent "had to go."[81] The Iowa Supreme Court concluded that a school board's role of "investigation, instigation, prosecution, and verdict rendering" denied a teacher an impartial hearing, since the board used no witnesses and relied solely on its personal knowledge of the case in reaching a decision.[82] A lack of impartiality or inferences of partiality may include board members testifying as witnesses, prior

---

[77]426 U.S. 482 (1976).

[78]*Id.* at 496–497. *See also* Batagiannis v. W. Lafayette Cmty. Sch. Corp., 454 F.3d 738 (7th Cir. 2006) (finding that school board members did not exhibit bias that would disqualify them from conducting the superintendent's termination hearing, even though board members disagreed with the superintendent about how the schools should be run).

[79]*See, e.g.,* Beischel v. Stone Bank Sch. Dist., 362 F.3d 430 (7th Cir. 2004); Martin v. Sch. Dist. No. 394, 393 F. Supp. 2d 1028 (D. Idaho 2005); Sekor v. Bd. of Educ., 689 A.2d 1112 (Conn. 1997). *But see* Crump v. Bd. of Educ., 378 S.E.2d 32 (N.C. Ct. App. 1989), *aff'd*, 392 S.E.2d 579 (N.C. 1990) (ruling that prehearing knowledge of the board members coupled with denial of such knowledge at the hearing substantiated impermissible bias).

[80]*Ex parte* Greenberg v. Ala. State Tenure Comm'n, 395 So. 2d 1000 (Ala. 1981). *But see* Danroth v. Mandaree Pub. Sch. Dist. No. 36, 320 N.W.2d 780 (N.D. 1982) (holding that a teacher was not denied fair and proper hearing even though a board member's wife was the primary critic); Katruska v. Dep't of Educ., 767 A.2d 1051 (Pa. 2001) (concluding that the testimony of a board member's wife against her principal created the appearance of bias in a hearing, but the Secretary of Education's *de nova* review met due process).

[81]Staton v. Mayes, 552 F.2d 908 (10th Cir. 1977). *But see* Welch v. Barham, 635 F.2d 1322 (8th Cir. 1980) (finding that statements by two board members at trial that they could not think of any evidence that would have changed their minds about terminating the individual did not show the degree of bias necessary to disqualify a decision maker).

[82]Keith v. Cmty. Sch. Dist., 262 N.W.2d 249, 260 (Iowa 1978).

announcements by board members of views and positions showing closed minds, and board members assuming adversarial or prosecutorial roles.[83]

Evidence. Under teacher tenure laws, the burden of proof is placed on the school board to show cause for dismissal. The standard of proof generally applied to administrative bodies is to produce a *preponderance of evidence.*[84] Administrative hearings are not held to the more stringent standards applied in criminal proceedings (i.e., clear and convincing evidence beyond a reasonable doubt). Proof by a preponderance of evidence simply indicates that the majority of the evidence supports the board's decision or, as the New York high court stated, "such relevant evidence as a reasonable mind might accept as adequate to support a conclusion."[85] If the board fails to meet this burden of proof, the judiciary will not uphold the termination decision. For example, the Nebraska Supreme Court, in overturning a school board's dismissal decision, concluded that dissatisfaction of parents and school board members was not sufficient evidence to substantiate incompetency charges against a teacher who had received above-average performance evaluations during her entire term of employment.[86]

The objective of school board hearings is to ascertain the relevant facts of the situation; the board hears evidence from both the teacher and the district officials recommending termination. These hearings are not encumbered by technical judicial rules of evidence, even if charges also carry criminal liability. Termination proceedings are separate from the criminal proceedings, and, as such, dismissal might be warranted based on the evidence presented, even though such evidence would not satisfy the more stringent requirements to sustain a criminal conviction. For example, a teacher could be dismissed on evidence of drug use, even though criminal charges are dropped due to a defective search warrant.

Only relevant, well-documented evidence presented at the hearing can be the basis for the board's decision.[87] Unlike formal judicial proceedings, hearsay evidence

[83]*See, e.g.*, McClure v. Indep. Sch. Dist. No. 16, 228 F.3d 1205 (10th Cir. 2000); Cook v. Bd. of Educ., 671 F. Supp. 1110 (S.D. W. Va. 1987); Buckner v. Sch. Bd., 718 So. 2d 862 (Fla. Dist. Ct. App. 1998); Johnson v. Pulaski County Bd. of Educ., 499 S.E.2d 345 (Ga. Ct. App. 1998); Riter v. Woonsocket Sch. Dist. #55-4, 504 N.W.2d 572 (S.D. 1993).

[84]*See, e.g.*, Lacks v. Ferguson Reorganized Sch. Dist. R-2, 147 F.3d 718 (8th Cir. 1998); Rivers v. Bd. of Trs., 876 So. 2d 1043 (Miss. Ct. App. 2004); *In re* Termination of Kibbe, 996 P.2d 419 (N.M. 1999).

[85]Altsheler v. Bd. of Educ., 464 N.E.2d 979, 979-980 (N.Y. 1984). *See also* Johanson v. Bd. of Educ., 589 N.W.2d 815 (Neb. 1999).

[86]Schulz v. Bd. of Educ., 315 N.W.2d 633 (Neb. 1982). *See also* Weston v. Indep. Sch. Dist. No. 35 of Cherokee County, 170 P.3d 539 (Okla. 2007) (ordering school district to reinstate a teacher because officials did not prove by a preponderance of evidence that dismissal was warranted).

[87]*See, e.g.*, Goldberg v. Kelly, 397 U.S. 254, 271 (1970). *See also* Atwater Elem. Sch. Dist. v. Cal. Dep't of Gen. Servs., 158 P.3d 794 (Cal. 2007) (finding four-year limitation in state law to introduce evidence of teacher sexual misconduct not an absolute bar); Packer v. Orange County Sch. Bd., 881 So. 2d 1204 (Fla. Dist. Ct. App. 2004) (holding that school board could not terminate a teacher when the administrative law judge did not find credible evidence to support charges); Arriola v. Orleans Parish Sch. Bd., 809 So. 2d 932 (La. 2002) (finding that a teacher was afforded adequate due process in termination for drug use even though he was not able to cross-examine the laboratory technician who conducted the chemical analysis).

may be admissible in administrative hearings.[88] Courts have held that such evidence provides the background necessary for understanding the situation. Comments and complaints of parents have been considered relevant, but hearsay statements of students generally have been given little weight.[89]

Findings of Fact.   At the conclusion of the hearing, the board must make specific findings of fact. A written report of the findings on which the board based its decision is essential. Without a report of the findings of fact, appropriate administrative or judicial review would be impeded. The Minnesota Supreme Court noted "if the trial court were to review the merits of the case without findings of fact, there would be no safeguard against judicial encroachment on the school board's function since the trial court might affirm on a charge rejected by the school board."[90] Similarly, the Oklahoma Supreme Court held that a probationary teacher's statutory entitlement to a hearing includes the right to know the rationale for the board's decision. The court admonished that "an absence of required findings is fatal to the validity of administrative decisions even if the record discloses evidence to support proper findings."[91] The findings of fact need not be issued in technical language but simply in a form that explains the reasons for the action.

    If an independent panel or hearing officer conducts the hearing, the school board is bound by the panel's findings of fact but can accept or reject the panel's conclusions and recommendations.[92] Accordingly, the board can decide to terminate an individual who has been supported by the panel as long as the board bases its decision on the evidence included in the panel's factual findings.

Dismissal for Cause

Tenure laws are designed to assure competent teachers continued employment as long as their performance is satisfactory. With the protection of tenure, a teacher can be dismissed only for cause, and only in accordance with the procedures specified by

---

[88]*See, e.g.*, Rogers v. Bd. of Educ., 749 A.2d 1173 (Conn. 2000); Hierlmeier v. N. Judson-San Pierre Bd., 730 N.E.2d 821 (Ind. Ct. App. 2000); Walthart v. Bd. of Dirs., 694 N.W.2d 740 (Iowa 2005).

[89]*See, e.g.*, Daily v. Bd. of Educ., 588 N.W.2d 813 (Neb. 1999).

[90]Morey v. Sch. Bd., 128 N.W.2d 302, 307 (Minn. 1964).

[91]Jackson v. Indep. Sch. Dist. No. 16, 648 P.2d 26, 31 (Okla. 1982).

[92]*See, e.g.*, Rogers v. Bd. of Educ., 749 A.2d 1173 (Conn. 2000); Raitzik v. Bd. of Educ., 826 N.E.2d 568 (Ill. App. Ct. 2005); Oleske v. Hilliard City Sch. Dist. 764 N.E.2d 1110 (Ohio Ct. App. 2001); Montgomery Indep. Sch. Dist. v. Davis, 34 S.W.3d 559 (Tex. 2000). *But see* City Sch. Dist. v. Campbell, 798 N.Y.S.2d 54 (App. Div. 2005) (noting that an arbitrator's award may not be vacated unless it is clearly irrational or against public policy; court found hearing officer's reinstatement of a teacher, who pled guilty to drug charges, as coordinator of a program to deter drug use of students to defy common sense).

law.[93] Tenure rights accrue under state laws and therefore must be interpreted in light of each state's requirements.

Where grounds for dismissal of a permanent teacher are identified by statute, a school board cannot base dismissal on reasons other than those specified. To cover unexpected matters, statutes often include a catch-all phrase such as "other good and just cause." Causes included in statutes vary considerably among states and range from an extensive listing of individual grounds to a simple statement that dismissal must be based on cause. The most frequently cited causes are incompetency, immorality, insubordination, and neglect of duty.

Since grounds for dismissal are determined by statute, it is difficult to provide generalizations for all teachers. The causes are broad in scope and application; in fact, individual causes often have been attacked for impermissible vagueness. It is not unusual to find dismissal cases with similar factual situations based on different grounds. In addition, a number of grounds often are introduced and supported in a single termination case.[94] Illustrative case law is examined here in relation to the more frequently cited grounds for dismissal. Educators should consult state laws and judicial rulings in their respective states to gain an understanding of their specific employment rights.[95]

Incompetency

Courts have broadly defined *incompetency*. Although it usually refers to classroom performance, it has been extended in some instances to a teacher's private life. The term is legally defined as "lack of ability, legal qualifications, or fitness to discharge the required duty."[96] Incompetency has been challenged as unconstitutionally vague, but courts have found the term sufficiently precise to give fair warning of prohibited conduct. Incompetency cases often involve issues relating to teaching methods, grading procedures, classroom management, and professional relationships. In general, dismissals for incompetency are based on a number of factors or a pattern of behavior rather than isolated incidents. In a Minnesota case, indicators of incompetency included poor rapport with students, inappropriate use of class time, irrational grading of students, and lack of student progress.[97] A Pennsylvania court interpreted

---

[93]*See* Michael Long, "Studying the 'Dismissal Gap': Research on Teacher Incompetence and Dismissals," *Macro International* (March 2007). In a paper presented at the National Center for Education Statistics's (NCES) Symposium on Data Issues in Teacher Supply and Demand, Long synthesized research on teacher dismissals and reported on his analysis of NCES's Schools and Staffing Survey with both showing that less than 1 percent of teachers are terminated each year.

[94]*See, e.g.*, Hellmann v. Union Sch. Dist., 170 S.W.3d 52 (Mo. Ct. App. 2005) (supporting incompetency, inefficiency, and insubordination in the termination of a teacher).

[95]Claims that dismissals impair constitutional rights are discussed in Chapter 9.

[96]Henry Black, *Black's Law Dictionary*, 8th ed. (St. Paul, MN: West, 2004).

[97]Whaley v. Anoka-Hennepin Indep. Sch. Dist. No. 11, 325 N.W.2d 128 (Minn. 1982).

incompetency as deficiencies in personality, composure, judgment, and attitude that have a detrimental effect on a teacher's performance.[98] Incompetency in this case was supported by evidence that the teacher was a disruptive influence in the school; could not maintain control of students; and failed to maintain her composure in dealing with students, other professionals, and parents.

Dismissals for incompetency have included a wide range of charges and occasionally have involved only a single incident. To illustrate, dismissals have been upheld for incompetency where a teacher brandished a starter pistol in an attempt to gain control of a group of students[99] and an assistant principal permitted teachers to conduct a strip search of a fifth and sixth grade physical education class against explicit board policy.[100] A Louisiana court of appeals, however, held that a social studies teacher could not be dismissed for showing two R-rated movies; the court viewed the penalty as too harsh for a teacher with a 14-year unblemished teaching record.[101] Similarly, the South Dakota high court did not find a teacher's indiscreet answer to a fourth-grader's question about homosexual activity following a sex education video to be the type of "habitual and ongoing action" needed to support a charge of incompetency.[102]

Frequently, school boards have based charges of incompetency on teachers' lack of proper classroom management and control. Such dismissals have been contested on the grounds that the penalty of discharge was too severe for the offense. Courts have generally held that school boards have latitude in determining penalties, and their decisions will be overturned only if disproportionate to the offense. As long as evidence is presented to substantiate the board's charge, poor classroom management can result in termination.[103]

Termination for incompetency usually requires school officials systematically to document a teacher's performance. Providing opportunities and support for a teacher to achieve expected performance standards can be an important component in substantiating that a teacher had adequate notice of deficiencies.

[98]Hamburg v. N. Penn Sch. Dist., 484 A.2d 867 (Pa. Commw. Ct. 1984).

[99]Myres v. Orleans Parish Sch. Bd., 423 So. 2d 1303 (La. Ct. App. 1983).

[100]Rogers v. Bd. of Educ., 749 A.2d 1173 (Conn. 2000).

[101]West v. Tangipahoa Parish Sch. Bd., 615 So. 2d 979 (La. Ct. App. 1993).

[102]Collins v. Faith Sch. Dist. No. 46-2, 574 N.W.2d 889, 893 (S.D. 1998). *See also In re* Termination of Kibbe, 996 P.2d 419 (N.M. 1999) (ruling that a school board did not provide substantial evidence to show that a teacher's arrest for driving under the influence of alcohol was rationally related to his competence to teach).

[103]*See, e.g.,* Jones v. Jefferson Parish Sch. Bd., 688 F.2d 837 (5th Cir. 1982); Linstad v. Sitka Sch. Dist., 963 P.2d 246 (Alaska 1998). *See also* Ketchersid v. Rhea County Bd. of Educ., 174 S.W.3d 163 (Tenn. Ct. App. 2005) (finding that a teacher exhibited incompetence, defined as evident unfitness for service, by grabbing the faces of students and hitting them over the head with books to gain their attention).

Immorality

Immorality, one of the most frequently cited causes for dismissal, is generally not defined in state laws. In defining the term, the judiciary has tended to interpret *immorality* broadly as unacceptable conduct that affects a teacher's fitness. Traditionally, the teacher has been viewed as an exemplar whose conduct is influential in shaping the lives of young students.

Sexually related conduct *per se* between a teacher and student has consistently been held to constitute immoral conduct justifying termination of employment. The Supreme Court of Colorado stated that when a teacher engages in sexually provocative or exploitative conduct with students, "a strong presumption of unfitness arises against the teacher."[104] Similarly, a Washington appellate court found that a male teacher's sexual relationship with a minor student justified dismissal.[105] The court declined to hold that an adverse effect on fitness to teach must be shown. Rather, the court concluded that when a teacher and a minor student are involved, the board might reasonably decide that such conduct is harmful to the school district. An Illinois appellate court, however, noted that damage to the students, faculty, or the school must be shown; the fondling of third grade female students by a male teacher presented such damage.[106]

Teachers discharged for sexually related conduct have challenged the statutory grounds of "immorality" or "immoral conduct" as impermissibly vague. An Alabama teacher, dismissed for sexual advances toward female students, asserted that the term *immorality* did not adequately warn a teacher as to what behavior would constitute an offense. The court acknowledged the lack of clarity but rejected the teacher's contention, reasoning that his behavior fell "squarely within the hard core of the statute's proscriptions."[107] The court noted that the teacher should have been aware that his conduct was improper, and the claim of vagueness or overbreadth could not invalidate his dismissal. A Missouri federal district court conceded that the term immoral conduct is abstract, but, when construed in the overall statutory scheme, can be precisely defined as any conduct rendering a teacher unfit to teach.[108]

A New York case highlights the delicate balance between a teacher's First Amendment expressive rights and the need to protect students from a self-described

---

[104]Weissman v. Bd. of Educ., 547 P.2d 1267, 1273 (Colo. 1976). *See also* Hamm v. Poplar Bluff R-1 Sch. Dist., 955 S.W.2d 27 (Mo. Ct. App. 1997); *In re* Morrill, 765 A.2d 699 (N.H. 2001); Andrews v. Indep. Sch. Dist. No. 57, 12 P.3d 491 (Okla. Civ. App. 2000).

[105]Denton v. S. Kitsap Sch. Dist. No. 402, 516 P.2d 1080 (Wash. Ct. App. 1973). *See also* DeMichele v. Greenburgh Cent. Sch. Dist. No. 7, 167 F.3d 784 (2d Cir. 1999) (ruling that termination of a teacher for sexual misconduct with students occurring 24 years earlier did not violate his due process rights).

[106]Fadler v. Ill. State Bd. of Educ., 506 N.E.2d 640 (Ill. App. Ct. 1987). *But see* Youngman v. Doerhoff, 890 S.W.2d 330 (Mo. Ct. App. 1994) (concluding that a male teacher's hugging of a 14-year-old male student was motivated by caring and concern, not by a sexual motive substantiating immoral conduct).

[107]Kilpatrick v. Wright, 437 F. Supp. 397, 399 (M.D. Ala. 1977).

[108]Thompson v. Southwest Sch. Dist., 483 F. Supp. 1170 (W.D. Mo. 1980).

pedophile.[109] In this instance, a 30-year, successful teacher was terminated for advocating sexual activity between men and young boys. He was a long-term member of the North American Man/Boy Love Association (NAMBL) and closely involved with editing and writing the group's publication. With public notoriety, the school board found that the teacher could no longer be effective in the classroom. Even though no evidence existed that he had been illegally involved with young boys, the Second Circuit upheld the dismissal, noting that the school board did not base its decision on membership in NAMBL but on the disruption his activities caused.

Sexual harassment involving inappropriate comments, touching, and teasing may result in termination for immorality.[110] The West Virginia high court upheld the termination of a teacher for repeated comments of a sexual nature to students; the comments had continued in spite of warnings to desist.[111] Similarly, the Supreme Court of Missouri supported a board's dismissal of a teacher for sexual harassment of the only female member of his class and for permitting male students also to harass her.[112]

In addition to sexual improprieties with students, which clearly are grounds for dismissal, other conduct that sets a bad example for students may be considered immoral under the "role model" standard. Courts, however, generally have required school officials to show that misconduct or a particular lifestyle has an adverse impact on fitness to teach. They have recognized that allowing dismissal merely upon a showing of immoral behavior without consideration of the nexus between the conduct and fitness to teach would be an unwarranted intrusion on a teacher's right to privacy. For example, an Ohio appellate court found that school officials had not produced evidence to show that an adulterous affair with another school employee constituted immorality when it did not have a hostile impact on the school community.[113]

Teachers' sexual orientation has been an issue in several controversial dismissal cases. Although these cases often have raised constitutional issues related to freedom of expression and privacy, courts also have confronted the question of whether sexual orientation *per se* is evidence of unfitness to teach or whether it must be shown that this lifestyle impairs teaching effectiveness.[114] Courts have rendered

---

[109]Melzer v. Bd. of Educ. of City of N.Y., 336 F.3d 185 (2d Cir. 2003). *See* text accompanying note 185, Chapter 9.

[110]*See* text accompanying notes 159–165, Chapter 8, and notes 76–89, Chapter 10, for further discussion of sexual harassment.

[111]Harry v. Marion County Bd. of Educ., 506 S.E.2d 319 (W. Va. 1998). *See also* Forte v. Mills, 672 N.Y.S.2d 497 (App. Div. 1998) (ruling that a teacher's inappropriate touching of fourth and fifth grade girls was sexually harassing conduct justifying termination for insubordination and conduct unbecoming to a teacher; he had received repeated warnings to desist).

[112]Ross v. Robb, 662 S.W.2d 257 (Mo. 1983).

[113]Bertolini v. Whitehall City Sch. Dist. Bd. of Educ., 744 N.E.2d 1245 (Ohio Ct. App. 2000).

[114]*See* text accompanying note 98, Chapter 10, for a discussion of claims of discrimination based on sexual orientation; note 145, Chapter 9, for constitutionally protected privacy rights.

diverse opinions regarding gay, lesbian, bisexual, and transgendered (GLBT) educators. According to the Supreme Court of California, immoral or unprofessional conduct or moral turpitude must be related to unfitness to teach to justify termination.[115] Yet, the Supreme Court of Washington upheld the dismissal of a teacher based simply on the knowledge of his homosexuality.[116] The court feared that public controversy could interfere with the teacher's classroom effectiveness. In recent years, however, courts have been reluctant to support the dismissal of a GLBT educator simply because the school board does not approve of a particular private lifestyle. For example, an Ohio federal court concluded that the nonrenewal of a teacher because of his homosexuality did not bear a rational relationship to a legitimate government purpose, thereby violating the Equal Protection Clause.[117] The Court ordered reinstatement with a two-year contract and assessed damages against the school board.

Whereas many dismissals for immorality involve sexual conduct, immorality is much broader in meaning and scope. As one court noted, it covers conduct that "is hostile to the welfare of the school community."[118] Such hostile conduct has included, among other things, dishonest acts, criminal conduct, and drug-related conduct. The following cases reflect the range of misconduct involving charges of immorality.

Frequently, criminal conduct has resulted in dismissals for immoral behavior. For example, Alaska statutes define *immorality* as "an act which, under the laws of the state, constitutes a crime involving moral turpitude."[119] The state high court held that a conviction for unlawfully diverting electricity was such a crime. Under Georgia law, conviction for submitting false tax documents was sufficient grounds to dismiss a principal for moral turpitude.[120] Other dishonest acts found to substantiate charges of immorality include misrepresenting absences from school as illness,[121] being

[115]Morrison v. State Bd. of Educ., 461 P.2d 375 (Cal. 1969). *See also* Sch. Comm. v. Civil Serv. Comm'n, 684 N.E.2d 620 (Mass. App. Ct. 1997). *But see* Rowland v. Mad River Local Sch. Dist.,730 F.2d 444 (6th Cir. 1984) (upholding the nonrenewal of a guidance counselor who revealed her homosexuality); text accompanying note 182, Chapter 9.

[116]Gaylord v. Tacoma Sch. Dist. No. 10, 559 P.2d 1340 (Wash. 1977).

[117]Glover v. Williamsburg Local Sch. Dist., 20 F. Supp. 2d 1160 (S.D. Ohio 1998).

[118]Jarvella v. Willoughby-Eastlake City Sch. Dist., 233 N.E.2d 143, 145 (Ohio 1967). *See also* Winters v. Ariz. Bd. of Educ., 83 P.3d 1114 (Ariz. Ct. App. 2004) (upholding the revocation of a teaching certificate for aggressive, threatening, and violent off-campus behavior; nexus existed between teacher's conduct and fitness to teach).

[119]*See* Kenai Peninsula Borough Bd. of Educ. v. Brown, 691 P.2d 1034, 1036 (Alaska 1984). *See also* Toney v. Fairbanks N. Star Borough Sch. Dist., Bd. of Educ., 881 P.2d 1112 (Alaska 1994) (finding that a teacher's sexual relationship with a 15-year-old student occurring prior to his employment by the school district was a crime of moral turpitude supporting termination; the court commented that it is questionable whether such a crime could ever be too remote to be considered in determining a teacher's fitness to teach).

[120]Logan v. Warren County Bd. of Educ., 549 F. Supp. 145 (S.D. Ga. 1982).

[121]Riverview Sch. Dist. v. Riverview Educ. Ass'n, 639 A.2d 974 (Pa. Commw. Ct. 1994). *See also* Dohanic v. Commonwealth Dep't of Educ., 533 A.2d 812 (Pa. Commw. Ct. 1987) (holding that lying to school officials constituted immoral conduct).

involved in the sale of illegal drugs,[122] possessing cocaine,[123] pleading guilty to grand larceny,[124] reporting to school under the influence of marijuana,[125] and falsely claiming to be an agent of a school district for personal gain.[126]

In the absence of a statutory specification, however, the West Virginia Supreme Court held that a school board could not conclude that a conviction for a misdemeanor was *per se* immoral conduct.[127] A Pennsylvania court held that a conviction for threatening an individual did not substantiate immoral conduct; the court cautioned that not all unprofessional conduct is automatically immoral conduct.[128] Similarly, the Supreme Court of Oklahoma concluded that a teacher's verbal threats on school grounds against a school superintendent and another teacher may have been unprofessional and inappropriate but the comments did not rise to the level of moral turpitude under state law to justify dismissal.[129]

Although *immorality* is an abstract term that can encompass broad-ranging behavior, it is understood to refer to actions that violate moral standards and render a teacher unfit to teach. Courts consistently hold that school officials must link the challenged conduct to impairment of the teacher's effectiveness in the classroom to justify termination for immorality.

Insubordination

Insubordination, another frequently cited cause for dismissal, is generally defined as the willful disregard of or refusal to obey school regulations and official orders. Teachers can be dismissed for violation of administrative regulations and policies even though classroom performance is satisfactory; school officials are not required to establish a relationship between the conduct and fitness to teach.

With the plethora of regulations enacted by school districts, wide diversity is found in types of behavior adjudicated as insubordination. Dismissals based on insubordination have been upheld in cases involving refusal to abide by specific school directives, unwillingness to cooperate with superiors, unauthorized absences, and numerous other actions. Because conduct is measured against the existence of a rule or policy, a school board may more readily document insubordination than most other legal causes for dismissal.

Many state laws and court decisions require that acts be "willful and persistent" to be considered insubordinate. A Florida teacher's continuous refusal to provide

[122]Woo v. Putnam County Bd. of Educ., 504 S.E.2d 644 (W. Va. 1998).

[123]Gedney v. Bd. of Educ., 703 A.2d 804 (Conn. App. Ct. 1997).

[124]Green v. N.Y. City Dep't of Educ., 793 N.Y.S.2d 405 (App. Div. 2005).

[125]Younge v. Bd. of Educ. of City of Chi., 788 N.E.2d 1153 (Ill. App. Ct. 2003).

[126]Ahmad v. Bd. of Educ. of City of Chi., 847 N.E.2d 810 (Ill. App. Ct. 2006).

[127]Golden v. Bd. of Educ., 285 S.E.2d 665 (W. Va. 1981) *But see* Zelno v. Lincoln Intermediate Unit No. 12 Bd. of Dirs, 786 A.2d 1022 (Pa. Commw. Ct. 2001) (finding that a teacher could be terminated for immoral conduct based on three drunken driving convictions and two convictions for driving without a license).

[128]Horton v. Jefferson County-Dubois Area Vocational Technical Sch., 630 A.2d 481 (Pa. Commw. Ct. 1993).

[129]Ballard v. Indep. Sch. Dist. No. 4 of Bryan County, 77 P.3d 1084 (Okla. 2003).

lesson plans during school absences resulted in termination for insubordination. A Florida appellate court, upholding the dismissal, noted insubordination under state law as "constant or continuing intentional refusal to obey a direct order, reasonable in nature, and given by and with proper authority."[130] A severe or substantial single incident, however, may be adequate for dismissal action.[131] The Wyoming Supreme Court found that repeated refusals to obey orders were not required to justify dismissal.[132] The court concluded that termination of a teacher who refused a split assignment between two schools was proper; repeated refusals were unnecessary if other elements of insubordination were present, such as reasonableness of the order and direct refusal to obey. Similarly upheld were a Missouri teacher's termination after she refused to teach an assigned course[133] and a Colorado teacher's dismissal for showing an R-rated movie without submitting a request for approval under the district's controversial materials policy.[134]

Insubordination charges often have resulted from conflicts arising from the administrator/teacher relationship. For example, a North Carolina teacher's refusal to discontinue a classroom project that the principal and curriculum specialist determined to be lacking in any educational value and her subsequent refusal to develop and implement a professional growth plan supported dismissal.[135] The South Dakota Supreme Court upheld the dismissal of a teacher who refused to submit to the principal's authority; the teacher's actions were characterized as disobedient, confrontational, adversarial, insolent, and defensive.[136] However, a Tennessee teacher, who was unable to work because of stress, fear, and intimidation resulting from incidents in the school, could not be terminated for insubordination when she failed to return to work as directed by the superintendent.[137]

[130]Dolega v. Sch. Bd. of Miami-Dade County, 840 So. 2d 445, 446 (Fla. Dist. Ct. App. 2003). *See also* Hall v. Gary Cmty. Sch. Corp., 298 F.3d 672 (7th Cir. 2002) (holding evidence showed a teacher's frequent tardiness and disregard for rules and regulations was the basis for his dismissal rather than retaliation for filing a discrimination charge with the EEOC).

[131]*See, e.g.*, Ware v. Morgan County Sch. Dist., 748 P.2d 1295 (Colo. 1988) (finding one-time use of profanity, after being ordered not to use profanity with students, supported termination); Gaylord v. Bd. of Educ., 794 P.2d 307 (Kan. Ct. App. 1990) (upheld termination of a teacher for taking sick leave after his request for a one-day leave was denied). *But see* Trimble v. W. Va. Bd. of Dirs., 549 S.E.2d 294 (W. Va. 2001) (concluding that termination for a minor incident of insubordination denied individual constitutional due process).

[132]Bd. of Trs. v. Colwell, 611 P.2d 427 (Wyo. 1980).

[133]McLaughlin v. Bd. of Educ., 659 S.W.2d 249 (Mo. Ct. App. 1983).

[134]Bd. of Educ. v. Wilder, 960 P.2d 695 (Colo. 1998). *But see infra* text accompanying note 154.

[135]Hope v. Charlotte-Mecklenburg Bd. of Educ., 430 S.E.2d 472 (N.C. Ct. App. 1993).

[136]Barnes v. Spearfish Sch. Dist. No. 40-2, 725 N.W.2d 226 (S.D. 2006). *See also* Yukadinovich v. Bd. of Sch. Trs., 278 F.3d 693 (7th Cir. 2002).

[137]McGhee v. Miller, 753 S.W.2d 354 (Tenn. 1988). *See also* Brawner v. Marietta City Bd. of Educ., 646 S.E.2d 89 (Ga. Ct. App. 2007) (finding that a teacher on disability leave who voluntarily returned to school for a summer preplanning day could not be terminated for insubordination for failure to provide a certificate of fitness for duty).

Teachers cannot ignore reasonable directives and policies of administrators or school boards. If the school board has prohibited corporal punishment or prescribed procedures for its administration, teachers must strictly adhere to board requirements. In upholding the termination of a Colorado teacher, the state supreme court ruled that tapping a student on the head with a three-foot pointer supported termination because the teacher had been warned and disciplined previously for using physical force in violation of school district policy.[138] Repeatedly failing to follow official directives in administering corporal punishment resulted in the termination of a Texas teacher.[139] The Eleventh Circuit found that insubordination was established when a teacher refused to undergo urinalysis within two hours of the discovery of marijuana in her car in the school parking lot, as required by school board policy.[140] The Eighth Circuit upheld the dismissal of a teacher for violating a school board policy that prohibited students' use of profanity in the classroom; students had used profanity in various creative writing assignments such as plays and poems.[141] Other instances of failure to follow administrative directives justifying dismissal for insubordination include failing to follow directives designed to improve instruction, continuing to emphasize sexual aspects of literature, and failing to acquire board approval of supplementary materials used in the classroom.[142]

Generally, the key factor in dismissal for insubordination is whether a teacher has persisted in disobeying a reasonable and valid school policy or directive.[143] That is, school officials must show that specific requests have been made related to the teacher's classroom performance or other professional matters and the teacher failed to comply.

Neglect of Duty

Neglect of duty arises when an educator fails to carry out assigned duties. This may involve an intentional omission or may result from ineffectual performance. In a Colorado case, neglect of duty was found when a teacher failed to discipline students

---

[138]Bd. of Educ. v. Flaming, 938 P.2d 151 (Colo. 1997). *See also* Daily v. Bd. of Educ., 588 N.W.2d 813 (Neb. 1999) (upholding a 30-day suspension for "smacking" a student on the head in violation of a state law that prohibited corporal punishment).

[139]Burton v. Kirby, 775 S.W.2d 834 (Tex. Ct. App. 1989).

[140]Hearn v. Bd. of Pub. Educ., 191 F.3d 1329 (11th Cir. 1999).

[141]Lacks v. Ferguson Reorganized Sch. Dist. R-2, 147 F.3d 718 (8th Cir. 1998).

[142]*See, e.g.*, Fisher v. Fairbanks N. Star Borough Sch., 704 P.2d 213 (Alaska 1985) (supplemental materials); *In re* Proposed Termination Johnson, 451 N.W.2d 343 (Minn. Ct. App. 1990) (teaching deficiencies); *In re* Bernstein and Norwich City Sch. Dist., 726 N.Y.S.2d 474 (App. Div. 2001) (sexual aspects of literature).

[143]A Tennessee appellate court noted that insubordination cannot be substantiated without an order that is disregarded; a principal had discouraged a teacher from entertaining students in his home but had not ordered him to cease the activity. Morris v. Clarksville-Montgomery County Consol. Bd. of Educ., 867 S.W.2d 324 (Tenn. Ct. App. 1993).

consistent with school policy.[144] Similarly, the Louisiana high court ruled that a teacher repeatedly sending unescorted students to the principal's office in violation of school policy substantiated willful neglect of duty.[145] The Oregon appellate court concluded that a teacher's failure to maintain "harmonious relations with students, parents, staff and other teachers" constituted neglect of duty.[146]

The United States Supreme Court upheld the dismissal of an Oklahoma teacher for "willful neglect of duty" in failing to comply with the school board's continuing education requirement.[147] For a period of time, lack of compliance was dealt with through denial of salary increases. Upon enactment of a state law requiring salary increases for all teachers, the board notified teachers that noncompliance with the requirement would result in termination. Affirming the board's action, the Supreme Court found the sanction of dismissal to be rationally related to the board's objective of improving its teaching force through continuing education requirements.

The Supreme Court of Nebraska addressed what constitutes neglect of duty when a teacher allegedly had failed on several occasions to perform certain duties and at other times had not performed duties competently.[148] Evidence revealed that the teacher had not violated any administrative orders or school laws, had received good evaluations, and had been recommended for retention by the administrators. The court concluded that the facts did not support just cause for dismissal. In addition, the court cautioned that in evaluating a teacher's performance, neglect of duty is not measured "against a standard of perfection, but, instead, must be measured against the standard required of others performing the same or similar duties."[149] It was not demonstrated that the teacher's performance was below expectations for other teachers in similar positions.

In a later case, the Nebraska high court held that a superintendent's failure to file a funding form did not constitute neglect of duty to support the termination of his contract.[150] Similarly, a Louisiana appellate court held that a teacher's showing of an

---

[144]Bd. of Educ. v. Flaming, 938 P.2d 151 (Colo. 1997). *See also* Flickinger v. Lebanon Sch. Dist., 898 A.2d 62 (Pa. Commw. Ct. 2006) (concluding that principal's failure to immediately respond to a report of a gun in the middle school established willful neglect of duty; school procedures specified that such a crisis situation must be handled without delay).

[145]Wise v. Bossier Parish Sch. Bd., 851 So. 2d 1090 (La. 2003).

[146]Bellairs v. Beaverton Sch. Dist., 136 P.3d 93 (Or. Ct. App. 2006).

[147]Harrah Indep. Sch. Dist. v. Martin, 440 U.S. 194 (1979). *See also* Dolega v. Sch. Bd. of Miami-Dade County, 840 So. 2d 445 (Fla. Dist. Ct. App. 2003).

[148]Sanders v. Bd. of Educ., 263 N.W.2d 461 (Neb. 1978). *See* Baker v. Bd. of Educ., 534 S.E.2d 378 (W. Va. 2000).

[149]*Sanders*, 263 N.W.2d at 465. *See also* Eshom v. Bd. of Educ., 364 N.W.2d 7 (Neb. 1985) (ruling that dismissal was supported by detailed evaluations comparing a terminated teacher with other teachers).

[150]Boss v. Fillmore Sch. Dist. No. 19, 559 N.W.2d 448 (Neb. 1997). *But see* Smith v. Bullock County Bd. of Educ., 906 So. 2d 938 (Ala. Civ. App. 2004) (ruling that principal's failure to establish procedures to prevent the theft of about $25,000 of athletic funds was neglect of duty).

R-rated film did not warrant dismissal for neglect of duty and incompetence.[151] The Louisiana high court concluded that a teacher bringing a loaded gun to school in his car did not substantiate willful neglect of duty to support termination.[152] The court commented that his action was certainly a mistake and possibly endangered students, but it did not involve a failure to follow orders or an identifiable school policy required for dismissal under state law.

Teachers can be discharged for neglect of duty when their performance does not measure up to expected professional standards in the school system. Often, charges relate to a failure to perform but also can be brought for ineffective performance. Again, as with other efforts to terminate employment, documentation must substantiate that performance is unacceptable.

Unprofessional Conduct

A number of states identify either unprofessional conduct or conduct unbecoming a teacher as cause for dismissal. A teacher's activities both inside and outside of school can be used to substantiate this charge when they interfere with teaching effectiveness. Dismissals for unprofessional conduct, neglect of duty, and unfitness to teach often are based on quite similar facts. Facts that establish unprofessional conduct in one state may be deemed neglect of duty in another state. Although causes for dismissal are identified in state statutes, they are defined through case law and administrative rulings in individual states.

Most courts have defined *unprofessional conduct* as actions directly related to the fitness of educators to perform in their professional capacity. The working definition adopted by the Supreme Court of Nebraska specified *unprofessional conduct* as breaching the rules or ethical code of a profession or "unbecoming a member in good standing of a profession." Under this definition, the court reasoned that a teacher engaged in unprofessional conduct when he "smacked" a student on the head hard enough to make the student cry, thereby violating the state prohibition against corporal punishment.[153]

Courts have upheld dismissal for unprofessional conduct based on a number of grounds, such as permitting students to kick or hit each other for violations of classroom rules,[154] engaging in sexual harassment of female students,[155] wrapping a student

---

[151]Jones v. Rapides Parish Sch. Bd., 634 So. 2d 1197 (La. Ct. App. 1993).

[152]Howard v. W. Baton Rouge Parish Sch. Bd., 793 So. 2d 153 (La. 2001). *But see* Spurlock v. E. Feliciana Parish Sch., 885 So. 2d 1225 (La. Ct. App. 2004) (ruling that a teacher could be terminated for willful neglect of duty for making misbehaving second grade students simulate a sex act in front of the class; the teacher did not violate a specific policy or fail to follow orders, however, the court opined that she should have known that her egregious behavior was improper).

[153]Daily v. Bd. of Educ., 588 N.W.2d 813, 824 (Neb. 1999). Following a hearing to consider termination of employment, the school board instead imposed a 30-day suspension on the teacher.

[154]Roberts v. Santa Cruz Valley Unified Sch. Dist. No. 35, 778 P.2d 1294 (Ariz. Ct. App. 1989).

[155]Conward v. Cambridge Sch. Comm., 171 F.3d 12 (1st Cir. 1999).

in an electrical cord and verbally humiliating him in front of other students,[156] losing complete control of the classroom,[157] taking photos of a female student nude above the waist,[158] showing a sexually explicit film to a classroom of adolescents without previewing it,[159] and stealing pills labeled methylphenidate (generic name for Ritalin) from the school office.[160] As with dismissals based on incompetency, courts often require prior warning that the behavior may result in dismissal.

Other Good and Just Cause

Not unexpectedly, "other good and just cause" as grounds for dismissal often has been challenged as vague and overbroad. Courts have been faced with the task of determining whether the phrase's meaning is limited to the specific grounds enumerated in the statute or whether it is a separate, expanded cause. An Indiana appellate court interpreted it as permitting termination for reasons other than those specified in the tenure law, if evidence indicated that the board's decision was based on "good cause."[161] As such, dismissal of a teacher convicted of a misdemeanor was upheld, even though the teacher had no prior indication that such conduct was sufficient cause. A Connecticut court found *good cause* to be any ground that is put forward in good faith that is not "arbitrary, irrational, unreasonable, or irrelevant to the board's task of building up and maintaining an efficient school system."[162] Terminating a teacher for altering students' responses on state mandatory proficiency tests was held to be relevant to that task.

The Second Circuit found *other due and sufficient cause* as a ground for dismissal to be "appropriate in an area such as discipline of teachers, where a myriad of uncontemplated situations may arise and it is not reasonable to require a legislature to elucidate in advance every act that requires sanction."[163] The court declined to rule on

[156]Johanson v. Bd. of Educ., 589 N.W.2d 815 (Neb. 1999).

[157]Walker v. Highlands County Sch. Bd., 752 So. 2d 127 (Fla. Dist. Ct. App. 2000).

[158]Dixon v. Clem, 492 F.3d 665 (6th Cir. 2007).

[159]Fowler v. Bd. of Educ., 819 F.2d 657 (6th Cir. 1987).

[160]Lannom v. Bd. of Educ., No. M1999-00137-COA-R3-CV, 2000 Tenn. Ct. App. LEXIS 133 (Tenn. Ct. App. Mar. 6, 2000).

[161]Gary Teachers Union, Local No. 4, AFT v. Sch. City of Gary, 332 N.E.2d 256, 263 (Ind. Ct. App. 1975). *See also* Hierlmeier v. N. Judson-San Pierre Bd., 730 N.E.2d 821 (Ind. Ct. App. 2000) (ruling that sexual harassment of female students and other inappropriate conduct toward students substantiated good and just cause for termination); Sheldon Cmty. Sch. Dist. Bd. of Dirs. v. Lundblad, 528 N.W.2d 593 (Iowa 1995) (finding frequent sarcastic remarks to adolescents to establish "just cause" under Iowa law). *But see* Trs. Lincoln County Sch. Dist. No. 13 v. Holden, 754 P.2d 506 (Mont. 1988) (concluding that two instances of calling students crude names did not support good cause for dismissal).

[162]Hanes v. Bd. of Educ., 783 A.2d 1, 6 (Conn. App. Ct. 2001). *See* Cooledge v. Riverdale Local Sch. Dist., 797 N.E.2d 61 (Ohio 2003) (ruling that a teacher receiving temporary total disability compensation under state law could not be discharged for absenteeism; termination of the teacher for "other good and just cause" violated public policy).

[163]diLeo v. Greenfield, 541 F.2d 949, 954 (2d Cir. 1976).

the vagueness of the term, but rather noted that courts generally assess the teacher's conduct in relation to the statutory grounds for dismissal. That is, if the specific behavior is sufficiently related to the causes specified in state law, it is assumed that the teacher should have reasonably known that the conduct was improper. In this case, where a teacher repeatedly humiliated and harassed students (and school administrators had discussed the problem with him), the court concluded that the teacher was aware of the impropriety of his conduct.

The Supreme Court of Iowa supported the termination of a teacher for shoplifting under a statute permitting teachers to be terminated during the contract year for "just cause."[164] Although the teacher claimed that her compulsion to shoplift was related to a mental illness, the court found the weighing of the teacher's position as a role model, the character of the illness, and the school board's needs provided substantial evidence to terminate the teacher's employment. In a subsequent case, the Iowa high court ruled "just cause" existed to terminate a teacher who had knowledge of her son and his high school friends drinking at a campsite on her property. She failed to monitor their activities, and four students who left to buy more beer died in a car crash. The court agreed with the school board that the teacher's effectiveness as a role model was significantly diminished.[165]

Reduction-in-Force

In addition to dismissal for causes related to teacher performance and fitness, legislation generally permits the release of teachers for reasons related to declining enrollment, financial exigency, and school district consolidation. Whereas most state statutes provide for such terminations, a number of states also have adopted legislation that specifies the basis for selection of released teachers, procedures to be followed, and provisions for reinstatement. These terminations, characterized as *reductions-in-force (RIF)*, also may be governed by board policies and negotiated bargaining agreements.

Unlike other termination cases, the employee challenging a RIF decision shoulders the burden of proof. There is a presumption that the board has acted in good faith with permissible motives. Legal controversies in this area usually involve questions related to the necessity for the reductions, board compliance with mandated procedures, and possible subterfuge for impermissible termination (such as denial of constitutional rights, subversion of tenure rights, discrimination).[166]

---

[164]Bd. of Dirs. v. Davies, 489 N.W.2d 19 (Iowa 1992). *See also* Snyder v. Jefferson County Sch. Dist. R-1, 842 P.2d 624 (Colo. 1992) (holding that expiration of a teacher's certificate constituted other good and just cause for termination).

[165]Walthart v. Bd. of Dirs., 694 N.W.2d 740 (Iowa 2005).

[166]*See, e.g.*, Impey v. Bd. of Educ., 662 A.2d 960 (N.J. 1995) (holding that a school board did not need to eliminate programs or services to eliminate teaching positions; all services were provided less expensively through a contract with an external agency).

If statutory or contractual restrictions exist for teacher layoffs, there must be substantial compliance with the provisions. One of the provisions most frequently included is a method for selecting teachers for release. In general, reductions are based on seniority, and a tenured teacher, rather than a nontenured teacher, must be retained if both are qualified to fill the same position. Some state statutes require that both licensure and seniority be considered; a teacher lacking a license in the area would not be permitted to teach while a permanent teacher with proper credentials, but less seniority, was dismissed.[167] Along with seniority, merit-rating systems may be included in the determination of reductions. School districts in Pennsylvania use a combination of ratings and seniority; ratings are the primary determinant unless no substantial difference exists in ratings, and then seniority becomes the basis for the layoff.[168] Both the Montana and Nebraska high courts concluded that school boards have broad discretion in deciding what factors to use in their RIF policies and how to weigh those factors.[169] Guidelines and criteria established by state law or state and local education agencies, however, must be applied in a uniform and nondiscriminatory manner. For example, under New Mexico law, the school board must determine that no other positions exist for teachers targeted for release.[170]

The Fourteenth Amendment requires minimal procedural protections in dismissals for cause, but courts have not clearly defined the due process requirements for RIF. The Eighth Circuit noted that tenured teachers possess a property interest in continued employment, and thereby must be provided notice and an opportunity to be heard.[171] Specific procedural protections for employees, however, vary according to interpretations of state law, bargaining agreements, and board policy. The District of Columbia Circuit held that due process did not require pretermination hearings when posttermination proceedings were available.[172] A Michigan court found no need for a hearing over staff reductions, because there were no charges to refute.[173] The court emphasized that the law protected the released teacher, who, subject to qualifications, was entitled to the next vacancy. In contrast, a Pennsylvania commonwealth court held that a hearing must be provided to assure the teacher (1) that termination

---

[167]*See, e.g.*, DeGeorgeo v. Indep. Sch. Dist. No. 833, 563 N.W.2d 755 (Minn. Ct. App. 1997); Summers County Bd. of Educ. v. Allen, 450 S.E.2d 658 (W. Va. 1994).

[168]Pa. Stat. Ann. tit. 24 § 11-1124 (2007).

[169]Scobey Sch. Dist. v. Radakovich, 135 P.3d 778 (Mont. 2006); Nickel v. Saline County Sch. Dist. No. 163, 559 N.W.2d 480 (Neb. 1997).

[170]Aguilera v. Bd. of Educ. of Hatch Valley, 132 P.3d 587 (N.M. 2006).

[171]Boner v. Eminence R-1 Sch. Dist., 55 F.3d 1339 (8th Cir. 1995). *See also* Chandler v. Bd. of Educ., 92 F. Supp. 2d 760 (N.D. Ill. 2000) (ruling that a teacher must be provided a notice describing the reasons for termination of employment); Westport Sch. Comm. v. Coelho, 692 N.E.2d 540 (Mass. App. Ct. 1998) (interpreting state-level arbitration to apply to performance-based dismissals not budget-induced layoffs).

[172]Washington Teachers' Union v. Bd. of Educ., 109 F.3d 774 (D.C. Cir. 1997).

[173]Steeby v. Sch. Dist. of Highland Park, 224 N.W.2d 97 (Mich. Ct. App. 1974).

was for reasons specified by law and (2) that the board followed the correct statutory procedures in selecting the teacher for discharge.[174]

State law or other policies may give employment preference to teachers who are released due to a reduction-in-force. Typically, under such requirements, a school board cannot hire a nonemployee until each qualified teacher on the preferred recall list is reemployed.[175] Although statutes often require that a teacher be appointed to the first vacancy for which licensed and qualified, courts have held that reappointment is still at the board's discretion. A Michigan appeals court recognized that a teacher could be licensed in an area, but in the opinion of the board, not necessarily qualified.[176] Additionally, a board is generally not obligated to realign or rearrange teaching assignments to create a position for a released teacher.[177]

Remedies for Violations of Protected Rights

When established that school districts or officials have violated an employee's rights protected by federal or state law, several remedies are available to the aggrieved individual. In some situations, the employee may seek a court injunction ordering the unlawful action to cease. This remedy might be sought if a school board has unconstitutionally imposed restraints on teachers' expression. Where terminations, transfers, or other adverse employment consequences have been unconstitutionally imposed, courts will order school districts to return the affected employees to their original status with back pay.

In addition to these remedies, educators are increasingly bringing suits to recover damages for actions that violate their federally protected rights. Suits are usually based on 42 U.S.C. Section 1983, which provides that any person who acts under color of state law to deprive another individual of rights secured by the federal Constitution or laws is subject to personal liability. This law, originally enacted in 1871 to prevent discrimination against African American citizens, has been broadly interpreted as conferring liability on school personnel and school districts, not only for racial discrimination but also for actions that may result in the impairment of other federally protected rights.[178]

---

[174]Fatscher v. Bd. of Sch. Dirs., 367 A.2d 1130 (Pa. Commw. Ct. 1977). *See* Harris v. Trs. of Cascades County Sch. Dist., 786 P.2d 1164 (Mont. 1990).

[175]*See, e.g.*, Bd. of Educ. v. Owensby, 526 S.E.2d 831 (W. Va. 1999). *See also* Davis v. Chester Upland Sch. Dist., 786 A.2d 186 (Pa. 2001) (ruling that teachers who challenged the district's failure to recall them must exhaust collective bargaining grievance procedure before filing for judicial review).

[176]Chester v. Harper Woods Sch. Dist., 273 N.W.2d 916 (Mich. Ct. App. 1978).

[177]*See, e.g.*, Hinckley v. Sch. Bd. of Indep. Sch. Dist. No. 2167, 678 N.W.2d 485 (Minn. Ct. App. 2004); Hanson v. Vermillion Sch. Dist., 727 N.W.2d 459 (S.D. 2007). *But see* Pennell v. Bd. of Educ., 484 N.E.2d 445 (Ill. App. Ct. 1985) (ruling that restructuring positions is not required, but bad faith realignment of positions to avoid existence of a position for a tenured teacher is prohibited).

[178]Maine v. Thiboutot, 448 U.S. 1 (1980).

Suits alleging Section 1983 violations can be initiated in federal or state courts,[179] and exhaustion of state administrative remedies is not required before initiating a federal suit.[180] When a federal law authorizes an exclusive nondamages remedy, however, a Section 1983 suit is precluded.[181] This section focuses on the liability of school officials and districts for the violation of protected rights and on the types of damages available to aggrieved employees.

Liability of School Officials

Under Section 1983, public school employees acting under color of state law can be held personally liable for actions abridging students' or teachers' federal rights. The Supreme Court, however, has recognized that government officials cannot be held liable under Section 1983 for the actions of their subordinates, thus rejecting the doctrine of *respondeat superior*, even where school officials have general supervisory authority over the activities of the wrongdoers. In order to be held liable, the officials must have personally participated in, or had personal knowledge of, the unlawful acts or promulgated official policy under which the acts were taken.[182] Furthermore, the Supreme Court in 1998 ruled that public officials are absolutely immune from suit under Section 1983 for their legislative activities.[183] These actions involve discretionary, policy-making decisions, enactment of regulations, often with budgetary implications. Subsequently, courts have clarified that employment decisions related to individual employees (such as hiring, dismissal, or demotions) are administrative, not legislative, in nature.[184]

The Supreme Court has recognized that in some circumstances school officials can claim qualified immunity to shield them from personal liability when they have acted in good faith. The burden of establishing good faith immunity clearly resides with the official claiming the protection; the plaintiff does not have to prove that immunity is not applicable.[185] In a 1975 student discipline case, *Wood v. Strickland*, the Supreme Court declared:

> A school board member is not immune from liability for damages under Section 1983 if he knew or reasonably should have known that the action he took within his sphere of

---

[179]The Supreme Court has rejected the assertion that school officials are immune from a § 1983 suit initiated in a state court. Howlett v. Rose, 496 U.S. 356 (1990).

[180]Patsy v. Bd. of Regents, 457 U.S. 496 (1982).

[181]*See, e.g.*, Gonzaga Univ. v. Doe, 536 U.S. 273 (2002); Blessing v. Freestone, 520 U.S. 329 (1997).

[182]*See* Am. Mfrs. Mut. Ins. Co. v. Sullivan, 526 U.S. 40 (1999); Rizzo v. Goode, 423 U.S. 362 (1976).

[183]Bogan v. Scott-Harris, 523 U.S. 44 (1998).

[184]*See, e.g.*, Canary v. Osborn, 211 F.3d 324 (6th Cir. 2000); Harhay v. Town of Ellington Bd. of Educ., 323 F.3d 206 (2d Cir. 2003).

[185]Gomez v. Toledo, 446 U.S. 635 (1980).

official responsibility would violate the constitutional rights of the student affected, or if he took the action with the malicious intention to cause a deprivation of constitutional rights or other injury to the student.[186]

Subsequently, in *Harlow v. Fitzgerald* the Court eliminated the subjective test (i.e., an assessment of whether the defendants acted with malicious intentions) from the qualified-immunity standard. Under *Harlow*, "government officials performing discretionary functions generally are shielded from liability for civil damages insofar as their conduct does not violate clearly established statutory or constitutional rights of which a reasonable person would have known."[187] The Second Circuit, noting that unlawfulness must be apparent, stated:

> A right is clearly established if the contours of the right are sufficiently clear that a reasonable official would understand that what he or she is doing violates that right. The question is not what a lawyer would learn or intuit from researching case law, but what a reasonable person in the [school official's] position should know about the constitutionality of the conduct.[188]

The Ninth Circuit recognized the difficulty of determining a "clearly established" violation when confronted with applying the balancing tests of *Pickering v. Board of Education*[189] for protected speech and *Mathews v. Eldridge*[190] for procedural due process in a teacher-termination case. Concluding that the specific facts in this case did not show a violation of established law, the court found the school officials entitled to qualified immunity.[191] More recently, the Supreme Court has emphasized that the overriding issue is whether the law at the time an individual acted gave "clear and fair warning" that rights were established.[192]

The Seventh Circuit noted that the individual alleging violation of a clearly established right bears the burden of demonstrating the existence of the right.[193] In determining whether a right is clearly established, the court stated that first it examines controlling Supreme Court precedent and its own circuit decisions related to the case and then reviews all relevant case law. According to the appellate court, a split among courts in assessing similar conduct points to unsettled law.

[186]420 U.S. 308, 322 (1975).

[187]457 U.S. 800, 818 (1982).

[188]McCullough v. Wyandanch Union Free Sch. Dist., 187 F.3d 272, 278 (2d Cir. 1999).

[189]391 U.S. 563 (1968).

[190]424 U.S. 319 (1976).

[191]Brewster v. Bd. of Educ., 149 F.3d 971 (9th Cir. 1998). *See also* Townsend v. Vallas, 256 F.3d 661 (7th Cir. 2001); Ulichny v. Merton Cmty. Sch. Dist., 249 F.3d 686 (7th Cir. 2001).

[192]Hope v. Pelzer, 536 U.S. 730 (2002).

[193]Denius v. Dunlap, 209 F.3d 944 (7th Cir. 2000). *See also* Beard v. Whitmore Lake Sch. Dist., 402 F.3d 598 (6th Cir. 2005); Thomas v. Roberts, 323 F.3d 950 (11th Cir. 2003).

School officials have been denied qualified immunity when they disregard well-established legal principles in areas such as due process, protected expression, and privacy. For example, school board members violated a superintendent's procedural due process by failing to provide him a fair hearing.[194] Similarly, a superintendent was not protected by qualified immunity for refusing to recommend a teacher's reemployment based on constitutionally impermissible reasons pertaining to her involvement in a divorce.[195] The Third Circuit, in remanding a case for further proceedings, noted that a superintendent who appeared to have maliciously prosecuted a teacher for theft in retaliation for the exercise of her First Amendment activities was not entitled to qualified immunity.[196] Public officials are not expected to predict the future course of constitutional law, but they are expected to adhere to principles of law that were clearly established at the time of the violation.

Liability of School Districts

In 1978, the Supreme Court departed from precedent and ruled that local governments are considered "persons" under Section 1983.[197] In essence, school districts can be assessed damages when action taken pursuant to official policy or custom violates federally protected rights. To prevail against a school district, an individual must present evidence that the district acted with deliberate indifference in establishing and maintaining a policy, practice, or custom that directly deprived an individual of constitutionally protected rights.[198]

The governmental unit (like the individual official), however, cannot be held liable under the *respondeat superior* doctrine for the wrongful acts committed solely by its employees. Liability under Section 1983 against the agency can be imposed only when execution of official policy by an individual with final authority impairs a federally protected right.[199] The Supreme Court has held that a single egregious act of

---

[194]Baird v. Bd. of Educ., 389 F.3d 685 (7th Cir. 2004).

[195]Littlejohn v. Rose, 768 F.2d 765 (6th Cir. 1985).

[196]Merkle v. Upper Dublin Sch. Dist., 211 F.3d 782 (3d Cir. 2000). The court also noted that injury to reputation alone does not violate the Fourteenth Amendment; however, if the teacher is able to show damage to her reputation during the deprivation of a constitutional right, she can establish liability under § 1983 for a Fourteenth Amendment violation. *See also* Evans-Marshall v. Bd. of Educ. of Tipp City Sch. Dist., 428 F.3d 223 (6th Cir. 2005).

[197]Monell v. Dep't of Soc. Servs., 436 U.S. 658 (1978).

[198]Thomas v. Bd. of Educ., 467 F. Supp. 2d 483 (W.D. Pa. 2006) (rejecting plaintiff's claim that school district was aware of teacher's previous abuse of corporal punishment but had taken no action, thereby establishing an unconstitutional custom).

[199]*See, e.g.*, Collins v. City of Harker Heights, 503 U.S. 115 (1992); St. Louis v. Praprotnik, 485 U.S. 112 (1988); Pembaur v. City of Cincinnati, 475 U.S. 469 (1986); Seamons v. Snow, 206 F.3d 1021 (10th Cir. 2000).

a low-level employee does not infer an official policy of inadequate training and supervision,[200] but an agency can be liable if "deliberate indifference" in ensuring adequately trained employees is established.[201]

Although school officials can plead good faith immunity, this defense is not available to school districts. The Supreme Court has ruled that school districts and other governmental subdivisions cannot claim qualified immunity based on good faith actions of their officials. The Court acknowledged that under certain circumstances, sovereign immunity can shield municipal corporations from state tort suits, but concluded that Section 1983 abrogated governmental immunity in situations involving the impairment of federally protected rights.[202]

To avoid liability for constitutional violations, school districts have introduced claims of Eleventh Amendment immunity.[203] The Eleventh Amendment, explicitly prohibiting citizens of one state from bringing suit against another state without its consent, also has been interpreted by the Supreme Court to preclude federal lawsuits against a state by its own citizens.[204] A state can waive this immunity by specifically consenting to be sued, and Congress can abrogate state immunity through legislation enacted to enforce the Fourteenth Amendment. Such congressional intent, however, must be explicit in the federal legislation.[205]

School districts have asserted Eleventh Amendment protection based on the fact that they perform a state function. Admittedly, education is a state function, but it does not necessarily follow that school districts gain Eleventh Amendment immunity against claims of constitutional abridgments. For the Eleventh Amendment to be invoked in a suit against a school district, the state must be the real party

---

[200]Okla. City v. Tuttle, 471 U.S. 808 (1985). *See also* Back v. Hastings on Hudson Union Free Sch. Dist., 365 F.3d 107 (2d Cir. 2004); Wilson *ex rel.* Adams v. Cahokia Sch. Dist. No. 187, 470 F. Supp. 2d 897 (S.D. Ill. 2007).

[201]City of Canton, Ohio v. Harris, 489 U.S. 378 (1989). For a discussion of school district liability in connection with sexual abuse of students by school employees, see text accompanying note 160, Chapter 8.

[202]Owen v. City of Independence, Mo., 445 U.S. 622 (1980). *See* Chapter 13 for a discussion of governmental immunity under tort law.

[203]Under certain circumstances, school districts may be able to use other defenses to preclude liability in a § 1983 suit. Claims that have already been decided in a state case (*res judicata*) or could have been litigated between the same parties in a prior state action (*collateral estoppel*) may be barred in a federal suit under § 1983. *See* Migra v. Warren City Sch. Dist., 465 U.S. 75 (1984); Allen v. McCurry, 449 U.S. 90 (1980).

[204]*See, e.g.*, Hans v. Louisiana, 134 U.S. 1 (1890). *See also* Will v. Mich. Dep't of State Police, 491 U.S. 58 (1989) (holding that § 1983 does not permit a suit against a state; Congress did not intend the word person to include states).

[205]The Supreme Court held that the Family Educational Rights and Privacy Act of 1974 does not explicitly confer individually enforceable rights. Gonzaga Univ. v. Doe, 536 U.S. 273 (2002). Also, in deciding whether an individual can sue a state for money damages in federal court under the Americans with Disabilities Act of 1990, the Supreme Court ruled that Congress did not act within its constitutional authority when it abrogated Eleventh Amendment immunity. Bd. of Trs. v. Garrett, 531 U.S. 356 (2000). *See also* text accompanying note 149, Chapter 3 and note 170, Chapter 10.

in interest. The Third Circuit identified the following factors in determining if a governmental agency, such as a school district, is entitled to Eleventh Amendment protection: (1) whether payment of the judgment will be from the state treasury, (2) whether a governmental or proprietary function is being performed,[206] (3) whether the agency has autonomy over its operation, (4) whether it has the power to sue and be sued, (5) whether it can enter into contracts, and (6) whether the agency's property is immune from state taxation.[207] The most significant of these factors in determining if a district is shielded by Eleventh Amendment immunity has been whether the judgment will be recovered from state funds. If funds are to be paid from the state treasury, courts have declared the state to be the real party in interest.[208]

For many states, the Eleventh Amendment question with respect to school district immunity was resolved in the *Mt. Healthy* case.[209] The Supreme Court concluded that the issue in this case hinged on whether, under Ohio law, a school district is considered an arm of the state as opposed to a municipality or other political subdivision. Considering the taxing power and autonomy of school district operations, the Supreme Court found school districts to be more like counties or cities than extensions of the state. Thus, the Court ruled that school districts could not claim Eleventh Amendment immunity.

Remedies

Depending on employment status, judicial remedies for the violation of protected rights may include compensatory and punitive damages, reinstatement with back pay, and attorneys' fees. The specific nature of the award depends on federal and state statutory provisions and the discretion of courts. Federal and state laws often identify damages that may be recovered or place limitations on types of awards. Unless these provisions restrict specific remedies, courts have broad discretionary power to formulate equitable settlements.

Damages. When a school official or school district is found liable for violating an individual's protected rights, an award of damages is assessed to compensate the

---

[206]*Governmental functions* are those performed in discharging the agency's official duties; *proprietary functions* are often for profit and could be performed by private corporations.

[207]Urbano v. Bd. of Managers, 415 F.2d 247, 250-251 (3d Cir. 1969).

[208]Eleventh Amendment immunity covers only federal suits; it does not have any bearing on immunity in state actions.

[209]Mt. Healthy City Sch. Dist. v. Doyle, 429 U.S. 274 (1977). *See, e.g.,* Missouri v. Jenkins, 495 U.S. 33, 56 (1990); Woods v. Rondout Valley Cent. Sch. Dist. Bd. of Educ., 466 F.3d 232 (2d Cir. 2006); Febres v. Camden Bd. of Educ., 445 F.3d 227 (3d Cir. 2006); Black v. N. Panola Sch. Dist., 461 F.3d 584 (5th Cir. 2006); Crenshaw v. Eudora Sch. Dist., 208 S.W.3d 206 (Ark. 2005). *But see* Belanger v. Madera Unified Sch. Dist., 963 F.2d 248 (9th Cir. 1992) (holding that California school boards are indivisible agencies of the state and thus entitled to Eleventh Amendment immunity).

claimant for the injury.[210] Actual injury must be shown for the aggrieved party to recover damages; without evidence of monetary or mental injury, the plaintiff is entitled only to nominal damages (not to exceed one dollar), even though an impairment of protected rights is established.[211] Significant monetary damages, however, may be awarded for a wrongful termination if a teacher is able to demonstrate substantial losses. At the same time, individuals must make an effort to mitigate damages by seeking appropriate employment.[212]

The Supreme Court held in 1986 that compensatory damages could not be based on a jury's perception of the value or importance of constitutional rights.[213] In this case, involving the award of compensatory damages to a teacher for his unconstitutional dismissal, the Supreme Court declared that although individuals are entitled to full compensation for the injury suffered, they are not entitled to supplementary damages based on the perceived value of the constitutional rights that have been abridged. The Court remanded the case for a determination of the amount of damages necessary to compensate the teacher for the *actual* injury suffered.

In some instances, aggrieved individuals have sought punitive as well as compensatory damages. The judiciary has ruled that school officials can be liable for punitive damages (to punish the wrongdoer) if a jury concludes that the individual's conduct is willful or in reckless and callous disregard of federally protected rights.[214] Punitive as well as compensatory damages were assessed against a principal and superintendent who, without authority, discharged a teacher in retaliation for the exercise of protected speech.[215]

---

[210]*See, e.g.*, McGee v. S. Pemiscot Sch. Dist. R-V, 712 F.2d 339 (8th Cir. 1983) (concluding that even though a teacher-coach, who was dismissed for exercising protected speech, found a higher-paying job, he was entitled to $10,000 in damages for mental anguish, loss of professional reputation, and expenses incurred in obtaining new employment).

[211]*See, e.g.*, Farrar v. Hobby, 506 U.S. 103 (1992) (concluding that an award of nominal damages is mandatory when a procedural due process violation is established but no actual injury is shown); Carey v. Piphus, 435 U.S. 247 (1978) (holding that pupils who were denied procedural due process in a disciplinary proceeding would be entitled only to nominal damages unless it was established that lack of proper procedures resulted in actual injury to the students).

[212]*See, e.g.*, McClure v. Indep. Sch. Dist. No. 16, 228 F.3d 1205 (10th Cir. 2000); McDaniel v. Princeton City Sch. Dist., 45 Fed. Appx 354 (6th Cir. 2002) Boone v. Atlanta Indep. Sch. Sys., 619 S.E.2d 708 (Ga. Ct. App. 2005).

[213]Memphis Cmty. Sch. Dist. v. Stachura, 477 U.S. 299 (1986).

[214]*See, e.g.*, Smith v. Wade, 461 U.S. 30 (1983). In 1991, the Supreme Court refused to place a limit on the amount of punitive damages that properly instructed juries can award in common-law suits, but it did note that extremely high awards might be viewed as unacceptable under the Due Process Clause of the Fourteenth Amendment. Pac. Mut. Life Ins. Co. v. Haslip, 499 U.S. 1 (1991). *See also* Standley v. Chilhowee R-IV Sch. Dist., 5 F.3d 319 (8th Cir. 1993) (holding that evidence did not support evil motive or reckless or callous indifference).

[215]Fishman v. Clancy, 763 F.2d 485 (1st Cir. 1985). *See* Ciccarelli v. Sch. Dep't of Lowell, 877 N.E.2d 609 (Mass. App. Ct. 2007).

In 1981, the Supreme Court ruled that Section 1983 does not authorize the award of punitive damages against a municipality.[216] Recognizing that compensation for injuries is an obligation of a municipality, the Court held that punitive damages were appropriate only for the *individual* wrongdoers and not for the municipality itself. The Court also noted that punitive damages constitute punishment against individuals to deter similar conduct in the future, but they are not intended to punish innocent taxpayers. This ruling does not bar claims for punitive damages for violations of federal rights in school cases, but such claims must be brought against individuals rather than against the school district itself.

The following cases illustrate the diverse circumstances that have resulted in awards of damages. An Illinois school board was required to pay a teacher $750,000 in compensatory damages for wrongfully terminating her for an out-of-wedlock pregnancy.[217] A principal's failure to respond adequately to a student's complaints of sexual abuse by a teacher resulted in an award of $350,000 against the principal.[218] An Ohio teacher's wrongful termination resulted in reinstatement, back wages (including retirement contributions and health insurance costs), and attorneys' fees for a total award of $172,675.[219] A North Carolina teacher received $78,000 in damages based on mental distress evidenced by depression and insomnia following procedural violations in his termination.[220]

Given the success teachers have had in securing damages to compensate for the violation of constitutional rights, school officials should ensure that dismissals or other disciplinary actions are based on legitimate reasons and accompanied by appropriate procedural safeguards. Courts, however, have not awarded damages unless the evidence shows that a teacher has suffered actual injury. As the Supreme Court has noted, compensatory damages are intended to provide full compensation for the loss or injury suffered but are not to be based simply on a jury's perception of the value of the constitutional rights impaired.[221]

---

[216]City of Newport v. Fact Concerts, 453 U.S. 247 (1981).

[217]Eckmann v. Bd. of Educ., 636 F. Supp. 1214 (N.D. Ill. 1986). *See also* Peterson v. Minidoka County Sch. Dist., 118 F.3d 1351 (9th Cir. 1997) (upholding a damage award of $300,000 as well as attorneys' fees for the school board's reassignment of a principal because he proposed to home school his children); Welton v. Osborn, 124 F. Supp. 2d 1114 (S.D. Ohio 2000) (awarding $177,000 in compensatory damages, $65,625 in punitive damages, and $77,747 in attorneys' fees and costs against the superintendent for retaliation toward the principal for exercising constitutionally protected speech).

[218]Baynard v. Malone, 268 F.3d 228 (4th Cir. 2001).

[219]McDaniel v. Princeton City Sch. Dist. Bd. of Educ., 45 Fed. Appx. 354 (6th Cir. 2002). *See also* Glover v. Williamsburg Local Sch. Dist. Bd. of Educ., 20 F. Supp. 2d 1160 (S.D. Ohio. 1998) (awarding compensatory damages of $71,494 and reinstatement for two years for impermissible nonrenewal based on sexual orientation).

[220]Crump v. Bd. of Educ., 392 S.E.2d 579 (N.C. 1990) (awarding damages for procedural violation even though discharge was upheld). *See also* Dishnow v. Sch. Dist. of Rib Lake, 77 F.3d 194 (7th Cir. 1996) (upholding a damages award for humiliation and injury to reputation in the firing of a teacher based on the exercise of his free speech rights).

[221]Memphis Cmty. Sch. Dist. v. Stachura, 477 U.S. 299 (1986).

Reinstatement. Whether a court orders reinstatement as a remedy for school board action depends on the protected interests involved and the discretion of the court, unless specific provision for reinstatement is specified in state law. If a tenured teacher is unjustly dismissed, the property interest gives rise to an expectation of reemployment; reinstatement in such instances is usually the appropriate remedy. A nontenured teacher wrongfully dismissed during the contract period, however, is normally entitled only to damages, not reinstatement.

A valid property or liberty claim entitles a teacher to procedural due process, but the teacher can still be dismissed for cause after proper procedures have been followed. If a teacher is terminated without proper procedures and can establish that the action is not justified, reinstatement will be ordered.[222] If proven that the actual reason for the nonrenewal of a teacher's contract is retaliation for the exercise of constitutional rights (e.g., protected speech), reinstatement would be warranted, although substantiation of such a claim is difficult.

The failure to comply with statutory requirements in nonrenewals and dismissals may result in reinstatement. When statutory dates are specified for notice of nonrenewal, failure to comply strictly with the deadline provides grounds for reinstatement of the teacher. Courts may interpret this as continued employment for an additional year[223] or reinstatement with tenure if nonrenewal occurs at the end of the probationary period. In contrast to the remedy for lack of proper notice, the remedy for failure to provide an appropriate hearing is generally a remand for a hearing, not reinstatement.

Attorneys' Fees. Attorneys' fees are not automatically granted to the teacher who prevails in a lawsuit but are generally dependent on statutory authorization. At the federal level, the Civil Rights Attorneys' Fees Award Act gives federal courts discretion to award fees in civil rights suits.[224] In congressional debate concerning attorneys' fees, it was stated "private citizens must be given not only the right to go to court, but also the legal resources. If the citizen does not have the resources, his day in court is denied him."[225]

To receive attorneys' fees, the teacher must be the prevailing party; that is, damages or some form of equitable relief must be granted to the teacher. The Supreme Court has held that a prevailing party is one who is successful in achieving some benefit on any significant issue in the case, but not necessarily the primary issue. At a minimum, the Court ruled, "the plaintiff must be able to point to a resolution of the dispute which changes the legal relationship between itself and the

---

[222]*See, e.g.,* Brewer v. Chauvin, 938 F.2d 860 (8th Cir. 1991); McDaniel 45 Fed. Appx. 354. *But see* Hanover Sch. Dist. No. 28 v. Barbour, 171 P.3d 223 (Colo. 2007) (awarding back pay but not reinstatement).

[223]*See, e.g.,* Kiel v. Green Local Sch. Dist. Bd. of Educ., 630 N.E.2d 716 (Ohio 1994).

[224]42 U.S.C. § 1988 (2007).

[225]122 Cong. Rec. 33,313 (1976).

defendant."[226] If a plaintiff achieves only partial success, the fees requested may be reduced.[227]

Because Section 1983 does not require exhaustion of state administrative proceedings before initiating litigation, the Supreme Court has denied the award of attorneys' fees for school board administrative proceedings conducted prior to filing a federal suit. Unlike Title VII's explicit requirement that individuals must pursue administrative remedies, plaintiffs can bring a Section 1983 claim directly to a federal court. In a wrongful termination case, a Tennessee teacher was awarded attorneys' fees as a prevailing litigant for the time spent on the judicial proceedings but was unsuccessful in persuading the Supreme Court that the local administrative proceedings were part of the preparation for court action.[228]

Although it has been established that the plaintiff who prevails in a civil rights suit may, at the court's discretion, be entitled to attorneys' fees, the same standard is not applied to defendants.[229] When a plaintiff teacher is awarded attorneys' fees, the assessment is against a party who has violated a federal law. Different criteria are applied when a prevailing defendant seeks attorneys' fees. The Supreme Court has held that such fees cannot be imposed on a plaintiff unless the claim was "frivolous, unreasonable, or groundless."[230] Although awards of damages to prevailing defendants have not been common, in some situations such awards have been made to deter groundless lawsuits.

Conclusion

Through state laws and the federal Constitution, extensive safeguards protect educators' employment security. Most states have adopted tenure laws that precisely delineate teachers' employment rights in termination and disciplinary proceedings. Additionally, in the absence of specific state guarantees, the Fourteenth Amendment ensures that teachers will be afforded procedural due process when property or liberty interests are implicated. Legal decisions interpreting both state and federal rights in dismissal actions have established broad guidelines as to when due process

---

[226]Tex. State Teachers Ass'n v. Garland Indep. Sch. Dist., 489 U.S. 782, 792 (1989). *See also* Sutton v. Cleveland Bd. of Educ., 958 F.2d 1339 (6th Cir. 1992); Farner v. Idaho Falls Schs. Dist., 17 P.3d 281 (Idaho 2000).

[227]*See, e.g.*, Standley v. Chilhowee R-IV Sch. Dist., 5 F.3d 319 (8th Cir. 1993).

[228]Webb v. Bd. of Educ., 471 U.S. 234 (1985). *See also* N.C. Dep't of Transp. v. Crest St. Cmty., 479 U.S. 6 (1986) (ruling that attorneys' fees could not be recovered in administrative proceedings independent of enforcement of Title VI of the Civil Rights Act of 1964).

[229]*But see* Daddow v. Carlsbad Mun. Sch. Dist., 898 P.2d 1235 (N.M. 1995) (applying state law that entitles the prevailing party to an award of costs unless the court rules otherwise).

[230]Christiansburg Garment Co. v. EEOC, 434 U.S. 412, 422 (1978). *See also* Jefferson v. Jefferson County Pub. Sch. Sys., 360 F.3d 583 (6th Cir. 2004); Bisciglia v. Kenosha Unified Sch. Dist. No. 1, 45 F.3d 223 (7th Cir. 1995).

is required, the types of procedures that must be provided, and the legitimate causes required to substantiate dismissal action. Generalizations applicable to teacher employment termination are enumerated here.

1. A teacher is entitled to procedural due process if dismissal impairs a property or liberty interest.

2. Tenure status, defined by state law, confers upon teachers a property interest in continued employment; tenured teachers can be dismissed only for cause specified in state law.

3. Courts generally have held that probationary employment does not involve a property interest, except within the contract period.

4. A probationary teacher may establish a liberty interest, and thus entitlement to a hearing, if nonrenewal implicates a constitutional right, imposes a stigma, or forecloses opportunities for future employment.

5. When a liberty or property interest is implicated, the Fourteenth Amendment requires that a teacher be notified of charges and provided with an opportunity for a hearing that includes representation by counsel, examination and cross-examination of witnesses, and a record of the proceedings; however, formal trial procedures are not required.

6. An adequate notice of dismissal must adhere to statutory deadlines, follow designated form, allow the teacher time to prepare for a hearing, and specify charges.

7. The school board is considered an impartial hearing tribunal unless bias of its members can be clearly established.

8. The school board bears the burden of proof to introduce sufficient evidence to support a teacher's dismissal.

9. Causes for dismissal vary widely among the states, but usually include such grounds as incompetency, neglect of duty, immorality, insubordination, unprofessional conduct, and other good and just cause.

10. Incompetency is generally defined in relation to classroom performance—classroom management, teaching methods, grading, pupil/teacher relationships, and general attitude.

11. Immoral conduct, as the basis for dismissal, includes dishonest acts, improper sexual conduct, criminal acts, drug-related conduct, and other improprieties that have a negative impact on the teacher's effectiveness.

12. Dismissal for insubordination is based on a teacher's refusal to follow school regulations and policies.

13. Declining enrollment and financial exigencies constitute adequate causes for dismissing tenured teachers.

14. Wrongfully terminated employees may be entitled to reinstatement with back pay, compensatory and punitive damages, and attorneys' fees for the violation of constitutional rights.

15. An individual can recover only nominal damages for the impairment of constitutional rights unless monetary, emotional, or mental injury can be proven.

16. School officials can plead immunity to protect themselves from liability if their actions were taken in good faith; ignorance of clearly established principles of law is evidence of bad faith.

17. School districts cannot plead good faith as a defense against Section 1983 liability for compensatory damages in connection with the impairment of federally protected civil rights.

18. Punitive damages to punish the wrongdoer can be assessed against individual school officials but not against school districts.

19. Most courts have not considered school districts an arm of the state for purposes of Eleventh Amendment immunity from federal suits initiated by the state's citizens.

12

Labor Relations

Historically, boards of education had unilateral control over the management and operation of public schools. Teachers, as employees of the school board, were only minimally involved in decision making. To achieve a balance of power and a voice in school affairs, teachers turned to collective action during the 1960s and acquired significant labor rights. Labor laws and judicial rulings governing this shift in power were modeled after private-sector bargaining, resulting in labor relations in schools taking on an adversarial character.[1]

At the most fundamental level, collective bargaining pits teachers' demands for improved wages, hours, and conditions of employment against school boards' efforts to retain authority over educational policies and school operations. However, since the emergence of formalized collective bargaining in the early 1960s, negotiated contracts have evolved from a few pages addressing salaries to lengthy agreements that frequently are complex and impenetrable. Moreover, labor relations also are controlled by numerous other documents interpreting or amending the contract such as state labor relations board decisions, arbitration rulings, and memoranda of understanding related to the operation of the contract that often lead to limited flexibility for teachers and administrators.[2]

Diversity in labor laws and bargaining practices among the states makes it difficult to generalize about collective bargaining and teachers' labor rights. State labor laws, state employment relations board rulings, and court decisions must be consulted to determine specific rights, because there is no federal labor law covering public school employees.[3] Over two-thirds of the states have enacted bargaining laws,

---

[1]Pressures to reform schools have focused attention on creating collaborative negotiation processes that reduce the adversarial nature of conventional bargaining. While some innovations have been implemented in the bargaining process, the basic legal structure explored in this chapter remains unchanged and shapes labor relations in school districts.

[2]For an analysis of this "contract behind the contract," *see* Howard Fuller, George Mitchell, and Michael Hartmann, *The Milwaukee Public Schools' Teacher Union Contract: Its History, Content, and Impact on Education* (Milwaukee, WI: Institute for Transformation of Learning, Marquette University, 1997).

[3]*See infra* text accompanying note 19.

438

varying widely in coverage from very comprehensive laws controlling most aspects of negotiations to laws granting the minimal right to meet and confer. Still other states, in the absence of legislation, rely on judicial rulings to define the basic rights of public employees in the labor relations arena. This chapter examines the legal structure in which bargaining occurs and public school teachers' employment rights under state labor laws.[4]

Employees' Bargaining Rights in the Private and Public Sectors

Although there are basic differences in employment between the public and private sectors, collective bargaining legislation in the private sector has been significant in shaping statutory and judicial regulation of public negotiations. Similarities between the two sectors can be noted in a number of areas, such as unfair labor practices, union representation, and impasse procedures. Because of the influence of private-sector legislation on the public sector, a brief overview of its major legislative acts is warranted.

Prior to the 1930s, labor relations in the private sector were dominated by the judiciary, which strongly favored management. The extensive use of judicial injunctions against strikes and boycotts effectively countered employee efforts to obtain recognition for purposes of bargaining.[5] Consequently, courts reinforced the powers of management and substantially curtailed the development and influence of unions. To bolster the position of the worker, Congress enacted the Norris-LaGuardia Act in 1932.[6] The purpose of this federal law was to circumscribe the role of courts in labor disputes by preventing the use of the injunction, except where union activities were unlawful or jeopardized public safety and health. In essence, the legislation did not confer any new rights on employees or unions but simply restricted judicial authority that had impeded the development of unions.

Following the Norris-LaGuardia Act, in 1935 Congress passed the National Labor Relations Act (NLRA), commonly known as the Wagner Act.[7] This act created

---

[4]As collective bargaining has matured in the public sector, state labor relations board decisions have become a substantial source of legal precedent for each state with courts rendering fewer decisions in the labor arena. In fact, courts defer to the boards' rulings unless they are clearly contrary to law. While specific rulings of labor boards are not included in this chapter, educators are encouraged to examine that extensive body of law if a board governs negotiations in their state.

[5]For a historical discussion of the use and control of labor injunctions, *see* Fred Witney and Benjamin Taylor, *Labor Relations Law*, 7th ed. (Englewood Cliffs, NJ: Prentice Hall, 1996).

[6]29 U.S.C. § 101 (2007). This act also rendered "yellow dog" contracts, which required employees to promise not to join a union, unenforceable by courts.

[7]The Wagner Act states that "employees shall have the right to self-organization, to form, join or assist labor organizations, to bargain collectively through representatives of their own choosing, and to engage in concerted activities, for the purpose of collective bargaining or other mutual aid or protection." 29 U.S.C. § 157 (2007).

substantial rights for private-sector employees, but one of the most important outcomes was that it granted legitimacy to the collective bargaining process. In addition to defining employees' rights to organize and bargain collectively, the act established a mechanism to safeguard these rights—the National Labor Relations Board (NLRB). The NLRB was created specifically to monitor claims of unfair labor practices, such as interference with employees' rights to organize, discrimination against employees in hiring or discharge because of union membership, and failure to bargain in good faith.[8]

Congress amended the NLRA in 1947 with the enactment of the Labor Management Relations Act (commonly known as the Taft-Hartley Act).[9] While the Wagner Act regulated employers' activities, the Taft-Hartley Act was an attempt to balance the scales in collective bargaining by regulating abusive union practices, such as interfering with employees' organizational rights, failing to provide fair representation for all employees in the bargaining unit, and refusing to bargain in good faith. Since 1947 other amendments to the Taft-Hartley Act have further limited union abuses. Federal legislation has restricted interference from both the employer and the union, thereby ensuring the individual employee greater freedom of choice in collective bargaining.

Although the NLRA specifically exempted bargaining by governmental employees, a number of state public employee statutes have been modeled after this law, and judicial decisions interpreting the NLRA have been used to define certain provisions in public-sector laws. The recognition of the sovereign power of public employers, however, is clearly present in public labor laws. For example, many public laws require employers to bargain over wages, hours, and other terms and conditions of employment as in the NLRA, but this requirement then is restricted by management rights clauses limiting the scope of bargaining.

---

[8]The application of private-sector labor laws to private schools, most of which are church related, has been controversial. Only private schools with a gross annual revenue of $1 million or more come under the jurisdiction of the NLRB; however, the majority of private schools do not reach this income level. Furthermore, the United States Supreme Court has held that the NLRB does not have jurisdiction over lay faculty in parochial schools in the absence of a clear expression of congressional intent to cover teachers in church-related schools under the NLRA. Nat'l Labor Relations Bd. v. Catholic Bishop of Chi., 440 U.S. 490 (1979). The Second Circuit, however, concluded that Catholic schools in New York come under the jurisdiction of the state labor relations board. Since the ruling involved bargaining activities of lay teachers regarding only secular employment practices, no infringement of the Establishment Clause or Free Exercise Clause of the First Amendment was found. Catholic High Sch. Ass'n v. Culvert, 753 F.2d 1161 (2d Cir. 1985). See also S. Jersey Catholic Sch. Teachers Org. v. St. Teresa, 696 A.2d 709 (N.J. 1997) (finding that the state labor law was a generally applicable law, neutral in its application and not intended to regulate religious conduct or belief); N.Y. State Employment Relations Bd. v. Christ the King Reg'l High Sch., 682 N.E.2d 960 (N.Y. 1997) (ruling that the state labor relations law in its application to lay teachers did not violate the Free Exercise Clause or Establishment Clause). But see M.E.A. v. Christian Bros. Inst., 706 N.W.2d 423 (Mich. Ct. App. 2005) (deciding that the legislature did not grant the Michigan Employment Relations Commission jurisdiction over lay teachers in parochial schools).

[9]29 U.S.C. §§ 141 *et seq.* (2007).

There are several basic differences in bargaining between the public and private sectors. First, the removal of decision-making authority from public officials through bargaining has been viewed as an infringement on the government's sovereign power, which has resulted in the enactment of labor laws strongly favoring public employers. Public employees' rights have been further weakened by prohibitions of work stoppages. Whereas employees' ability to strike is considered *essential* to the effective operation of collective decision making in the private sector, this view has been rejected in the public sector because of the nature and structure of governmental services.

Bargaining rights developed slowly for public employees, who historically had been deprived of the right to organize and bargain collectively. President Kennedy's Executive Order 10988 in 1962, which gave federal employees the right to form, join, and assist employee organizations, was a significant milestone for all public employees. The granting of organizational rights to federal employees provided the impetus for similar gains at the state and local levels.

Until the late 1960s, however, public employees' constitutional right to join a union had not been fully established. A large number of public employees actively participated in collective bargaining, but statutes and regulations in some states prohibited union membership. These restrictions against union membership were challenged as impairing association freedoms protected by the First Amendment. Although not addressing union membership, the Supreme Court held in 1967 that public employment could not be conditioned on the relinquishment of free association rights.[10] In a later decision, the Seventh Circuit clearly announced that "an individual's right to form and join a union is protected by the First Amendment."[11] Other courts followed this precedent by invalidating state statutory provisions that blocked union membership.[12]

Similar to other public employees, the judiciary acknowledged teachers' constitutional rights to participate fully in union activities. School officials have been prohibited from imposing sanctions or denying benefits to discourage protected association rights. For example, the Sixth Circuit overturned a school board's dismissal of a teacher because of union activities.[13] The Eighth Circuit held that a teacher's allegation that the superintendent placed her on probation to punish her for union activities was sufficient to establish a claim against the superintendent.[14] Similarly, the Connecticut Federal District Court found that the transfer of a teacher to

[10]Keyishian v. Bd. of Regents, 385 U.S. 589 (1967).

[11]McLaughlin v. Tilendis, 398 F.2d 287, 289 (7th Cir. 1968). *See also* St. Clair County Intermediate Sch. Dist. v. St. Clair County Educ. Ass'n, 630 N.W.2d 909 (Mich. Ct. App. 2001) (ruling that a school district violated a school nurse's rights when a supervisor told her either not to join the union or face losing her job).

[12]*See, e.g.*, Atkins v. City of Charlotte, 296 F. Supp. 1068 (W.D.N.C. 1969); Dade County Classroom Teachers' Ass'n v. Ryan, 225 So. 2d 903 (Fla. 1969).

[13]Hickman v. Valley Local Sch. Dist. Bd. of Educ., 619 F.2d 606 (6th Cir. 1980). *See also* Cent. Sch. Dist. 13J v. Cent. Educ. Ass'n, 962 P.2d 763 (Or. Ct. App. 1998) (ruling that teacher could not be discharged for exercising association rights protected under state law).

[14]Springdale Educ. Ass'n v. Springdale Sch. Dist., 133 F.3d 649 (8th Cir. 1998).

another school in retaliation for using the negotiated grievance procedure was constitutionally prohibited.[15]

The United States Constitution has been interpreted as protecting public employees' rights to organize, but the right to form and join a union does not ensure the right to bargain collectively with a public employer; individual state statutes and constitutions govern such bargaining rights. Whether identified as professional negotiations, collective negotiations, or collective bargaining, the process entails bilateral decision making in which the teachers' representative and the school board attempt to reach mutual agreement on matters affecting teacher employment. This process is governed in 34 states by legislation granting specific bargaining rights to teachers and their professional associations. Courts, viewing collective bargaining as within the scope of legislative authority, have restricted their role primarily to interpreting statutory and constitutional provisions. The judiciary has been reluctant to interfere with legislative authority to define the collective bargaining relationship between public employers and employees unless protected rights have been compromised.

Because of the variations in labor laws, as well as the lack of such laws in some states, substantial differences exist in bargaining rights and practices. A few states, such as New York, have a detailed, comprehensive collective bargaining statute that delineates specific bargaining rights. In contrast, negotiated contracts between teachers' organizations and school boards are prohibited in North Carolina. Under North Carolina law, all contracts between public employers and employee associations are invalid.[16] Similarly, the Virginia Supreme Court declared that a negotiated contract between a teachers' organization and a school board is null and void in the absence of express enabling legislation.[17] The board maintained that its power to enter into contracts allowed it also to bargain collectively with employee organizations, but the court concluded that such implied power was contrary to legislative intent.

In contrast to North Carolina and Virginia, other states without legislation have permitted negotiated agreements. The Kentucky Supreme Court ruled that a public employer may recognize an employee organization for the purpose of collective bargaining, even though state law is silent regarding public employee bargaining rights.[18] The decision does not impose a duty on local school boards to bargain but

---

[15]Stellmaker v. DePetrillo, 710 F. Supp. 891 (D. Conn. 1989). *See also* Morfin v. Albuquerque Pub. Sch., 906 F.2d 1434 (10th Cir. 1990) (recognizing teacher's right to associate with a union and to file a grievance); Rockville Centre Teachers Ass'n v. N.Y. State Pub. Employment Relations Bd., 721 N.Y.S.2d 112 (App. Div. 2001) (holding that employees must establish a connection between an adverse employment decision and union activity); State Employment Relations Bd. v. Adena Local Sch. Dist. Bd. of Educ., 613 N.E.2d 605 (Ohio 1993) (finding retaliation prohibited under public bargaining law).

[16]N.C. Gen. Stat. § 95–98 (2007).

[17]Commonwealth v. County Bd. of Arlington County, 232 S.E.2d 30 (Va. 1977).

[18]Bd. of Trs. of Univ. of Ky. v. Pub. Employees Council No. 51, 571 S.W.2d 616 (Ky. 1978). *See also* Independence-Nat'l Educ. Ass'n v. Independence Sch. Dist., 223 S.W.3d 131 (Mo. 2007), *overruling* City of Springfield v. Clouse, 206 S.W.2d 539, 542 (Mo. 1947) (holding that state constitutional provision guaranteeing "employees" the right to organize and bargain collectively includes both public and private employees).

merely allows a board the discretion to negotiate. This ruling is consistent with a number of other decisions permitting negotiated contracts in the absence of specific legislation. The board's power and authority to enter into contracts for the operation and maintenance of the school system have been construed to include the ability to enter into negotiated agreements with employee organizations.

Unless bargaining is mandated by statute, courts have not compelled school boards to negotiate. Whether to negotiate is thus at the school board's discretion. Once a school board extends recognition to a bargaining agent and commences bargaining, however, the board's actions in the negotiation process are governed by established judicial principles. Although the employer maintains certain prerogatives, such as recognition of the bargaining unit and determination of bargainable items, specific judicially recognized rights also are conferred on the employee organization. For example, there is a legal duty for the board to bargain in good faith. Furthermore, if the negotiation process reaches an impasse, the board may not unilaterally terminate bargaining. Also, after signing a contract, the board is bound by the provisions and cannot abrogate the agreement on the basis that no duty existed to bargain. Hence, the school board is subject to a number of legal constraints after it enters into the negotiation process.

The diversity across states in protected bargaining rights for public employees has led many individuals and groups to advocate a federal bargaining law for all state and local employees. Several national organizations have supported such a proposal, including the National Education Association, the American Federation of Teachers, and the American Federation of State, County, and Municipal Employees. Although it appears that a federal law would be within congressional authority under the Commerce Clause,[19] for the immediate future, bargaining rights seem destined to be controlled either by individual state legislation or, in the absence of such legislation, by court rulings.

Teachers' Statutory Bargaining Rights

In the states that have enacted statutes governing teachers' bargaining rights, school boards must negotiate with teachers in accordance with the statutorily prescribed process. Generally, public employee bargaining laws address employer and employee rights, bargaining units, scope of bargaining, impasse resolution, grievance procedures, unfair labor practices, and penalties for prohibited practices. Many states have established labor relations boards to monitor bargaining under their statutes. Although the specific functions of these boards vary widely, their general purpose is to resolve questions arising from the implementation of state law. Functions assigned to such boards include determination of membership in bargaining units, resolution of union recognition claims, investigation of unfair labor practices, and interpretation of the general intent of statutory bargaining

---

[19]*See* Garcia v. San Antonio Metro. Transit Auth., 469 U.S. 528 (1985).

clauses. Usually, judicial review cannot be pursued until administrative review before labor boards is exhausted. Thus, decisions of labor boards are an important source of labor law, since many of the issues addressed by boards are never appealed to courts. When the boards' decisions are challenged in court, substantial deference is given to their findings and determinations.[20]

State laws generally provide that the school board will negotiate with an exclusive representative selected by the teachers. Procedures are specified for certification of the bargaining representative, election of the representative by employees, and recognition by the employer. Once the state labor relations board recognizes an exclusive representative, the employer must bargain with that representative. In addition to certification, state laws address cause and process for decertification of the exclusive representative.

Like the NLRA, state statutes require bargaining "in good faith." Good faith bargaining has been interpreted as requiring parties to meet at reasonable times and attempt to reach mutual agreement without compulsion on either side to agree. A number of states have followed the federal law in stipulating that this "does not compel either party to agree to a proposal or to require the making of a concession."[21] However, it does mean that an employer cannot make unilateral changes in a term or condition in the contract to circumvent its obligation to bargain collectively.[22] Good faith bargaining has been open to a range of interpretations, and judicial decisions in the public sector have relied extensively on private-sector rulings that have clarified the phrase.

Statutes impose certain restrictions or obligations on both the school board and the employee organization. Violation of the law by either party can result in an *unfair labor practice* claim with the imposition of penalties. Allegations of unfair labor practices are brought before the state public employee relations board for a hearing and judgment. Specific unfair labor practices, often modeled after those in the NLRA, are included in state statutes. The most common prohibited labor practice in both public and private employment is that an employer or union will not interfere with, restrain, or coerce public employees in exercising their rights under the labor law.[23] Among other prohibited *employer* practices are interference with union operations, discrimination against employees because of union membership,

---

[20]*See, e.g., In re* Laconia Sch. Dist., 840 A.2d 800 (N.H. 2004); Dodgeland Educ. Ass'n v. Wis. Employment Relations Comm'n, 639 N.W. 2d 733 (Wis. 2002).

[21]29 U.S.C. § 158(d) (2007). *See also* Bd. of Educ. v. Sered, 850 N.E.2d 821 (Ill. App. Ct. 2006) (finding that a tentative oral agreement made by the board's representatives was valid; the board could not disregard or modify the terms of the agreement).

[22]Educ. Minn.-Greenway v. Indep. Sch. Dist., 673 N.W.2d 843 (Minn. Ct. App. 2004).

[23]*See, e.g.,* Fort Frye Teachers Ass'n v. SERB, 809 N.E.2d 1130 (Ohio 2004) (ruling the nonrenewal of teacher's contract for union activities constitutes an unfair labor practice; SERB was directed to act upon court's finding); Uniontown Area Sch. Dist. v. Pa. Labor Relations Bd., 747 A.2d 1271 (Pa. Commw. Ct. 2000) (concluding that the school district committed an unfair labor practice when it did not promote a teacher to principal because of concerns about her union activities).

refusal to bargain collectively with the exclusive representative, and failure to bargain in good faith. *Unions* are prevented from causing an employer to discriminate against employees on the basis of union membership, refusing to bargain or failing to bargain in good faith, failing to represent all employees in the bargaining unit, and engaging in unlawful activities such as strikes or boycotts identified in the bargaining law.

Upon completion of the negotiation process, the members of the bargaining unit and the school board must ratify the written agreement (usually referred to as the *master contract*). These agreements often contain similar standard contract language and clauses, beginning with recognition of the exclusive bargaining representative and union security issues (i.e., fair share fees). Management rights and association rights also are detailed. Management clauses emphasize the board's control over the establishment of educational policies, and union clauses may include the right to use school facilities or communication systems. The remaining provisions relate to the scope of bargaining, which is defined by the state's labor law or common law. These items include not only salary and fringe benefits but also may address grievance procedures, employee evaluations, preparation time, length of workday, class size, procedural process for employee discipline, transfers, layoff and recall procedures, assignment of duties, and procedures for filling vacancies. The range in the negotiability of these issues can be seen in the next section.

Scope of Negotiations

Should the teachers' organization have input into class size? Who will determine the length of the school day? How will extra-duty assignments be determined? Will reductions in force necessitated by declining enrollment be based on seniority or merit? These questions and others are raised in determining the scope of negotiations. *Scope* refers to the range of issues or subjects that are negotiable, and determining scope is one of the most difficult tasks in public-sector bargaining. Public employers argue that issues must be narrowly defined to protect the government's policy-making role, whereas employee unions counter that bargaining subjects must be defined broadly for negotiations to be meaningful.

Restrictions on scope of bargaining vary considerably among states. Consequently, to determine a particular state's negotiable items, the state's collective bargaining law, other statutes, and litigation interpreting these laws must be examined. The specification of negotiable items in labor laws may include broad guidelines or detailed enumeration. Many states have modeled their bargaining statutes after the National Labor Relations Act, which stipulates that representatives of the employer and employees must meet and confer "with respect to wages, hours, and other terms and conditions of employment."[24] A few states have elected to deal directly with the

[24]29 U.S.C. § 158(d) (2007).

scope of bargaining by identifying each item that must be negotiated.[25] Some states specify prohibited subjects of bargaining. For example, Michigan's prohibited subjects include decisions related to the establishment of the starting date for the school year, composition of site-based decision-making bodies, interdistrict and intradistrict open enrollment opportunities, authorization of public school academies, use of volunteers in providing services at schools, and establishment and staffing of experimental programs.[26] Generally, statutory mandates cannot be preempted by collective bargaining agreements;[27] however, in a few states, the negotiated agreement prevails over conflicting laws, unless the laws are specifically exempted.[28]

All proposed subjects for negotiation can be classified as mandatory, permissive, or prohibited. Mandatory items must be negotiated.[29] Failure of the school board to meet and confer on such items is evidence of lack of good faith bargaining. Permissive items can be negotiated if both parties agree; however, there is no legal duty to consider the items. Furthermore, in most states permissive items cannot be pursued to the point of negotiation impasse, and an employer can make unilateral changes with respect to these items if a negotiated agreement is not reached. Prohibited items are beyond the power of the board to negotiate; an illegal delegation of power results if the board agrees to negotiate regarding these items. Since most statutory scope provisions are general in nature, courts or labor relations boards often have been asked to differentiate between negotiable and nonnegotiable items.[30] The following sections highlight issues related to governmental policy and specific bargaining topics.

[25]*See, e.g.,* Iowa Code § 20.9 (2007); Nev. Rev. Stat. § 288.150 (2007). *See also* Blount County Educ. Ass'n v. Blount County Bd. of Educ., 78 S.W.3d 307 (Tenn. Ct. App. 2002) (ruling that the state legislature did not intend to give "working conditions" a broad interpretation when it specifically listed eight mandatory bargaining topics).

[26]Mich. Comp. Laws § 423.215(3)(4) (2007). *See also* Mich. State AFL-CIO v. Mich. Employment Relations Comm'n, 551 N.W. 2d 165 (Mich. 1996).

[27]*See, e.g.,* Bd. of Educ. v. Ill. Educ. Labor Relations Bd., 649 N.E.2d 369 (Ill. 1995); Lucio v. Sch. Bd., 574 N.W.2d 737 (Minn. Ct. App. 1998); Mifflinburg Area Educ. Ass'n v. Mifflinburg Area Sch. Dist., 724 A.2d 339 (Pa. 1999). Furthermore, collective bargaining agreements cannot deprive individuals of rights guaranteed by federal laws. Abrahamson v. Bd. of Educ. of Wappingers Falls Cent. Sch. Dist., 374 F.3d 66 (2d Cir. 2004).

[28]*See, e.g.,* Streetsboro Educ. Ass'n v. Streetsboro City Sch. Dist., 626 N.E.2d 110 (Ohio 1994). *See also* State Dep't of Admin. v. Pub. Employees Relations Bd., 894 P.2d 777 (Kan. 1995) (holding that collective bargaining agreement takes precedence over conflicting civil service regulations).

[29]Wages definitely fall within the mandatory category. A wage-related area that has received recent attention is the payment of "signing bonuses" to attract teachers for difficult to fill positions. Failure to bargain these payments may constitute an unfair labor practice. *See, e.g.,* Ekalaka Unified Bd. of Trs. v. Ekalaka Teachers' Ass'n, 149 P.3d 902 (Mont. 2006); Crete Educ. Ass'n v. Salie County Sch. Dist., 654 N.W.2d 166 (Neb. 2002).

[30]*See* Junction City Educ. Ass'n v. Bd. of Educ., 955 P.2d 1266 (Kan. 1998) (ruling that issues of negotiability should be determined initially by the state administrative agency rather than through a declaratory judgment action in a district court).

Governmental Policy

Defining managerial rights is one of the key elements in establishing limitations on negotiable subjects at the bargaining table. State laws specify that public employers cannot be required to negotiate governmental policy matters, and courts have held that it is impermissible for a school board to bargain away certain rights and responsibilities in the public policy area.[31] Generally, educational policy matters are defined through provisions in collective bargaining statutes, such as "management rights" and "scope of bargaining" clauses. Policy issues (e.g., class size and decisions related to the granting of tenure) are totally excluded as negotiable items in a few states; however, most states stipulate only that employers will not be *required* to bargain policy rights.

Public employee labor laws requiring the negotiation of "conditions of employment" can include far-reaching policy matters since most decisions made by a school board either directly or indirectly affect the teacher at the classroom level. The difficulty in distinguishing between educational policy and matters relating to teachers' employment was noted by the Maryland high court: "Virtually every managerial decision in some way relates to 'salaries, wages, hours, and other working conditions,' and is therefore arguably negotiable. At the same time, virtually every such decision also involves educational policy considerations and is therefore arguably nonnegotiable."[32] In many states, the interpretation of what is negotiable resides with the labor relations board. Often, these boards as well as courts employ a balancing test, beginning with an inquiry into whether a particular matter involves wages, hours, and terms and conditions of employment. If it does, then the labor board or court must determine if the matter also is one of inherent managerial policy. If the response is *no* to this second question, the matter is a mandatory subject of bargaining. However, if the response is *yes*, then the benefits of bargaining on the decision-making process must be balanced against the burden on the employer's authority.[33] Accordingly, this process entails a fact-specific analysis.

Judicial decisions interpreting negotiability illustrate the range in bargainable matters. The Supreme Court of New Jersey narrowly interpreted "conditions of employment" to mean wages, benefits, and work schedules, thereby removing

---

[31]*See, e.g.*, Montgomery County Educ. Ass'n v. Bd. of Educ., 534 A.2d 980 (Md. 1987); Bd. of Educ. v. N.Y. State Pub. Employment Relations Bd., 554 N.E.2d 1247, 1251 (N.Y. 1990); Raines v. Indep. Sch. Dist. No. 6, 796 P.2d 303 (Okla. 1990). *See also* City Univ. of N.Y. v. Prof. Staff Cong., 837 N.Y.S.2d 121 (App. Div. 2007) (holding that employer could not bargain away its right to inspect teacher personnel files; agreement was against public policy to investigate discrimination complaints).

[32]*Montgomery County Educ. Ass'n*, 534 A.2d at 986.

[33]*See, e.g.,* Cent. City Educ. Ass'n v. Ill. Educ. Labor Relations Bd., 599 N.E.2d 892 (Ill. 1992); City of Beloit v. Wis. Employment Relations Bd., 242 N.W.2d 231 (Wis. 1976); Dodgeland Educ. Ass'n v. Wis. Employment Relations Comm'n, 639 N.W. 2d 733 (Wis. 2002*). See also* Sherrard Cmty. Unit Sch. v. Ill. Educ. Labor Relations Bd., 696 N.E.2d 833 (Ill. App. Ct. 1998) (finding that reassignment of teachers involves exercise of managerial discretion that generally is not a mandatory bargaining subject; actions of school board in directly negotiating with a teacher made it a mandatory subject).

governmental policy items such as teacher transfers, course offerings, and evalua-tions.[34] A number of courts, however, have construed conditions of employment in broader terms. As such, the Nevada Supreme Court ruled that items *significantly* related to wages, hours, and working conditions are negotiable.[35] Similarly, the Penn-sylvania Supreme Court concluded that an issue's *impact* on conditions of employ-ment must be weighed in determining whether it should be considered outside the educational policy area.[36]

Even though courts are in agreement that school boards cannot be *required* to negotiate inherent managerial rights pertaining to policy matters, these rights are viewed as *permissive* subjects of bargaining in some states. That is, the board may agree to negotiate a particular "right" in the absence of statutory or judicial prohibi-tions.[37] If the board does negotiate a policy item, it is bound by the agreement in the same manner as if the issue were a mandatory item.[38]

Selected Bargaining Subjects

Beyond wages, hours, and fringe benefits, there is a lack of agreement among states as to what is negotiable. Similar enabling legislation has been interpreted quite dif-ferently among states, as illustrated by the subjects discussed below.

---

[34]Ridgefield Park Educ. Ass'n v. Ridgefield Park Bd. of Educ., 393 A.2d 278 (N.J. 1978). *See also* Polk County Bd. of Educ. v. Polk County Educ. Ass'n, 139 S.W.3d 304 (Tenn. Ct. App. 2004) (ruling that a dress code policy constituted a "working condition," not a managerial prerogative); Carter County Bd. of Educ. v. Carter County Educ. Ass'n, 56 S.W.3d 1 (Tenn. Ct. App. 1996) (holding that authority to appoint principal was not subject to collective bargaining).

[35]Clark County Sch. Dist. v. Local Gov't Employee-Mgmt. Relations Bd., 530 P.2d 114 (Nev. 1974). *See also* Oak Hills Educ. Ass'n v. Oak Hills Local Sch. Dist., 821 N.E.2d 616 (Ohio Ct. App. 2004) (ruling that a tuition reimbursement program for university course work could not be unilaterally implemented by school board).

[36]Pa. Labor Relations Bd. v. State Coll. Area Sch. Dist., 337 A.2d 262 (Pa. 1975). *See also* Local 1186 of Council No. 4 v. State Bd. of Labor Relations, 620 A.2d 766 (Conn. 1993); Tualatin Valley Bargaining Council v. Tigard Sch. Dist., 840 P.2d 657 (Or. 1992).

[37]*See, e.g.,* Blount County Educ. Ass'n v. Blount County Bd. of Educ., 78 S.W.3d 307 (Tenn. Ct. App. 2002). *But see* Colonial Sch. Bd. v. Colonial Affiliate, 449 A.2d 243 (Del. 1982) (holding that the state law does not recognize bargaining of permissive subjects; *Montgomery County Educ. Ass'n,* 534 A.2d 980 (finding no provision for permissive subjects to be bargained).

[38]*See, e.g., In re* White Mountain Reg'l Sch. Dist., 908 A.2d 790 (N.H. 2006); DiPiazza v. Bd. of Educ., 625 N.Y.S.2d 298 (App. Div. 1995). *See also* Univ. of Haw. Prof'l Assembly v. Cayetano, 183 F.3d 1096 (9th Cir. 1999) (noting that in interpreting the requirements of a negotiated agreement past practices are probative; holding that the employer changing the timing of the payroll schedule raised such an issue); Malahoff v. Saito, 140 P.3d 401 (Haw. 2006) (ruling that no constitutional violation regarding collective bargaining occurred with the state shifting pay dates by one to four days a month since employees did not experience any loss of wages; however, implementation of change was impermissible because the statute providing for such a shift had expired); Bd. of Educ. v. Ward, 974 P.2d 824 (Utah 1999) (finding that school boards have substantial discretion to interpret their policies, but do not have that discretion if the policy is part of a negotiated collective bargaining contract).

Class Size. This has been one of the most controversial policy subjects, and one that courts and state legislatures have been reluctant to designate as negotiable. Only a few states specifically identify class size as a mandatory bargaining item,[39] and the majority of courts reviewing the issue have found it to be a nonmandatory item.[40] The Nevada Supreme Court interpreted the state collective bargaining statute as including class size among mandatory subjects by implication,[41] but the legislature responded by revising the state law to exclude class size from a detailed list of bargainable items.[42] An Illinois appellate court, however, held that class size is a mandatory issue for bargaining,[43] and several other courts have found it to be a *permissive* subject of bargaining.[44] Although the Wisconsin Supreme Court found class size to be such a permissive subject, the court held that negotiations on the *impact* of class size (e.g., more projects to supervise, potential for more disciplinary problems, etc.) on teachers' conditions of employment would be mandatory.[45] Similarly, a Florida appellate court concluded that class size and staffing levels were not mandatorily bargainable but noted that bargaining on the impact or effect of the implementation of these decisions would be mandatory.[46]

School Calendar. Establishment of the school calendar generally has been held to be a managerial prerogative.[47] Reflecting the judicial trend that it is a nonnegotiable managerial decision, the Maine high court stated, "The commencement and termination of the school year and the scheduling and length of intermediate vacations during the school year, at least insofar as students and teachers are congruently involved, must be held matters of 'educational policies' bearing too substantially upon too many and important non-teacher interests to be settled by collective bargaining."[48] An Indiana appellate court agreed, noting that the impact of the school calendar on students and

[39]*See, e.g.,* Mass. Gen. Laws ch. 150E § 6 (2007).

[40]*See* Cent. State Univ. v. Am. Ass'n of Univ. Professors, 526 U.S. 124 (1999), *on remand* 717 N.E.2d 286 (Ohio 1999) (upholding an Ohio statute excluding faculty workload in public universities from collective bargaining).

[41]Clark County Sch. Dist. v. Local Gov't Employee Mgmt. Relations Bd., 530 P.2d 114 (Nev. 1974).

[42]Nev. Rev. Stat. 288 § 150.3 (2007).

[43]Decatur Bd. of Educ., Dist. No. 61 v. Ill. Educ. Labor Relations Bd., 536 N.E.2d 743 (Ill. App. Ct. 1989).

[44]*See, e.g.,* Nat'l Educ. Ass'n-Kan. City v. Unified Sch. Dist., Wyandotte County, 608 P.2d 415 (Kan. 1980); Fargo Educ. Ass'n v. Fargo Pub. Sch. Dist., 291 N.W.2d 267 (N.D. 1980); City of Beloit v. Wis. Employment Relations Comm'n, 242 N.W.2d 231 (Wis. 1976).

[45]*City of Beloit*, 242 N.W.2d 231. *See also* Tualatin Valley Bargaining Council v. Tigard Sch. Dist., 840 P.2d 657 (Or. 1992) (holding that class size was not automatically a mandatory subject under "other conditions of employment" because it related to a teacher's workload; an assessment must be made relative to its effect on working conditions).

[46]Hillsborough Classroom Teachers Ass'n v. Sch. Bd., 423 So. 2d 969 (Fla. Dist. Ct. App. 1982).

[47]*See, e.g.,* Pub. Employee Relations Bd. v. Wash. Teachers' Union Local 6, 556 A.2d 206 (D.C. Cir. 1989); Piscataway Twp. Educ. Ass'n v. Piscataway Twp. Bd. of Educ., 704 A.2d 981 (N.J. 1998); W. Cent. Educ. Ass'n v. W. Cent. Sch. Dist., 655 N.W.2d 916 (S.D. 2002).

[48]City of Biddeford v. Biddeford Teachers Ass'n, 304 A.2d 387, 421 (Me. 1973).

other public interests outweighed teachers' interests.[49] Notwithstanding that the establishment of the school calendar is a managerial prerogative, the Supreme Court of New Jersey ruled that decisions impacting the days worked and compensation for those days implicates a term and condition of employment.[50] Departing from the prevailing view, the Wisconsin Supreme Court upheld a ruling of the Wisconsin Employment Relations Commission declaring the school calendar mandatorily bargainable; calendar issues were found to be more closely related to terms of employment than to policy matters.[51]

Teacher Evaluation. Employee unions have made significant gains in securing the right to negotiate various aspects of teacher performance evaluations. Most states have not specified evaluation as a mandatory bargaining item, but a number of courts have found it to be significantly related to conditions of employment and thus negotiable. Although courts have been receptive to union proposals to negotiate the technical and procedural elements of evaluation, they have been reluctant to mandate the negotiation of evaluation criteria. In ruling that teacher evaluation was not a prohibited bargaining subject, the Supreme Court of New Hampshire noted that the contested evaluation plan provided only the procedures for evaluations, not the standards by which the teachers would be reviewed.[52] Similarly, the Supreme Court of Kansas distinguished between managerial policies and the mechanics of such policies; the mechanics of developing the evaluation procedures were found to be mandatorily negotiable but not the evaluation criteria, which were designated as a managerial prerogative.[53] The Supreme Court of Iowa, however, found a statutory requirement to negotiate *evaluation procedures* to encompass substantive criteria for evaluation because the term *procedures* had been interpreted broadly in previous judicial rulings.[54]

---

[49]Eastbrook Cmty. Sch. Corp. v. Ind. Educ. Employment Relations Bd., 446 N.E.2d 1007 (Ind. Ct. App. 1983).

[50]Troy v. Rutgers, 774 A.2d 476 (N.J. 2001).

[51]City of Beloit v. Employment Relations Comm'n, 242 N.W.2d 231 (Wis. 1976). *See also* Lincoln County Educ. Ass'n v. Lincoln County Sch. Dist., 67 P.3d 951 (Or. Ct. App. 2003) (finding that amount of student contact time each day for teachers was a mandatory subject of bargaining and could not be changed without negotiation). *But see* Racine Educ. Ass'n v. Wis. Employment Relations Comm'n, 571 N.W.2d 887 (Wis. Ct. App. 1997) (upholding the Wisconsin Employment Relations Commission's (WERC) determination that the implementation of a pilot year-round school calendar was not subject to mandatory bargaining; in balancing the employer and employee interests in this specific situation, WERC found the year-round program primarily related to educational policy).

[52]*In re* Pittsfield Sch. Dist., 744 A.2d 594 (N.H. 1999). In a later case, the New Hampshire court held that a school district breached the collective bargaining contract when it implemented new procedures under a change in state law; the previously negotiated procedures were to remain in effect until the expiration of the contract. *In re* White Mountain Reg'l Sch. Dist., 908 A.2d 790 (N.H. 2006).

[53]Bd. of Educ. v. NEA-Goodland, 785 P.2d 993 (Kan. 1990).

[54]Aplington Cmty. Sch. Dist. v. Iowa Pub. Employment Relations Bd., 392 N.W.2d 495 (Iowa 1986). *See also* Atl. Educ. Ass'n v. Atl. Cmty. Sch. Dist., 469 N.W.2d 689 (Iowa 1991) (concluding that the collective bargaining contract did not provide for arbitration of performance evaluation in the absence of negotiated performance criteria; the negotiated agreement addressed only procedural aspects, which were not contested by the teacher); Snyder v. Mendon-Union Local Sch. Dist. Bd. of Educ., 661 N.E.2d 717 (Ohio 1996) (ruling that, in the absence of a collective bargaining agreement specifying otherwise, state law governs the evaluation of a nontenured teacher).

Reduction-in-Force. With declining student enrollments and financial exigency faced by many school districts, staff reductions-in-force (RIF) have become a threat to tenured as well as nontenured teachers. The threat has resulted in employee unions demanding input into decisions to reduce staff, criteria for reductions, and procedures for selecting teachers for release. Courts generally have held that the decision to reduce staff and the criteria used to make that decision are educational policy matters and thus are not negotiable.[55] State laws also may specifically prohibit collective bargaining of reduction-in-force decisions.[56] The *impact* of reductions on employee rights, however, may necessitate negotiation of procedures for the reduction. The Supreme Court of South Dakota held that the decision to reduce teaching positions was a nonnegotiable managerial decision, but concluded that the mechanics of staff reductions, such as how staff would be selected and procedures for recall, were mandatorily negotiable.[57] The Supreme Court of Wisconsin found that notice and timing of layoffs had to be bargained as they were primarily related to employees' interest and had "a direct impact on wages and job security."[58]

Procedures agreed to in the collective bargaining contract must be followed. An Idaho school district argued that its contract agreement specifying notification by May 15 conflicted with a statutory requirement that districts provide notice by June 15. The state supreme court ruled that the Idaho Code gives school trustees broad authority to negotiate "matters specified in any such negotiation agreement," which expressly enabled the district to bind itself to the earlier date.[59] Teachers, however, may possess independent statutory rights that cannot be subordinated to collective bargaining agreements. A Massachusetts appellate court held that a teacher possessed "bumping" rights across the school system under statutory law, not merely within her bargaining unit as specified in the collective bargaining agreement.[60] The

---

[55]*See, e.g.,* Thompson v. Unified Sch. Dist. No. 259, 819 P.2d 1236 (Kan. Ct. App. 1991); N. Star Sch. Dist. v. N. Star Educ. Ass'n, 625 A.2d 159 (Pa. Commw. Ct. 1993); Blount County Educ. Ass'n v. Blount County Bd. of Educ., 78 S.W.3d 307 (Tenn. Ct. App. 2002). *But see In re* Hillsboro-Deering Sch. Dist., 737 A.2d 1098 (N.H. 1999) (ruling that the decision to release all employees in a bargaining unit to contract with a private company did not constitute a true layoff involving managerial rights and therefore it was subject to bargaining).

[56]*See* Chi. Sch. Reform Bd. of Trs. v. Educ. Labor Relations Bd., 741 N.E.2d 989 (Ill. App. Ct. 2000) (affirming the state labor board's decision upholding an arbitrator's order to reinstate a reserve teacher; the court agreed that the decision did not involve a prohibited subject since the termination of the reserve teacher was not a "layoff" involving a lack of funds or work).

[57]Webster Educ. Ass'n v. Webster Sch. Dist., 631 N.W.2d 202 (S.D. 2001). *See* Davis v. Chester Upland Sch. Dist., 786 A.2d 186 (Pa. 2001); Hanson v. Vermillion Sch. Dist., 727 N.W.2d 459 (S.D. 2007).

[58]The court developed a balancing test for weighing employees' interests in wages, hours, and conditions of employment against the employer's right to make managerial policy decisions. If an item is "primarily related" to wages, hours, and conditions of employment, it is a mandatory subject of bargaining; if not, there is no duty to bargain. W. Bend Educ. Ass'n v. Wis. Employment Relations Comm'n, 357 N.W.2d 534, 543 (Wis. 1984). *See also* Cent. City Educ. Ass'n v. Ill. Educ. Labor Relations Bd., 599 N.E.2d 892 (Ill. 1992).

[59]Hunting v. Clark County Sch. Dist. No. 161, 931 P.2d 628, 633 (Idaho 1997).

[60]Ballotte v. City of Worcester, 748 N.E.2d 987 (Mass. App. Ct. 2001). *See also* Marino v. Bd. of Educ, 691 N.Y.S.2d 537 (App. Div. 1999).

school district argued that she could not bump a less senior teacher in another high school that involved a different bargaining unit. Ruling that state law prevailed, the appellate court noted that the legislature did not list the statute protecting seniority rights as subordinate to negotiated agreements.

Procedures negotiated by the employer and the teachers' union for staff reductions, however, must not violate the constitutional rights of any employees. The Supreme Court overturned a collective bargaining agreement that was designed to protect members of certain minority groups from layoffs.[61] The agreement ensured that the percentage of minority teachers would not fall below the percentage employed before any reduction-in-force. Without evidence that there had been prior employment discrimination, the Court held that the plan violated the equal protection rights of nonminority teachers.

Nonrenewal and Tenure Decisions.   Decisions to retain a teacher or grant tenure clearly are managerial rights and are not mandatorily bargainable.[62] If a school board negotiates procedural aspects of these decisions, however, the provisions generally are binding. For example, collective bargaining agreements may entitle nontenured teachers to procedural protections that ordinarily would not be required under state laws or the Fourteenth Amendment.[63] The Supreme Court of New Hampshire held that state law did not prevent a school board from agreeing to provide probationary teachers with a statement of reasons for nonrenewal; the board retained its managerial prerogative not to renew the teacher's contract.[64] An Illinois federal district court ruled that under Illinois law a teacher's failure to exhaust his contractual remedies under the collective bargaining agreement prevented him from challenging his nonrenewal in court.[65]

Failure of school boards to follow negotiated procedures has resulted in arbitrators' ordering reinstatement of discharged teachers. Permissibility of such awards,

---

[61]Wygant v. Jackson Bd. of Educ., 476 U.S. 267 (1986). *See also* Milwaukee Bd. of Sch. Dirs. v. Wis. Employment Relations Comm'n, 472 N.W.2d 553 (Wis. Ct. App. 1991); text accompanying note 49, Chapter 10.

[62]Under most state laws, reemployment of probationary teachers and tenure decisions has been found to be a prohibited subject of bargaining. *See, e.g.,* Chi. Sch. Reform Bd. v. Ill. Educ. Labor Relations Bd., 721 N.E.2d 676 (Ill. App. Ct. 1999); Honeoye Falls-Lima Cent. Sch. Dist. v. Honeoye Falls-Lima Educ. Ass'n, 402 N.E.2d 1165 (N.Y. 1980); Mindemann v. Indep. Sch. Dist. No. 6, 771 P.2d 996 (Okla. 1989). *But see* State *ex rel.* Rollins v. Bd. of Educ., 532 N.E.2d 1289 (Ohio 1988) (holding that under the collective bargaining law a negotiated agreement prevails over another conflicting law).

[63]*See* text accompanying note 53, Chapter 11. *See also* Kentwood Pub. Sch. v. Kent County Educ. Ass'n, 520 N.W.2d 682 (Mich. Ct. App. 1994). *But see* Bd. of Educ. v. Round Valley Teachers' Ass'n, 914 P.2d 193 (Cal. 1996) (ruling that negotiated procedures beyond statutory minimum for not rehiring probationary employees were preempted by the Education Code; when exclusive discretion is vested in the board to determine scope of procedures, the subject matter may not be subjected to mandatory or permissive bargaining).

[64]*In re* Watson, 448 A.2d 417 (N.H. 1982).

[65]Lombardi v. Bd. of Trs. Hinson Sch. Dist., 463 F. Supp. 2d 867 (N.D. Ill. 2006).

however, depends on how a school board's authority is interpreted under state law. The Supreme Court of Alaska rejected an arbitrator's reinstatement of a teacher, reasoning that school boards "possess the exclusive power, not subject to *any* appeal, to decide whether to 'nonrenew' a provisional employee."[66] The court noted that a range of other remedies was available for the board's violation of the negotiated nonretention procedures. In contrast, the Supreme Court of Montana concluded that reinstatement of teachers by an arbitrator did not usurp school board authority but simply provided appropriate relief for the board's failure to abide by negotiated procedures.[67]

Under Maine law, school boards can enter into negotiated agreements containing binding grievance arbitration for employee dismissal. The state high court ruled that a school board voluntarily negotiating such an arbitration process could not then seek to overturn an arbitrator's reinstatement decision by arguing that the decision causes the board to violate its duty to provide a safe learning environment. By agreeing to submit the dismissal to an arbitrator, the board agreed to abide by the arbitrator's interpretation of the law.[68]

Union Security Provisions

To ensure their strength and viability, unions attempt to obtain various security provisions in the collective bargaining contract. The nature and extent of these provisions will depend on state laws and constitutional limitations. In this section, provisions related to union revenue and exclusive privileges are addressed.

Dues and Service Fees

In bargaining with employees, unions seek to gain provisions that require all employees either to join the association or to pay fees for its services. Since a union must

[66]Jones v. Wrangell Sch. Dist., 696 P.2d 677, 680 (Alaska 1985). *See* Sch. Comm. v. Johnston Fed'n of Teachers, 652 A.2d 976 (R.I. 1995).

[67]Savage Educ. Ass'n v. Trs., 692 P.2d 1237 (Mont. 1984). *See also* N. Miami Educ. Ass'n v. N. Miami Cmty. Schs., 746 N.E.2d 380 (Ind. Ct. App. 2001) (ruling that the Indiana Code allows school districts and associations to agree to binding arbitration regarding teacher nonrenewal but does not give arbitrators such authority unless specifically included in the negotiated agreement).

[68]Union River Valley Teachers Ass'n v. Lamoine Sch. Comm., 748 A.2d 990 (Me. 2000). *See* Clark County Sch. Dist. v. Riley, 14 P.3d 22 (Nev. 2000) (finding that teacher's termination was subject to statutory law and thus could be reviewed by the court; there was no agreement to submit postprobationary actions to arbitration); Juniata-Mifflin Counties Area Vocational-Technical Sch. v. Corbin, 691 A.2d 924 (Pa. 1997) (upholding arbitrator's determination that the language of the negotiated agreement evidenced intent to incorporate the statutory code, thus rendering teacher dismissal subject to grievance arbitration); Montpelier Bd. of Sch. Comm'rs v. Montpelier Educ. Ass'n, 702 A.2d 390 (Vt. 1997) (ruling that in the review of a nonrenewal decision the arbitrator was not limited to the substantive performance of the teacher but also could include the violation of evaluation procedures within the negotiated contract in ordering reinstatement).

represent all individuals in the bargaining unit, it is argued that such provisions are necessary to eliminate "free riders"—the individuals who receive the benefits of the union's work without paying the dues for membership. Union security provisions take several forms. The *closed shop*, requiring an employer to hire only union members, does not exist in the public sector and is unlawful in the private sector under the National Labor Relations Act and the Taft-Hartley amendments. The *union shop* agreement requires an employee to join the union within a designated period of time after employment to retain a position. Even though union shop agreements are prevalent in the private sector, they are not authorized by most public-sector laws and are limited or proscribed in a number of states under "right-to-work" laws.[69] The security provisions most frequently found in the public sector are *agency shop* and *fair share* agreements—terms that often are used interchangeably. An agency shop provision requires an employee to pay union dues but does not mandate membership, while a fair share arrangement requires a nonmember simply to pay a service fee to cover the cost of bargaining activities.

Nonunion teachers have challenged mandatory fees as a violation of their First Amendment speech and association rights. The Supreme Court, however, has held that the payment of fair share fees by public employees is constitutional. In *Abood v. Detroit Board of Education*, the Court rejected the nonunion members' First Amendment claims, noting the importance of ensuring labor peace and eliminating "free riders."[70] Nonetheless, the Court concluded that employees could not be compelled to contribute to the support of ideological causes they may oppose as a condition of maintaining their employment as public school teachers. Accordingly, the fee for nonmember teachers who object to forced contributions to a union's political activities must be adjusted to eliminate costs not related to unions' collective bargaining functions.[71]

Under the *Abood* ruling, the nonunion employee bears the burden to object to the union's use of the agency fee,[72] and the union then must establish the proportionate service fee share related to employee representation. The Supreme Court noted the difficulty in drawing the line between collective bargaining activities and ideological activities unrelated to collective bargaining. In subsequent cases, the Supreme

---

[69]Twenty-two states have laws that specifically declare that an individual's employment cannot be conditioned on joining a union or paying fees to a union.

[70]431 U.S. 209 (1977).

[71]Under Title VII of the Civil Rights Act of 1964, an employee who objects to payment of a service fee on religious grounds must be allowed to substitute a contribution to a charitable organization. *See* Katter v. Ohio Employment Relations Bd., 492 F. Supp. 2d 851, 862 (S.D. Ohio 2007) (holding Ohio Revised Code § 4117.09(C), which provides for religious exemptions, unconstitutional in its application to employees based on formal church membership with a long history of objection to labor unions; law needed to be "more closely tailored . . . by providing protection to all employees who hold *bona fide* religious beliefs without regard to membership in a particular religious organization").

[72]*Abood*, 431 U.S. 209. The Supreme Court ruled in 2007 that a state law requiring unions to obtain affirmative authorization from nonmembers prior to spending agency fees for election-related purposes is not unconstitutional. The state gave the unions the right to collect the fees and could also place limitations on the use. Davenport v. Wash. Educ. Ass'n, 127 S. Ct. 2372 (2007).

Court and other courts have attempted to define this dividing line as well as the procedural protections necessary to respond to nonmembers' objections.

In *Ellis v. Brotherhood of Railway, Airline, and Steamship Clerks*, a private-sector case, the Supreme Court advanced a standard for determining which union expenditures can be assessed against objecting employees:

> The test must be whether the challenged expenditures are necessarily or reasonably incurred for the purpose of performing the duties of an exclusive representative of the employees in dealing with the employer on labor–management issues. Under this standard, objecting employees may be compelled to pay their fair share of not only the direct costs of negotiating and administering a collective-bargaining contract and of settling grievances and disputes, but also the expenses of activities or undertakings normally or reasonably employed to implement or effectuate the duties of the union as exclusive representative of the employees in the bargaining unit.[73]

In applying this test, the Court upheld the assessment of costs related to union conventions, social activities, and publications, but disallowed expenditures related to organizing activities and litigation unrelated to negotiations, contract administration, and fair representation.

In 1991, however, the Supreme Court in *Lehnert v. Ferris Faculty Association* limited some of the *Ellis* charges in a Michigan public-sector case.[74] Expenditures for conventions, selected sections of union publications, preparations for a strike,[75] and chargeable activities of state and national affiliates were upheld. But the Court ruled that unions may not assess nonmembers for lobbying and other political activities that are unrelated to contract ratification or implementation, for litigation that does not involve the local bargaining unit, and for public relations efforts to enhance the image of the teaching profession. Significant for unions, however, was the recognition that contributions to the state and national affiliates are chargeable expenditures even in the absence of a "direct and tangible impact" on the local bargaining unit.

The constitutionality of union procedures adopted to respond to nonmembers who object to the fair share fee continues to create debate. Generally, after a nonmember raises an objection, unions have provided a rebate of the portion of the fee unrelated to bargaining activities. In the *Ellis* decision, however, the Supreme Court found a *pure rebate* procedure inadequate. Characterizing this approach as an "involuntary loan," the Court stated that "by exacting and using full dues, then refunding months later the

---

[73]466 U.S. 435, 448 (1984).

[74]500 U.S. 507 (1991). *See also* Bromley v. Mich. Educ. Ass'n-NEA, 82 F.3d 686 (6th Cir. 1996) (ordering that defensive organizing activities designed to protect and strengthen the status of the union be treated as nonchargeable).

[75]Although strikes are illegal in Michigan, preparation for a strike was viewed as an effective bargaining tool during contract negotiations. *Lehnert*, 500 U.S. 507. *But see* Belhumeur v. Labor Relations Comm'n, 735 N.E.2d 860 (Mass. 2000) (finding that expenses related to implementing a statewide strike and a demonstration highlighting lack of funding for negotiations were not chargeable to nonunion members).

portion that it was not allowed to exact in the first place, the union effectively charges the employees for activities that are outside the scope of the statutory authorization."[76] Because other alternatives such as advance reduction of dues and escrow accounts exist, the Court found even temporary use of dissenters' funds impermissible.

In *Chicago Teachers' Union, Local No. 1 v. Hudson*, the Supreme Court provided further guidance in determining the adequacy of union procedural safeguards to protect nonmember employees' constitutional rights in the apportionment and assessment of representation fees. According to the Court, constitutional requirements for the collection of an agency fee include "an adequate explanation of the basis for the fee, a reasonably prompt opportunity to challenge the amount of the fee before an impartial decision maker, and an escrow for the amounts reasonably in dispute while such challenges are pending."[77] The contested Chicago union's plan included an advance reduction of dues, but it was found to be flawed because nonmembers were required to file an objection in order to receive any information about the calculation of the proportionate share, and they were not provided sufficient information to judge the appropriateness of the fee. The Court held that adequate disclosure required more than identification of expenditures that did not benefit objecting employees; reasons had to be provided for assessment of the fair share. The Court went further than the *Ellis* prohibition on a pure rebate procedure and held that, even if an advance reduction is made, any additional amounts in dispute must be placed in escrow. This was found to be necessary to minimize the risk that any funds of an objector would be used for impermissible ideological activities. Subsequently, most federal appellate courts have found that escrow schemes adequately protect an individual's constitutional rights.[78]

The adequacy of unions' financial reporting practices, as required in *Hudson*, has been contested. According to the Supreme Court, financial disclosure must be adequate or sufficient, not an exhaustive and detailed list of all expenditures. The Court specifically stated in *Hudson* that the union must provide enough detail to enable nonmembers to make an informed decision about the "propriety of the union's fee."[79] The Sixth Circuit held that this does not require unions to provide financial

---

[76]*Ellis*, 466 U.S. at 444. *See also* Anderson v. E. Allen Educ. Ass'n, 683 N.E.2d 1355 (Ind. Ct. App. 1997) (ruling that the negotiated agreement that set the fair share fee at the full union dues amount violated teachers' First Amendment rights; because of changes in Indiana law, unions can no longer negotiate fair share agreements).

[77]475 U.S. 292, 310 (1986).

[78]*See, e.g.*, Grunwald v. San Bernardino City Unified Sch. Dist., 994 F.2d 1370 (9th Cir. 1993); Gibson v. Fla. Bar, 906 F.2d 624 (11th Cir. 1990); Crawford v. Air Line Pilots Ass'n Int'l, 870 F.2d 155 (4th Cir. 1989); Hohe v. Casey, 868 F.2d 69 (3d Cir. 1989). *But see* Tavernor v. Ill. Fed'n of Teachers, 226 F.3d 842 (7th Cir. 2000) (ruling that collecting 100 percent of the union dues from nonmembers and placing the funds in an escrow account was impermissible when the association's calculation showed that fair share generally was approximately 85 percent of full dues).

[79]*Hudson*, 475 U.S. at 306. *See also* Harik v. Cal. Teachers Ass'n, 326 F.3d 1042 (9th Cir. 2003) (finding that the employer has "no specific duties to employees" to ensure that each receives a proper *Hudson* notice before fees are deducted).

information audited at the "highest" available level of audit services.[80] In that case, the court concluded that the union's financial disclosure, including budgets, audited financial statements, and audited supplemental schedules of the state and national associations, was constitutionally adequate. Other courts have emphasized that although a formal audit may not be required, unions, regardless of size, must provide independent verification of expenses incurred.[81]

Although the Supreme Court has upheld fair share arrangements, they may not be permitted under some state laws. The Maine high court held that forced payment of dues was "tantamount to coercion toward membership."[82] The Maine statute ensures employees the right to join a union *voluntarily*, and the court interpreted this provision as including the right to *refrain* from joining. Similarly, the Vermont Supreme Court held that fees were prohibited under the Vermont Labor Relations for Teachers Act, which specified that teachers have the right to join or not to join, assist, or participate in a labor organization.[83] Under some state labor laws, collection of fees may be forbidden. For example, Indiana amended its labor law to prohibit the payment of fair share fees or any other representation fees on all contracts negotiated after July 1, 1995.[84]

Representation fees do not violate the federal Constitution and have been upheld in most states, but legal controversy surrounds enforcement of the provisions. Some collective bargaining agreements require employers to discharge teachers who refuse to pay the fees. In Pennsylvania, an appellate court overturned the dismissal of two teachers, stating that refusal to pay dues did not constitute "persistent and willful violation of the school laws" to justify dismissal.[85] Several courts have attempted to reconcile labor laws that authorize the negotiation of fair share fees as a condition of employment with tenure laws that permit dismissal only for specified causes. The Supreme Court of Michigan ruled that the state labor law prevails when it conflicts with another statute.[86] Accordingly, a tenured teacher who fails to pay the agency service fee can be discharged without resort to procedural requirements of the teacher tenure law. Similarly, the California Public Employment Relations Board

---

[80]Gwirtz v. Ohio Educ. Ass'n, 887 F.2d 678 (6th Cir. 1989).

[81]*See* Otto v. Penn. State Educ. Ass'n-NEA, 330 F.3d 125 (3d Cir. 2003); *Harik*, 326 F.3d 1042; Wareham Educ. Ass'n v. Labor Relations Comm'n, 713 N.E.2d 363 (Mass. 1999).

[82]Churchill v. Sch. Adm'r Dist. No. 49 Teachers Ass'n, 380 A.2d 186 (Me. 1977).

[83]Weissenstein v. Burlington Bd. of Sch. Comm'rs, 543 A.2d 691 (Vt. 1988). *But see* Nashua Teachers Union v. Nashua Sch. Dist., 707 A.2d 448 (N.H. 1998) (interpreting state law that permits negotiation of "other terms and conditions of employment" as authorizing agency fees to promote labor peace; rejecting the argument that the fees were an unfair labor practice "encouraging" union membership).

[84]Ind. Code § 20-7.5-1 (2007).

[85]Langley v. Uniontown Area Sch. Dist., 367 A.2d 736 (Pa. Commw. Ct. 1977). *But see* Belhumeur v. Labor Relations Comm'n, 589 N.E.2d 352 (Mass. App. Ct. 1992) (affirming the five-day suspension of three teachers who refused to remit an agency service fee; teachers did not follow procedures for protesting the fee).

[86]Bd. of Educ. v. Parks, 335 N.W.2d 641 (Mich. 1983).

held that state law authorizing a service fee permits termination of a teacher's employment.[87]

Exclusive Privileges

The designated employee bargaining representative gains security through negotiating exclusive rights or privileges such as dues checkoff, the use of the school mail systems, and access to school facilities. Although exclusive arrangements strengthen the majority union and may make it difficult for minority unions to survive, courts often support these provisions as a means of promoting labor peace and ensuring efficient operation of the school system.

The exclusive privilege most often found in collective bargaining contracts is dues checkoff, a provision that authorizes employers to deduct union dues and other fees when authorized by employees. Over half of the states with public employee bargaining laws specify dues checkoff as a mandatory subject for bargaining. The Supreme Court, however, has held that employee unions do not have a constitutional right to payroll deductions.[88] The Fourth Circuit ruled that state legislation permitting payroll deductions for charitable organizations but not labor unions was not an infringement of the First Amendment; the law did not deny the union members the right to associate, speak, publish, recruit members, or express their views.[89] Unless prohibited by state law, most courts have upheld negotiated agreements between the designated bargaining representative and the employer that deny rival unions checkoff rights.

In 1983, the Supreme Court clarified one of the most controversial security rights—exclusive access to school mail facilities.[90] The case focused on an agreement between the exclusive bargaining representative and an Indiana school board denying all rival unions access to the interschool mail system and teacher mailboxes. One of the unions challenged the agreement as a violation of First and Fourteenth Amendment rights. The Supreme Court upheld the arrangement, reasoning that the First Amendment does not require "equivalent access to all parts of a school building in which some form of communicative activity occurs."[91] The Court concluded that the school mail facility was not a public forum for communication, and thereby its use could be restricted to official school business. The fact that several community

---

[87]King City Joint Union High Sch. Dist., Cal. Pub. Relations Bd., Order No. 197 (March 1982). Unions also have pursued enforcement of fair share agreements in civil actions against nonmember teachers.

[88]City of Charlotte v. Local 660, Int'l Ass'n of Firefighters, 426 U.S. 283 (1976).

[89]S.C. Educ. Ass'n v. Campbell, 883 F.2d 1251 (4th Cir. 1989).

[90]Perry Educ. Ass'n v. Perry Local Educators' Ass'n, 460 U.S. 37 (1983). *See also* San Leandro Teachers Ass'n v. Governing Bd., 65 Cal. Rptr. 3d 288 (Ct. App. 2007) (ruling that state law prohibits unions from using school mailboxes to distribute political endorsement information); Unified Sch. Dist. No. 233 v. Kan. Ass'n of Am. Educators, 64 P.3d 372 (Kan. 2003) (finding that a school district could not permit a rival professional association to distribute its membership materials through the district's internal mail system when the collective bargaining representative had negotiated exclusive use of the mail system); text accompanying note 50, Chapter 9.

[91]*Perry Educ.* Ass'n, 460 U.S. at 44.

groups (e.g., Scouts, civic organizations) used the school mail system did not create a public forum. The Court noted that, even if such access by community groups created a limited public forum, access would be extended only to similar groups—not to labor organizations. The Court's emphasis on the availability of alternative channels of communication (e.g., bulletin boards and meeting facilities), however, indicates that total exclusion of rival unions would not be permitted.

The Fifth Circuit subsequently ruled, and the Supreme Court affirmed, that denial of access to the school mail to all teacher organizations did not violate the First Amendment when other channels of communication were available.[92] However, the Court found unconstitutional a policy prohibiting individual teachers from discussing employee organizations during nonclass time or using the internal mail system or bulletin boards to mention employee organizations. Such limitations on an individual employee's expression would be permissible only if a threat of material and substantial disruption were shown.

Although a school board may provide access to mailboxes and school facilities, a school board cannot deliver a union's mail through its interschool mail delivery system. Under the federal Private Express Statutes,[93] an employer is permitted to deliver only mail related to its business through the "letters of the carrier" exception to the federal law. In 1988, the United States Supreme Court held that this exception did not permit a union attempting to organize faculty in a university to use the university's internal mail system; the activity did not relate to the university's "current business."[94] Subsequently, the Seventh Circuit ruled that the delivery of mail of the exclusive bargaining representative did not relate to the school's current business, but rather to the union's business.[95] The case was remanded for further review to determine if some correspondence related to joint school/union committees could be characterized as the school's business.

In most states, school boards negotiate only with the designated bargaining representative. Under this exclusive recognition, other unions and teacher groups can be denied the right to engage in official exchanges with an employer. The Supreme Court has held that nonmembers of a bargaining unit or members who disagree with the views of the representative do not have a constitutional right "to force the government to listen to their views."[96] The Court concluded that a Minnesota statute requiring

---

[92]Tex. State Teachers Ass'n v. Garland Indep. Sch. Dist., 777 F.2d 1046 (5th Cir. 1985), *aff'd*, 470 U.S. 801 (1986).

[93]18 U.S.C. §§ 1693 *et seq.* (2007); 39 U.S.C. §§ 601 *et seq.* (2007). These laws establish a postal monopoly and, in general, prohibit the private delivery of letters without payment to the United States Postal Service.

[94]Univ. of Cal. v. Pub. Employment Relations Bd., 485 U.S. 589 (1988).

[95]Fort Wayne Cmty. Schs. v. Fort Wayne Educ. Ass'n, 977 F.2d 358 (7th Cir. 1992).

[96]Minn. State Bd. for Cmty. Colls. v. Knight, 465 U.S. 271, 283 (1984). *See also* Sherrard Cmty. Unit Sch. Dist. v. Ill. Educ. Labor Relations Bd., 696 N.E.2d 833 (Ill. App. Ct. 1998) (ruling that a school board's direct negotiation with a nonunion teacher regarding her proposed involuntary reassignment was an unfair labor practice).

employers to "meet and confer" only with the designated bargaining representative did not violate other employees' speech or associational rights as public employees or as citizens since these sessions were not a public forum. According to the Court, "the Constitution does not grant to members of the public generally a right to be heard by public bodies making decisions of policy."[97]

Nonetheless, if a public forum, such as a school board meeting, is involved, a nonunion teacher has a constitutional right to address the public employer, even on a subject of negotiation. The Supreme Court concluded in a Wisconsin case that a nonunion teacher had the right to express concerns to the school board.[98] In this case, negotiation between the board and union had reached a deadlock on the issue of an agency shop provision. A nonunion teacher, representing a minority group of teachers, addressed the board at a regular public meeting and requested postponement of a decision until further study of the issue. The Court reasoned that the teacher was not attempting to negotiate, but merely to speak on an important issue before the board— a right any citizen possesses. The Court further noted that teachers have never been "compelled to relinquish their First Amendment rights they would otherwise enjoy as citizens to comment on matters of public interest in connection with the operation of the public school in which they work."[99]

While union security provisions such as fair share arrangements and exclusive use of specific school facilities can be negotiated, nonunion teachers' constitutional rights cannot be infringed. Teachers must be ensured an effective mechanism for challenging financial contributions that might be used to support ideological causes or political activities to which they object. If specific communication channels for nonmembers are restricted through the negotiation process, alternative options must remain open.

Grievances

Disputes concerning employee rights under the terms of a collective bargaining agreement are resolved through the negotiated grievance procedures, which generally must be exhausted before pursuing review by state labor relations boards or courts.[100] The exhaustion requirement sustains the integrity of the collective bargaining process, encouraging the orderly and efficient settlement of disputes at the local level. Grievance procedures usually provide for a neutral third party, an arbitrator, to

---

[97]*Knight*, 465 U.S. at 283.

[98]City of Madison v. Wis. Employment Relations Comm'n, 429 U.S. 167 (1976). *See also* Ohio Ass'n of Pub. Sch. Employees v. State Employment Relations Bd., 742 N.E.2 696 (Ohio Ct. App. 2000) (ruling that association representatives' comments at a school board meeting did not constitute negotiations under state law; the board had argued that bypassing the board's bargaining representative and negotiating directly with the board was an unfair labor practice).

[99]*City of Madison*, 429 U.S. at 175 (quoting Pickering v. Bd. of Educ., 391 U.S. 563, 568 (1968)).

[100]*See, e.g.*, Reynolds v. Sch. Dist. No. 1, 69 F.3d 1523 (10th Cir. 1995); Hokama v. Univ. of Haw., 990 P.2d 1150 (Haw. 1999); Milton Educ. Ass'n v. Milton Bd. of Sch. Trs., 759 A.2d 479 (Vt. 2000).

conduct a hearing and render a decision. *Grievance* arbitration, which addresses enforcement of rights under the contract, is distinct from *interest* arbitration, which may take place in resolving an impasse in the bargaining process.[101]

Depending on state law and the negotiated contract, the decision in grievance arbitration may be advisory or binding. Public employers, adhering to the doctrine of the sovereign power of government, have been reluctant to agree to procedures that might result in a loss of public authority. Allowing grievance procedures to include final decision making by a third party significantly lessens a school board's power, effectively equating the positions of the teachers' organization and the school board. Nevertheless, as bargaining has expanded, legislative bodies have favored binding arbitration as a means of settling labor disputes. About half of the states have enacted laws permitting school boards to negotiate grievance procedures with binding arbitration, and several states require binding arbitration as the final step in the grievance procedure.[102] With the widespread use of grievance arbitration, it has become one of the most contested areas in collective bargaining. Suits have challenged the arbitrator's authority to render decisions in specific disputes as well as the authority to provide certain remedies.

One of the primary issues in establishing a grievance procedure is the definition of a grievance—that is, what can be grieved. In the private sector, a grievance is usually defined as any dispute between the employer and the employee. Teachers' grievances, on the other hand, are generally limited to controversies arising from the interpretation or application of the negotiated contract. Arbitrability of a dispute then depends on whether the school board and union agreed to settle the issue by arbitration, or whether the agreement shows such intent.[103] Arbitrators generally make decisions as to arbitrability, and the decisions are presumed to be valid when derived from the construction of the negotiated agreement. The Supreme Court of Iowa noted that because the law favors arbitration, the court's duty is to construe the agreement broadly, recognizing arbitrability "unless it may be said with positive assurance that the arbitration clause is not susceptible to an interpretation that covers the asserted dispute. Doubts should be resolved in favor of coverage."[104]

Disputes held to be arbitrable based on specific negotiated contracts include unsatisfactory teacher performance, procedural aspects of performance evaluation,

[101]As noted in the next session, binding interest arbitration has met with resistance in the public sector as a method to resolve negotiation impasses. If it were permitted regarding monetary issues, school boards would relinquish control of the power to determine the budget.

[102]States requiring binding grievance arbitration are Alaska, Florida, Illinois, Minnesota, and Pennsylvania. *See* Palmer v. Portland Sch. Comm., 652 A.2d 86 (Me. 1995) (holding that discharged teacher could not compel arbitration of his dispute where he failed to exhaust his procedural remedies under the collective bargaining agreement; arbitration was the last step in the process).

[103]*See, e.g.*, Bd. of Educ. v. Wallingford Educ. Ass'n, 858 A.2d 762 (Conn. 2004); *In re* Bd. of Educ., 710 N.E.2d 1064 (N.Y. 1999); Davis v. Chester Upland Sch. Dist., 786 A.2d 186 (Pa. 2001); Mount Adams Sch. Dist. v. Cook, 81 P.3d 111 (Wash. 2003).

[104]Postville Cmty. Sch. Dist. v. Billmeyer, 548 N.W.2d 558, 560 (Iowa 1996) (quoting Sergeant Bluff-Luton Educ. Ass'n v. Sergeant Bluff-Luton Cmty. Sch. Dist., 282 N.W.2d 144, 147-148 (Iowa 1979)). *See also* E. Assoc. Coal Corp. v. United Mine Workers, 531 U.S. 57 (2000) (reaffirming the strong federal policy of judicial deference to arbitration in labor disputes).

eligibility for continuing contract, reinstatement of a reserve teacher, contribution to health insurance premiums, involuntary transfer of a teacher, and transfer of students to other districts on a tuition basis.[105] Although a range of issues has been found to be arbitrable, courts have ruled that issues related to nondelegable policy matters under state law are outside the scope of arbitration. For example, impermissible issues have involved tenure decisions, employee dismissal, reappointment of nontenured teachers, evaluation of teacher qualifications, transfer of teachers, curriculum content, teacher discipline, reinstatement of an eliminated teacher position, and provision of health services to special education students.[106] Also, issues that are specifically excluded in the contract cannot be submitted to arbitration.

Moreover, arbitration awards or remedies have been challenged. Again, as with arbitrability, courts have adopted a narrow scope of review, with many courts presuming the validity of awards. The deference afforded an arbitrator's award is evident from the Supreme Court's statement that "unless the arbitral decision does not 'draw its essence from the collective bargaining agreement,' a court is bound to enforce the award and is not entitled to review the merits of the contract dispute."[107] As long as an arbitrator's award can be interpreted as rationally derived from the language and context of the agreement, courts have found that it "draws its essence" from the agreement.[108] Courts do not interfere with arbitration awards simply because they would have provided a different remedy.[109]

---

[105]*See, e.g.,* Chi. Sch. Reform Bd. of Trs. v. Ill. Educ. Labor Relations Bd., 741 N.E.2d 989 (Ill. App. Ct. 2000) (reserve teacher reinstatement); Sch. Comm. v. United Educators of Pittsfield, 784 N.E.2d 11 (Mass. 2003) (involuntary transfer of teacher); Sch. Comm. v. Boston Teachers Union, 664 N.E.2d 478 (Mass. App. Ct. 1996) (evaluation procedures); *In re* Bd. of Educ., 710 N.E.2d 1064 (N.Y. 1999) (health insurance); State *ex rel.* Williams v. Belpre City Sch. Dist. Bd. of Educ., 534 N.E.2d 96 (Ohio Ct. App. 1987) (continuing contract); Midland Borough Sch. Dist. v. Midland Educ. Ass'n, 616 A.2d 633 (Pa. 1992) (transfer of students).

[106]*See, e.g.,* Chi. Sch. Reform Bd. of Trs. v. Ill. Educ. Labor Relations Bd., 721 N.E.2d 676 (Ill. App. Ct. 1999) (dismissal of teachers); Sch. Admin. Dist. No. 58 v. Mount Abram Teachers Ass'n, 704 A.2d 349 (Me. 1997) (curriculum content); Sch. Comm. v. Peabody Fed'n of Teachers, 748 N.E.2d 992 (Mass. App. Ct. 2001) (teacher transfers); Raines v. Indep. Sch. Dist. No. 6, 796 P.2d 303 (Okla. 1990) (teacher discipline); Mindemann v. Indep. Sch. Dist. No. 6, 771 P.2d 996 (Okla. 1989) (teacher nonrenewal); Sch. Dist. v. Erie Educ. Ass'n, 873 A.2d 73 (Pa. Commw. Ct. 2005) (teaching position); Woonsocket Teachers' Guild v. Woonsocket Sch. Comm., 770 A.2d 834 (R.I. 2001) (health services to special education students).

[107]W. R. Grace and Co. v. Local 759, United Rubber Workers of Am., 461 U.S. 757, 764 (1983).

[108]*See, e.g.,* Sch. Comm. v. Hull Teachers Ass'n, 872 N.E.2d 767 (Mass. App. Ct. 2007); Danville Area Sch. Dist. v. Danville Area Educ. Ass'n, 754 A.2d 1255 (Pa. 2000). *See also* Sch. Comm. v. Hanover Teachers Ass'n, 761 N.E.2d 918 (Mass. 2002) (finding that arbitrator exceeded his authority when he did not follow the plain language of the agreement); *In re* Liberty Cent. Sch. Dist., 808 N.Y.S.2d 445 (App. Div. 2006) (finding arbitrator's award of back pay and health insurance costs in nonrenewal of teacher to be irrational); Rochester Sch. Dist. v. Rochester Educ. Ass'n, 747 A.2d 971 (Pa. Commw. Ct. 2000) (finding arbitrator's decision that school board must work with association in developing all policies, such as standards for student honor roll in this case, did not draw its essence from the agreement; the board had preserved the right to develop inherent managerial policies when it signed the negotiated agreement).

[109]*See, e.g.,* Union River Valley Teacher Ass'n v. Lamoine Sch. Comm., 748 A.2d 990 (Me. 2000).

Negotiation Impasse

An impasse occurs in bargaining when an agreement cannot be reached and neither party will compromise. When negotiations reach such a stalemate, several options are available for resolution—mediation, fact-finding, and arbitration. As discussed in the final section of this chapter, the most effective means for resolving negotiation impasse—the strike—is not legally available to the majority of public employees. Most comprehensive state statutes address impasse procedures, with provisions ranging from allowing impasse procedures to be negotiated to mandating detailed steps that must be followed. Alternatives most frequently employed to resolve impasse are identified below.

Mediation is often the first step to reopening negotiations. A neutral third party assists both sides in finding a basis for agreement. The mediator serves as a facilitator rather than a decision maker, thus enabling the school board's representative and the teachers' association jointly to reach an agreement. Mediation may be optional or required by law; the mediator is selected by the negotiation teams or, upon request, appointed by a public employee relations board.

Failure to reach agreement through mediation frequently results in fact-finding (often called advisory arbitration). The process may be mandated by law or may be entered into by mutual agreement of both parties. Fact-finding involves a third party investigating the causes for the dispute, collecting facts and testimony to clarify the dispute, and formulating a judgment. Because of the advisory nature of the process, proposed solutions are not binding on either party. However, since fact-finding reports are made available to the public, they provide an impetus to settle a contract that is not present in mediation.

In a number of states, the final step in impasse procedures is fact-finding, which may leave both parties without a satisfactory solution. A few states permit a third alternative—binding interest arbitration. This process is similar to fact-finding except that the decision of the arbitrator, related to the terms of the negotiated agreement, is binding on both parties. States that permit binding arbitration often place restrictions on its use.[110] For example, Ohio, Oregon, and Rhode Island permit binding arbitration on matters of mutual consent;[111] Maine allows binding arbitration on all items except salaries, pensions, and insurance.[112]

It is generally agreed that mediation and fact-finding, because of their advisory nature, do not provide the most effective means for resolving negotiation disputes. Since strikes are prohibited among public employees in most states, conditional binding arbitration has been considered a viable alternative in resolving deadlocks. Although a greater balance of power is achieved between the school board and the teachers' association with binding arbitration, public-sector employers, who often view it as an illegal

[110]To avoid strikes among certain groups of public employees, interest arbitration may be mandatory. *See, e.g.*, Ohio Rev. Code § 4117.14 (D)(l) (2007).

[111]Ohio Rev. Code § 4117.14 (C) (2007); Or. Rev. Stat. 243 § 712 (2)(e) (2007); R.I. Gen. Laws 28 § 9.3-9 (2007).

[112]Me. Rev. Stat. 26 § 979.D(4)(D) (2007).

delegation of power, have not readily embraced it. As a result, interest arbitration generally has occurred in the educational setting only on a voluntary or conditional basis.

If a collective bargaining agreement expires while the employer and the union are attempting to reach an agreement, the *status quo* must be maintained. Adhering to this principle means that all terms and conditions of employment remain in effect during the continuing bargaining process.[113] Unless restricted by state law, the majority of courts have held that this means the continuance of annual salary increments for teachers.[114] After the exhaustion of all required impasse resolution procedures, generally an employer can implement its best and last offer,[115] or state law may allow employees to strike in a few instances.

Strikes

While it is argued that there can be no true collective bargaining without the right to withhold services, which characterizes the bargaining process in the private sector, most teachers are prohibited from striking by either state statute or common law. In those states that have legislation granting public employees a limited right to strike,[116] certain conditions, specified in statute, must be met prior to the initiation of a work

---

[113]*See* NLRB v. Katz, 369 U.S. 736 (1962) (establishing in the private sector that unilateral changes in terms and conditions of employment are unlawful; this principle has been applied broadly in the public sector); Denver Classroom Teachers Ass'n v. Sch. Dist. No. 1, Denver, 921 P.2d 70 (Colo. Ct. App. 1996) (ruling that school district's failure to deduct association dues from the salaries of dues-paying nonmembers altered the conditions of employment); St. Croix Falls Sch. Dist. v. Wis. Employment Relations Comm'n, 522 N.W.2d 507 (Wis. Ct. App. 1994) (holding that school district was required to maintain *status quo* regarding sick leave). *But see* Providence Teachers Union v. Providence Sch. Bd., 689 A.2d 388 (R.I. 1997) (deciding that the grievance arbitration provisions in the expired contract were not applicable to disputes arising after expiration of the agreement and unrelated to vested rights in the expired contract).

[114]*See, e.g.*, Jackson County Coll. Classified and Technical Ass'n v. Jackson County Coll., 468 N.W.2d 61 (Mich. Ct. App. 1991); *In re* Cobleskill Cent. Sch. Dist., 481 N.Y.S.2d 795 (App. Div. 1984). *But see* Bd. of Trs. v. Assoc. Colt Staff, 659 A.2d 842 (Me. 1995) (finding that maintenance of the *status quo* is freezing salaries at the level existing at the expiration of the contract); *In re* Alton Sch. Dist., 666 A.2d 937 (N.H. 1995) (ruling that under state law teachers receive the annual salary increment for experience at the expiration of the negotiated contract only if the contract contains an automatic renewal clause; however, salary increases for additional training must be recognized and health benefits must be continued to maintain *status quo*).

[115]*See, e.g.*, Mountain Valley Educ. Ass'n v. Me. Sch. Admin. Dist. No. 43, 655 A.2d 348 (Me. 1995); Ranta v. Eaton Rapids Pub. Schs., 721 N.W.2d 806 (Mich. Ct. App. 2006); Kenmare Educ. Ass'n v. Kenmare Pub. Sch. Dist., 717 N.W.2d 603 (N.D. 2006).

[116]A limited right to strike exists under state law for public employees in Alaska, Colorado, Hawaii, Illinois, Minnesota, Montana, Ohio, Oregon, Pennsylvania, Vermont, and Wisconsin. Alaska law has been interpreted as prohibiting teachers from striking even though most other public employees are permitted to strike. Anchorage Educ. Ass'n v. Anchorage Sch. Dist., 648 P.2d 993 (Alaska 1982). *See also* Martin v. Montezuma-Cortez Sch. Dist., 841 P.2d 237 (Colo. 1992) (interpreting Colorado's Industrial Relations Act to include a limited right to strike); Reichley v. N. Penn Sch. Dist., 626 A.2d 123 (Pa. 1993) (upholding constitutionality of the statute allowing strikes by public educators; the court noted that this is a policy consideration for the legislature rather than an issue for the judicial system).

stoppage. Designated conditions vary but usually include: (1) the exhaustion of statutory mediation and fact-finding steps, (2) expiration of the contract, (3) elapse of a certain time period prior to commencing the strike, (4) written notice of the union's intent to strike, and (5) evidence that the strike will not constitute a danger to public health or safety. In contrast to the few states permitting strikes, most states with public employee collective bargaining statutes have specific "no-strike" provisions.[117]

Courts consistently have upheld "no-strike" laws and generally have denied the right to strike unless it has been affirmatively granted by the state.[118] Several early cases are still representative of the dominant judicial posture on public teachers' strikes. In a Connecticut case, the state high court stated that permitting teachers to strike could be equated with asserting "they can deny the authority of government."[119] The court in this case denied teachers the right to strike, emphasizing that a teacher is an agent of the government, possessing a portion of the state's sovereignty. The Supreme Court of Indiana issued a restraining order against striking teachers, affirming the same public welfare issue.[120] Addressing the legality of strikes, a New Jersey appellate court declared that legislative authorization for bargaining did not reflect the intent to depart from the common law rule prohibiting strikes by public employees.[121] In contrast to the prevailing common law position, the Louisiana high court declared strikes permissible for some public employees, including teachers. The court found under state law "an intent to afford public employees a system of organizational rights that parallels that afforded to employees in the private sector."[122]

A strike is more than simply a work stoppage; states define the term broadly to include a range of concerted activities such as work slowdowns, massive absences for "sick" days, and refusal to perform certain duties. For example, the Massachusetts high court found that refusal to perform customary activities, such as grading papers and preparing lesson plans after the end of the school day, constituted a strike.[123] A Missouri appellate court upheld the right of the St. Louis school superintendent to

---

[117]*See, e.g.*, Mich. State AFL-CIO v. Employment Relations Comm'n, 551 N.W.2d 165 (Mich. 1996) (upholding statutory prohibition on strikes protesting unfair labor practices; provision does not violate First Amendment free speech guarantee regardless of the employees' motivation for the strike).

[118]*See, e.g.*, Passaic Twp. Bd. of Educ. v. Passaic Twp. Educ. Ass'n, 536 A.2d 1276 (N.J. Super. Ct. App. Div. 1987); Jefferson County Bd. of Educ. v. Jefferson County Educ. Ass'n, 393 S.E.2d 653 (W. Va. 1990).

[119]Norwalk Teachers Ass'n v. Bd. of Educ., 83 A.2d 482, 485 (Conn. 1951).

[120]Anderson Fed'n of Teachers v. Sch. City of Anderson, 251 N.E.2d 15 (Ind. 1969).

[121]Passaic Township Bd. of Educ. v. Passaic Township Educ. Ass'n, 536 A.2d 1276 (N.J. Super Ct. App. Div. 1987).

[122]Davis v. Henry, 555 So. 2d 457, 464–465 (La. 1990).

[123]Lenox Educ. Ass'n v. Labor Relations Comm'n, 471 N.E.2d 81 (Mass. 1984). "Concerted activity" may extend beyond activities related to the negotiation of the contract. *See* Cent. Sch. Dist. 13J v. Cent. Educ. Ass'n, 962 P.2d 763 (Or. Ct. App. 1998) (ruling that concerted activity to enforce the rights in a union contract is protected under state law; a teacher bringing a representative of his choice to a meeting that could have disciplinary consequences was such a protected activity).

request documentation from 1,190 teachers that a "sick" day was not related to a labor dispute surrounding the negotiation of a new contract.[124] In the absence of documentation from the teachers, the school district could deny payment for the day.

State laws, in addition to prohibiting work stoppages, usually identify penalties for involvement in strikes. Such penalties can include withholding compensation for strike days, prohibiting salary increases for designated periods of time (e.g., one year), and dismissal. Penalties for illegal strikes also are imposed on unions. Sanctions may include fines, decertification of the union, and loss of certain privileges such as dues checkoff.[125]

Despite statutory prohibitions against strikes, many teachers, as well as other public employees, participate in work stoppages each year. Public employers can request a court injunction against teachers who threaten to strike or initiate such action. Most courts have granted injunctions, concluding, as did the Supreme Court of Alaska, that the "illegality of the strike is a sufficient harm to justify injunctive relief."[126] Failure of teachers and unions to comply with such a restraining order can result in charges of contempt of court, with resulting fines and/or imprisonment. For example, teachers in a Maryland school district who refused to obey an injunction were found guilty of criminal contempt.[127] In issuing an injunction, a New Jersey court ordered incarceration rather than monetary penalties for teachers who failed to return to work; the court noted that monetary fines had not been effective in the state in forcing teachers to return to work.[128] In South Bend, Indiana, refusal to comply with an injunction resulted in a contempt-of-court charge and fines totalling $200,000 against two unions.[129] Establishing the level of fines involves a consideration of factors such as the magnitude of the threatened harm and the association's financial condition. A Massachusetts appellate court remanded a case in which the trial court

[124]Franklin v. St. Louis Bd. of Educ., 904 S.W.2d 433 (Mo. Ct. App. 1995).

[125]*See, e.g.*, Buffalo Teachers Fed'n v. Helsby, 676 F.2d 28 (2d Cir. 1982); Nat'l Educ. Ass'n-S. Bend v. S. Bend Cmty. Sch. Corp., 655 N.E.2d 516 (Ind. Ct. App. 1995); E. Brunswick Bd. of Educ. v. E. Brunswick Educ. Ass'n, 563 A.2d 55 (N.J. Super. Ct. App. Div. 1989).

[126]Anchorage Educ. Ass'n v. Anchorage Sch. Dist., 648 P.2d 993, 998 (Alaska 1982). *See also* Carroll v. Ringgold Educ. Ass'n, 680 A.2d 1137 (Pa. 1996) (holding that an injunction could include provisions for court-monitored bargaining between the parties). *But see* Wilson v. Pulaski Ass'n of Classroom Teachers, 954 S.W.2d 221 (Ark. 1997) (requiring proof of irreparable harm to issue a preliminary injunction). In the Arkansas case, the Eighth Circuit also declined to issue an injunction requested by the school board in order to enforce a desegregation consent decree. The court did not find that its power to enforce the consent decree gave it authority to resolve other disputes arising in the district. Knight v. Pulaski County Special Sch. Dist., 112 F.3d 953 (8th Cir. 1997).

[127]Harford County Educ. Ass'n v. Bd. of Educ., 380 A.2d 1041 (Md. 1977).

[128]Bd. of Educ. v. Middletown Twp. Educ. Ass'n, 800 A.2d 286 (N.J. Super. Ct. App. Div. 2001).

[129]Nat'l Educ. Ass'n-S. Bend v. S. Bend Cmty. Sch. Corp., 655 N.E.2d 516 (Ind. Ct. App. 1995). *See also* Franklin Twp. Bd. of Educ. v. Quakertown Educ. Ass'n, 643 A.2d 34 (N.J. Super. Ct. App. Div. 1994) (holding that the school board could be awarded attorneys' fees and damages associated with a strike and that the trial court could impose additional monetary sanctions to pressure compliance with a court order to return to work).

judge failed to consider relevant factors in imposing a $20,000 fine for each day the union refused to return to work.[130]

Even though the injunction has been the most effective response to strikes, courts have been reluctant to impose this sanction automatically. Other factors have been considered, such as whether the board bargained in "good faith," whether the strike constituted a clear and present danger to public safety, and whether irreparable harm would result from the strike.[131] The Supreme Court of Arkansas ruled that the party requesting an injunction must "establish irreparable harm."[132] The court found this to be true regardless of whether the strike is illegal *per se*. Evidence required by school boards to demonstrate sufficient cause for an injunction has varied according to the legal jurisdiction and the interpretation of applicable state statutes.

The procedures required for dismissal of striking teachers have received judicial attention. Courts have held that due process procedures must be provided, but questions arise as to the nature and type of hearing that must be afforded. The Wisconsin Supreme Court ruled that striking teachers must be provided an impartial and fair hearing, and that the board of education was not sufficiently impartial to serve as the hearing panel. Reversing this decision, the United States Supreme Court maintained that the board's involvement did not overcome "the presumption of honesty and integrity in policymakers with decision-making power."[133] The Court further held that "permitting the board to make the decision at issue here preserves its control over school district affairs, leaves the balance of power in labor relations where the state legislature struck it, and assures that the decision whether to dismiss the teachers will be made by the body responsible for that decision under state law."[134] While noting that the Fourteenth Amendment guarantees each teacher procedural due process, the Supreme Court concluded that a hearing before the school board satisfies this requirement.

State legislatures and courts generally have refused to grant public school teachers the right to strike. Even in the few states where a limited right to strike has been gained, extensive restrictions have been placed on its use.[135] Teachers participating in an illegal strike are subject to court/imposed penalties and, in most states, to statutory penalties. Refusal of teachers to return to the classroom can result in dismissal.[136]

---

[130]Labor Relations Comm'n v. Salem Teachers Union, 706 N.E.2d 1146 (Mass. App. Ct. 1999).

[131]*See, e.g.*, Jersey Shore Area Sch. Dist. v. Jersey Shore Educ. Ass'n, 548 A.2d 1202 (Pa. 1988); Jefferson County Bd. of Educ. v. Jefferson County Educ. Ass'n, 393 S.E.2d 653 (W. Va. 1990); Joint Sch. Dist. No. 1 v. Wis. Rapids Educ. Ass'n, 234 N.W.2d 289 (Wis. 1975).

[132]Wilson v. Pulaski Ass'n of Classroom Teachers, 954 S.W.2d 221, 224 (Ark. 1997). *See* Niles Twp. High Sch. Dist. v. Niles Twp. Fed'n of Teachers, 692 N.E.2d 700 (Ill. App. Ct. 1997).

[133]Hortonville Educ. Ass'n v. Hortonville Joint Sch. Dist., 225 N.W.2d 658 (Wis. 1975), *rev'd*, 426 U.S. 482, 497 (1976). See also text accompanying notes 77–78, Chapter 11.

[134]*Id.*, 426 U.S. at 496.

[135]*See supra* text accompanying note 116.

[136]National Labor Relations Act, in the private sector, preserves the employer's right to permanently replace economic strikers; this right offsets employees' right to strike. 29 U.S.C. §§ 151 *et seq.* (2007). *See also* Van-Go Transp. Co. v. N.Y. City Bd. of Educ., 53 F. Supp. 2d 278 (E.D.N.Y. 1999).

Conclusion

Because of the diversity in collective bargaining laws among states, legal principles with universal application are necessarily broad. Generalizations concerning collective bargaining rights that are applicable to most teachers are set forth below.

1. Teachers have a constitutionally protected right to form and join a union.
2. Specific bargaining rights are conferred through state statutes or judicial interpretations of state constitutions, thus creating wide divergence in teachers' bargaining rights across states.
3. School boards are not required to bargain with employee organizations unless mandated to do so by state law.
4. Collective bargaining must be conducted "in good faith," which means that the school board and teachers' organization attempt to reach agreement without compulsion on either side to agree.
5. The scope of negotiations is generally defined as including wages, hours, and other terms and conditions of employment, such as teaching load, planning time, and lunch periods.
6. Governmental policy matters are not mandatorily bargainable but may be permissive subjects unless prohibited by law.
7. State legislation permitting the negotiation of a service fee (fair share) provision for nonunion members is constitutional; however, if a public employee objects to supporting specific ideological or political causes, the fee must be adjusted to reflect chargeable bargaining costs.
8. To collect a fair share fee from a nonunion teacher who raises First Amendment objections, the union must provide adequate information regarding the basis of the fee, independent verification of union expenses, procedural safeguards to ensure a prompt response to employees who may object, and an escrow account for challenged amounts.
9. Unions may constitutionally negotiate exclusive privileges such as the use of the school mail and dues checkoff; other communication options, however, must be available to rival unions.
10. Nonunion teachers have the right to express a viewpoint before the school board on an issue under negotiation between the board and union.
11. Negotiated agreements generally include a grievance procedure for resolving conflicts that arise under the terms of the contract; the procedures may provide for either advisory or binding arbitration, depending on state law.
12. Impasse procedures for public-sector bargaining are generally limited to mediation and fact-finding, with the public employer retaining final decision-making authority.
13. Teacher strikes, except in limited situations in a few states, are illegal and punishable by dismissal, fines, and imprisonment.

13

Tort Liability

Tort law offers civil rather than criminal remedies to individuals for harm caused by the unreasonable conduct of others. A *tort* is described as a civil wrong, independent of breach of contract, for which a court will provide relief in the form of damages. Tort cases primarily involve state law and are grounded in the fundamental premise that individuals are liable for the consequences of their conduct that result in injury to others.[1] Most school tort actions can be grouped into three primary categories: negligence, intentional torts, and defamation.

Negligence

Negligence is a breach of one's legal duty to protect others from unreasonable risks of harm. The failure to act or the commission of an improper act, which results in injury or loss to another person, can constitute to negligence. To establish negligence, an injury must be avoidable by the exercise of reasonable care. Additionally, each of the following four elements must be present to support a successful claim:

- The defendant has a *duty* to protect the plaintiff,
- The *duty is breached* by the failure to exercise an appropriate standard of care,
- The negligent conduct is the *proximate or legal cause* of the injury, and
- An actual *injury* occurs.

[1]Similar claims also have been brought under 42 U.S.C. § 1983 (2007), which entitles individuals to sue persons acting under color of state law for damages in connection with the impairment of federally protected rights. In such controversies, there is no *respondeat superior* liability and state action is required. *Compare* Preschooler II v. Clark County Sch. Bd. of Trs., 479 F.3d 1175 (9th Cir. 2007) (denying qualified immunity when public school educators were directly responsible for the physical abuse of a 4-year-old child with disabilities) *with* Harry A. v. Duncan, No. 05-35206, 2007 U.S. App. LEXIS 7474 (9th Cir. March 27, 2007) (finding no state action where three boys videotaped activity in the girls' locker room and then circulated the tape among their peers). *See* text accompanying note 178, Chapter 11.

Duty

School officials have a common law duty to anticipate foreseeable dangers and to take necessary precautions to protect students entrusted in their care.[2] Among the specific duties school personnel owe students are to:

- Provide adequate supervision;
- Give proper instruction;
- Maintain equipment, facilities, and grounds; and
- Warn of known dangers.

Supervision.   Although state statutes require educators to provide proper supervision, school personnel are not expected to have every child under surveillance at all times during the school day or to anticipate every possible accident or incident that might occur. Moreover, there is no set level of supervision required under common law (i.e., there is no predetermined student/teacher ratio mandated by courts) for each activity or population. The level of supervision required in any given situation is determined by the aggregate of circumstances, including the age, maturity, and prior experience of the students; the specific activity in progress; and the presence of external threats. Accordingly, there may be situations in which no direct temporary supervision is needed (e.g., when a nondisruptive student is permitted to leave the classroom to use adjacent restroom facilities in a building with no known dangers[3]), where close supervision is prudent (e.g., when students with a history of inappropriate behavior are assigned to the same activity-oriented classroom), and even where one-to-one supervision is required (e.g., aquatic exercise class involving students with significant physical disabilities).

In assessing if adequate supervision has been provided, courts will determine whether the events leading up to the injury foreseeably placed the student at risk and whether the injury could have been prevented with proper supervision. Two student injury cases involving rock-throwing incidents illustrate this point. In one instance, when student rock throwing had continued for almost 10 minutes before the injury occurred, the court found the supervising teacher liable for negligence.[4] But, where a teacher aide had walked past a group of students moments before one child threw a rock that was deflected and hit another child, no liability was assessed.[5] The court concluded that the teacher aide had provided adequate supervision and had no reason to anticipate the event that caused the injury.

[2]*See, e.g.,* Carr v. Sch. Bd. of Pasco County, Fla., 921 So. 2d 825 (Fla. Ct. App. 2006).

[3]*But see* Miami-Dade County Sch. Bd. v. A.N., 905 So. 2d 203 (Fla. Ct. App. 2005) (affirming jury verdict when the board failed to warn a substitute teacher of the sexually aggressive history of a student; the student was permitted to go to the restroom unsupervised and while there attacked another student).

[4]Sheehan v. Saint Peter's Catholic Sch., 188 N.W.2d 868 (Minn. 1971).

[5]Fagan v. Summers, 498 P.2d 1227 (Wyo. 1972). *See also* Stephenson v. Commercial Travelers Mut. Ins. Co., 893 So. 2d 180 (La. Ct. App. 2005) (determining that when a soccer player incurred a fractured leg, her injury was not foreseeable or preventable).

Proper supervision is particularly important in settings that pose significant risks to students, such as vocational shops, gymnasiums, science laboratories, and school grounds where known dangers exist. In these settings, it is critical that school personnel provide both proper instruction and adequate supervision to reduce the likelihood of injury to children and staff. Even when such care is provided, accidents will occur. In a New York case, an 11-year-old student attempted to get off a slide when he was only halfway down.[6] He caught his foot under another student and fell to the ground. In ruling for the school district, the court observed that the events were sudden and unforeseen and that no amount of supervision could have prevented the injury.

The school district's duty to supervise also includes the responsibility to protect pupils and employees from foreseeable risks posed by other students or school personnel, as well as persons not associated with the district. Depending on the circumstances of a particular case, districts can meet this duty by warning potential victims, increasing the number of supervisory personnel, or providing increased security where assaults, batteries, or other violent acts are reasonably foreseeable. Courts do not expect schools to ensure the safety of students but do require that officials respond promptly and professionally when confronted with potentially dangerous circumstances.[7]

In Georgia, school employees failed to intercede prior to an altercation between two students or to call 911 following the severe beating one of the students received.[8] The teacher had heard at least part of a verbal exchange between the two, but failed to discipline or provide further supervision as he had not been informed that one of the students had an extensive history of explosive violent behavior. Moreover, school officials failed to seek emergency aid following the beating, even though the victim was covered in blood, writhing in pain, begging for help, and unable to say how his injuries were sustained. Aid eventually was summoned 49 minutes following the battery, but only after the mother had arrived at the school and called her husband

[6]Swan v. Town of Brookhaven, 821 N.Y.S.2d 265 (App. Div. 2006). *See also* Reardon v. Carle Place Union Free Sch. Dist., 813 N.Y.S.2d 150 (App. Div. 2006) (determining that when an 11-year-old student jumped from a swing and was injured in the fall, the accident occurred suddenly and without warning and could not have been prevented by any reasonable degree of supervision).

[7]*Compare* David XX v. Saint Catherine's Ctr. for Children, 699 N.Y.S.2d 827 (App. Div. 1999) (denying summary judgment where a 6-year-old was sexually abused by a 13-year-old during transport to school; the parents had informed officials on numerous occasions that an aide had not accompanied the driver, as was required, and that the older child had a history of aggressive sexual dysfunction) *with* Johnson v. Carmel Cent. Sch. Dist., 716 N.Y.S.2d 403 (App. Div. 2000) (finding no notice that a student would attack another student; school personnel could not be expected to guard against all spontaneous acts).

[8]Bajjani v. Gwinnett County Sch. Dist., 630 S.E.2d 103 (Ga. Ct. App. 2006). *See also* Wood v. Watervliet City Sch. Dist., 815 N.Y.S.2d 360 (App. Div. 2006) (concluding that fact issues remained regarding foreseeability when a student with an extensive disciplinary record, including 10 reported prior charges, battered yet another classmate with the teacher standing outside the classroom door). *But see* Peretin v. Caddo Parish Sch. Bd., 889 So. 2d 1190 (La. Ct. App. 2004) (finding no foreseeability where one student injured another student by placing her pencil in his chair as he was sitting down; the act was found unexpected and spontaneous).

who then demanded immediate medical assistance. To make matters even worse, school officials failed to make hospital personnel aware of the severity of the attack, delaying even longer the provision of needed services. The plaintiff suffered from severe head trauma, a subdural hematoma, a temporal skull fracture, and three facial fractures. School officials were reluctant to notify the police given administrative directives strongly discouraging the reporting of violence for fear that the school would be classified as "persistently dangerous" under the federal No Child Left Behind Act. The appeals court reasoned that the case should proceed to a jury, as the parents provided support for their claim of willfulness, corruption, and malice so that a jury might find the school district's immunity defenses abrogated.

When the alleged violator is a school employee, most courts have rejected claims of school district liability, finding conduct such as battery and sexual assault to represent independent acts outside an individual's scope of employment.[9] Generally, the conduct of the individual violator is the proximate cause of injury and not the negligent supervision of the district. Nonetheless, districts may be found liable for negligence in hiring or in retaining employees where school officials had knowledge of prior or continuing misconduct.[10]

Notwithstanding the general requirement to provide supervision, there may be times when students pass out of the "orbit of school authority," even though they may remain on school property. This often occurs today, given the wide range of uses of school buildings and the variety of activities. In such a case, an Indiana appeals court found that a district had no duty to supervise male students who secretly videotaped female lifeguards in their locker room in various stages of undress.[11] The tape later was circulated at the school, and the victims claimed that the school district's negligence caused their emotional distress. The lifeguard class, although held in school facilities, was not part of the public school curriculum (i.e., it was sponsored by the Red Cross after school hours), and school employees neither taught nor supervised the course. When school officials learned what had transpired, they investigated the incident, identified and suspended those responsible, and confiscated the one remaining tape. The taping was found to be unforeseeable, and no special duty was established for the district either to provide security or to supervise the class.

Supervision of students en route to and from school also has generated considerable litigation. Over the years, parents have argued that school officials are responsible for their children from the time they leave home until the time they return.[12] Although such a bright-line test would assist courts in rendering uniform decisions, it

---

[9]*See, e.g.*, Bratton v. Calkins, 870 P.2d 981 (Wash. Ct. App. 1994).

[10]But, failure to conduct a background check before hiring a staff member will result in liability only if such failure is shown to be the proximate cause of the injury. *See, e.g.*, Kendrick v. E. Delavan Baptist Church, 886 F. Supp. 1465 (E.D. Wis. 1995).

[11]Roe v. N. Adams Cmty. Sch. Corp., 647 N.E.2d 655 (Ind. Ct. App. 1995).

[12]Also, some parents have unsuccessfully asserted that their respective school districts should provide supervision during private transport to school functions. *See, e.g.*, Gylten v. Swalboski, 246 F.3d 1139 (8th Cir. 2001).

clearly would result in the placement of an unrealistic demand on school resources and an unfair burden on personnel. Courts instead focus on whether:

- The events that caused the injury were foreseeable;
- The district had an express or implied duty to provide supervision on and off school grounds both before and after school hours; and
- The child was injured due to a breach of that duty.

In cases where the district is responsible for providing transportation, officials should ensure that involved staff are properly trained and that district procedures are communicated and practiced. Personnel should strictly adhere to transportation requirements, including those related to licensure; background checks; vehicle maintenance; driving, loading, and unloading practices; conduct during transport; and criteria for when an aide is to be assigned. Designated procedures were not followed when a Washington bus driver was found negligent in the death of a 13-year-old who was killed by a car after she had exited the bus.[13] The driver failed to use either the stop sign or flashing lights as the student was discharged and then permitted the student to cross behind the bus instead of in front, as required by state law.

In addition, school officials have a duty to provide supervision during school-sponsored off-campus activities. As with other supervisory roles, school officials accompanying the students need to assess foreseeable risks associated with each activity and be aware of the abilities of participating students. However, when the activity is neither curricular nor school sponsored, liability is less likely, given the difficulty of identifying a continuing duty on the part of school officials to provide supervision. No continuing duty was identified when Washington school officials failed to supervise students participating in a party during "senior release day."[14] A student left the party intoxicated and was killed in an accident on her way home. School personnel were not involved in planning or financing the party nor did they attend. Knowledge that there would be a party did not create a duty to supervise.

In those instances in which districts are not responsible for transporting children to and from school, proper supervision still should be provided at the pick-up and drop-off area; crossing guards should be stationed at nearby intersections for "walkers"; and assistance should be provided to parents and children to help identify safe routes to and from school. Moreover, parents need to be informed about the earliest time supervision will be provided before school so that students will not arrive prior to school personnel. No duty to supervise existed where a 12-year-old Kansas boy ran off school property before school and was hit by a car. The court reasoned that the school did not owe a duty to the student to provide supervision 25 to 40 minutes prior to the beginning of the school day.[15]

---

[13]Yurkovich v. Rose, 847 P.2d 925 (Wash. Ct. App. 1993).

[14]Rhea v. Grandview Sch. Dist., 694 P.2d 666 (Wash. Ct. App. 1985).

[15]Glaser v. Emporia Unified Sch. Dist. No. 253, 21 P.3d 573 (Kan. 2001).

As a general rule, school districts are not expected to protect truant and nonattending students, or students who are injured in their homes.[16] This is true for those who never arrive at school as well as for those who exit school grounds during the school day without permission, notwithstanding an appropriate level of surveillance of the school building and grounds as determined by the age and ability of the students. A New York student left school detention to go joyriding with five friends. They were involved in a high-speed police chase resulting in a crash at approximately 5:00 p.m., well after school hours. The plaintiff lost part of an arm, in addition to other injuries, and the parents sued the school claiming negligent supervision. The court declared that "nothing short of a prison-like atmosphere with monitors at every exit could have prevented [the student] from leaving the school grounds."[17] The court refused to require such extreme measures to detain students or to require the district to provide supervision of truant students off school property and after the school day.

Moreover, extreme measures to keep students at school may themselves result in liability. A Kentucky teacher chained a student by the ankle and later, when he "escaped," chained him by the neck to a tree to prevent him from leaving school grounds again. The student had arrived late or skipped class on numerous occasions. The appeals court determined that the lower court erred in granting a directed verdict to the teacher and that proof of emotional damages should be submitted to the jury on remand.[18]

Instruction.   Teachers have a duty to provide students with adequate and appropriate instruction prior to commencing an activity that may pose a risk of harm—the greater the risk, the greater the need for proper instruction.[19] Following such instruction, effort should be made to determine whether the material was heard and understood. This can be accomplished through assessments such as paper and pencil tests, oral tests, or observations, as appropriate for the activity. Proper instruction was not given when a Nebraska freshman was severely burned in a welding course when his flannel shirt ignited.[20] The school failed to make protective leather aprons available to the students, as was recommended for such activities, and the instructor had informed the students simply to wear old shirts. Perhaps most damaging to the district's case was the

[16]*See, e.g.*, Maldonado v. Tuckahoe, 817 N.Y.S.2d 376 (App. Div. 2006).

[17]Palella v. Ulmer, 518 N.Y.S.2d 91, 93 (Sup. Ct. 1987). *See also* Doe v. San Antonio Indep. Sch. Dist., 197 Fed. Appx. 296 (5th Cir. 2006) (determining that when a student left school without permission and was later sexually assaulted by her alleged uncle, her injury was not foreseeable and was not due to any disciplinay action taken by the district or to its lack of supervision); Chalen v. Glen Cove Sch. Dist., 814 N.Y.S.2d 254 (App. Div. 2006) (finding no duty to protect a student beyond the boundaries of school property or liability in a wrongful death claim in which a student and family friend ingested poison and died; noting that officials had no knowledge that the visitor posed a danger or that the student would leave campus without permission).

[18]Banks v. Fritsch, 39 S.W.3d 474 (Ky. Ct. App. 2001).

[19]*See, e.g.*, Traficenti v. Moore Catholic High Sch., 724 N.Y.S.2d 24 (App. Div. 2001).

[20]Norman v. Ogallala Pub. Sch. Dist., 609 N.W.2d 338 (Neb. 2000).

testimony of the instructor, when he stated on four separate occasions that it was not his responsibility to ensure that students wore protective clothing. "Safety garments" as a topic was briefly mentioned in one of many handouts distributed in class, but no effort was made to determine whether students read or understood the material and on no occasion did the instructor prevent a student from participating based on the type of clothing worn.

Maintenance of Buildings, Grounds, and Equipment.   Some states by law protect frequenters of public buildings from danger to life, health, safety, or welfare. These *safe place statutes* may be used by individuals to obtain damages from school districts for injuries resulting from defective conditions of school buildings and grounds. Moreover, school officials have a common law duty to maintain facilities and equipment in a reasonably safe condition. Districts can be held liable when they are aware of, or should be aware of, hazardous conditions and do not take the necessary steps to repair or correct the conditions. For example, school districts are responsible for the removal or encasement of asbestos materials;[21] failure to do so can result in injury and accompanying tort suits when injuries are shown to be related to exposure. The fear of future disease appears insufficient to base a claim, however.[22] Because state and federal support for asbestos removal has been limited, numerous districts have sued asbestos manufacturers and suppliers to recover extraction costs.[23] Such providers typically failed either to test the materials to determine whether they were hazardous or to warn consumers of potential dangers.

The duty to provide reasonable maintenance of facilities does not place an obligation on school personnel to anticipate every possible danger or to be aware of and correct every minor defect as soon as the condition occurs. For example, a Louisiana student was unsuccessful in establishing a breach of duty in connection with an injury sustained on a defective door latch.[24] The state appeals court concluded that there was no evidence that any school employee had knowledge of, or should have had knowledge of, the broken latch. Because the risk was unforeseen, a duty to protect the student could not be imposed. Similarly, two Alabama teachers were not found negligent for an injury that occurred when a student slipped on a puddle of water during a physical education class; the teachers were unaware of the puddle and the condition in the roof that led to the accumulation of water.[25]

If dangers are known, damages at times may be awarded when injuries result from unsafe building or grounds conditions. A Michigan student was successful in obtaining damages for the loss of sight in one eye; the injury was sustained while

[21]Asbestos School Hazard Detection and Control Act, 20 U.S.C. § 3601 *et seq.* (2007); Asbestos Hazard Emergency Response Act of 1986, 15 U.S.C. § 2641 *et seq.* (2007).

[22]Brooks v. Stone Architecture, 934 So. 2d 350 (Miss. Ct. App. 2006).

[23]*See, e.g., In re* Asbestos Sch. Litig., Pfizer, 46 F.3d 1284 (3d Cir. 1994); Adam Pub. Sch. Dist. v. Asbestos Corp., 7 F.3d 717 (8th Cir. 1993).

[24]Lewis v. Saint Bernard Parish Sch. Bd., 350 So. 2d 1256 (La. Ct. App. 1977).

[25]Best v. Houtz, 541 So. 2d 8 (Ala. 1989).

playing in a pile of dirt and sand on the playground after school hours.[26] The area was not fenced, and prior to the incident parents had complained to school officials about "dirt fights" among children. The state appeals court concluded that the school district breached its duty to maintain the school grounds in a safe condition. In contrast, a parent fell on a sidewalk on school property and was injured.[27] Officials did not cancel an athletic contest held in the evening, even though school had been cancelled that day due the accumulation of ice and snow. In granting immunity to the West Virginia school district, the court distinguished between conditions caused by the weather and those caused or exacerbated by the district (e.g., placement of snow on the walkway in an effort to clear the roadway), with liability assigned only in the latter.

In addition to maintaining buildings and grounds, school personnel are required to maintain equipment and to use it safely, such as in woodshop, science labs, athletics, or transportation.[28] A Kentucky coach was found liable for the electrocution death of a student who had been using a whirlpool. The coach had "modified" the equipment but had failed to install a ground fault interrupter, although one was required by the national electric code. His negligence was found to be the substantial factor causing the student's death.[29] Similarly, the Texas appeals court determined that immunity would be waived in part where a 5-year-old child fell asleep on her way to school and was locked in the bus for the remainder of the school day. The court reasoned that although the district was immune for its alleged failure to supervise the unloading of the children, the district could be sued for the negligent locking of the door, given that such an act did not qualify as the "operation or use of a motor vehicle" for which immunity is granted.[30]

Duty to Warn.   Courts in nearly all states today have recognized either a statutory or common law duty to warn students, parents, and at times educators and staff of known risks they may encounter. This duty has been identified in areas such as physical education and interscholastic sports, vocational education, laboratory science, and other occasions when a student uses potentially dangerous machinery or equipment.[31] Informing, if not warning, those involved of known dangers is necessary so that they then may appreciate the risk and be in a better position to decide whether to assume it.

In addition to the somewhat traditional warnings connected with sports or the use of equipment, educators, school psychologists, and counselors have a duty to warn when they learn through advising, counseling, or therapy that students intend to harm themselves or others. Those in receipt of such information are required to inform potential victims or to notify parents if the student threatens to self-injure. This requirement supersedes claims of professional ethics, discretion, therapist/client

---

[26]Monfils v. City of Sterling Heights, 269 N.W.2d 588 (Mich. Ct. App. 1978).

[27]Porter v. Grant County Bd. of Educ., 633 S.E.2d 38 (W. Va. 2006).

[28]*See, e.g.*, Arteman v. Clinton Cmty. Unit Sch. Dist. No. 15, 740 N.E.2d 47 (Ill. App. Ct. 2000).

[29]Massie v. Persson, 729 S.W.2d 448 (Ky. Ct. App. 1987).

[30]Elgin Indep. Sch. Dist. v. R.N., 191 S.W.3d 263 (Tex. App. 2006).

[31]*See, e.g.*, Mangold v. Ind. Dep't of Natural Res., 720 N.E.2d 424 (Ind. Ct. App. 1999).

privilege, or confidentiality. In California, a university psychotherapist failed to warn a patient's former girlfriend of a death threat he made against her. Campus police interviewed the patient after they were notified of his intentions, but released him following a brief interrogation. Neither the police nor the psychotherapist took further action and the patient carried out his threat. The court held that the psychotherapist had not exercised reasonable care, particularly given his knowledge of both the seriousness of the threat and the identity of the potential victim.[32]

Typically, however, school officials will not be found liable when the act of suicide is unforeseeable (i.e., the threat of suicide was neither explicitly stated nor apparent), even if they knew that a particular student was under stress or seemed depressed or preoccupied. The Third Circuit found no school district liability when a student committed suicide while at home.[33] The decedent had briefly dated a female student. After hearing rumors of her involvement with a new boyfriend, he gave her a note indicating that the gossip "almost made me want to go kill myself."[34] The former girlfriend gave the note to a school counselor, indicating that although she did not feel that he would harm himself, she nonetheless was tired of him bothering her. The counselor discussed the matter with the young man and was satisfied that he showed no indications of committing suicide. As a result, the counselor elected not to inform the school psychologist or his parents. A little over a week later, following an altercation with his mother, the youth hanged himself. The school district and its employees were found entitled to immunity, given that the counselor's conduct did not amount to actual malice, willful misconduct, fraud, or a crime. She did not believe the student was at risk, nor did she create or enhance the danger.[35]

School officials also have a duty to warn employees of known dangers, whether structural, environmental, or human. Accordingly, a Florida court reversed a lower court grant of summary judgment in a case in which district officials had failed to warn a teacher about a student's propensity for violence.[36] On remand, to overcome the general rule of workers' compensation[37] immunity, the battered teacher will have to show that the employer engaged in conduct that was substantially certain to result in injury.[38] To aid the lower court in reaching its decision, the appeals court noted that

---

[32]Tarasoff v. Regents of the Univ. of Cal., 551 P.2d 334 (Cal. 1976).

[33]Sanford v. Stiles, 456 F.3d 298 (3d Cir. 2006).

[34]*Id.* at 301.

[35]*See also* Carrier v. Lake Pend Oreille Sch. Dist., 134 P.3d 655 (Idaho 2006) (finding no duty to warn as the student's conduct did not qualify as "suicidal tendency" under state law—i.e., a present aim, direction, or trend toward taking one's own life).

[36]Patrick v. Palm Beach County Sch. Bd., 927 So. 2d 973 (Fla. Ct. App. 2006).

[37]*See, e.g.*, Wyble v. Acadiana Preparatory Sch., 956 So. 2d 722 (La. Ct. App. 2007) (determining that a school employee was eligible for workers' compensation when injured at work moving a desk at work, it did not matter that the task was routine rather than an accident).

[38]Workers' compensation immunity protects employers from liability when employees are injured on the job while involved in performing job-related responsibilities. To avoid the application of this form of immunity, the employee is required to show that the employer intended to injure the employee or in the alternative required the employee to engage in conduct that was substantially likely to result in injury.

the student had (1) been classified as severely emotionally disabled with a multiple personality disorder, (2) been involved in numerous acts of violence, (3) previously threatened teachers, and (4) been ordered by a court to undergo inpatient treatment for slamming his mother's head against the floor. Moreover, the district had either concealed or misrepresented these facts in its effort to place the student in his current school.

Breach of Duty/Standard of Care

Once a duty has been established, the injured individual must show that the duty was breached by the failure of another to exercise an appropriate standard of care.[39] The degree of care teachers owe students is determined by:

- The age, experience, and maturity level of the students;
- The environment within which the incident occurs; and
- The type of instructional or recreational activity.

For example, primary grade students will generally require closer supervision and more detailed and repetitive instructions than will high school students, and a class in woodwork will require closer supervision than will a class in English literature. Variability in the level of care deemed reasonable is illustrated in a Louisiana case in which a mentally retarded student was fatally injured when he darted into a busy thoroughfare while being escorted with nine other classmates to a park three blocks from the school.[40] The state appellate court noted that the general level of care required for all students becomes greater when children with disabilities are involved, particularly when they are taken away from the school campus. The court found the supervision to be inadequate and the selected route to be less safe than alternate routes. The reasonableness of any given action will be pivotal in determining whether there is liability.

Reasonable Person.   In assessing whether appropriate care has been taken, courts consider whether the defendant acted as a "reasonable person" would have acted under the circumstances. The reasonable person is a hypothetical individual who has:

- The physical attributes of the defendant;
- Normal intelligence, problem-solving ability, and temperament;
- Normal perception and memory with a minimum level of information and experience common to the community; and
- Such superior skill and knowledge as the defendant has or purports to have.

Courts will not assume that a defendant possesses any predetermined physical attributes (e.g., size, strength, agility), but rather will consider each defendant's

---

[39]*See, e.g.*, Weber v. William Floyd Sch. Dist., 707 N.Y.S.2d 231 (App. Div. 2000).

[40]Foster v. Houston Gen. Ins. Co., 407 So. 2d 759, 763 (La. Ct. App. 1981).

actual physical abilities and disabilities in determining whether the defendant was responsible in whole or in part for an individual's injury. Accordingly, if a child requires physical assistance to avoid injury (e.g., when being attacked by another student), a different expectation will exist for a large, physically fit teacher as compared to a small, frail teacher.

Although a defendant's actual physical characteristics and capabilities are used in determining whether his or her conduct was reasonable, that is not the case when considering mental capacity. Courts will assume all adult individuals have normal intelligence, problem-solving ability, and temperament, even when the evidence indicates that they do not possess such attributes.[41] Although this may initially appear unfair, any other approach is likely to result in defense claims that are judicially unmanageable. For example, if defendants' own intellect were used, they could argue that consideration should be given to factors such as their inability to make good or quick decisions, lack of perception or concentration, poor attention to detail, confrontational personality, or inability to deal with stress. Trying to determine each person's mental abilities and capabilities would be impractical, if not impossible, given the dearth of valid and reliable assessment instruments or techniques and the ease of those being assessed to misrepresent their abilities. The current approach of assuming normal intelligence provides a more objective procedure and requires defendants to be responsible for injuries they cause others.

Courts also attempt to ascertain whether a defendant "discovered that which was readily apparent"[42] in that the defendant is required to have a normal perception of the environment (e.g., be aware that the rear of the school yard is bordered by a small river) and an accurate memory of what has occurred previously within that environment (e.g., recalling that the playground floods following a heavy rain). This requirement does not assume that the defendant will know all facts, foresee all risks, or be aware of all things. Instead, it is based on the position that there exist certain facts that a reasonable adult, with normal intellect, should know.

In an effort to determine whether the defendant acted as a reasonable person, courts also consider whether the defendant had or claimed to have had any superior knowledge or skill. Teachers, who are college graduates and state licensed, are expected to act like reasonable persons with similar education. In addition, any special training an individual has received may affect whether a given act is considered reasonable. Accordingly, a physical education instructor who is a certified lifeguard or a teacher with an advanced degree in chemistry may be held to higher standards of care than others with lesser skills and knowledge when a student is drowning or when chemicals in a school laboratory are mixed improperly and ignite.

Invitee, Licensee, and Trespasser. In reaching a decision on whether an appropriate standard of care has been provided, courts also determine whether an injured

---

[41]W. Page Keeton, Dan B. Dobbs, Robert E. Keeton, & David G. Owen, *Prosser and Keeton on Torts*, 5th ed. (St. Paul, MN: West, 1984), p. 177.

[42]*Id.* at 182.

individual was an invitee, licensee, or trespasser, with invitees receiving the greatest level of care and trespassers receiving the least. In a school setting, an invitee is one who enters the school premises on the expressed or implied invitation of the school district or one of its agents. The district then has an affirmative duty to exercise reasonable care for the safety of invitees commensurate with the risks and circumstances involved. Furthermore, invitees must be protected against known dangers as well as those that might be discovered with reasonable care. Under most circumstances, students, teachers, and administrators are invitees of the district. Students who break into a school after hours, however, have exceeded the "period of invitation" and become trespassers.[43]

Where permission to be on school premises is requested and permitted, the person becomes a licensee (e.g., requests by unsolicited visitors, salespersons, parents, newspersons). Even schoolchildren may qualify as licensees under certain circumstances (e.g., while engaged in activities of a local nonschool organization that has been permitted evening or weekend use of a school classroom). Such persons enter the building or grounds facing the same conditions and threats as the occupier. Nevertheless, districts still need to warn licensees of known dangers and not injure intentionally or by willful, wanton, or reckless conduct.

When the individual has neither been invited nor received consent, the person is guilty of trespass upon accessing school property. Although state laws often blur the distinction between licensee and trespasser, less care has to be provided for the safety of trespassers. Adult trespassers in particular have no right to a safe place and must assume the risk of what they may encounter. Generally, the owner owes no duty to trespassers other than to refrain from willfully or wantonly injuring them (e.g., by setting traps). In selected jurisdictions, however, if the owner knows that trespassers are on the premises (e.g., vagrants living in an abandoned school building), the owner must use reasonable care not to expose the trespasser to an environment that is known to be dangerous. When the trespasser is a child, as often is the case on school property, it is prudent to take additional steps to restrict access or to remove known dangers. In such narrow instances, there is little legal distinction between a trespasser and a licensee in regard to the standard of care provided.

Proximate Cause

For liability to be assessed against a school district, the negligent conduct of school personnel must be the proximate or legal cause of injury. *Proximate cause* has been defined as "that which in a natural and continuous sequence, unbroken by any efficient

---

[43]*See, e.g.,* Howard County Bd. of Educ. v. Cheyne, 636 A.2d 22 (Md. Ct. App. 1994) (holding that a 4-year-old was an invitee when she initially entered a gymnasium to attend a sports function, but that a question remained for the jury to determine whether she had exceeded the "scope of her invitation" at the time of the injury—following a school basketball game, the child was injured while retrieving basketballs her mother had shot). *See also* Tincani v. Inland Empire Zoological Soc'y, 875 P.2d 621 (Wash. 1994) (remanding a case in which a student sued a zoo after falling off a cliff during a field trip; the court questioned whether he became a licensee when he strayed beyond the "area of his invitation").

intervening cause, produces the injury, and without which the result would not have occurred."[44] In determining proximate cause, courts consider factors other than the defendant's conduct that contributed to producing the injury, ascertain whether the challenged conduct created a force that was in operation up to the time of the injury, and assess the lapse of time between the conduct and the occurrence of the injury. Accordingly, not every seemingly negligent act results in liability, even when an injury results, unless the act was in fact the cause of the injury. The New York appellate court affirmed summary judgment for a school district when the sole proximate cause of the appellant's injuries was his attempt to do a back flip dismount from the playground equipment while his teacher's back was turned; the act was sudden and unforeseeable.[45] Likewise, the Montana Supreme Court affirmed a jury verdict finding no negligent supervision on the part of a special education assistant when a child let go and fell two to three feet from playground equipment, breaking her tibia. Two adult supervisors were overseeing 11 special needs students, but by the time the supervisors saw the child falling, it was too late to intervene. The alleged failure to supervise was not found to be the proximate cause of the child's injury.[46]

Injury

Legal negligence does not exist unless actual injury is incurred either directly by the individual or by the individual's property. Most often, an individual will know of the injury as soon as it occurs; in some instances, however, the individual may not be aware of the injury for many months or even years (e.g., development of asbestosis due to exposure to asbestos 20 years previously). In most states, there is a statute of limitations of one to three years on tort claims, although the actual time can be greater if the limitations period does not begin until the plaintiff reaches the age of majority or becomes aware of the injury.

When students are injured in the school setting, school personnel have a duty to provide reasonable assistance commensurate with their training and experience. Where reasonable treatment is provided, no liability will generally be assessed, even if the treatment later is proven to be inappropriate or inadequate.

Defenses against Negligence

Several defenses are available to school districts when employees have been charged with negligence. At times, districts have identified procedural defects (e.g., the failure to adhere to statutory requirements regarding notice of claim), or have proposed that an individual's injury was caused by uncontrollable events of nature (i.e., an act

[44]Anselmo v. Tuck, 924 S.W.2d 798, 802 (Ark. 1996).

[45]Ascher v. Scarsdale Sch. Dist., 700 N.Y.S.2d 210 (App. Div. 1999).

[46]Morgan v. Great Falls Sch. Dist., 995 P.2d 422 (Mont. 2000). *See also* Williamson v. Liptzin, 539 S.E.2d 313 (N.C. Ct. App. 2000) (reasoning that the alleged negligence by the psychiatrist was not the proximate cause of plaintiff's actions—i.e., killing two people eight months after his last session).

of God) in an effort to thwart liability claims. More commonly, defenses such as immunity, contributory negligence, comparative negligence, and assumption of risk have been asserted.

Governmental Immunity.   In rare cases in which governmental immunity is comprehensively applied, governmental entities including school districts cannot be sued for any reason. But, this defense is available to employees only when state law specifically confers such immunity for acts within the scope of employment, or courts interpret the law to do so.[47] However, immunity is seldom comprehensively applied today, as nearly all states have limited its use by considering factors such as whether (1) the claim was related to the maintenance of the school building or property, (2) acts were governmental or proprietary, (3) decisions qualified as discretionary or ministerial, (4) school property was being used for recreational purposes, or (5) the injury was compensable under the state's workers' compensation laws (employees only).

In most jurisdictions, school districts can be held liable for injuries arising from a dangerous realty condition if authorities have knowledge of a defect and do not take corrective action or if they maintain an attractive nuisance.[48] An *attractive nuisance* is a facility, structure, or piece of equipment that entices the public to engage in activity that is potentially dangerous. Swimming pools and ponds on school property often are classified as attractive nuisances. Because of the potential for serious injury, school districts may claim immunity only if proper precautions are taken to prevent public access to such areas.

In some states, a distinction has been made between governmental and proprietary functions in determining whether a school district is immune. *Governmental functions* are those that are performed in discharging the agency's official duties (e.g., hiring faculty) that are generally considered immune from liability. On the other hand, *proprietary functions* are those that are only tangentially related to the curriculum, can as easily be performed by the private sector, and often require the payment of a fee (e.g., community use of school pool); these activities have been permissible targets for tort actions. Except in the most extreme cases, however, it may prove difficult to identify activities that are proprietary, because most school endeavors in some way can be linked to the mission of the district.

In other states, the distinction between discretionary and ministerial functions is used to determine whether liability exists. As with governmental and propriety functions, differentiation between those that qualify as discretionary and ministerial will be obvious only when assessing extreme examples.[49] By definition, *discretionary*

---

[47]*See, e.g.*, Brown v. Fountain Hill Sch. Dist., 1 S.W.3d 27 (Ark. Ct. App. 1999); Coonse v. Boise Sch. Dist., 979 P.2d 1161 (Idaho 1999).

[48]*See supra* text accompanying notes 21–30.

[49]*See, e.g.*, Univ. of Tex. at San Antonio v. Trevino, 153 S.W.3d 58 (Tex. App. 2002) (distinguishing discretionary and ministerial functions where a 3-year-old died when she fell between the railings of the bleachers by applying the design/maintenance test for structures and equipment—i.e., immunity is granted for the design of the bleachers but not for their maintenance or operation).

functions are those that require consideration of alternatives, deliberation, judgment, and the making of a decision (e.g., the discretion used in the selection of a new teacher). In contrast, *ministerial functions* are those performed in a prescribed manner, in obedience to legal authority, and without discretion (e.g., procedures used for stopping a school bus at a railroad crossing).[50] As a rule, districts will be liable for negligence involving ministerial duties but be immune from liability for negligence associated with those that are discretionary.[51]

Some states also differentiate between policy-level discretionary acts (for which immunity is granted) and operational-level discretionary acts that deal with policy implementation (for which immunity is not granted).[52] For example, in a case in which an individual was injured when knocked from her bike by a powerful water sprinkler,[53] a Texas appeals court determined that the decision of whether to water the grounds of a university was an immune policy decision. However, placement of the sprinkler system near the running and riding path and turning it on during a time when there foreseeably would be traffic constituted policy implementation for which liability could be assessed.

A similar grant of discretionary-function immunity was provided in an Ohio case.[54] A coach elected to have the girls' basketball team practice with older boys, given his belief that the boys used sound skills and would help take the girl's team to the next level athletically. During practice, one of the girls incurred a broken arm when a boy attempted to slap the ball from her hands. There was no personal contact and had the slap of the ball occurred during a game, no foul would have been called. The court determined that the coach had exercised discretionary authority with the intent to improve his team's skills and competitive ability.

Another type of immunity defense exists for *recreational use*. Such statutes were passed to encourage property and landowners (including public-sector entities) to open their lands and waters for public recreational use. School gymnasiums, playgrounds, and athletic fields at times have been labeled as recreational facilities or areas, although state laws vary considerably.[55] Immunity for injuries incurred while

---

[50]*See, e.g.*, Harrison v. Hardin County Cmty. Unit Sch. Dist. No. 1, 730 N.E.2d 61 (Ill. App. Ct. 2000).

[51]*See, e.g.*, Pauley v. Anchorage Sch. Dist., 31 P.3d 1284 (Alaska 2001); Trotter v. Sch. Dist. 218, 733 N.E.2d 363 (Ill. App. Ct. 2000).

[52]Norman v. Ogallala Pub. Sch. Dist., 609 N.W.2d 338 (Neb. 2000).

[53]Stephen F. Austin State Univ. v. Flynn, 202 S.W.3d 167 (Tex. App. 2004).

[54]Schnarrs v. Girard Bd. of Educ., 858 N.E.2d 1258 (Ohio Ct. App. 2006). *See also* Worthington v. Elmore County Bd. of Educ., 160 Fed. Appx. 877 (11th Cir. 2005) (granting immunity when a student claimed to have been sexually abused by another student while being transported on a bus for special needs children, and reasoning that the supervision of students was a discretionary, rather than ministerial, function and that even if it were not, there was insufficient evidence to find the driver negligent; his alleged failure to properly supervise the students was found not to be the "moving force" behind the assault).

[55]*See, e.g.*, Fear v. Indep. Sch. Dist. 911, 634 N.W.2d 204 (Minn. Ct. App. 2001) (holding that a district was not necessarily entitled to immunity when an elementary school child fell from piled snow and was injured; whether recreational immunity applied was a question to be answered at trial by applying the child trespasser standard); Auman v. Sch. Dist., 635 N.W.2d 762 (Wis. 2001) (concluding that the recreational immunity statute did not shield the district from liability for injuries to a student during mandatory recess).

on the property is provided unless the entrant was charged a fee for admission or was injured because of the owner's willful or wanton misconduct. In Kansas, a football player collapsed at the end of his first mandatory practice and died the following day; plaintiffs claimed that his death was caused by the failure to provide proper supervision. The court applied recreational-use immunity in regard to the ordinary negligence claim, but remanded the case for a determination of whether the defendant's conduct amounted to gross or wanton negligence.[56] If the defendant's conduct were found gross or wanton, neither recreational use nor discretionary function immunity protect the district from liability.

Immunity also may be used as a defense when an injury is compensable under the state's workers' compensation statute. Workers' compensation laws are intended to reduce or eliminate negligence litigation (i.e., they do not protect employers or employees who engage in intentional torts), encourage employer interest in safety and rehabilitation, and promote the study of the causes of accidents rather than concealment of fault, thereby reducing the occurrence of preventable accidents.[57] Under workers' compensation, liability exists regardless of negligence or fault on the part of the employer or employee, provided that the injury was accidental *and* arose out of and in the course of employment. Note, however, that not all injuries that occur at work are necessarily "work related." A teacher's widow was unsuccessful in securing benefits after her adulterous husband was shot at school by another teacher's jealous husband. The New Mexico court ruled that the action was taken for purely personal reasons and that the death did not arise out of, was not incident to, and did not occur in the course of the teacher's employment.[58]

A corollary issue in some states has been whether the purchase of liability insurance has impliedly waived immunity, notwithstanding explicit state statutes granting it. Courts have been divided on the matter with some maintaining immunity (in whole or in part) and others abrogating it.[59] In some states, it is clear that public school districts may be sued, but often only to the extent of insurance coverage.[60]

In addition to purchasing insurance to protect district funds, a number of states have enacted legislation requiring school systems to indemnify or save harmless educators for potential monetary losses associated with negligent conduct that occurred during the performance of assigned duties. Although funds for such purposes can be derived from a variety of sources (e.g., sinking funds, current operations, endowments), it is common for districts to purchase insurance to help manage the financial

---

[56]Barrett v. Unified Sch. Dist. No. 259, 32 P.3d 1156 (Kan. 2001).

[57]For a related discussion, *see* Stephen B. Thomas, *Students, Colleges, and Disability Law* (Dayton, OH: Education Law Association, 2002), pp. 270–272.

[58]Gutierrez v. Artesia Pub. Sch., 583 P.2d 476 (N.M. Ct. App. 1978).

[59]*Compare* Brock v. Sumter County Sch. Bd., 542 S.E.2d 547 (Ga. Ct. App. 2000) (holding that the district had not waived sovereign immunity through the purchase of motor vehicle liability insurance) *with* Crowell v. Sch. Dist. No. 7, Gallatin County, 805 P.2d 522 (Mont. 1991) (holding that the purchase of insurance constituted a waiver of immunity).

[60]*See, e.g.*, Helena-W. Helena Sch. Dist. v. Monday, 204 S.W.3d 514 (Ark. 2005).

risk associated with employee negligence. Generally, these laws require districts to assume the cost of legal representation and any resulting liability if negligence is proven.

Contributory Negligence. Under the contributory model, only the injured party bears financial responsibility if ultimately found responsible for the act leading to an injury; it makes no difference that the defendant was negligent and also at fault. Over the years, the contributory defense has been modified and weakened by courts due to a number of factors, including its harshness to injured plaintiffs, the ease of negligent defendants to avoid liability, and a change in social viewpoint (i.e., from the need to protect new industries early in the twentieth century to the desire to compensate injured persons).[61] As a result, in most jurisdictions today, a slight degree of fault will not prevent a plaintiff from prevailing.

In assessing whether contributory negligence exists, children are not necessarily held to the same standard of care as adults. Rather, their actions must be reasonable for persons of similar age, maturity, intelligence, and experience. Many courts make individualized determinations as to whether a minor plaintiff appreciated the risks involved and acted as a reasonable person of like characteristics and abilities. Other courts have established age ranges in an effort to more objectively and uniformly determine whether children have the capacity to contribute to or cause their own injuries. Although courts vary greatly and designated ages may seem arbitrary (often based on biblical scripture or criminal law, with little or nothing to do with child development), the most commonly used ranges are:

- Children below the age of 7 are considered incapable of negligence;
- Children between the ages of 7 and 14 are considered incapable of negligence, but this presumption can be rebutted;[62] and
- Students age 14 and over are generally presumed capable of negligence, although this presumption too can be rebutted.[63]

When adults are injured on school grounds or at school functions, courts will assess the nature of the risk involved and whether such a risk was known to the injured party or reasonably should have been known. An Indiana court upheld a grant of summary judgment where a father fell from backless bleachers while watching his son participate in a basketball game. The court found the plaintiff to be contributorily

---

[61]Keeton, *et al. supra* note 41, pp. 452–453.

[62]*See, e.g.*, Agnor v. Caddo Parish Sch. Bd., 936 So. 2d 865 (La. Ct. App. 2006) (determining that an 8-year-old was 25 percent liable for the injury she sustained when sliding on the routinely wet floors in the girls' restroom; when she lost her balance and fell, a pencil penetrated her face and lodged beneath her eye).

[63]*See, e.g.*, Doe v. LaFayette Sch. Corp., 846 N.E. 2d 691 (Ind. Ct. App. 2006) (observing that although children over the age of 14 generally are responsible for exercising the standard of care of an adult, a 15-year-old student who was seduced by her teacher was found not to have been engaged in contributory negligence).

negligent in that he failed to exercise the degree of care that an ordinary, reasonable, and prudent person in a similar situation would exercise.[64] Similarly, a California appeals court concluded that a district was not liable for the death of a student on school grounds after regular school hours.[65] Although the playground was accessible to the public, unsupervised, and in disrepair, the court concluded that the student's death resulted from his own conduct in attempting to perform a hazardous skateboard activity, not from defective playground conditions.

Comparative Negligence.   With the comparative model, the plaintiff and/or one or more defendants bear responsibility in proportion to fault. For example, a Louisiana school bus driver permitted two girls to exit his bus even though he knew one had threatened to injure the other. He initially left the bus with them, held them apart, and told a teacher to summon the principal. Instead of waiting for the principal or a teacher to arrive, however, he reentered the bus to move it, because he was blocking traffic. When he pulled away, one student proceeded to stomp the other student's ankle; the injury was so severe as to require three screws to align the broken bones. The court reasoned that the driver should not have left the students unsupervised under the circumstances and assessed 15 percent liability against him and 85 percent of liability to the student responsible for the attack.[66] Similarly, an Arizona appeals court upheld a jury verdict where a student was hit by a car when he ran into the street trying to flee another student after he safely exited a school bus on his way home. Liability was apportioned to the injured boy (45 percent), his parents (40 percent), and the district (15 percent) in a $6 million award. Although the school district was not responsible for escorting the child home, school officials were aware of the conduct of the students at the bus stop, a nearby busy street with fast-moving traffic, and the availability of an alternative and safer bus stop.[67]

Assumption of Risk.   This defense can be either express or implied. *Express assumption* occurs when the plaintiff consents in advance to take his or her chances of injury, given a known danger. On the other hand, *implied assumption* occurs without an express written or oral agreement, yet is logically assumed, given the plaintiff's conduct. For example, implied assumption would exist where spectators at a baseball game elect to sit in unscreened seats; such persons assume the risk of possible injury even if they failed to sign an agreement.

   Inherent risks are associated with athletics or recreation, but it cannot be assumed that all participants, regardless of age, maturity, and experience, understand those risks. As a result, school personnel must exercise reasonable care to protect students from unassumed, concealed, or unreasonably high risks. This duty can be met when participation is voluntary and the student is knowledgeable of and assumes the

---

[64]Funston v. Sch. Town of Munster, 849 N.E.2d 595 (Ind. 2006).

[65]Bartell v. Palos Verdes Peninsula Sch. Dist., 147 Cal. Rptr. 898 (Ct. App. 1978).

[66]Bell v. Ayio, 731 So. 2d 893 (La. Ct. App. 1999).

[67]Warrington v. Tempe Elementary Sch. Dist. No. 3, 3 P.3d 988 (Ariz. Ct. App. 1999).

risks associated with the activity. For instance, in Indiana a football player died following extensive conditioning in hot and humid weather. His mother had signed a release form providing permission for him to participate in organized athletics and acknowledging that injuries and even death may result.[68] The appeals court concluded that the lower court was correct in permitting the admission of the form as part of the district's defense. The athlete had several years of general football experience and in prior years had participated in the conditioning program of the current coach.

In regard to sports, however, student athletes assume only those risks that occur during normal participation; they do not assume unknown risks associated with a coach's negligence. Moreover, they are not assuming that they will be exposed to intentional torts or conduct that represents a reckless disregard for the safety of others. But, penalties and poor judgment by other participants generally will not qualify as intentional torts and most often will be viewed as occurring commonly, if not routinely, in the sport (e.g., being clipped in football). In an illustrative case, the Ohio appeals court affirmed summary judgment for a school district where one soccer player collided with another, causing an injury. The student responsible for the collision was removed from the game, and her team was penalized. The court, nevertheless, reasoned that the risk of being subjected to an illegal slide tackle was a foreseeable risk of playing soccer, even if it represented a rules violation.[69]

A slightly different perspective was taken by the Maryland appeals court when it reviewed a case involving the sport of weightlifting—a particularly high-risk sport when lift levels exceed 500 pounds.[70] The court concluded that the student assumed the risks typically associated with the sport, even the improper positioning of spotters. However, the court further reasoned that the student did not assume that the spotters would fail to intervene or come to his aid unless signaled by an official to do so.[71]

Intentional Torts

Among the more common types of intentional torts are assault, battery, false imprisonment, and intentional infliction of mental distress. Each of these torts is discussed briefly below.

[68]Stowers v. Clinton Cent. Sch. Corp., 855 N.E.2d 739 (Ind. Ct. App. 2006). *See also* Ross v. New York Quarterly Meeting of the Religious Soc'y of Friends, 819 N.Y.S.2d 749 (App. Div. 2006) (determining that the athlete had assumed the risks associated with playing softball when she was injured when practicing her slide).

[69]Bentley v. Cuyahoga Falls Bd. of Educ., 709 N.E.2d 1241 (Ohio Ct. App. 1998). In *dicta* the court opined that had the conduct been so extreme so as to qualify as "reckless" (i.e., exceeds negligence and creates an unreasonable risk of physical harm), the penalized athlete could have been found liable.

[70]*See, e.g.*, Cotillo v. Duncan, 912 A.2d 72 (Md. Ct. Spec. App. 2006).

[71]*See also* Milea v. Our Lady of Miracles Roman Catholic Church, 736 N.Y.S.2d 84 (App. Div. 2002) (finding that a student assumed the risk of injury when he landed on a metal cross bar attached to a portable basketball hoop, as the risk did not exceed the usual dangers inherent in the sport).

Assault and Battery

Assault consists of an overt attempt to place another in fear of bodily harm; no actual physical contact need take place. Examples include threatening with words, pointing a gun, waving a knife, or shaking a fist. For there to be an assault, the plaintiff needs to be aware of the threat, and the person committing the assault needs to be perceived as having the ability to carry out the threat. In contrast, a *battery* is committed when an assault is consummated. Examples include being shot, stabbed, beaten, or struck. Actual injury need not result for a battery claim to succeed (e.g., the person could have been punched but not injured due to a comparatively weak blow). For the plaintiff to prevail in either an assault or a battery case, the act must be intentional; there is no such thing as a negligent assault or battery.

Some school-based assault and battery cases have involved the administration of corporal punishment and other forms of discipline that require physical touching. Generally, courts have been reluctant to interfere with a teacher's authority to discipline students and have sanctioned the use of reasonable force to control pupil behavior. The Oregon appeals court ruled that a teacher was not guilty of assault and battery for using force to remove a student from the classroom. After the pupil defiantly refused to leave, the teacher held his arms and led him toward the door. The student extricated himself, swung at the teacher, and broke a window, thereby cutting his arm. The court concluded that the teacher used reasonable force with the student and dismissed the assault and battery charges.[72] In contrast, a Louisiana student was successful in obtaining damages.[73] The pupil sustained a broken arm when a teacher shook him, lifted him against the bleachers in the gymnasium, and then let him fall to the floor. The court reasoned that the teacher's action was unnecessary either to discipline the student or to protect himself.

Although comparatively uncommon, school personnel may initiate battery suits against students who injure them.[74] Suits are not barred simply because the person committing the tort is a minor. A Wisconsin appeals court awarded damages to a teacher when he was physically attacked outside the school building while attempting to escort a student to the office for violating a smoking ban. The court held that the student, who had five previous fighting violations, acted with malicious intent in repeatedly striking the teacher and in pushing the teacher's face into the corner of a building. Both actual and punitive damages were awarded, notwithstanding the fact that the student was a minor at the time of the battery or that the student's

---

[72]Simms v. Sch. Dist. No. 1, 508 P.2d 236 (Or. Ct. App. 1973). *See also* Frame v. Comeaux, 735 So. 2d 753 (La. Ct. App. 1999) (finding no battery when a substitute teacher grabbed a confrontational eighth grade student by the arm and escorted him out of the room—the student had been talking during a test).

[73]Frank v. Orleans Parish Sch. Bd., 195 So. 2d 451 (La. Ct. App. 1967).

[74]In addition, some negligence suits are filed by school personnel against their districts when they have been battered at work. In most cases, however, courts have found that the incidents were unforeseen and that no special duty existed on the part of the district to prevent the battery. *See, e.g.,* Genao v. Bd. of Educ., 888 F. Supp. 501 (S.D.N.Y. 1995).

psychiatrist purported that a punitive award would not be a deterrent for his impulsive conduct.[75] The court also was unpersuaded by the argument that the student's violence and anger were due to his poor self-control or that he had a learning disability. In conclusion, the court noted that if the student expected to continue to live freely in society, he would have to learn to control his assaultive behavior, or "appreciate" the consequences.

Self-defense often has been used to shield an individual from liability for alleged battery. An individual need not wait to be struck to engage in defensive acts, although reasonable grounds must exist to substantiate that harm is imminent. The "test" in such cases is to determine whether the defendant's conduct was that in which a reasonable person may have engaged given the circumstances. Consideration should be given to the magnitude of the existing threat, possible alternatives to physical contact, and the time frame available to make a decision (i.e., whether the defendant acted instantaneously or had time for contemplation and deliberation).[76] Even where contact is justified, the defendant must use only force that is reasonably necessary for self-protection. Furthermore, if the alleged aggressor is disarmed, rendered helpless, or no longer capable of aggressive behavior, the defendant may not take the opportunity to engage in revenge or to punish.

In addition to self-defense, individuals accused of battery also may claim that they were acting in the defense of others. This type of tort defense is of particular importance in a school setting where educators often are called on to separate students who are fighting or to come to the aid of someone being attacked. Most jurisdictions not only permit such action on behalf of others but also consider it to be a responsibility or duty of educators, assuming good faith and the use of reasonable and necessary force.

False Imprisonment

All restrictions on the freedom of movement or the effort to enter or exit will not qualify as false imprisonment. For example, the court found no false imprisonment where a student was placed for seven minutes in a holding cell in a county detention facility for continually disrupting a tour of the building—the student's behavior jeopardized the safety of the children and disrupted an otherwise orderly environment.[77] Also, a student who was taken out of class to be questioned by the principal and a magistrate judge regarding sexual activities on the Internet could not claim false imprisonment.[78] Interestingly, to be falsely imprisoned, one need not be incarcerated; walls, locks, and iron bars are not required. Rather, imprisonment can result from being placed in a closet, room, corner, automobile, or even a circle in the middle of a

[75]Anello v. Savignac, 342 N.W.2d 440 (Wis. Ct. App. 1983).

[76]American Law Institute, *A Concise Restatement of Torts* (St. Paul, MN: American Law Institute 2000), p. 19.

[77]Harris *ex rel*. Tucker v. County of Forsyth, 921 F. Supp. 325 (M.D.N.C. 1996).

[78]Howard v. Yakovac, No. CV04-202-S-EJL, 2006 U.S. Dist. LEXIS 27253 (Idaho May 2, 2006).

football field; it can occur when confined to an entire building or when forced to accompany another person on a walk or trip. The taking of a purse, car keys, or other property with the intent to force the person to remain also may qualify as imprisonment. Imprisonment results when physical action, verbal command, or intimidation is used to restrain or detain persons against their will. Tone of voice, body language, and what was reasonably understood or even implied from the defendant's conduct will be considered.

In imprisonment cases, the plaintiff need not show that physical force was used; it will suffice that the plaintiff submitted given the apprehension of force. The plaintiff must be aware of the restraint, but need not show damages beyond the confinement itself to prevail at trial. Accordingly, any time children are unjustifiably restrained against their will, tied or taped to chairs, or bound and gagged, the tort of false imprisonment (as well as other possible violations[79]) may be claimed.

Although there are times when the use of physical restraints may be necessary, educators need to document the circumstances requiring such actions and provide a narrative explaining why restraint is an appropriate and reasoned response to the behavior. Where explanations are insufficient, liability will be possible, if not probable. For example, an Oklahoma court denied summary judgment for the school district where a child with mental disabilities and cerebral palsy was locked in the school bathroom for three hours by her teacher to clean the "mess" she created. The court concluded that there was sufficient evidence for a reasonable jury on remand to conclude that the teacher who confined the child acted unreasonably. Furthermore, if the teacher's conduct was perceived as "reckless," the court projected that she also could be found liable for the intentional infliction of emotion distress.[80]

Intentional Infliction of Mental Distress

This area of tort law is relatively new because of the historic resistance to awarding damages for a mental injury when it was not accompanied by a physical injury (e.g., pain and suffering associated with a broken leg). This reluctance purportedly was due to the difficulty of generating proof of both injury and proximate cause and then determining the appropriate amount of damages to be awarded. Nevertheless, a tort claim of intentional infliction of mental distress now is available to individuals who have experienced severe mental anguish. This claim, however, does not provide a remedy for every trivial indignity, insult, bad manners, annoyance, or sexist or racist comment, even if disturbing to the plaintiff.

Some forms of communication can result in an assault claim (e.g., a threat to strike another) or defamation suit (e.g., an unfounded claim that a teacher has been

---

[79]For example, plaintiffs also may claim a Fourth Amendment "seizure" violation that could be accompanied by 42 U.S.C. § 1983. *See* Gray v. Bostic, 458 F.3d 1295 (11th Cir. 2006) (determining that the handcuffing of a compliant 9-year-old girl for the sole purpose of punishing her represented a constitutional violation), *cert. denied*, 127 S. Ct. 2428 (2007).

[80]Gerks v. Deathe, 832 F. Supp. 1450 (W.D. Okla. 1993).

sexually involved with students). Other communications might provide a basis for discrimination suits under federal laws (e.g., sexual or racial harassment). For the conduct to result in intentional infliction of mental distress under tort law, it must be flagrant, extreme, or outrageous; it must go beyond all possible bounds of decency and be regarded as atrocious and utterly intolerable in civilized society.[81] No reasonable person should be expected to endure such conduct (e.g., severe and extreme acts of stalking, harassment, and assault). Moreover, in most instances, the conduct needs to be prolonged and recurring, since single acts seldom meet the necessary threshold.

Given the difficulty of meeting this stringent standard, it is not surprising that few school-based claims succeed. Numerous claims have involved injured feelings or reputations, appearing trivial at best. In one such claim that bordered on disingenuous, a sixth grade Oregon student claimed intentional infliction of mental distress when two of her teachers refused to use her nickname, Boo. "Boo" also is the street name for marijuana and was recognized as such by other students. Neither teacher had ever stated that the student used or condoned the use of drugs. In granting summary judgment for the teachers, the court concluded that no juror could reasonably find that the conduct of the teachers was an "extraordinary transgression of the bounds of socially tolerable conduct."[82] Other unsuccessful claims include a school supervisor who was callous and offensive when he ridiculed a subordinate's speech impediment;[83] a program faculty that removed a student teacher based on her unacceptable performance, unprofessional conduct, and erratic and disturbing behavior;[84] and a school administrator who sent a letter to parents and students indicating that a teacher who had made racially offensive remarks that perpetuated negative stereotypes was returning to work following a 10-day suspension.[85] None of these cases was found to have met the necessary threshold to qualify as outrageous or extreme.

In contrast, a Florida teacher was found to have supported a claim of intentional infliction of mental distress against two students.[86] The youths had planned, edited, written, printed, copied, and distributed a newsletter that referred to the teacher in racially derogatory and sexually vulgar ways; threatened to rape her, her children, and their cousins; and threatened to kill her. The court distinguished the

---

[81]Keeton, et al. *supra* note 41, pp. 54–66. *See also* Ott v. Edinburgh Cmty. Sch. Corp., 189 Fed. Appx. 507 (7th Cir. 2006) (concluding that a former coach was not defamed when a school board member disclosed to the superintendent that the coach had a criminal record).

[82]Phillips v. Lincoln County Sch. Dist., 984 P.2d 947, 951 (Or. Ct. App. 1999). *See also* Green v. San Diego Unified Sch. Dist., 226 Fed. Appx. 677 (9th Cir. 2007) (determining that defendant's conduct was neither extreme nor outrageous and plaintiff failed to meet the standard for emotional distress).

[83]Shipman v. Glenn, 443 S.E.2d 921 (S.C. Ct. App. 1994).

[84]Banks v. Dominican Coll., 42 Cal. Rptr. 2d 110 (Ct. App. 1995).

[85]Elstrom v. Indep. Sch. Dist. No. 270, 533 N.W.2d 51 (Minn. Ct. App. 1995).

[86]Nims v. Harrison, 768 So. 2d 1198 (Fla. Dist. Ct. App. 2000). *See also* Smith v. Jackson County Bd. of Educ., 608 S.E. 2d 399 (N.C. Ct. App. 2005) (denying defendant's motion to dismiss in a case seeking damages based on emotional distress in which a teacher encouraged the 14-year-old female plaintiff to have a sexual relationship with an 18-year-old male student; made his office, home, and car available for the relationship; and attempted to videotape the two having sex).

case from those that involved mere name-calling, embarrassing photos, or harassment and concluded that the conduct was extreme and went beyond all possible bounds of decency.

Defamation

Most tort actions have involved claims for damages that were due to physical or mental injuries, but plaintiffs also have claimed injury to their reputations in the form of defamation. School districts may be liable for the defamatory acts of their employees, but only when they are engaged in district work and their conduct is within the scope of their authority.[87] Otherwise, claims may be filed only against the individual responsible for the alleged defamation. *Slander* is the term generally associated with spoken defamation (but also includes sign language), whereas *libel* often is used to refer to written defamation (but also includes pictures, statues, motion pictures, and conduct carrying a defamatory imputation—e.g., hanging a person in effigy).[88] In determining whether defamation has occurred, courts will consider whether:

- The targeted individual was a private or public person,
- The communication was false,
- The expression qualified as opinion or fact, and
- The comment was privileged.

Private and Public Persons

To prevail in a defamation case, private individuals need prove only that a false publication by the defendant was received and understood by a third party and that injury resulted. Receipt of potentially defamatory information that is not understood (e.g., receiving an unintelligible encrypted message on a computer, hearing Morse code over a radio, receiving a phone call in an unknown language) cannot adversely affect the plaintiff's reputation, dignity, or community standing and does not qualify as defamation. Individuals considered public figures or officials additionally must show that the publication was made with either malice or a reckless disregard for the truth. Although definitions vary considerably by state, public figures generally are those who are known or recognized by the public (e.g., professional athletes, actors), whereas public officials are those who have substantial control over governmental affairs (e.g., politicians, school board members).

Although the trend in recent years has been to broaden the class of public officials and figures, it is fortunate for teachers that the vast majority of courts have not found them to be "public," in large part because their authority typically is limited to

---

[87]*See, e.g.*, Henderson v. Walled Lake Consol. Schs., 469 F.3d 479 (6th Cir. 2006).

[88]Keeton, et al. *supra* note 41, p. 786.

students.[89] Some courts, however, have found school administrators and coaches to be either public officials or figures.[90] This does not mean that all administrators and coaches, even within the same jurisdiction, will qualify as public persons; such a determination is made on an individual basis and is dependent on the role, responsibility, degree of notoriety, and authority of the specific individual.

Veracity of Statements

In assessing defamation claims, courts also consider whether a statement is true or false. If the statement is found to be true, or at least substantially true, judgment will generally be for the defendant, assuming that critical facts have not been omitted, taken out of context, or otherwise artificially juxtaposed to misrepresent.[91] Educators must be particularly careful, however, when discussing students and must avoid making comments in bad faith that will result in liability. For example, if a teacher were to comment in class that a particular female student was a "slut," the comments would qualify as defamation *per se*.[92] In such cases, no proof of actual harm to reputation is required.

In addition to proving a communication to be false, the individual must show that he or she was the subject addressed. Interestingly, the individual's identity need not be clear to all third parties (i.e., readers, viewers, or hearers of the defamation); as long as at least one third party can identify the individual, the claim is actionable even though the individual is not mentioned by name.[93] Furthermore, the defamatory content need not be explicit; it may be implied or may be understood only by third parties with additional information.

Fact versus Opinion

Most opinions receive constitutional protection, particularly when public figures or officials are involved or the issue is one of public concern. To qualify as opinion, the communication must not lend itself to being realistically proven as true or false and must be communicated in such a way as to be considered a personal perspective on

[89]McCutcheon v. Moran, 425 N.E.2d 1130 (Ill. App. Ct. 1981). *But see* Elstrom v. Indep. Sch. Dist. No. 270, 533 N.W.2d 51 (Minn. Ct. App. 1995) (concluding that a teacher was a public official).

[90]*See, e.g.*, Jordan v. World Publ'g Co., 872 P.2d 946 (Okla. Ct. App. 1994) (principal); Johnson v. Southwestern Newspapers Corp., 855 S.W. 2d 182 (Tex. App. 1993) (football coach). *But see* O'Connor v. Burningham, No. 20060090, 2007 Utah LEXIS 139 (Utah July 31, 2007) (determining that a coach was not a public official as school athletics did not affect in any material way the civic affairs of a community).

[91]Determining whether something is true can be difficult, as perspectives and standards will vary. *See, e.g.*, Woodruff v. Ohman, 166 Fed. Appx. 212 (6th Cir. 2006) (concluding that plaintiff's former boss defamed her in letters stating that she had not been a productive scholar; finding the defendant's statements to be false, defamatory, and malicious since the plaintiff had accumulated the necessary data for a paper and presented her research in the form of an abstract, even if she had no actual product).

[92]*See, e.g.*, Smith v. Atkins, 622 So. 2d 795 (La. Ct. App. 1993).

[93]*See, e.g.*, McCormack v. Port Wash. Union Free Sch. Dist., 638 N.Y.S.2d 488 (App. Div. 1996).

the matter.[94] Parents may express critical opinions about a teacher (verbally or in writing) and may submit such opinions to a principal or school board.[95] Moreover, parents may even express negative views directly to the teacher, assuming that the expression does not amount to "fighting words"[96] or qualify as an assault.

Notwithstanding these examples, allegations that "the teacher sold drugs to a student" or that "the superintendent stole school funds" are factual statements that are capable of being substantiated and therefore may qualify as defamation unless proven true. The appeals court in Ohio reversed a lower court dismissal where letters and a news article stated that a football coach had his entire team batter one of the players on the team. On remand, in reexamining the facts of the case, the lower court was directed to assess the totality of circumstances, including the specific language used in the statement, whether the statement was verifiable, and the general context of the statement.[97] Similarly, an Oregon appeals court affirmed a damage award against parents who accused a school bus driver of sexual abuse. Even though there were no facts or evidence that supported the claim, the parents persisted in making accusations over an extended period of time by writing letters, uniting parents in protest, and attending board meetings. Their unsupported claims injured the driver's reputation, adversely affected his employability, and caused him to suffer emotional distress.[98]

Privilege

Whether a communication qualifies as "privileged" also may affect whether defamation is supported. Statements that are considered *absolutely privileged* cannot serve as a basis for defamation under any circumstance, even if they are false and result in injury.[99] An absolute privilege defense has been selectively applied in cases involving superintendents and school board members, although it is less common in education than qualified privilege. For example, a North Dakota court held that a board member's statements at a school board meeting about a superintendent were absolutely

---

[94]*Compare* Milkovich v. Lorain Journal Co., 497 U.S. 1 (1990) (observing that statements made by a newspaper about a high school wrestling coach implied that the coach committed perjury in a judicial proceeding; because the statements could be proven true or false, they did not qualify as opinion) *with* Maynard v. Daily Gazette Co., 447 S.E.2d 293 (W. Va. 1994) (holding that a former athletic director was not defamed by an editorial identifying him as one of several parties responsible for the poor graduation rates of athletes; statements expressed in the newspaper were constitutionally protected opinions regarding topics of public interest).

[95]*See, e.g.*, Nodar v. Galbreath, 462 So. 2d 803 (Fla. 1984); Ansorian v. Zimmerman, 627 N.Y.S.2d 706 (App. Div. 1995).

[96]"Fighting words" are by their nature likely to result in an immediate breach of the peace and do not qualify as First Amendment protected speech. *See* text accompanying note 12, Chapter 4.

[97]Rich v. Thompson Newspapers, Inc., 842 N.E.2d 1081 (Ohio Ct. App. 2005).

[98]Kraemer v. Harding, 976 P.2d 1160 (Or. Ct. App. 1999).

[99]*See, e.g.*, Gallegos v. Escalon, 993 S.W.2d 422 (Tex. App. 1999).

privileged.[100] Similarly, a New York court held that a superintendent's written reprimand to a coach for failure to follow regulations in the operation of the interscholastic athletic program was protected by absolute privilege.[101]

Communication between parties with qualified or conditional privilege also may be immune from liability if made in good faith, "upon a proper occasion, from a proper motive, in a proper manner, and based upon reasonable or probable cause."[102] But, conditional privilege may be lost if actual malice exists (i.e., a person made a defamatory statement that was known to be false, acted with a high degree of awareness of probable falsity, or entertained serious doubts as to whether the statement was true). Qualified privilege was supported where a board member during a board meeting commented on the suspension of a student for marijuana possession,[103] administrators rated school personnel,[104] and a teacher informed school officials about the inappropriate conduct of another teacher during a European trip.[105]

Qualified privilege was not supported where an Iowa superintendent stated during an open session board meeting that a former employee, with whom he had numerous disagreements, had created an unsafe workplace and was dangerous. Only a single incident substantiated the superintendent's position—a staff member had received a minor bruise when she came into contact with the plaintiff as they both rushed to a file cabinet that contained "secret" records about the plaintiff. The jury found that this accidental injury did not support the superintendent's claim and held that the plaintiff had been defamed; that opinion and a $250,000 award were upheld on appeal.

Damages

Damages in tort suits can be either compensatory or punitive, and many include attorneys' fees that are typically calculated as a percent of the total award (often one-third if the case settles prior to trial and 40 percent if the case is tried). Compensatory damages include past and future economic loss, medical expenses, and pain and suffering. These awards are intended to make the plaintiff whole, at least to the degree

---

[100]Rykowsky v. Dickinson Pub. Sch. Dist. No. 1, 508 N.W.2d 348 (N.D. 1993). *But see* Overall v. Univ. of Pa., 412 F.3d 492 (3d Cir. 2005) (determining that statements made in a private internal university grievance proceeding were not quasi judicial and not, therefore, entitled to absolute privilege.

[101]Santavicca v. City of Yonkers, 518 N.Y.S.2d 29 (App. Div. 1987).

[102]Baskett v. Crossfield, 228 S.W. 673, 675 (Ky. 1920). *See also* Phillips v. Winston-Salem/Forsyth County Bd. of Educ., 450 S.E.2d 753 (N.C. Ct. App. 1994) (holding that a board did not defame a discharged assistant superintendent since the board's communications with the superintendent were protected by qualified privilege).

[103]Morrison v. Mobile County Bd. of Educ., 495 So. 2d 1086 (Ala. 1986).

[104]*See, e.g.*, Malia v. Monchak, 543 A.2d 184 (Pa. Commw. Ct. 1988).

[105]Rocci v. Ecole Secondaire MacDonald-Cartier, 755 A.2d 583 (N.J. 2000).

that money is capable of doing so. If a plaintiff's previous injury has been aggravated, the defendant is generally liable only for the additional loss.

Although damages vary by state, it is common to cap intangibles (e.g., pain, suffering, loss of consortium, mental anguish) but not to cap actual loss. When plaintiffs prevail, it is important to note that school district assets are not subject to execution, sale, garnishment, or attachment to satisfy the judgment. Instead, judgments are paid from funds appropriated specifically for that purpose, acquired through revenue bonds, or available because of insurance. If sufficient funds are not forthcoming, it is common for states to require fiscal officers to certify the amount of unpaid judgment to the taxing authority for inclusion in the next budget. When the amounts are significant, many states permit districts to pay installments (at times up to 10 years) for payment of damages that do not represent actual loss.[106]

Furthermore, in most states, educators can be sued individually unless they are "save harmlessed" by their school district. Under save harmless provisions, the school district agrees to provide legal representation and pay any resulting liability. When educators are not "save harmlessed" and do not have personal insurance coverage, their personal assets (e.g., cars, boats, bank accounts) may be attached, their wages may be garnished, and a lien may be placed on their property. Where a lien is filed, the property may not be sold until the debt is satisfied. Moreover, debtors are not permitted to transfer ownership to avoid attachment (i.e., this would represent *fraudulent conveyance*). It is common for persons in law enforcement (e.g., a county sheriff) to be authorized to seize the property and hold it for sale at public auction. Because the debtor's financial worth is not a factor in calculating actual damages, the award may exceed the debtor's ability to pay. If the debtor is eventually successful in filing for bankruptcy, the plaintiff/creditor is typically paid in the same manner as other creditors.

Punitive damages are awarded to punish particularly wanton or reckless acts and are in addition to actual damages. The amount is discretionary with the jury and is based on the circumstances, behaviors, and acts. Unlike the calculation of actual damages, the debtor's financial worth may be a factor in determining punitive amounts. When jury verdicts are seemingly out of line, the court may reduce (*remittitur*) or increase (*additur*) the amount where either passion or prejudice is a factor.

Conclusion

All individuals, including educators, are responsible for their actions and can be liable for damages if they intentionally or negligently cause injury to others. Educators have a responsibility to act reasonably, but some negligent conduct is likely to occur. Consequently, educators should be knowledgeable about their potential liability under applicable state laws and should ensure that they are either protected by their school districts or have adequate insurance coverage for any damages that might

---

[106]Jonathan E. Buchter, Susan C. Hastings, Timothy J. Sheeran, & Gregory W. Stype, *Ohio School Law* (Cleveland, OH: West, 2001), p. 862.

be assessed against them. To guard against liability, teachers and administrators should be cognizant of the following principles of tort law.

1. The propriety of an educator's conduct in a given situation is gauged by whether a reasonably prudent educator (with the special skills and training associated with that role) would have acted in a similar fashion under like conditions.
2. Educators owe students a duty to provide proper instruction and adequate supervision; to maintain equipment, buildings, and grounds in proper condition; and to provide warnings regarding any known dangers.
3. Educators are expected to exercise a standard of care commensurate with the duty owed.
4. Foreseeability of harm is a crucial element in determining whether an educator's actions are negligent.
5. If an educator has information that a student poses a danger to self or others, parents and identifiable victims must be notified.
6. An intervening act can relieve a teacher of liability for negligence if the act caused the injury and the teacher had no reason to anticipate that it would occur.
7. The common law doctrine of governmental immunity has been abrogated or qualified in most states (e.g., "safe place" statutes).
8. Where recognized, contributory negligence can be used to relieve school personnel of liability if it is established that the injured party's own actions were significant in producing the injury.
9. Under comparative negligence statutes, damages may be apportioned among negligent defendants and plaintiffs.
10. If an individual knowingly and voluntarily assumes a risk of harm, recovery for an injury may be barred.
11. School personnel can be held liable for battery if it is determined that they used excessive force with students.
12. Unnecessary restraint and excessive detainment of students can result in false imprisonment charges.
13. In severe cases in which conduct qualifies as "extreme" or "outrageous," educators or students can be found liable for the intentional infliction of mental distress.
14. Public officials can recover damages for defamation from the media for statements pertaining to public issues only if malice or an intentional disregard for the truth is shown.
15. Educators generally are protected from defamation charges by "qualified privilege" when their statements about students are made to appropriate persons and are motivated by proper intentions.

14

Summary of Legal
Generalizations

In the preceding chapters, principles of law have been presented as they relate to specific aspects of teachers' and students' rights and responsibilities. Constitutional and statutory provisions, in conjunction with judicial decisions, have been analyzed in an effort to depict the current status of the law. Many diverse topics have been explored, some with clearly established legal precedents and others about which the law is still evolving.

The most difficult situations confronting school personnel are those without specific legislative or judicial guidance. In such circumstances, educators must make judgments based on their professional training and general knowledge of the law as it applies to education. The following broad generalizations, synthesized from the preceding chapters, are presented to assist educators in making such determinations.

Generalizations

The Legal Control of Public Education Resides with the State as One of Its Sovereign Powers. In attempting to comply with the law, school personnel must keep in mind the scope of the state's authority to regulate educational activities. Courts consistently have held that state legislatures possess plenary power in establishing and operating public schools; this power is restricted only by federal and state constitutions and civil rights laws. Of course, where the federal judiciary has interpreted the United States Constitution as prohibiting a given practice in public education, such as racial discrimination, the state or its agents cannot enact laws or policies that conflict with the constitutional mandate. In contrast, if the federal Constitution and civil rights laws have been interpreted as permitting a certain activity, states retain discretion in either restricting or expanding the practice. Under such circumstances, standards vary across states, and legislation becomes more important in specifying the scope of protected rights. For example, the Supreme Court has rejected the assertion that probationary teachers have an inherent federal right to due process prior to contract nonrenewal, but state legislatures have the authority to create such a right under state law. Similarly, the Supreme Court has found no Fourth Amendment violation in blanket or random drug testing of public school students who participate in extracurricular activities; however, state law may place restrictions on school authorities in conducting such searches. Also, the Supreme Court has found no Establishment Clause violation in the participation of sectarian schools in state-supported voucher programs to fund education, but these programs might run afoul of state constitutional provisions prohibiting the use of public funds for religious purposes.

Unless constitutional rights are at stake, courts defer to the will of legislative bodies in determining educational matters. State legislatures have the authority to create and redesign school districts, to collect and distribute educational funds, and to determine teacher qualifications, curricular offerings, and minimum student performance standards. With such pervasive control vested in the states, a thorough understanding of the operation of a specific educational system can be acquired only by examining an individual state's statutes, administrative regulations, and judicial decisions that interpret such provisions.

Certain prerequisites to public school employment are defined through statutes and state board of education regulations. For example, all states stipulate that a teacher must possess a valid teaching license based on satisfying specified requirements. State laws also delineate the permanency of the employment relationship, dismissal procedures for tenured and nontenured teachers, and the extent to which teachers can engage in collective bargaining.

State laws similarly govern conditions of school attendance. Every state has enacted a compulsory attendance statute to ensure an educated citizenry. These laws are applicable to all children, with only a few legally recognized exceptions. In addition to mandating school attendance, states have the authority to prescribe courses of study and instructional materials. Courts will not invalidate such decisions unless constitutional rights are abridged.

Comparable reasoning also is applied by courts in upholding the state's power to establish academic standards and graduation requirements. To determine whether students and school districts are progressing in a manner consistent with state standards and federal expectations, students are being subjected to more testing than ever before. Assessments determine the level and type of instruction provided; whether the child should be promoted from grade to grade or is eligible for graduation; and if the local school district has achieved required outcomes.

It is a widely held perception that local school boards control public education, but local boards hold only those discretionary powers conferred by the state. Depending on the state, a local board's discretionary authority may be quite broad, narrowly defined by statutory guidelines, or somewhere in between. School board regulations enacted pursuant to statutory authority are legally binding on employees and students. For example, school boards can place conditions on employment (e.g., continuing education requirements, residency requirements) beyond state minimums, unless prohibited by law.

In some states, policy-making authority in certain domains (e.g., curriculum, personnel) has been delegated to school-based councils, and the relationship between local boards and school-based councils is still being defined. Courts will not overturn decisions made by school boards or site-based councils unless clearly arbitrary, discriminatory, or beyond their scope of authority. School board and/or council discretion, however, may be limited by negotiated contracts with teachers' associations. Negotiated agreements may affect terms and conditions of employment in areas such as teacher evaluation, work calendar, teaching loads, extra-duty assignments, and grievance procedures. It is imperative for educators to become familiar with all these sources of legal rights and responsibilities.

All School Policies and Practices That Impinge on Protected Personal Freedoms Must be Substantiated as Necessary to Advance the School's Educational Mission.   The state and its agents have broad authority to regulate public schools, but policies that impair federal constitutional rights must be justified by an overriding public interest. Although courts do not enact laws as legislative bodies do, they significantly influence educational policies and practices by interpreting constitutional and statutory provisions. Both school attendance and public employment traditionally were considered privileges bestowed at the will of the state, but the Supreme Court has recognized that teachers and students do not lose their constitutional rights when they enter public schools. The state controls education, but this power must be exercised in conformance with the federal Constitution.

It is important to keep in mind that the Bill of Rights places restrictions on governmental, not private, action that interferes with personal freedoms. To illustrate, public schools may have to tolerate private student expression under certain circumstances, but expression representing the school can be censored for educational reasons. Similarly, the Establishment Clause prohibits public school employees from directing or condoning devotional activities in public education, whereas student-initiated religious groups in secondary schools must be treated like other student groups in terms of school access during noninstructional time. Furthermore, community religious groups, even those involved in religious instruction targeting elementary school children, must be treated like other community groups in terms of access during nonschool hours.

In balancing public and individual interests, courts weigh the importance of the protected personal right against the governmental need to restrict its exercise. For example, courts have reasoned that there is no overriding public interest to justify compelling students to salute the American flag if such an observance conflicts with religious or philosophical beliefs. In contrast, mandatory vaccination against communicable diseases has been upheld as a prerequisite to school attendance, even if opposition to immunization is based on religious grounds. Courts have reasoned that the overriding public interest in safeguarding the health of all students justifies such a requirement.

Restrictions can be placed on students' activities if necessary to advance legitimate school objectives. For example, the judiciary has recognized that students' constitutional rights must be assessed in light of the special circumstances of the school. Consequently, school authorities can impose dress codes, and even student uniforms, if shown to advance legitimate educational objectives, such as reducing disciplinary problems and gang influences, and the requirement is not intended to stifle expression. School authorities, although considered state officials, can conduct warrantless searches of students based on reasonable suspicion that contraband posing a threat to the school environment is concealed. Similarly, vulgar speech or expression promoting illegal activity that might be protected by the First Amendment for adults can be curtailed among public school students to further the school's legitimate interest in maintaining standards of decency. As noted, student expression that gives the appearance of representing the school also can be censored to ensure its consistency with educational objectives. And even personal student expression of ideological views that merely happens to take place at school can be restricted if linked to a disruption of the educational process.

Similarly, constraints can be placed on school employees if justified by valid school objectives. Prerequisites to employment, such as examinations and residency requirements, can be imposed if necessary to advance legitimate governmental interests. Furthermore, restrictions on teachers' rights to govern their lifestyles and appearance can be justified when their behavior impinge on their effectiveness in the classroom. Although teachers enjoy a First Amendment right to express views on matters of public concern, expression pursuant to job responsibilities is not protected by the First Amendment. Even if educators are speaking as private citizens, expression relating to private employment grievances, rather than a public concern, can be the basis for disciplinary action. And even teachers' expression on public issues can be curtailed if it impedes the management of the school, work relationships, or teaching effectiveness.

Every regulation that impairs individual rights must be based on valid educational considerations and be necessary to carry out the school's mission. Such regulations also should be clearly stated and well publicized so that all individuals understand the basis for the rules and the penalties for infractions.

School Policies and Practices Must Not Disadvantage Selected Individuals or Groups.   The inherent personal right to remain free from governmental discrimination has been emphasized throughout this book. Strict judicial scrutiny has been applied in evaluating state action that creates a suspect classification, such as race. In school desegregation cases, courts have charged school officials with an affirmative duty to take whatever steps are necessary to overcome the lingering effects of past discrimination. Similarly, intentional racial discrimination associated with testing methods, suspension procedures, employee hiring, and promotion practices has been disallowed. Whether voluntary race-based school/program assignments that further the goal of diversity will be upheld in *de facto* segregated school districts will depend on the ability of school officials to devise sufficiently narrowly tailored means to achieve their desired objective.

In contrast, neutral policies, uniformly applied, are not necessarily unconstitutional, even though they may have a disparate impact on minorities. For example, prerequisites to employment, such as tests that disqualify a disproportionate number of minority applicants, have been upheld as long as their use is justified by legitimate employment objectives and not accompanied by discriminatory intent. Also, the placement of a disproportionate number of minority students in lower instructional tracks is permissible if such assignments are based on legitimate educational criteria that are applied in the best interests of students. Likewise, school segregation that results from natural causes rather than intentional state action does not implicate constitutional rights.

In addition to racial classifications, other bases for distinguishing among employees and students have been invalidated if they disadvantage individuals. Federal civil rights laws, in conjunction with state statutes, have reinforced constitutional protections afforded to various segments of society that traditionally have suffered discrimination. Indeed, the judiciary has recognized that legislative bodies are empowered to go beyond constitutional minimums in protecting citizens from discriminatory practices. Accordingly, laws have been enacted that place specific responsibilities on employers to ensure that employees are not disadvantaged on the basis of race, sex, age, religion, national origin, or disabilities. If an inference of discrimination is established, employers must produce legitimate nondiscriminatory reasons to justify their actions. School officials can be held liable for damages if substantiated that benefits have been withheld from certain individuals because of their inherent characteristics.

Federal and state mandates also stipulate that students cannot be denied school attendance or be otherwise disadvantaged based on characteristics such as race, sex, disability, national origin, marriage, or pregnancy. Eligibility for school activities, such as participation on interscholastic athletic teams, can be restricted only narrowly because of factors such as age, sex, or disability. In addition, disciplinary procedures that disproportionately disadvantage identified groups of students are vulnerable to legal challenge. Educators should ensure that all school policies are applied in a nondiscriminatory manner.

Courts will scrutinize grouping practices to ensure that they do not impede students' rights to equal educational opportunities. Nondiscrimination, however, does not require identical treatment. Students can be classified according to their unique needs, but any differential treatment must be justified in terms of providing more appropriate services. Indeed, judicial rulings and federal and state laws have placed an obligation on school districts to provide appropriate programs and services to meet the needs of children with disabilities and to eliminate the language barriers of those with English-language deficiencies.

Due Process Is a Basic Tenet of the United States System of Justice—the Foundation of Fundamental Fairness. The notion of due process, embodied in the Fifth and Fourteenth Amendments, has been an underlying theme throughout the discussion of teachers' and students' rights. The judiciary has recognized that due process guarantees protect individuals against arbitrary governmental action impairing life, liberty, or property interests and ensure that procedural safeguards accompany any governmental interference with these interests.

In the absence of greater statutory specificity, courts have held that the United States Constitution requires, at a minimum, notice of the charges and a hearing before an impartial decision maker when personnel actions impair public educators' property or liberty rights. A property claim to due process can be established by tenure status, contractual agreement, or school board action that creates a valid expectation of reemployment. A liberty claim to due process can be asserted if the employer's action implicates constitutionally protected rights, damages the teacher's reputation, or imposes such a stigma that the opportunity to obtain other employment is foreclosed.

Many state legislatures have specified procedures beyond constitutional minimums that also must be followed before a tenured teacher is dismissed. The provision of federal and state due process procedures does not imply that a teacher will not be dismissed or that sanctions will not be imposed. But it does mean that the teacher must be given the opportunity to refute the charges and that the decision must be made fairly and supported by evidence.

Students, as well as teachers, have due process rights. Students have a state-created property right to attend school that cannot be denied without procedural requisites. The nature of the proceedings depends on the deprivation involved, with more serious impairments necessitating more formal proceedings. If punishments are arbitrary or excessive, students' substantive due process rights may be implicated. Children with disabilities have due process rights in placement decisions as well as in disciplinary matters. Since school authorities are never faulted for providing too much due process, at least minimum procedural safeguards are advisable when making any nonroutine change in a student's status.

Inherent in the notion of due process is the assumption that all individuals have a right to a hearing if state action impinges on personal freedoms. Such a hearing need not be elaborate in every situation; an informal conversation can suffice under some circumstances, such as brief student suspensions from school. Moreover, such an informal hearing can serve to clarify issues and facilitate agreement, thus eliminating the need for more formal proceedings. The crucial element is for all affected parties to have an opportunity to air their views and present evidence that might alter the decision.

Educators Are Expected to Follow the Law, to Act Reasonably, and to Anticipate Potentially Adverse Consequences of Their Actions. Public school personnel are presumed to be knowledgeable of federal and state constitutional and statutory provisions as well as school board policies affecting their roles. The Supreme Court has emphasized that ignorance of the law is no defense for violating clearly established legal principles. For example, being unaware of the Supreme Court's interpretation of Title IX restrictions under the Education Amendments of 1972 would not shield a school district from liability for school authorities' failure to respond to student complaints of sexual harassment.

Educators hold themselves out as having certain knowledge and skills by the nature of their special training and certification. Accordingly, they are expected to exercise sound professional judgment in the performance of their duties. To illustrate, in administering pupil punishments, teachers are expected to consider the student's age, mental condition, and past behavior as well as the specific circumstances surrounding the rule infraction. Failure to exercise reasonable judgment can result in dismissal or possibly financial liability for impairing students' rights.

Moreover, teachers are expected to make reasonable decisions pertaining to academic programs. Materials and methodology should be appropriate for the students' age and educational objectives. If students are grouped for instructional purposes, teachers are expected to base such decisions on legitimate educational considerations. In addition, educators are held accountable for reasonable actions in supervising students, providing appropriate instructions, maintaining equipment in proper repair, and warning students of any known dangers. Teachers must exercise a standard of care commensurate with their duty to protect students from unreasonable risks of harm. Personal liability can be assessed for negligence if a school employee should have foreseen that an event could result in injury to a student.

Educators also are expected to exercise sound judgment in personal activities that affect their professional roles. Teachers do not relinquish their privacy rights as a condition of public employment, but private behavior that impairs teaching effectiveness or disrupt the school can be the basis for adverse personnel action. As role models for students, teachers and other school personnel are held to a higher level of discretion in their private lives than expected of the general public.

Conclusion

One objective of this book has been to alleviate educators' fears that the scales of justice have been tipped against them. It is hoped that this objective has been achieved. In most instances, courts and legislatures have not imposed on school personnel any requirements that fair-minded educators would not impose on themselves. Reasonable policies and practices based on legitimate educational objectives have been consistently upheld by courts. If anything, legislative and judicial mandates have clarified and supported the authority as well as the duty of school personnel to make and enforce regulations that are necessary to maintain an effective and efficient educational environment.

The federal judiciary in the late 1960s and early 1970s expanded constitutional protection of individual liberties against governmental interference. Since the 1980s, however, federal courts have exhibited more restraint and reinforced the authority of state and local education agencies to make decisions necessary to advance the school's educational mission, even if such decisions impinge on protected personal freedoms. Courts do continue to invalidate school practices and policies if they are arbitrary, unrelated to educational objectives, or impair protected individual rights without an overriding justification.

Because reform is usually easier to implement when designed from within than when externally imposed, educators should become more assertive in identifying and altering those practices that have the potential to generate legal intervention. Internet censorship, peer sexual harassment, anti-harassment policies, bullying, hazing, and other intimidating behavior are a few issues now requiring educators' attention. Furthermore, school personnel should stay abreast of legal developments, since new laws are enacted each year and courts are continually reinterpreting constitutional and statutory provisions.

In addition to understanding basic legal rights and responsibilities, educators are expected to transmit this knowledge to students. Pupils also need to understand their constitutional and statutory rights, the balancing of interests that takes place in legislative and judicial forums, and the rationale for legal enactments, including school regulations. Only with increased awareness of fundamental legal principles can all individuals involved in the educational process develop a greater respect for the law and for the responsibilities that accompany legal rights.

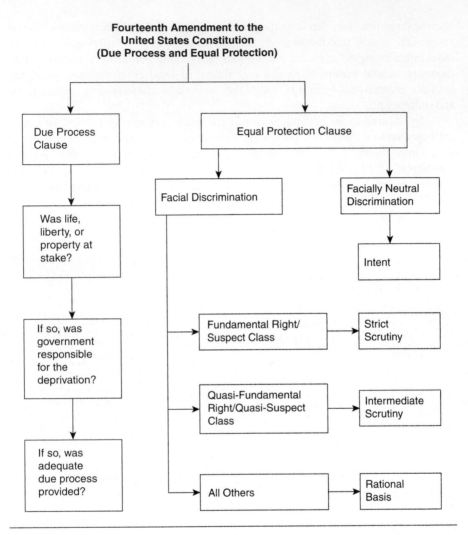

**Fourteenth Amendment to the
United States Constitution
(Due Process and Equal Protection)**

FIGURE 1A

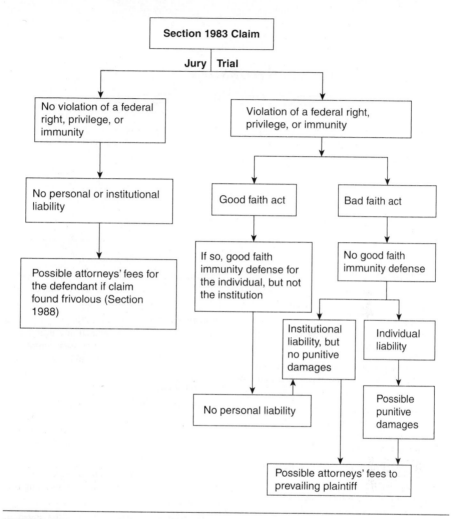

FIGURE 2A

Glossary

absolute privilege protection from liability for communication made in the performance of public service or the administration of justice.

appeal a petition to a higher court to alter the decision of a lower court.

appellate court a tribunal having jurisdiction to review decisions on appeal from inferior courts.

arbitration (binding) a process whereby an impartial third party, chosen by both parties in a dispute, makes a final determination regarding a contested issue.

assault the placing of another in fear of bodily harm.

battery the unlawful touching of another with intent to harm.

certiorari a writ of review whereby an action is removed from an inferior court to an appellate court for additional proceedings.

civil action a judicial proceeding to redress an infringement of individual civil rights, in contrast to a criminal action brought by the state to redress public wrongs.

civil right a personal right that accompanies citizenship and is protected by the Constitution (e.g., freedom of speech, freedom from discrimination).

class action suit a judicial proceeding brought on behalf of a number of persons similarly situated.

common law a body of rules and principles derived from usage or from judicial decisions enforcing such usage.

compensatory damages monetary award to compensate an individual for injury sustained (e.g., financial losses, emotional pain, inconvenience) and restore the injured party to the position held prior to the injury.

concurring opinion a statement by a judge or judges, separate from the majority opinion, that endorses the result of the majority decision but offers its own reasons for reaching that decision.

consent decree an agreement, sanctioned by a court, that is binding on the consenting parties.

consideration something of value given or promised for the purpose of forming a contract.

contract an agreement between two or more competent parties that creates, alters, or dissolves a legal relationship.

criminal action a judicial proceeding brought by the state against a person charged with a public offense.

damages an award made to an individual because of a legal wrong.

declaratory relief a judicial declaration of the rights of the plaintiff without an assessment of damages against the defendant.

de facto segregation separation of the races that exists but does not result from action of the state or its agents.

defamation false and intentional communication that injures a person's character or reputation; slander is spoken and libel is written communication.

defendant the party against whom a court action is brought.

de jure segregation separation of the races by law or by action of the state or its agents.

de minimis something that is insignificant, not worthy of judicial review.

de novo a new review.

dictum a statement made by a judge in delivering an opinion that does not relate directly to the issue being decided and does not embody the sentiment of the court.

directed verdict the verdict provided when a plaintiff fails to support a prima facie case for jury consideration or the defendant fails to produce a necessary defense.

discretionary power authority that involves the exercise of judgment.

dissenting opinion a statement by a judge or judges who disagree with the decision of the majority of the justices in a case.

en banc the full bench; refers to a session where the court's full membership participates in the decision rather than the usual quorum of the court.

fact finding a process whereby a third party investigates an impasse in the negotiation process to determine the facts, identify the issues, and make a recommendation for settlement.

friend-of-the-court briefs briefs provided by nonparties to inform or perhaps persuade the court (also termed *amicus curiae* briefs).

governmental function activity performed in discharging official duties of a federal, state, or municipal agency.

governmental immunity the common law doctrine that governmental agencies cannot be held liable for the negligent acts of their officers, agents, or employees.

impasse a deadlock in the negotiation process in which parties are unable to resolve an issue without assistance of a third party.

injunction a writ issued by a court prohibiting a defendant from acting in a prescribed manner.

in loco parentis in place of parent; charged with rights and duties of a parent.

liquidated damages contractual amounts representing a reasonable estimation of the damages owed to one of the parties for a breach of the agreement by the other.

mediation the process by which a neutral third party serving as an intermediary attempts to persuade disagreeing parties to settle their dispute.

ministerial duty an act that does not involve discretion and must be carried out in a manner specified by legal authority.

negligence the failure to exercise the degree of care that a reasonably prudent person would exercise under similar conditions; conduct that falls below the standard established by law for the protection of others against unreasonable risk of harm.

per curiam a court's brief disposition of a case that is not accompanied by a written opinion.

plaintiff the party initiating a judicial action.

plenary power full, complete, absolute power.

plurality opinion an opinion agreed to by less than a majority of the court; the concurring judges agree as to which party prevails, but disagree as to reasoning; plurality opinions carry less weight under stare decisis than do majority opinions.

precedent a judicial decision serving as authority for subsequent cases involving similar questions of law.

preponderance of evidence a standard that requires more evidence to support than refute a claim; it also is termed the *51 percent rule.*

prima facie on its face presumed to be true unless disproven by contrary evidence.

probable cause reasonable grounds, supported by sufficient evidence, to warrant a cautious person to believe that the individual is guilty of the offense charged.

procedural due process   the fundamental right to notice of charges and an opportunity to rebut the charges before a fair tribunal if life, liberty, or property rights are at stake.

proprietary function   an activity (often for profit) performed by a state or municipal agency that could as easily be performed by a private corporation.

punitive damages   a monetary punishment where the defendant is found to have acted with either malice or reckless indifference.

qualified immunity   an affirmative defense that shields public officials performing discretionary functions from civil damages if their conduct does not violate clearly established statutory or constitutional rights.

qualified privilege   protection from liability for communication made in good faith, for proper reasons, and to appropriate parties.

reasonable suspicion   specific and articulable facts, which, taken together with rational inferences from the facts, justify a warrantless search.

remand   to send a case back to the original court for additional proceedings.

respondeat superior   a legal doctrine whereby the master is responsible for acts of the servant; a governmental unit is liable for acts of its employees.

save harmless clause   An agreement whereby one party agrees to indemnify and hold harmless another party for suits that may be brought against that party.

stare decisis   to abide by decided cases; to adhere to precedent.

statute   an act by the legislative branch of government expressing its will and constituting the law within the jurisdiction.

substantive due process   requirements embodied in the Fifth and Fourteenth Amendments that legislation must be fair and reasonable in content as well as application; protection against arbitrary, capricious, or unreasonable governmental action.

summary judgment   disposition of a controversy without a trial when there is no genuine dispute over factual issues.

tenure   a statutory right that confers permanent employment on teachers, protecting them from dismissal except for adequate cause.

tort   a civil wrong, independent of contract, for which a remedy in damages is sought.

ultra vires   beyond the scope of authority to act on the subject.

vacate   to set aside; to render a judgment void.

verdict   a decision of a jury on questions submitted for trial.

Selected Supreme Court Cases

Index